The Sports Card EXPLOSION

Sports Collectors Digest
1973-1993
20 YEARS

Two Decades of America's
Hottest Hobby as Seen
Through the Pages of
Sports Collectors Digest

Edited by Mark K. Larson

Published by:

**krause
publications**

700 E. State Street • Iola, WI 54990-0001
Telephone: 715/445-2214

Library of Congress Catalog Number 93-77541
ISBN: 0-87341-254-0

Printed in the United States of America

Contents

1) News & Trends.. 6

All-time baseball team; Goudey reprints; Fake T206 Wagner card; Negative press; Monopoly busters; PVC "crisis;" Card restoration; Trading returns; SCD's beginnings; A season of errors; Fake Rose rookie cards; Happy anniversary; Rated Rookies; Up Autograph Alley; To the dump; Proof sheets found; Counterfeit Mattingly cards; Best and worst from Topps; Dealer survey I; Collector issues banned; What we like; September 1970; From swapping to big business; Cops and robbers; The 1980s in review; X-rated mania; Dealer survey II; Price Guide Report; Bogus Bos; $910,000 worth of 1980s cards; "Find" of the decade; Opening a 1952 wax pack; Top hobby developments of the 1980s; Trends of the 1990s; Minor league cards go big league; Nolan and Shoeless Joe; Act Now — Or Else; Major T206 collection found; The National Convention; What happened to baseball card shows?; The rest of the story.

2) Trivial Tidbits.. 56

3) Dollar Signs... 68

4) Columns & Letters... 74

5) Voices from the Past.. 123

J. Adcock, J. Antonelli, J. Augustine, J. Baldschun, Y. Berra, J. Bouton, R. Bridges, L. Brock, B. Cain, J. Callison, B. Carbo, R. Clemens, R. Colavito, G. Conley, C. Connors, R. Duren, M. Fidrych, A. Gionfriddo, V. Gomez, D. Grate, Reggie Jackson, F. Jenkins, S. Johnson, N. Jones, R. Kiner, M. Krukow, D. Larsen, B. Lee, B. Leonard, D. Liddle, D. Long, F. Malzone, M. Mantle, E. Mathews, J. Mize, B. Newsom, W. Nixon, J. Oates, T. Oliva, J. Palmer, J. Pepitone, J.W. Porter, B. Powell, V. Power, J. Reuss, B. Robinson, E. Robinson, B. Ruth, R. Schoendienst, D. Schofield, T. Seaver, R. Sewell, R. Sievers, T. Simmons, S. Sisti, E. Slaughter, W. Spahn, T. Stallard, R. Stennett, D. Sutton, G. Thomas, M. Throneberry, B. Uecker, G. Varsho, A. Vazquez, C. Veal, H. Walker, H. Washington, B. Werle, B. Will, B. Williams, T. Williams, A. Wilmore, D. Womack, C. Yastrzemski

6) Feelings... 150

H. Aaron, S. Abner, H. Arft, J. Augustine, D. Baker, J. Baldschun, E. Banks, J. Barfield, J. Bench, P. Blair, S. Blass, W. Boggs, B. Boone, G. Brett, L. Brock, E. Broglio, A. Bumbry, R. Campanella, J. Canseco, H. Caray/J. Buck, C. Cardenas, R. Carew, S. Carlton/G. Perry, G. Carter, O. Cepeda, C. Chambliss, R. Clemens, R. Colavito, D. Cone, P. Corrales, S. Coveleski, D. Crandall, J. Crutchfield, B. Davidson, G. Davis, A. Dawson, D. Denkinger, B. Dent, J. DiMaggio, D. Drabek, D. Drysdale, B. Feller, M. Fidrych, R. Fingers, W. Ford,

J. Garagiola, R. Gardenhire, S. Garvey, B. Gibson, A. Gionfriddo, T. Glavine, K. Griffey Jr., O. Guillen, T. Gwynn, P. Harnisch, T. Harrah, R. Henderson, B. Hitchcock, F. Howard, J. Hunter, M. Irvin, Randy Jackson, Reggie Jackson, G. Jefferies, F. Jenkins, T. John, N. Jones, J. Kaat, H. Killebrew, R. Kiner, C. Koonce, M. Krukow, T. Kubek, H. Kuenn, R. Kuntz, C. Lansford, D. LaPoint, D. Larsen, T. Lasorda, V. Law, M. Lemke, B. Leonard, M. Lolich, G. Luzinski/M. Marshall, M. Mantle, B. Martin, E. Martinez, E. Mathews, D. Mattingly, W. Mays, T. McGraw, F. McGriff, M. McGwire, G. Michael, M. Minoso, G. Minton, D. Money, J. Morgan, B. Murcer, D. Murphy, S. Musial, G. Nettles, H. Newhouser, P. Niekro, M. Nokes, J. Oates, J. Odom, T. Oliva, D. Pall, R. Palmeiro, J. Palmer, D. Parker, L. Parrish, R. Patterson, T. Pendleton, G. Perry, B. Powell, K. Puckett, D. Rasmussen, J. Reuss, B. Richardson, C. Ripken Jr., M. Rivers, B. Robinson, F. Robinson, P. Rose, M. Schmidt, T. Seaver, R. Sierra, T. Simmons, E. Slaughter, D. Snider, W. Spahn, T. Steinbach, G. Steinbrenner, S. Stone, R. Sutcliffe, D. Sutton, F. Tanana, F. Thomas, A. Thornton, M. Torrez, A. Trammell, B. Uecker, G. Varsho, R. Ventura, B. Watson, B. Werle, F. White, B. Will, B. Williams, D. Williams, T. Williams, E. Wynn

7) Other Sports...................................... 199

Football: NFL souvenirs, Metal detectors?, The Hulkster, T. Aikman, B. Baschnagel, S. Baugh, B. Bell, K. Bowman, T. Canadeo, V. Ferragamo, F. Gregg, E. Hirsch, E.J. Holub, P. Hornung, R. Ismail, J. Kapp, D. Lane, D. Maynard, D. Meggett, C. Miller, A. Monk, E. Smith, B. St. Clair, J. Stenerud, D. Thomas, T. Thomas, C. Turner, J. Unitas, R. White, D. Williams. Hockey: Hockey brawls, J. Bucyk, G. Howe, B. Hull, E. Lindros, B. Orr, J. Roenick. Basketball: NBA's nicest signers, 1973-74 Topps cards, The worst, K. Abdul-Jabbar, S. Augmon, R. Barry, L. Carnesecca, B. Cousy, K. Gill, L. Johnson, M. Jordan, B. Lanier, E. Macauley, G. Mikan, C. Mullin, S. O'Neal, J. Paxson, S. Pippen, J. Pollard, T. Porter, I. Thomas, J. West, J. Wooden/Dale Brown. Others: J. Douglas, G. Foreman, E. Holyfield, F. Patterson, B. Shoemaker.

8) Dealers/Hobby Personalities...................................... 216

B. Barker, M. Berkus, S. Berger, G. Brace, L. Brown, L. Denny, L. Fritsch, F. Fulop, R. Gallo, T. Galovich, B. Goodwin, W. Hall, R. Hawksley, M. Jordan, R. Lifson, D. Lepore, R. Lewis, G. Martin, R. Medeiros, G. Moll, Morganna, B. Newton, B. Parker, F. Pemper, J. Petruzzelli, C. Pursley, A. Rosen, G. Rothstein, R. Salvino, K. Savage, R./P. Schiflett, R.J. Smalling, J. Spalding, F. Steele, R. Wochnick, L. Woodcock, K. Young

9) Show Time...................................... 270

10) Memories...................................... 293

Hostess card caper; The ultimate collectible; The summer of '71; Home run #755; St. Louis Cardinals keep collectors in mind; Searching for those elusive Hartland statues; Autograph hound usually gets his man; Maris fan is remembered for his catch; Kiecker's Walnut Shop; Growing up with Nolan Ryan; Obsessed with Cracker Jack cards; The Famous Chicken; The Phoenix Suns Gorilla; Wrigley Field Ballhawks; The last autographed ball.

These are some of the pages from the first issue of Sports Collectors Digest.

Introduction

As some of our Krause Publications promotional staff sat around one day discussing the marketing strategies for this book, it was hard for me to offer a few flashy, catchy, attention-getting adjectives to describe what this book represents. The best I could come up with, and the working title in the back of my mind as I scanned every page of 625 consecutive issues through 1992, was "The Best of SCD," because that's what it is — a book commemorating the 20th anniversary of Sports Collectors Digest. It's 20 years of the collecting hobby, 20 years of memories, reprinted from the pages of SCD, the voice of the hobby, and the hobby's oldest and largest publication.

From penny cards to $451,000 investments, The Sports Card Explosion revisits the news, events and people that have shaped the hobby into the booming, multi-million dollar business it is today. You'll read about the trends which have occurred since 1973, and the dealers who have tracked them while building their successful businesses and promoting attendance-breaking shows. You'll relive the experiences we've had in assembling our collections, and hopefully cherish those moments.

You'll also hear players' thoughts regarding signing autographs and collecting memorabilia, and a few anecdotes about historic baseball, basketball and football moments, as told by the athletes who were there. Plus, you'll learn a few trivial tidbits about cards, and a few opinions about the hobby are tossed in, too.

Each of the 10 chapters has an introductory page which captures the essence of its following pages. Stories which have been reprinted in their entirety have headlines. Some stories have been condensed into various excerpts from the original story, as indicated with the ellipsis at the end of some paragraphs and the beginning of the next. Other stories have had bits and pieces paraphrased or quoted from. Each contributing writer has been recognized with attribution.

The Sports Card Explosion is unlike most of KP's other sports books, which are reference books occasionally used to determine a card's value. Although those books have text which accompanies the price lists, they aren't necessarily intended to be read from cover to cover. The Sports Card Explosion is. It's entertaining and informative, and something you will have to sit down with in the easy chair and read, perhaps when it's raining outside, and your favorite team's ball game has been postponed.

To quote one of my old journalism professors, I think this book is "a good read," one that, once you pick it up, you won't want to put it back down, except maybe to dig out your card collections...

Acknowledgements

These editors helped lay the groundwork for this book: the original editors, John and Phil Stommen, and their families and helpers, who launched the publication in 1973; Bob Lemke, who continued its tradition when Krause Publications purchased it in 1981; Steve Ellingboe, Ted Taylor, Vic Knight and Tom Owens, who have had their turns thereafter as editors; Dan Albaugh, Jeff Kurowski and Don Butler, who have filled the roles of price guide editors; and the current editor, Tom Mortenson.

Those who have contributed stories and columns are too numerous to mention here, but they have been acknowledged; their material has been attributed to them.

An all-encompassing thanks goes to all those who have done work behind the scenes over the years, too.

Certain individuals deserve recognition for making my role in this book easier: Chris Williams, who photocopied hundreds of pages from back issues; Wendy Liter, who lent me her back issues; Marge Larson, who input material so it could be edited; Mary Sieber, who helped coordinate the production process; Kevin Ulrich, who designed the cover; Jeff Walker, who's promoted the book and teased readers with his time-bomb ads in SCD; the photo department; and Tom Nelsen, Patsy Morrison, Shelly Domask and Ethel Thulien, who designed and laid out the pages for this book.

Chapter 1 revisits the past 20 years of collecting — from penny cards to $451,000 investments; from Goudey reprints to fake Bo Jackson minor league cards; from bubble gum to holograms; from rookie card mania to Billy Ripken error card obsessions; from national conventions to $1.6 million auctions; from 1952 Topps wax packs to competition from Score, Fleer, Donruss and Upper Deck; from the increased demand in football, basketball and hockey cards to the interest in all types of memorabilia; from the rest of the story about the famous T206 Honus Wagner card, to President George Bush's Topps card.

If it made news, Sports Collectors Digest was there, every step of the way, capturing the sports card explosion.

* * *

One of the most significant hobby finds in years, a previously unknown 1932 U.S. Caramel card, was noted Steve Ellingboe's Oct. 28, 1988, SCD story.

The card, which pictures Hall of Famer Fred Lindstrom, is #16 in the scarce 32-card set of famous athletes, issued by the U.S. Caramel Co. of East Boston, Mass. Collectors had assumed that card #16 was never issued, until Allentown, Pa., dealer Joshua Evans, of Lelands Inc., announced he had purchased the card, thought to be the only one of its kind in existence.

Evans didn't disclose details of the purchase, made at a show in San Francisco over the Labor Day weekend in 1988, but hinted at what he hoped to get for the card by dubbing it "a million-dollar card."

His "one-of-a-kind treasure" compares to a "Rembrandt or Van Gogh that is suddenly discovered in some attic," he told SCD.

"If the T206 Honus Wagner card is worth over $100,000, and there are 40 or 50 of them in existence, then this card ought to be worth a million," Evans said.

Several advanced collectors, however, scoffed at the million-dollar estimate, calling the price "crazy," "imbecilic," "unrealistic," and "moronic." Several believed if one Lindstrom card exists, there's surely another one around.

Said Lew Lipsett, an authority on older card sets, "It has always been my feeling that if you find one, you'll probably find another."

Evans said his card was in Excellent condition, although it was stamped "CANCELLED" on the back and had two punch holes in it, probably indicating the promotional card was sent back to the company, along with the rest of the set, to be redeemed for either a baseball or fielder's glove (three complete sets). Sets would be returned along with the gifts, the cards promised.

For years many assumed the caramel company didn't issue a card #16, purposely duping Depression-era youngsters into buying more caramels, hoping to find a card that didn't exist. But Evans revealed the Lindstrom card had been owned by a farmer in Illinois, who sold it to another party, who in turn sold the card to Evans.

The third edition of the Sports Collectors Digest Standard Catalog of Baseball cards lists the card at $25,000 in Near Mint condition.

* * *

The primary function of any newspaper or magazine is to keep its readers informed about current events and issues, and in Sports Collectors Digest's case, new products. This chapter provides a chronological look at the newsworthy events in the hobby, as reported in the pages of SCD.

SCD readers made Lou Gehrig their top choice.

In 1975, Lou Gehrig topped the balloting in Coffin Corner columnist John Stirling Jr.'s survey of SCD readers regarding baseball's all-time team. Stirling asked readers to select a 25-man baseball team plus a manager. Ninety responses were tabulated, with 174 players receiving at least one vote.

"In addition to picking their all-time team, many of the collectors sent along other ballots, such as for all-time mascot, stadium, announcer, National Anthem singer, groundskeeper, trainer, sponsor, spring training city, scandal, etc., so you can see that it certainly has been a long winter for some collectors," Stirling wrote in his April 15, 1975, column.

Players who had at least five votes were: Pitchers — Walter Johnson 83, Christy Mathewson 73, Sandy Koufax 68, Lefty Grove 54, Bob Feller 54, Warren Spahn 51, Cy Young 47, Pete Alexander 46, Carl Hubbell 29, Satchel Paige 23, Hoyt Wilhelm 23, Bob Gibson 21, Dizzy Dean 18, Eddie Plank 16, Whitey Ford 14, Rube Waddell 12, Mike Marshall 9, Kid Nichols 9, Ed Walsh 7, Elroy Face 7, Juan Marichal 6, Three Finger Brown 6 and Nolan Ryan 6.

Infielders receiving votes — Lou Gehrig 87, Honus Wagner 80, Rogers Hornsby 76, Pie Traynor 64, Stan Musial 54, Brooks Robinson 53, Jimmy Foxx 30, Eddie Collins 25, George Sisler 23, Nap Lajoie 23, Jackie Robinson 21, Ernie Banks 19, Charlie Gehringer 18, Frankie Frisch 14, Luke Appling 14, Eddie Mathews 13, Joe Cronin 12, Luis Aparicio 9, Maury Wills 6, Arky Vaughn 5, Rabbit Maranville 5 and Cap Anson 5.

Outfielders receiving votes — Babe Ruth 85, Ty Cobb 81, Willie Mays 69, Ted Williams 68, Hank Aaron 67, Joe DiMaggio 51, Tris Speaker 39, Mickey Mantle 26, Roberto Clemente 17, Joe Jackson 10, Mel Ott 8, Harry Heilmann 6, Frank Robinson 5 and Sadaharu Oh 3.

Catchers receiving votes — Mickey Cochrane 48, Bill Dickey 38, Johnny Bench 29, Roy Campanella 25, Josh Gibson 19, Yogi Berra 19, Gabby Hartnett 6, Ray Schalk 5 and Smoky Burgess 5.

Managers receiving votes — Connie Mack 12, John McGraw 12, Casey Stengel 8, Joe McCarthy 8 and Walter Alston 7.

In 1976, many collectors also voiced their opinions about a Goudey and Diamond Star reprint set which wasn't marked as being reprinted. "Letters and calls continue to come in — all unanimous in their opinion that issuance of the set without the reprint label is a needless risk that could easily have been avoided," wrote SCD Editor John Stommen in the March 15, 1976, issue.

"Dr. Dan Turner called from New York very concerned about the overall harm that issuance of the set can cause and reported that he had informed the prestigious Antique Trader paper of the fact and that publication has agreed to warn dealers of the possible appearance of these cards.

"It is good to see that hobbyists are 'up in arms' over this particular issue. Evidence is clearly present that many hobbyists DO CARE about the future of sports collecting," Stommen wrote.

In a letter to the editor in the March 31, 1976, issue, reader Tom Tuschak presented the other side of the story. "As one of the people advertising the Goudey reprint set in your paper I feel that it is time to answer some of the criticism that several people have seen fit to toss at the issuer of the set, Charles Brooks.

"When the idea of the sets was first conceived it was agreed that the word reprint was to appear on the back of the card. The months went by and we waited and waited for the printer to give us the finished product. When the cards finally came the word reprint had been left off, much to our surprise. We knew that the quality of the cards would cause some eyebrows to raise but we felt that the 'fuzzy' tone of the front of the card was enough to tell it from the real thing.

"We have since had a second printing of the set and instead of reprint stamped on the card the thickness of the paper used has been reduced from 24 point to 15 point, which we feel should bring an end to the 'problem' of fakes once and for all. For all those that have inquired, a second and a third set of 32 are in the works and will be made available very soon," Tuschak wrote.

Andy Waldman wrote in his May 15, 1976, Sport Talk column, "the biggest news to hit the hobby this year has been the Goudey reprint set, as everyone knows...Many beginners, like myself, for example, would not know the difference between an original and a reprint just by looking at the card. The word reprint, or some other thing, should have been issued on the cards before they were distributed to collectors, or anyone, for that matter. Not only do you have people selling reprints as originals, but the people holding the originals might have trouble finding any buyers now, with the controversy going on. About the only bright side of this mess is that it should serve as a lesson for other collectors issuing reprints."

Dealer Wilfred F. Jonske, Detroit, Mich., offered his solution to the problem. "On all of the Goudey reprints he sells he is stamping the world REPRINT in 1/4" high red letters to designate that the card is a reprint," SCD reported in its May 31, 1976, issue. Jonske added that he didn't think the stamp could be erased without noticeably damaging the card, which would, in turn, arouse suspicion as to what was done to it.

Chuck Brooks' solution to the issue was reported in the June 15, 1976, SCD. His subsequent 32-card reprint set was clearly marked Reprint 123, and the backs were done in black ink rather than the original green ink.

"The first set of 32 cards, as you recall, caused a good deal of controversy in the hobby because the cards were 'too good' — that is, they so closely resembled the originals that the possibility existed for future chicanery. This newest series leaves no possibility for such thinking...It has been said that the emergence of reprinted items on the market shouldn't cause too much concern because the true collector can generally tell the difference between an original and a reproduction. But how easy it is to do away with any possibility of cards being sold as reprints just by adding that simple word," Brooks wrote.

* * *

Even the hobby's granddaddy card of them all, the T206 Honus Wagner, was subject to being faked. In the May 31, 1976, SCD, Dick Reuss offered his theory, which, one might say, does hold water, on why the Wagner card he found was a fake.

New T206 Wagner Card Turns Out To Be A Fake

By Dick Reuss

The "new" rare T206 tobacco card of Honus Wagner, discovered late last fall by Tom Wickman, Bob Rathgeber and myself, has turned out out to be a "fake" after all. This conclusion is based on my own further investigation of the physical properties of the card and not on any hypothetical arguments advanced by critics of our find.

The card is a composite of the E95 Wagner, front and back, with a Piedmont back glued to the back of the former. The two sections were glued together unusually skillfully, leaving no out-of-the-ordinary seam marks. (All T206 style cards are ply products in that they are reprised of at least two layers of paper glued together in the factory.)

Two sets of government paper experts had examined the card and pronounced it authentic in one case and "probably genuine" in the other. When we displayed the card at the Indianapolis convention in February, about 80 percent of the advanced collectors who viewed it accepted it as real, another 10 percent were openly skeptical, and the rest offered no opinion. I personally remained convinced the card was real until two weeks ago.

Meanwhile, a number of people challenged the card's authenticity based on its slight variations in format and the reputed history of the T206 issue. For example, a number of collectors pointed to the word "Natl" after the Pittsburgh team designation next to Wagner's name as an indication the card could not be from T206, but was instead of E95 origins. Some declared it impossible for Wagner to have been issued with a Piedmont back or in the "350" series.

Surprising at this late date, yes, but by no means impossible as far as I was — and am — concerned. In spite of our Wagner card's clearly non-genuine character now, I still flatly reject all arguments similar to the above as lacking substance, or moot, since conclusive evidence concerning the production history of T and E cards proving or disproving the card's validity is lacking.

For example, the word "Natl" on the face obviously could be explained by the fact that an E95 photo plate (including the name and the team designation underneath) was combined by the printer with a cigarette back; the presumption that Wagner could not have been issued on a Piedmont back or in the 350 series is simply a hypothesis, not a fact. Isn't it possible, to cite a counter-hypothesis, that T206 and E95, similar in format and design in many respects, were manufactured by the same printer who for whatever reason mixed a caramel Wagner portrait with a cigarette back?

My point is we simply don't know the printing and distribution histories of most cards, especially back in 1910, nor what sorts of errors, variations and experimental creations were produced, then destroyed (?) in the manufacturing process.

What's more, nobody has really tried to find out. Instead we take it on blind faith that there was only one T206 Wagner since thus far we have seen only the one portrait pose, much as we presume on the basis of what we have experienced, but do not know for a fact — that there are only 29 cards in the Dan Dee regional baseball set instead of 30.

Logic and the American preference for order and symmetry suggests that there ought to have been at least a 'drawing board' plan for an action pose of Wagner (since most of the stars in T206 were issued in both portrait and action views) as well as well as for a 30th Dan Dee player. Certainly the serious possibility even now should not be ruled out in the case of Wagner, since Bill Mastro recently acquired — and then sold — a T206 proof card (blank back) of Eddie Collins batting — another picture of a superstar from the same set previously unreported.

Except for the frustration and anxiety it causes collectors who already have "complete" T206 sets, why is it so unreasonable to accept the notion of a second Wagner card?

OK, so what led me to the positive conclusion that the "new" Wagner was a "fake?" The answer simply is soaking the card in water, an absurdly easy test suggested by a conversation with Cliff Lambert, an Ironton, Ohio, collector, at the Indianapolis convention. (All chemical tests, we were told, would have destroyed the card itself.)

At breakfast one morning, Lambert mentioned that he had acquired a similar type of card in a collection purchased some time before from an Arkansas man. The cards were all pasted in an album, and in order to get them out, Lambert soaked them in water. The 60-year-old glue used to hold the front and back of the Wagner card failed to hold together and Lambert found himself the proud owner of a disintegrated E95 Wagner composite worth nothing to anybody. He gave his "rare" find to a neighborhood kid.

The possibility of our own Wagner find being a composite of course was present in our minds from the very beginning, hence our unusual efforts to determine the card's authenticity by consulting paper experts, etc. Until I talked with Lambert, however, no one to my knowledge had suggested soaking the card as a test, particularly since it wasn't glued to anything. In fact, Frank Nagy and others stated that I ought not to "experiment" with the card in such fashion, but I finally decided go ahead anyway in the interest of establishing the card's legitimacy as fully as possible.

Soaking the card might not prove it authentic any more than previously, but if the card fell apart that would be ample evidence that it indeed was a phony. I have, after all, soaked hundreds of T206 cards out of albums with no damage to the cards themselves; if the Wagner card was real it ought to easily sustain the water test, even in its present marginal (fair) condition.

When I removed the Wagner item from the water after allowing it to soak for a half hour, I found that the glue had loosened sufficiently in one corner, already worn, for me to catch a glimpse of the E95 back inside the ply. Even more conclusively, once the card was wet the caramel back print showed right through the Piedmont cigarette paper since the latter was so thin. Much like invisible ink, the E95 back "disappeared" once the card dried.

My guess is that the composite was "manufactured" by some collector 50 or more years ago. It seems likely anyway, given the worn and stained appearance of the card, and total absence from the hobby scene insofar as we could determine its personal history. Wagner was perhaps the premiere player of his era as far as public adulation went, and no doubt it was as frustrating to collectors then as now to have nearly every player but the best or most famous current individual in his collection. There certainly is no evidence to suggest that the card was deliberately created as a counterfeit to defraud anybody. Someone just did an unusually good job creating a "homemade" Wagner for himself.

So, our "valuable" card is no more, at least not in terms of big money. However, we probably won't be giving the card away to any neighborhood kid. Perhaps some collector will want to buy the card as a historic — non-authentic — Americana souvenir. But probably we will opt to keep the card ourselves as a relic of a memorable sports hobby experience. — Dick Reuss

* * *

Reprints and fakes were hobbyists' early concerns, but the May 15, 1977, SCD posed another concern — the criminal element. In one of its first cops-and-robbers stories, SCD reported that collector Tom Koppa, from Texas, was offering a reward for information regarding the whereabouts of several of his albums of quality autographed gum cards he said were stolen from a card convention in Indianapolis. Koppa said he was missing Topps, Bowman, Post and tobacco cards of players such as Warren Spahn, Yogi Berra, Willie Mays, Sandy Koufax, Stan Musial, Whitey Ford, Rube Marquard, Luke Appling and several other Hall of Famers.

But the hobby press also recognized the good guys in the hobby, too. The July 15, 1977, SCD paid tribute to Charles (Buck) Barker of St. Louis, Mo. Barker, one of the hobby's best-known, best-loved and most knowledgeable in the field of baseball cards and postcards, won the third annual Frank Jock Memorial Award, sponsored by Bob Jaspersen's Sport Fan magazine. The award, an engraved plaque given annually to the collector voted number one for contributions to the hobby, honors the memory of a pioneer collector who died in 1968 in Kezar Falls, Maine.

A collector since 1922, Barker, an authority on card issues and baseball postcards, was the associate editor of the American Card Catalog and had written many articles about baseball cards for various hobby magazines. Other 1976 candidates included H.R. Shapley, George Miller, George Martin, Dan Even and Mike Bondarenko. Previous winners were Don Schlaff of Lincoln Park, Mich., and Frank Nagy of Grosse Ile, Mich.

Another fan favorite was emerging on the scene in 1977, too, a character nicknamed after Big Bird, a creature who lives on Sesame Street. "Judging from dealers, Mark Fidrych seems to be the most popular player in the 1977 set. Seems that many dealers are saving him, this being his first full photo on a card or selling him as a star," reported Andy Waldman in his Dec. 15, 1977, Sport Talk column.

But, while Fidrych was generating interest in the hobby in 1977 after his successful 19-9 rookie season in 1976, and drawing national publicity for his antics on the mound, the national press picked up on another story which put the hobby in a bad light, again. The April 15, 1978, SCD cited an Associated Press story about a Jerry West basketball jersey being stolen from a display at the Basketball Hall of Fame in Springfield, Mass.

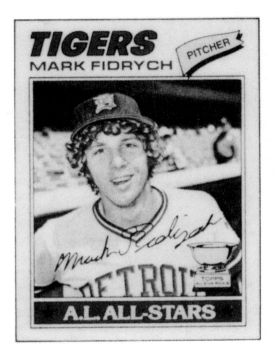

Mark Fidrych generated tremendous interest in 1977.

That same SCD issue cited a United Press International story from Ft. Lauderdale, Fla., regarding jersey thefts from the New York Mets and Philadelphia Phillies from their spring training quarters. Although the 46 Mets shirts and 25 Phillies uniforms were not recovered at the time of arrest in March, a suspect was charged with possession of stolen property and jailed after "discarded coat hangers belonging to the club were found. Two bus shipping tickets were also found," SCD reported.

SCD later reported in its Nov. 30, 1978, issue that a dispatch from Clearwater, Fla., reported "Baseball fever has earned a 33-year-old California man 60 days in jail and a $1,500 fine for stealing 31 jerseys from the Phillies during spring training earlier this year. And sentencing by Pinellas Circuit Judge John Andrews could be only the beginning of a losing streak for Warren Winkler of Los Angeles. St. Petersburg police officers, sitting in the rear of the courtroom, interrupted proceedings to serve Winkler with a warrant for his arrest for allegedly stealing 47 baseball jerseys from the New York Mets training camp in the spring as well."

Photographer Mel Bailey, Riverside, Calif., also captured the negative aspect of sports collecting with his Nov. 30, 1978, SCD cover photo of Chicago White Sox third baseman Eric Soderholm at bat during the team's season finale at California. Soderholm is wearing an Angels batting helmet; the White Sox's helmets were stolen the first night of the series. A Bailey photo inside the issue also shows New York Yankee slugger Reggie Jackson struggling to keep his batting helmet from a fan during a World Series victory celebration.

The preceding stories, although negative and few and far between, did however, illustrate there were interests in other collectibles besides baseball cards. And there was an interest in collectibles from other sports, too. But back to card collecting, and the woes thereof. In his Dec. 15, 1978, Sport Talk column, Andy Waldman lamented about how hard it is becoming to complete Topps sets from 1968-1973, due to the number of star cards, scarcity and the higher prices on the last series cards in those years.

"The one that comes to mind right away is the 1970 No. 660 Johnny Bench. This is the number one card that collectors are finding hardest to obtain. It is not included among the star and superstar cards in dealer's albums, but it's in a class itself. Also, the 1972 No. 695 Rod Carew has become a prize for those holding one and a headache for those needing it," Waldman wrote.

However, Waldman could find consolation in schedule collecting. In 1978 there were more than 500 variations of Major League Baseball team schedules. "This is certainly a banner year for baseball schedule collectors as there are a record number of different variations of schedules to collect. Some teams have more than 10 variations and each day seems to turn up a new one...A few years ago SCD ran a listing of all schedule collectors. Since then schedule collecting has grown to an enormous level whereby many collectors are joining every day because of the cheapness and popularity of the pocket schedule," he wrote in his Aug. 15, 1978, column.

Two months into the 1979 baseball season, John R. Goldberg, in his May 15, 1979, Observations column, expressed his disappointment that the 1979 Topps baseball set didn't have rookie trophy cards, or an A.L. All-Star card for shortstop Fred Patek. In addition to the prospects cards, there were several players making their first card appearances, including Johnny Sutton, Shane Rawley, Mike Parrott, Bob Welch, Mike Proly, Gary Serum, Roger Erickson, Ozzie Smith, John Henry Johnson, Bob Horner, and many others, Goldberg noted.

Goldberg also shared his feelings about autographs. "There seem to be more and more forgeries popping up. I've heard of collectors with certain peculiarities — recently, I heard of one who only wants autographs signed in blue Sharpie! Speaking of Sharpies, I've found that the purple one stands out the best, with blue next, and red last (especially when the pen is old)...I feel that the action in 'selling' Mickey Mantle's autograph at $10 a pop at the recent New York show is setting a bad precedent, as well as a high price for Mantle autographs. If a player cannot be persuaded to appear and autograph, either for nothing or for a reasonable honorarium, don't ask him. At least, that's my opinion," he wrote.

In a letter to the editor in the June 15, 1979, SCD, Jerry Ahrens warned readers about what he considers "the latest rip-off" — chain letters asking readers to send 25 basketball cards to the first name on the list, to remove that name and then put theirs on the bottom. By sending between 5-25 copies to friends, as little as five letters will bring back 3,000 cards in only a few weeks, claimed the letter Ahrens received.

It's illegal, and impractical, said Ahrens, who noted that "to send out the minimum of five letters would entail mailing 125 cards. At an average of 3 cents per card, that is $3.75, plus another 75 cents for postage, and it brings the cost to $4.50. Stringing that out to 25 letters it would then cost $22.50."

Ahrens concluded that "after speaking to friends who are collectors and others who are not, I find that none of these people answer such letters. At that rate, the expense is too high and the rewards too low. Only a fool or a compulsive gambler with the desire to lose would fall for this type of rip-off. Unfortunately, there are two many rip-off artists around. Luckily, with the large number of highly decent collectors and dealers in the hobby, they are in the vast minority."

And in his Aug. 15, 1979, Cartophilic News Notes, Steve Freedman provided another caveat to collectors. "Topps is on the lookout for uncut sheets disappearing from its distribution points. These items are not legitimately entering the collectors' market and hobbyists should be leery of these items," he wrote.

Hobby awareness continued to increase in the public's eye, changing the public's opinion about collectors, wrote Roland Chapdelaine in his Aug. 15, 1979, Chap's Chatter column. "People no longer consider it odd for mature adults to collect baseball cards. In fact, baseball cards are referred to, from time to time, in movies and on TV shows," he wrote.

"Usually during a detective story there's the scene where Augie and Joey, childhood pals who now travel different roads, are in a dingy warehouse; and it becomes increasingly obvious to the audience, and to Joey, why Augie has brought him here. Augie reaches into his jacket for his revolver as Joey starts moving away, pleading, 'Oh, No Auge, not me! This is Augie. You remember how we wuz kids together, don't you Augie? We used ta sit on the stoop tradin baseball cards; remember Augie?' Augie remembers. Joey always saved his Yankees and Dodgers, trading only his Browns and Senators. Blam! 'Sorry Joey,'" Chapdelaine wrote, also noting Sweet Caporals were used as props in the movie "Pride of the Yankees" and Topps cards were used in an "Alfred Hitchcock Presents" episode entitled "The Doubtful Doctor."

The Wall Street Journal mentioned baseball cards, too, as Steve Freedman noted in his Sept. 15, 1979, Cartophilic News Notes column, referring to the Aug. 6, 1979, Journal story entitled "If you never made a buck out of baseball, take a look at those bubble gum cards."

"Quoted in the article, which will surely cause greater price rises because of it, are the 1954 Topps Hank Aaron — $100; 1952 Topps Mickey Mantle — $680, with a printed prediction of $1,200 for this card; 1959 Topps Lew Burdette error card — $2; 1969 Aurelio Rodriguez error card — 50 cents," Freeman wrote. Also featured, he noted, were Hartland baseball statues, with prices between $55-$300 each.

"I have already heard of one businessman in Philadelphia who has located a batch of Hartland statues in his attic as a direct result of this article. In addition, a walk-in shopper at a recent mall show told me he pulled an old shoebox out of his attic as a result of the Wall Street Journal article.

"Another card mentioned in the Journal for price speculation is the 1970 Topps Johnny Bench, currently at $10. A corresponding price explanation on this card states 'in anticipation of the catcher's induction into the Baseball Hall of Fame and a sharp increase in the demand for his cards.' It was also pointed out that investments in cards are comparable to the stock market where prices are bid up according to supply and demand, and that baseball cards have fared better than stocks!" Freedman wrote.

The demand for cards was growing, and a new company, the Fleer Corp., the company which claimed to have invented bubble gum in 1928, had been waiting in the wings for more than two decades, hoping to break Topps' stranglehold on the market.

Bob Bartosz, of Pennsauken, N.J., informed SCD about Fleer's plans and that the company's president, Donald Peck, had met in New York with Marvin Miller, executive director of the players' association. Peck, the Aug. 31, 1980, SCD, reported, expressed confidence that Fleer would soon be licensed by the players' association to make and sell baseball cards; photographers would be hired to take color pictures of all 700 major leaguers and statisticians would be hired.

The story Bartosz sent SCD quoted Peck as saying "We can't wait to compete, we're very excited about the opportunity because it's been a long time coming."

Peck, the story said, also praised Topps' performance in the card market, saying, "Topps has done a doggone good job with baseball trading cards." He added, "They've developed the marketing model. We think there are things that can be done better and we're going to try them. They would dearly love to know what our next move is."

Peck, the story said, expected to sell "less than Topps and more than Topps thinks." Fleer would be expected to receive a deal similar to the deal the players' association has with Topps — the players' association gets 8 percent of the first $4 million in sales and 10 percent thereafter, SCD reported.

In his Wirt's Words column Aug. 31, 1980, Wirt Gammon credited U.S. District Judge Clarence Newcomer in Philadelphia for reaching a verdict against Topps for "monopoly of the bubblegum baseball card market," although triple damage amounted to only $3.

Fleer, based in Philadelphia, had "filed suit in 1975 as a result of Topps' policy since 1966 of signing players to contracts for exclusive use of their pictures on cards. In 1974 Fleer tried and failed to win approval of the Major League Baseball Players Association to market large satin baseball patches. Judge Newcomer's ruling was that Topps and the MLBPA violated the anti-trust laws. He ordered the latter to consider carefully any applications it receives for licenses, to enter into at least one new one by January 1 and to give Fleer first shot. His reason for the small nominal award of damages was that it was 'guess-work' to determine Fleer's losses," Gammon wrote.

Steve Freedman, in his Aug. 31, 1980, Cartophilic News Notes, said healthy competition to sign baseball players for the purpose of issuing baseball cards would perhaps mean "we have entered a new era or taken a 'good' step backwards to the days of Topps vs. Bowman vs. Leaf. In other words, we have a choice and the manufacturers will have to compete for our business by issuing the best product for the lowest possible price."

Topps would be the sole producer of cards for the last time in 1980, but was prepared for the strong sales heading into competition in 1981. Freedman, in his Sept. 15, 1980, column, shared the results of Topps Chewing Gum's annual report for the fiscal year ending March 1, 1980, quoting the report as saying "During the fiscal year which ended March 1, 1980, Topps incurred a huge loss of $8,850,000, or $4.98 per share...Baseball bubblegum cards started strongly this season and appear to be headed for record sales. Football cards will be the second item in the sports line we will issue this year and they are expected to continue the improved performance of this line when they are marketed during the second quarter."

Although Fleer paved the way for competition against Topps, Donruss, a Memphis-based firm which made "Super Bubble" and was best known for its cards based on television shows, became the first new entry into the baseball card printing production field by signing an agreement with the Major League Baseball Players Association late in September.

Donruss, noted SCD Editors John and Phil Stommen in their Our Hobby column Nov. 15, 1980, planned to distribute cards via the mail order route. The two wondered if this meant collectors would be able to purchase sets directly, or would they have to purchase cases?

"Donruss has not announced the number of cards in their planned set, but the company feels it will be an effective force in improvement of the baseball card collecting hobby," the Stommens wrote.

Collectors, who would enter the 1981 collecting season anticipating improvement in card quality, would close out the 1980 collecting season dreaming of dollar figures. Money Magazine, noted Tom Gregg in his Dec. 31, 1980, Off the Top of My Head column, listed the most valuable "heavy hitters" in baseball cards: 1. American Tobacco Honus Wagner, issued 1909, $12,500; 2. Goudey Napoleon Lajoie, issued 1934, $6,500; 3. American Tobacco Eddie Plank, issued 1919, $5,000; 4. Topps Jim Konstanty standup, issued 1951, $2,500; 5.

Topps Mickey Mantle, issued 1952, $1,700; 6. Bowman Ted Williams, issued 1954, $1,075; 7. American Tobacco Sherry Magee, issued 1919, $950; 8. Topps Willie Mays, issued 1953, $700; 9. Topps Henry Aaron, issued 1954, $300; 10. Topps Roger Maris Yankees variation, issued 1967, $300.

"Thanks to much similar sensationalisitic news coverage (invariably mentioning the Wagner and the Mantle cards), the general public now thinks that any 10 year-old-card in any condition ought to be worth at least a few bills. Which means you can offend people but good merely by offering a fair, full Beckett price for stuff they've dredged up from the attic," Gregg wrote.

Debby Jennings, sports information director for the University of Tennessee's women's teams, informed SCD of what was perhaps the first set of cards issued for women's athletics. The 144-card set, according to the Stommens in their Feb. 28, 1981, column, pictures staff members and athletes from basketball, volleyball, swimming and diving, track and tennis, with special attention given to Olympians and Hall of Famers.

Early reactions on the 1981 card sets from newcomers Fleer and Donruss and mainstay Topps were mixed, reported Ted Taylor in the March 20, 1981, SCD.

"At this time there is no clearcut winner, but Topps seems to be coming off in third place among collecting consumers. Another trend seems to be the willingness of hobbyists to forgive mistakes made by Fleer and Donruss and to scold Topps for not doing anything new or innovative this time out," wrote Taylor, who quoted several readers who responded to a readers poll:

"Obviously, the question is who will survive and who will succumb," wrote Elliott Irving from Farmville, Va. "It would be nice if the hobby could support three major sets, but I have my doubts that this will occur."

"I would pick the Donruss card as the most attractive," wrote Robert Zollo, from West Babylon, N.Y., "The Topps and Fleer cards look almost identical, the only difference being that Topps has a silly hat with the team name. Frankly, I believe that the baseball cap looks ridiculous and am not impressed with it on the (Topps) card."

"Who wants a silly looking baseball cap pulling your eyes down to the bottom of the card?" asked Jim Smedley of Baltimore, Md., "and who wants a large 'Topps' printed on your cards? I believe that Donruss has made an appeal to the younger collectors (which is where the profits are made). First off, a youngster does not particularly care about heavy card stock or excellence in coloring. Chances are that a less expensively produced card by Donruss will mean that they can sell their cards cheaper and that means more will be available for a youngsters' money," he said.

Irving added "under the circumstances I don't believe that any collector is expecting anything miraculous from Donruss this year. Actually I've been more impressed by this card than I thought I would be."

David Hunt, of Elkview, W.Va., made his feelings known about Donruss: "I don't plan to buy this set for the simple reason I don't like the quality. I also don't like the multiple poses of players. One card for each player is enough."

Bud Lynch, from Winchester, Mass., was angry with Donruss. "Somebody should take a collection and buy them a new blade for their cutting machine," he wrote.

Irving praised Fleer's quality. "The company's experience in sports cards should help them even though this is a return after many years absence from baseball...the Fleer card seems to be the one I am favoring at this point. Fleer's is a much sturdier stock, the front picture is sharp and is a much neater card."

Smedley added, "Fleer has attempted to produce a 'professional' card. The true collector or hobbyist will value the Fleer cards. The neatly-written team name inside the baseball border adds a touch of art to the bottom of the card."

Zollo remained a traditionalist in his support of Topps. "I guess I'll stick with Topps as my favorite and let a few years pass before I pass judgement on the other two. Who knows, Topps may have enough muscle to push them both out of business as they did with Bowman and Berk Ross."

"I think Topps will be the most active set on the market," added Hunt. "Topps has already proven it can turn out top-quality cards. I also like the fact that it is the largest set out."

Smedley summed up the competitive field for 1981 by saying, "I've got a feeling it's like picking a pennant winner. You're so sure of the winner and the loser but when the season is over you couldn't have been more wrong. We'll see, huh??"

 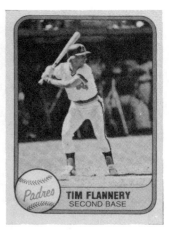

Kurt Bevacqua and Tim Flannery were victims of reversed negatives for the 1981 Fleer set.

In its second run in 1981, Fleer, correcting errors made in its first run, reversed photos for card No. 382 Kurt Bevacqua, to have the "P" on his Pirates cap facing correctly, and card No. 493, Tim Flannery, who was now shown batting from the correct side of the plate. "Padres" on his shirt was also now running in the right direction, reported Ted Taylor in the March 31, 1981, issue.

The second run also had the correct spelling on card No. 436 Darryl Evans, and an altering in the ink color on the word "Royals" on Hal McRae's card, No. 42.

"The anxiously-awaited second printing of Fleer cards has hit the market with the double-edged results of driving up the per-pack and per-box price," Taylor wrote. In making the show circuit, Taylor had seen prices range from first-run Fleer counter boxes selling from a low of $10 each at King of Prussia, Pa., to a high of $40 each at Alexandria, Va.

* * *

In the April 30, 1981, SCD, Taylor called for end to the preoccupation with "error" cards.

Enough With This Preoccupation Let's Get On With It

By Ted Taylor

OK, that's enough. Let's cut it out now and get on to something else.

What I'm referring to is the absolute preoccupation with "error cards" this year and the total domination that topic has had in our conscious, semi-conscious and unconscious states of being since late January.

Sure, it was fun for a while. It was good, too, for the hobby to have instant collectibles attached to a brand new issue and it made everybody pay more attention than usual to just what those new little works of art we all collect really said and what they really looked like.

But enough is enough and it really is time that we move along now to other topics and stop this absolute compulsion we feel to dub anything that isn't quite jake in our eyes as an "error."

I guess it was the phone call I got recently telling me that the color shading in the word "Royals" on a card differed from one press run to another, hence it must be an "error," and wasn't I excited. But it did get me to thinking about what was really going on here and it dawned on me that I was reading about nothing but errors in all the hobby publications. It struck me that a newcomer to the hobby could easily get the impression that the major companies producing the card sets this year were staffed with incompetent clods, guys who just couldn't get it flat right and who really didn't care about what their product said or looked like. — Ted Taylor.

* * *

Two teachers from Wayne City, Ill., were attempting to give collectors a voice in their hobby by forming a national group, the National Card Collectors Association, reported Ted Taylor in the March 31, 1981, SCD. The two, David Beehn and Stephen White, announced their intentions in a series of advertisements purchased in the hobby press.

"The NCCA feels it is time for the hobby to be organized and to look out for what is best for the collector. After all, the collector is the hobby. Even though there are collectors of all ages and we would like to have them all as members, our main interest is in the younger collectors. The hobby is getting very big and commercialized, and look what has happened to Christmas. Where do these youngsters, that we as educators work with every day, have a voice in what is going on? We feel with a strong organization behind them, they would have a voice," Beehn and White said.

As an example of a change that could be made for the better, a united base of collectors' could alert the card companies that they were "depriving today's youth of the opportunity to renew the collecting excitement every few weeks of the summer by turning out their entire sets at once," they said.

The two, realizing previous attempts to form a national group had failed, said times were changing; the hobby was now ready to have a need filled. "We are not professional organizers and we are sure we have made mistakes, and will make more," they wrote. "But, as long as we put the collector first in our thoughts and efforts, we are sure it will come through that the collectors' interest is our foremost concern. We want our sons to enjoy the hobby as we have and are sure many fathers feel the same."

The NCCA's statement of purpose was to "advocate the collecting of cards for pleasure and educational benefits. A secondary consideration is that of investment, the profits from which are realized over a long term based on wise selection and intelligent purchases of the best conditioned cards."

To secure those future profits, Ted Taylor, in the April 30, 1981, SCD, advocated another idea whose time had come — hobby insurance.

"One of the unfortunate aspects of the tremendous growth of our hobby is that its increasing value has made it attractive to society's shady element, and the day is rapidly approaching when any collection of substance should be insured," he wrote.

"While many of the larger collections in the hobby are currently insured, it is likely that the great majority of them are not and in the case of a major fire, theft or other loss the owner would be reimbursed for only a small fraction of the true value," he wrote, noting standard homeowners policies have limits and provide for low pay backs on collectibles, such as a maximum loss on a stamp collection is $500. Additional "floaters" coverage, he wrote, provides coverage ranging from 30 cents to $1.60 per $100 of value.

Thus, the Cornell and Finkelmeier Insurance Agency in Wapakoneta, Ohio, created the original "Sports Memorabilia Insurance Policy," underwritten by the St. Paul Fire & Marine Insurance Co. According to Thomas S. Finkelmeier, "the policy is designed especially for the dealer and/or collector covering sports memorabilia including, but not limited to, baseball and football cards, non-sport cards, autographs, uniforms, programs and all sports collectibles along with the books, pages and mountings."

"There is no deductible except for theft and then you pay only the first $100," he added. Collectors, Taylor wrote, select a "blanket limit based on your inventory. You schedule only those individual cards and items with values over $250 each and the policy also covers 10 percent of your 'blanket inventory' in transit or at shows or conventions. Scheduled items means that if you value your 1952 Topps Mantle card at $2,000 and it is stolen that is the amount you get back (because you paid your premium on that amount).

"On unscheduled inventory you get current 'market value' in case of loss. As you acquire material you must keep the insurance company advised, however, the policy automatically extends up to 10 percent of your inventory for additional acquisitions," Taylor wrote, noting Finkelmeier pointed out that the policy "requires that you insure your collection at 100 percent of its market value and that you maintain an adequate inventory to substantiate loss."

Taylor also quoted the Journal of American Insurance as suggesting collectors have their collections professionally appraised, and photographed or video taped, while keeping a copy of the negatives or video at an off-premise site such as in a safe-deposit box.

* * *

Actually protecting the cards themselves drew questions from readers concerned with storing cards in plastic sheets, as Taylor noted in a May 31, 1981, story.

An Editorial Viewpoint
PVC "Crisis" Casts Doubt
On Plastic Sheets,
Seems To Sell Magazines

By Ted Taylor, SCD News Editor

The recent article in a nationally distributed magazine entitled "Card-Killing Album Pages: Is PVC Destroying Your Cards?" sent waves of panic throughout our hobby, shed doubt on the safety of our beloved card collections and, ultimately sold copies of the new magazine for the publisher.

The volume of mail received regarding the evils of Polyvinyl Chloride (PVC) indicates a real worry on the part of collectors who now have cause to question the wisdom of using plastic sheets and exactly what to do next? Take all cards out of plastic sheets? Buy a specific brand? Or, just what?

One of the nation's largest distributors of plastic sheets for baseball cards told us that while there may be some basis for allegations as they apply to other hobbies the charge that they are destroying baseball cards is not only "ridiculous but absolutely irresponsible."

Ted Pina of the Sports Franchise in Callahan, Fla., was disturbed about the magazine article because "all facts relate to experiences with coins and stamps and no facts are given as to damage to cards. The magazine sensationalizes the story and leads readers to believe that great damage has been done to card when, in reality, no proof at all exists."

The key to the problem seems to be in the plastic composition. "All sheets contain PVC," said Pina, a long-time dealer in plastic sheets, "if someone tells you that his sheet doesn't have it, it isn't a plastic sheet."

"We've had 20th Century Plastics do testing for us and they have not come up with anything conclusive with regard to damage to baseball cards," Pina reported.

He also pointed out, however, that there is really no way to tell if any damage will be done to cards 20 to 30 years from now. "You just can't accelerate time tests," he added.

Denny Eckes, a former research chemist and leading hobby author and dealer, points out that time testing is a problem in that you often create abnormal conditions when you try to accelerate the passage of time. "If you create abnormal conditions you often get abnormal results," Eckes commented, "just as you do with rats in laboratories. Stress and long-term climatic conditions as they apply to plastic sheets just cannot be duplicated in a laboratory."

Pina, who estimates that he's sold enough sheets to cover 830 million cards since 1975, has had just one complaint of a damaged card in all that time. "I question the conditions under which the card was damaged," he said, "and I wonder why the seven others made of the same substance were not damaged under the same circumstances."

The card in question was a regional issue that was, in fact, a photograph and the sheet in which it was placed was damp at the time. "I suspect there was a chemical reaction between the photo and the sheet, but I don't think it is a valid example," he said.

Rotman Plastic Sheets of Worcester, Mass., recently took out full page ads in the hobby press to list a 12-point "Statement of Quality" that, among other things, points out that five million sheets have been sold under their specifications and they have not had one single complaint.

Common sense, of course, is a necessity in the use and storage of plastic sheets. Several authorities have pointed out that it isn't reasonable to expect the sheets to stand up to adverse heat or cold and one should not expect to escape damage if they store their sheeted cards in the trunk of their car in the hot summer months and in an unheated attic in the colder climates in the winter.

PVC itself is not the culprit, it is the plasticizers that are used for clarity where a lot of the problems are encountered. "There are no sheets that could be called 100 percent safe," Pina said, "because the conditions under which they are used and stored could make the safest sheet on the market a risk."

Most of the people we spoke with cautioned against "cheap" sheets which may not be as well made as some of the better and more commonly accepted brands on the market. "A good price isn't always a good buy," Pina said.

Hobby shop owner Andy Stoltz of Philadelphia called the article "stupid" and said that he hadn't noticed any drop in plastic sheet sales as a result of it. "It has resulted in a lot of stupid questions, though," he said.

Stoltz, who sells mostly the P.O.P. (Photo Organizer Plus) sheets in his store, added, "I haven't had any complaints at all from people using my sheets. In fact, I have all my own cards in plastic from most of the different manufacturers and haven't noticed any problems either. I did notice one thing, though," he continued, "people are sore at the magazine for printing such an article and I have copies in my store that people won't buy because of that particular article."

Pina, who deals in both wholesale and retail plastic sheets, has noticed a marked increase in mail inquiries as to the safety of the sheets. "I have one customer who has spent well over $1,000 on plastic with me and he wants me to assure him that everything is all right," Pina said, "and my reply to him was that the sheets are safe at this time. What happens in the future is still unknown."

Ironically, Pina's wholesale plastic sheet business has shown a steady gain in the past several months but his retail trade has dropped slightly, a drop he lays at the doorstep of the magazine article.

Hobbyists are generally agitated by the article and in the Spring 1981 issue of the EPSCC newsletter Editor Bob Schmierer says, "damaging and of questionable responsibility is the story on plastic sheets. Their claim that PVC in sheets ruins baseball cards is a very sensationalized approach, with awesome implications, that lacks facts and research."

Elkins Park, Pa., collector/dealer Allan Becker is a long-time user of the sheets and feels the magazine article went "off the deep end" in its article.

"I'll continue to keep my cards in plastic until somebody can show me proof that they are being damaged," Becker commented.

And that seems to be the bottom line.

All evidence and testimony seems to point to the fact that there is no evidence to support the theory that "PVC is destroying your cards" and that most knowledgeable people in the hobby, while maintaining a careful watch on the situation, will continue to buy and use plastic sheets to store and display their cards.

Just as there is no guarantee that someday somebody will prove that milk is bad for you, there is no way of knowing what effects plastic sheets will have on cards, 20, 30 or more years down the road.

We all have to "go" with our best judgement and that seems to be that, unconclusively proven otherwise, we'll stick with plastic sheets.
— Ted Taylor

* * *

Collectors were also inquiring about the restoration of cards. William Sarill, College of Ephemera, Cambridge, Mass., in Reader Reaction, Aug. 31, 1981, informed readers that he's been restoring paper collectibles for some years.

Collectibles he's restored have included comic books; a 12th century illuminated manuscript page (removing tape stains); a 1953 Willie Mays Topps card (rebuilding corners and mending a tear); valuable magazines such as Playboy No. 1 and Weird Tales No. 1; movie posters such as Chaplin's The Kid; lobby cards such as Casablanca and King Kong; movie press books (the exceptionally rare original Frankenstein); and original art work (three pencil drawings by Maxfield Parrish).

Sarill explained the cautious and conservative approach used in restoration is "built upon a foundation of painstaking research, patient experimentation and a dedication to ethical principles. We are proud of our reputation for performing the finest quality work, and we are constantly striving to maintain that reputation. Our staff includes highly-trained professionals who have come to us with backgrounds in archival and in fine arts conservation."

The staff, he said, has achieved a major breakthrough in the restoration of cards — developing a process for the complete removal of first order creases, which are those which do not break the surface of the card and maintain all of the original color. In second order creases, some of the lithographic inks are missing, and the crease shows up as a white line.

"We can now remove all first order creases without a trace. Removal of second order creases involves the same process, but also requires retouching of the missing colors. As a result we will not promise that we can make second order creases completely invisible, although we can come close," he said.

"Now that we've succeeded in removing creases, we've decided to accept work from a larger segment of the card-collecting public. In addition to crease removal, our services include rebuilding corners, filling in holes, removing tape and tape stains, cleaning off dirt and pencil marks, sterilizing mold, mending tears, retouching colors, removing oil and water stains and pen marks, and deacidifying cards to ensure their longevity."

Sarill said his services are definitely not cheap, at a base rate of $30 per hour. Most jobs, he said, take at least an hour or more, so cards worth less than $50 or $75 are probably not worth being restored.

"Nevertheless, we are confident that we can increase the value of certain cards many times, at a price which is reasonable relative to this increase," he concluded.

Meanwhile, Los Angeles Dodgers pitcher Fernando Valenzuela was capturing the hearts of fans and collectors during the 1981 strike-shortened season. As Larry Shenk, in his Aug. 20, 1981, The Baron's Corner column, reported, "Fernando Valenzuela is the biggest pitching splash to hit the majors since Mark (The Bird) Fidrych came on the scene in 1976 with the Detroit Tigers...To say Valenzuela is a hot item is putting it mildly. He's already had a book written about him, he's doing commercials for a soda company in both English and Spanish, there's a record on the market, plus a poster, and two movie studios are negotiating with him on doing a life story."

The baseball strike did cut into collecting, at least of club-issued cards, reported Dan Even in his Aug. 31, 1981, The Postcards and W Corner column.

Fernando Valenzuela captured the hearts of fans in 1981.

"Among the no replies I got during the strike was a nice letter from the Blue Jays that said in part 'Due to the players strike and the drop in fan mail for the players, we were not in need of additional postcards this season.' Thus, no Blue Jays issue. And some teams didn't even bother answering their mail during the strike," Even reported.

Later, Even, in his Jan. 1, 1982, column said, 1981 was "a bad year for postcard and team issue collectors. But it could have been worse.

"The strike forced several clubs — Kansas City, Toronto and Detroit — to cancel their usual sets, while several others — notably Baltimore and the Cardinals — waited until late in the season to issue their sets, and, of course, there were no updates as in past years.

"And even the teams that got their sets out early, such as the Indians and Phillies, didn't bother to add late-season additions as they have in past years. In that respect, the 1981 team issues won't have as many 'hard to get' cards as some of the previous years."

Just about the time the baseball strike was ending and play was set to resume on Aug. 10, the Stommen reign over SCD was ending, too, as the two editors announced in their Aug. 31, 1981, Our Hobby column:

"This column is a little tougher to write than most because after 200 issues (190 regular SCD and 10 SCD Express) it is also our last. We have sold the publications to Krause Publications of Iola, Wis., the publishers of Baseball Cards Magazine as well as many other publications in the hobby field.

"After eight years serving the hobby with its largest publication, both page-wise and in paid circulation, we bow out of the business and the hobby with mixed emotions. It has been fun, but a whale of a lot of work for a small family operation. We'll miss it, but we won't — as you might understand if you are or have been in a similar circumstance.

"The friendships with collectors throughout the country have been priceless and the support you have given us has been terrific. It would be impossible to list everyone who helped so much, but we naturally give special thanks to all who have at anytime contributed editorially and shared their hobby information with all of us, and your subscription and advertising support have been what made the publications possible. We sincerely thank you one and all," they wrote.

In his initial column, the Sept. 20, 1981, Coach's Box, new Editor Bob Lemke assured collectors they need not be alarmed about the sale of SCD to Krause Publications.

"This is the same SCD in a new package. Those among our fellow hobbyists who are not familiar with Krause Publications from our national newsstand magazine Baseball Cards might be understandably a bit concerned that the sports collectors periodical which they made number one in publishing frequency, page count and paid circulation has been sold.

"I think our two unofficial company mottos allay any misgivings you might have on that score. From this issue on, Sports Collectors Digest will be published with these two statements our foremost consideration:

For collectors, by collectors and On time, every time.

"That first motto means SCD is going to continue to be the voice for the hobby. We don't plan any great changes in SCD's content in the future. You've made us number one because you like what you've been reading in these pages for the past eight years. Our company has been publishing magazines, newspapers, books and catalogs for hobbyists since the days a 1952 Topps Mickey Mantle could be bought for a penny with a stick of gum. We've learned that 'you don't mess with success.'"

Lemke concluded by inviting readers to drop him a line if they had any questions. "As a collector of more than 27 years' standing, I'm the guy who's the happiest with the change of ownership for SCD. The only thing I can think of that is better than sitting in my easy chair at home reading SCD is sitting in my office chair creating it," he wrote.

* * *

Although it was an old concept, another refreshing development was also occurring within the hobby, too, as Ted Taylor reported in a Sept. 25, 1981, feature story about swapping cards.

Trading Is Coming Back

By Ted Taylor

While baseball cards are often referred to as "trading" cards, very little of that really has gone on in recent years within the hobby. Now, thanks to the state of the economy and the tight money situation, the pendulum seems to be swinging back toward the trade and away from the cash transaction.

While the Pennsylvania Turnpike hardly seems like a place to swap baseball cards, that's exactly what happened on a Monday night in August when a car driven by hobbyist Mike Galella was the mid vehicle in a five-car crackup just short of the Willow Grove exit.

"We were on the way to the R&B Baseball Auction in Warrington when a chain-reaction collision happened all around us," Galella commented. "Fortunately, while mine was the middle car in the event, we escaped with no damage."

Galella and his passengers, Brian Wolfson and Max Silberman, pulled off to the side of the road to offer assistance and to await the arrival of police. "We saw who did it and how it happened and thought we'd better stick around," Mike said.

After a while, however, the novelty of waiting for the police began to wane so Mike, Brian and Max decided to take advantage of this lull in their activity and began to swap cards among one another. Before long other people involved in the accident had joined in the session and the trades had developed a substantial audience and not a cent, but a considerable number of cards, had changed hands.

Trades consummated, police informed and accident victims accounted for, the trio headed off, again, toward Warrington, but not before Mike had informed the passenger in the lead car as to the value of 1972 Rod Carew and Steve Garvey cards which the latter had recently discovered among his possessions.

"It's amazing how many people are aware of the hobby. You'll never know who you might run into," Galella quipped with tongue firmly in cheek.

Another Pennsylvanian, Bill Bossert, who runs the Mid-Atlantic Coin Exchange in Swarthmore, is approaching the resurgence in trading full speed ahead.

"Trading in the hobby is a new concept," Bossert said, "we've found especially at shows that we can do quite well swapping what other people want for what we want.

"You've got to go with the flow in this hobby," Bill added, and it seems that people today have more material than they have ready cash. "So it makes sense that if they have wants that I can fill and, conversely have material I can use, we should make a trade," he went on.

As a large-scale dealer, Bossert usually has large quantities of recent issues that he is willing to swap for older common cards that he can use to build complete sets.

With superstar mania of the last few years it is amazing how difficult it has become to acquire common cards, especially those issued in the 1960s, an era that, until recently, was regarded with only passing interest.

Now that the rookies of the 1960s (Rose, Stargell, Seaver, Carew, etc.) are nearing the end of careers that will eventually lead them to the Hall of Fame, cards of their early days are getting extremely scarce. With scarcity comes price increases and sill most collectors will tell you that the best way to have a Pete Rose rookie card is as a part of the complete 1963 set. Consequently, cards of Howie Koplitz, Ed Hobaugh, Al Luplow, Ed Bauta and other "who's he?" of 1963 are necessary to round out that particular Topps set.

"The new Squirt (soft drink) sets are plentiful here and we find a lot of trade interest in them in other parts of the country," Bossert explained. "We set unit values on older common cards and then trade accordingly."

The trick, of course, to trading is to make both sides happy with the outcome of the deal. "If a person wants to trade something that I don't particularly need I'd better make sure that I get a two-for-one value out of the deal," he said, "but if he has something I want and I have something he wants, the best trade, then, is value for value." — Ted Taylor

* * *

One SCD reader, Shawna Burkham, Columbus, Ohio, expressed a concern about the value of cards, in particular those being offered in a baseball card starter set offered in the 1981 J.C. Penney Christmas catalog. In the Oct. 23, 1981, Reader Reaction, she wrote:

"As a dealer, I am excited to see that one of the country's largest retailers (J.C. Penney) has chosen to include a baseball card starter set in its Christmas catalog. I do not see this as a threat to us 'little dealers,' but rather as an indication of the kind of growing this hobby has done in recent years.

"Great! So what's the problem? The problem lies in their description of the items offered. For a very modest price, they are offering an assortment of cards, a book, some sheets, etc. What they picture are various late '70s cards, and a group of Goudey, Cracker Jack, T-cards, and other miscellaneous pre-fifties issues. Nowhere in the copy does it mention that these are reprints.

"Now, to those of us who are aware of the value of even the 'commonest' Cracker Jack card, that is no big deal. But to the many mothers, Grandmas, Grandpas and such, who will be ordering for their young collectors, it is misleading. They will have no idea that the cards are reprints of much more valuable originals.

"I don't think that selling these reprints is a problem, but not representing them for what they are is a problem to me. It is obviously too late to do anything about this now, as I doubt Penneys has any intention of recalling who knows how many books. I suppose the best we can do is to educate people, who might be considering ordering them, as to what they are getting.

"It is still a pretty good deal, and an excellent way for a youngster to learn what cards looked like before baseball cards came with that tasty pink stuff that messes up teeth. I just hope no one is disappointed and in turn, 'turns off' our hobby before they get started," she concluded.

As the year drew to a close, Ted Taylor, in a Dec. 18, 1981, recap of the year, noted "both Fleer and Donruss announced their return to the baseball card wars by signing agreements with Marvin Miller and the Players Association to issue 660-card sets each with products other than gum."

On Aug. 23, Fleer and Donruss had been tossed a curve ball when the Third U.S. District Court of Appeals ruled that "things were just fine, thank you, with the state of baseball cards before Judge Clarence Newcomer had allowed the two other companies to compete with Topps, and all things had to revert to before," Ted Taylor recapped in the Dec. 18 story.

"In other words, Topps had the market all to itself again and, despite successful years by all three companies, judicial wisdom had decided that such was not necessary — or even legal — anymore.

"Fleer President Donald Peck was not pleased with the decision and promised to battle 'all the way to the Supreme Court' to resolve the issue," Taylor concluded.

Tom Gregg, in his Nov. 6, 1981, Off the Top of My Head column, summarized reader survey results on the 1981 card sets:

1. Which set (s) did you collect at least 500 cards of in 1981?

Collected Topps — 95.6 percent. Collected Fleer — 92.6 percent. Collected Donruss — 68.1 percent.

2. Did you buy mainly from a dealer or a drugstore? Dealer — 50.3 percent. Drugstore — 44.9 percent. Wholesale Grocer Outlet — 4.8 percent.

3. Did the strike hurt card sales?

Yes, lots — 4.4 percent. Yes, some — 30.4 percent. No, little — 43.5 percent. Not sure — 21.8 percent.

4. Please rank the issues from 1 (best-liked) to 3 (least-liked).

Fleer 71 percent — 1; 26 percent — 2; 3 percent — 3.

Topps 24.6 percent — 1; 47.1 percent — 2; 28.3 percent — 3.

Donruss 4.4 percent — 1; 26.9 percent — 2; 68.7 percent — 3.

5. Did any of the '81 sets make your top five all-time favorite list?

Fleer — 29 percent; Topps — 10.1 percent; Donruss — 1.4 percent.

6. Assuming you didn't collect Donruss, what factor (s) led to this decision? (percent of total respondents)

Didn't want to spend the money to collect three sets — 13.1 percent; Had heard of uneven distribution problems — 20.3 percent; Didn't like the card thinness — 29 percent; Didn't like the card design — 7.2 percent.

7. Were Fleer errors intentional on the first printing?

Yes — 33.3 percent; No — 27.5 percent; Not sure — 39.2 percent.

8. Would you like to see facsimile autographs used?

Always — 14.8 percent; Occasionally — 42.6 percent; Never — 42.6 percent.

Ted Taylor offered readers a preview of what to expect during the 1982 collecting season. In his Jan. 1, 1982, Off the Cuff column, he wrote "the flurry of trades during the recent winter meetings in Hollywood, Fla., give promise to rendering the 1982 baseball card sets obsolete before they hit the candy counters.

"Last year close to 100 players were initially issued in wrong uniforms. This year the count could be even higher. That, of course, paves the way for more 'traded' sets, like Topps' '81 effort. And, speaking of Topps sets, it appears to be getting scarce already," Taylor concluded.

Autographs were becoming difficult to obtain, too, suggested Bill Dod in his Jan. 15, 1982, No Dod About It column.

Rod Carew responded to autograph requests with a letter saying he'd sell his autographs for just under $10.

"The autograph-collecting world is becoming more difficult in some ways — the price of stamps continues to rise and some superstars refuse to autograph through the mails, especially if cards are sent to their homes.

"But some players are coming out and handling autograph requests in a different manner. Rod Carew recently joined the ranks of Willie Stargell and Tim Raines and a cast that seems to be growing ever larger.

"Carew is responding to requests for autographs with a letter offering to sell merchandise from a signed autograph for just under $10 to an autographed bat for just under $100.

"Interesting! What do you think of this trend in our hobby? I like it for one main reason — you can be sure the autograph you're getting is of the person it is suppose to be," he wrote.

* * *

The second issue of 1982, dated Jan. 15, traced the history of Sports Collectors Digest.

From Milan To Iola
A Look At The Start Of SCD

The second week of October 1973...Oakland fans were celebrating the A's second straight World Championship, Pete Rose and Reggie Jackson had just completed seasons that earned them MVP awards, Henry Aaron, soon to turn 40, ended the year one short of tying Babe Ruth's career home run record, and card collectors across the country were reading the first issue ever of Sports Collectors Digest.

It seemed almost natural at the time for John Stommen to launch the new magazine, which back then was published in a tabloid-newspaper format.

"Our family had owned the weekly newspaper here in town (Milan, Mich.) for about 15 years when we decided to start SCD," Stommen recalled in a recent interview.

"We had five boys, who at that time were between 8 and 17. We were all interested in card collecting and thought it would be kind of fun. Since we were already involved in the publishing business, we just decided to get something in print and go from there."

That premiere issue of SCD — dated Oct. 12, 1973 — was begun with a simple philosophy: "We just enjoyed doing it," Stommen said. "We were all collectors and we just decided to give everyone a chance to advertise their buy, sell and trade items as reasonably as possible."

And reasonable it was. A year's subscription to SCD (24 issues) cost just $6 that first year, and classified advertising was free.

"We figured we'd run the ads while we could," Stommen said, "but then it kind of got out of hand and reached the point where either we had to start getting something for them, or we couldn't afford to do it."

Still, then as now, SCD offered its readers and advertisers more than anyone else. Right from the start, the magazine was published twice a month.

"We were just trying to give as much service to readers as we could," Stommen said, "and we figured if we came out twice as often as anyone else, it would be twice as much service."

Stommen soon learned, however, that it was twice as much work, too. And so did the rest of his family.

John and his son Phil handled most of the writing and editing, while his wife, Barbara, was in charge of circulation and the rest of the family was involved in mailing.

"Mailing was probably the biggest bottleneck," Stommen admitted, "coming out twice a month and just being a family operation."

But all that hard work paid off, as the Stommen family learned after publishing just the first issue.

"It was well received right away," Stommen said. Our circulation just continued to grow. Every issue we published always had more subscribers than the previous one." (A trend that continues even today.)

Sports Collectors Digest continued to grow both in subscriptions and in number of pages. After about two years, the newspaper was changed to a magazine format, similar to the current SCD, but slightly smaller.

And as the magazine changed, so did the hobby.

"The major changes have been the growth of the hobby and the values connected with it," Stommen said. "The tremendous number of people that have gotten involved. It's just wild how the hobby has grown. Prices, of course, went out of sight. If you look back at those first issues we published, some of those prices seem unbelievable.

"Neither of the changes is bad," Stommen continued. "It's nice to have the material be worth more money, but it's also nice if the prices are not out of the range of collectors, either. You don't like to have things priced so out of sight that it shuts people out of the hobby.

"That was one thing we really tried to deal with," Stommen said. "We tried to keep our price structure as low as possible to keep as many people interested and allow them to participate in the hobby. You don't always accomplish everything you set out to do, but I think we did accomplish that.

"We got a lot of people interested in the hobby, and they were able to get two issues a month for the price that anyone else was getting for one issue," Stommen said. "And we did keep our ad rates relatively low. I think those were the things we were most proud of during the time we had SCD," he concluded.

Just as it seemed almost natural for Stommen to start SCD in 1973, it also seemed almost natural that when he decided to give up the magazine eight years later, that he would sell it to someone like Chester Krause of Krause Publications in Iola, Wis.

After all, Krause has been publishing books, newspapers, magazines and catalogs for hobbyists for 30 years, and when Chester Krause published his very first hobby paper back in 1952, it was with much the same simple philosophy that John Stommen had when he began publishing SCD. — feature story

* * *

In the March 5, 1982, SCD, Editor Bob Lemke, in the Coach's Box, challenged readers not to participate in error mania this year:

Are You Going To Be A Chump?

By Bob Lemke

Are You a Chump?: If you fall for Fleer's error game this year you're a chump. Sure, last year it was cute when they made all those little mistakes; and when they created a "rare" variety by correcting the Craig Nettles error, many of us felt the company was just honestly trying to make a decent baseball card. BULL!

They were out to sucker us for our hobby dollar. It worked so well they're back at it again. The deliberate creation of errors and varieties serves no other purpose than to fleece the collector. Those that play their game this time around will only reinforce Fleer's conception of baseball card collectors as mindless idiots who blindly pursue any piece of cardboard with a player's picture on it.

I refuse to do business with a company that has no respect for its customers. We bought a Fleer set for the office photo file, but I swear that is the last dime the company will ever get out of me for their 1982 baseball cards. I wouldn't put a set of '82 Fleer into my personal collection if they were the only baseball cards on the market. — Bob Lemke

* * *

Just six pages later, in the same issue, SCD's associate editor, Steve Ellingboe, recapped the errors already known at that time.

Here We Go Again Another Season Of Errors

By Steve Ellingboe, Associate Editor

Although the 1982 collecting season is only a few weeks old — and the real baseball season hasn't even begun yet — it has already become agonizingly evident that '82 is going to be another year of errors.

Early reports from collectors indicate that Fleer — the company that led the error parade last year — is back, ready to defend its title.

Fleer's proofreaders apparently spent the off-season repeating some of last year's blunders — and even compounding them — to come up with a roster of errors that grows as each new pack is opened.

The list already includes one card with three confirmed variations, and the strong possibility of a fourth.

First reported by SCD reader Tom Penzkowski of Racine, Wis., the card — No. 438 of Al Hrabosky — may turn out to be this year's version of the famous 1981 C. Nettles error.

Penzkowski reports that while sorting through a couple of boxes of Fleer cards purchased in the Milwaukee and Racine, Wis., area, he came up with seven Hrabosky cards. On four of them Hrabosky's first name was incorrectly spelled "All." The other three had the name spelled correctly, but on all seven cards, Hrabosky's height was erroneously listed as 5'1 (a repeat of last year's error).

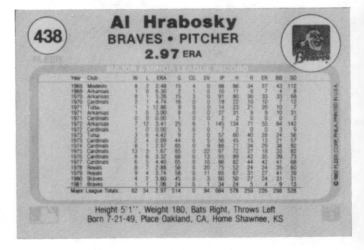

Al Hrabosky comes in all shapes and sizes.

And, with help from columnists Steve Freedman and John Dieroff, SCD uncovered a third '82 Hrabosky card with the first name spelled "Al" and the height corrected to 5'10". That results in three confirmed variations and the possibility of a fourth, if a Hrabosky card turns up with the first name "All" and the correct height.

More Fleer errors reported by Freedman and others include card No. 603 of Lee Smith, which shows the Chicago Cubs team insignia printed backwards on the back of the card. Freedman reports that the error was found in store packs, but that a corrected version showed up in Fleer's dealer vendor boxes.

And, as reported in an earlier SCD, Fleer also repeated last year's error on the Kent Tekulve card, which lists Tekulve as playing in both the years 1071 and 1078, instead of 1971 and 1978. There have been no reports of that error being corrected — yet.

In addition, other spelling errors have been detected on the backs of some Fleer cards. Card No. 561 of Chuck Baker, for example, refers to the team that plays in Minnesota as the "Twns," rather than the Twins. And there is every indication that there are more errors out there still waiting to be uncovered and reported.

Fleer president Donald Peck's position on the error situation is bluntly evasive.

"I have no comment on it," Peck told SCD in a recent phone interview.

"We're into a new year now, and I don't plan to talk about our errors — or anyone else's. I don't mean to sound stiff about it," he continued, "but that kind of talk is unproductive. The industry went through a year of that last year, and that's enough."

Peck then held firm to his promise, refusing to answer any further questions regarding the Hrabosky error or any others.

He did, however, react to another interesting surprise that many collectors discovered while searching their '82 Fleer and Topps sets — both companies used the exact same photograph of Rod Carew.

The photo, which shows Carew fielding a ground ball, appears on card No. 455 in the Fleer set and on No. 501 in the Topps set (the "In Action" card).

"It's obviously the same photograph," Peck admitted, explaining that a free-lance photographer apparently sold the same photo to both companies.

"I had to laugh a little bit when I first saw it," Peck said. "Obviously I would have preferred that they weren't the same photo, but the free world is not going to cave in over it," he concluded.

Topps spokesman Norman Liss, however, prefers to think that the photos "came from adjoining frames" on the same roll of film, and are not the exact same photograph. — Steve Ellingboe

* * *

In a May 28, 1982, story Ted Taylor wondered if the cards were issued too early by the card companies, saying the early press dates "resulted in a nightmare of omissions and wrong team designations, making the collection of current 'team sets' an impossibility.

"An incredible 108 players are portrayed in the wrong major league uniform and another 79 are not portrayed at all. In other words almost 30 percent of the current opening day rosters are not available to the team set collector in either the correct or any uniform at all.

"Chicago Cubs fans are in for a particularly hard time of it as only 40 percent (10 players) are portrayed in Cub uniforms. And, to make matters worse, the Cubs are one of a few teams that Donruss didn't issue a manager card for.

"The numbers would also indicate that it doesn't pay for Seattle Mariners fans to get too attached to anybody since only 11 of their team comes up in the correct doubleknits this season.

"Of course we realize all the marketing reasons for early press dates but find it hard to comprehend that trades and player switches made in late fall couldn't have been reflected on at least one of the three major sets," he concluded.

Reader Gene Borowski, Staten Island, N.Y., in the June 11, 1982, Reader Reaction, was disgusted with whole situation of collectors on seemingly never-ending quests for the "error card." He blasted the card companies.

"I could certainly understand the hullabaloo that would be created should, for example, a Pete Rose photo be substituted on a Mike Schmidt card (or any other major error.) But I will never understand why nowadays it seems that collectors (with magnifying glass in hand) are going over every card they come across, nitpicking for errors they might find.

"I really don't think that anybody is interested that the 1980 Joe Schmoe Topps cards has him listed as a member of the Pirates in 1977 when he was really on the Expos, or that the 1982 Joe Schmoe Donruss card has him listed as a LHP when really he is a RHP.

"Cards with slight errors have little interest or value. I firmly believe that the card companies have been making error cards on purpose. Not only for all the free publicity they've been receiving, but I sure would like to know how much money was put into the pockets of the boys at Fleer by collectors who were running all over the country buying up packs of cards in hopes of finding a C. Nettles or any of the other 'ERROR' cards.

"So, I'm sure that I am not alone when I say that the next time a collector picks up his pen and thinks about writing SCD to announce his latest miniscule error discovery, I wish he would give us all a break and not waste our time, because nobody cares!!!" he wrote.

* * *

The June 25, 1982, SCD carried details about an investigation into the manufacturing and selling of counterfeit 1963 Topps Pete Rose rookie cards. An arrest was made in the case, as SCD reported:

California Dealer Charged Arrest In Rose Rookie Case

A second arrest has been made in connection with the manufacture and sale of counterfeit 1963 Topps Pete Rose rookie cards.

Sheldon Jaffe, a 41-year-old collector and part-time card dealer from Calabasas, Calif., was charged with grand theft after he turned himself in to police in Fullerton, Calif., May 27. Jaffe was released on his own recognizance, pending a court appearance.

The investigating officer, Fullerton Detective Jack Petruzzelli, told SCD that Jaffe is accused of masterminding the printing of 10,000 of the fake Rose rookie cards, which were done by a printer in Chatsworth, Calif.

A 17-year-old youth who allegedly did the "leg work" for Jaffe was questioned by police, but will not be prosecuted, according to Petruzzelli.

Another part-time dealer, 29-year-old Mike Nathan of Woodland Hills, Calif., was arrested earlier and also faces grand-theft charges for his alleged involvement in the scheme. (See June 11 SCD)

"They apparently just looked up printers in the Yellow Pages of the phone book," said Petruzzelli.

He said of the 10,000 bogus cards printed, only 175 to 200 were ever sold and the rest were destroyed.

"We know who has possession of about 165 of those cards," Petruzzelli said. "There are maybe 25 or 30 or so still floating around out there somewhere."

The largest block of the counterfeit cards was sold to Rick Hamilton, a Salem, Ore., dealer who bought 113 of them in late February. Hamilton, in turn, sold several of the cards at a Philadelphia show in early March, but discontinued sales after learning the cards were counterfeits.

Hamilton's attorney told SCD that Hamilton is being refunded his money and is also in the process of reimbursing collectors who bought cards from him.

In addition, according to Petruzzelli, about 23 of the fake cards were sold at a show in Indianapolis the same weekend.

He said both Nathan and Jaffe are being prosecuted on misdemeanor grand theft charges which carry a maximum penalty of one year in jail, but added that the district attorney's office has begun plea bargaining negotiations that could result in probation if full restitution is made.

"In the mind of the D.A.'s office," Petruzzelli said, "because the case has civil overtones, any plea bargaining must contain full restitution as a condition of probation."

Petruzzelli said both Nathan and Jaffe have been "very cooperative" with police and have indicated a willingness to make restitution. He said Nathan, in fact, has already returned money to two collectors who purchased a total of seven counterfeit cards. Petruzzelli said Jaffe indicated to the police that his intent was not to ruin the hobby, but to sell the cards to investors who would put them away and bring them out years later. "He didn't plan on it getting this far out of hand," Petruzzelli said.

Petruzzelli, himself an advanced collector and part-time dealer, had one of the fake Rose rookie cards on display at his table at a Los Angeles show during the Memorial Day weekend. — news story

* * *

Ten months after the story of the arrest appeared, Paul Richman, in the April 15, 1983, SCD, told readers the worst was over concerning the fake Rose rookie cards:

An Update
On The Fake Rose Rookies
"The Phony Thing Is Over"

By Paul Richman

Like a rampant fire, counterfeit baseball cards swept through the hobby last summer causing a temporary hysteria and a longer lasting suspicion of what is real and what is fake.

The 1963 Pete Rose rookie card created most of the commotion when more than 100 bogus cards were uncovered in Philadelphia.

California hobbyist Jack Petruzzelli has an insight into the counterfeit card spectrum, and he feels the worst of it is over. Petruzzelli is a police detective and was an important figure in the arrests of the bogus Rose card issuers.

"I don't think you're going to see any more of that stuff," Petruzzelli said. "The phony thing is over."

Apparently, the hobby's foundation was strong enough to withstand the negative publicity the fake Rose cards created.

"I don't think people want to risk making counterfeit cards now," Petruzzelli continued. "If they start messing with that they know they're going to get caught; there are just too many experts out there who can tell if a card is fake and then they'll nail the dealer. I don't think anyone wants to get stuck with a 'crook' label."

Petruzzelli also explained briefly about the penalties a fake baseball card producer risks.

"First of all, if they are making cards with the purpose of ripping off people it is a definite crime: theft by trickery. If you buy a Pete Rose rookie from a guy for $300 and it turns out to be fake, he has just stolen $300 from you," he said.

"The law depends a lot on what state you are in. It could be a felony or misdemeanor depending on the amount," Petruzzelli continued. "But what the police can do is get an arrest warrant and arrest the offender. If it is a felony the police don't even need the warrant."

Those accused in the Rose rookie card case were given a court-ordered restitution and put on probation, according to Petruzzelli. They were not given a jail sentence because this was their first offense and they had no criminal record.

"This was the first case of its kind, though," Petruzzelli said. "No one knew what to expect. I think if it happens again the people involved will get a stiffer penalty — a fine and probably jail."

Before you go thinking that the Rose card counterfeiters got off easy, it must be pointed out that they are also facing civil lawsuits.

"And don't forget counterfeit cards are a copyright violation," Petruzzelli added. "Topps could also sue and they wouldn't mess around either. They'd go for the guy's car, his house and everything else."

Petruzzelli doesn't believe that there is a counterfeit card problem in the hobby anymore.

"Ninety-nine and nine-tenths percent of the cards that are available to collectors are real," he said. "The Rose thing made national headlines and that scared a lot of people who might have had the idea."

Still, with the improved printing techniques, it seems nearly impossible for someone not to duplicate a card to near perfection.

"It's possible to counterfeit cards," Petruzzelli said. "But they'd have to know ink coloring, paper thickness, lettering, and other printing styles. Since Topps doesn't make this information public, it would be very hard to make a card that would fool experts."

OK, but what if you are not an expert. What if you are just Joe average collector?

"Well, I would be a little suspicious of a large quantity of quality, mint cards at one table," Petruzzelli warned. "Older cards in perfect mint condition are even more suspicious. If you are not sure about a card ask another dealer about it, or find another card of the same player and compare them."

Buying from reputable dealers is always a safeguard against getting ripped off. These dealers have built up too good a reputation to risk ruining with fake cards.

Petruzzelli also suggests other methods of determining authenticity, such as observing the card under a magnifying glass.

"You can see if the printing symbols are the same this way," he explained. "Like the Topps asterisk — that was larger on one fake card I saw."

If a collector is really on his toes he should have no trouble distinguishing the rotten apples from the good ones.

"Everyone is aware," Petruzzelli said. "It's good for the hobby. From the shows I've been to, dealers are always willing to check over a card a collector has purchased to tell him if it is a good card or if the collector has been ripped off. People are in this hobby to help you get it rolling along."

If you, as the buyer, feel you have been burned by a fake card, and a dealer or more knowledgeable collector confirms it, rest assured the dealer who sold it to you will be blacklisted.

"If there is ever a guy selling fake cards at a show and some dealers find out about it they'll be over at his table so fast..." Petruzzelli said. "The hobby would do the guy in before the police even got there."

Maybe baseball card collecting will remain a hobby after all. People like Jack Petruzzelli are working to keep it that way. — Paul Richman

* * *

SCD Editor Steve Ellingboe, in his Coach's Box column in the same SCD issue, offered collectors a solution to another dilemma in the hobby — storing cards in plastic sheets.

A Safe "Plastic" Sheet?

By Steve Ellingboe

A safe "plastic" sheet? In the premiere issue of our sister publication, Baseball Cards magazine, two years ago, Editor Bob Lemke shook the hobby with his grim warning about the dangers of storing cards in plastic sheets. Ever since, collectors and dealers have been debating the controversy and asking the same questions.

Are plastic sheets safe? What are the alternatives?

Our position has always been that as long as plastic sheets contained PVC (Polyvinyl Chloride), we could not recommend them for long-term storage.

You have to be a chemist to fully understand what PVC is and why it will eventually destroy your valuable cars. I'm not a chemist, but I have read enough to be convinced that, over a period of time, conventional plastic sheets would ruin my collection.

By the same token, we also recognized the value of plastic sheets for short-term storage and transportation of cards. Just don't put all your '52 Topps cards in vinyl sheets and leave them there for 10 years. The results could be disastrous — and expensive.

But now comes the good news. We are happy to report that collectors finally have a safe alternative to conventional plastic sheets.

The Enor Corp. of Cresskill, N.J., has just introduced a new "non-vinyl" sheet made of polyethylene, which contains no PVC, no plasticizers and, according to the company, is the "safest sheet on the market."

Spokesman Steve Udwin told SCD that Enor has devoted many months to the project and has spent "tens of thousands of dollars" developing the machinery and technology to produce the sheets.

Right now, they are available only in a nine-pocket, top-loading page, but Udwin said other sizes and styles will be coming out shortly.

The sample page we've seen looks good. It's 5 1/2 gauge — thicker than most vinyl sheets on the market, but lighter in weight.

We haven't seen a price list for the new sheets yet, but Udwin said they will be priced competitively with the conventional sheets we're used to buying.

Even if they aren't, we think most collectors would be willing to pay a little more for the peace of mind in knowing their collections are safe.

At least collectors will now have an alternative.

To the best of our knowledge, Enor is the first to develop a polyethylene sheet. According to Udwin, one of the reasons they did so is because of that article that appeared in Baseball Cards magazine two years ago. We take pride in that, and we salute the Enor Corp. for its pioneering efforts. We hope that others will follow. — Steve Ellingboe

* * *

Meanwhile, on the card front, the Feb. 4, 1983, SCD reported Topps ended months of speculation and bowed to increased pressure from the sports collecting hobby by announcing details of its planned 1952 reprint set. The limited-edition set, which would carry a dealer price of about $27.50 per set, had 402 of the 407 cards from the original set.

"The announcement by Topps," the story reported, "ended speculation about one of the most controversial issues to face the hobby in recent years. Some dealers and collectors have objected to the proposed set because of fears it will have an adverse effect on the market for the original '52 Topps set.

"Norman Liss (Topps spokesman), however, said Topps doesn't think it will ruin the demand for the original. 'The classic set is the classic set,' Liss said. 'Topps feels this is an opportunity for collectors to have the next best thing to the original.'

"He said there will be no chance of mistaking a reprint card for the 'real thing.' They will be smaller, on different card stock, have white backs, and the word 'reprint' will be prominently displayed on the bottom of the back of each card, Liss said. 'It will be very obvious,' he concluded."

Collectors were also following the career progress of a "Toy Cannon" Jimmy Wynn lookalike — Kirby Puckett, as Irwin Cohen reported in his May 27, 1983, On the Baseball Beat column:

"The Visalia Oaks sent Kent Hrbek to the Twins and now they have another slugger in right fielder Kirby Puckett. The 5-8 right fielder is known as 'The Toy Cannon' after lookalike Jim Wynn. Scouts rate Puckett as being blessed with blazing speed, a good arm and the ability to hit for average and with power. Sounds like he can count on a mighty sound financial future. Also sounds like a very hot rookie card in 1985."

Kirby Puckett would later lead the Twins to titles in two World Series appearances. About the time the Baltimore Orioles and the Philadelphia Phillies were squaring off in the 1983 World Series, SCD Editor Steve Ellingboe, in his Oct. 14, 1983, column, marked SCD's milestone 10th anniversary with a reminiscent column which asked readers to look back in time 10 years.

* * *

Kirby Puckett was a top prospect with the Visalia Oaks,

Where Were You Ten Years Ago?

By Steve Ellingboe

What were you doing 10 years ago?

That's a question I've been asking around the SCD office this week because, with this issue, Sports Collectors Digest celebrates its 10th anniversary.

Granted, it's not as dramatic as when recalling what you were doing when you learned that President Kennedy was shot or when Neil Armstrong first stepped onto the moon, but for sports collectors, the date Oct. 12, 1973, has special significance. That was the date of the very first SCD, a new twice-a-month tabloid published by the John Stommen family of Milan, Mich.

I wasn't familiar with SCD in those early days. As a matter of fact, it was another five years before I even learned that SCD existed.

Back in October, 1973, I was working as a radio and television news reporter in Green Bay, Wis., having graduated with a journalism degree from the University of Wisconsin-Milwaukee two years earlier. I was, of course, a devoted baseball fan, loyal Packer backer and Bucks fan (we still had Lew Alcindor back then, although by now he was already Kareem Abdul-Jabbar.)

As a kid growing up in Milwaukee in the Fifties and Sixties I had been a baseball card junkie, but like many of you, the baseball card and autograph collecting that I pursued so actively as a youngster gradually took a backseat to my education, career and other interests.

But then, in 1978, it happened! While searching through fellow reporter Bob Rockstroh's desk for some misplaced film we had shot, I stumbled across a copy of Sports Collectors Digest. Unbeknown to me, Bob was a baseball card collector and an SCD subscriber. I borrowed that copy of SCD, read it from cover to cover and was hooked. A born-again collector. I couldn't wait to see Bob's new copy of SCD every two weeks. It was like being a kid back in Milwaukee again, rooting for Aaron and Mathews and Spahn and even Felix Mantilla. I never knew such a magazine existed. Every baseball card I ever had as a kid was in there — and I wanted all of them back.

I started ordering cards through the mail, going to shows, and finally, to Bob's relief, got my own subscription to SCD.

I continued my job at the radio and TV station, later became a radio news director, and was working for a Green Bay newspaper in the summer of 1981 when I learned that Krause Publications in nearby Iola had purchased Sports Collectors Digest and needed an associate editor.

It was a job I had to have. I never even wrote a letter, just drove over one afternoon and told Krause's personnel director that I was showing up for work the next Monday whether they hired me or not.

Well, actually, I didn't come that next Monday because that was Labor Day, but I did come on Tuesday — and I've been here, and been happy, ever since.

Coincidentally, I ran into my old friend Bob Rockstroh at a card show in Los Angeles last month. He's still a card collector and he's still a subscriber. By the way, thanks, Bob, for leaving that copy of SCD lying around the WBAY newsroom five years ago. — Steve Ellingboe

* * *

Bob Lemke, now the paper's publisher, was also nostalgic in the same issue in his column The Bleacher Bum.

As We Begin Our Second Decade

By Bob Lemke

Happy Birthday to Us: With this issue, Sports Collectors Digest celebrates completion of its 10th year of service to sports memorabilia hobbyists.

SCD and the hobby have come a long way together since that first 16-page issue dated Oct. 12, 1973. Most of our current readers probably have never seen a copy of the premiere issue of SCD, but we were a tabloid newspaper in those days, published in Milan, Mich., by John Stommen and his family. It was not until 1976 that SCD adopted the magazine-format style that we have today.

If you can manage not to start crying over the prices of baseball cards and sports collectibles advertised a decade ago, it is quite interesting to read the back issues. You'll find a lot of the same names prominent in the hobby. There's also a lot written about the same "hot" topics — card grading, prices, variations, the need for a national organization, etc. I guess some things never change.

Know what else hasn't changed in the 10 years since SCD made its debut? The purpose of the magazine. I couldn't put it any better than founding editor John Stommen did in his initial "Our Hobby" column in that first issue: "We feel that bringing sports collectors in touch with each other is the chief function of a sports collecting publication," Stommen wrote.

He continued, "In addition to serving current collectors, it is our intention to reach as many new sports collectors as possible."

John also voiced the sentiments of the current SCD staff when he wrote, "Combining the fun of collecting itself, along with writing about, it isn't really what you'd call work."

The front page of the Oct. 12, 1973, SCD carried a story of the recently-concluded New York convention sponsored by Mike Aronstein (one of the sponsors of the upcoming 1984 national convention), along with a preview article about the first Cincinnati Area Sports Collectors convention.

Doug Watson and I will be traveling to the 11th annual Cincy show in early November, and we'll be renewing acquaintances with many of the same people who were responsible for the first show in the Queen City: Stanley McClure, Bob Rathgeber, Tom Pfirrman and Tim Turner. Long-time SCD advertiser Don Steinbach was auctioneer at the first Cincy convention.

Speaking of long-time SCD advertisers, when paging through that first issue, I came across the name of many collectors and dealers who still advertise in our pages today: Jack Urban, Tom Koppa, Ed Budnick, Kermit Tanzey and Mike Wheat were advertisers in that first issue.

Who was the first of SCD's current writers to appear in the magazine? It looks to me like Bill Dod captures that distinction. He had an article on collecting sports photos in issue #3. Irwin Cohen received a favorable mention in the very first issue of SCD for his new column in TEAM magazine, but "Mr. Baseball" didn't actually begin writing for SCD on a regular basis until 1981.

From the first issue of SCD, it was evident that the paper was destined to become the news source and marketplace for the hobby. John Stommen encouraged the average collector to use the pages of SCD to advertise his wants and his duplicates by offering free classified ads. Then, as now, SCD's twice a month frequency meant that readers got the first report of new issues and discoveries and other important hobby information.

SCD quickly became known as the place to sell the truly rare or unusual cards and memorabilia. That reputation continues today. When someone has a T206 Honus Wagner or a 1933 Goudey Nap

Lajoie card to sell, they do it in our pages. I am continually amazed by the quality, quantity and diversity of collectibles to be found in each issue of SCD.

Our last issue, Sept. 30, was a good example. There was material from the estate of 1920s major league catcher Wally Schang, there were uniforms of all eras, from Hank Aaron's 1958 tomahawk jersey to Paul Molitor's 1982 Brewer shirt. There was not one, but two offers of the very rare Post cereal baseball card albums — I've never even seen one. You can't find that kind of diversity in any other sports hobby paper. And the classified ads, although they are no longer free, still provide you and me with the best place to buy, sell and trade sports collectibles, reaching the greatest number of readers at the lowest possible cost.

Speaking of cost, when SCD premiered, a one-year (24-issue) subscription cost $7.50. Today, that figure is exactly doubled, though you get 26 issues now. You know what's interesting, though? In 1973, you could buy brand new set of that year's Topps baseball cards for about the price of an SCD subscription — and that situation holds true today. A single pack of baseball cards also doubled in price from 1973 to today, from 15 cents to 30 cents. The cost of enclosing an SASE with your autograph request or want list more than doubled; what required an 8 cent stamp in 1973 now requires a 20-center. Some other prices you might find interesting from that first issue of SCD were reported as part of the first Cincinnati convention; tables were $5 apiece, and a double room at the host hotel was $21.

Prices have changed in the past decade, but the basic structure hasn't really shifted, nor has SCD's stated purpose of serving all of the collectors, from the most novice to the most advanced.

I'm especially proud to sit in the publisher's seat as SCD begins its second decade of hobby service. I'd like to take this opportunity to especially thank my predecessors, John Stommen and Doug Watson, as well as the man who brought SCD here to Iola, Chet Krause.

Thanks also go to you, our readers and advertisers, the folks who support SCD. Without you, we wouldn't be able to do what we do. — Bob Lemke

* * *

In his Nov. 11, 1983, Bleacher Bum column, Lemke speculated on how many baseball cards Topps issues in any given year. Although the number of cards Topps produces is a "secret more closely guarded than Satchel Paige's true age," Lemke said the starting point for determining that figure is the company's yellow "Winning Line-Up Baseball Game" scratchoff cards available in in 1983 wax packs.

The "Odds Chart" on the back of the cards, Lemke noted, said there were 40 million game cards distributed; thus, 40 million packs of 1983 Topps baseball cards. At 15 cards per pack, that makes 600 million cards, he said. Since the set has 792 different cards, that boils down to more than 75,000 for each card, he figured, also cautioning that that number does not include cards which were included in vendor boxes and cello packs.

By the end of the year, the companies were already gearing up for their 1984 sets. Donruss was the first out of the gate to print its cards, of which samples were shown on the Dec. 9, 1983, SCD cover. But Donruss' efforts left Editor Steve Ellingboe puzzled.

Duke Snider is featured on the 1984 Donruss puzzle.

"Donruss wins this year's race as the first company to reveal the design of its 1984 set," Steve Ellingboe reported in his Coach's Box column. "The cards, themselves, won't be released for a couple of months yet, and I've only seen the fronts of nine cards and the backs of none — but, so far, I like them. I wish we could show them to you in full color, because the photographs are sharp and the colors are crisp. I'm anxious to see the rest of the set.

"I'm a little surprised about Donruss' selection of Duke Snider for this year's puzzle. Snider is a popular Hall of Famer, of course, and was a great player, but after starting the puzzle series with legends like Babe Ruth and Ty Cobb, I just expected someone different.

"Apparently so did most collectors. An SCD advertiser who was running a contest to guess the subject of Donruss' 1984 puzzle received no correct answers," Ellingboe wrote.

* * *

In Ted Taylor's July 20, 1984, Off the Cuff column, a Donruss consultant explained another unique company innovation making its debut in 1984 — Rated Rookies cards:

Donruss Consultant Explains 'Rated Rookies' Selections

By Ted Taylor

Pittsburgh Pirates rookie outfielder Doug Frobel is quoted as saying that things have gone so bad for him this year that he called his Mom on Mothers Day and she hung up on him.

Frobel, who was hitting .148 at the time of the phone call, was one of 20 Donruss "Rated Rookies" this year, and one of the eight who remain in the major leagues.

In the June 8 issue of SCD, I commented that being a "Rated Rookie" wasn't exactly the best thing that could happen to a young ballplayer this season since a majority of them are spending the year in places like Indianapolis, Edmonton, Tidewater, Toledo and even Japan.

Well, there are two sides to every viewpoint and the opposite side of mine was recently shared with me by nationally-known sportswriter Bill Madden.

"Ordinarily, I don't get involved in 'official' replies to criticism of the Donruss baseball cards because I am not an official memmber of the Donruss family — merely a paid consultant," Madden began.

"However, since you and I are both hobbyists and apparently share the same passion — getting cards of as many players each year to keep them in team sets — I felt I should take the time to answer some of your salient complaints about the Donruss 'Rated Rookies,'" Madden continued.

Bill takes credit (or responsibility) for the Rated Rookie idea, which, by the way, I feel is a terrific one and the most innovative thing to happen in baseball cards in years.

"I felt it would catch the fancy of collectors such as you and me, of which I hope there are many," Bill added. And, he was right. My mail tells me that there is a reasonably large number of us out there who collect players by a team and keep them current almost on a day-to-day basis.

Bill admits that the omission of Juan Samuel from the crop of 20 this year and was "my biggest complaint — (and) as a Phillies fan might surely be justified." But he then recounted to me the great pains he went to and his efforts in getting Samuel included from the word go.

Madden says that he felt omitting Samuel "would make our entire program a travesty," which might have been a bit harsh, but most experts agreed that Samuel might well be the N.L. Rookie of the Year and how can you miss him among your Rated Rookies?

The problem at Donruss was not an oversight, Bill states, but rather a lack of a decent picture.

"We had three and all were so dark you wouldn't have known if it was Juan Samuel or Juan Valdez," Madden reported. "Give Fleer credit for having a picture, yes, but I seriously doubt if they had any idea that Juan Samuel would be a significant entry in their set.

"Believe me, I did — and you can ask the people at Donruss who, by December, had grown very weary of my attempts to get Samuel into the set," he went on.

'As for missing the boat on so many other 'rated rookies' I say this "You show me a scout who can call the tune on 25 'sure shots' in one year and I'll show you the next Branch Rickey.'

"I go further to say Brad Komminsk, Tony Fernandez, Joel Skinner, Sid Fernandez and even Mike Brown (now up) will be heard from soon — if not this year, then next. The point is, you have a card of them now! And, nobody else thought to issue one," Bill said.

And, he's correct. The only cards that existed before on people like Komminsk, Sid Fernandez, Mike Brown, Joel Skinner, Doug Frobel, etc., came from the likes of TCMA. But, then, those of us who collect team sets did, indeed, have cards of all those people (Along with thousands who haven't made it since TCMA began in the early 1970s) in our collections.

The next biggest point of criticism in the "Rated Rookie" column was the inclusion of noted Japanese slugger Chris Smith.

Chris Smith went to Japan, but made the Rated Rookies team.

"As for Chris Smith, I take full blame," Madden said, "I knew he was going to Japan and still gave the go-ahead to run him. I couldn't believe that some American League team wouldn't take a shot at him as a DH. The guy's a born hitter as all my scouts informed me. I still think he'll be back in the U.S., some say a la Terry Whitfield — and if he is, you'll have a card of him."

"The bottom line here is, I thought he'd be more interesting to run in the set than say, Julio Gonzalez," he added.

All the info I've read on Smith says he can hit. The rap on him is that he gets about as much use out of his one glove as Michael Jackson does.

Bill concluded by saying that he hoped I'd pass along the facts to my readers so that people don't get the idea that he (and Donruss) deliberately blundered on both Samuel and Smith and that they were, to quote Bill, "idiots." That there was good reasons for both and both reasons were based on sound information.

Agreed. I never implied that they were "idiots." In fact the idea, as I said before, was innovative and refreshing. Perhaps a better label than "Rated Rookies" may well have been "Stars of the Future," which would have allowed some further seasoning in the minors of a top prospect.

Remember, if Donruss had been around in 1951 and printed a "Rated Rookie" card of both Mickey Mantle and Willie Mays they would have been open to criticism because both men, after opening in the majors that season, spent some AAA time in Kansas City and Minneapolis, respectively. Bowman, you may recall, printed them both! — Ted Taylor

* * *

Dave Miedema, in his April 13, 1984, Up Autograph Alley column, reassured collectors that ballplayers were still willing to sign baseball cards, despite the doomsayers who were saying that aspect of the hobby would soon die a painful death, due to an alleged large number of players who were refusing to sign and the lack of customers purchasing autographs at shows.

"The collector who chooses to go this route will have an interesting challenge in completing his or her sets, although achieving a desired goal will, in most cases, be far from impossible," Miedema wrote.

One collector Miedema heard from on this subject made it sound as though there were more players who wouldn't sign cards than there were those who would.

"For my answer to all this: pure poppycock," wrote Miedema, who then presented his research on the subject, based on the approximately 780 players, managers and coaches currently employed in the major leagues.

"Now, how many of these 780 baseball individuals do you think will normally refuse to sign a gumcard? Fifty? One hundred? Two hundred? Let's take a head count. All in attendance please respond by sneering at the nearest autographed gumcard collector.

"From the Mets, we have Rusty Staub. The Phillies have Garry Maddox, and had Pete Rose. Pirate Bill Madlock has been known to refuse in recent months, as has Indian Bake McBride and White Sox hurler Ron Reed. You could also include Angel slugger Fred Lynn, and former Sox hurler Early Wynn, now an announcer with the Pale Hose.

"After growing up on Sesame Street, Mister Rogers and Zoom, I think I am intellectually capable of counting up to eight. Heck, I don't even have to use all my fingers!

"The number of players who refuse to sign certain gumcards is also minimal. Ron Davis won't sign Yankee cards, Ozzie Smith won't sign Padre cards, Garry Templeton won't sign Cardinal cards, and Pete Vuckovich won't sign Blue Jay cards. Bob Stinson, Steve Stone, and a few other players won't sign their 1976 SSPC cards, and Gaylord Perry won't sign his Donruss Action All-Stars card.

"There may be a few more instances, and in fact, I'd be willing to bet on it. However, it's hardly cause to signal the doom of a very popular sub-hobby," he wrote.

Other players, he noted, simply refuse to sign autographs on anything, period. These players include John Denny, George Brett, Willie Wilson and Steve Carlton, he said.

Others, Miedema said, are more selective as to who they'll sign for. "A small but slowly growing number of players tend to pick and choose in regards to whom they will sign for. Some players will reserve signing for female fans. I've written about Lou Piniella in this regard, but can also recall several occasions in the mid-70s when catcher Jerry Grote would ignore a whole group of collectors and fans at Wrigley Field, mostly male and mostly young, only to stop a few sections down and pen his name on a ball for a cute blonde who was egged on by her boyfriend. Or, you can take Bake McBride, who, last year at Comiskey Park, signed a ball for a girl who was with her boyfriend, then scurried off as several kids and adults, bearing cards, programs, or whatever, approached," he wrote.

"Other players seem to be in a mindframe that all adults asking for autographs are doing so out of a profiteering motive, rather than for personal collections. Subsequently, these players will ignore adults in favor of children, figuring the kids aren't going to turn around and sell the items for a quick profit.

"The number of players of this nature is also small, and also growing by inches, rather than by miles. I have been quick to point out the tendencies of Rickey Henderson and Dave Parker to act in this manner. Based on other collectors' reports, and eyewitness accounts, other players, such as Ron Reed, Harold Baines, George Hendrick, Mickey Rivers, and Johnny Bench have acted thusly," he wrote.

Miedema also said he's had people express their appreciation to him for having signed cards for sale at card shows, because no one else had them; few dealers stock up on them. He added that his sales of autographed cards have sometimes comprised more than half of his total sales at shows.

In July, SCD reported the sale of the hobby's most valuable card, the T206 Honus Wagner, for $23,000. The July 6, 1984, SCD reported the card was in Near Mint condition, had oversize borders and was described as "the equal of any in the hobby." The buyer and seller wanted to remain anonymous.

* * *

Meanwhile, in New York, a pair of collectors found several baseball treasures at a Long Island dump. The Aug. 3, 1984, SCD told their story:

Baseball Treasures Found In New York Dump

By Steve Ellingboe

A pair of New York collectors surprised the hobby last month when they revealed that they were holding the original plaster casts used to make 75 of the plaques at the Baseball Hall of Fame in Cooperstown.

No one was more stunned by the announcement than Hall of Fame officials, who thought the molds had all been destroyed years ago.

The unique pieces are owned by Howie Levy and Bob Garrett, operators of Blue Chip Sport Cards in Lake Grove, N.Y. They were alerted to the treasure by one of their customers, an attorney, who stumbled onto 39 of the molds at an antique shop on Long Island three years ago. The antique dealer said he found the casts during a routine search of the Long Island dump. They apparently had been discarded by the foundry which made the plaques for the Hall of Fame years ago.

"At first we didn't even know what they were," Garrett told SCD in a recent phone interview. But soon after figuring it out, Garrett and Levy went searching for more, visiting several foundries in the New York area.

Their search paid off, turning up 36 additional casts, including Mickey Mantle.

"After seeing that, I really didn't care what the price was," Garrett said. "He gave me a price and I bought them."

The molds are made of either hard wax or plaster and include some of the biggest names in baseball history — Grover Cleveland Alexander, Honus Wagner, Lou Gehrig, Christy Mathewson, Lefty Grove, Rogers Hornsby, Ted Williams, Cy Young and many others.

The molds show only the face from the Hall of Fame plaques and do not include any of the printing.

Many of them are in excellent condition, some perfect, but others are chipped or have parts missing, according to Garrett, who said that all of the molds will soon be offered for sale to the general hobby.

That is upsetting to officials at Cooperstown, who feel the material does not belong on the open market where reproductions of the plaques could be made. The molds were offered to the Hall of Fame by Garrett and Levy, but officials balked at the $25,000 asking price — $350 for each of the 75 molds.

"We felt that was more than fair," Garrett said, explaining that they arrived at the price after being told by the foundries that the sculptors were paid between $350 and $500 to make the molds. "These are one-of-a-kind items, works of art," Garrett said. "We didn't know what they were worth, we still don't." Levy told SCD that "we've got a bid on one of them for $5,000."

Garrett and Levy defend their decision to release the treasures to the open market. "We have been talking with the Hall of Fame constantly over the past few months to see if they would be interested in buying the entire lot," Garrett said. "Our effort was more than generous. We did not go to the Hall of Fame to hold them up. We weren't wearing guns."

Hall of Fame spokesman William Guilfoile told SCD that Cooperstown officials are "very disappointed" with the situation. "We assumed the casts had been destroyed," he said. "It was our understanding that that is what is usually done in cases like this."

Guilfoile said it was the Hall of Fame that had originally paid for the production of the casts, and that it is now "ironic that a third party is trying to sell them back to us."

He said the officials tried, without success, to find a benefactor to buy the molds from Levy and Garrett and then donate them to the Hall of Fame.

"Even if we had them, we would just destroy them," Guilfoile said. "They're not something that we would want to display." — Steve Ellingboe

* * *

In his Sept. 28, 1984, Coach's Box column, Ellingboe alerted readers of a new "grab bag" marketing approach being used to sell 25 to 50 assorted "older" cards in rack packs for between $2.50 to $5 per pack.

A sample pack of 25 cards, offered by Hyman Products for about $4, contained cards worth $1.24, and the oldest card included was a 1972 card of Montreal catcher John Boccabella, despite the St. Louis company's claims that the cards inside could be worth up to $400 and could include cards from as far back as 1957, Ellingboe noted after opening the pack. The only star card was a 1983 Topps "Super Veteran" card of Carl Yastrzemski, he said, adding it's worth about 25 cents.

The rest of the pack contained these cards (all in Ex-Mint condition): 1979 Topps: Rennie Stennett and Jamie Quirk; 1980 Topps: Phil Garner, Dale Murray and Brewers Future Stars; 1981 Donruss: Jim Frey; 1982 Fleer: Bill Gullickson, Dick Ruthven, Shooty Babitt, Billy Sample and Lee May; 1982 Donruss: Jerry Augustine and Alex Trevino; 1983 Fleer: Ozzie Virgil, Rick Mahler, Rick Dempsey, Jim Wohlford, Bruce Berenyi, Champ Summers, Doc Medich, Aurelio Rodriguez, Steve Trout and Peter Ladd; 1983 Topps: Alan Wiggins.

"It's an interesting idea, and if you like to gamble you may be tempted to try a package or two. But to me, it's kind of like playing a slot machine that you know is rigged against you. I'd rather spend three bucks on something a little more solid. And I don't mean a Darryl Strawberry rookie card," Ellingboe wrote.

With the new card collecting season underway, the April 26, 1985 Price Guide Report estimated it would cost collectors about $900 to collect all the new 1985 sets on the market at the time, including the super-expensive silver and bronze Topps replica sets and the full Topps glossy set. Without those high-ticket items, the "regular" issues would cost about $260.

The report listed the sets and average prices as determined from display ads in the April 12, 1985, issue: regular Topps set (792 cards), $18; regular Donruss set (660), $18; regular Fleer set (660), $12; Donruss/Leaf Canadian set (264), $12; Topps All-Star Glossy (22), $4; Topps "Bonus Runs" Glossy (40), $12; Topps "Supers", $10.50; Topps 3-D set, $14; Topps sticker set with album (376), $18; Donruss 5x7 Diamond Kings (27), $10; Donruss Action All-Stars (60), $7; Fleer stickers with album (132), $8; Topps bronze replicas (12), $99; Topps silver replicas (12), $419; Topps "limited-edition" glossy (924, with update), $119; Fun Food buttons (133), $18; Slurpee coins (6 regional sets, 12-14 coins each), $12-$14 per set; and Gardner's Brewers (22), $15.

The list did not include the Woolworth's set, the Circle K set, or Topps Rub-downs, for which prices had not yet been firmly established.

* * *

In the Aug. 16, 1985, SCD, Keith Olbermann reported about a major hobby discovery of items for which prices really couldn't be determined:

Major Hobby Discovery Proof Sheets Found In Garage

By Keith Olbermann

A previously undiscovered stash of Topps proof sheets and printing plates, comparable in volume and significance to a small archaeological dig, has turned up in the garage of a Connecticut house.

The collection, consisting of approximately 75 uncut sheets and 100 aluminum plates, has already been nearly totally absorbed into the hobby. Two of the most important items — a pair of 1962 Topps Baseball 6th Series proof sheets containing a total of eleven previously unreported proof varieties went to private collectors, with the bulk of the remaining items going to dealers.

While the sheets and plates run the gamut from baseball to hockey to non-sports, all of them date from just one year, 1962. Topps did at least half of its printing at a private firm near New Haven in the '60s, and the items were discarded from that operation.

The 1962 variations include versions of each of the American League All-Star cards which lack the player's positions, and a blank 7th Series checklist. Among the other highlights of the remarkable find:

- 1962 Topps football sheets showing 44 cards, with each player incorrectly identified (the Alex Karras card, for instance, features the picture of Billy Kilmer).

- 1962 Topps baseball sheets which lack card borders, the "wood grain paneling" effect, and indeed all artwork, and show only a series of 2 1/2" x 3 1/2" photographs.

- A 1962-63 Topps hockey sheet showing the photographs on the cards of Bruce Gamble and Doug Mohns switched, and a card of Rangers' trainer Frank Paice featuring Paice's picture, but goalie Marcel Paille's name. This proof sheet, unlike any other previously discovered, has printed backs, which also feature a full write-up of Paille where Paice's biography should be.

- A sheet of 24 different, apparently unissued "Hockey Bucks," in the style of the 1962 Baseball and Football "Bucks" inserts.

- A printing plate for part of the scarce 1962 Bazooka Baseball set, sadly without the accompanying proof sheet.

For those unfamiliar with the terms "proofs" and "plates," proof sheets are the preliminary versions of series of cards, printed to test color, format, etc.

Subtle — and sometimes blatant — changes are made between the proof and issued stages. Proof sheets rarely make their way into the hobby, and are responsible for such unique items as the 1977 Reggie Jackson card showing him in an Oriole's uniform. The plates, thin sections of aluminum identical in size and design to the sheets, are used in the production of the cards. While rarer even than the cardboard sheets, proof plates such as those found in Connecticut are not considered very desirable to the average collector. The faintness of the ink against the shiny metallic surface often renders the plates aesthetically displeasing.

The staggering number of sheets and plates discovered owes to the fact that a plate and a sheet are made at each stage of the printing process. Therefore, there are sheets and plates which show only red printing, others show only blue, only yellow, and only black. Versions are also made for the yellow-blue combination, and for the three-color stage of yellow, blue and red. The finalized version of a sheet, of course, features all four colors. Considering that for the 1962 Topps cards the whole process was repeated twice — first without artwork, and then with — there are some card patterns that repeat on no fewer than 14 different sheets, and an equal number of plates.

Most historically intriguing of all the sheets are the handful that show a strip of six 1962 Baseball 2nd Series cards on one side, and a selection of a dozen photos used in the 1959 set on the other. These sheets were made only to match the color accuracy of the '62 set to that of the '59. Collectors familiar with the '62 Topps will recall that the 2nd Series was printed twice, after eight apparently "bad" photos ruined the color balance of the entire series. In the first print, skies often came out green and grass, brown. The eight photos were replaced and the series then reprinted. These particular sheets in the Connecticut collection were used to re-test the troubled '62 color printing process.

* * *

Interest continued in the rookie card craze, as reported in the May 9, 1986, Price Guide Report, which cited the Jose Canseco Donruss card as the hottest new card, listed at $3, but selling for even more. The Fleer version, which Canseco shares with Eric Plunk, is listed at $2.

Cards of Brewer pitcher Juan Nieves were listed at 75 cents, while many other rookie cards' prices were also increasing, including cards for Earnest Riles, Billy Joe Robidoux, Teddy Higuera, Ozzie Guillen, Mariano Duncan, Chris Brown, Oddibe McDowell and Floyd Youmans.

Bert Blyleven's first card, from the 1971 Topps set, had jumped to $3 in Ex-Mint condition, and Jim Presely's card was also rapidly rising, according to the report.

In his June 6, 1986, Coach's Box column, Steve Ellingboe reported that yes, Topps would be getting on the Canseco band wagon by including the A's rookie slugger in its Traded set. Rumors had been racing throughout the hobby that Canseco might not have signed a contract with Topps to produce the card, but Ellingboe squashed the rumor by getting Topps spokesman Norman Liss to confirm that the set included Canseco.

Meanwhile, rookie card prices continued to increase, as noted in the June 6, 1986, Price Guide Report. The Dwight Gooden 1984 Fleer "Update" card had reached $40, bringing the value of the 132-card, two-year-old set to $75. The 1984 Topps Traded Gooden card had hit $30, bringing the price of that set to $45. Gooden's other cards were also increasing dramatically, to $6 for the '85 Topps and Donruss Goodens, and $5 for the '85 Fleer. His current Topps card had hit $2.50.

Jose Canseco's '86 Donruss card had reached $3.50, while his Fleer card was at $2.25. Other recent rookie cards showing big price hikes included Bret Saberhagen, Darryl Strawberry, Teddy Higuera, Kirby Puckett and Roger Clemens.

"While rookie cards are still the hottest and most active part of the hobby, interest continues to grow in 'errors and variations.' Recognizing that fact, we have added another variation to the Price Guide. Under the 1982 Topps listing you will now find the Pascual Perez 'no position' variation (#383). We have set the value at $27.50, although that may be conservative," the report concluded.

The Aug. 1, 1986, SCD reported Donruss and Topps were catering to the rookie card mania by including two-sport star Bo Jackson in their update sets. Jose Canseco, who was in the regular Donruss set, would also be included in the company's update "The Rookies."

Meanwhile, the October 24, 1986, Price Guide Report asked readers to guess who's rookie card price had shown the biggest increase, percentage-wise.

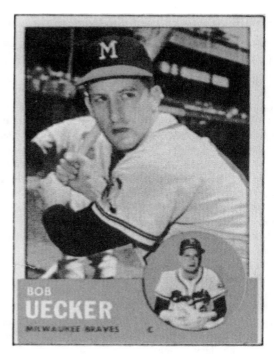

Guess whose card was one of the hottest in October 1986?

"It's not Aaron, Mays, Feller, Koufax or even Mickey Mantle. Their cards have gone up in value, for sure, but the player showing the biggest jump is none other than Bob 'I must be in the front row' Uecker! We can't deny it any longer. Uecker is HOT. He always was here in Wisconsin. Being a former Milwaukee Brave and now a broadcaster for the Milwaukee Brewers, Uecker has always been a local hero, and his cards have long been in demand at area card shows. But, because of his recent beer commercials, Tonight Show appearances and his role on Mr. Belvedere, Uecker is now loved nationwide. And his card values reflect that. How many other career .200 hitters have rookie cards worth $12.50? Even his '63 card is hard to find at $1.50.

"Turning to slightly more serious matters, in addition to increasing the values of many stars and superstars, we have also raised the values of most commons and complete sets from the '50s and '60s.

"There's also a lot of interest in Bowmans, too, and many of them carry display + signs," the report said.

For those interested in buying every card set issued in 1986, the Nov. 21, 1986, SCD reported there were 172 different sets produced, including the various regionals, police sets and major card company issues. Reader Lee Temanson, who compiled the list, estimated it would cost about $3,055 to purchase all the sets, based on advertising prices.

* * *

SCD rang in the new year with a story in the Jan. 30, 1987, issue about counterfeit Don Mattingly rookie cards invading the hobby:

Where Did The Fake Mattinglys Come From? A Special SCD Investigative Report Counterfeit Cards Invade Hobby

By Kit Kiefer

Donruss-Leaf is considering taking legal action against a 14-year-old boy who allegedly counterfeited and sold 1984 Donruss Don Mattingly cards, a D-L spokesman said.

"We're still investigating, but we feel our rights have been violated," said D-L's Neil Lewis after learning that between 900 and 1,000 high-quality fake Mattinglys were printed and passed off as genuine specimens of the hobby's hottest card.

"We feel like we've been ripped off a little," Lewis said. "It's our reputation, and it's our property that's at stake here. We'll do whatever it takes to uphold the reputation of our product."

The counterfeit cards first surfaced prior to a Dec. 20 Fort Lauderdale show, according to Hollywood, Fla., dealer Rich Altman.

"We (Altman and show promoter Lou Scalia) made an announcement before the show, before the public was let in, warning the dealers that these cards were out there," Altman said. "During the show, if anyone from the public came over to my table and asked to see the card, I was happy to show it to them."

After the show, Altman sent a sample of the counterfeit to SCD.

From the best sources available to SCD, here is how the counterfeiting plan allegedly worked: A 14-year-old boy convinced a printer — either by claiming he was Don Mattingly's cousin or saying he needed them for a party — to print the cards.

According to two different sources, the boy allegedly had the cards printed at a quick-print shop. SCD was not able to locate the exact shop, but did contact the manager of one such business who confirmed that any quick-printing shop could produce the cards.

"You have an AB Dick machine, a web like most shops have, and any shop can make this sort of thing," the printer said. "It won't be great, but 95 percent of the people won't be able tell it from the real thing."

After getting them printed, the boy allegedly sold the cards at school — persuading one friend to buy 40 of them at $30 each — and at shows, being careful to avoid situations where the counterfeits could be compared side by side with the real thing.

The largest reported sale was an $1,800 transaction between the boy and a coin and baseball card shop.

The shop owner, who did not want to be identified, said he bought the cards from the youth, who came into his store and offered him the cards for $38 each. "He had 25," the shop owner said, "and said he could get 40.

"I said, 'For that price, it's a good deal, I'll pay you $37.50 cash.'"

The shop owner said he didn't discover the cards were counterfeit until later that evening. "That night I called another dealer and said, 'I bought a bunch of Mattinglys.' He said, 'Are they glossy? There are some fakes out there, and they're glossy.' I looked at my cards and, sure enough, they were glossy."

The shop owner said he then confronted the boy's mother, who wrote him a check to cover a portion of his loss. The remainder is being contested.

However, the shop owner said prosecution is not an option.

"Prosecute? What for?" he said. "I just want my money back."

"As far as the state is concerned, if it's a juvenile, it's not fraud; it's an act of God," he added. "And what am I going to do? Break the kid's legs?"

He also said he blames himself for buying the cards in a hurry and not taking them out of the plastic to inspect them.

The youth also allegedly tried to trade off some of the counterfeit Mattingly cards to dealer John J. Pluta as partial payment for 1985 Topps rack cases and 1987 Fleer cases. But Pluta said he refused to take the cards.

"When I went to collect I could tell right away something wasn't right," Pluta said. "I said I could not accept these cards in trade, and I notified other dealers about these cards."

The youth allegedly used a different approach to rip off another dealer and show promoter, Joe Sokoloff.

Said Sokoloff, "This kid called me and said, 'My mother just put down on a deposit on some 1987 Donruss cases. Would you like a couple cases? If you would, just put down a deposit' — and he quoted me a price — 'and what you want, I can get it.' He goes around to three, four, 10 different dealers and gets them to put two-thirds down. Then he skips town."

When Sokoloff demanded payment, the youth allegedly tried to pay him in counterfeit Mattinglys.

Attempts by Sokoloff to track down the youth and his parents, who recently moved, have been unsuccessful. Sokoloff said he is in the process of obtaining a forwarding address through the Freedom of Information Act.

However, Sokoloff added that the youth himself was conned out of 100 of the counterfeit Mattinglys by another young dealer, who said he was going to do a show in another state and would dispose of the fakes there.

"Then once he had the cards he said 'OK, now try to get them back. You complain and I'll tell them you had the counterfeits printed.'"

SCD has also learned that the fake cards were spread to other parts of the country through a juvenile dealer who obtained some of them from the 14-year-old.

"I was suckered in like everyone else," the young dealer said, and added he was going through the process of trying to get back the 15 cards he had sent out.

"I'm just like any other dealer," he said. "I get the cards, make $8 or $9 on them and move on. I don't want any of my customers having any counterfeit cards."

Mike Stolicny of Connecticut Card Investors, who bought five of the counterfeits from the young dealer, said he's convinced the dealer was just an unwitting intermediary: "He sounded fairly honest, like he was caught in the middle, if what he told me was right."

However, Stolicny is not returning the counterfeits he was sent.

"I knew they were fake as soon as I opened then," Stolicny said. "But I paid C.O.D., and stopped payment on the check right away, so I'm only out the $12.50 it cost to stop payment on the check."

Stolicny also said he called a Connecticut FBI office and was told they would handle a fraud case such as this provided there was a provable loss of $5,000.

Curiously, Stolicny — who said he was "devastated" by the discovery that the cards were counterfeit — was not advertising to buy or sell Mattingly cards.

"He must have just been going through the SCD and calling dealers around the country," he said.

Among the other dealers that bought counterfeit Mattinglys were Blake Meyer of Lone Star Sports Cards and John Digulio.

Meyer said he received a call from the dealer Dec. 28.

"He said he had these Mattinglys for sale, and said he'd sell them to me at $40 apiece," Meyer said. "I couldn't figure out why he was selling them to me at $40 when guys are advertising in SCD to buy at

$60. Then between the time he called me and the time I got them, I heard there were counterfeits out there so I knew right away what I had."

Digiulio's story matches the one told by Jeff Bauer of Bauer Baseball, Williamsport, Pa., as well as Meyer's. Bauer said he received two fake Mattinglys — and could have had as many as four — from the dealer. All three said they wouldn't have been able to tell the cards were counterfeit if they hadn't been warned in advance.

Both Digiulio and Stolicny said they received "distressed" calls from the young dealer looking to retrieve the cards after he spoke with SCD.

Although the particulars of the case are muddled, the issues are very clear to Donruss' Lewis.

"It's actually a crime," Lewis contends. "It's an infringement of our copyright, and it's an infringement of our agreement with the owners and the players' association," he said.

However, when it comes to prosecuting, Lewis admits, "Sure, it's tough for us to police. When we find someone duplicating cards, we'll take some action, sure. But hobby people are their own breed. Everyone buys and sells, and everyone is presumed to have some degree of knowledge about what it is they're buying and selling. I doubt whether we'll ever be able to monitor every nook and cranny."

The biggest surprise to come out of this case, according to the principals involved, is not that the cards were counterfeited but that more cards aren't counterfeited.

"The hobby is so hot right now that I thought more of these professionals would come out of the woodwork," Stolincy said. "It's sad; it makes people real hesistant about buying these cards."

"With cards moving so fast, I'm leery," Altman said. "If a 14-year-old kid can do it and get away with it, and get one of his friends who's a little older to peddle them for him, what's going to happen if some pros, with real knowledge of printing, get ahold of it? It's a real scary situation."

Editor's note: Although for obvious reasons, the above report does not name juveniles involved in the alleged counterfeiting scheme, SCD was able to determine their identities rather easily. Their names are being kept on file, and SCD will cooperate with authorities investigating the situation.

This report again emphasizes the need for dealers and collectors to examine everything closely for authenticity before buying, and it also demonstrates that, although it may be relatively easy to counterfeit a modern card, it is also easy to get caught at it! — Kit Kiefer

* * *

In February, SCD Publisher Bob Lemke had an announcement for the paper's readers — Sports Collectors Digest would begin publishing on a weekly basis, instead of every two weeks. He explained why in the Feb. 13, 1987, issue:

"The tremendous growth in the baseball card hobby in the past year has shown that we are ready for a weekly publication. Publishing SCD on a weekly frequency will allow buyers and sellers to get together twice as quickly as well as allowing you to receive the latest hobby news twice as fast.

"I have no doubt that baseball card collecting is the country's fastest-growing hobby. Even better, it is growing at all levels of interest. And best of all it is growing from the grass roots up.

"Let me illustrate. Sports Collector's Digest, long regarded as the publication for the more advanced, serious collector, grew from a paid circulation of 22,767 on Jan. 1, 1986, to a circulation of 31,758 on Jan. 1, 1987 — a 39.5 percent growth.

"Baseball Card News, our monthly newspaper for the more casual or newer collector, gained 70 percent in calendar 1986, from a paid circulation of 10,882 to 18,507.

"And at the most basic level, our newsstand-oriented Baseball Cards magazine, geared to introducing the hobby to the new collector, went from circulating 92,416 copies on Jan. 1, 1986, to a circulation of 114,390 at the first of this year, an increase of more than 20.000 copies.

"This growth pattern shows that while more and more collectors are coming into the hobby at the beginning level, most of them seem to be sticking with us and becoming more involved with each passing month.

"The hobby's growth is also apparent outside the pages of our collector periodicals. There are more baseball card sets being issued with each passing year — from the big national gum companies to major league teams to small regional issuers. There are more, larger and more active card shows than ever before. There are more dealers — part-time, full-time, mail order and retail store — than at any time in the hobby's history. And I don't see any sign of slowdown on the horizon."

Lemke added that the weekly circulation would cut back in the number of pages per issue; the publication was nearing its 400-page cutoff for being acceptable for being stapled together. And, he said, a change in deadlines would result in the issue arriving in readers' hands a day earlier.

* * *

SCD readers were called upon again to participate in a survey to select the worst and best sets ever produced by Topps. Jeff Zeigler shared the results in the March 20, 1987, SCD:

SCD Readers Cast Their Votes For The Best And Worst Sets Ever Produced By The Granddaddy Of The Card Companies

By Jeff Zeigler

And so, the results are in. You, the readers of SCD, have voted for the best Topps set and the worst Topps set of all time. The drum roll please...Actually, the results of the poll, in my judgment, are not very surprising. The set which came out the king of the mountain was the 1957 Topps issue with 15 percent of the vote. The 1953 Topps set finished second with 8 percent and third place was a tie between 1955, 1963 and 1967, all with 6 percent of the total votes cast.

Much to my displeasure, the 1972 Topps set (one of my favorite sets) took the booby prize with 20 percent of the votes for worst set. The second worst set with 11 percent was the year 1982, and the 1975 and 1962 sets tied for third worst with 9 percent each.

As far as decades go, the Topps sets from the '50s proved to be the favorite with 49 percent of all the "best" votes cast. The 1970s topped the worst voting list with 43 percent of the "worst" votes.

The trend in voting seemed to go with the more conservative designs — 1957, 1967, 1963 and 1953 are all simple designs. In comparison, the sets that were voted the worst were the issues that were colorful or loud. The '75, '72, '82 and '58 Topps sets all fit into this category, although the '75s received almost as many "best" votes as it did "worst" votes.

The main reason for the 1957 set's top tally seemed to be overall design, but answers ranged from "they are most like the '53 Bowmans" to "they have old stadium backgrounds."

Rand D. Laramie of South Egremont, Mass., picked the '57s for best set because of the non-cluttered photos which include many action shots.

R.P. Lekosta, of Elmwood Park, Ill., chose the 1957 Topps issue because of the backgrounds of Ebbets Field, the Polo Grounds and Yankee Stadium, and because the players wore flannel uniforms.

And, Gordon Sutla loves the 1957 cards because they are the closest to the 1953 Bowman set, which he claims is the all-time best. As a side note, Surney James Steele of Boulder, Colo., thinks cards #400, Dodger Sluggers, and #407, Yankee Power Hitters, in the 1957 set are "baseball at its finest."

Of course, the 1957 Topps set wasn't the only one with supporters. There were good reasons for voting for another set.

Clay Clatur from Framington, Mass., is a 1953 Topps supporter, claiming "hi-tech photography can never match the art and classic backs of these cards." Others quoted an all-around good effort by Topps for their 1953 vote and claimed that this was due to the presence of Bowman cards during that era.

A strong front was put up for the 1967 Topps issue, a set which is close in looks to the 1957 set.

John J. Halonka perhaps described the '67s best by saying "the pictures are large...the backs are easy to read...and the player write-ups are colorful and heroic as opposed to the bland facts of recent years. Descriptions such as Boog Powell's card (#230)...'His massive frame is enough to strike fear into the heart of any opposing pitcher'...is more likely to inspire dreams and spur the imagination of youngsters than, say, Don Mattingly's '86 card (#180) which says, 'First major league Home Run: 6-24-86.'"

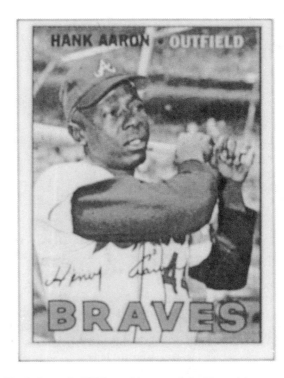

Hank Aaron's 1967 card is one of the Topps' best ever, says reader Dave Spock.

Dave Spock, of State College, Pa., gave several reasons for picking the '67s, including clean, economical design, full-length photos and good specialty cards. Also, he sites the '67 Aaron and Gibson as the two best Topps cards of all time.

The 1955 set had a strong showing, including a vote from Ray Isham, of Granger, Ind., who said the color sharpness, dual photos, team logo and near perfect back make it a well thought out set.

Debra Thorpe of Glen Allen, Va., thought the '55s deserved best ranking because of the horizontal design, good cartoons and white paper stock, among other things.

The 1963 offering had some advocates, including Ken Leonhardt of Pawling, N.Y., who said "it was one of the last sets made where you could get Musial, Snider, Hodges, Berra, etc., as players and also includes Mantle, Mays, Aaron, Clemente, Koufax, Gibson and Banks. Today's stars just don't seem to have that legendary greatness..."

Tom Smith from Chesterfield, Ohio, is absolutely ecstatic about the '63 set, claiming "this set has outstanding design, fantastic color, full stats, good photos, a great mix of former stars and stars to be, good special cards (especially numbers 412 and 138), high value and an overall challenge to collect."

How about a minority opinion? James McMahon of El Paso, Ill., chose the 1958 issue, which received only one "best" vote, because "the cards really stand out at a show surrounded by other cards" and "the players back then played ball for the love of the game rather than love of money, etc."

All the comments for best set were great, but perhaps the best comments came for the worst sets.

Comments about the "psychedelic '72s" usually included bad overall design, but also contained several other words of wisdom.

John Gustafson of Hinsdale, Ill., said the cards look more like rock star cards besides being gaudy and having small photos.

Richard Borgerson from Bellingham, Minn., said the lettering on top was too much, there were no player positions and to make matters worse, 1972 was the year he graduated high school!

Paul Casey of Staten Island, N.Y., said "the '72s had so many gaudy colors on them, they should be stuck on sticks and made into pinwheels!"

Other adjectives used to describe the '72s included putrid, outrageous and horrid. Enough said.

The 1982 Topps release made a strong bid for worse set near the end of the poll. Some collectors said when the '82s first came out, they thought they were hockey cards because of the hockey stick design. Others said useless action shots, unreadable backs and blurry, shaded photos were good reasons to vote the '82 Topps set the worst.

The 1975 Topps issue was another set with a lot of critics. Scott Salvice of Syracuse, N.Y., blasted the '75 set saying, "The people at Topps must have been on something. Horrendous color choice, both in terms of colors and color matchup, bad layout and off-center cards make them the all-time classic worst."

Brett Goodman of Livingston, N.J., thought the '75s looked like somebody wrote over them with magic maker and also said the red and green backs make the stats illegible.

The '62 Topps set also received a bunch of worst set votes including Todd Thibedeau from Whitteman Air Force Base in Missouri, who claimed the wood grain background and curled up photos added to his displeasure along with bad artwork on the in-action cards.

Charles Thorpe of Glen Allen, Va., cast one of the few "worst" votes for the '68 set, claiming "the card borders look like paper you'd line the bottom of drawers with." And the 1969 issue picked up a worst set vote from S.L. Toth of Morenci, Ariz., who said "with all the retouched photos in the set, it appears they tried to use as many shortcuts as possible to grind out this product."

On the subject of a worst set that could have been a best set, several respondents said that the 1958 set, which received six "worst" votes and only one "best" vote, could have been a lot better if it had normal background rather than the colored background.

The "winning" 1957 set consists of 407 cards valued at $1,875 in Near Mint.

Some of the more expensive cards in the set are #95 Mickey Mantle at $130, #302 Sandy Koufax at $80, #328 Brooks Robinson at $80, #1 Ted Williams valued at $55 and #20 Hank Aaron at $43. The four unnumbered checklists, which may be the hardest cards to find in Mint, range from $25 to $65.

The rookie card crop in the '57 issue is fairly good with #18 Don Drysdale, #35 Frank Robinson, #212 Rocky Colavito, #286 Bobby Richardson, #312 Tony Kubek, #328 Brooks Robinson and #338 Jim Bunning leading the way.

The set, which was the first to have the now standard 2 1/2" x 3 1/2" measurements, features a full-card length photo, with writing reproduced over the photo.

The backs contain full career stats for each player in a red and gray layout with blue lettering.

None of the photos, which include 24 airbrushes, are in-action game shots.

The Topps '72 "losers" consist of 787 cards with a price tag of $675 in Near Mint.

The team name dominates the '72 fronts, along with the bright colors, and at times seem to take away from the posed photos. The backs, layed out in orange and gray with black lettering, include full career stats, a quiz question and, for some players, a short biography.

The 1972 release features several subsets — a traded subset, an in-action subset and an awards card subset were all new in 1972.

Topps 1972 rookie cards are few and far between. Carlton Fisk, Dave Kingman, George Hendrick, Ben Oglivie, Ron Cey, Jose Cruz and Chris Chambliss are the notables.

One extreme drawback to the set, in my opinion, is that it contains 76 air-brushed photos and has many head-shots. Some of the less appealing cards in the set are #8 Ron Swoboda, #104 Toby Harrah, #140 Pat Dobson, #193 Kurt Bevacqua, #309 Roberto Clemente, #350 Frank Howard and #730 Rick Monday.

So, there you have it folks, the best and the worst Topps sets. For you who voted for the year 1957, congratulations — you are a baseball connoisseur. For those who voted for 1972 (the best set for two of you), cheer up. Maybe 1987 will be Topps' worst and then you'll be out of the cellar! — Jeff Zeigler

* * *

The results of 25 dealers who responded to a survey given during a show in Hawaii in February were given in the March 27, 1987, SCD:

1. One of the monthly price guides lists a 1984 Topps Mattingly at a value of $35. How do you feel about the price?

A. Sounds about right. He's easily the best player in the game today.

B. Should be higher. He's the greatest Yankee since Lou Gehrig.

C. A bit high. He's not worth twice as much as Boggs or four times as much as Gooden.

D. $35 for a 1984 card? Who is this guy listing the prices...Mattingly's agent?

Answers: A) 8% B) 4% C) 13% D) 35%

Comments: "This price does not reflect actual market value. It is prematurely priced."

"$20-$25 is about right."

"I think $15 is too much for an '84 card, but the buying public obviously disagrees."

You could buy Don Mattingly's rookie card for $35 in 1987.

2. The same guide lists a rookie Kirby Puckett at $5.50. Any thoughts?

A. Should be higher. He's a fantastic player — a superstar of the future.

B. Sounds about right. Eric Davis is listed at $1 less, but Puckett's already had a great season.

C. Sounds a bit high. $2-3 might be more accurate until he has two or three good seasons.

D. How can a two-year old card be worth $5.50? Is this guy Puckett's agent, too?

Answers: A) 0% B) 9% C) 21% D) 70%

Comments: "If he's $5.50, what are Kuenn, Oliva, Rosen worth? Does this guy have a pipeline to 10,000 Pucketts?"

3. Which players' cards are the hottest selling right now? (Space was given for up to four answers.) Mattingly 26, Eric Davis 9, Boggs 7, Cory Snyder 6, Mantle 6, Canseco 4, Joyner 3, '50s cards 3, Clemens 2, Ruth 2. The following received one mention each: Cobb, Gehrig, Gooden, gum packs, Bo Jackson, Raines, T. Williams, Valenzuela. (Note: Not a single mention of Pete Rose!)

4. How much do you get for a 1984 Donruss set?

Answer: Average was $162; high quote was $250, low $135.

5. What will the value of a 1984 Donruss set be at the end of 1987?

Answer: Average was $180; high quote was $325, low $90.

6. Baseball cards are considered a great investment by a number of collectors. What percent of all card sales are to collectors and what percent are bought primarily for investment?

Answers: Collect 51% Invest 48%

7. How much were your hobby sales in 1986?

Less than $50,000 — 20%; $50,000-$100,000 — 4%; $100,000-$200,000 — 16%; $200,000-$350,000 — 24%; $350,000-$600,000 — 24%; $600,000-$1,000,000 — 0%; $1,000,000 or more — 12%

8. How did your 1986 sales compare to 1985?

Answer: (Averaged) Up 115%

9. How will 1987 compare?

Answer: (Averaged) Up 49%

31

10. Donruss Co.'s new "dealer network" is now in place. Is it working?

Yes 29% No 71%. Are they printing enough material? Yes 21% No 79%. Is this network good for the hobby? Yes 50% No 50%.

Comments: "I need more cards."

"My allocation is three cases; that's too few to even bother with."

"Because of hobby growth it's the only way to be sure everybody gets some."

"It's easier to obtain cocaine."

11. How many collectors do you think there are in the country?

Answer: Under 100,000 — 25%; 100,000-199,999 — 10%; 200,000-499,999 — 40%; 500,000-999,999 — 5%; Million or more — 20%;

12. A major publisher, SCD, has decided to publish weekly. Any thoughts?

A. Fantastic. A great sign that the hobby is growing like crazy.

B. Once every two weeks seems right the way it is.

C. Enough is enough. I love cards, but I'll barely be able to dig through the present issue before another one shows up.

Answers: A) 32% B) 32% C) 36%

13. Advertisers: Does this weekly format appeal to you?

A. It's terrific. I'll have fresh ads hitting the mail every seven days — sales will rise.

B. I think ads every two weeks is enough. Besides, it takes enough of my time preparing ads that often.

C. Nice idea, but I'm afraid it will cut the "life" of my ad to just seven days. Besides, who has money to buy cards every seven days?

Answers: A) 14% B) 36% C) 50%

14. How many 1952 Topps Mantles do you think still exist?

Answers: Fewer than 1,000 — 21%; 1,000-1,999 — 11%; 2,000-4,999 — 26%; 5,000-9,999 — 11%; 10,000 or more — 32%

15. How many '85 Goodens?

Answers: Under a million — 42%; One to two million — 16%; More than two million — 42%

16. How many full-time dealers are there today? (We don't know either — take a guess.)

Answers: Under 100 — 14%; 100-250 — 24%; 250-500 — 19%; 500-1,000 — 9%; 1,000-5,000 — 29%; Over 5,000 — 5 %

17. How many dealers will there be two years from now?

Answers: Under 100 — 6%; 100-250 — 11%; 250-500 — 22%; 500-1,000 — 28%; 1,000-5,000 — 33%; Over 5,000 — 0 %

18. The promoters of one of the largest shows tries to stop "walk-ins" from entering the convention hall and then tries to buy their cards themselves. Any thoughts?

A. It's their show — they take the risks and rewards. Besides, no one asked you to take a table.

B. It's not fair. One reason I do shows is to buy material coming in off the street.

C. It's OK for promoters to buy cards, but others should be given a chance to buy them (plus the seller will get a fairer price for his cards).

D. Who cares? I'm there to sell cards and besides, nothing good ever comes in off the street anymore.

Answers: A) 24% B) 52% C) 24% D) 0%

19. More and more coin and stamp dealers are entering the card business. How do you feel about this development?

A. Let them stick to coins and stamps — they don't know a Bowman from a Donruss.

B. Their involvement is all positive. They bring new investor money into the game, creating new business for all of us.

C. Let them do what they want. This is a free enterprise system we've got.

D. Hey, they are causing a lot of "price hype" today and they'll abandon the business when it cools off.

Answers: A) 22% B) 13% C) 31% D) 34%

20. A recent ad in a hobby publication showed one dealer calling himself "America's Most Reliable Dealer," two are its "Best Dealer" and three more say they are the country's largest. Any thought?

A. Who cares? My business is fine without calling myself a big gun or bragging about my sales.

B. It's a free market, let them do what they want. Besides, you can't prove them wrong anyway.

C. It's good for the hobby to know who's who and the information is usually accurate.

D. Who needs to show a tax return or brag about the 10 billion cards they have? The bottom line is how much is in the bank at the end of the year.

Answers: A) 42% B) 29% C) 0% D) 29%

21. Other than yourself, of course, which dealer do you think is the country's largest? Take two or three educated guesses, if you like.

Answers: Renata Galasso — 12 votes; Larry Fritsch Cards — 11; Mr. Mint-Alan Rosen — 4; Rotman — 3; Pacific Coast Trading Card — 3; Card Collectors Co.-R. Gelman — 2; Tony Galovich — 2; TCMA — 1; Scott Bradshaw — 1; Steinbach/Quinn — 1; Tom Daniels — 1

22. For years complete sets of cards have been valued at considerably less than the individual cards in the set. What do you think?

A. It's crazy — a premium should be placed on a complete set. It should be a lot more than the single cards.

B. Sets are getting too high. Single cards are good sellers because of the stars themselves (Mantle, Rose, etc.). It's tough to sell Pinsons, Powells, and Luzinskis and a set is a great way to dump quantities of commons and minor stars.

C. The pricing seems about right. It takes a lot of individual sales to produce as much money as a set goes for. Besides, few collectors have $1,000 to pay for a set at one time.

Answers: A) 42% B) 8% C) 50%

* * *

In the June 5, 1987, SCD issue, Lee Temanson reported there had been 119 different baseball card sets issued in 1987. But his list didn't include any unauthorized collector-issue cards. As the issue's cover story proclaimed, SCD was banning them from the publication.

SCD Bans 'Collector Issues'

By Bob Lemke, Publisher

Effective June 1, 1987, the advertisement of all unauthorized collector-issue baseball cards depicting current players will be prohibited in the pages of Sports Collectors Digest, Baseball Card News, Baseball Cards Magazine and all other periodicals and books produced by Krause Publications.

The ban will apply to, but not be limited to, those issues commonly known in the hobby as "Broders" "Cunninghams" "Piedmont Productions" etc.

While this policy is going to cost us thousands of dollars per year in advertising revenues, we feel it is in the best long-range interests of the hobby.

Simply put, we feel the recent rash of unauthorized collector-issue baseball cards is bad for the hobby. First and foremost, they siphon money away from legitimate collectibles — the authorized baseball card issues that have formed the backbone of this hobby for more than a century.

Secondly, they are causing the baseball establishment — everybody from individual players to the players' union to the commissioner's office — to take a hard look at the hobby, a study that too often gives the image of a hobby which doesn't care for the legal and moral rights of others, but is only concerned with lining the pockets of selected individuals.

Like you, we find it hard to dish up any sympathy for the $2 million per year player who doesn't get his 1/4 cents-per-card royalty from a bootleg baseball card. We can, however, empathize with the legitimate card set producers — from the biggest bubble gum company to the smallest potato chip company — who do pay royalties — up to mid six-figure and more — to the players and teams for the right to use photos and trademark team logos.

Our real sympathy, though, is for the beginning collector who hasn't yet learned there is a difference between a legitimately issued baseball card which — the occasional K-Mart issue aside — will increase in value year after year as increasing demand chases diminishing supply, and the unauthorized collector issue, which, should value ever rise significantly, is always subject to reprinting by the same parties who produced them in the first place.

The situation wasn't so bad when collector issues used to he confined to team sets of old-timers that sold for a nickel or dime per card; it was easy for even the most novice collector to differentiate between such issues and the "real" baseball cards produced by Topps, Kellogg's and a handful of others in the 1970s.

Today, however, the producers of unauthorized collector cards concentrate on the latest rookie phenoms and hottest superstars. Some are turning out products that are more attractive than anything the bubble gum companies can do. The photos are often sharp and clear, the designs and artwork can be as good as anything ever done in the golden age of 1950s baseball cards, and they are usually well printed. However, they now sell for as much as $1, $2, $5 — even $15 apiece. How is the beginning collector to differentiate the unauthorized collector card from the 100 or so other sets being legitimately produced each year? How is he to know that once the supply of $15 Don Mattingly photo cards dries up, the printing presses may roll again and a new supply emerge?

If the hobby is to continue to grow and prosper, it's up to you and us to curb the abuses and nurture the hobby at the grassroots level by affording some protection to the newer collector.

Similarly, if the sports memorabilia industry is to gain the respect of the baseball establishment, we must clean up the bootleg products that give a bad name to all.

We're going to keep a sharp eye on the ads submitted to our periodicals and I'm going to exercise my right as publisher to delete advertising reference to any baseball card issues which I feel have not been properly licensed by the players, teams or major league baseball, as necessary.

Moreover, we are going to place the burden of proof on the potential advertiser to provide us with copies of such authorizations upon demand. If you want to sell cards to our readers, you must obtain the necessary documentation of their legitimacy from your supplier so that you can provide it to us if called upon to do so.

Obviously, we can't do this job alone. We're asking our readers to help us police these pages. There are going to be unauthorized cards which slip by even the most watchful eyes. If you have reason to question the legitimacy of a baseball card, series or set you see advertised, contact us and we'll look into it.

This policy raises a number of questions and concerns, many of which don't have pat answers. Let's look at some of them:

OK, how about your own collector issues which you publish as inserts in your Baseball Cards magazine?

Those cards are produced as part of the editorial content of the magazine. As such, they are protected under the doctrines of fair editorial use of the player's photos or team logos, much as a picture of a ballplayer in the daily newspaper or monthly sports magazine.

They are not now, and never were, intended to be resold as collectors' items.

In fact, one of the straws which broke the camel's back is when I saw the 1983-style Don Mattingly cards from our April, 1987, BBC Magazine being advertised in our own pages and at shows at $4 and $5 a pair.

While we have maintained a policy of making print overruns of these insert cards available to dealers in the past, they will no longer be sold. All extra cards will be destroyed or given away at shows as table handouts, etc.

All right; how about collector-issue baseball cards of non-current players?

Since collectors are unlikely to confuse cards of "old-timers" with current issues, we will maintain a bit broader stance on collector-issue cards of non-current players. Those issues which have been advertised prior to June 1 will be allowed to continue for sale in our pages. New issues, however, will still be on a case-by-case basis. If, in our determination, any old-timers' card set appears to have the potential of confusing the hobbyist or otherwise being detrimental to our hobby goals, we will again reserve the publisher's prerogative to keep it from our pages.

Additionally, we have been currently, and are currently, involved in a series of meetings with Major League Baseball Players' Alumni Association and licensing agent for the estates of many deceased stars and of the Hall of Fame. While I personally have some reservations about the legal finepoints in this matter, it is our intention to work with them to curb abuses of the use of likenesses of former ballplayers on hobby items, while still maintaining their fair use.

What does your policy say about reprints of legitimate baseball cards of the past?

As long as they are well marked as reproductions and don't infringe on legal copyrights, we don't have a problem with their appearance in our pages.

Does this ban apply to photos, original artworks, statues, etc.?

Not currently. Our principal goal in banning unauthorized collector-issued cards of current players is to protect the legitimacy of the authorized issues with which they are too easily confused.

In the area of 8x10 photos, plates, statues, lithographs, plaques, etc., the potential for confusion between authorized and unauthorized issues is certainly present. However, since the hobby views all of these items — authorized and unauthorized — as made-for-collectors, most hobbyists don't seem to differentiate between legitimate issues and unauthorized issues.

Again, we have some doubts about the ultimate ability of an enforcement agent to prevent the public sale of a work of art depicting a baseball player. We will again fall back on the publisher's right to ultimately decide what material is offered to his readers in the pages of his publication.

We thank our advertisers for their cooperation in working with us on this matter for the good of the hobby. — Bob Lemke

* * *

In a follow-up story on the ban, Steve Ellingboe reported in the June 26, 1987, SCD that response had been very favorable towards SCD's new policy. The Eastern Pennsylvania Sports Collectors Club (EPSCC), which sponsors the annual "Philly" shows, became the first in the nation to ban such material from its shows, Ellingboe reported.

EPSCC President Bob Schmierer told SCD, "We've reached a time in this hobby/business where major shows must take a stand on the issue. There are enough legitimate, licensed products to make all dealers and collectors happy without encouraging or supporting the pirates who refuse to deal with Major League Baseball, the Players Association, the individual teams and players."

The ban, he said, would not affect many dealers at his shows because most dealt only in authorized products. The ban would also apply to photos, souvenir-type items and all other phases of sport and non-sport collectibles offered for sale, and would place responsibility on the dealer to provide written documentation that any questionable items have been authorized and are licensed.

"Legitimate issuers pay healthy fees to Major League Baseball and the Players Association," Schmierer said. "To permit the continued sale of unauthorized items at our shows is unfair to those who've paid fees. If we are to achieve the respectability we all want with the baseball establishment, those who legitimately serve baseball and the mass media, this is a logical step to clean up dealers' tables and operate within the same boundaries in which licensees have dealt for years.

"It's only a matter of time until the baseball establishment turns its enforcement powers in the direction of material that is offered for sale at shows," Schmierer concluded.

* * *

Another issue which was cropping up again was the ramifications of card restoration, which Alan Rosen addressed in his July 31, 1987, Mint Matters column. He wrote:

"It seems that an expert in paper restoration has been attempting for some time to restore these card classics, and, I should say, with extreme success. At one card show, I had occasion to examine these cards, and the work is really quite incredible. Unless you look extremely closely under magnification, it's nearly impossible to detect the restoration.

"This leads me to the following questions:

"Although on this dealer's table the cards were clearly marked as restorations, nothing could prevent a buyer from simply purchasing the card, removing it from its present holder and then reselling it as a Gem Mint original specimen. Would this be legal? Would it be ethical?

"The restorer uses the paper from original Goudey cards to restore the corners of the specimen he's working on. Is this deceiving the collecting public? The dealer and restorer tell me no, the cards are clearly marked restored.

"What price would you have to pay for a Gem Mint 1933 Goudey Babe Ruth card in restored condition? The answer is simple: $750, about the same as you'd pay for what I'll call an 'original' specimen.

"At a later show, I noticed what I considered to be a positive change in the marketing of these cards. Not only did the cards say 'restored' on the holders, but they were also clearly marked indelibly with a dot on the top right hand corner of the back.

"As far as I'm concerned, these cards are absolutely beautiful. The only thing I question is the resale value of these blazing beauties. Any comments from SCD readers would be welcome," Rosen concluded.

In that same column, Rosen also recapped card prices he had found in a December 1982 issue of Card Prices Update.

"Looking at the prices blew me away. Just five years ago, a 1958 Topps set was listed at $325; a '62 set was $312. Boy, have times changed! Thought you might like to reminisce a little, so here are a few of the prices of sets and singles from that 1982 (now-defunct) publication:

"1952 Topps: $6,725; 1953 Topps: $1,200; 1954 Topps: $675; 1955 Topps: $500; 1956 Topps: $425; 1957 Topps: $590; 1958 Topps: $325; 1959 Topps: $278; 1960 Topps: $310; 1961 Topps: $562; 1962 Topps: $312; 1963 Topps: $575; 1964 Topps: $210; 1965 Topps: $285; 1966 Topps: $375; 1967 Topps: $455; 1968 Topps: $200; 1969 Topps: $275;

"1948 Bowman: $250; 1949 Bowman: $1,750; 1950 Bowman: $560; 1951 Bowman: $985; 1952 Bowman: $580; 1953 Bowman: $1,050; 1953 Bowman (B&W): $640; 1954 Bowman: $400; 1955 Bowman: $290;

"1957 Williams: $27; 1958 Mantle: $23.50; 1959 Mantle: $17.50; 1960 Yaz: $40; 1963 Rose: $165; 1964 Mantle: $10; 1965 Carlton: $30; 1966 Perry: $22; 1967 Seaver: $55; 1968 Bench: $11; 1969 Jackson: $22."

In the July 10, 1987, Coach's Box, Editor Steve Ellingboe alerted readers about more counterfeit cards being produced. The six different cards, among the hottest cards in the hobby then, were all Donruss issues — the 1984 Don Mattingly, Joe Carter and Wade Boggs; and the 1985 Don Mattingly, Wade Boggs and Eric Davis. Earlier, in the March 13, 1987, SCD, readers were alerted that a small number of counterfeit Fleer Update cards of the high-demand $100 Dwight Gooden card had been circulating in the hobby. The 132-card set, listed at $225, also included first cards for Roger Clemens and Kirby Puckett.

* * *

One again, SCD readers were asked their opinions, this time on what they liked and didn't like about card sets issued by Topps, Fleer and Donruss. Ted Taylor reported the findings in his Aug. 7, 1987, Off the Cuff column:

SCD Readers Cast Their Votes

By Ted Taylor

In my July 3, SCD column we proposed a readers' suvery on what you like and what you don't like in the Topps-Fleer-Donruss issued card sets. Well, the vote is in, and a lot of you voted, with some very interesting results.

So here, without charge to marketing departments of "the big three," are our findings.

SCD readers prefer action shots over posed ones by a slim 65 to 50 margin. Respondents commented that, among other things, "most players are ugly" (says Joe Linder of Opa Locka, Fla.), "posed shots tend to be dull" (says David Milstead of Rock Hill, S.C.), "I like to see what the player looks like, so I prefer posed" (says Doug Long of Downers Grove, Ill.).

Manager cards got overwhelming support with 85 of 115 votes in favor of them. Additional suggestions included adding selected coaches cards each year — several people suggested Yogi Berra (Astros) and Willie Stargell (Braves) as people they'd like to see.

Multi-player cards got a close call, but readers did support them 60 to 55. What bugs several people is having two or more players to a card. Michael Oestreich of Hazelwood, Mo., voices a large negative toward "cute" cards. "Such things as (Fleer's) 'Holland-Tunnell' are poor," he writes. Many others agree.

"Cute" cards such as these get negative marks from some readers.

Checklist cards also get a slim OK (60 to 55), but even those who voted for them said that more than one or two such cards per set is overkill and takes away from other potential player cards that could have been included. Mike Gillen of East Grand Forks, Minn., expresses the main sentiment against them by saying "every collector has a guide of some sort anyway and if you mark a checklist card it's considered ruined." Good point.

Multi-player rookie cards are considered good by 75 of 115. "How else would you get two rookie cards of Mickey Klutts or Don Aase?" asks reader Steve Birmingham. Gordon Pelzek, on the other hand, says "they are a waste...no place to keep them unless you cut them up, as I did back in the early days of collecting." Me too.

While readers gave a slim edge to specialty cards (65 to 50) they were pretty unanimous in one thing they didn't like — Donruss Diamond Kings. "I like the Rated Rookies, but not Diamond Kings," said Richard Abel. "Diamond Kings are getting old...if Donruss wants to use Dick Perez's artistic talents they should do a subset of the prior year's Hall of Fame inductees," says David Milstead. "I like the speculation involved in Rated Rookies, but do not like Diamond Kings," says Pelzek. Birmingham says "Diamond Kings were nice once, now they're boring."

One thing that is being offered now that the readers really don't like at all are inserts. "Puzzles, I hate 'em," says Doug Long. "I hate puzzles," says Carmen Ianelli. "Stickers are great — if you happen to be under 10 years of age," says Bill Watson of Ponte Vedre, Fla. Jim Smith, of Woonsocket, R.I., says "puzzles, I don't like 'em...my 4-year-old son likes the stickers." Mike Gillen says "inserts are a big waste." David Wheeler of Baxter, Tenn., says "who buys cards for the inserts?" The total vote was 80 to 35 against them.

Readers did prefer team cards by a 65 to 50 margin, but several qualified their support. "Subsets and team cards are good and a vital part of the hobby," says Christopher Beck of Clymer, N.Y. "I like team pictures with a checklist on the back," says Mike Terry of Indianapolis, Ind. Robert Lekostaj of Elmwood Park, Ill., votes as follows, "subsets like All-Stars, 'Record Breakers' or 'Turn Back the Clock' are fun additions to the sets."

Gary Mills of Milwaukee, Wis., carried the survey to its logical conclusion and spelled out his idea of what would constitute the "perfect" set and, in considering it, I tend to pretty much agree with him.

Starting with the premise of a 660-card set, Gary would divide the distribution of subjects as follows:

509 regular baseball cards — this would depict, roughly, 80 percent of the players on the 24-man roster of the 26 teams; 26 team photo cards with a checklist on the back; 26 manager cards; 26 coaches cards (four per team, per card); 26 stadium photo cards; 26 hot prospect cards — one per team; 10 A.L. umpires; 10 N.L. umpires; 1 baseball commissioner.

If you were to scrap the umpires — because the last time anyone did this was 1955 Bowman and those cards aren't exactly in great demand — you could either add 20 more prospects or, perhaps, an assortment of "final" cards for players who retired after the prior season and some prospects. — Ted Taylor

* * *

In the Dec. 4, 1987, SCD, Tom Owens reported prospects were having their minor league cards counterfeited. The 1982 Columbus Clippers Don Mattingly and the 1975 International League All-Star Gary Carter cards were cropping up as fakes among legitimate issues, he said.

Jim Hawkins, in his Feb. 26, 1988, Eye of the Hawk column, noted just how big the hobby was becoming:

Look At How Our Hobby Has Grown!

By Jim Hawkins

How huge has our hobby grown? Well, to give you some idea, I'd like to share with you an excerpt from an article that appeared in the Detroit News in September, 1970, reporting on the First Annual Midwest Sports Collectors Convention, forerunner of the popular Plymouth show:

"By Ted Goczkowski

"Detroit News Staff Writer

"DETROIT, MICH. — More than 50 persons — many of them businessmen or teachers — gathered in the Detroit Hilton Hotel yesterday for several bargaining sessions. They came from all over the country, having planned for months for the meeting. You could see the emotion in their faces as they got down to the business at hand — trading baseball cards."

Can you imagine a show today at which "50 persons" would be considered a significant — and satisfactory — crowd? Can you imagine dealers coming "from all over the country" for such a show?

Incredible as it may sound in this era of 200-table shows and crowds that are counted by the thousands, a little publication called Sport Fan out of Rosemont, Pa., was able to print the names and hometowns of nearly every collector who attended that inaugural Midwest Sports Collectors Convention.

I think you'll find this list most interesting. I know I did:

Tom Altshuller, Oak Park, Mich.; Jay Barry, Oak Park, Mich.; Dennis Graye, Detroit; Ed Lotz, Flint, Mich.; Dick Reuss, Detroit; Lloyd Toerpe, Flint, Mich.; Paul Frisz, Terre Haute, Ind.; Ed Broder, La Habra, Calif.; John Taylor, Portage, Mich.; Allen Denny, Minneapolis, Minn.; Ed Budnick, Detroit; John England, Fort Smith, Ark.; Owen Ricker, Waterloo, Ontario, Canada; Dave Lewis, Oak Park, Mich.; Richard Egan, Mundelein, Ill.; Ray Billbrough, Flushing, Mich.; Bob Ikins, Jackson, Mich.; Gary Dunstone, Flint, Mich.; Jack Daniels, Flint, Mich.; Al Peterjohn, Columbus, Ohio; Dick Ockomon, Pendleton, Ind.; Steve Hepter, Anderson, Ind.; Andy Richardson, Detroit; Wilfred Jonske, Detroit; Don Steinbach, Joliet, Ill.; Alan Graver, Toledo, Ohio; William Loechel, Birmingham, Mich.; Bob Santino, Flint, Mich.; Colin Sinclair, Tecemseh, Ontario, Canada; Jim McConnell, Pomona, Calif.; John Sterling, Indianapolis, Ind.; Elliott Harvith, Southfield, Mich.; Tom Wickman, Frostburg, Md.; John Ryan, Detroit; Mike Cramer, Phoenix, Ariz.

These men, and others like them, are the true pioneers of our industry. Some of the names, of course, you recognize. They are still involved. I wonder what they and others think of the state of our hobby today. — Jim Hawkins

* * *

Midway through the 1988 baseball season, columnist Ted Taylor picked the year's best baseball cards and listed them in his June 17, 1988, Off the Cuff column.

"There is nothing particularly objective about judging art and beauty. One man's masterpiece is another's piece of junk. What I perceive as a beautiful woman may be perceived by others as a plain Jane.

"And so, armed with those premises, I boldly venture forth with my opinions concerning the best-looking baseball cards of 1988.

"I started out to rate the top 20. Next I extended that to the top two dozen. Finally, I settled on 26, and though that is the same number as there are Major League teams, there will not be one card per team. Things never work out that way," he wrote.

Topps had 13 cards in the list, Fleer had five, and Donruss and Score each had four: 1. Dewayne Buice, Topps #649; 2. Kelly Downs, Topps #629; 3. Doc Edwards, Topps #374; 4. Tommy Hinzo, Topps #576; 5. Roger Clemens, Donruss #51; 6. Pete Incaviglia, Fleer #470; 7. Carlton Fisk, Topps #385; 8. Bruce Ruffin, Score #492; 9. Tim Birtsas, Topps #501; 10. Jeff Treadway, Fleer #249; 11. Ron Darling, Score #141; 12. Gary Carter, Score #325; 13. Chris Bando, Fleer #601; 14. Phil Lombardi, Topps #283; 15. Wade Boggs, Donruss #BC-7; 16. Sam Horn, Topps #377; 17. Carmen Castillo, Topps #341; 18. Roy Smalley, Fleer #22; 19. Kevin Seitzer, Donruss #BC-17; 20. Tom Brunansky, Score #194; 21. Wally Joyner, Donruss BC-13; 22. Jim Acker, Topps #678; 23. Benny Santiago, Topps #693; 24. Billy Ripken, Topps #352; 25. Mike Loynd, Topps #319; and 26. Curt Young, Fleer #296.

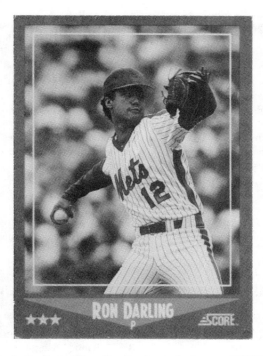

Ted Taylor selected Ron Darling's card as one of 1988's best.

The July 1, 1988, SCD announced Hartland Plastics Inc. was planning to release limited-edition replica player statues honoring the 25th anniversary of the original 18 well-loved baseball statues made during the late 1950s and early '60s.

The statues, in copies of their original boxes, would be branded (and individually numbered) clearly as 25th anniversary replicas. Each figure would be limited in production to 10,000 units worldwide, available for $23.95 each.

In that same SCD issue, Tom Mortenson, in his Coach's Box column, posed the question who's to blame for high prices for Joe DiMaggio's autograph?

DiMaggio, he said, received an enormous sum of money to make a one-day appearance at the show to sign autographs, so show promoters charged $3.50 admission, and $15 to $19 per autograph.

Who's to blame for such high prices, he asked, offering these answers:

"A. Joe DiMaggio. He's ripping off the public for all he can get.

"B. Promoter Allan George. Charging $3.50 admission and $15 and $19 for autographs is ridiculous.

"C. The dealers. They're only adding to the problem by adding to the already-inflated prices in the market. And they should respect Joe's wishes.

"D. The public. Anyone dumb enough to spend that much deserves what they get.

"E. All of the above.

"F. None of the above. Hey, it's America. People charge and spend whatever they please. If fans want to spend $19 for an autograph and it makes them happy, who are we to criticize?"

* * *

The collecting hobby was growing in leaps and bounds, transforming from swap meets into big business. Mark K. Larson interviewed dealer Mike Jaspersen, the press secretary for the hobby's national convention, about how the hobby had changed in the last 15 years:

From Swapping To Big Business Dealer Recalls The Way It Was, The Way It Is

By Mark K. Larson

Comparing the first organized memorabilia shows to today's conventions is like comparing a Little League game to a World Series game, says dealer Mike Jaspersen.

Jaspersen, the press secretary for this year's National Convention July 8-10 in Atlantic City, N.J., says sports memorabilia collecting shows in the early 1970s were swap meets. But today the hobby is a big business, says Jaspersen.

The old shows, he said, were more personable and educational. Cards, stories and tales about the trades made with the guy next door, articles on the hobby and checklists were swapped at the early shows, he said.

About 20 people attended the first organized show Jaspersen attended. It was a one-day event in 1970 in a home in Yorktown Heights, N.Y.

"It was great," Jaspersen said, noting the show was the second largest organized sports collectors show at the time, compared to a show in Los Angeles in 1969.

At the early shows — before 1973 when shows began appearing at Legion Halls — dealers and collectors "would have their material with them. They'd open up their briefcases. It was more of a swap. Very little cash changed hands," he recalls.

Today, trading is becoming a lost art. Jaspersen's trick in trading was to never go first. You always wanted to give the other guy the edge, give him the better deal by throwing in something extra, he said.

Trading was fun, but even then, "people were still concerned about values...everybody had it in the backs of their minds," he said.

Today, kids, "when they go to a show, it's dollars and cents...that came with the price guides. If they can get something for 25 cents that was worth 50 cents, they'd be ecstatic," he said.

Price guides are beneficial for collectors and dealers when they are buying and selling, but have been a factor in the escalation of prices, he said.

When there was just one price guide, "that was it. That was the word. But now prices seem to go up real fast with two," Jaspersen said.

People won't buy the guide if the prices inside always stay the same, he explained, so the competition for sales between different guides has resulted in card price changes.

As the talk spreads about high prices, "the dealers are creating their own fears. Everyone thinks it's going to bust, the bottom is going to fall out," he said.

But the demand will continue — and in some cases the supply will remain high — and prices will continue to rise.

To keep the hobby growing, the base of collectors must be expanded, he said, adding it would be nice if the 50,000 projected to attend the show this year includes 10,000 new collectors, who in turn sell the hobby to another 10,000 to keep the base growing.

"There are a lot of baseball fans out there. It was embarrassing to admit they collect cards. They wouldn't tell anyone. But now they do because of the prices," he said.

Sports memorabilia, excluding cards, is incredibly undervalued because there are no price guides, Jaspersen said. Unlike cards, there is a new piece of memorabilia that pops up everyday that isn't catalogued, he said.

Pennants and stadium souvenirs will be popular, he said, noting cards are kept in boxes or sheets, but memorabilia can be used to decorate the hobby room.

Some junk has flooded the market, causing some dealers to take their lumps and walk away. But others come back, he said.

The hobby is growing so big and quickly it will need organization to control fakes and rip-offs, he said, adding perhaps a review board could be created to protect collectors and dealers. Major League Baseball's crackdown on licensing will also help keep "the garbage" out, he said.

Jaspersen said he'd like to see the hobby foster a professional image.

"You want the hobby to look professional, which is one of the things that is definitely needed," he said.

Conventions are just like any other trade show, he explained, so those participating in them should work on their displays and appearance and take pride in what they are doing.

"It's not just a backyard thing or just a game. It's a business," he said.

This year's convention in Atlantic City "is going to be tough for someone to top it. They (promoter Ron Durham and his staff) have pulled out all the stops," he said.

A new twist is the use of corporate sponsorship for the convention from such companies as the New Jersey Nets, Parker Brothers and New York Yankees. "It's the greatest thing that could happen to the national," Jaspersen said.

"It makes the business legitimate. You see these big corporations and you know that it is legitimate. It adds credibility and exposure to the hobby," he added.

Scheduled guests include Joe DiMaggio, Ralph Branca, Bobby Thomson, Ray Dandridge and Lou Dials.

In 1970, at the second annual Southern California show in a home in Los Angeles, about 30 people, including some 12 and 13 year olds, attended to see Cleveland Indian/Kansas City Athletic/New York Yankee pitcher Bud Daley, the first player to ever appear at a show, Jaspersen said.

"It was pretty impressive to be that close. He wasn't a superstar. But still, he was a major league ballplayer" he recalls.

Today the demand for some players is excessive.

"Mark McGwire was everywhere (last year). So what is that going to do to the value of his autograph?" he asked, noting the A's slugger signed 35,000 autographs in the off-season.

Don Mattingly, however, has priced himself out of shows and has stayed in the background, Jaspersen said, noting his will become more valuable.

It's OK for promoters to charge for autographs, he said, because the players will still sign at the ball park, charity golfing events and in restaurants.

If a person has four dozen balls signed and then resells them, a player should be able to capitalize on the fan who is capitalizing on him, Jaspersen said.

The public doesn't realize the player only receives a small percentage of the fees and thinks, "Boy, the guy must be broke and having a lot of problems...but 75 percent of the autographs being sold at the shows are being resold. There's nothing wrong with players taking a cut," he said.

"Having players there brings people in," Jaspersen said.

Promoters must "make it sound exciting as far as what's there. You have to educate the people on the promotions. You have to do something to entice them," he said.

Atlantic City is a resort, which means if the family becomes disinterested, there's always the beach. The city and convention have "all the right ingredients. The beach. The boardwalk. The site that is big enough to hold a very big crowd," he said.

Jaspersen expects the show to draw 50,000 people this year, topping the record crowd of about 25,000 who attended the National Convention last year in San Francisco.

"The average collector is probably the smaller spender. But he is going to find something for his collection...the average guy is going to find what he wants," he said. — Mark Larson

* * *

Krause Publications didn't like the way a certain aspect of the hobby was headed. In the Aug. 5, 1988, issue the company announced it was banning sports card restoration ads in SCD.

The reason for the ban on the sale of restored cards and any item or service which attempts to teach readers how to restore cards was simple, according the SCD's advertising manager, Hugh McAloon: "We don't like the direction in which card restoration is heading, and we don't feel it is in the long-term best interest in our hobby. Restoration is an accepted practice in many other areas, but there is a large price variance between the original and a restored product. In baseball cards, we feel that it would be too easy to pass a restored card as an original, and we all know what that could do to our hobby."

The criminal element had entered the hobby again, as the Aug. 5, 1988, SCD reported about an armed robbery of a card shop.

Mantle, Schmidt Cards Taken In Armed Robbery

By Matt Chaney

Larry and Nancy White recently entered the baseball card business in Springfield, Mo., because today's popularity of cards can make operating a store worthwhile.

The hobby's impact as a big business has also attracted the attention of criminal elements. Counterfeiting, burglaries and thefts of baseball cards are now widely reported.

But a rare, perhaps unheard-of occurrence has been the armed robbery of a baseball card store. This is what happened to Nancy White on May 25 as she worked alone in the family store, Triple Play Baseball Collectibles.

Springfield police say shortly before 2 p.m. a man and woman carrying a briefcase entered Triple Play, and told White they wanted her most expensive baseball cards.

"When he opened up the briefcase, I could see a sawed-off shotgun in it," White said during a recent interview in Triple Play.

"I walked up to (a display case) where I had all the expensive ball cards; the (Mickey) Mantles and such. I just figured that was what he was talking about.

"I started handing out all the expensive ones."

Atop the counter, White placed Mantles from 1955, '56, '58, two '59s, '61, '67 and '69. She sweetened the pot with a pair of Mike Schmidt rookies, a '56 Ted Williams, a Carl Yastrzemski rookie and a '66 Yaz. The cards' condition include strong excellent, near-mint and mint, with a $2,200 total retail price on the lot, she said.

As she placed the last few cards on the counter, White said she "looked up, and the man had closed the briefcase. He'd had it open until then, where I could see the gun."

The display case was the closest one to the front of Triple Play, five feet from the entrance door. White made a break for it.

"When he closed the briefcase, I felt like I could get out before he could get the gun out, so I ran out the door, and ran screaming into the office next door," she said.

The robbers, a 31-year-old man and 21-year-old woman, according to police, were taken by surprise. They yelled 'Hey!' but did little more than also run as White bolted from the store.

The woman did manage to throw the cards in her purse before departing through the front door, seconds after White.

The duo rushed past the office White had fled into, and headed for a getaway car and driver waiting about 100 feet away, at the west end of a string of single-story storefronts that includes Triple Play. But the scheme had gone awry.

"When the (getaway driver) saw me and the robbery going bad, he left (the robbers)," said White. The suspects disappeared in the storefronts, and police were called.

Minutes later, as White and other merchants stood outside the rear of Triple Play, the duo came walking around the buildings, pretending to be "passing through," White said.

The robbers saw White and the others, then ran east of the store and into woods that are scattered around east central Springfield, a newer area in the growing city of about 140,000.

Nancy said a merchant trailed them in his car, and police had little difficulty arresting the robbers a short time later near railroad tracks, confiscating the loaded shotgun and a handgun, and recovering the stolen cards.

Local police and some news media apparently had trouble taking the armed robbery seriously, according to John Hoogesteger, the reporter assigned to the case by The News-Leader, Springfield's daily newspaper.

"It doesn't add up," police Sgt. Bruce Headley told Hoogesteger.

"It's one of the sillier armed robberies I've seen, as far as having a goal and getting through with it. Of course, the people who were victimized took it very seriously."

Hoogesteger, a Michigan native who, coincidentally, collects baseball cards, told his skeptical editors the robbery made more sense than some others.

"I tried to tell them how valuable cards were, how hard they would be to trace, and the fact (the robbers) could probably get a lot for the old ones, especially the Mantles," he said.

"Most fences (dealers of stolen items) only pay 10 cents on the dollar (value) for hot goods. A card dealer someplace else would've had a hard time knowing those cards were stolen, and probably would've paid a lot for them."

White agreed with Hoogesteger. "I think they felt they could get enough money out of the cards to make (the robbery) worthwhile," she said.

"I guess it's hard to imagine somebody pulling off an armed robbery in the middle of the day for baseball cards, but when you think about it, everybody wants the older cards, and they probably could have taken them on to Kansas City and easily gotten $1,000 for them."

In initial hours following the robbery, the suspects told police they were "Fred and Wilma Flintstone."

Later, they were identified as Karl Edwin Smith, 31, of Titusville, Fla., and his sister-in-law, Teresa Cooper Smith, 21, of Ocala, Fla., according to Springfield Police Detective Sgt. Dan Wilson.

The next day, the alleged getaway driver, Keith Ashley Smith, 33, the husband of Teresa, was arrested at a local motel, according to Wilson.

All three suspects face a charge of first-degree robbery, with Karl Smith also charged with armed criminal action.

They are being held in the Greene County jail on $150,000 bond each, according to Rhonda Taylor, a spokeswoman for the county prosecuting attorney's office. The three are scheduled to appear in county associate court this month.

The Smith's are also wanted by Florida, Ohio and Arkansas authorities for questioning in other May robberies, according to Wilson.

The sawed-off shotgun used in the Triple Play robbery was identified as one of 11 guns taken May 9 at a Palatka, Fla., K-Mart, where bandits tied up an employee after the store had closed for the day, according to Hoogesteger.

On May 19, an undetermined amount of cash was taken in the robbery of a Freedom Federal Savings and Loan in Columbus, Ohio, when a man and a woman passed a threatening note to an employee.

May 23, in Little Rock, Ark., armed robbers of a First Federal Savings and Loan threatened to detonate an explosive device, and left with a large sum of cash before exploding dye pellets in bank bags forced them to drop the money in the bank's parking lot, according to Hoogesteger.

Springfield, located in southwest Missouri, is 200 miles north of Little Rock.

Karl Smith and Teresa Smith had first entered Triple Play on May 24, said White.

"They said they wanted to sell some old cards," she recalled. "I told them to come back the next day when my son Bryan would be in. So when they walked in (May 25) with a briefcase, I didn't think anything about it. My son wasn't in yet, so I said I would call him."

38

In a shaking voice, the man told White "it wouldn't be necessary" to call Bryan. "He told her that he hated to do this, but he had to have all of my expensive ball cards," said White.

She remembered the man had been nice the day before, which, she said, played a big part in her dangerous decision to run from the robbers.

"I guess that's why I felt like I could get out, because he wasn't a real mean looking type," she said. "You had to be there." — Matt Chaney

***

As the 1988 season drew to a close, Lee Temanson again supplied his list of how many card sets were issued so far in 1988. More than 200 new sets had been issued, he reported in the Sept. 30, 1988, SCD.

To ring in the new year, and close out the last year of collecting in the 1980s, Ted Taylor, in his Jan. 20, 1989, Off the Cuff column, recapped the decade, calling it the era the hobby came of age.

The 1980s — The Era The Hobby Came Of Age

By Ted Taylor

As we near the end of the 1980s, it's interesting and sobering to think about the tremendous changes that have taken place in our hobby since this decade dawned.

I recall quite vividly that there was much apprehension in 1980. There was a general feeling that the hobby had gotten as big as it possibly could and the high prices we were paying were artificial — the bottom could drop out at any moment.

Specifically, I can recall a conversation with my then show partner Bob Schmierer in January or February of 1980. We toyed with the prospect of selling our substantial personal collections for the current high prices, with all likelihood of being able to repurchase them at some time in the future for about half of what we sold them for.

Of course, that was just conjecture, and we didn't do it. But the climate was uncertain.

A few weeks before our scheduled Willow Grove show in March 1980, the annual Indianapolis show reported extremely light sales, little auction interest and a decline in attendance. We suspected the end was drawing near.

Yet the Philly show that March was dynamite. I was able to auction off three 1952 Topps Mickey Mantle cards for about $3,000 each and the show dealer business was probably the best ever.

In the months following that show the market did, in fact, soften a bit, but nothing like we had forecast. In fact, it remained healthy for the rest of that year.

What really launched the decade, though, was the 1981 decision of Judge Clarence Newcomer in U.S. District Court in Philadelphia that allowed Fleer and Donruss into the baseball card arena.

Things have never been the same since. The hobby just keeps getting bigger and bigger.

For those of us who have been along for the ride since the organized hobby flexed its muscles in the early 1970s, the 1980s have been, at times, uncomfortable.

It's not our private little hobby anymore. It's everybody's hobby.

Some say it's the fastest growing hobby in the country. I tend to agree with that thought. People from every walk of life are interested in it and, frankly, most of them are having fun.

This past Christmas season has shown just how visible the hobby really is. Remember all those sets you saw for sale?

The myriad hobby books in every popular book store? The hobby supplies? Yes, the hobby as we used to know it has grown up in the 1980s.

There are baseball card shops in most major shopping centers and people are speculating in cards like they used to do on Wall Street.

Is that good? I don't know. But I do know it's a fact.

One note of caution might be that we just may have streamlined the hobby right out of the reach of the very people it was first intended to entertain — the kids.

Sure, some of them have more money then Donald Trump when it comes to buying at the card shows. But how many kids who used to save up their lunch money to buy a wax pack or two on the way home from school now even bother?

We've told them they can't flip the cards — it ruins their value. We've told them they can't put them in rubber band packs anymore. It dents the sides of the cards.

We've told them to keep their cards in plastic sheets so that no one will touch them.

Does that sound like fun to you?

But all that aside, and maybe the hobby's growth has claimed some casualties, what the 1980s mostly did was refine the hobby, make it more visible and more accessible. And that isn't so bad.

There's one year left in this decade. It'll be interesting to see where we go next. — Ted Taylor

***

Things were interesting right off Billy Ripken's bat to start the new collecting season. Several readers informed SCD about the vulgarity printed on the 1989 Fleer card #616 of Bill Ripken. The card contains an obscenity on the bottom of the bat Ripken is holding.

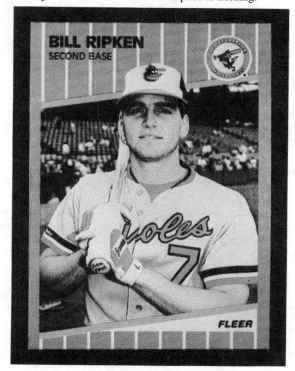

Billy Ripken's bat does some talking of its own.

The Feb. 3, 1989, SCD reported the national news media picked up on the mistake: "An article in the Baltimore Sun reported that Ripken knew nothing about the bat or how the obscenity got there. The report stated that Ripken was 'angry and disappointed' he was portrayed in such a disrespectful way.

"In a prepared statement from Fleer, the company regrets the occurrence of the incident. The statement is as follows: 'Fleer Corporation became aware of the printing mistake on Bill Ripken's card on Tuesday, Jan. 17. The company has affected the necessary changes to correct the card. Fleer sincerely regrets that this incident has occurred.'

"A spokesperson for Fleer would not comment on how many cards may have been printed with the obscenity," SCD reported.

In the Feb. 10, 1989, SCD, Steve Ellingboe summed up the Ripken situation:

X-Rated Ripken Card Sparks Hobby Hysteria

By Steve Ellingboe

No two words have ever had such a dramatic and sudden impact on the baseball card market as the two four-letter words that appeared on the knob of Billy Ripken's bat on his 1989 Fleer card.

The obscenity, which was first reported in the Feb. 3 SCD, sent the price of the Ripken card from two cents to over a hundred dollars overnight, and sent thousands of collectors scurrying to find the X-rated variation for their own collections.

Since its discovery, the value of the card has been bouncing around like a bad-hop grounder — first soaring, then dropping slightly following the initial collector hysteria, and then running up again, fueled by national media coverage that has attracted even non-collectors who want the card simply for its novelty.

Several hobby shops reported that dozens of new customers — people they've never even been before — are coming in to buy the scandalous Ripken card or just sneak a peek at it — a scenario that is undoubtedly being repeated at baseball card shops across the country as word of the naughty novelty spreads.

It's still too early, of course, to predict where the value of the card will eventually settle, or to speculate on how many are out there, but judging from the number of phone calls, reports and rumors to hit our office, the Ripken card has sparked more interest and controversy than any other hobby development in recent memory.

Fleer is, understandably, embarrassed by the situation. In a carefully-worded statement issued almost immediately after the obscenity was discovered, company President Vincent J. Murray said that Fleer regrets the incident and is correcting the card for future print runs. Although reluctant to discuss details of the situation, Murray's concern is obviously sincere.

"The less we fan this fire, the better," he said in a telephone interview, also acknowledging that "our proofreaders just missed it. It was a very unfortunate thing."

For his part, Billy Ripken claims he was the innocent victim of a teammate prankster. In a Baltimore Sun article, Ripken said he was "angry and disappointed" about being shown in "such a disrespectful way," and added that he is sorry so many young people were exposed to the obscenity.

Ripken has the reputation of being a prankster himself, among Oriole players and, as such, is a likely target of teammate jokes. Still, some collectors wonder, if Ripken wasn't in on the prank, is it just a coincidence that the offensive words appear exactly straight up — not sideways or upside-down? According to Ripken, who stopped in at a suburban Baltimore baseball card shop several days after the story broke, it is a coincidence. Sonny Vaughan, who operates Arundel Coins and Cards, just south of Baltimore, said a very "subdued" Billy Ripken was in his store on Saturday, Jan. 21, and "conveyed sincere regret over the incident."

In various news stories, Ripken has denied any knowledge of the bat or how the offensive words got there.

SCD was first notified of the situation by a sharp-eyed collector on Tuesday, Jan. 17, the same day that Fleer officials were shocked with the news.

"Once we were aware of it," said Murray, "we stopped the presses immediately and blackened out the offensive words. All cards printed after Jan. 17 have been corrected."

Murray would not comment, however, on how many of the X-rated cards were actually printed — a factor which will ultimately determine their collector value. He did acknowledge, though, that all of the Fleer factory-collated sets — which are printed after the wax, rack and cello packs — will contain the corrected version of the card.

Murray also said that Fleer is offering collectors who would rather not display the X-rated card in their own collection the opportunity to exchange it for a corrected version.

With the card currently selling for anywhere from $25 to $125, it doesn't seem likely, however, that too many collectors will accept Fleer's offer of a one-for-one exchange. SCD has, though, received calls from some concerned parents who would rather not have their children exposed to the obscenity, and there is also an unconfirmed report that one dealer who sold a Fleer pack containing the Ripken card to a minor is already being sued by the boy's parents.

Reports that Fleer was trying to recover some of the wax cases already shipped could not be substantiated and seem unlikely.

In addition to driving up the price of the Ripken card, the situation has caused the price of 1989 Fleer wax boxes and cases to soar. At the peak of the hysteria, SCD received reports of six-dollar wax packs, $125-wax boxes and $1,800-cases (20 boxes per case). Within a few days, however, most prices had tumbled to about half that, although they are still fluctuating wildly and vary greatly from day to day and place to place.

Based on the number of cards that are trading hands, the Ripken card does not seem at all "scarce," but then again no previous error card has ever sparked such a frantic frenzy and no variation has ever been in such great demand. — Steve Ellingboe

* * *

In March, Upper Deck informed SCD that it was correcting card errors it had made in its first print run. The errors involved a flipped negative on Dale Murphy's card and an omission of a position designation on the front of Pat Sheridan's card. Fewer than 20,000 of each card were printed and inserted into foil packs before the errors were detected and the presses were stopped, and corrected cards were inserted, according to Jay McCracken, Upper Deck's vice president of sales.

The Murphy card passed through more than 10 proofreading stages without being detected, McCracken told SCD for its March 31, 1989, issue.

"It's a tough one," he said. "He's got his arms crossed and it's just not that easy to spot," he said.

Upper Deck noticed the Sheridan error before printing began, but instead of shutting down the presses for the two days needed to rectify the mistake, the company let it ride, McCracken said.

"Our printer said, 'Why not leave the card out of the set?'" McCracken said. "We explained to him there was no way we were going to put out a 699-card set."

With its debut set in 1989, Upper Deck offered a new innovation to each baseball card — a small laser 3D hologram on the back, making the card counterfeit-proof.

In July, an old familiar card company name returned to the hobby — Bowman. Topps released a 484-card "Comeback Edition" set of Bowman Baseball Bubble Gum Cards. The set marked the return of the Bowman brand for the first time since 1955.

* * *

Several dealers at a Honolulu show in February were surveyed by Dan Albaugh on their thoughts about problems in the hobby. Albaugh reported his findings in the May 5, 1989, SCD:

1) The hottest selling single cards right now are the following: 1) Jefferies; 2) Sheffield; 3) Ripken error; 4) Canseco; 5) Greenwell; 6) Mantle; 7) Grace. (The preceding mainly refer to rookie cards).

2) What percent of your card sales are to collectors and what percent are primarily for investment purposes? Collectors 60%, investors 40%.

3) How much were your hobby sales in 1988? Less than $100,000 — 5 responses; $100,000-$250,000 — 4 responses; $250,000-$500,000 — 8;

$500,000-$750,000 — 6; $750,000-$1,000,000 — 3; $1,000,000-$1,500,000 — 3; $1,500,000-$2,000,000 — 2; over $2,000,000 — 4. (Two reported sales over $4,000,000).

4) How did your 1988 sales compare to 1987? Up 10-15% — 4 responses; up 20-25% — 7 responses; up 30-40% — 9; up 50-60% — 7; up 120% 2.

5) How will this year (1989) compare? Down 15% — 1 response; up 15% — 3 responses; up 20-25% — 12; up 30-40% — 7; up 50-60% — 4; up 100% — 1.

6) What card shows are the country's best for selling cards? 1) Willow Grove — 15 votes; National Convention — 10 votes; San Francisco — 9 votes; Los Angeles — 7 votes.

6) How about buying? 1) National Convention, Plymouth, St. Louis, Willow Grove — 7 votes each; Chicago — 5 votes; Cincinnati — 4.

7) "Mega Conventions" (with many autograph guest stars) are cropping up all over. Are they good for the hobby? Do they help or hurt dealers sales? How do they affect the quality of other "traditional card shows?" At least half of the responses felt mega-conventions were good for the hobby. They help bring in many new collectors into the hobby. The chief negative concern was that too much money is diverted from card sales and goes into the promoter's pocket.

8) What is the future of the National Convention? How can the National be made better? Over 60% felt the National is very special and will remain distinct from other large shows. Many believed the National could be improved by having better organized seminars and lectures.

9) How good a job are the hobby's price guides doing? How can they improve? 1) Doing a good job — 60%; cannot be improved much — 25%; need improvement — 15% Guides can improve by utilizing more dealer input.

10) What is the hobby's best investment today? 1) 1980s wax packs — 12 votes; 1960s cards — 10 votes; 1950s cards — 8; complete sets — 8; 1960s sets — 4.

11) What are the hobby's most overpriced cards? 1) 1980s rookies — 9 votes; 2) 1980s stars — 8 votes; 3) 1951 Bowman Mantle — 5; all Mantle cards — 4.

12) How about its most undervalued cards? 1) Tobacco cards — 8 votes; 2) 1960s commons — 6 votes; 3) Goudey cards — 6; 4) 1960s stars — 4.

13) How many full-time dealers are there today? 100-200 — 6 votes; 200-500 — 3 votes; 800-1,000 — 4; 1,500-2,000 — 7; 2,000-3,000 — 5; over 3,000 — 4.

14) How many dealers will there be two years from now? 1) 75% of the responses said 25-50% more; 2) 25% said "less."

15) Is the hobby headed for a big fall in the near future? 1) 95% of the responses said no; 2) 5% said yes.

16) What do you see for card values — will they increase or fall off? 1) 51% said increase; 2) 41% said prices will stabilize; 3) 8% said prices will fall slightly.

16) Do you feel there is any manipulation of card prices in the hobby? 1) 55% said yes; 37% said no; 8% said "to a minor degree."

17) How are card prices being manipulated? 1) Big dealers have an inordinate ability to affect prices — 8 votes; 2) buying ads — 7 votes; 3) price guides — 5.

18) What do you see for the hobby in 1989? Most responses were bullish. Dealers anticipated greater sales due in part to the tremendous publicity the hobby has received from the media and the popularity of the game of baseball. (One Texas dealer stated that in their recession environment, sales are greater than ever.)

19) Are 1980s cards overpriced? Over 75% of the responses felt 1980s cards were overpriced 50-100%.

20) Are tobacco cards, Goudeys and Play Balls valued correctly? 1) Correctly valued — 20%; 2) incorrectly valued — 55%; 3) greatly undervalued — 25%. (Over 30% of the responses stated that prices were too low but demand was still modest.)

21) What do you see for future prices on Mickey Mantle cards? 1) Prices up — 50%; 2) prices down — 25%; 3) prices stable — 25%.

22) What are your thoughts on the T206 Honus Wagner that reportedly sold for $100,000? 1) 85% of the responses were critical of the transaction and the price; 2) 15% thought the deal involved a fair price.

23) How do you feel about card restoration? 1) 100% of the responses felt that card restoration was a current hobby problem with the potential to become greater; 2) 5% were in favor of restored cards, even if they were properly identified as such.

24) Are the new card companies such as Score and Upper Deck good or bad for the hobby? Will the proliferation of card sets have a positive or negative effect? 1) 70% of the responses felt that the additional competition in the card market was good; 2) 30% believed it was bad for the hobby.

25) The number of minor league and dealer-produced sets is an ever-growing one. Has the hobby gone overboard on this? 1) Yes — 70%; 2) no — 30%. (Several dealers surveyed responded by saying the market will take care of itself.)

26) Baseball cards are now being sold by national retailers such as J.C. Penney, K-Mart, Toys R Us, etc. Will this pose a threat to dealers? 1) No — 82%; 2) yes — 18%. (Most believed the national chains helped bring many new collectors into the hobby.)

27) Some people feel that sky-high card prices have forced many collectors out of the hobby. Is this a real problem? 1) major problem — 25%; 2) no problem — 50%; 3) slight problem — 25%.

28) Could a foreign market become a significant factor in our business? 1) Yes — 33%; 2) no — 67%. (45% of the responses mentioned the potential of Japan.)

29) Are "card societies" and their investment programs bad for the hobby? 1) Bad for the hobby — 72%; 2) good for the hobby — 9 %; 3) no major effect on hobby — 19%.

30) Is our hobby ripe for ripoffs? Most felt that with hobby growth comes some ripoff schemes. Our hobby has experienced no more ripoffs than any other hobby — perhaps less.

31) What are your main hobby concerns? 1) Card restoration — 10 votes; 2) need for a national dealers association — 7 votes; 3) role/quality of card shows — 6; 4) card pricing — 4; 5) price manipulation — 4. — Dan Albaugh

* * *

In the fall of 1989, the ultimate complements for Mickey Mantle and Willie Mays cards' were making the rounds across the country.

The 1953 Topps Mickey Mantle and Willie Mays artwork, auctioned off during Topps' summer auction, was displayed in eight sports bars called Champions, each housed in Marriott Hotels. The two 3 1/4-by-4 1/2-inch paintings, which garnered combined bids of $209,000, were to be framed together, along with examples of the cards created from the paintings.

The 1953 Topps Mickey Mantle card displayed with the artwork is priceless to its owner, Champions founder Michael O'Harro, who got it out of a wax pack in 1953.

"I nearly refused to go on vacation with my parents to San Diego until I got that last card I needed to complete the set — Mickey Mantle," O'Harro told SCD for its Sept. 22, 1989, issue.

"This was my first year collecting and I just could not find it. We must have stopped at every five-and-dime and grocery store along the way, buying packs of baseball cards.

"Finally, on Aug. 22, 1953, I bought a whole box and in the very last pack there it was.

"I bought another '53 Mantle years later to go with my set, but I will keep that one forever. It's very special to me."

* * *

The Price Guide Report, Nov. 3, 1989, presented five cards that had shown the greatest price increases since the Price Guide Report had debuted five years earlier.

Five Years And Counting

This report marks the fifth anniversary of the SCD Price Guide and Price Guide Report. The Price Guide has experienced several changes since its debut in the Oct. 26, 1984, SCD. Although there have been several format changes, none of the changes are more evident than the great price increases.

The original price guide consultants included Mid-Atlantic Coin Exchange, Hall's Nostalgia, Kit Young, Pittsburgh Sports Collectibles, Blue Chip Sportcard Inc., Joe Szeremet, David Festberg and Marty Perry.

The price guide listed fewer cards per set in 1984, and also used a sentence under the respective card photo to highlight the top features of each set. Originally, the common card price was listed above the complete set price.

Another difference between the original price guide and the present guide is the different grading scale. An EX-MT and VG grade was presented for pre-1980 cards, and a MINT and EX-MT grade for the 1980-84 cards. Once again, these are all minor changes compared to the price increases.

I have chosen what I consider five of the most significant single card price differences between the original price guide and their present values. They are presented in no particular order:

1) 1968 Topps Nolan Ryan rookie: 1984 ($25), 1989 ($550); 2) 1954 Topps Henry Aaron rookie: 1984 ($130), 1989 ($1,000); 3) 1967 Topps Tom Seaver rookie: 1984 ($73), 1989 ($675); 4) 1984 Donruss Don Mattingly rookie: 1984 ($1.50), 1989 ($65); 5) 1952 Topps Mickey Mantle rookie: 1984 ($1,000), 1989 ($6,500.).- Jeff Kurowski

* * *

The Nov. 17, 1989, SCD broke news about counterfeit Bo Jackson minor league cards.

Bogus Bo Jackson Cards Found!

By Steve Ellingboe

SCD has learned that a counterfeit Bo Jackson minor league card is being circulated in the hobby.

The bogus card pictures Jackson as a member of the Memphis Chicks, and is a direct copy of the Chicks' team-authorized 1986 minor league card set — with one major difference. The counterfeit card has the identical design, the same silver border and the same back as the legitimate card, but the phony version is easy to spot because the photo on the front is different. The genuine card shows Jackson in his home uniform with the word "Chicks" on the front; the counterfeit card pictures Jackson wearing an away jersey with "Memphis" on the front. Except for that very obvious difference, the fake card is designed to appear exactly like it's part of the legitimate 1986 Memphis Chicks set.

SCD was informed of the counterfeit cards by Mary Huston, publisher of the Minor League Monthly Price Guide and one of the hobby's foremost experts on minor league cards. Although the source of the bogus cards is unknown, they were apparently printed in fairly large quantities — perhaps as many as 5,000, according to a minor league specialist who has been investigating the situation. The bogus cards have shown up at baseball card shops and shows throughout the country, and have also appeared in the ads of at least two SCD advertisers who unwittingly purchased some of the cards for resale. (The ads were immediately pulled from the publication when SCD was made aware of the situation.) The fake cards were generally selling in the $7 to $8 range.

Peter Kass, the producer of the original, team-authorized Memphis set in 1986, is understandably quite shaken by the development.

"It's a very aggravating thing," he said. "I have a reputation to protect." With Huston's help, Kass is trying to track down the source of the fake cards, although he admits that even if he finds the perpetrator he couldn't "afford to take any legal action." Kass adds, however, that he has informed Bo Jackson's agent of the situation, and he may have an interest in pursuing the case.

Kass was a 16-year-old high school student when he produced the 1986 Chicks set, which was fully authorized by the Memphis club. Kass said he initially produced 6,000 sets with the silver border, and then, shortly afterward, produced another 10,000 sets with a gold border. He said the second printing corrected two errors that had appeared in the silver bordered set — one of them on the back of the Bo Jackson card, where the word "contract" is misspelled. The back of the counterfeit Jackson card is identical to the legitimate one, including the misspelling.

Kass said when the sets were produced in 1986, the Memphis Chicks ball team received about 1,000 of each of the silver-border and gold-border sets to sell at their souvenir stands, and each player on the team was given approximately 100 of his own card. The photos for the cards were provided by the club.

Kass sold the remainder of the sets to dealers and through ads in the hobby papers. He said the silver-bordered sets are entirely sold out, while a small number of gold-bordered sets are still available. At the original time of issue, the sets sold in the $5 to $7 range. They now sell for between $35 and $50 on the collector market.

Kass assured collectors that he would never reprint either of the Memphis sets. "I certainly want to maintain the integrity of the set as a legitimate collectible," he said, "and I would never want to tarnish my reputation as a dealer." — Steve Ellingboe

* * *

In December, the first error in the 1990 card sets was found. In a letter to the editor in the Dec. 29, 1989, SCD, reader Jason Schuster, Linden, N.Y., wrote: "I found the first error in the 1990 Fleer baseball set. That's right, 1990. It says on the back of the Jose Canseco Player of the Decade card that Reggie Jackson won the MVP as a unanimous choice in 1983. It should read 1973."

To start the new year, Price Guide coordinator Jeff Kurowski, in the Jan. 5, 1990, issue, speculated on where minor league cards were headed: "A new method of distributing minor league baseball cards was introduced in 1989. The Star Co. released its 120-card minor league set in wax boxes. From speaking with minor league collectors I discovered that both supporters and detractors exist with regard to the new minor league cards.

"Some collectors believe that not issuing minor league cards through team sets only destroys the uniqueness minor league card collecting possessed. Others are happy to have minor league cards more available. Both sides have cases for which method of distribution is better, but team set distribution is definitely more desirable with regard to prices.

"The 1977 Modesto team set features Rickey Henderson. This team set sells for prices in the $350-$500 range. Even though Henderson is the top draw of the set, no single card prices are assigned. The set was issued as a team set and is priced as a team set. Henderson fans will be interested to know that the 1979 Ogden team set retails at around $70. The new Star minor league cards will not carry comparable price tags to the team set cards due to the fact that more were produced and wide distribution eliminates the rarity aspect."

On the East Coast, a dealer made news buy paying what was believed to be a record price for a Nolan Ryan rookie card. The dealer, who was buying for a client, paid $2,700 for a gem-mint, perfectly-centered 1968 Topps Ryan rookie card which was auctioned off on the Sports Collectors Digest Baseball Card Phone Shoppers' line Dec. 11. The Jan. 5, 1990, SCD had the story about the card.

The dealer, who along with his client wished to remain anonymous, said his client "only invests in premier cards and he collects a number of (premier rookies). He's not so much into sets as he is in premier rookie cards, all the way back to a 1939 Ted Williams Play Ball."

His client, who was buying for his own personal inventory, was willing to pay $5,000 for the Ryan and a 1967 Topps Seaver rookie card, he said.

The dealer expected the price on the Ryan card to be high, but, since there were two premium cards offered, that put the brakes on the price for the Seaver card. Thus, he was able to purchase both.

Bidding on the Ryan card, listed at $875 in the current Baseball Card Price Guide Monthly, started at $900 and was sold to the dealer after 25 bids. The Seaver card, also listed at $875 and in similar condition, went for $1,700.

* * *

Another record-setting purchase was made shortly before Christmas, 1989. The Feb. 9, 1990, SCD had the details:

Trio's Purchase Nets $910,000 In 1980s Cards

By Mark Larson

It would take two full-size semis to haul away the possible record-setting purchase a trio of dealers made shortly before Christmas.

The $910,000 transaction, involving the Magazine Exchange, of Grants Pass, Ore., San Diego Sports Collectibles, of San Diego, and Richard Howard Inc., of Leipsic, Ohio, who collaborated to purchase the massive holdings of an unnamed Kansas investor.

It's the "largest single transaction on the secondary market," according to Barry Young, of the Magazine Exchange.

Young defines secondary market as a deal made between dealer to collector, a dealer to dealer, or a collector to a dealer, as opposed to someone, such as K-Mart, or a dealer, buying directly from the manufacturer.

The trio purchased mostly cases of Fleer, Topps and Donruss wax boxes from the 1980s, including 700 cases of 1987 Donruss, and 1986 Topps, 1987 Fleer, 1986 and 1987 Fleer Traded, and 1984 Topps Traded.

The cards, "in beautiful condition," totaled approximately 14 million, said Young.

According to Tony Schroeder, a sales representative from Richard Howard Inc., 80 percent of the purchased goods was divided about equally between the Magazine Exchange and Richard Howard Inc. San Diego Sports Inc. purchased the remaining 20 percent.

Young, who's surprised at how fast the material has been absorbed into the hobby, said he has virtually sold all of what he bought. "Shoot, just a few phone calls and it was gone," he said.

Schroeder said William Goepner, from San Diego Sports Collectibles, contacted the other two companies to join in on the deal.

"Goepner didn't feel he could handle the whole thing himself...and we basically let him pick what he wanted since it was his deal to start with," he said.

Richard Howard Inc. also had connections to move the merchandise. "We basically had everything sold when we went to close out the deal," Schroeder said.

The deal was closed after about 45 days of negotiations with the sellers accountant.

"The party that we bought it from was not a long-term collector...he was basically an investor," said Young.

The seller, Young said, paged through buy ads in hobby publications and saw all the high buy prices. But he found that many of the dealers could only buy five to 20 cases, not 500, he added.

The investor wanted to sell the entire lot in one lump sum and, after calling some of the dealers listed in the ads, "realized then that he was going to have to find a larger dealer" and contacted Goepner, said Schroeder.

Young, who was happy with his purchase, said, "needless to say, we'd love more deals like this. Obviously they don't come along too often. We were just happy to be involved in the purchase."
— Mark Larson

* * *

While T206 cards were fetching record prices at recent auctions, a printer's proof strip of famous T206 cards, believed to be the only one in existence, was being offered by Alan "Mr. Mint" Rosen for $2 million, the Feb. 9, 1990, SCD reported.

The proof features five cards: Honus Wagner, Mordecai "Three Fingers" Brown, Boston catcher Frank Bowerman, Denton True "Cy" Young, and Cubs catcher Johnny Kling. The proof had several creases; the Kling, Brown and Wagner cards were heavily creased, and the Young card was creased down the right side. The Bowerman card appeared almost untouched.

The strip, which came from Pittsburgh Sports, was purchased by noted collector and Yankee minority owner Barry Halper. Rosen planned to announce his purchase during a press conference on Feb. 6 at Mickey Mantle's Restaurant in New York.

In the February 1990 Trader Speaks supplement to the Jan. 26, 1990, SCD, Publisher Bob Lemke reported about what he called the hobby's most significant find:

Old Judge/Gypsy Queen 100-year-old Find Is Hobby's Most Historically Significant

By Bob Lemke

While its dollar value does not approach many of the fabulous baseball card "finds" of the decade, the last great hoard discovery of the 1980s surely ranks as the most historically significant. The true hobbyist will also find considerably more charm in the tale than in the stories associated with more commercially valuable discoveries of recent years.

The box itself is unremarkable. Though obviously of quality manufacture a century ago, this child's wooden lap desk shows the effects of generations of use. The fine oak is dried, cracked and separating. There are guages and chips in both the woodwork and the slate center. A heavy black garter, probably cut from an inner tube, holds the 18x12" box together. The top is still firmly held in place by rusting brass hinges.

If you saw the desk at a flea market or antique shop you would probably not give it a second glance. Unless...the eye happens to catch the scraps of yellowing newspaper once glued, then partially torn from, the top of the desk. Apparently cut from a contemporary issue of The Sporting News or The Sporting Life, the remnants reveal rosters of baseball teams of the late 1880s.

No real card collector could resist a peek inside.

It is a find, no doubt about it. A find — at least — of cigarette boxes. There must be three dozen "Duke's Cameo" boxes; bright with pastel flowers, feathers and a gaily colored portrait of a Victorian era beauty. There's another 10 or 12 "Dog's Head" boxes, in more somber shades of brown. Boxes like this can bring $100-150 in the tobacco collector's market.

Inside, the desk top is pasted with more scraps of newsprint; more team rosters, from the National League, American Association, Western Association and other minor leagues. On some of the rosters there is a bold red ink mark to the left of most names. Many of the names have other pencilled marks following.

This old desk contained a treasure of Old Judge cards.

A scrap of paper in the bottom of the box draws the eye. Neatly inked thereon is "Louisville." Hello! Each of the cigarette boxes has a similar paper strip glued to a side. Some bear a penned notation, some typed: "Washington," "New York," "Hamilton," "Chicago," "Buffalo/Detroit," "Jersey City...'

Each box bears a label repeating the team names pasted to the desk's lid.

Picking up one of the cigarette boxes, a rattle is heard from inside. Another box, another rattle.

It couldn't be...could it?

How do these damn things open? Ah! "To open this Box Push this End" reads the printing at one end of the cigarette box. An inner tray slides forward at the other end of the box, along with a small stack of cards inside. A familiar black cartouche is seen at the top: "OLD JUDGE Cigarettes." Underneath, the top of another card is visible. The words "Gypsy Queen" surmount a familiar tombstone-shaped photo of a baseball player with a striped cap and a laced jersey that reads "St. Louis."

At this juncture, most of us would expect to awaken from a pleasant, though frustrating, dream. And while this is no dream, there is a frustrating realization to come.

As each of the cigarette boxes is emptied and piles of Old Judge and Gypsy Queen cards begin to build on the table, there is a gnawing feeling that something is not quite right.

When one of the boxes disgorges a card that seems so much larger than the rest, a terrible realization hits home — these cards are trimmed.

Out of just over 500 Old Judge cards and more than 60 Gypsy Queens, only a handful remain in their original size. All the rest have suffered the application of the razor; cut down on the sides and tops to nearly the borders of the photos, though the cigarette brand names have been left mercifully intact.

Who? When? Why?

Those are just about the only substantive questions for which the current owner of this hoard offers no answers. He is exceedingly well versed on the rest of the history of this collection. It has been in his family for over 100 years.

The current owner, who wishes to remain annonymous, became aware of the cards' existence about four years ago when the lap desk was found in the attic of the ancestoral home in Maine.

Judging from the player rosters glued to the lid of the desk, the assembly of the collection appears to have peaked in 1888. At that time, according to the owner, his grandfather would have been 10 years old.

A decade later, the original collector moved into a huge new house. The lineal descendents of the original owner have inhabited the house since 1898. With some 20,000 square feet of home, and the family never moving, it is not hard to imagine how the desk — and collection — survived intact for a century. The mobility of most American Families in the past hundred years created many opportunities for similar collections to have been trashed at least once per generation.

The discovery of so many N-172s (the American Card Catalog designation for Old Judge and Gypsy Queen baseball cards) in a collection untouched for 100 years at first glance seemed like it must rewrite the checklist, if not the price guide, for this most popular of the 19th century issues.

Significantly, however, the hoard adds virtually nothing to the existing cataloging done by the Cartophilic Society of Great Britain over the years. According to the cards' owner, there are no new players among the 560+ cards. Cursory comparison of the discovery with the N-172 checklist in the Standard Catalog of Baseball Cards has revealed only a few pose and/or team variations for previously known players. A complete card-by-card analysis of the hoard has yet to be undertaken by a knowledgeable hobbyist.

For the most part, the photos on the cards remain in bright, sharp contrast. Only a small percentage exhibit the characteristic fading exhibited by many of Old Judge cards known within the hobby. No doubt the fact the cards were sealed away from damaging light rays for a century contributed to the remarkable state of the images' preservation.

Too bad the cards could not have been preserved from the knife, as well. The owner professes no knowledge of who trimmed the cards, why or when. There does exist several untrimmed cards in the hoard. The characteristic slightly rounded corners on those few undamaged specimens might give a person pause to consider that the cards were only recently trimmed, perhaps to conform to a non-hobbyist's view of baseball card aesthetics. The survival of at least one card in the collection with thumbtack holes in each corner also makes plausible the theory that the cards were later trimmed to remove the holed corners, though none of the trimmed cards exhibit the indentations of the tacks' rounded edge, as is usually seen.

Too, it must be considered that trimming this many N-172s would be no easy task. Essentially photographic prints affixed to stiff, multi-layered cardboard backs, the Old Judge cards are not easily trimmed, especially so as to yield the clean, sharp edges which these cards exhibit.

Despite the fact the cards are housed in cigarette boxes that do not bear the Old Judge or Gypsy Queen brand name, and in the case of the Duke's Cameo boxes are not even of the Goodwin & Co. family, there was no need to trim the cards to fit the boxes; a normal-sized N-172 fits inside with room to spare.

While condition freaks will argue that the trimming has destroyed most of the cards' market value, they would be overlooking the true nature of the Old Judge market.

Part of the historic significance of this find is that in many cases the cards in this hoard double the known examples of a particular N-172. The collector who has been searching in vain for years for a particular player, pose or team designation within this set may have seen the pool of potential specimens available double from its previous level — if he is willing to accept a trimmed card. However, since many col-

lectors of N-172 will accept a card in any condition, unless or until something better comes along, the trimmed nature of these cards may not have all that disastrous effect on market value.

As of now, however, the market value of this collection is only theoretical because the owner has not determined whether or not he will sell the find. He currently holds the commercial element of the baseball card hobby in little regard, the result of a negative contact made at a show when the cards first came into his possession. The cards' owner visited one of the larger Anaheim shows several years ago and approached a self-proclaimed Old Judge expert with a handful of cards. He was rudely brushed off by the dealer who, not realizing the extent of the find, told him the cards were worthless in their trimmed state.

It was several years before the owner looked into the matter again, after having purchased a copy of the SCD Baseball Card Price Guide annual, and realizing that even in their damaged condition, the cards would have some value.

Whether that value will be enough to induce the owner to part with a collection that has been in his family for three generations is an open question at this point. — Bob Lemke

* * *

Another rare find was made in Champaign, Ill., by card shop owner Lee Hull, who found one of Topps' rare George Bush baseball cards — number USA 1 — in a wax pack he purchased from a woman around Christmas. The wax box he obtained the pack from was in what was believed to be a salesman's sample.

Topps, which had given President Bush 100 copies of the special card picturing him from his Yale University playing days, were certain every Bush card was given to the president, the March 2, 1990, SCD reported.

Hull, who initially thought the card was probably a regular card from the new 1990 Topps set, displayed it in his shop. When he learned only 100 George Bush cards were printed, and that all were presented to the president, Hull called Topps and SCD.

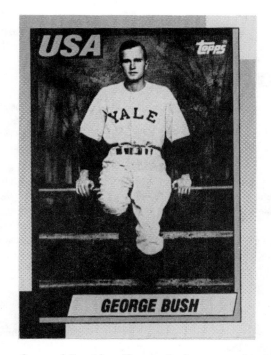

Topps featured President George Bush on a card in 1990.

45

Topps, the story said, told Hull it would be impossible to discover one of the Bush cards in a pack because normally the cards are printed at a plant in Duryea, Pa., while the Bush cards were specially-made in New York.

Phil Carter, sports director at the Brooklyn-based Topps Co., told Hull that if he had a Bush card, Topps wanted it back because the card was probably stolen internally, the story said. Topps, the story reported, threatened to sue if the card was not returned; Hull's attorney advised Hull to keep the card.

"We have informed the gentleman (Hull) that he is in possession of stolen property. We need to determine all the facts before any action would be taken. We feel that it would be impossible that the card could be found in a wax pack," Topps spokesman Ken Liss told Hull.

Hull, claiming he had done nothing wrong, said he was the rightful owner of the card, and planned to keep the card.

Topps decided to make a George Bush card after the president publically stated his grandson said he wanted to be a baseball player when he grew up "because politicians don't get their pictures on bubble gum cards."

Another card company, Score, was taking action against counterfeit Bo Jackson cards, #697 in its 1990 set. The July 13, 1990, SCD reported Score had taken action against a dealer and a seller, who agreed to the entry of a permanent injunction against the continued sale or distribution of the counterfeit cards.

The black-and-white card, selling for between $8 to $20 at the time, features Jackson in his football shoulder pads, holding a baseball bat. The card back reads "BO" in blue and black boldface letters. The counterfeit reads "BO" in black letters only.

"The main issue here, although an unfortunate incident, is to prevent Score card collectors from being fooled by a fake," Randy Friedberg, an attorney for Score, told SCD. "Collectors should be taking extra care when they purchase the Bo card and check that it's authentic."

Not only did collectors have to be wary of Bo Jackson cards, but, as the Aug. 31, 1990, SCD reported, altered T206 Joe Doyle and Sherry Magee cards had surfaced in New York.

The extremely deceptive alterations of two scarce variations in the tobacco card set involved changes in the player name (in Magee's case) and team designation (in Doyle's case). The cards appear to have been altered by having the original line of type at the bottom removed and replaced with similar type to give the appearance of rare variations.

During the initial press run of the T206 cards, the T206 Magee card was spelled incorrectly as "MAGIE." This card, which is the one the altered one was made to look like, is listed in the second edition of the Standard Catalog of Baseball cards as being worth $15,000 in Near Mint condition. The corrected Magee version was listed at $175.

On the genuine Doyle card the N is larger than the A, T, and L in NAT'L at the bottom of the card. The apostrophe is flush with the tops of the letters. The altered cards showed all four letters to be the same size, with the apostrophe rising above the letters.

According to the Standard Catalog, a genuine Doyle NAT'L card is valued at $30,000 in top grade, while the variation, a league-less verision, is a $100 card.

* * *

In the fall, excitement was building on the West Coast, as three dealers at a San Francisco show prepared to open up three 1952 Topps wax packs. The Sept. 28, 1990, issue had the story:

What's It Like To Open A 1952 Topps Wax Pack?

Baseball card collectors love opening up wax packs — the anticipation of getting a key rookie card, the thrill of finding a superstar. Even the disappointment of getting all commons. It's all part of the fun of collecting.

Opening a 1990 wax pack is one thing, but opening a 1952 wax pack is something different entirely.

Just ask Darren Prince of Baseball Card City in Livingston, N.J., Greg Heim of the Greg Manning Co. in Montville, N.J., and Mark Murphy of the Baseball Card Kid in Greenwich, Conn., three dealer friends who were set up at Bob Lee's Labor Day Weekend show in San Francisco. In what may be the ultimate baseball collecting lark, the three, during the course of the busy show, each opened a pack of 1952 Topps cards.

Mark Murphy, Darren Prince and Greg Heim experience what it's like to open a 1952 Topps wax pack.

The packs, which came from Prince's display case, carried a price tag of $2,500 each. They were all first-series 1952 wax packs. Collectors of early Topps sets know that even commons in that first series sell for a minimum of $50 each in Near Mint condition, and that the series also contains cards of Duke Snider, Warren Spahn, Phil Rizzuto and the valuable Johnny Sain and Joe Page variations. Plus there's the possibility of getting the #1 Andy Pafko card, one of the most elusive condition scarcities in the hobby and valued at more than $1,200 in Near Mint.

At precisely 5 p.m. on Saturday, as the second day of the four-day show was winding down, Prince reached into his case, pulled out three of the scarce packs, kept one for himself and handed the others to fellow dealers Heim and Murphy. And then, before a small, but appreciative crowd of nearby tableholders, curious collectors and an SCD photographer, the three, with hands shaking slightly, opened their treasures.

Considering the combined $7,500 price tag, the action didn't take long. In just a matter of minutes it was over. The first pack yielded Grady Hatton, Billy Loes, Eddie Robinson, Bob Mahoney and Andy Hansen. The second pack produced Luke Easter, Don Mueller, Irv Noren, Preacher Roe and a second Bob Mahoney. The third pack contained Gene Hermanski, Leo Kiely, Monty Basgall, a second Don Mueller and a third Bob Mahoney.

Three packs, three Mahoneys. No stars, no major rookies. The only card better than a common was the Billy Loes rookie card, valued at about $125. The total value of the 15 cards was estimated to be somewhere between $850 and $900.

But the three dealers weren't quite done yet. To fully appreciate the experience, they also had to try the gum. After all, how often do you get the chance to chew 38-year-old bubble gum? Even if it is brown?

Somewhat reluctantly, each of the three gave it a try, biting off only small chunks and then offering the remaider to those standing nearby. Most probably wisely passed up the opportunity. — news story

* * *

In early November, with approximately 150 members in the fold, a newly organized dealer association association began a membership drive with the hopes of having 1,000 members by July, the Dec. 7, 1990, SCD reported.

The association, the Sports Collectibles Association International (SCAI) had been proposed in February at a Hawaii trade show and was officially formed in August. Since August, the group had established a set of bylaws, adopted a formal code of ethics and hired an executive director.

The association's mission statement said: "The mission of this association shall be to promote the best interests of the dealers in sport and non-sport trading cards and hobby-associated merchandise and to unite the professional members of this industry for its common good."

Michael Keighley, a representative of Communications & Show Management Inc., designed the membership club for the organization. He told SCD "The association stands for honesty, integrity and professionalism. It's a very strong code of ethics, and we require all members to sign it and abide by it. What we are saying to dealers is that if you're not willing to sign this statement, then we don't want you as a member. It's as simple as that. The message that we want to go out to the public is that when you deal with one of our members, you're dealing with someone who is fair, honest and ethical."

SCAI would discipline, including expulsion, those who violated the code. In addition to monitoring the business conduct of its members, SCAI planned to offer a newsletter, access to resources in a hobby data bank, a unified voice in the hobby, public relations efforts, and the authorization to use the association's logo in advertising.

In a survey of potential members, dealers said establishing a uniform code of business ethics was the greatest goal of the association, followed by self-regulation and policing, combined buying power and establishing a credit network.

In the Dec. 14, 1990, SCD, readers learned Score's 1991 baseball card set would be the largest set ever produced by a licensed card manufacturer. The 893-card set would be available in two series, with factory rets containing an additional seven exclusive bonus cards.

As the 1991 cards began appearing, Ted Taylor had a little bit of unfinished business to take care of regarding the 1990 cards. In his Dec. 28, 1990, Off the Cuff column Taylor presented the results of his readers' poll for the favorite card of the year. The cards selected were:

Rick Cerone, Score #139; Randy Bush, Upper Deck #493; John Olerud, Donruss #711; Doc Gooden, Bowman insert card; Don Zimmer, Topps #549; Ben McDonald, Upper Deck #54; Nolan Ryan, Donruss #166; Billy Ripken, Fleer #186; Mike Scott, Bowman #71; Carlton Fisk, Score #290; Hal Morris, Donruss #514; Ken Oberkfell, Topps #488; Mariano Duncan, Topps #224; Greg Blosser, Bowman #278; Randy Ready, Donruss #396; Mike Hartley, Score #641; Bobby Bonilla, Fleer #462; Bill Doran, Upper Deck #198; Dave Dravecky, Score #550; Bobby Thigpen, Donruss #266; Rick Honeycutt, Upper Deck #151; Bill Schroeder, Upper Deck #149; Stan Javier, Upper Deck #209; Steve Sax, Upper Deck #172; Rickey Henderson Rips the Jays, Score #698; and Chad Kreuter, Upper Deck #609.

* * *

As a new decade of card collecting approached, the SCD editorial staff, in a Jan. 5, 1990, column, had already summarized the top five most important developments in the hobby during the 1980s and then predicted five trends to watch in the 1990s:

The Five Most Important Developments In The Hobby

1. The "demonopolization" of Topps, 1981. If Fleer hadn't sued to break into the market, or if the company hadn't won, there is no way the baseball card market would be even close to what it is today. A mere eight years after the courts ruled other companies could combine confectionery with baseball cards, there are at least five major companies producing cards. Different companies means a variety of cards and card styles, plus increased competition to improve the product. In short, it's been a bonanza for collectors.

2. The football/basketball boom of '89. Once classified in the same derogatory category as non-sport cards (another market which is seeing increased interest and growth), football and basketball cards came into their own in 1989. Prices and interest in older football cards seemed to triple overnight. Fleer's 1986 basketball set exploded from $20 to up to $175. Companies such as Pro Set and Score dramatically improved the quality and stature of football cards, and the '90s should see more expansion of this market. NBA Hoops provided true competition in the basketball card market for the first time in memory.

3. The Topps/Guernsey's auction. Other auctions have shown that either the timing in the August 1989 auction in New York was perfect or that buyers were in a frenzy. The incredible prices exceeded all expectations at this auction — nearly $200,000 for the 1953 originals of Mantle and Mays was probably $150,000 more than anyone expected them to sell for. Despite the slower sales in other memorabilia auctions, the Topps auction proved that investors are in the market for quality memorabilia and are here to stay.

4. The advent of the investor. Pins. Programs. Autographed balls. Items and more items became available to investor/collectors who bought them up big time and resold them quickly or hung onto them strictly for investment purposes. Card dealers sold card lots for investment purposes. The current rage in football seems to see buyers sinking thousands into such sets as the 1984 Topps and simply holding them.

5. Success of the huge autograph show. The utilization of former or current players as autograph guests to attract attention and promote shows has progressed from one and two player shows to huge extravaganzas with as many as 20 Hall of Famers appearing together at a show. Theme shows, such as reunions of several living members of the '57 Brooklyn Dodgers, '69 Mets, '84 Olympians, 500 home run hitters, and Ralph Branca/Bobby Thomson, have become popular. — SCD editorial staff

Five Trends To Watch In The '90s

1. Hockey/non-sport card boom. There are enough quality sets out there — and at wonderfully low prices — to interest any card collector, especially the younger set. Since prices on baseball, football and even basketball seem to be rising daily and make it difficult for collectors with modest income to buy sets backward, it wouldn't take much for them to shift their attention to the more affordable, just as interesting, and grossly overlooked segments of the card game.

2. The grading controversy. This will reach its peak in the next five years. Despicable as it sounds to most collectors, investors will demand it for higher-priced, rare cards. This may become a secondary market to card collecting.

3. Cataloguing of memorabilia. The demand of quality memorabilia has led to some amounts of forgery, and we think the hobby will mobilize itself to find out what items are real and rare — and what aren't.

There is currently a huge market available for someone willing to do a little homework to verify the authenticity of memorabilia — especially autographs. Don't be surprised if within the year a service is offered to authenticate signatures.

4. Abating of demand for autographs. There's been a lot of evidence toward fake autographs and wife/clubhouse boy signatures. The inability to authenticate autographs will turn off collectors, unless they can have items autographed at card shows or other personal appearances. Mail signings will drop off dramatically as other older players demand fees. Much like baseball itself, superstar signers will have contract disputes with dealers and will hold out for more money and bigger shows. We don't like the way it's going, either — we'd much rather wait for players in the parking lot after the game — but you can hardly blame the players, who are usually swarmed the moment they appear everywhere in public. Maybe if autograph interest wanes, we can once again wait for players in the parking lot.

5. At least one card company could die out. The hobby grew so fast everybody could make money, but when (if?) it ever stabilizes and investors or "quickie collectors" ever leave the hobby, some companies may perish. Right now it doesn't look probable, as everybody seems to be enjoying the card boom of 1989. But will it continue? How much money can people spend, especially since economists say a recession is due to hit sometime in the near future? — SCD editorial staff

* * *

Upper Deck started the new year, 1991, with aggressive hockey card advertising. The company, Robert Wimmer noted in his Jan. 4, 1991, Point Shot column, had gotten several National Hockey League teams to put its logo on the rink boards located inside the blue lines, thus getting maximum television exposure. The logo was on the boards in Los Angeles, Edmonton, Chicago, Detroit and in the Madison Square Garden. The company, which also advertised during the teams' broadcasts, planned to attend the NHL All-Star Game in Chicago, too.

Awareness was increasing in Japanese baseball cards, too, thanks in part to Cecil Fielder's accomplishments with the Detroit Tigers during the 1990 season, when he hit 51 home runs. Rich Marazzi, in his Feb. 1, 1991, Batting the Breeze column, interviewed Larry Fuhrmann, a Japanese baseball expert, about that aspect of the hobby:

"SCD: What changes have you seen in the Japanese card and memorabilia hobby since we last met?

"Fuhrmann: The biggest change has been an increased awareness of Japanese cards and a corresponding increase in demand. Thanks to the interview you did last year and other publicity we got, I received close to 1,000 inquiries in the past year.

"Another big factor was that Cecil Fielder had such a tremendous season last year. Almost every story about him mentioned that he played in Japan in 1989.

"Not only has Cecil done a lot for Japanese baseball cards, but most importantly, he has given the Japanese game some much-deserved credibility."

Furhmann said most of the card collectors in Japan were boys ages 10 and 11, but adults were slowly increasing in number. Although there were only two shops in Japan which sold American cards, Upper Deck foil packs were sold at stadiums throughout the country, he said.

"The problem is exposure. Major League games are not shown on regular Japanese television and there is not much print coverage given to U.S. baseball, so the players are not well-known," Furhmann said.

Score recruited one well-known Hall of Famer for a blockbuster promotion of its series two 1991 baseball cards. Mickey Mantle autographed and numbered 2,493 Mickey Mantle cards from a seven-card collection being randomly inserted into series two packs. Seven other cards were signed and to be used in a mail-in sweepstakes, the April 5, 1991, SCD reported.

The promotion marked the first time a licensed card manufacturer had offered in-pack, instant-win prizes, featuring autographed cards of a current Hall of Famer.

"There's been a lot of anticipation for Score's Series II baseball," said Lou Costanzo of Champion Sports in California. "By far, Mickey Mantle is the most sought-after collectible. Anything he touches, people want. I imagine just one of his autographed Score cards will go for a minimum of $1,500, while the collection of seven could be close to $10,000."

In May, Dave Platta told how minor league card collecting was going big league. In his May 3, 1991, story, Platta described the new working agreement between the National Association of Professional Baseball Leagues and Major League Baseball which would give MLB a greater say in how minor league teams operate.

In the past, he said, minor league teams set up their own deals with companies to make team sets, and became a big source of revenue for the teams. They were also given a cut of television money revenues to be, in effect, subsidized by the MLB. But, as billion-dollar TV contracts were being signed, the National Association sought more TV revenues for its minor league teams, Platta said.

MLB, however, thought they'd been lied to about the profitability of minor league teams, and the Association was taking money from their pockets, Platta reported.

When the MLB negotiators threatened to form their own independent minor league system, 59 minor league teams would be left without player agreements with big league clubs, thus forcing those teams to face the prospect of signing their own players, which they couldn't afford to do. As a result, the Association agreed to the demands of the MLB negotiators, Platta reported.

One part of the agreement was that Major League Properties, a $45 million business, would act as agent for the National Association and would receive an 8.5 percent royalty on all merchandise sold. MLBP would get a cut for commission; the rest would be returned to the minors, Platta reported.

Baseball cards were an exception. Agreements teams had in force before March 15 would be honored in full with no royalty payment and no commission to MLBP. However, all minor league card manufacturers in the future would need to be licensed by the MLBP.

As a result, several of the nine companies which did more than one minor league team set in 1990 got out of the business in 1991. Grand Slam's Mike Feder, who would be busy running the Triple A Tucson Toros, told SCD he wasn't going to cry about the agreement which ultimately led to his departure from the minor league card business, which he'd been in since 1987. He wanted to do sets for AA teams, but three other companies beat him to the punch, and it wouldn't be worthwhile to be the fourth, he said.

Bill Pucko, who'd been doing New York/Penn League sets since 1987, was also closing up shop. "I have no regrets, nor are there any bad feelings. The teams I did business with were always happy with their product, and we've parted on the best of terms," he told SCD.

"What I liked most about having been a card producer is the lasting aspect of the work. I ran 15 sets, all exclusives, and those sets will last as long as the hobby.

"They'll always look good. They will always reflect positively on my contributions to the hobby. Few have the opportunity to create such an impact," Pucko said.

Rick Smith's Cal League Cards was one of the companies to survive the changes in the industry. He said the jury is still out as to what would happen to the industry.

"When you have more competition, the consumer benefits because of lower price and higher quality. I can't see how this new setup will help. I'm afraid that with the elimination of the small card manufacturers the hobby will be hurt," he told SCD.

John Metzger of Pro Cards was a proponent of the changes; his company had been licensed by Major League Baseball Properties since 1987.

"The others got around it, and that will stop. It's fairer when everyone plays under the same rules," he told SCD, adding he expected 1991 to be the company's biggest year ever.

Best Classic Cards owner Don White was excited about the new card season. "We're excited about it. We did real well last year. We're going to blow the doors off everyone this year.

"Minor league cards are a hotter commodity than basketball or football cards. Rather collect 'em myself. You see, baseball will always be there. Football, basketball, hockey — they're all seasonal and regional.

"The difference between us and the NBA is baseball card collecting is a 12-month a year deal. Basketball lasts maybe six months," White told SCD.

White said the new arrangement will benefit everyone. "MLB Properties will make the ballclubs more money, and it'll make life easier for the card companies and for the collectors. If Topps and Fleer had to deal with each big league team on an individual basis, there wouldn't be any baseball cards. MLBP understands whole and retail marketing. They'll do a good job. The ballclubs didn't understand wholesaling at all. They seemed to think we got the price guide for every set we sold. They figured we got $15 for every Birmingham set with Frank Thomas that we sold. All I can say is I wish we got guide price!" he told SCD.

The only problem caused by the arrangement was that card companies were delayed in planning their sets. Metzger told SCD, "We're running late right now. The delays in awarding contracts has us a month behind in scheduling photography sessions. But that's minor." He added that "what it comes down to is that no matter how much some teams complain about the deal, it's to their benefit. We're dealing with MLBP, people no one pushes around. They're strong in dealing with infringements and violations. They'll pursue those who break the rules, and, in the end, it makes everyone stronger."

In July, a controversial "$12" Nolan Ryan rookie card was in the hands of an Illinois collector who bid $5,000 for it in a charity auction in June, the July 12, 1991, SCD reported.

Tony Del Angel outbid all others to win the card, which made headlines when an 11-year-old collector bought the $1,200 1968 Topps card for $12 from an inexperienced store clerk at Ball Mart in Addison, Ill., in April 1990. The store owner, Joe Irmen, later sued the youngster, Bryan Wrzesinski, to get the card back, claiming the youngster purposely deceived the clerk. After a year-long court battle, both parties agreed to auction the card for charity.

Irmen told SCD he filed the lawsuit to prove a point.

"I did it to open a lot of eyes to what's going on in the world. There's not enough parental discipline. If I had done what Bryan did when I was a kid, my father would have cracked me, made me return the card, then sent me out to mow the lawn."

Wrzesinski didn't plan to bid on the card during the auction, but did bring down the house when the auction started by making an initial bid of $12. Irmen participated, and kept flashing bid cards until he reached $4,700. When the auctioneer said he'd end the auction if the

bidding reached $5,000, Del Angel made the final, winning bid. Del Angel said he'd keep the card "In my bedroom. That way I can see it and enjoy it."

Irmen was disappointed the bidding was cut off at $5,000. "I was prepared to go higher. The card should have brought more." The auctioneer, Chicago sports radio broadcaster Chet Coppock, defended his actions. "Hey, when you take a baseball card and raise $5,000 for charity, you can't be too disappointed," he said. The money was split between Ronald McDonald House and Alhambra, a fund for the mentally retarded.

Another high-ticket sale, a Joe Jackson signature for $23,100, triggered the interest of Bernhard Kleinhans, who claimed he had a baseball signed by six members of the 1919 Chicago White Sox, including "Shoeless" Joe Jackson. In April, Kleinhans, from Secor, Ill., sold the ball for an undisclosed price to Gary Gearhart.

Chicago White Sox historian Pat Quinn, however, did not agree the signature was real. Quinn, who the White Sox brass consider the expert on the 1919 White Sox, believes there are only two known Jackson signatures in existence — one from a driver's license and one from an income tax return, the July 12, 1991, SCD reported in a story by Kenneth Brown. Jackson was believed to be illiterate for much of his life; he signed his contracts with an "X" and only later in life did he learn to write his name.

The Jackson signature on the ball did not match the two he knows are authentic, Quinn told SCD, although the others — of Eddie Collins, John Collins, Dick Kerr, Buck Weaver and Oscar "Happy" Felsch, seemed authentic.

Quinn believes Kleinhans, when he had the ball autographed in 1919, "didn't actually see Joe Jackson sign the ball. I feel someone was just covering for him (Jackson). He just said, 'Here,' and signed Joe's name."

Kleinhans told SCD he, as a 12-year-old, went to Comiskey Park in 1919. During batting practice, someone hit a foul ball which landed near where he was sitting behind the White Sox dugout, Kleinhans said. When a long-armed guy swatted the ball away from him, Buck Weaver, who saw the incident, said "Why don't you let the kid have it?"

So Weaver let Kleinhans onto the field, into the dugout, and had some players sign a ball for him. He later had the ball lacquered and kept the ball in a safety deposit box. The bank president put Kleinhans in touch with Gearhart, a La Salle attorney who has one of the most impressive sports memorabilia collections imaginable.

If the Jackson signature is genuine, the ball could be worth at least $25,000.

In the July 19, 1991, SCD, it was reported the National Basketball Association was going after card counterfeiters, the first action against card counterfeiters by any major sport. The NBA announced its plan to combat non-licensed card manufacturers in a paid ad placed in several hobby publications. In part, the ad read:

"On January 23, 1991, NBA Properties, Inc. ("NBPA") commenced suit against several defendants for federal trademark counterfeiting/infringement and unfair competition with respect to manufacture, distribution, and sale of unauthorized and unlicensed trading cards bearing one or more of the National Basketball Association ("NBA") trademarks, names and/or logos and/or the NBA players' likeness ("Counterfeit NBA Trading Cards"). The suit has been reduced to a final judgement with permanent injunction against all named defendants therein on May 13, 1991.

"As a result thereof, NBAP has learned of the existence of additional manufacturers, printers, distributors, wholesalers and retailers of Counterfeit NBA Trading Cards. WE KNOW WHO YOU ARE."

NBAP offered those involved in counterfeit trading cards a one-time opportunity to avoid certain civil prosecution, "if and only if you immediately cease any manufacture, printing, distribution, promotion and/or sale of such Counterfeit NBA Trading Cards."

The NBA also asked for a list of information regarding how many sets they produced and sold, amounts received from such sales, the name of the printer, source of photographs, and sources of other counterfeit cards. Then the NBA would contact those involved to confirm the accuracy of the information they supplied.

"Be advised that any response which contains less than the demanded information and materials shall be deemed insufficient and shall be interpreted to mean that you intend to continue selling Counterfeit NBA Trading Cards in violation of the law. If you disgard the provisions of the Amnesty Program you will be subject to civil prosecution and will be potentially responsible to us for treble your profits and our damage plus the costs and expenses of the attendant action. "We Know Who You Are — Be Smart — Act Now — Or Else! NBA Properties, Inc."

A 1952 Mickey Mantle Topps card made news during the summer when it was sold for a record price — $58,000, which surpassed the previous high of $50,000 obtained during Sotheby's auction. Tom Strauss, from Wisconsin, purchased the card from Boynton Beach, Fla., dealer Rick Kohl, who said in the Aug. 9, 1991, SCD he thinks the card will be worth at least $100,000 within the next year.

* * *

In the Nov. 1, 1991, SCD, Rick Hines reported about a major find of T206 cards in Kentucky.

Major T206 Collection Found In Eastern Kentucky

By Rick Hines

Remember back in the early-to-mid-1980s when discoveries of rare baseball card or memorabilia collections occurred with some regularity? Maybe it happened to you, or your next door neighbor. Someone would be cleaning out the attic and find "the collection," or maybe it was stumbled on at a garage sale.

Well, some 11 years after the baseball card hobby took off, another find, just like the good old days, has been made. It doesn't rank up there in importance with the discovery of America or a vaccine for polio, but in the baseball card hobby, it's a major discovery.

Chicago area dealer-collector Bill Mendel (Porter, Ind.) recently purchased what he accurately described as "the motherlode" in T206s, some 400 of the desirable 1909-11 tobacco cards in all, including 100 near mint to mint specimens.

Just how did Mendel come across these 80-year-old beauties? He explains:

"In mid-August I set up at the Kentucky State Fair and I was about the only tableholder at the show with anything older than 1990 cards (laughs), or so it seemed. Because of that, my table attracted a lot of attention. So much, in fact, that I was interviewed on local television two or three times.

"The people who had the cards, a 93-year-old man and his granddaughter, from Olive Hill, Ky., contacted me through a dealer there to see if I'd be interested in purchasing their cards. I agreed to meet with them and I drove to the meeting place, a motel, in Sandy Hook, Ky., in the eastern part of the state."

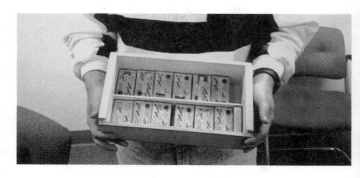

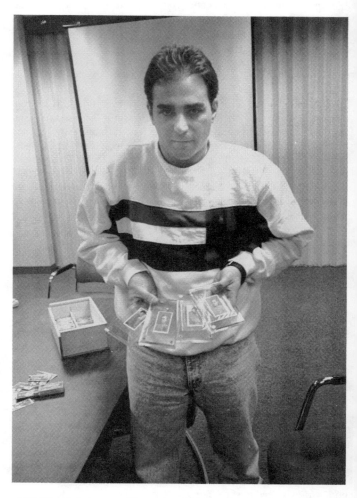

Bill Mendel shows off a major T206 collection he purchased.

Mendel admits that when the old gentleman and his granddaughter (who asked for anonymity) brought the cards into the room his mouth started watering. He couldn't believe what he was seeing.

"They brought the cards in a wooden box and they (the cards) were still inside the Piedmont tobacco boxes just as they came 80 years ago. The 93-year-old man collected the cards when he was about 12. A neighbor smoked Piedmont cigarettes and he gave the cards to the young neighbor boy. This man was a very organized collector as a youth and he asked for the boxes to keep the cards in. This is what I like. He labeled each box by city, not team (for instance, he kept both Browns and Cardinals cards in the same box), by putting a piece of adhesive tape on the front of the box and he wrote the name of the city on the tape. The boxes themselves are worth about $100 each and he had 26 of them, including minor league teams.

"The Piedmont cards were in meticulous condition, but he also had some cards with Sweet Caporal and Old Mills backs which weren't as nice. He told me he traded with other kids in the neighborhood and that's why the non-Piedmont cards are in worse shape."

Mendel told SCD the man didn't sell the cards because he needed the money, but he realized their popularity and he wanted to get them in the hands of a collector or collectors. "He didn't want to sell them to a dealer, but to a collector. (Mendel is both, and he plans to keep many of the cards he purchased.) He and his granddaughter had rediscovered the cards when they were cleaning their home and found the wooden box."

Although Mendel didn't disclose what he paid for the cards, he said the Kentuckians didn't budge from their asking price. "They had already basically decided on how much they wanted for the cards, but when I got there we got a price guide out, ordered a pizza, and went through each card individually, examining the condition.

"The sale wasn't made immediately. I returned home after they rejected my offer, but a week or so later we corresponded again and I bought the cards. I just can't believe the condition they're in," said Mendel, who had trouble containing his enthusiasm.

Mendel said the collection proves that Ty Cobb was a popular player at that time because the man he bought them from had traded for all four Cobb variations. "The Cobb cards were the key to the buy," said Mendel, "especially in their condition (near mint). Of the 100 near mint to mint cards, 20 to 25 of them were Hall of Famers and 75 were commons."

One of the rarest cards in the set, the Bill Dahlen Brooklyn card, was also included in the collection, in mint condition. All together, of the 523 cards in the set, the collection included 385 different cards with a retail value of about $60,000.

Mendel said the collection of T206s also disproves a lot of the dealer stories of how the tobacco cards have been trimmed. "A lot of dealers are wary when they buy these cards, getting a ruler out and measuring them and everything, but that's nonsense. They (the cards) don't size up; they're all different sizes. I stacked 60 of them up and they're all different. They just weren't cut like the cards are today."

Mendel probably thought he was in baseball card heaven that week, but actually he was in Eastern Kentucky the whole time. "That same week I purchased a 1933 Goudey Benny Bengough (number one card in the set) in near mint to mint condition ($8,500 book value); a large collection of R316s (1929 black-and-white cards), including multiples of Ruth and Gehrig; and a 1952 Topps collection, including a near mint to mint run of high numbers with a near mint and centered Mantle card.

"All of the buys were in Eastern Kentucky. I had the help of a local dealer and show promoter who arranged for me to meet with the sellers."

Mendel says he's on a buying roll and he is going to attend a card show in San Juan, Puerto Rico, later this month, where he hopes to find similar rare memorabilia and cards. "I'm going where no one has ever gone before," he said. "Hopefully, I'll turn up something rare and unusual." — Rick Hines

* * *

A 1954 Topps cello pack made history when it sold for $25,000, a record for any type of unopened pack in hobby history, the Dec. 6, 1991, SCD reported. Tony Galovich, who sold the card to a Canadian collector, said the amount more than doubled the previous record.

"The key factor was that Hank Aaron's rookie card was the top card of the pack. Also, this is the only known 1954 Topps cello pack to still exist in the hobby. And none of the major players' rookie cards — such as Mantle, Mays, Cobb or Ruth — ever came in any type of cello pack. This is the most desirable rookie cello pack in the entire hobby today," said Galovich, president of American Card Exchange.

The buyer said he thinks items such as the cello pack have been overlooked in the hobby; now is the time to purchase hobby rarities before the prices go through the roof.

"Cello packs with stars showing on top have been gaining slowly but surely with collectors for the past few years. When collectors start realizing how truly scarce many pre-1970 packs are, I anticipate a far stronger demand than we are seeing today," Galovich told SCD.

Also in December, the Dec. 13, 1991, SCD reported officials of SCAI were pleased and encouraged following the group's first annual meeting and conference held in St. Louis, Nov. 11-14.

More than 300 dealers, distributors and card company representatives attended the conference, sponsored by Sports Collectibles Association International in part to help unite the sports collectibles industry and bring honesty and integrity to all dealer members through its stringent code of ethics.

"Attendance even surpassed our highest expectations," said SCAI President Andy Rapoza. "The incredible success of this conference has been key for all levels of the hobby, including the manufacturers, the licensors, the dealers and the press. The fact that they were all here, all participating, made this a watershed event. I see nothing but important progressive actions intermingling those four groups continually from now on."

Gene Upshaw spoke at SCAI's first annual meeting in 1991.

51

The event was the first time industry leaders and dealers met in a forum that included educational seminars, celebrity speakers, question-and-answer sessions, round-table discussions, and face-to-face meetings with card manufacturers. Corporate sponsors included Action Packed, Pro Set, Impel Marketing (NBA Hoops), Fleer, Topps and the NFL Players Association.

Another noteworthy event, the sale of a Bob Cousy basketball card set for $5,000, was reported in Dec. 27, 1991, SCD. Anthony Taylor purchased the #1 set of 100,000 personally-numbered sets called the Bob Cousy Card Collection Preview Edition. The set, which was selling for $25, spotlights the life and career of the former Boston Celtics great.

Taylor told SCD he bought the #1 set because he thinks the Cousy set was going to become a prototype classic for future sets spotlighting sports super heroes; the #1 set will always be regarded as the most important.

Sets numbered 1,891, and 1,991 of the set were donated to the Basketball Hall of Fame in commemoration of the 100th-year anniversary of basketball. Cousy and Milton Kahn own the Bob Cousy Card Collection Co.

Two brothers from Michigan purchased what was called "the most expensive wax pack in the world," the Jan. 10, 1992, SCD reported.

The two purchased a 1934 Goudey wax pack, believed to be the only one of its kind, for $20,000 in an SCD auction in October. The pack, according to dealer Darren Prince of Baseball Card City in Livingston, N.J., tops the previous record for a wax pack of $8,000. Six cards are included in the pack, which has the #1 Jimmie Foxx card showing through the back. That card is valued at $2,000.

* * *

In the July 10, 1992, SCD Dave Miedema recapped the previous 12 National Sports Collectors Convention.

Past Nationals At A Glance

1. Los Angeles, Aug. 28-Sept.1, 1980 — hosted by Gavin Riley, Mike Berkus and Steve Brunner.

2. Detroit, July 9-12, 1981 — hosted by Lloyd and Carol Toerpe.

3. St. Louis, Aug. 26-29, 1982 — hosted by Paul Marchant, B.A. Murray, Bill Stone and Mimi Alongi.

4. Chicago, July 7-10, 1983 — hosted by Bruce and Bonita Paynter.

5. Parsippany, N.J., Aug. 9-12, 1984 — hosted by Mike Aronstein, Lew Lipset and Mike Gordon.

6. Anaheim, Calif., July 11-14, 1985 — hosted by Mike Berkus, Steve Brunner, Bill Heitman, Gavin Riley, Jerry Williams and Jack Petruzzelli.

7. Arlington, Texas, July 24-27, 1986 — hosted by John and Wanda Marcus.

8. San Francisco, July 10-12, 1987 — hosted by Bob Lee.

9. Atlantic City, July 6-10, 1988 — hosted by Ron and Maureen Durham.

10. Chicago, June 28-July 2, 1989 — hosted by Bruce and Bonita Paynter.

11. Arlington, Texas, July 4-8, 1990 — hosted by John and Wanda Marcus.

12. Anaheim, Calif., July 9-14, 1991 — hosted by Jack and Patti Petruzzelli.

Facts, Trivia From Past, Present Nationals

By Dave Miedema

Good times are ahead in Atlanta, as the National Sports Collectors Convention hits its 13th edition under the direction of Smith-Bucklin Associates.

The previous 12 years of hobby show promoter direction of the NSCC has had a lot of high points, but has always been at the forefront of hobby news.

One could even derive a bit of trivia and historical pleasure from those previous 12 events.

What? No waiting list: Those trying in vain to gain booth space for the 1992 National would have found the situation at the 1982 National 10 years ago an eye-opener.

As soon as the week prior to the event, that year's National (held in St. Louis) had table space available for dealers wishing to set up.

No jackpot here: Twice, in 1982 and again in 1988, promoters representing Las Vegas, Nev., have placed bids for the following year's National.

Both times, the Vegas bids were defeated by the same promoter (Bruce Paynter) from Chicago.

The only difference in each scenario was the identity of the unsuccessful Las Vegas promoter bidding — Californian Will Davis the first time around and former Las Vegas resident Joel Hellman on the second occasion.

Both bids were of fine quality and professionalism, but both times voters were swayed, in part, by the cities' respective populations, and concerns over whether large numbers of collectors in southern California, Arizona, etc., would travel to Las Vegas for the event.

State of affairs: Of the 12 previous Nationals, seven were located in one of three states: California (three Los Angeles/Anaheim, one San Francisco), Illinois (two Chicago) and New Jersey (one each in Parsippany and Atlantic City).

Sales pitch: No National seemed to match the 1988 Atlantic City event, before or after, in terms of collector and dealer disappointment.

Numerous dealers complained of slow sales in an era of freewheeling hobby spending.

What doesn't get mentioned much is one possible reason why some of those dealers fared so poorly at the cash box.

That reason is made apparent by the conversations I had at a midwestern show some two months earlier with the female half of a husband/wife dealer team that makes the rounds at a number of midwestern shows.

It seems that the couple, according to the wife, planned to double the prices on most of their inventory, explaining the action by flippantly commenting, "It's the New York crowd, they'll pay anything."

Several other dealers indicated to me intentions of raising prices to take advantage of presumed liberal spending policies of East Coast hobbyists.

And, of course, some of the same dealers gleefully reaffixing price tags in the week before the National were the ones whining the loudest about their empty wallets in the week after.

From despair to delight: Probably no National was preceded by as much uncertainty and trepidation as the 1987 event, held in San Francisco.

The promoter was faced with numerous accusations and criticisms from various points of the hobby's political world, on a variety of issues.

That, coupled with an unusually slow flow of information from the promoter regarding the show, led more than a few folks with at least some feeling of the hobby pulse to wonder aloud if the National would even take place.

When all was said and done, however, the San Francisco National was of similar quality to the other top events in the show's history, and very few problems of even a minor nature were experienced.

Major cities that have never hosted a National: New York, Philadelphia, Houston, Boston, Cleveland and Washington D.C.

Cities that have bid unsuccessfully for the National (besides Las Vegas): Minneapolis-St. Paul, San Diego, Milwaukee, New York and Philadelphia.

National held closest to major league baseball stadium: Arlington, Texas, 1986 and 1990, both at the Arlington Convention Center, within walking distance of the Texas Rangers' home park.

National held chronologically closest to major local baseball event: Chicago, 1983, which ran the weekend following the All-Star game held at Comiskey Park the preceding Thursday. Many National dealers attended.

Most prolific instance of a player going ballistic at a national: Arlington, 1986, when the Cleveland Indians were playing a series against the Rangers, and staying at the host hotel for the National dealers.

One dealer, who was told Indians pitcher Phil Niekro was in a nearby gift shop, asked Niekro to autograph a Yankee jersey once used by him.

Niekro complied, and all was fine until Friday, when Niekro became highly upset after teammate Scott Bailes, roaming around the show, told Niekro he saw the same jersey for sale at the dealer's table.

Biggest unloading mess at a National: Atlantic City, 1988, when dealer vehicles stretched for nearly a mile on the boulevard outside the convention center awaiting permission to drive into the convention facility to unload.

One dealer, impatient with the slowness of the line, hand-carried some of his stock to the opposite entrance on the Boardwalk side of the building.

Dropping off his luggage, he emerged, descended a ramp from the Boardwalk, and spotted a private parking lot on a side street, with spaces available.

Returning to the car, he instructed his wife to pull out of the long stretch of dealer vehicles. She did, much to the surprise of those in line ahead of them.

Dealer, wife and car hung a right onto the side street, pulled into the lot, paid the fee most gratefully, and drew reactions ranging from shock to anger as those dealers entered the show and found the couple fully set up and ready to go.

(P.S.: I'd do it again in a minute if I had to.)

Most disappointing autograph no-show: St. Louis, 1982, as ex-shortstop Marty Marion unthinkingly decided that a golf outing was more essential than an advertised appearance at the National.

Bring it back to the coasts: A bylaw passed after the first selection of Chicago as National host stipulated that the National could not be held within 500 miles of the current year's site in the succeeding year; nor could it be held in a state with an adjoining border to the state hosting the current year's National in the year after.

The reason is a lot of East Coast and West Coast types were grumbling about the shows having (at the time) come home to roost in the Midwest (before Chicago, the previous two events were held in Ply-

mouth, Mich., and St. Louis, in order), and, more importantly, collectors in the eastern and western states were being deprived of a chance to attend a National affordably.

Overkill?: Interestingly, four of the next five Nationals were held in either California or New Jersey, with the fifth held in Arlington.

The once-overdone Midwest did not see another National until it returned to Chicago in 1989.

Oh, those politics: How competitive can National bidding get, or should I say, did get, in the pre-Smith-Bucklin days?

Several years ago, one dealer was urging associates to vote against a bid from a rival promoter in his home area!

The eventual result, had it gone as he hoped, would have been for the individual to place his own bid the following year, hoping to personally bring home the bacon for his native area.

A Big Mac, fries and an 8x10 of Musial, please: The 1989 Chicago edition found some of the most unique National advertising the show has seen.

Any Chicago-area McDonald's customers ordering dine-in meals for the month or so before the show received a liner on their food tray that carried an advertisement for the show.

Show guests off the beaten path: Not every National Convention autograph signer has been a sports star of renowned acclaim.

A few have been known for something other than hitting, pitching and fielding.

Cases in point: 1991, Anaheim, where one of the corporate sponsors featured Spider-Man at its booth, and 1983, Chicago, where one of the dealers (in the days before dealers were prohibited from bringing in surprise autograph guests to lure customers to their displays) produced Cubs ballgirl Marla Collins.

A note of progress: Dealers in 1992 will be offered all sorts of services and furniture possibilities to enhance their booth displays as part of the package of forms and notes they receive in periodic mailings from NSCC headquarters.

It is definite progress from 1985, when a dealer needing a clothes-rack for his table display was told by a member of the Anaheim staff that it was not available.

When reminding the staff person that he had asked for one in correspondence mailed three months earlier, the dealer was told by the show staffer, "We don't make mistakes."

Cities hosting National convention and World Series in same year: St. Louis, 1982.

Stupidest reason for not attending a National: "This idea will never get off the ground," spoken by dozens of hobby dealers prior to the first event held in Los Angeles.

Consensus choice, worst National: 1988 in Atlantic City. Slow sales, mass disorganization, allegedly padded attendance announcements, lack of courtesy by much of the staff, and the whole Convention Center/Taj Mahal mess left few overly positive impressions about the event.

Consensus choice, best National: The all-time greatest National would be hard to single out.

Of the veterans of the circuit I've spoken to, most would put their vote to one of the many listed: 1980 (Los Angeles), for initiating the concept; 1983 (Chicago) for establishing the National, once and for all, as the show of shows in the hobby; 1989 (Chicago), either Arlington show, 1987 (San Francisco), or 1985 (Anaheim), mostly due to massive transacting of business.

Consensus choice, most anticipated National: This year's in Atlanta, as many are anxious to see if Smith-Bucklin can balance corporate, collector, and dealer interests, handle with smoothness some of the problems that have caused consternation at some recent Nationals, from promo card distribution to loading/unloading, and improve upon the many contributions made to the event over the years.

I wish them luck. — Dave Miedema

* * *

In the July 31, 1992, SCD, Editor Tom Mortenson provided some tidbits from the recently-concluded 13th National Sports Collectors Convention:

"Among the biggest news at the 13th National Sports Collectors Convention, held in Atlanta at the World Congress Center on July 9-12, was the vote at the National Convention Committee (NCC) meeting held Saturday evening, July 11. By a total of just five votes (234 to 229) the show management firm of Smith-Bucklin and Associates (Chicago), promoters of the 13th National Convention, was not retained to promote the 15th National Convention. Smith-Bucklin was seeking to extend its contract with the NCC for 1994 and beyond before losing out in the narrowest of vote margins. The company will, however, be promoting the 14th National, to be held at McCormick Place in Chicago in 1993.

"Three cities are being proposed as possibilities by Smith-Bucklin for the '94 National prior to the vote dismissing the firm of its services. Cities in the running were Philadelphia, Houston and Los Angeles. Whether or not these cities, or others, are in consideration for hosting the '94 event is now up in the air.

"Pam Stevens of Smith-Bucklin, show manager of the 13th National, told SCD that, although all the tickets had not been officially counted, the company estimated that more than 65,000 collectors attended the convention in Atlanta.

By comparison, last year's 12th National Convention in Anaheim, with its large population base in Southern California, drew some 91,000 sports collectors"...

..."Bert Price, an auto worker from Sandusky, Ohio, was the big prize winner in the 1992 Topps Match the Stats insert game. Price's name was selected July 8 as the winner of a $100,000 shopping spree at the National. The only stipulation for Price, 39, was that he select $100,000 worth of Topps or Bowman products from dealers' tables in a five-hour time span.

"Price's first selection was a complete 1952 Topps set (which includes the Mickey Mantle rookie) from Colorado Cards. He spent 10 minutes dickering before settling on a $37,000 sale price.

"Price also selected a 1982 case of Topps Traded cards for $31,000 and a 1967 Topps set for $7,000. The '82 Traded set contains the first major league card of Cal Ripken Jr.

"Some of Price's other picks in his shopping spree incuded a 1991 Topps Desert Shield set for $3,600, a 1981 Topps baseball case for $3,200, a 1991 Stadium Club Series I case for $2,400, three 1992 Topps Gold baseball cases for $2,200, a 1968 Nolan Ryan/Jerry Koosman rookie for $1,750 and a 1991 Stadium Club Series II baseball case for $1,000.

" As the clock was approaching 3:30 p.m. and time was running out on his shopping spree, Price ended up selecting a box of Topps micro baseball for $96, 13 packs of 1982 football cards at $81, three sets of Beverly Hills 90210 cards for $30 and two Desert Shield cards for $25."

* * *

In September 1992, Suzanne Wimmer, daughter of Robert "Red" Wimmer (known by SCD readers for his column Point Shot) reminisced about how it used to be on the card show circuit.

What Happened To Baseball Card Shows?

By Suzanne Wimmer

What the heck happened to baseball card shows?

Three years ago I began college and started to skip the shows. They'll always be there, I thought. They never change, I thought.

Yeah, right.

Baseball card shows were like fraternity-sorority parties.

The men, all clad in T-shirts and worn-out jeans that exposed a plumber's butt, nicknamed each other things like "Skinny Freddy," "Fast Eddie," and "Crazy Teddy."

They all spoke the same lingo, they had secret clicks. And most like a fraternity party, the beer flowed continuously.

The women, on the other hand, displayed more of a sorority sister-type image. They hung out together, shopped together and talked about each other together.

But when it came down to it, they were all good friends.

Now, I ask again, what the heck happened?

Dealers used to hang signs that said "Buy! Sell! Trade!" Now it's "Visa! MasterCard! American Express Gold Card!"

I think I even saw one dealer at the last show offering a reasonable fixed mortgage to finance purchases at his table.

It's no longer a hobby, it's big business. Before you know it, the government will be regulating for vertical monopolies and things of the sort.

And just think, many kids started buying cards for the free gum.

And what is this I hear about promotional receptions to introduce new cards at the National? They apparently served hors d'oeuvres and cocktails.

Excuse me?

It wasn't too long ago that the dealers I knew pronounced hors d'oeuvres as hoover-doovers and considered bottled beer instead of a canned ritzy cocktail.

In fact, I thought most dealers considered a seven-course meal to be a hot dog and a six-pack.

I find it hard to believe these same dealers, who will spend four straight days talking about the "hobby" at a card show without even taking a breath, would refrain from adding their two cents through an entire presentation about high-gloss cards.

So what does this say about the future of the hobby? Frankly, I'm not sure.

Maybe in 10 years, the national will be a black-tie affair. Maybe it will become the hobby of the elite.

Then again, maybe it will be strictly a business venture. Kind of like the stock market of baseball cards — strictly for investment purposes.

But maybe, just maybe, it will revert back. Yeah, I like the way that sounds.

Just think, the men's pants will start creeping down as the plumber's butts start creeping up.

The smell of cigar smoke will again permeate the air. Credit cards will be outlawed.

And best of all, the kegs will be tapped again. — Suzanne Wimmer

* * *

The Oct. 23, 1992, SCD reported that a recent article in the Chicago Tribune listed baseball cards, desktop publishing and message therapy as the fastest-growing businesses in 1991, based on the number of businesses listed under those categories in 5,000 telephone books nationwide.

The number of listings under the heading "baseball cards" increased from 3,274 in 1990 to 5,755 in 1991, a 76 percent increase, according to the American Business Institute, a market-research firm that compiled the data.

But, baseball cards probably won't make the list again in 1992 because the market has cooled, according to comments from card dealers in the Modesto, Calif., area.

While some dealers were predicting an eventual cooling off period in the hobby, in September another milestone was reached. As reported in the Dec. 11, 1992, SCD, a complete 1952 Topps set was sold for a record price of $215,000.

The set, described as gem mint, almost doubled the previous record for a 1952 set. Approximately 377 of the 407 cards in the set were gem mint, according to Bill Hughes, who represented the buyer in the sale. The cards had perfect corners, full gloss and 50/50 centering. The rest, Hughes said, were mint with 60/40 centering.

The buyer, who wished to remain anonymous, was described as "one of America's most advanced and sophisticated card collectors." The seller, who also wanted to remain anonymous, was identified as a "prominent foreign collector" who had assembled the set over a five-year period by buying and selling several 1952 sets, taking the best cards from each.

* * *

In October, SCD told the rest of the story on the hobby's most famous card — the T206 Honus Wagner card, the likes of which brought $493,000 at an auction last summer. Rick Hines interviewed Wagner's granddaughter for the Oct. 23, 1992, SCD, for the real story behind the card.

"The story most often heard as to why the card was rare was that Wagner was opposed to tobacco, objected to a tobacco company (Piedmont tobacco) putting his likeness on a baseball card and demanded that it be removed from all packages. I often wondered about that, because his 1960 Fleer card shows him with a big chew of tobacco in his jaw," Hines wrote.

Other theories were that Wagner didn't get paid for the card or didn't like the photograph.

But Hines interviewed the granddaughter of the late Hall of Fame shortstop, Leslie Blair, who explained the real reason why the card is rare, and admitted her grandfather always chewed tobacco.

"He chewed tobacco and spat. He called it 'chewbacca,' he always had a wad of chewbacca in his mouth, and he wasn't against tobacco at all. His concern was he didn't want children to have to buy tobacco in order to get his card. He would not have minded if they printed the card and gave them out, but he just didn't want the children to have to buy anything to get the card. That's the fact behind it. It wasn't he didn't get paid for it, or he was against tobacco, he just didn't want children to have to buy tobacco at a young age in order to get his cards," Blair said.

Blair, who wished she had a card of her grandfather, said it was her understanding that only about 12 cards, not 25 or 30, were not returned to the company, thus making the card so scarce.

If her grandfather were still living, she said, he would be amazed, and embarrassed, at the value of his memorabilia today. When she heard the Wagner card sold for $493,000, Blair said "I couldn't believe it.

"I could not believe a piece of paper about three inches by two inches would be able to bring something like that. Anything you collect is only worth as much as someone is willing to pay for it, but again, I, like Buck, am honored that someone, whether it be something to have or whether they really admired the man or cared about Buck (Honus) himself or the record or whatever was behind their buying and they're going to save it and display it, I'm happy for them if

indeed they're happy. And I'm honored; it makes me feel very proud of him. I could get very emotional after all these years and there's someone still remembering him and keeping his name alive. That to me is very wonderful."

Leslie Blair is kept alive, too, as part of the statue of Honus Wagner at Three Rivers Stadium in Pittsburgh. The girl pictured on the base is Leslie as a child.

Her grandfather, she said, was polite and friendly, especially toward kids who were seeking his autograph.

The little girl at the base of this Honus Wagner statue is a likeness of his granddaughter, Leslie Blair.

"After he played a ball game, he would not just run into the locker-rom and change and take off; he would talk to the people; he would talk with children. There's a beautiful picture that we have in the auction of him with a little black boy who was starting out in the little league.

"The story behind the photo was he had come up to Buck and asked him for some pointers, and Buck was giving him some pointers, and that's when the photographer from the press took the picture. It's a darling picture, but he always had time for people. I wish today people had more time for people instead of rushing around and being in a hurry to do anything; he always took time."

* * *

U L WASHINGTON SHORTSTOP

ANDY VAN SLYKE OF-1B

Bob Costas

MICKEY MANTLE — OUTFIELD NEW YORK YANKEES

Chapter 2 contains a potpourri of trivial information, ranging from U.L. Washington's toothpick to Gaylord Perry's peanuts, from Joe Jackson's ghost-written autograph to Pedro Guerrero's autographed batting helmet, from Andy Van Slyke's favorite baseball card to Kevin Seitzer's most embarrassing.

* * *

In 1948, Yale University's team captain was a good-field, no-hit, left-handed first baseman who admired Yankee Hall of Fame first baseman Lou Gehrig. Although captain Bush didn't realize his dreams of becoming a big league ball player, he did become a big-time politician — President George Bush, who would eventually have a 1990 Topps card made of him in his Yale University uniform.

The June 28, 1991, Sports Collectors Digest presented an interview with Bush, conducted through the mail by George Vassallo, a collectibles columnist with the Washington Times. Bush collected cards as a kid, but alas, as the story goes, he, too, was one of many youngsters who eventually threw them away:

SCD: Have you saved any sports memorabilia? If so, what?

Bush: I still have my left-handed first baseman's glove from Yale. I also collected baseball cards as a kid, but, unfortunately, in all of my travels, my cards did not keep up with me. We keep the balls I have thrown out at the start of games, and I keep the shirts, balls and jackets that visiting sports teams give me when they visit the White House. These will go to the Presidential Library.

President Bush also had some advice for young collectors.

SCD: Do you have any recommendations for American youngsters in the sports collecting field?

Bush: I know that kids still have their ticket stubs as a memento of a day at the ballpark. And, if you get the chance, have the ticket stub signed by one of the players, write the score along with the signature and you will have a treasure for life.

Collecting sports memorabilia is a fun hobby. Some of the neatest things you can save cost very little, like a program, ticket stub, or, if you are really lucky, a foul ball.

* * *

One inexpensive collectible, a Toronto Blue Jays Opening Day program, actually blocked a potentially big trade for the Blue Jays, one which would have sent Yankee pitcher Ron Guidry to the Jays for veteran Bill Singer. As Rich Marazzi reported in his Dec. 13, 1991, Batting the Breeze column interview with Blue Jays play-by-play announcer Don Chevrier:

SCD: If there was a prized collectible from Blue Jays history that you don't have and would like to have, what would it·be?

DC: The Blue Jays had a deal on the table with the New York Yankees. Bill Singer, a veteran, was going to the Yankees for a younger pitcher named Ron Guidry. The deal was made. Pat Gillick (general manager) went to Peter Bavasi, then the president of the team, one week before the beginning of the season.

Bavasi nixed the deal because Singer was on the cover of the Opening Day program with 45,000 copies made. The deal was turned down for that reason. Bavasi laughed about it later. So a program cover blocked a potentially big trade for the Blue Jays.

* * *

Another play-by-play voice, NBC's Bob Costas, says he isn't a collector, per se, although he does have a lot of magazines, Sports Illustrateds, and yearbooks from his childhood years in the 1950s and '60s, and, he does have one card which he covets — a 1958 Topps Mickey Mantle, which, up until early 1989, he carried in his wallet.

"I carried it with me every single day for years, but just within the last few months, I've stopped carrying it because everybody asked me about it," Costas told Ross Forman for an Aug. 18, 1989, SCD article.

"And then I'd have to take it out and it was getting battered. It was literally falling apart. So, I have put it in a drawer (of my desk) at home. And now, I only pull it out for special occasions. My standard answer (on why I carried it) was, 'You should have a religious artifact on you at all times.'"

* * *

That's actually Gene Tenace being congratulated, not Joe Rudi.

Joe Rudi surprised us when he informed those in attendance that the player being congratulated on his 1973 Topps card (supposedly Rudi) is actually Gene Tenace. — Dave Miedema, Up Autograph Alley, 12/15/75

* * *

Thoughts On Collecting

It was ironic that some of the negotiating between pro baseball players and owners was done beneath huge cardboards hanging on the wall showing gum cards. This was illustrated in Sports Illustrated. It was the Players Association Office.

To me this underlines that fans and collectors are represented by the cards and the cards have just to hang there and say nothing, when all that the fans want is "Play Ball." — Wirt Gammon, Wirt's Words, 4/15/76

* * *

The April 24 issue of The Sporting News came last Saturday and it contained the rosters of all the major league teams. I looked closely at the Detroit roster and glanced at the others, mostly at the coaches. Then I turned to the daily paper and looked at the box scores. Detroit had played the Angels Friday night and gotten whipped by 6 to 5. Nothing particularly startling about that except that the Tigers showed a player named "Noname." This was startling so I went back to TSN and looked at the Tigers roster again and there was no player by that name listed. He was probably some late recall from Evansville, I guessed. Noname is apparently a speedster as he went in as a pinch runner for Sutherland and stole a base and scored a run. If you do not see him in the box score the rest of the season, you can assume he was just a one-game flash-in-the-pan, but be sure to watch for him in the final averages at the end of the season. We can expect he will be listed in Mr. Smalling's next edition of his Baseball Address List.

Editor's note: Good old Noname had to be Ron LeFlore we'd guess and the steal was one of six he has at this writing. Wonder how Ron viewed this brief period of anonymity? — Eugene Wood, The Wandering Wood-Chopper, 5/15/76

* * *

As noted by Bill Dod, this seems to be a banner year for autographers. With the usual exceptions, most of the players I have written to so far have responded rapidly. I guess that Dave Meiners was right, perhaps I do have something to contribute to other collectors. I have found in the last few years that most of the Spanish-speaking players that I have written to in Spanish will honor requests. Remember, not everyone who plays baseball speaks English. (My experiences in obtaining an autographed photo of Sadaharu Oh can attest to that.)

Following is a sample of the letter that I use in requesting autographs from Spanish-speaking players:

Estimado Sr.

Podria tener usted la amabilidad de autografiar para mi las postales anexas? Agradeceriale su autografo al frente, asi como tambien me envie estas de vuelta en el sobre anexo. Querria una foto autografiada, si es posible.

Muchas gracias Senor. Reitero a usted mi admiracion y deseos por una exitosa temporada. Pidiendo excusar la brevedad de esta.

de usted atentamente,

(sign your name)

It has worked fine. Naturally, I can not guarantee that any given player will respond, but I find that a ball player who speaks little or no English is more apt to if he can read the autograph request. — John R. Goldberg, More Observations, 6/15/76

* * *

Quotable Quote

By Mark McCarter, Chattanooga News-Free Press, writing about the manager of the Chattanooga Baseball Club, Rene Lachemann:

"It was back in the middle '60s, back when trading baseball cards was at its peak in the neighborhood. The haggling and the lying and the stealing was great to pass away the boring times and to develop the valuable skills needed when summer passed and it was time to return to school.

"In an all-out effort to field a starting lineup from every team in the majors, two-a-day excursions were made to the nearest store, pockets jingling with pennies as bicycles raced down the street. Cigar box after cigar box was filled with cardboard heroes.

"It seemed though there were two regulars in each pack purchased — Hank Aaron and an obscure catcher for Kansas City, a baby-faced blond player with both cheeks jutting out like a chipmunk, stuffed full of chewing tobacco. His name: Rene Lachemann.

"After that summer, the last time I saw Rene Lachemann's name, with the exception of an occasional "L'ch'm'nn,'c" in eye-straining, abbreviated box score type, was in huge headline type. "Rene Lachemann Named Manager of Lookouts." — Wirt Gammon, Wirt's Words, 10/15/76

* * *

Topps baseball cards, by the way, are being featured permanently as part of a major new exhibition that has opened in the Smithsonian Institution in Washington, D.C. The cards appear as part of an eight minute continuous film and slide presentation that highlights sports personalities. They are projected at both sides of the film, depicting famous names in the history of sports. Baseball cards are included in another part of the exhibit, in the section called "Shared Experiences." — Our Hobby, 11/15/76

* * *

I've noticed a lot of comment on the stupid remarks regarding players on the backs of the 1977 Topps baseball set. Can anyone top the one on the back of card number 586, Steve Renko, which reads: "Steve hurled 7 innings and got credit for victory as Cubs beat Braves, 8-28-78." Was that the highlight of his eight-year career in the majors? Anyone know of one more stupid than that? — Lionel Carter, 9/30/77

* * *

Suggestion

Dear Mr. Stommen:

I am writing this letter to the editor hoping to fill a large void in our hobby — a name. In this day and age, we tend to label everything. Why not label sports collectors? Coin collectors are numismatists. Stamp collectors are philatelists. Ball card collectors are...?

An appropriate name might be an "olympichartist." This word is derived from a combination of the Greek words "olympikos" and "chartres." Olympicos means the great sport games of ancient Greece. Chartes means a leaf of paper. Therefore, an olympichartist is one who collects cards depicting sports game heroes.

I would appreciate your readers' comments. — Wayne J. Kleman, Columbus, Ohio, Reader Reaction, 12/15/77

* * *

The People's Almanac, The Book of Lists (about almost everything) pays our hobby attention with a list of the eight most valuable baseball cards. The author of the list is not given. It has Wagner T206; Plank T206; Lajoie Goudey 1933; Lowdermilk, Recruits; Houtteman, Glendale Meats 1953; Gil Hodges, Dormand mid-1950s; any player, Briggs hot dogs mid-1950s; and any player, George Miller Candy 1932. — Wirt Gammon, Wirt's Words, 4/15/78

* * *

Writer Recognizes Our Hobby

Dick Young, lively writer of the New York Daily News, reports some collectors' doings. He says collectors have flooded the Mets' office with bids for Tom Seaver's old equipment. Offers run as high as $500 for the full uniform (original cost $80). Also, he reports that the Cincinnati Reds have worked their souvenir merchandising to a science, with a stand at their spring training complex of between 20 and 25 items. And Dick says, "Jerry Morales' Cardinal locker is trimmed with bubble gum cards of his baseball buddies: Fuentes, Moret, Velez, Cardenal, Concepcion, DeJesus and brother Jose. Atop them is Jerry's card, on which a St. Loo teammate had drawn a beard and written the word "Mullion" — baseballese for funny looking."

It's nice that the writers take notice of our hobby. The Young lines were in The Sporting News, as was this item by Jerry Holtzman recently: "Dennis Lamp has an unusual hobby for a player. The Cubs' pitcher collects baseball bubble gum cards." — Wirt Gammon, Wirt's Words, 4/30/78

* * *

Debits And Credits

Credit to America's Number One rated sports writer, Jim Murray, of Los Angeles, for doing the impossible — finding something really nice to say about Howard Cosell: "Underneath all the bluster is the soul of a knotholer. Howard Cosell remembers every bubble gum card he ever collected. He's probably a closet autograph hound."

Credit to our hobby for hitting a record high in attendance of 15,000 at the recent four-day Midwest Sports Collectors Convention in Detroit. — Wirt Gammon, Wirt's Words, 9/30/78

* * *

Joe Has His Own Card

NBC sportscaster Joe Garagiola has his own Topps baseball card which was printed for him in 1976 by Topps.

The card, numbered 1, lists him as a catcher for the NBC All-Stars and lists his New York City NBC address, which is 30 Rockefeller Plaza, New York, N.Y. 10020. — News brief, 10/31/78

* * *

Before parting company, I teased Denny (Walling) about having his picture on the rookie outfielders card in the Topps baseball set in 1977. For all of you card collectors, it is #473, and for agreeing to have his picture placed on the card, Topps gave Denny a color TV and he hopes that for next year he will get a wide-angle camera and movie screen so that he can take pictures of his baby daughter, Heather Marie, whom he predicts will be the first female center fielder in the Astrodome in 1998. — Bud Hullett, Interview Corner, 3/31/79

* * *

Feedback

More on the Dave Collins No. 431 Topps 1977 card.

Perry Kinney, of Arlington, Wash., writes that when Collins was with the Mariners he had the opportunity to talk to Collins after a game. Shown that card, Collins told Kinney that the picture was of Bob Jones, who played with California along with Dave the preceding season. Kinney says he has several of the cards and thinks it is not rare. Kinney thinks Collins and Jones do look alike.

Bob Decker, Grand Rapids, Mich., says he asked Collins to sign the card in spring training and Collins told him the picture was of Bob Jones, and refused to sign. About the glasses, Collins said Jones wore the same type glasses that Collins wears.

Bill Haber, Brooklyn, N.Y., writes that the error was brought to the attention of Topps by Collins himself and as a result Topps was able to correct the Collins card in the 1977 O-Pee-Chee series. — Wirt Gammon, Wirt's Words, 7/31/79

* * *

Credit to Coca Cola for its award-winning TV commercial based on uniform collecting. You've seen it, no doubt. Mean Joe Greene is entering the dressing room and a kid offers him a Coke. Joe at first says "no thanks," then takes the Coke, tosses the kid his uniform jersey and downs the drink with one gulp. Incidentally, I read where they shot this commercial some 20 times before it suited everyone. — Wirt Gammon, Wirt's Words, 6/15/80

* * *

Debit And Credits

Credit to Rick Honeycutt's mother, Rena, who is manager of a branch bank of Fort Oglethorpe (Ga.) State Banks in Fort Oglethorpe for answering my request for a card of Rick. She sent the 1980 Topps and a 1979 Seattle club issue, autographed. As far as I can find out, this is his first time on a Topps card. But it won't be his last, the way he is pitching. — Wirt Gammon, Wirt's Words, 7/31/80

* * *

Debits And Credits

Credit to Sports Illustrated for taking notice of baseball card collectors and the prices of some rarer cards. It traces the surge in Mantle 1952s from $1,200 over a year ago to $3,250 in July and then — after more such cards surfaced — down to $1,765. It noted that other superstar cards had experienced similar trends, and now the market has bottomed out and is on the upswing. SI notes that attention is suddenly paid to rookie cards, with Bob Horner last year (prices at $2.50 now) and George Brett's card, which is now $7 though it was only 75 cents four months ago. — Wirt Gammon, Wirt's Words, 1/20/81

* * *

U.L. Washington of Kansas City got extra attention because of keeping a toothpick in his mouth during the Playoffs and World Series. At the Cincinnati convention of collectors in November, a dealer offered toothpicks from U.L. as souvenirs at $7.50, but he was doing so with tongue (I mean toothpick) in cheek.

U.L. is missing a bet here if he doesn't somehow actually come up with toothpick souvenirs. The question is: How could this be done?

Is there any question about the legality of a ballplayer keeping a toothpick in his mouth while batting? The American League office received a query about it and replied that there is no rule against it, just as there is no rule against gum or tobacco in the mouth, but if a batter came up with a lollipop or pipe in his mouth, it is the umpire's judgment whether a safety factor is involved. — Wirt Gammon, Wirt's Words, 1/20/81

* * *

Well, it's that time of year again.

Springtime officially arrived, for me, on Jan. 31, when I saw the first packs of Topps and Fleer baseball cards in the candy store.

Personally, I think that's rushing things quite a bit. If I ruled the world, baseball cards would go on sale between Feb. 15 and 28 each year, at just the precise moment when you get that ominous feeling that the winter is never going to end. Then the enthusiasm for collecting would pick up as the weather got warmer. As it is now, even with three sets available, it's possible to have all the cards collected and all the sets completed before Opening Day; and there's something un-American about that. — Roland Chapdelaine, Chap's Chatter, 4/20/81

* * *

'Got To Get Some Cards For Mom'

If you wrote to Tim Raines for autographs recently and didn't get back as many cards as you sent him, there's a reason.

"I snitched one or two," confided Raines. "Where do they get those cards anyway?" he asked. "I bought a bunch of packs and got cards of everybody but me."

It seems that Raines has dozens of friends and relatives who want to add his baseball cards to their collections of Raines memorabilia. The list includes his number one fan, as well.

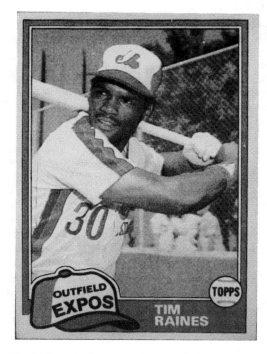

Tim Raines has to save some cards for his mom.

"Hey man, I've got to get some cards for my mom," Raines said.

To deal with this situation, Gary Taylor, a sports collector from Raines' home town of Sanford, Fla., has come up with a unique plan that should please both Raines and autograph seekers.

For every two cards sent to Taylor, along with an SASE, Taylor will have one of the cards autographed by Raines and return it.

"There's no limit," Taylor said. "Send two of the same card and one will be returned autographed. Send 50 cards and 25 will be returned. Just make sure you include the proper postage."

If you have another item you would like autographed, send a card along with it and include proper return postage.

"I know I have items that I would like to have autographed, but sometimes I won't send them to a player because I'm afraid they won't be returned," Taylor said. "If you have such a Raines item, this is an excellent way to send it off for an autograph and be sure of getting it back.

"If your package will require any special handling to return, such as going to the post office to send it insured, make sure to include enough money to cover the cost, and include one additional Raines card to cover the special handling," Taylor said. — Bill Dod, No Dod About It, 1/1/82

* * *

1973 Error Discovered

The big craze in 1981, of course, was the error card, and that may have been on my mind as I was absorbing some baseball history while looking through my 1973 set of Topps cards. I came across card number 135 — Houston star Lee May, who led the Astros in homers and RBI after being traded by the Reds.

At the bottom of the stats on the back of the card, where you're supposed to find his career batting average, you find .000. As far as errors go, this one is as good as any. — Norman Holtzman, West Babylon, N.Y., Reader Reaction, 1/15/82

* * *

Who Are BB's Toughest Autographs?

I still would like to compile a list of the toughest autographs to get among active players, but I need your help. So far, the list includes: Reggie Jackson, Jim Palmer, Yaz, Jim Rice, Rod Carew, George Brett, Gary Templeton, Pete Rose, Mike Schmidt, Steve Carlton, Dave Parker and Johnny Bench. Who would you include? I would like to list the top 100 in a future column before the start of next season. — Bill Dod, No Dod About It, 1/29/82

* * *

The Story Behind The Errors

To this moment there have been at least four error cards discovered among the very nice 1982 Donruss baseball card set, and in the case of one of the mistakes, the perpetrator has actually admitted his mistake.

"Yeah, I blew it," Frank Steele quipped candidly, "I left out one "L" in Alan Trammell's last name. It was my fault, I copied it wrong and when we sent the finished mechanicals to Memphis it was wrong, period."

Trammell is one of the 26 "Diamond Kings" presented as the first 26 players in the '82 Donruss entry, and that segment was created and produced by Steele's Fort Washington, Pa., based operation.

The other errors, for which Frank takes no credit, include Phil Garner reversed in a Pirate uniform as a member of the Astros, a statistical error on Oscar Gamble's card (his hat size? the wrong name for his barber?) and the wrong player on Juan Eichelberger's card.

"You know who Juan Eichelberger is?" Steele asked.

I replied that I did.

"He's black, right?" Steele continued.

And I replied in the affirmative.

"Not on the '82 Donruss he isn't," Steele said.

Obviously, it is the wrong Juan on the card. — Ted Taylor, Off the Cuff, 4/2/82

* * *

Why Not Umpires?

Why hasn't anyone ever put out a nice set of past and present umpires? I suppose I'll get booed for this!

P.S. I played, I didn't umpire. — Robert Gibson, Indiana, Pa., Reader Reaction, 5/14/82

* * *

Hart to Hart for Hobby: The episode of the ABC-TV program "Hart to Hart" which aired May 4 dealt with the baseball card hobby. While some aspects of the program were not representative of the "real" hobby, it was overall a nice national television plug for our hobby.

The show opened with a nice grouping of collectibles, from a '52 Mantle and '51 Mays in nice plastic cases, to uniform jerseys, pennants and bats. The plot of the show revolved around the theft of a 10,000-card collection worth $250,000 — honest, that's what the dealer who gave the appraisal over the phone told Jonathon Hart. There were some great close-up shots of Fifties vintage cards and even some 1982 Topps. There was a black tie card flipping contest using such items as '58 Mantle and Mays, '53 Topps Reese, '55 Bowman Campy, etc. There were lots of good group shots of 1956 Topps cards. There was even a baseball card convention. Though the long shots were actually of an antique show, the more detailed convention

scences were reasonably accurate; except when they had a dealer pay $250,000 cash for a collection right there at the show. The dealer was later stabbed with a 1947 Washington Senators jacknife.

All in all, it was nice to see so many nice cards there on the screen in living color and I think the overall impression on the non-collector would have been favorable for our hobby.

Watch for it in the reruns. — Bob Lemke, The Coach's Box, 5/28/82

* * *

Cleveland Indians

...One strange paradox involves shortstop Jerry Dzybinski. He is very tough in the mail, although, in person, he is probably the nicest guy on the team. Other good guys for signing include Len Barker, Jack Perconte, and manager Dave Garcia.

Barker, however, is reluctant to sign the 1982 Fleer card which pictures Bo Diaz, rather than Ron Hassey, as his perfect game catcher. — Dave Miedema, Up Autograph Alley, 8/6/82

* * *

Autograph antics: It looks like you can add Boston Red Sox Jim Rice's and Carney Lansford's names to the list of those who have "ghost writers" taking care of their clubhouse autographing. In an article in the Aug. 15 Boston Globe, sportswriter Peter Gammons said he observed clubhouse boys Dean and Danny Lewis sitting at a big table "pulling pictures and baseball cards out of envelopes and autographing them. Dean had Jim Rice's stack, Danny had Carney Lansford's." — Coach's Box, 10/1/82

* * *

The 'Real' Story About Steve Garvey

The reason is not residuals: A few issues ago, I mentioned that Steve Garvey is not signing his 1982 Fleer card. A reason was offered to me by a local collector, one that was apparently in error. The local hobbyists claimed that Garvey was not paid for the use of his '82 Fleer photo, and took out "revenge" by refusing to autograph the card. In response to my area buddy: Next time you've got information for me, don't call me; I'll call you.

Four collectors wrote or phoned to explain their stories on the '82 Fleer mystery. All four stories tend to fit together, and I will hereby accept them as the legitimate truth.

The apparent fact is that Garvey, for some unkown reason, decided to autograph just one 1982 Fleer card, which was to be auctioned off for charity in the New York City area. To help preserve the rarity, and the value, of the one card, Garvey agreed not to sign any others for any reason. So, if you've got a signed 1982 Fleer Garvey in your possession, chances are strong that the seller pulled the wool over your eyes, unless, of course, you got it straight from Garvey himself, which, according to the situation, appears to be highly improbable. — Dave Miedema, Up Autograph Alley, 2/4/83

* * *

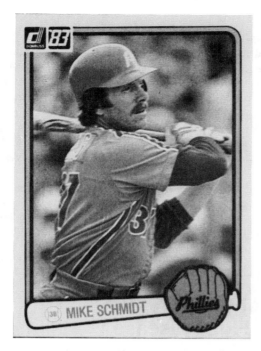

Mike Schmidt is apparently wearing a minor league jersey.

We have received a number of letters to the editor noting that Donruss' Mike Schmidt card (#168) does not picture him in the old familiar uniform No. 5. Instead, it looks like he's wearing No. 37, and the last letter in the name is a "G." Word around the hobby is that when the picture was taken in spring training, Schmidt's jersey had been stolen, and he was wearing a minor league version. Otherwise it's not a bad card, if you like Mike Schmidt. I don't know why, though, they spelled "caliber" the British way, "calibre," in the career highlights. — Bob Lemke, 3/4/83

* * *

Hall Of Fame Balloting — The Winner Is...

If SCD readers were in charge of selecting new members to the Baseball Hall of Fame, Harmon Killebrew would be joining Brooks Robinson and Juan Marichal in Cooperstown this summer.

And Luis Aparicio would be standing just outside the door.

Those are the highlights of SCD's own Hall of Fame balloting, which brought responses from many of our readers — some of them very opinionated.

You'll recall that in the Jan. 21 issue we printed a copy of the official Hall of Fame ballot and invited our subscribers to make their own choices for Cooperstown. Forget what the baseball writers did — we encouraged — this was your chance.

Well, 448 of you accepted our invitation — a number we think is pretty good for a poll of this kind — and the results are interesting...

...Our poll did agree with the professional baseball writers that Brooks Robinson was the most deserving man on the ballot. Robby was picked by 94 percent of SCD readers and by 92 percent of the writers.

But, surprisingly, after that the two lists start to look a little different.

We chose Killebrew second and Marichal third and gave both players enough votes to be elected. The writers reversed the order and Killebrew came up 12 votes short...

...You'll notice that Luis Aparicio finished in fourth place on both lists, but was much closer to election on ours, missing out by just five votes. (Shame on you five Aparicio fans who were too lazy to mail in your ballots.) — Steve Ellingboe, The Coach's Box, 3/4/83

* * *

The next morning's edition of the Los Angeles Times sports section carried the much heralded full page advertisement by Garvey, thanking fans for their support. The ad reportedly cost $15,000, and as Terry Kennedy joked, "That's just like him to pay $15,000 to thank the fans. I would have bought myself a new BMW."

In the ad, which featured a photograph of a smiling Garvey, the man of the weekend expressed his sincere gratitude to all fans for their "inspiration." Garvey dedicated the record (National League consecutive games played) to the fans.

The advertisement drew criticism from many, but it was something Garvey did not intend to be controversial. That has been a long story in his life, though. Because he was so clean-cut, many players expressed their dislike for him. Garv was just being Garv, though. That's the only man he knows how to be, and "Steve Garvey Weekend" proved that he is still a hero. — Paul Richman, 5/27/83

* * *

Gaylord Perry, Dealer

You may have already been told of this, but it is something of interest, especially in light of the recent controversy over players selling their items. I was at the show in Seattle in June at the Seattle Center, and Gaylord Perry had a table at it. He was selling autographed pictures, jerseys, balls, posters, etc., of himself, as well as autographed Mariners baseballs, autographed pictures of his brother and various items he had gotten from other players. He was also taking orders for bags of peanuts from his farm.

I believe this may be the first time a player has actually had a table at a show, and other readers might be interested in this. He did man the table for part of each day until he had to go to the park. — Mike Squire, Victoria, B.C., Reader Reaction, 8/19/83

* * *

Notes: The latest collector mania among kids at the Vet (Philadelphia's Veterans Stadium) is getting players' "tire tracks" on paper. The kids stick a clean piece of white paper under the wheels of players' cars as they drive by and then note the name of the player next to the tread mark. What next? — Ted Taylor, Off the Cuff, 11/11/83

* * *

Do players collect autographs of other players? Pedro Guerrero, after being beaned by a Nolan Ryan fastball, had no hard feelings and asked Ryan to autograph his shattered helmet. — Irwin Cohen, On the Baseball Beat, 12/23/83

* * *

The Story Behind The Hubbard Card!

Have you seen the '84 Fleer card of Glenn Hubbard yet? If not, make sure you do. It's got a picture of Hubbard standing in Philadelphia's Veterans Stadium with a huge boa constrictor wrapped around his neck!

We wondered about it, too, and went to Braves' P.R. man Doak Ewing for an explanation. It seems Philadelphia had a "snake handler" in as a part of a pregame publicity stunt, according to Ewing, and "the guy took the snake into both locker rooms before the start of the game.

"Most of the players wouldn't get near the thing," Ewing said. "But a few started petting it and stuff, and then Hubbard apparently picked it up, put it around his shoulders and walked out onto the field, where his picture was taken."

You can tell it's Veterans Stadium because the "Phillie Phanatic" is in the background of the photo. It's an interesting photo, but I'm not sure it belongs in a baseball card set! — Steve Ellingboe, The Coach's Box, 2/3/84

* * *

Smile, Here Comes The Topps Photographer

UPI had a story about baseball cards this past spring that I found interesting and informative. It was out of Oakland and centered around photographer Doug McWilliams, who takes many of the photos for Topps each year.

McWilliams explained that it started out as just a hobby for him, but turned into a profession 10 years ago after the folks at Topps were impressed with a color postcard that McWilliams had done for Vida Blue. The rest of the year McWilliams is chief photographer for the Lawrence Berkeley Laboratory at the University of California in Berkeley. But each spring he works for Topps, taking photos at spring training sites. According to the story, Topps uses seven photographers in all, during the spring and regular season.

They're always shooting pictures a year ahead of time. In other words, the photos shot this spring will appear on next year's cards. The players each receive a standard fee of $250 for the use of their likeness on a baseball card.

McWilliams is quoted as saying that despite the money, some players are still a little camera shy and don't enjoy posing for the photos. He singles out Rod Carew as being one of the toughest.

Rookies, on the other hand, are easy. They love having their picture taken for their first baseball card, McWilliams said.

He added that he takes about 10 photos of each player to make sure there are enough photos for Topps to choose from. — Wirt Gammon, Wirt's Words, 7/20/84

* * *

When you look at card number 407 of Herb Washington you have to think of Charlie Finley. Washington's card features pinch running statistics on the back, since Finley employed him to do nothing else except run.

Of course, Washington's appearance on a baseball card gave track stars new hope that someday they could be on a card, too...

...There are some great player cards, too. The Bert Blyleven card shows Blyleven blowing a bubble, tempting the collector to want to burst it in Bert's face. — Paul Richman, Around the Horn, 8/3/84

* * *

Sax Jersey Winner Announced

If you are one of the more than 3,000 collectors who is receiving this free sample copy of Sports Collectors Digest, it's our way of letting you know who won the Steve Sax rookie jersey in the contest announced in the June 1984 issue of Baseball Cards magazine. Each person who entered the Sax jersey contest, and who is not already an SCD subscriber, is receiving this issue as a consolation prize.

Altogether, more than 5,000 persons entered the BBC contest, attempting to guess what Steve Sax's batting average would be at the All-Star break. The prize was a genuine, game-used L.A. Dodgers home uniform worn by Steve Sax during his rookie of the year season in 1982.

Of the entries in the contest, a total of 49 persons correctly guessed that Sax would be batting .249 on July 9. Our computer then randomly selected a winner from among the correct entries, and the Sax jersey went to Gloria Sanborn of Joplin, Mo. — News brief, 9/14/84

* * *

Murphy Card Sales Help Fight Disease

Collectors wanting to help find a cure for Huntington's Disease can now make a contribution to the cause and get a Dale Murphy card along with it.

The card is an aluminum rendering of the 1977 Topps Murphy rookie card. Through the cooperation of Topps and the support of Murphy, the card was produced to raise funds to find a cure for the hereditary neurological disorder.

The cards are the same size as the original 1977 Murphy rookie. The aluminum renderings will sell for $10 each and are sequentially numbered. The back is identical to the original also, with brief sketches of the four players that are featured on the card front.

Proceeds from the sale will go to the Huntington's Disease Foundation of America to help find a cure for the disorder which now affects over 100,000 individuals in the United States.

Collector Charlie Adams of the Atlanta Sports Collectors Association is administering the unique campaign.

Murphy has also publically announced his support for the program and the sale of the card stating, "I am pleased and proud to be a part of the team fighting to discover a cure for Huntington's Disease. I hope you will enjoy the team effort and that you will enjoy this addition to your sports memorabilia collection."

To order the card send $10 per card plus $1 postage and an additional 25 cents for each additional card ordered to Huntington's Disease Foundation, Dale Murphy Rookie Card, P.O. Box 88004-B, Dunwoody, Ga. 30356. — News brief, 12/7/84

* * *

Effective Ads

This is just a short note to inform you that for every dollar I spent on advertising in your magazine for the years 1984 and 1983, I had $107 in sales. — Michael Rivet, Manchester, N.H., Reader Reaction, 1/18/85

* * *

Jim Bouton created Big League Cards.

Paul Green: It's no secret that you have a baseball card company which makes cards for people. How did that happen?

Jim Bouton: The baseball card company was one of several products I developed recently. The first was Big League Chew shredded bubble gum. That came out of my comeback. I was playing in Portland, Ore., with a bunch of kids in Class A. I was sitting on the bench one night and the guys were all chewing tobacco which was making them sick. So I asked them why they chewed it if it made them sick and they said, "We need if for our image." We laughed about it a little bit and later on the kid sitting next to me by the name of Rob Nelson, who is now my partner, said, "It's too bad there isn't something that looks like tobacco but tastes good like gum." I thought that was a great idea, shredded gum in a pouch.

A couple months went by and I couldn't get the idea out of my head so I called Rob and suggested we become partners on that idea. I told him I would put the money up and he should see if he could put some gum in a pouch and we would see if we could sell the idea to a gum company. That's what we did. After about a year and a half we licensed it to a company called Amurol Products and they turned it into a $15 million a year brand.

I took the royalties from the gum and invested them in my own business product development company. One of the first products was Big League Cards because I wanted to let people fantasize that they were like big league players. Players have their own baseball cards, so why can't everybody have their own cards with their picture on the front and any information they want on the back?

Green: And many of our readers have done exactly that.

Bouton: Sure, and they are having fun with the cards. You can tell by the things they write on them. They are really having a good time.

Green: Some are pretty creative. It must be fun to see what they send.

Bouton: It is. Every time our printer sends a finished plate it's amusing to see what people have ordered. I like thinking of products which let people be stars, which give people a chance to celebrate themselves like the players. — Paul Green, 2/15/85

* * *

One Box, No Doubles!

I wish to report an occurrence that is absolutely unprecedented in my 20 years of collecting: I bought a box of baseball cards which did not contain a single duplicate.

The flawless box contained Fleer wax packs, and when they opened I found myself with 540 different cards. Curious and disbelieving, I bought a second Fleer box from the same store. While not getting quite the same results, I was still impressed to find only 42 doubles in that box.

Someone ought to straighten Fleer out. In this time of card inflation, hoarding and rumors of Topps "star-pulling," providing nearly 100 percent effective distribution and one-and-a-half complete sets per every two boxes is bad business. — Keith Olbermann, Hastings-on-Hudson, N.Y., Reader Reaction, 3/15/85

* * *

Would You Believe $7 Million?

It's no secret that the baseball card hobby is a big business. The card companies produce millions of cards every year and there are thousands of serious collectors who buy them.

There are also lots of people who depend on the hobby for their full-time livelihoods. I happen to be one of them. That's one of the reasons I'm so pleased to see our hobby continuing to prosper.

There was evidence of that as we compiled the results of our reader survey earlier this year. As we told you in the Jan. 4 "Coach's Box," we surveyed 500 of our subscribers at random, gathering information about their age, education, income levels, what they collect, things they like about SCD, things they don't like, etc. We reported some of the results in earlier columns.

Since then, we have come up with some interesting — and impressive — figures on just how big a business this hobby has become. One of our survey questions asked readers how much money they spend with SCD advertisers during a typical year.

Would you believe $7 million? Based on our survey, that's the total amount that SCD readers spend with SCD advertisers in a given year. Divide that by approximately 20,000 readers, and you can see that the average reader spends about $350 a year answering ads in SCD.

Of course, some of our readers spend less; others spend more. Some spend a lot more. About eight percent said they spend more than $1,000 a year with SCD advertisers, and three percent said they spend more than $3,000 per year.

At all levels, though, our survey indicates that collectors spend a good share of their hobby budget with SCD advertisers. That makes the advertisers happy — and us, too.

Perhaps some collectors don't like to think of our hobby as a business; after all, most of us are in it for the fun, not the money. But let's face it, isn't it good to know that our hobby is firmly established and continues to grow and prosper? — Steve Ellingboe, The Coach's Box, 5/10/85

* * *

No Superstars

This weekend I opened six boxes of Topps' new 3-D cards. Each box has 24 individually wrapped cards. The set consists of 30 different players. Out of the six boxes (144 cards), I received: no Mike Schmidts, no Eddie Murrays, no Ryne Sandbergs and no Don Mattinglys.

How can this be? Did Topps print the same number of each player? Did someone pull these four? — Dick Goddard, Jackson, Tenn., Reader Reaction, 5/10/85

* * *

Baseball people tell me that Jose Canseco is the Real McCoy. Save anything you can lay your hands on that depicts the young A's prospect in card form. He burned up AA with Huntsville, found AAA a piece of cake with Tacoma. Big league stardom, they say, is right around the bend. He's a "gimme" for Donruss "Rated Rookies" in '86. — Ted Taylor, Off the Cuff, 10/11/85

* * *

NBC's Bob Costas idolizes Mickey Mantle so much that he still carries his 1958 Mantle card in his wallet. — Irwin Cohen, On the Baseball Beat, 6/20/86

* * *

They say that Mickey Mantle gets $10,000 just to show up at autograph shows. Now you know why they charge so much for autographs... — Irwin Cohen, On the Baseball Beat, 5/22/87

* * *

"Lefty" Carlton is signing with his right hand!

Steve Carlton was a surprise "substitute" guest at the recent St. Louis show to replace Jack Clark. Notice that "Lefty" signs autographs with his right hand! — Photo cutline, 2/26/88

* * *

Good question: Check out the feature on page 132 from reporter Pete Dobrovitz. Pete recently attended a Rochester, N.Y., baseball card show featuring Joe DiMaggio as a guest signer.

DiMaggio received an enormous sum of money to make a one-day appearance at the show to sign autographs. As a result, show promoters charged $3.50 admission, and $15 to $19 per autograph.

After reading the report, readers should attempt to answer the following multiple-choice question:

Who's to blame for such high prices?

A. Joe DiMaggio. He's ripping off the public for all he can get.

B. Promoter Allan George. Charging $3.50 admission and $15 and $19 for autographs is ridiculous.

C. The dealers. They're only adding to the problem by adding to the already-inflated prices in the market.

D. The public. Anyone dumb enough to spend that much deserves what they get.

E. All of the above.

F. None of the above. Hey, it's America. People charge and spend whatever they please. If fans want to spend $19 for an autograph and it makes them happy, who are we to criticize? Tom Mortenson, Coach's Box, 7/1/88

* * *

It's Mind Boggling

I would like to know why Score photographers can't come up with a better picture of one of the greatest hitters of the '80s, Wade Boggs.

His 1988 card shows him missing the ball and his 1989 card shows him looking at a strike. I think they could have done a lot better for a man who rarely misses the ball when he swings. — John Hefflefinger, Sarasota, Fla., Reader Reaction, 1/6/89

* * *

Andy's favorite: Pittsburgh Pirates star Andy Van Slyke's favorite baseball card is his 1984 Topps rookie card #206. "They got the swing with which I hit a home run off Tom Seaver," says Van Slyke. — Tom Mortenson, Coach's Box, 3/31/89

* * *

A batboy's perspective: The March 22 issue of The Milwaukee Sentinel has an interesting article about Jason Schulist, a former visiting batboy who worked for the Milwaukee Brewers in 1986. The article gives insights into the personal habits and idiosyncracies of some players.

Terry Forester, then of the California Angels, was considered the best tipper for stadium workers. He once gave Schulist $20 to get him a bratwurst.

Jose Canseco seemed to get egotistical in his rookie year, according to the story Schulist told the Sentinel. "Canseco the first time in town he was a little modest. The second time he was charging for his autograph," Schulist recalled.

"Jim Gantner was one of the nicest players I met," Schulist said. "He loved signing autographs. Paul Molitor was the same way. The most difficult one was Cecil Cooper. We weren't supposed to ask Cecil even if we knew him.

"Kirk Gibson (then with Detroit) was the most unlikable. He was really (upset) because he had to sign some baseballs. Even other players didn't seem to care for him.

"I felt Wade Boggs was a really nice guy. He'd sign 30 or 40 balls every time. He seemed to be a really nice person."

"Don Baylor was a really nice guy, but he wouldn't sign his New York Yankee cards because he had a rough time there."

The article goes on to relay Schulist's first-hand accounts of the amount of ego displayed by various stars. According to Schulist, Roger Clemens would walk around with a T-shirt that said "20 K" on it, in celebration of his fabulous strikeout game against the Seattle Mariners. The Angels' Wally Joyner, despite 100 RBI in his rookie year, simply walked up to batboys and said, "Hi, I'm Wally Joyner," and shook hands. — Tom Mortenson, The Coach's Box, 4/7/89

* * *

One Every 15 Minutes
For 43 Years

In your March 31 issue, Hall of Famer Ralph Kiner is quoted as saying he must have signed "over a million" autographs since he broke into the major leagues as a player.

Since that was exactly 43 years ago, I decided to punch some buttons on the calculator to see if his estimate was possible. It's not.

Dividing a million autographs by 15,702 (43 years, including seven leap years), he'd have had to sign more than 63 autographs per day to make a million.

Give the man eight hours off for sleep, and that comes to just about four autographs an hour. That's an autograph every 15 minutes of every waking hour of every day for 43 years.

I'm sure some ballplayers feel like they've signed a million times, but it's virtually impossible. — Robert L. Parker, Waupaca, Wis., Reader Reaction, 4/14/89

* * *

I'll Give You Eight Blausers For...

I thought you and the other SCD readers might be interested in a record purchase I made. I bought a pack of '88 Fleer cards from a local store.

When I opened the pack, I discovered that the pack contained nine of the same card — the nine cards were Jeff Blauser of the Atlanta Braves.

I have never come across anything so out of the ordinary, and I have been in the business since 1981. — William H. Gainer Jr., Parma, Ohio, Reader Reaction, 5/19/89

* * *

What's Your Choice
For All-time Silliest Card?

Craziest ever?: The 1973-74 Topps basketball card #220 of Warren Jabali is SCD staff writer Don Butler's choice as the worst sports card ever produced. In Don's column, The Butler Did It, which debuts this week on page 60, he offers an opinion of why the Jabali card is the most ridiculous card ever produced.

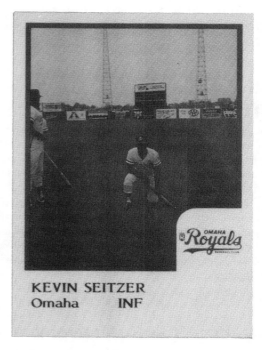

Is this one of the silliest baseball cards ever?

We thought it might be fun if SCD readers expressed their own personal favorites for the craziest, funniest or most ridiculous card ever produced. Any individual sports card is fair game. We'll purposely eliminate non-sport cards, such as Garbage Pail Kids, Trash Can Tots, etc., for obvious reasons. Let's eliminate the Bill Ripken #616 1989 Fleer card while we're at it too. We hope none of the card manufacturers will be offended, because its intent is just fun.

My own personal choice in this category is the 1986 ProCards Inc. Omaha Royals card of Kevin Seitzer. Granted, it's a minor league card, but how far away was the photographer standing when the picture was taken? The pose itself is a fairly common staged baseball pose of a player waiting "on deck." There's another player standing to Seitzer's right (we can only assume that it is indeed Kevin pictured) who appears to be hitching up his belt, apparently waiting in line to have his picture taken next. Perhaps the photographer was trying to show us the comparative size between a ballplayer and the huge utility standards beyond the outfield? Bizarre. — Tom Mortenson, Coach's Box, 9/15/89

* * *

Mays' Autograph Rate Jumps
To $4,000 Per Hour

It was reported in SCD (May 26, 1989) that Willie Mays established a flat rate of $3,000 per hour, plus expenses, for card show appearances. At the Madison Avenue 18 show Sept. 23-24 in New York City, a Pennsylvania show promoter said Mays has jacked up his rate to $4,000 an hour, plus expenses.

"Willie demands first-class airplane travel, and a fancy hotel suite, and all that made his total bill for one appearance at my show come to nearly $14,000," the promoter said. "I lost money on that deal and cannot invite him for another appearance. As far as I'm concerned, Willie Mays has priced himself out of the market." Robert Obojski, 10/20/89

* * *

SCD's 1990 Baseball Card Shop Directory contains more than 2,000 listings of shops across the country. — 4/6/90

* * *

Finally: A Remedy
For The Dreaded Wax Backs

Jeff pulled out a Mitch Webster card. Very waxy on the back. He placed the card face down on the table, put a piece of paper toweling over it, and ironed the card. (He also discovered that it's smarter to keep the iron on a low setting because too much heat causes the card to curl a little.) After his ironing the wax had disappeared.

I tried it Jeff's way too but after 10 cards or so, I got to thinking: why do we need to cover the card with toweling? I put the toweling on the table, placed the card on top, and started rubbing the iron directly over the card. No sweat. After five or six seconds, the wax was gone. Then I rubbed the card with the toweling and end of problem. — Tim Sullivan, 4/6/90

* * *

Several Big League Umpires
Are Collectors Too

Sportswriter Furman Bisher once said of umpires, "They're submerged in the history of baseball like idiot children in a family album." Unfairly labeled as sightless villans with Stone Age intelligence, umpires have been the target of abuse since the first pitch was ever thrown.

But believe it or not, umpires are human. And like fans and players, they enjoy collecting memories along the way. Take Bill Jackowski, the former N.L. umpire who was behind the plate in Game Seven of the 1960 World Series when the Pirates' Bill Mazeroski hit his epic home run against the Yankees. As a remembrance from that game, Jackowski has the batting helmet worn by "Maz" that immortal day.

Jackowski is not the only arbiter who has kept some form of memorabilia. I found that most umpires who I have talked to (past and present) enjoy collecting bits and pieces, reminders of the more pleasant moments they encountered.

Here is a sampling of what some of the men in blue collect.

Jerry Crawford: "I was behind the plate for Mike Schmidt's 500th home run. Mike signed the picture for me."

Ken Kaiser: "I worked Gaylord Perry's 300th win. I've got the last ball. They think the Hall of Fame has it. But when the last strikeout was made, I got the (game) ball and gave Gaylord another ball. I've got the 300th win ball and nobody knows that — but they do now."...

...Mike Reilly: "I have a ticket enclosed in glass from the first game ever played in Exhibition Stadium in Toronto, a game in which I opened. And I also opened (umpired) the SkyDome in Toronto. Hopefully we'll get something so that we can reflect on that game."...

...Rocky Roe: "I opened the SkyDome. I worked the first plate job there so I kept the lineup cards. I have lineup cards and baseballs from special ball games. For instance, I worked in Boston the night (Carl) Yastrzemski got his 3,000th hit, so we all got a ball that night."...

...Al Clark: "The most treasured thing I have from my career is my one World Series ring.

"I save some lineup cards for collectors in my area because they get a kick out of having them.

"I have a couple of sets of uniforms at home. If the right situation comes and somebody asks me for them for a charity that I believed in where there's sentiment involved, I would probably donate them."...

...Mark Johnson:..."I save the number two patch we wore in 1989 in honor of Nick Bremigan who passed away just before the start of the season. I also have one of Nick's hats that will never be worn again. I have fond memories of that man."...

...Joe Shulock: "I can't say I'm a collector. I get signed balls occasionally that I put aside.

"I've got a ball when (Tom) Seaver won his 300th game. I worked the plate so I got the ball for that."...

...Jerry Neudecker: "I've had the opportunity of sitting and chatting with five different presidents and have had baseballs autographed by them.

"I worked the perfect game behind the plate that 'Catfish' Hunter pitched. From that game I have a ball that has lots of drawings and a complete box score. It was given to me by former umpire George Sosnick." — Rich Marazzi, Batting the Breeze, 8/10/90

* * *

Bonds' Actions
Toward Injured Fan Lauded

Barry Bonds once stopped a game to check on an injured fan.

Pirates in person: The Bucs were OK in their most recent visit to the Friendly Confines.

Most were signing at least to some extent but, as happens with other teams, a few surprises were in store for collectors.

Andy Van Slyke did little signing (no surprise) but did kid around with fans during batting practice the night I attended.

He even slid a broken bat toward a group of fans standing near the wall by his team's on-deck circle.

Those fans within potential reach of the prize were delighted, until a security guard who liked like Dorothy, but had the personality of the Wicked Witch of the West, huffily threatened to confiscate the bat from any collector who retrieved it (despite that being Van Slyke's obvious intention).

She shoved the bat back out towards the slightly startled Pirate slugger, who then handed the chipped stick to a batboy (perhaps Ms. Personality's younger brother?)

Among the better signers were Jose Lind, Jay Bell, Neal Heaton, Tommy Sandt (a coach who went unrecognized until I produced a 1977 Topps card of him in Oakland garb), Steve Blass (an announcer who, like Sandt, nearly went unnoticed), Doug Drabek, Bob Kipper, Ted Power, Don Slaught, Jeff King, and Ray Miller (coach, and ex-skipper of the Twins).

Bobby Bonilla signed for kids, but made himself scarce when too many (translated: more than one) adults showed up with pen and photo.

The few outright refusals came from Dann Billardello (notorious for declining at the hotel, but a complete shock as a "not now" type at the park), Bill Landrum (another refusal which turned a few heads), and (not surprising here) outfielder Barry Bonds.

One needs to remember, though, that autograph signing does not always make a player a saint, and, likewise, saying "no" doesn't automatically brand a player as a creep, either. Regarding this, consider Bonds.

A few collectors, mostly younger ones, muttered less-than-endearing comments behind Bonds' back or out of B.B.'s earshot after being told "no."

The next day, however, a truer mark of Bonds' worth as a man was displayed to nearly a full house at the park and countless viewers on the Cubs' cable-ready flagship station, WGN.

Bonds, batting in a Wednesday day game, hit a foul shot that smacked a youngster in the stands on the head.

Rather than be "professional" and continue batting with no thought of the situation, Bonds, totally oblivious and unconcerned about the game, made a beeline for the buzzing in the stands, watching at the wall, concerned for the stricken youth.

At one point, still not realizing the degree of the boy's injury, Bonds gave a family member his bat. After the game, Bonds was deeply moved as to the severity of the boy's injury.

One news report indicated Bonds said the game was then unimportant at that point. He later indicated that, had he known the full scope of the injury at the time, he would have walked off the field and "would have carried him (the boy) off myself, if I had to."

The kids who were turned down by Bonds, and the guy who chose to accentuate numerous negatives in a Sports Illustrated story about him recently, can keep their opinions, as far as I'm concerned.

Putting the boy's welfare over the game he's paid to play may not have been "professional," but it was very human and most admirable and laudatory.

That day, I was surely rooting for the Cubs to win (which they did), but Bobby Bonds' superstar son in Pirate doubleknits won himself at least one new fan that August afternoon. Way to go, Barry!

For those who seek autographs from Bonds, Van Slyke and Bonilla, and aren't terribly picky about the item that gets signed, all three Bucs stars do respond to fan requests with a team-issued postcard-signed photo, actually signed. But your enclosures will be returned unsigned.

Still, a response on a collectible photo is far better than no response at all. Bonilla was the swiftest of the trio (just over a month) to reply; Van Slyke was the slowest (a bit over three months). — Dave Miedema, Up Autograph Alley, 8/31/90

* * *

Why Not Fishermen?

Please find enclosed newspaper clipping describing "Big League Bass Cards."

Why not? With baseball, football, basketball, hockey, golf, why not fishermen?

Wasn't Ted Williams a champion angler as well?

And how about horse jockeys, billiard players, auto racing drivers, chess players, bridge players, tennis players, etc? — Herman Krabbenhoft, Schenectady, N.Y., Reader Reaction, 9/14/90

* * *

Wreckers, Chisox At Odds Over Old Seats

Demolition of Comiskey Park in Chicago has raised a serious question. Who gets the seats?

According to an article in the Sept. 28 Chicago Tribune, Irv Kolko, president of Speedway Wrecking, says the bid of $1,237,500 made by his company to tear down the park was partly based on the memorabilia value of the wreckage. The attorney representing the company, Michael Roche, said the memorabilia value was something carefully weighed into the bid. The contract was signed in 1988 with Illinois Sports Authority.

"The contract couldn't be clearer," said Roche. "The contract specifically gives us fixtures, which is even more inclusive than bricks and seats. We receive all salvageable materials with two exceptions: the scoreboard and the color matrix (Diamond Vision)."

The dispute arose after the White Sox announced plans to donate the revenue from the sale of Comiskey Park salvage to charity. Howard Pizer, White Sox executive vice president, said the team's contract is obvious.

"Any contention that seats and other memorabilia (are the property of someone else) are totally without merit," he said in the Tribune article. "Typically, salvage means what is left over when someone leaves, and there were specific language identifying seats and other memorabilia as our property. The quote (in the contract) says: 'All seats, bases, pitching rubbers and other items of memorabilia.' That's pretty specific, isn't it?"

According to Roche, the mixup is the fault of the Illinois Sports Authority, which owns both the old and new stadiums, and negotiated contracts with both the White Sox and the wrecking company.

Julian D'Esposito, attorney for the Sports Authority, said it's hoped that the matter can be resolved soon. — News brief, 10/19/90

* * *

How about this price for a celebrity spouse-signed autograph?

One dealer had at his table a Joe Jackson autograph dated 1951 for $200. It had the notation that Jackson, himself, didn't sign it, but his wife did. What did Mrs. Jackson ever do to merit a $200 charge for her autograph (as Joe)? — Ted Taylor, Off the Cuff, 1/18/91

* * *

Chapter 3
Dollar Signs

Marriott's Matt Jones with the winning Mantle bid.

John Rue of the Rarities Group bought three of six paintings.

Although Chapter 3 does reflect some card prices in it (such as results of Topps' $1.6 million auction in 1989 and who the top 10 basketball card leaders are — based on the combined totals for all their regular card/sticker prices) — it mainly reminds us that this is a hobby, and we shouldn't take ourselves too seriously with things which perhaps are priceless — the memories we've attained collecting throughout the years.

In the Dec. 18, 1992, SCD, Russ Waterman reported Michael Jordan flies high at the top of the list. His 59 cards total $3,135, based mainly on his $1,200 1984-85 Star Co. rookie card. The others are: 2) George Mikan, one card, 1948 Bowman, $3,000; 3) Bill Russell, three cards, $2,440; 4) Wilt Chamberlain, 18 cards, $2,270.50; 5) Kareem Abdul-Jabbar, 53 cards, $1,680.50; 6) Julius Erving, 31 cards, $1,115; 7) Jerry West, 25 cards, $1,013; 8) Magic Johnson, 56 cards, $1,012.65; 9) Larry Bird, 53 cards, $766; 10) Oscar Robertson, 13 cards, $622.50.

Steve Ellingboe's report on the $1.6 million Topps auction in 1989 appeared in the Sept. 8, 1989, SCD. The auction, he said, proved two things: baseball memorabilia had moved into the big leagues of the investment world, and Mickey Mantle is its undisputed king.

The auction of treasures from Topps archives was conducted in New York in August by Guernsey's and grossed more than $1.6 million, including $121,000 for the original 3 1/4" x 4 1/2" painting used to create the 1953 Topps Mickey Mantle card. Artwork for the 1953 Willie Mays card went for $88,000.

The Marriott Hotel chain became the proud owners of both paintings, and displayed them on a rotating basis across the country at the chain's 10 "Champions" sports lounges.

"Mantle, Mays and Marriott. I love the alliteration," said Marriott's marketing director, Roger Conner, who was delighted with the purchase. "This is the most fun I've had in New York on a weekday. This is true baseball Americana."

The losing bidder on the Mantle and Mays pieces was John Rue, of The Rarities Group, a diversified collectibles wholesaler from Marlboro, Mass. However, Rue did successfully bid on card artwork for Whitey Ford ($35,200), Bob Feller ($33,000), and Roy Campanella ($16,500).

Artwork of the Jackie Robinson card went to an unidentified collector for $71,000.

A run of Topps contracts, cancelled checks, documents and letters with Mickey Mantle's signature went for prices ranging from $1,000 to $17,000 per lot, while Willie Mays' first contract with Topps sold for $3,000. Dozens of other player contracts sold for between $50 and $2,000.

In a three-part series on bargain investments (running in the Dec. 11, 1987, Dec. 25, 1987, and Jan. 8, 1988, issues), Tol Broome selected Topps rookie cards of 10 active, future Hall of Famers to invest in: Eddie Murray (1978, $28), Dave Winfield (1974, $20), Tim Raines (1981, $7), Jim Rice (1976, $10) Ted Simmons (1971, $5), Ozzie Smith (1979, $4), Andre Dawson (1977, $6), Jack Morris (1978, $4.25), Tommy John (1964, $12) and Bert Blyleven (1971, $5.50).

Retired superstars included: Joe Morgan (1965, $27), Tony Perez (1965, $29), Ron Santo (1961, $4.50), Orlando Cepeda (1958, $15.50), Dick Allen (1964, $8.50), Fergie Jenkins (1966, $17.50), Jim Kaat (1960, $15.50), Rollie Fingers (1969, $13) and Luis Tiant (1965, $4).

Players with three to six years experience included: Cal Ripken (1982, $8.50), Tony Fernandez (1984 Donruss, $2.50), George Bell (1982, $5.25), Ryne Sandberg (1983, $6), Tony Gwynn (1983, $11), Darryl Strawberry (1984, $8), Juan Samuel (1984 Fleer, $2.25), Wally Joyner (1987, $2.25), Dwight Gooden (1985, $5) and Bret Saberhagen (1985, $3.25).

Introducing: The SCD Price Guide

By Steve Ellingboe

The entire staff at Sports Collectors Digest has been working extra hard the past couple of weeks putting together the first edition of the new SCD Price Guide. We're excited about this new venture and we hope you share our enthusiasm.

It's a step we've been considering for many months. During the past year, we've heard from many of our subscribers — either through the mail or in person — who have told us they would like to see a price guide in SCD. And when we've given out sample copies to nonsubscribers at various shows around the country, the most frequently asked question has always been "Does it contain a price guide?"

Now the answer is "yes." From now on the new SCD Price Guide will appear in each and every issue. We believe you'll find it to be the most accurate and reliable price guide in the hobby. And because we publish it every two weeks, you can be sure it will be the most up-to-date...

...Values for cards are listed in two different grades — the two grades most popular with collectors and most frequently seen in dealers' buy and sell ads.

Because of space limitations, only cards that command a significant premium are listed individually. You'll find "common" players' cards grouped together by number at the beginning of each year's listing.

All values listed are retail prices — the price a dealer would sell the card for. Buy prices — the price a dealer would pay for a card — are less, ranging from about one-fourth the price listed for recent common cards to one-half or sometimes slightly more for higher value cards.

All prices are listed only as a guide to assist collectors and are not solicitations on the part of the publisher or anyone else to buy or sell cards.

Because of the high interest in "rookie" cards, the SCD Price Guide lists all rookies in italic type.

Many of the major "variations" (such as the "yellow letter" variations in the 1958 Topps set) are included in the listings.

To help illustrate trends in the hobby, we have used a + sign behind certain prices to signal cards that are rising in value, or a - sign to indicate cards that are falling.

SCD determines its prices using various sources, including buy and sell ads, auction results, price lists of reputable dealers and input from an experienced panel of card pricing experts.

Regional factors can cause the value of a card to vary from one city to another. A Robin Yount card, for instance, is naturally in higher demand and of more value in Milwaukee than in Houston.

Finally, we are always open to hear suggestions and are anxious to hear from our readers. If you care to comment on the new SCD Price Guide, please use the form on page 124 or send us a letter. — Steve Ellingboe, The Coach's Box, Oct. 26, 1984

* * *

Pie With Whipped Cream!

I am a subscriber to your wonderful magazine. Adding the price guide is like putting whipped cream on the pie. — Ray Becker, Ferguson, Mo., Reader Reaction, Nov. 9, 1984

* * *

Milestone Catalog Offers Hobby's Complete Reference

A three-year project has resulted in what will become the major and most comprehensive reference source in the baseball card collecting hobby.

Krause Publications, the nation's largest hobby publisher, has produced the Standard Catalog of Baseball Cards, a 624-page catalog designed to answer such questions as what do 1911-1938 Zeenuts cards look like, to how much is a Jose Canseco rookie card worth.

Highlights of the book include a hobby first, a checklist for the leading minor league sets produced since 1974, plus complete coverage of collectible major league issues and listings, discussions, and prices for dozens of obscure and unusual cards from 1887 to 1988.

Illustrations are also included for 98 percent of the major league card sets listed in the book.

The catalog's editor, Dan Albaugh, who is also the price guide coordinator for SCD's price guide, says there's a need for the reference book; there's an abundance of information on baseball cards that can overwhelm the unprepared collector.

Serious collectors, he says, need to know prices and how the prices vary, depending on the card's condition and amount in circulation.

"There are a lot of obscure cards out there and collectors are confused a lot of the time. Serious baseball card collecting poses a lot of questions. This book answers most of them," Albaugh says.

The book will provide background information and price ranges for almost all collectible cards on the market; it covers 1,800 sets, or more than 120,000 cards, many of which are obscure or of retired stars, an aspect which will keep the book from aging overnight. (Prices for such cards do not generally change as rapidly as do new card prices).

Checklists and prices for 777 sets of minor league card issues are also included. "No one's bothered to do that before. These so-called 'pre-rookie' cards are more in demand all the time. Collectors need a reliable reference for them, and our catalog is just that," Albaugh says.

More than 3,600 black-and-white photographs of card fronts and backs, plus more than 360,000 card prices (three for each card) are included. The sets are listed by date and manufacturer, while the cards are listed by the original number in the set.

User aids include baseball card histories, individual card prices, prices for sets of cards and upgraded grading standards.

Albaugh and his coworkers spent nearly three years on the project. Albaugh relied on a number of veteran collectors and hobbyists. The information has been verified as accurate by experts in the United States, Canada and even England, says Albaugh. — News brief, Nov. 18, 1988

* * *

In his March 29, 1985, Coach's Box, Steve Ellingboe offered an insight into how the hobby had changed in the last 15 years, as reflected in the prices of several baseball card sets:

"Speaking of inflation: Ohio collector Scott Mingus sent along a bit of nostalgia that demonstrates how dramatically our hobby has changed in the past 15 years. It's a price list that was mailed out by a Connecticut card dealer back in 1969.

"That really doesn't seem all that long ago, but the prices sure do. Can you imagine buying a complete Red Heart set for under $5? You pay more than that for one card today. Or a complete 1953 Topps set for $38? How about a '53 Bowman color set for $30.95? The list goes on and on.

"If only I had known then what I know now! Do you suppose any of the current sets will show that kind of profit in the future?"

The list showed these prices, effective Sept. 1, 1969: 1967 Topps, $18.90; 1966 Topps, $18.90; 1965 Topps, $19.90; 1964 Topps, $19.90; 1963 Topps, $20; 1962 Topps, $28.95; 1961 Topps, $27.75; 1960 Topps, $29.95; 1959 Topps, $29.95; 1958 Topps, $29.50; 1957 Topps, $35; 1956 Topps, $29.95; 1955 Topps, $26.95; 1954 Topps, $28.95; 1953 Topps, $38; 1952 Topps, $not available; 1951 Topps, $23.95; 1955 Bowman, $29.50; 1954 Bowman, $28; 1953 Bowman b&w, $24.95; 1953 Bowman color, $30.95; 1952 Bowman, $45; 1951 Bowman, $59.50; 1950 Bowman, $not available; 1949 Bowman, $not available; 1948 Bowman, $27.95; 1963 Fleer, $4.45; 1961 Fleer, $19.95; 1960 Fleer, $9.95.

* * *

SCD's Top 20 Most Valuable Baseball Cards

Although most of us who collect baseball cards do so because we truly love baseball and the hobby, we also recognize the hobby's huge investment potential. Apparently so does everyone else.

With the hobby's tremendous growth over the past few years, more and more "mainstream" newspapers and magazines have been doing news and feature stories about baseball cards and their increasing values. Because of our close involvement in the hobby, many of these newspapers and magazines often contact SCD for interviews and other information. Despite our best attempts to convey the nostalgic and "fun" aspects of the hobby, their questions — and articles — invariably emphasize the financial side of baseball cards.

Perhaps the most frequent request is for a listing of the most valuable baseball cards — which we, of course, are more than happy to provide. After providing this list to various other publications over the past few weeks, we thought our readers might like to see it, too.

1) 1909 T206 Honus Wagner, $95,000; 2) 1932 U.S. Caramel Charles (Lindy) Lindstrom, $18,000; 3) 1909 T206 Joe Doyle (rare variation), $15,000; 4) 1933 Goudey Napoleon Lajoie, $15,000; 5) 1909 T206 Eddie Plank, $9,000; 6) 1909 T206 Sherry Magie, $8,000; 7) 1952 Topps Mickey Mantle, $6,500; 8) 1951 Topps Current All-Stars Stanky, $5,500; 9) 1951 Topps Current All-Stars Konstanty, $5,500; 10) 1951 Topps Current All-Stars Roberts, $5,500; 11) 1951 Bowman Mickey Mantle, $4,800; 12) 1911 T3 Ty Cobb, $3,500; 13) 1933 Goudey Babe Ruth #181, $3,300; 14) 1933 Goudey Babe Ruth #53, $3,100; 15) 1933 Goudey Babe Ruth #149, $3,100; 16) 1933 Goudey Babe Ruth #144, $2,800; 17) 1912 T207 Irving Lewis, $2,800; 18) 1912 T207 Louis Lowdermilk, $2,800; 19) 1912 T207 Ward Miller, $2,800; 20) 1911 T205 Ty Cobb, $2,500. — Dan Albaugh, Price Guide Report, June 30, 1989

* * *

The legendary T206 Honus Wagner card first topped the $100,000 mark when it was sold in early 1988 by a seller and buyer who wished to remain anonymous.

Dan Albaugh, SCD's price guide editor, said in his March 11, 1988, report that the card listed at $36,000 in NR MT in the 1988 edition of Sports Collectors Digest Baseball Card Price Guide.

"What will we set the price at now? Normally, we don't set prices on the basis of what one card sells for. However, in this instance the card may be one of a kind. A figure of $75,000 seems to be justified," he wrote.

But the price just kept going up. The Dec. 1, 1989, SCD reported a T206 Wagner garnered a winning bid of $115,000 in a Lelands Inc. auction in October. Chicago-area collector Bill Mastro told SCD he paid so much for the card because it is so widely known around the world.

"If you're going to be a collector of anything and you're going to be an advanced collector...there's always one item that everybody wants to have, that everyone wants to see. In this hobby, it's the Wagner card," Mastro told SCD.

A Sotheby's $4.6 million auction brought more attention to the T206 Wagner card in March 1991, when the card, graded as Mint and having a pre-estimate value of between $125,000 and $150,000, sold for a new record — $451,000. After the bidding, which started at $228,000, had ended with the purchase by an anonymous buyer, a Sotheby's spokeswoman told a reporter, "I may have some news for you later."

As Steve Ellingboe reported in the April 12, 1991, SCD, later "came within a few hours, and when it did, the news was a blockbuster: The valuable Wagner card had been bought by hockey superstar Wayne Gretzky, who made the purchase in partnership with Bruce McNall, a major Beverly Hills coin dealer and the owner of the team for which Gretzky plays, the Los Angeles Kings."

In the April 19, 1991, SCD, dealer Alan Rosen offered his opinion on the price: "I lost a bet on the Wagner card. I thought it would go for between $250,000 and $300,000. But really, $400,000 is peanuts. There are coins and stamps that go for millions. I think the Wagner card will be a millon card in two to three years."

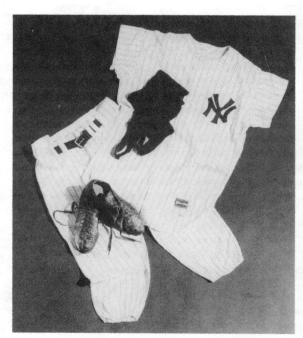

This Roger Maris uniform sold for $132,000.

In March 1992 a Sotheby's Auction House sale set another record — a 1961 Roger Maris New York Yankees uniform sold for $132,000. The uniform, a white wool flannel pinstripe (jersey, cap, socks and cleats) Maris wore during his 61-home-run season, topped the $111,100 paid for a 1960 Yankees jersey of teammate Mickey Mantle. The Mantle jersey, sold by Leland's in its "Heavy Hitters" auction in January 1992, topped the $82,500 paid for a Babe Ruth 1926 jersey in the same auction.

* * *

Rookie Fever —
How Far Will It Go?

By Paul Richman

At first it was just another aspect of our broad hobby; the goal — to collect the earliest card of every baseball star or star-to-be.

Now it has become an obsession to some, a business to others, and an investment in the future for many more. The rookie mania has swept the hobby, and the scars are just beginning to form.

It is disturbing for long-time hobbyists and true collectors, since it poses a threat toward the future success of the hobby. More than 35 percent of the recent ads in hobby publications have been dealing with buying or selling rookie cards.

A large portion of these cards are from recent sets, 1970-1982. The endless supply of 1975 Lynns and 1976 Guidrys have pushed the true memorabilia to the back.

Interestingly, it is the young and/or beginning hobbyists who are setting this trend. It is disheartening to see a kid spend his money on recent star cards that most people in his neighborhood still have.

Today, a boy leaves a convention $10 poorer after purchasing 10 Tim Raines rookie cards. A much more worthwhile collection could be built up with this money. Also one that would insure a future interest in the sports collecting spectrum.

Where will the future of our hobby lie after the rookie craze? Will there be 10,000 current rookie card dealers competing for the collectors' money?

Undoubtedly the rookie scene will eventually be hit by a crash in card values. This is due largely to the fact that the price structure of the 1960s and 1970s rookie cards revolves around the demand for quantity. (Selling the cards, in, say, lots of each).

When collectors wise up and realize that they only need one of each card for their collection, those who emptied their pockets on hoards of cards will have no person to sell to. They may end up eating 200 of each card for breakfast, lunch and dinner. Meanwhile, the rest of us continue to fulfill our collecting fantasies.

There are some rookie cards that have proved to be wise investments. I cite the 1963 Pete Rose and 1973 Mike Schmidt as good examples, since they have earned handsome profits for many overnight. Just one year ago, a person could have purchased the latter at about 25 percent of its current value.

Is anyone naive enough to think that the same thing will happen with the 1981 rookies? I mean, look how fast the 1981 error card craze simmered down.

Let's examine the facts. It took the Rose card 19 years to make a significant jump in value, and the Schmidt 9 years. Nowadays, every rookie card, no matter who of, is hoarded by thousands of amateur dealers.

More of each card are being printed, too. When it comes time 10 years down the road, for everyone to want a Mike Marshall rookie card after he has become a bonafide superstar, everyone will already have at least one.

Here's my question for the month: Why in the world would anyone pay $1.50 for a 1981 Fernando Valenzuela card, with the economy in the state it is?

Quite simply, I think it's absurd.

Don't go blaming the hobby scapegoat, Mr. full-time dealer, either. They're not dumb. They know that people will buy these cards at their outrageous prices. Nope, this one can be blamed on the thousands of aspiring dealers and fast-buck investors.

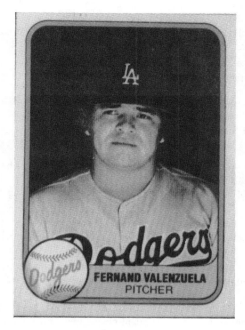

*How much would you pay
for Fernando Valenzuela's rookie card?*

I don't care if Fernando is the next Babe Ruth, I'm one of his biggest fans — but you'll never catch me dishing out that kind of money for his first card. I have as many as I need just by buying the gum packs at the local store.

It absolutely boggles my mind why someone would spend his money on these types of cards. My idea of a collection is an interesting and exciting display of memorabilia — not three plastic sheets full of Kirk Gibson cards. Obviously, my ideas are not shared by all.

Compared to the recent rookie card prices, the 1950s pricetags that we once scorned seem like bargains. For the price a person would pay to obtain all 26 rookie cards of last year, he could pick up at least two cards of Hall of Famers like Spahn and Koufax.

Unless that person is just a true fan of today's players, I think he'd prefer the older and more established cards. Every kid in town has a Raines rookie, but a 1964 Koufax separates the bubble gum blowing kid from the avid collector.

Personally, I don't even see what's so special about a rookie card. The "featured" player has to share his first card with one or two others who won't even make another card set.

It's always a small bust photo of the player, either 1/3, 1/2, or 1/4 the size of the card, depending on the particular year and set. The only write-up on the back is the players' vital statistics. Wow!

I think a real treasure of a rookie card is one with two or more big stars. Take the 1973 Schmidt; six-time All-Star Ron Cey is also on this card. (By the way, who is John Hilton?)

With all of the "no-names" appearing on rookie cards today, I wonder how Topps managed to overlook a true prospect named Maurice Wills, back in 1958.

If anything, this goes to prove that no matter how smart, nobody can pick'em all right. So it's about time people stopped trying, and beginners were once again directed toward the joy of real collecting. (To those who collect complete sets, rookie enthusiasts are a real pain.)

Please don't misunderstand me. I am proud to own a 1973 Mike Schmidt rookie card, a 1975 Fred Lynn, and yes, my 1981 Fernando. But it's a sad day when the hobby publications resemble the sports page with the constant chatter about money and value. I'd take a 1952 Topps Duke Snider over the aforementioned any day.

Let's face it. Enough is enough. Time to put the crystal balls away and participate in this great hobby with new goals. — Paul Richman

* * *

"Rookie Cards Ruin The Hobby"

I opened your November issue to see that a dealer was buying (not selling) 1984 Donruss Don Mattingly rookie cards for $22! A two-year-old card that was available in wax packs now is being bought by dealers for $22?

Give me a break! Rookie cards are ruining our hobby. Yes, that's right rookie cards, or, more precisely, those seeking a quick buck by buying and selling them are turning our "hobby" into the stock market.

A small kid, the kind that kept baseball cards going for years before it became only a business, now may want to buy a set (maybe an '84 Donruss set for that matter), but he must pay an exorbitant price simply because some so-called "collectors" are buying up all the key cards in the set in enormous quantities simply to make a fast dollar. Many probably don't care much about baseball cards, except for the money they can get out of them.

And don't think for a minute that the card companies aren't out to make a buck from the rookie card craze. Topps, Donruss, the Star Co., Sportflics and others are printing rookie card sets faster than newspapers.

Bo Jackson was on a major league card after being in the majors for less than a month. Wally Joyner and Jose Canseco had entire sets devoted to them before they had even played a full season. You have entire sets of nothing but rookies. And dealers are selling cards of one player in lots of 100 or more.

Sure, it's supply and demand in action, but the demand is coming from speculators — not from true hobbyists (who probably care to have only one Mattingly, Boggs or Gooden card, not 50!)

And the stock market approach doesn't stop with rookie cards. People are buying anything (sets, stars, old cards, commons) that they think might make them a little money. Many probably never even open or look at their cards. That's not a hobby.

Prices are rising incredibly fast. More and more cards are produced, but still people buy them in lots of 50, 100 or even 500. Do they really want 500 cards of Wade Boggs? I think not!

This is one hobbyist who doesn't like what he sees and wishes speculators would stay on Wall Street. I can only remind you of what role they played in the 1929 stock market crash and hope that the same doesn't happen to what used to be such a fun and simple hobby for so many. — Earl Thaxton, Phoenix City, Ala., Reader Reaction, Dec. 5, 1986

* * *

One reader was concerned 10 years earlier about what he called "Star Wars," "Whose Super Star Are You?" or "Will the Real Super Star Please Blow A Bubble Up At Me To Give Me A Clue." In his Sept. 15, 1977, column titled Star Wars, Gerald K. Shea wrote:

"Stopping at the first table, and trying not to look too disdainfully at those buyers bending over and groveling through the common cards, I asked the dealer if I could see his star books, 1950-present. The dealer, obviously unaware of my collecting stature, grumbled that they were somewhere, and went back to another customer.

"Unperturbed, I picked up a star book, and there on the first page was none other than a 1972T Len Randle — priced at a buck no less! Now, feeling a little less confident, and having absolutely nothing against Len Randle, I began to question myself.

"Did I miss this morning's sports page? Did he hit five triples in one game last night? Finally, seeing the dealer was free, I asked him very politely, 'Why is Len Randle in the star book?' 'I'm grabbing all the Randles I can get,' he answered.

"'I'm putting them away, and just letting a few go to the farsighted collectors. I haven't looked it up in the Encyclopedia of Baseball yet, but I'm sure that there are probably only two players who ever hit a manager and stayed in the big leagues. His cards are going to be worth plenty some day, and I'm in on the ground floor. You have to look ahead in this game, fella!'

"After having paused for a while to muse over my new found knowledge, I moved on to the next table, and picked up a star book labeled 1950-1959. I felt the need for the stability of the '50s to gather back my self assurance.

"And, there on the first page was a 1958T Herman Wehmeier for $1.25. While I pondered this, my second straight surprise, the dealer said, 'Can I help you, pal?' 'Yes,' I answered.

"'What makes Herman Wehmeier worth $1.25?' I asked. (Please God, don't let it be that he was the other player who punched a manager, and everyone knows but me.) 'Well,' said the dealer, 'He did a lot of good things, and it takes some players a while to get the recognition that they deserve. But, you're going to be hearing a lot more about Herman in days to come.'

"Putting down the urge to go back to rifling through the common cards where I felt safer, I moved on to the next dealer and his star books. There, once again, on the first page, was a 1972T of Frank Lucchesi at $1.25.

"'Well,' I said, 'I guess that former players who become managers make it big in the card world, eh?' 'Nah,' said the dealer, 'Did you ever hear of a guy named Len Randle?' 'Don't tell me! I don't want to know!' I yelled, and fled to the snack bar.

"After two cups of coffee, and a lengthy interval, I set out again. This time on the other side of the hall. Spotting a dealer who looked to be about 14, I boldly strode up to his table. 'I don't suppose you have a star book?' I said, while casually letting my well-marked checklist fall open, so as to let him know who he was up against.

"'I sure do, Mac. I've got some beauties in here.' Taking the book from him, and quickly putting it down so he would not notice my shaking hands, I opened the cover, and there on the first page (where else?) was a 1956T of Jim Rivera for $2. Silently vowing not to be beaten by this Little Leaguer, I quickly remarked, 'This Rivera is in great shape and not a bad buy for $2.'

"'Not a bad buy??' 'Not a bad buy?' 'It's worth $6,' he countered. 'Especially as more of us in the trade get to recognize who the guy in the brown suit, in the first row, trying to catch the ball, is.' I nodded knowingly, gave him the $2, and walked away with the buy of the day.

"Later that day, after I had purchased an $11 magnifying glass, I triumphantly identified the man in the brown suit.

"Now, all I have to do is to find out how all the in-the-know card collectors ever got to know my brother-in-law, Harry. — Gerald K. Shea

* * *

Robinson/Spahn Vs. Maris/Uecker

Wake up! For a few years now, card prices of certain baseball players have been escalating far out of proportion to their respective accomplishments on the field, while undervalued cards of certain bonafide superstars remain veritable bargains.

As a prime example, look at Roger Maris' career statistics. Granted, Maris beat the Babe in '61 and he had another one or two exceptional years.

However, Maris didn't even come close to hitting 300 career home runs, nor did he ever approach a .300 batting average in any year. Why the unbelievable demand?

Bob Uecker deserves "common card" status.

Yogi Berra and Roy Campanella had very good careers on great teams, but their card prices are insane when compared to other players with careers, like Lee May or Boog Powell. (Why are catchers' cards inflated, while pitchers' cards are deflated?)

Mickey Mantle performed on the superstar level, but $200 to $7,000 per card? Outrageous! Compare his career statistics sometime to those of Hank Aaron or Willie Mays.

Playing in New York can not justify the disproportional high prices. If it did, then what's the deal with Johnny Mize's undervalued Yankee cards?

Year after year Mize compiled superstar batting and slugging numbers that dominated the league. When the opportunity arises, look up his yearly statistics and notice his consistent, dominating performance with the rest of the league.

Speaking of wars, imagine if Ted Williams had not lost five prime years. Even without these years, Ted's career is still incredible, probably second only to the Babe (since Ruth was also an excellent pitcher). With those years, Williams could have had the opportunity to top Ruth's home run record.

Although Ted's cards are finally rising, they should be doubled, if not tripled. Try to find any player whose career compares with respect to league domination. Aaron, Mays and Mantle easily get lost in this legend's shadow.

Warren Spahn is another undervalued superstar. Spahn won 20 games year after year after year — 13 times total!

No pitcher in the "live ball" era comes close, nor is it likely that one ever will. Spahn's cards are amazing bargains.

Finally, compare Frank Robinson's career with Mickey Mantle's — they are quite similar. Why do Robinson's cards sell for less than one-tenth of Mantle's? Robinson's card values should be tripled across the board.

Open your eyes, fellow collectors! Examine the accomplishments of the players' cards you are purchasing. Give me a Frank Robinson or Warren Spahn card over a Roger Maris or Bob Uecker card any day. — Carl B. Schlenger, Pikesville, Md., Reader Reaction, 5/5/89

* * *

In The Eye Of The Beholder

An MS-63 Ruth!

Yes, that's what the ads are going to look like in this wonderful paper if we let these so-called "professional graders" ruin the card hobby as they did to coins.

I was into coins for about 25 years. It was a lot of fun in the beginning, when the grading was G, VG, F, VF, XF, UNC and Proof. Then, all of a sudden, a group of "dealers/professional graders" decided there should be more grades.

The dealer can tack the fee onto the coin and the collector, who's the last guy on the totem pole, will end up paying $50-$200 more than a coin is worth just because someone with a 200x microscope authenticated and graded it!

So they decided on the grades of VF-20, XF-40, Proof 59, 60, 61, 62, 63, etc.

How many people do you think can tell the difference between a Proof 62 and Proof 63 coin?

I can tell you many stories of people who have spent good money on a MS-65 coin, sent it to the "pro graders" and had it come back an AV, even AV-OBV, MS-62 REV! Come on now, did the coin wear more on one side than the other?

I hope my point is made. Don't let these "pro graders" get into the coin hobby. They'll ruin it just as sure as there's death and taxes!

Don't let some stranger tell you that your Mantle or Williams has a hairline crease only visible with a 200x microscope.

Who really cares? Do you want to show off your cards with a magnifying glass?

Cards are a trip back to your youth, or a chance to be next to your heroes. Keep the beauty of the cards in the eye of the beholder, not the holder that's made of a plastic, sealed slab! — Richard Gardeck, Dudley, Mass., Reader Reaction, May 19, 1989

* * *

Hold The Cheese, Please

Every card has its price. Cards from the 1952 Topps "find" had a price. The Lindstrom card has a price.

I'm sure that owners of a T-206 Wagner have a selling price in the back of their minds. Even rookie cards of a certain New York Met (currently batting below .200) have their price. So, if I wanted to buy a 1967 Topps Dave Ricketts, it would also have a price, right? Wrong!

I attended a late April show in a small southern Illinois town. I was looking through one dealer's "Cardinal" book when I found the 1967 Topps high number Dave Ricketts card.

I pulled it out, looked the card over, and said, "How much?"

Quickly, the dealer pulled out his trusty price guide. Ricketts wasn't listed, so he had to be a common.

But wait! Is he a common common or a short print common?

The "dealer" took the card around to other dealers and asked them if they knew. He finally came back and said he would have to wait until next year when the large price guides came out to see if it was deemed to be a short print or not.

Finally, he said "I don't want to sell it."

Let's see now; was Dave Ricketts known as the "Say Hey Kid" or the "Splendid Splinter?" Dave Ricketts, for crying out loud!

If you sold it for regular common price were you afraid you wouldn't be able to afford cheese on your burger at lunch?

I'll be darn. — Bruce G. Taber, Newburgh, Ind., Reader Reaction, May 19, 1989

* * *

Remember Him Before You Invest

The young phenom was first called up to the show in late August. He batted 96 times for a very respectable .281.

Today, would there be some interest in his rookie cards? Perhaps so.

The next year, his first full season, he banged out 219 hits, scored 101 runs, and batted a whopping .343.

Interest in his rookie cards today? Absolutely!

He missed about 30 games the next year due to injury, but still batted .325 with 180 hits. What would his rookie card be going for today?

The next year he continued his fine play with 200 hits and a .299 batting average. Perhaps his cards may have leveled off.

In his fourth full season he had a monster year. He batted .353, leading the league. He included, among his 214 hits, 24 doubles and 27 triples.

Would this be a $25 card today? $50?

Who am I talking about? Why of course, the infamous Ralph Garr.

Did anyone invest in his rookie cards? I suggest you remember him when you invest today. — Mike Parhomek, Topeka, Kan., Reader Reaction, April 26, 1991

* * *

Chapter 4
Columns & Letters

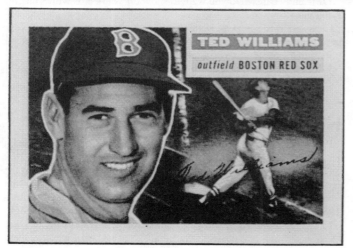

Although it was warm that day, it was a chilling moment, according to a collector who was present that magical day when Red Sox fans paid tribute to the Splendid Splinter. Josuha Evans wrote about that May 1991 day in his July 26, 1991, Balls in the Attic column:

I had the sheer joy of attending Ted Williams Day ceremonies in May during a warm Sunday Red Sox game at historic Fenway Park.

Because it took place where Williams originally created his magic, this event was magical.

As Williams approached the mike, a house packed full of Fenway fanatics gave him a five-minute standing ovation.

During the embarrassing but tender moment, he mimicked one of his trademarked swings, as if he was back in the batter's box for that one beautiful moment.

Hey, I never saw Williams play. But having seen films and photographs, there was no difference whatsoever between 1941 and 1991.

It was a chilling moment I'll never forget. I never saw Ted Williams play, but I did see him swing.

He spoke fondly of the past (even joked about his unusual relationship with the writers) and of the camaraderie with the special teammates there with him (and not with him) — Bobby Doerr, Dom DiMaggio and Johnny Pesky.

He mentioned the Yawkeys, his family and all who helped make him the greatest hitter who ever lived. Yes.

Finally, he spoke of never tipping his cap during his four-decade career as a legend. And then he did it.

"Opening Day at Denver Stadium"/"Night Game at Wrigley"

He took a crumpled Red Sox cap from his pocket and tipped it. He really did.

My only disappointment was with the gift they presented him — a framed, life-sized collage of memorabilia from his playing career.

Although it did contain a game-used Ted Williams bat and some nice photos, it was weak, for the most part. It even had a reproduction, the Ted Williams Root Beer bottle.

If the Red Sox had spent some more money and did a little more hunting, they could have found something fit for a king. Fit for Ted Williams.

* * *

Chapter 4 reflects on why our hobby is the greatest pastime since baseball itself, as seen through the eyes of SCD's columnists throughout the years. Or, some caution, perhaps it's in danger of losing that status...

The concerns and questions and thoughts and perspectives are all presented, as are the dismays and lamentations, thrills and spills, guilts and confessions, delights and dilemmas, and precious, priceless memories that we've experienced while losing ourselves in a world of memorabilia and cards.

And, letters, we get letters. Some of the best from SCD readers are presented here, too. Hopefully, this chapter keeps everything in perspective in this ever changing world in which we live in...

Would you rather have a Filer reprint, or this illustration?

Our Hobby

By John Stommen, editor

"Sports collecting — what's that?"

You can imagine the quizzical person's mind at work when he or she first reads about the hobby or learns of it from a friend or associate.

Sports fans — there are surely millions. But sports collectors — several thousand perhaps — maybe as many as 25,000. Quite likely, however, a good share of that number are still as yet unknown to one another.

We feel bringing sports collectors in touch with each other is the chief function of a sports collecting publication and we are happy to join with the other exciting sports collecting publications in attaining this end.

In addition to serving current collectors, it is our intention to reach as many new sports collectors as is possible. We feel strongly that there are many, many people out there who would just love the excitement of sports collecting and our mission is to let them know that there are many more folks just like themselves looking for them.

We who have been involved in the various facets of sports collecting for many years are the fortunate ones. We already know just how much fun it is and how many really great people you meet and become associated with in the course of pursuing sports collecting wants.

Sports collecting offers the novice any number of possibilities for getting started. If you desire, sports collecting really doesn't have to cost you a dime. You can have just as much fun collecting pocket schedules, autographs and ticket stubs in person for free or by trading with other collectors as you can paying top prices for the rare publications, cards and autographs.

That's the beauty of it! It is all up to you. Any individual can become involved to any extent he or she wishes.

In conclusion, we'd like to say that we believe our function is to serve you. What you want to read about in our publication is what is important to us. And we would like to hear from you in that regard either constructively or critically, however you desire.

We don't claim any super powers in being able to produce any better publication than the next fellow. All we can do is promise that we will give it our best effort and that in the long run, both you and we will be the better for it.

Perhaps the most encouraging part about starting a publication from scratch such as this is the terrific cooperation and assistance you get from other people. Our daily mail includes helpful advice, suggestions and information, plus — almost without fail — good wishes for future success.

We realize, of course, that there are and will be pitfalls — most of which we can not currently see — but combining the fun of collecting itself along with writing about it isn't really what you'd call work.

Thanks in advance for your assistance and we await hearing from those who have not already been in touch. And, most certainly, we welcome all of you new to the sports collecting hobby — your life has really just begun.

See you in our next issue, Friday, Oct. 26. — John Stommen's initial introduction, Oct. 12, 1973.

* * *

"I see too many people throwing too much money around for pieces of cardboard. If sports collectors were rated, a good statistic to keep would be the number of thrills per dollar output. Too many dealers might buy a rare card at $20, which really means nothing to them, except that it may be sold at $25. Is that really a hobby, or is it a second job? One group which I see at conventions which ticks me off more than some others are the kids who have a roll of money in their hands or pockets — they are not being introduced to a hobby, they are being introduced to a business!" — Bob Wait, Schenectady, N.Y., Letter to the Editor, Aug. 31, 1975

* * *

Letters

Dear Sir:

I recently purchased a set of the Goudey reprints and found them to be nearly excellent in every detail. I would recommend that the publishers of SCD refuse to print any advertisements pertaining to the selling of the reprints. I myself would not want to purchase a valuable card and then find out later it is worthless. For the benefit of the hobby, I believe strongly in this recommendation. — Richard Robinson, Lawrence, Mass., April 15, 1976

Sir:

I'm in total agreement with you on the Goudey reprint set. They should have been labeled as such. In the near and not too distant future, many innocent collectors will be taken in. They (the reprint set) should be boycotted by all.

Also, I believe that all people (and this should be SCD's policy) should list their names, no company names, inc., etc. — Alan Zucker, Wantagh, N.Y., April 15, 1976

Dear Editor:

At the last Chicagoland convention I attended, I had a chance to observe the Goudey reprint set. To me, it didn't seem like the originals at all.

The whole image of the front is a little blurry, not at all like the original. Secondly, most cards have uneven borders, something you don't see in the originals. The only thing that matches the two is the backs.

I hadn't seen the reprints before this, and when I saw the gentleman displaying them, I recognized them as the reprints.

However, I'll have to agree with my fellow collectors to place the word "reproduction" on the back just to be on the safe side. But in most cases it's hard not to notice the difference. — Scott Tomkowiak, Glendale Heights, Ill., April 15, 1976

* * *

Dr. Daniel Turner's Recent Experience With The Reprints

Dear Mr. Stommen

Much has already been said with regard to the Goudey reprints. For the past several days I have tried to decide whether or not I should write this letter. Finally, I reached a decision that this letter should not only be written but read by all.

My two sons and I have been collecting baseball cards for only a few years. We have found immense enjoyment, and have grown closer over this period of time due to our common hobby and working together.

Naturally, at moments, it becomes a monumental task to decide who gets what card. At this point a father really becomes a kid, and perhaps this is one of the benefits derived. Some people refer to this as nostalgia. It is nothing but a regression to age 12, but what fun it is.

Only a few days ago I took my sons to a memorabilia convention for comic books, sporting cards, etc. Let me tell you that walking into a ballroom filled with colorful comics is almost like Dorothy stepping out of her ramshackled farm house on to the "yellow brick road."

I was amazed by the number of children who were dealers and good businessmen. They really know how not to let you get away without a sale.

My boys called me over to a table that displayed baseball cards. My eyes struck two cards. A Goudey Ruth selling for $110 and a Goudey Gehrig selling for $75. I asked the young man, who was certainly no more than 15 years old, if I could see the cards closer. He handed them to me and it was obvious that these were the Goudey reproductions.

I immediately brought this to his attention. He was not overwhelmed with surprise. The dealer's comment was "perhaps they are, perhaps they are not."

No question about it, he knew!

To say the least, my boys and I were shocked to see this youngster starting out in the business world attaining an enduring reputation.

He is but one young dealer. I am sure others are doing the same thing. He is simply taking advantage of an unfortunate situation. Is he wrong for doing this?

I imagine that most of us would say yes. Nevertheless, he probably feels that others are doing it, so why shouldn't he? I honestly believe that he doesn't see the grave error of his choice.

Many of us have picked our brains for a solution to the problem of reproductions. In truth, nothing can be done legally. Perhaps if our hobby had a national organization our words would become more meaningful and a policy adopted that would at least make the manufacturer aware of the feeling of the hobby.

Let us remember that the young dealers of today will be the senior dealers in another 10 years or 15 years. Baseball is supposed to be a clean sport, so let us try to keep our hobby free from contamination.

I am making a request to the reprint manufacturer on behalf of all the collectors, dealers and youngsters that the word "reprint" should be placed where it belongs — on the card.

Thank you,

Daniel S. Turner, April 15, 1976

* * *

Steve Mitchell's Reprint Thoughts

Dear John:

Here's a second letter on a different subject, one which has also been receiving a good deal of attention in SCD, on the subject of reprints of baseball cards without marking them as such.

My point is, I feel, shared by many. Here it is:

According to one man who was instrumental in publishing the set, the word "reprint" was omitted by the printer. This is very believable. Personally, I have been the victim of numerous errors of similar nature made by printers in my time as an editor. In fact, I've made a good many more myself. My point: The printer's error should be accepted at face value.

Secondly, since the reprints were designed for collectors and through the hobby papers have been advertised as such, there appears to be no fraud involved. That antique dealers and other "garage sale" type operators may turn up with these cards and sell them without knowledge as to their authenticity should really be of little consequence to the organized hobby of sports collecting.

I say this because it is a well-known fact that there are hundreds of counterfeit stamps and coins in existence today. Whenever they are fraudulently passed off as the real thing, the offending party receives some sort of discipline. The fact is that fakes exist and some are even actively sought out by collectors — as fakes — and in some cases actually command a higher premium than the originals!

I think a few collectors have in this case greatly over-reacted. While I feel we certainly should denounce any collector who knowingly sells these reprints as originals, I believe that the ample publicity the set has received in the hobby journals, plus the additional cataloging it will receive in later years — as a reprint — should forewarn serious collectors sufficiently.

As for the non-collector, I find it extremely difficult to believe he would quickly part with any substantial sum of money for an "original" Babe Ruth, Lou Gehrig or other superstar when an attractive set of recently produced old-timers cards (Fleer '60 and '61, TCMA's numerous issues, etc.) can be purchased so cheaply.

Frankly, I am extremely leery of the authority some people seek to place in the hands of a very few. It seems to me that the dangers of accusing someone of fraud and then discovering we were in error pales to the insignificance any isolated cases of a non-collector being stuck with phoney cards for a few dollars.

Respectfully,

Stephen L. Mitchell, May 31, 1976

* * *

Beyond Collecting

By Bill Mastro

With our hobby growing in leaps and bounds and new faces coming and wrinkled ones being forgotten, it's nice to think that we've all made a few friends in the years gone by and hopefully will find more in the years to come.

But with articles on conventions, opening mail, letters to the editor, discrediting opinions of others, and just general news, it would be refreshing to write on an off-beat subject, one everyone seems to have forgotten — friendship.

I've grown very close to many people in my 10-plus years of serious collecting, but one person has touched me in a special way and so I'd like to let my mind wander on the good times with him for a moment.

There's one person in my youth as a collector who I admired most and who I was determined to meet.

So it was to be — at the second annual Detroit convention — that the little rich kid from Jersey (myself) was to first graze longingly upon the father of baseball card collecting — Frank Nagy.

He was a big man, but I strutted right up to him and immediately offered him $800 for his T206 Plank and Wagner.

He took me by the neck, sat me down, and I got my first lecture on baseball cards, and certainly not my last, from Frank.

I was invited to his home after the convention and my eyes are still buggy from that Sunday evening. My little sticky hands got into every drawer, cabinet, album and corner in the basement. I was so excited at times I forgot to breathe and the whole time Frank scurried around behind me closing lids on my paws, telling me I had no business in there. But he was a man with a big heart and a sucker for this little kid who wanted it all.

He filled my boxes, completed my wants and when I left I owed him my life. But in that basement that very night would start a friendship which would grow beyond collecting.

Well, the next two years saw rumor around the hobby of Frank's daughter (Brenda) and I getting married. We were very close as friends and we would both joke of how it would be the only way I'd ever get a T206 Wagner. But I eventually got my Wagner and Brenda married herself a real fine guy and we were both happy.

I would visit Frank's house every year after the Detroit show and it seemed as years went by we did less trading (as Frank would say, "I just took.") We would just lay around and watch baseball games, I'd get the heck beat out of me in those neighborhood football games that Frank's son, "little" Frank, would take me to play in, we'd drink pop (Oh so good) and generally relax after a long convention. I felt more like family than visitor each year and I've grown very close to them all.

Mom (as I call Mrs. Nagy) is a fancy little cook who is one of the best women I know. She's loved by everyone in the hobby for her good nature and sweetness. Never a minute went by when I didn't feel at home and comfortable with her by my side. We have shared a great deal of ourselves with each other over the years and do so now more than ever.

Well, the stories could go on for pages, but you see the whole joy in this for me is to let the hobby know of a good feeling I have for a friendship I've made in my travels, one which did not end after college, or dwindle because of my distance.

I'm proud to say I've made a friend, even more so, I love the Nagy family. They're the best thing which has ever happened to me in the hobby. I want collectors to read of a man and his family who mean a lot more to me as people. He's a good man with a whole lot of personality and he's made me feel terrific for years, and I think he's done the same for a lot of other folks.

So, for just this one short article I wanted people to look at themselves, look around them, and be thankful for the close friends they have made in this hobby because if we all try a little harder, it can go beyond collecting. — Bill Mastro, Aug. 31, 1976

* * *

Finds Own Way

Jeff Hein, Ipswich, Mass., thinks the whole idea of any national association is a ripoff. "I don't need a national association," he writes. "I've got my own. I find people from each state who will trade and sell at fair prices, grade items fairly, reply quickly, don't hype — and we try to keep money out of it." — Wirt Gammon, Wirt's Words, June 15, 1977

* * *

Chap's Chatter

By Roland Chapdelaine

With more and more collectors joining the hobby, everyone is looking for better methods of acquiring cards, preferably at the lowest prices. There are sports collector stores here and there, and conventions everywhere. The hobby papers have more subscribers and more ads than ever before. Collectors show up for every flea market and garage sale; and some run ads in local newspapers, trying to complete this set or that. But every now and then, cards come from the least likely places. Every now and then they come out of the sky...

It was 7 a.m. when my alarm clock went off. My first class was at eight, so I dragged myself out of bed and stumbled over to the window to check out the weather. My window faces the backyard of two adjoining apartment houses. It's quite a lovely view of fire escapes and clotheslines, but on this overcast fall day I noticed something unusual. It appeared that there were cards scattered all over the yard.

But being half asleep I attributed the apparition to the cold pizza I'd eaten at bedtime the night before. So I ate breakfast, got dressed and went on my way.

I never gave it another thought until I got home and happened to glance out the window. Whatever they were, they were still there. From the distance, I couldn't tell if they were really cards — they could have been torn up magazine pages. And even if they were cards, they could've been "Planet of the Apes" or something.

There was only one way to find out exactly what they were. I was soon walking around the block, on my way to the yard's entrance. My Bronx childhood had taught me one thing about exploring backyards: beware of hungry German Shepherds. But this was a different sort of yard than the ones I'd grown up in. It was much larger, squarer, almost the size of a Little League infield. Families had picnics here in the summer. And, with a large entrance from the street, there were always kids hanging around here in the afternoons, using the "No ball playing" sign for a strike zone when they played stickball.

The moment I entered the yard, I began living out one of the sports collector's favorite fantasies. A large yard, covered with hundreds of discarded baseball cards. Dave Hamiltons and Bud Harrelsons as far as the eye could see. A virtual cardboard carpet. And there was no one there but me.

There they were, a 1973 Ed Kranepool and Mickey Lolich.

The first card I picked up was a 1973 Ed Kranepool, and then a Mickey Lolich. I had to walk slowly, stooped over like a gorilla, scooping them all up. Face down, face up, sideways. "How many are here?" I wondered. "Hundreds? A thousand?" I had been collecting by mail for so long that I'd forgotten how good it felt to walk around with a stack of cards bulging out of my pocket.

"Who threw them out anyway? Was it a kid who just got tired of looking at them? A mother who got tired of picking them up off the floor? Or a father, angry about a bad report card or something? And I wonder what it must have looked like, all these colorful pasteboards floating down from the sky." I started humming, "Everytime it rains, it rains pennies from heaven."

But soon I was running out of pockets. "Let's see, coat's full. Pants? Sides are full; backs? Backs are full too. Oh, forgot the shirt pockets; still got room."

After some 15 minutes I had them all. And I must admit I also had some difficulty straightening up again. I brought them home and looked them over. Seven hundred eighty-three cards, mostly from 1973. Some of them were a bit creased and dogeared (you would be too if someone threw you out of a sixth-floor window) but I've never been fussy about condition.

I had been sorting for about 20 minutes when I happened to glance out the window again. The yard was covered with a light dusting of snow. Before the day ended, there was a snowfall of eight inches.

For the next few weeks I kept a watchful eye on the yard, wondering if anyone would have second thoughts about chucking away his collection. But even after the snow melted, no one ever showed up. I've often wondered if there's a kid somewhere who's going to go through life thinking that cardboard evaporates in snow.

In the four or five years since then, I've paid close attention to the yard every fall; but no cards have ever again appeared there. For all I know, that family may not even live there anymore.

But with collectors constantly trying to find new sources of cards, maybe it's a good idea to keep an eye on the neighborhood yard. The odds of finding anything are slim, but every now and then... — Roland Chapdelaine, March 31, 1979

* * *

An Open Letter To The Sports Collecting Hobby

With all the national attention our hobby has recieved recently through exposure in beer commercials, Life Magazine, and the Wall Street Journal, to say nothing of the numerous hobby publications, clubs local newspaper stories, and large gatherings around the country, it is almost redundant to say we are a force to be recognized in the hobby field. We have come so far, particularly in the last 10 years, that only one element is missing — a National Convention. That's right, a national convention! By this I don't mean another buy, sell, and auction "show" of which there are already too many, but a "convention" in its classic sense.

Personally having attended a dozen shows in the last couple of years and worked on the West Coast Convention committee for the last eight, I've noticed that they all have pretty much evolved, or degenerated if you will, into hobby swap meets.

When the very first hobby convention was held here in Los Angeles 11 years ago, the agenda included discussions of hobby issues, exhibits, a meal, souvenir program, and group outing to a major league game. Today virtually all of these activities have been scrapped in favor of carbon copy events distinguished only by locale. Shows have grown bigger, but I doubt if anyone can say better. It has been said that some of the older shows have been doing the same things for so long that apathy is setting in.

A national convention is therefore an idea whose time has come, not at some future date but in 1980, and more specifically at the Airport Marriott Hotel in Los Angeles beginning the Wednesday before the Labor Day Weekend.

I have engaged in preliminary discussions with the convention manager of the Marriott and he would be more than happy to make as much of the 1,100 room hotel, with 35,000 square feet of convention space, available to us as we can use. To get the ball rolling he would only need to know the number of hotel rooms that would be occupied with an expectation of three to five hundred.

The convention would include an opening evening informal reception; seminars on such same topics as regionals, uniforms, autograph collecting, etc.; round table discussions on a national organization, reprints, and/or hobby dishonesty; exhibits; workshops on such things as mounting, condition guide, and organizing a club or show; contests; a large banquet meal to also honor special hobby achievements during the year; convention program; chartered bus trips to Los Angeles attractions such as Disneyland, Universal Studios, or the Queen Mary, for family members wishing to get away from the convention for a while; hospitality suite; special section at an Angel or Dodger game;

and, of course, the usual three day show over the Labor Day Weekend with the potential of 300 tables. The cost of all these activities would be born by a single fee in the $150 range which would be less if the person did not wish a table.

The planning, coordination, and successful execution of such an enormous project would be staggering at least the first year, but Mike Berkus, Steve Brunner and I will "bite the bullet" to get the program off the ground. I have the added advantage as a teacher to have summer unemployment to spend working on the event.

The only element still to be heard from is the collecting community. If you are planning to stay in this hobby and your knowledge of card history consists of smoking habits of Honus Wagner, or the depth of your ideas about values are whatever a price guide says, and/or the only time you associate with fellow hobbyists is across a table of sports collectibles, then for you the time is ripe.

All I need is a postcard or letter stating that if planned you will be at the National Convention in 1980 and what particular activities you would like included in the agenda. If I can present hundreds of letters and postcards to the Marriott people we can gear up with nearly a year to plan. Don't let someone else do it; everyone take the five minutes or so to get a card or letter in the mail to me and we can launch our hobby into the decade of the 1980s with style. — Gavin Riley, Cerritos, Calif., Oct. 15, 1979

* * *

Chap's Chatter

By Roland Chapdelaine

As the hobby gets more and more sophisticated, I find myself feeling increasingly out of step with the times, like a dinosaur who has somehow managed to survive in a strange new world after all of his contemporaries have become extinct.

I guess I'm a relic from the Stone Age, as far as collecting is concerned. I still feel the best way to transport a small number of cards is to carry them in your hip pocket. But many of today's collectors shudder at the thought of this out of the fear that the precious bits of cardboard will become creased. Well, so what if they do? I was 18 before someone explained to me that "mint condition" does not mean cards that smell like bubble gum.

I still store my cards in the 500-count boxes Topps sells to dealers, which are slightly smaller than the old traditional shoebox; yet most modern hobbyists store their cards in plastic sheet binders. The first time a collector explained to me the advantages of the PS-900 sheet, I thought he was talking about an income tax form.

There was a time, not very long ago, when the large marjority of meetings among hobbyists took place in someone's basement, at casual little get-togethers known as "swap meets." The dialogue usually went something like, "OK, gimme him, him and him, and I'll give you him, him and him." Now it seems that every community in the country with a population of over 50 has at least one annual convention, often drawing collectors from across the country. This is great for the hobby itself and for those of us in it, but it is a bit overwhelming when you realize that almost all of these conventions have sprung up within the last five years.

When I first entered the organized hobby, the items on most want lists could be obtained from other collectors in exchange for some of your duplicate cards. Hobbyists were most interested in trading items than selling them, because most collectibles, especially cards, had little or no monetary value. Today, while trading cards usually won't be as welcome to a dealer or collector as cash is, credit cards are often accepted by dealers as a means of purchasing hobby items. Can you imagine that, credit cards because they tempt you to spend money you don't have. But I know myself well enough to know that, if I went to a convention with a credit card, I'd buy the whole place, then use the credit card to charge a plane ticket to Buenos Aires, and that would be the last you'd see of me.

I'm not really against the march of progress in the hobby; it's just that I find the sophistication of today different and often amusing, compared to what I grew up with. I enjoy watching many of the new trends, such as the recent interest in collecting baseball card wrappers. I honestly cannot say I remember what a single wrapper looked like from any of the years I bought cards in the candy store, basically because as soon as I bought the pack, I tore the wrapper apart, threw it and the gum away immediately, and excitedly examined the cards.

That's what we all did; and that's why some of those wrappers are now selling for $3 or $4 or more. No one thought to save them. But I'm just waiting to see an ad proclaiming "Auction: Slab of gum from 1957 Topps BB. Ex. MB-$5." And someone would probably buy it, too.

I do, however, find some trends in the hobby distressing. It is next to impossible to sell any kind of old (Spalding or Reach) guide or 1940s or '50s yearbook that is missing one or both covers. Why? I don't know; I'll gladly take them. All you're really missing are a few ads and one good cover picture; but the sketches on front covers of old guides and yearbooks aren't much to look at anyway.

Still, it seems that most hobbyists would rather spend $20 for a guide with both covers than pay $10 for one without a cover. That I'll never understand, especially since there aren't enough covered guides left in circulation to satisfy everyone who's left hoping to find one. And if we all refused to buy coverless guides, we'd be dismissing half of the guides in circulation simply because they lack one irrelevant page. But to each his own.

More basic to the hobby than a preoccupation with excellent condition is the problem of inflation. Obviously inflation isn't confined to the hobby alone; and if I could explain it, let alone solve it, I'd be writing for the Wall Street Journal instead of SCD. But I think we can fight inflation more successfully in everyday life than we can in the hobby. For example, a smart shopper can "beat the system" by buying winter clothing in the spring, summer clothing in the fall, Christmas decorations in January, etc. Department stores run sales on out-of-season stock which can save you a lot over the in-season prices.

And remember when sugar was so expensive a few years ago that supermarket managers hung signs on the shelves urging customers to refrain from buying sugar until the manufacturers reduced their prices? What happened? No one bought sugar, and the prices came down. The same thing happened with coffee. And once beef became too expensive, people switched to fish and hamburger. And what happened? Fish and hamburger prices went up, but beef came down slightly.

Unfortunately we can't "beat the system" in the hobby, because collecting is never out of season, and cards have never been known to spoil from sitting on the shelf too long. In fact, cards age like wine, increasing in value the longer they're around. It has gotten to the point where those annual (now monthly) price surveys are outdated shortly after publication. Any day now I expect to hear Walter Cronkite say "the New York Stock Exchange fell six points today, closing at its lowest level in six months; and 1952 Topps Mickey Mantle is now worth $1,000."

I think that's a very sobering thought, especially at the dawning of a new decade. Most of us got into the hobby when $1 would fill in a lot of boxes on your checklist. Today $1 won't even buy most dealers' price lists. Even the new sets being published about players of the recent past are being sold for $15. Ten years from now, will our chil-dren be able to afford the hobby we've enjoyed so much? Or will it become a rich man's club like autographs and Americana? Will our children have to become chairman of the board in order to afford the cards we bought as kids for a penny a piece?

I've heard it said that our hobby is still very inexpensive when compared to coin collecting, stamps or antiques. That's quite true, but how many 10-year-olds do you know who dream of owning a Louis XVI chair? And how many 30- or 40-year-olds do you know who try to recapture their youth through coins or stamps? We are in the business of collecting memories, and, the way I see it, recapturing the warm summers of our yesterdays should not cost our entire paycheck today. But then I'm an old dinosaur who still believes the hobby should be fun, within the reach of everyone. — Roland Chapdelaine, Dec. 31, 1979

* * *

Keeping It All In Perspective

By Wes Ruhrig

When is the last time you really enjoyed your hard-earned collection of baseball cards? Do you find yourself thinking that your wife, children, house, job and the dogs are roadblocks to the ultimate collection?

Do you lust (only in your heart, of course) for every baseball card ever printed — no, not just one of each, but every copy ever printed?

Well, if you exhibit some or all of these symptoms you are a collectaholic. You are suffering from collectivitis, an inflamed compulsion to collect, accumulate, hoard, stockpile and protect. But take solace in the knowledge that you are not alone. Millions of collectors of every conceivable item produced, from barbed wire, to corkscrews, are alive and well (except for suffering from collectivitis) and living in the United States.

We are a nation running head first in search of childhood dreams and remembrances. While the world gathers new problems by the day, we, the collectaholics, seek out our special something that somehow protects us from all that is crazy. And we, as baseball card collectors, know that long after the world forgets what an Ayatollah is it will remember the heroics of a Ruth, Gehrig, Cobb and Rose. But even so, have you found yourself collecting more lately, but enjoying it less? Perhaps it's not enough that we merely collect, categorize, file, store and ogle. Maybe we need to do something that hasn't been done for a long time.

The latest issue of Inside Sports magazine contained (yes, you guessed it) yet another article on BB card collecting. It was there that a sentence jumped off the page and hit me in my childhood. It was saying "this is why you don't enjoy card collecting as much as you did as a small boy." The sentence dealt with the current taboo against card flipping and all its various forms: fars-eeze, leaners, etc. Eureka!! When is the last time you took a pile of cards (note: not to include any of your good ones) and "flipped" away some time and relaxed? Why haven't card show organizers included as part of the day's festivities some card flipping competition with a few superstar cards on the side to sweeten the pot? Your local collectors organizations could do the same thing.

As a kid I never owned an excellent or mint card for long, and I don't remember that it detracted from the real fun of cards. The playground of Pershing Avenue Grammar School in Newark, N.J., featured some great flippers during the summers of 1954 and 1955. Chewy pink gum and a pocketful of cardboard faces with rounded corners transformed many an afternoon into Yankee Stadium, Ebbets

Field and the Polo Grounds. And whether it was the thrill of victory, or the agony of defeat, a fresh supply of ammunition was only a nickel away.

Maybe what we all need to do, as part of our therapy for collectivitis, is to grab a pile of 1980 Topps commons and organize the local playground. Anyone out there who wants to get up a game, with a few superstars on the side to sweeten the pot, let me know.

My therapist says I need the action. — Wes Ruhrig, June 15, 1980

* * *

Chap's Chatter

By Roland Chapdelaine

This is about collecting, sports collecting.

It's about the concept upon which our hobby used to be based, and what some of us still believe the hobby is all about. It's about pure collecting, for the sake of collecting and treasuring and remembering.

Nowhere in here is there any mention of condition, price guides, values or superstars, because these things are irrelevant to pure collecting. Pure collecting deals only with saving memories; and memories are priceless.

There's something magical about being on a team, wearing a bright, clean uniform with the team name on the front and your name and number on the back, knowing that, for once in your life, you're an integral part of something larger than yourself, a vital cog in an efficient machine, a member of a team.

Forget that you're not playing for the Yankees, that you never will. Whatever team you're on, whether it's somewhere in the low rungs of the minors, a high school league, or a store's softball team, that team IS the Yankees to you, the sandlot you play on IS Yankee Stadium, and your opponent IS the Red Sox.

For the time you're out on that field, nothing else in life exists, much less matters. When the sky is a brilliant blue, and a glorious summer sunlight is drenching a ballfield full of rich green grass, every practice, every pitch, each time bat meets ball and ball meets leather, it's an occurrence of monumental importance. The rest of the world may well be falling apart at the seams; but so what? You just popped one over the center fielder's head, or made a sensational basket catch. What else matters?

The desire to excel, to win, to prove superiority over every opponent pulls your team together so that you are no longer a group of individuals, but one single unit, a winning team. It's a feeling of union that defies description to anyone who hasn't been part of it. A family isn't even a proper analogy for a team, because members of many families pull in different directions, toward different goals. But a team has one single objective shared by all its members — winning. Sure, it's a game, and games are played for fun. But how can you have fun when you're losing?

Being a member of a team that has won in the face of adversity, that has won because it refused to give up, is something to treasure for a lifetime. Whether it be an entire season or a single important game, you will never forget precisely how bad the situation was, all of the circumstances which made your comeback seem impossible, and each of the details of how you came back, how you beat the odds and won.

And for as long as you live, that final inning will play over and over in your mind. Your pulse will quicken and the goose bumps will rise as that final out flashes before you time and again. Society may deem it advisable that you merely smile at the memory if you happen to be in a public place at the time. But inside you'll forever leap in the air, as you did when it happened, hugging your teammates and yelling, "Awright, We did it! We did it!"

But life is very much a fleeting thing. The most wonderful day lasts for only 24 hours, and then becomes a memory. Whatever circumstances brought your teammates together with you — a job, an education, a dream, luck — will all too quickly take them from you.

Today was never meant to be the final destination for any of us, only a brief stop on the way to somewhere else. And all too often, when tomorrow arrives, the magic you had hoped would go on forever, and the friends you loved, are gone. The memories you saved, thought to be insignificant at the time, are soon the only means of returning to that time and those people.

An empty, lonely-looking ballfield brings a melancholy smile to your face as you see and hear sights and sounds — and people you loved — who are no longer there. There's a bat and a glove that once upon a time helped win ball games; and there's your uniform shirt. There's also a wornout ball, signed by all of your teammates. At the time you gathered their signatures, it seemed so trivial; you were with them every day. But now that ball is all you've got left of them. And damn it, you miss them.

No one in the organized hobby of sports collecting would be interested in your uniform shirt. But even if they were, you couldn't part with it in exchange for a shirt of Babe Ruth's. And no one in the hobby would want the ball you've got, signed by all your teammates. But even if they did, you couldn't trade it for a ball signed by every member of the Hall of Fame.

Anyone who doesn't understand that just doesn't understand sports collecting, pure sports collecting. That's what it's all about — memories. Priceless memories. — Roland Chapdelaine, June 30, 1980

* * *

Chap's Chatter

By Roland Chapdelaine

The last few years have seen the prices of cards and other hobby items rise to the point where it became necessary to measure the monetary value of each card every few months. I can see that this is important; it gives everyone in the hobby accurate information to consider in their buying, selling and trading.

However, I think that many of us in the hobby have become preoccupied with the concept of monetary value. For instance, whenever a newspaper runs a feature on the hobby (many of which are reprinted in SCD), or whenever a radio or TV newscast interviews collectors, one of, if not the main point of the piece, is that collecting is economically profitable. Almost every one of these interviews mentions a) the T206 Wagner, b) the Goudey Lajoie, and c) the 1952 Topps Mantle, along with the current dollar value of each, as though this factor alone makes the hobby worthwhile.

It seems as though some of us are trying to justify our obsession with cardboard bubble gum cards by overstressing the fact that, in some cases, these cards are worth money. Didn't many of us enjoy the hobby before it was lucrative? Weren't we in it just for the fun of it? If cards suddenly became economically worthless, wouldn't many of us remain in the hobby simply because we enjoy it?

On the other hand, maybe all those value lists are valid. Maybe money is the only measure of something's worth. If so, then maybe we should all evaluate everything in life the same way.

If a 1952 Topps bubble gum card of Mickey Mantle is worth $3,000, then...

Taking a nap is worth $4,000. Being awakened is worth 14 cents; but waking up in the middle of the night to find you can sleep for three more hours is worth $3,500.

Finding a full mailbox is worth $1,000. Discovering that half of it is junk mail is worth $500. Discovering that the other half is bills is worth 50 cents.

A deserted beach in the summertime is worth $2,000. A deserted beach anytime is worth $1,000. A crowded beach anytime is worth $4.

Bing Crosby, Tony Bennett, Sinatra and Barry Manilow are worth $5,000 each. Disco and hard rock are worth five cents each.

Spring and summer are worth $6,000. Fall and winter are worth six cents. Summer vacation is worth $7,000. The end of summer vacation is worth seven cents. Sunrises and sunsets are worth $5,000. A starry night is worth $2,000. Rain is worth $5 and snow is worth 14 cents.

Cagney, Bogart and Garfield movies are worth $5,000 each. Most old Warner Brothers movies are worth $3,000. Musicals and science fiction are worth 25 cents. Bugs Bunny cartoons are worth $5,000.

People who never stop talking about their kids are worth $50. People who never stop talking about their pets are worth $25. People who never stop talking about their jobs are worth $12. People who never stop talking are worth 12 cents.

Reruns of "Harry O" and "Alfred Hitchcock Presents" are worth $5,000 each. Commericals for record album collections are worth 50 cents. Game shows, soap operas and newscasts are worth five cents each. Public TV is worth six cents. Pledge week on public TV is worth three cents. Poor reception during a ball game is worth 17 cents. Phone calls during a ball game or a movie are worth six cents. Most prime time network shows are worth five cents. The other prime time network shows are worth three cents.

Days off are worth $500. Rainy days off are worth $5. Sunday mornings are worth $100. Sunday nights are worth $50. Monday mornings are worth $5.

Doing the laundry is worth eight cents. Doing any household chores is worth eight cents. Letting it all slide until tomorrow is worth $50. Letting it all slide indefinitely is worth $100. Getting somebody else to do it is worth $500.

Rush hours are worth 21 cents. Long lines in the supermarket are worth three cents. Long lines anywhere are worth three cents. Long lines in the dentist's office are worth $300.

Root beer is worth $500. Chocolate milk shakes are worth $1,000. But a cold glass of water on a hot summer day is worth $5,000. Pizza is worth $500, chow mein is worth $300 and McDonald's is worth $5,000 ($10,000 if you work there).

Fashion fads are worth seven cents. Politicians are worth three cents (two cents in election years, one cent the rest of the time). Economists, corporate executives, and people who work behind a desk are worth $50. People who earn a living the hard way, getting their hands dirty, are worth $5,000 each.

People who agree with you (intelligent people) are worth $5,000 each. People who disagree with you (dumb people) are worth five cents each.

And people who think of baseball cards, and sports collecting, only in terms of their monetary value, are worth nothing at all. — Roland Chapdelaine, July 15, 1980

* * *

Off The Top Of My Head

By Tom Gregg

Boy, just a modest little survey in an off month like July, you don't know what you're getting yourself into.

For three solid weeks, the responses rolled in on my 7/31 SCD baseball card poll. 113 guys, girls, kids and couples from 36 states sent in their views via memos, printed stationery, scraps of looseleaf. The mailman, who isn't used to such a workout on this route, was giving me quizzical looks (ah, let him wonder). And I could have burned out a couple pocket calculators tabulating returns if I didn't favor a (t)rusty old slide rule.

But — whew — the results are finally in. Thanks awfully to all who participated. There were so many nice personal notes that after I doled out the door prize cards as advertised, I started sending out a few to each of those correspondents for as long as the supply lasted. Hope they're all happy. Anyway, let's look at the results.

Best Card Design (respondents asked to choose two; perecnt of ballots named on in parentheses): 1. 1956 (34); 2. 1957 (26); 3. 1967 (22); 4. 1960 (17); 5. 1953 (12).

As theorized, there is a collector consensus regarding card design. Out of 29 Topps issues, the above five pulled a whopping 56 percent of the votes. Another contention here was that the 1970s were steadiest but blandest of the three decades, and balloting backed this up too. 1956 alone got more bests than all the 1970s issues combined! What makes these sets work? Simple and complex style. Horizontal and vertical format. Year-by-year and season/career statistics. Maybe Topps can puzzle it out.

Worst Card Design (same arrangement as above): 1. 1968 (29); 1958 (18); 1962 (16); 4. 1971 (16); 5. 1972 (14). Fifty percent of the worst votes went to this quintet. What we collectors feel doesn't work is a lot less elusive than what will: each of these sets has an unusually prominent border or background. Many poll respondents pointed out that this detracts from the player photograph. Topps very probably reasoned this out for themselves, since they've avoided such a format in more recent years.

Should Topps Give Up Styling and Go Full Photo? Yes — 30 percent. No — 67 percent. No opinion — 3 percent. So, if borders are such a hassle, why not eliminate them altogether? If it's photos they like, give them 100 percent photo as the '53 Bowmans did. Logical, right? A majority of more than two to one says it's not that simple. "That'd be too boring; I like to see what new style they're going to come up with each year" was a typical comment. Styling stays, by popular demand.

Should Topps Recycle Design: Yes — 55 percent. No — 44 percent. No opinion — 1 percent. Some collectors took this to mean to the exclusion of new designs and said no. Others felt it would lead to confusion between sets and said no. To the former I say, how about once in a while? And to the latter, what if we mix fronts and backs, as several readers suggested? At any rate, the concept that in its extreme has kept Volkswagen afloat so long bears looking into.

Do You Prefer Year-By-Year Or Season Career Stats?: Y/Y — 73 percent. S/C 16 percent. Alternate — 5 percent. No opinion — 6 percent. No contest. Notice that four of the bottom five card issues featured either sketchy Y/Y or S/C stats? And why, a couple of collectors asked, can't stolen bases be included? A fair question. Another one might be why not include walks and strikeouts for hitters instead of games and runs scored? The former are useful, and difficult to get elsewhere.

Would You Be Interested In Improved Design At The Expense of Smaller Card Sets?: Yes — 62 percent. No — 36 percent. No opinion — 2 percent. The response to this question indicated both 1) a general dissatisfaction with design of the past decade or so, and 2) a willingness, an eagerness, even, to cut the size of the sets to concentrate greater effort and expense on design. "Let's have quality, not quantity," one reader writes. "Who needs Horace Speed (or marginal players like him)?" another wants to know. Of course, whether Topps will agree is something else again. Most players and fans see the baseball season as oversized, too, and you know how much of a difference that has made...

Should Topps Resurrect Fielding Stats?: Yes — 59 percent. No — 35 percent. No opinion — 6 percent. They disappeared after 1958, but glove men like Eddie Brinkman and Mark Belanger didn't.

Does It Bother You That A Player Just Traded Is Shown On His Own Team? i.e. Should Topps Airbrush Caps and Uniforms? Yes — 29 percent. No — 70 percent. No opinion — 1 percent. The state of the airbrushing art has gone from obvious to merely detectable, but collectors nevertheless laid into the practice. Descriptives like "terrible," "lousy," "horrible," and "ugly" popped up often. Actually, the question could have been phrased better, but many readers took time to explain that while they checked No, the didn't want airbrushing, yes, they were bothered by the player being depicted on his old team. Suggestions were to issue the cards later to accommodate more trades, issue a traded subset (i.e. 1974) or print a "traded" notation on the reverse. Just don't airbrush. — Tom Gregg, Sept. 15, 1980

* * *

A Letter To The Sporting News

Dear Sirs:

I just recently read in your publication about the autograph baseball collection that was stolen from pitcher Rick Wise. I have been a sports collector, mostly baseball items, for about 25 years now. After reading about this unfortunate incident, I became furious and wanted to do something about it. I am sending a photostat of the story to each of the three leading hobby publications and am asking them to publish a request to all collectors to be alerted of these stolen baseballs, especially the no-hitter ball that was also taken.

I have never met Rick Wise, but I know he probably feels the same way thousands of us "legitimate" sport collectors do about our items. There is a tremendous amount of sentimental value to our collectibles and a hell of a lot of grand memories that we cherish in each and every one of them. I still have the first baseball card I ever bought back in 1955. Its current value is only about 50 cents, but I would lose a very big item from my collection if it was ever stolen.

I'm sure these baseballs meant a lot more to Rick than most people would realize, especially his no-hitter ball. I'm hoping that at the very least he could somehow get that ball back. Maybe through the efforts of our fine trade journals, sport collectors across the country will be on the lookout for it. — Larry Dluhy, Houston, Texas, Letter to the Editor, Nov. 30, 1980

* * *

Early Reaction Positive To SCD Editorial On "National Show Format"

By Ted Taylor
SCD News Editor

In our Jan. 31 publication we editorially suggested the organization of a National Show format and invited replies from the hobby at large.

In the past weeks that have gone by since that editorial the response has been steady and, for the most part, supportive of the idea.

While we did not hear from as many promoters of small shows as we had hoped, the operators of three of the larger shows in the country — St. Louis, Cincinnati and Philadelphia — did offer interesting comments and many members of the general hobby felt it prudent to add their viewpoints by phone, letter and in person.

What follows, we hope, is a contribution of the dialogue necessary to reach some firm conclusions and guidelines. Your comments and viewpoints will be appreciated.

"Remember what happened to the early American settlers?" Frank Steele asked me the other day. I thought for a minute and replied, "the Indians killed them, didn't they?"

"Yes, they did," he replied, "it was the second band of pioneers who made it."

"What made you ask that question?" I countered.

"Well, I was reading your editorial about 'Let's Organize A National Show Format' and got to thinking that it was a noble pioneering effort, but I have a hunch the Indians might kill it."

Steele, who was recently described by the Philadelphia Daily News as "a real estate man and entrepreneur," is a longtime friend, collector, attorney, antique enthusiast and a valued counsel in things of a hobby nature, so his words had a semi-chilling effect.

Oddly enough, though, if the "Indians" are grouping for an attack, their advance scouts have done a remarkable job of doing so undercover and the initial reactions to our editorial have been most positive.

Perhaps the most encouraging letter of all came from Rich Hawksley, convention chairman of the 6th Annual St.Louis Cards' Baseball Card & Sports Memorabilia Show, who wrote, "I agree 100 percent and so do most of the members of the club here on your platform on conventions and shows. I hope you follow through with this platform except for some minor changes."

Hawksley finds fault only with the upper limits of tables in the various show categories, a feeling shared by several others, and pointed out that "major national shows" could function well with upwards of 100 tables or more assuming they met other criteria in representation, show hours and past track records.

Hawksley adds, "I certainly feel our show is a national show and I think other national conventions are Philadelphia, Gavin Riley's Los Angeles show, Chicago, Indianapolis, Cincinnati, Dearborn-Detroit and Kansas City. All of these shows have at least five years experience, except Dearborn."

Cincinnati show chief Phil Lachmeier was distressed by the fact that under the originally stated guidelines his show would not be considered "major" either nationally or regionally, though most hobbyists consider it one of the prime shows in the country.

Phil points out that Cincy usually has 115 tables and the last show had dealers from 23 states, but they do not invite baseball guests or run charity-related functions.

Steele agrees with Lachmeier on the charity aspect of the shows and feels that events claiming to be run in the name of charity should be "up front" with exactly what the percentage is that the charity will realize. "If it is proceeds from the auction, or a piece of the gate or just a contribution of some of the profits, I believe it is important that that fact be stated," Steele commented.

Bob Schmierer, co-chairman of the EPSOC-run Philadelphia Baseball Card & Sports Memorabilia Shows, shares Lachmeier's feeling on guest celebrities, but adds, "I feel we run a three-ring circus in Philly with the guest celebrity being one of the rings. In that context, I think it works to the advantage of all concerned. I'm more than a little concerned, however, when the guest celebrity becomes the be-all and end-all of the show — the single ring, so to speak — and takes away from the real purpose of the show, and that is the buying, selling and trading of baseball cards and related memorabilia."

Allan Voss from Belleville, N.J., who describes himself "as a fairly new member of the sports collectors fraternity" agrees with the basic thrust of organizing a national show format, but adds, "I disagree with the part about putting aside a national organization. I feel that in order to establish any rules that would govern shows and/or conventions a national organization would be a must."

Voss adds that he feels "shows" should be more than just dealer tables, acutions and celebrities and feels the need for more displays and educational seminars.

He adds that it would be helpful if educational seminars could be given by concerned dealers and collectors on various subjects, such as grading, authenticity of cards and hobby history.

One longtime show operator, who requested anonymity, responded to the idea of seminars, exhibits and the like, with the comment, "who will pay for them? In our current economy to cover costs of fringes like seminar rooms, exhibit space and the like we'd have to increase the cost of both our admission and our dealer tables. If I do that I run the risk of hurting hobby participation and cutting attendance. Neither prospect is very appealing."

Veteran hobbyist Jim Beckett commented that he feels there is a definite need for clarification of shows and remarked that poorly-run shows can have a devastating effect on the entire hobby. "If someone has a bad experience at one poorly-run show odds are we'll never again get him interested in attending another."

Harry Stubbs, owner of the Philadelphia Baseball Card Shop, added "the thing that's wrong with the negative impact of a poorly-run show can have on the hobby is the rippling effect. One person attends a show and is disillusioned. That person goes home and tells his neighbor that baseball card shows are a rip-off. That neighbor goes to work and tells his associates. The next thing you know one bad experience had cost us the respect and possible participation of a couple of dozen people."

Tung Chen, a collector from Darien, Ill., finds fault with the convention label and remarks that publications should quit listing "conventions" and start calling the events what they really are — sports memorabilia shows.

Another uniform criticism of shows is their failure to adhere to stated hours. "There is nothing more frustrating to an individual or family to show up for the Saturday evening hours of a weekend show and find 50 percent of the dealer's tables empty," commented Frank Steele. "We (he and his wife Peggy) attend many quality antique shows around the country and find that such things never happen at the 'better' shows. In fact, if a dealer packs up and leaves before the stated closing time of an antique show it is likely that he'll never get a table again at that show."

Schmeier points out that the Eastern Pennsylvania Sports Collectors Club has been telling dealers for the past several shows that early closing on Saturday nights will cost them their tables and his organization has recently begun enforcing that rule.

"We're also telling dealers who are planning to work our Ocean City, N.J., show this summer that the evening hours will be the best hours of the day and anyone who closes down early on Friday night will return Saturday night and find their table closed permanently!" — Ted Taylor, March 20, 1981

* * *

Feedback From You...
Let's Keep The Hobby Informal

Dear Ted,

A couple of years ago a prominent New York dealer had a disagreement with a dealer/collector who is very well thought of in New England. This New York "gentleman" threatened my fellow New Englander during the course of their debate with the exclusion from "any of the sanctioned conventions and card shows."

This, I believe, is what can be expected of a National Card Collectors Association. The "Johnny-come-latelys, the price-fixers and the gougers" would welcome an association. From what I've read and heard an organization would lend itself quite handily to these manipulators. With the advent of a formal organization it will be all too easy for those who wish to sanction or "black ball" someone or some event and to totally control the hobby's prices and trends.

As for the argument that an association will be able to "ride herd" on the disreputable or dishonest dealers, I ask if that's to be accomplished by a tax-supported hobby police force or what. Existing laws and postal regulations should be enough to discourage and punish wrongdoers. Price-fixing and false shortages are common in all commodities today and sports collectibles are no different. If collectors truly want to combat these trends they should simply forgo purchasing items from those people they believe to be falsely inflating prices.

What we really don't need are more bureaucrats and that's just what we're asking for with a national association. While it sounds nice in the concept stage, in reality it could be a frightening thing and create a whole new set of problems.

Rather than a formal organization, let's keep our hobby as informal as it is now and strive to deal in an honest and upright manner with our fellow hobbyists, at the same time ignoring the opportunists and would-be hobbyists who profess to "enjoy the hobby" but really couldn't tell you who played second base for the Orioles in 1966.

Thank you,

Bruce Skuce, Warwick, R.I.

Editor's Note: Don's letter reflects the growing sentiment among hobbyists. We already have one "Administration" in Washington, D.C. Who really needs to create another one? By the way, who did play second base for the 1966 Orioles? — Letter to the Editor, April 20, 1981

* * *

Rod Carew Responds

Like several other SCD readers, I sent a few items to Rod Carew for his autograph and received in my SASE his price list instead.

I wrote back to Mr. Carew explaining that he had not returned my items (signed or unsigned) and, hoping that this was an oversight on his part, I requested that he return my items.

A few days later I received the enclosed letter, along with my items — all of them signed. Perhaps others who feel they've been "burned" by Mr. Carew should also write to him and mention the items they had mailed.

Gary L. Stone, Rock Hill, S.D.

(Editor's note: Because SCD has received several letters and phone calls on this subject, we are printing the letter Rod Carew mailed out, hoping to clarify the situation. His letter follows.)

Dear Mr. Stone:

Due to an employee error, you have been sent an order form concerning autographed memorabilia of mine. These order forms have been printed to respond to serious baseball memorabilia collectors who have requested those extra items, not the general public or individuals requesting regular autographs. Unfortunately, this employee has sent these order forms to fans who have written me instead of the collecting hobby.

Please accept my apology for this inconvenience. There exists a large group who do collect expensive autographed items, and as a result, we have established a fund, out of the proceeds, to be donated to the Atwood Childrens Center in Placentia, Calif.

I am glad you described your enclosures so that I can return them to you.

As I have explained, this was not intened to be offered to the general public. Thank you for your understanding.

Very Truly Yours,

Rod Carew, Letter to the Editor, Feb. 12, 1982

* * *

A Special Kind Of Hobby Hero

Paul J. Richman

Like any other 8-year-old boy, Marcus Tracy of New Haven, Ind., collects sports cards and idolizes sports heroes. He dreams of tossing touchdown passes in the Super Bowl and driving home the winning runs in the World Series.

But unlike most youngsters, Marcus was born with an 0 and 2 count already against him. He suffers from leukemia, and while his family and friends pray for him each day, Marcus digs into the batters' box of life with the silent confidence of a DiMaggio or Mays. Two strikes or none, he is sure he will come through with the clutch hit.

"Marcus will probably never be able to be a good enough ballplayer to become as famous as many boys dream of," said his mother Elaine Tracy. She is Marcus' greatest inspiration and vice-versa.

Even if Marcus will never make people forget the Mantles or Granges, he has piled up nothing but wins so far in life's most challenging game.

"It was hard to accept the fact that our child has leukemia," Mrs. Tracy said of the illness that was first diagnosed last March. "My husband (Gary) and I were both bitter and angry, but we've learned to live with it and accept it."

"Marcus has been a fighter all of his life," Mrs. Tracy continued, "and I know he's not going to let this get the best of him. My husband and I have been the ones in tears, but Marcus has kept a positive attitude. He's the sick one, yet he's kept his mother and father's spirits up."

The Tracys have found out that they have a lot of great friends through Marcus' struggle.

"It certainly helps when you know that there are people out there who really care," Mrs. Tracy said.

One such caring person has been New York Jets fullback Mike Augustyniak, a former Purdue University star.

Augustyniak first heard about Marcus through one of his high school teachers whose wife works with Mrs. Tracy at a local bank.

"I heard about this boy in Fort Wayne who had leukemia," Augustyniak told George Honold of the Fort Wayne Journal-Gazette. "I didn't know the extent of his illness, but the whole thing got to me and I decided to do something."

What Augustyniak did was mail Marcus a football autographed by the Jets, a kicking tee, a Jets pennant, an autographed photograph, and a four-page handwritten letter.

"It was beyond Marcus' wildest dreams that he'd receive a letter from a professional football player," Mrs. Tracy said. "It was something he never expected."

Mrs. Tracy said Marcus was so excited when he received Augustyniak's package that he made her read it to him three times.

"He was tickled to death over it," she said.

In the letter, Augustyniak wrote such things as:

"I heard you were sick and I thought this letter from me might cheer you up...

"I don't know if you have ever talked to or met a pro football player before. The first time I ever met one was when I went to pre-season training camp. I thought they were pretty neat until they started tackling me, which doesn't always feel too good...

"I'm going to try and convert you into one of the many great Jets fans. We are playing on national television four times this year so everyone in Indiana can see the Jets play...

"It is very hard to understand why God would let you get sick and feel bad. I hope you get better soon...

"If you get bored you can take my picture and put it up on your dartboard for some target practice..."

"It was a tough letter to write," Augustyniak was quoted as saying. "It took about a week for me to finish it because I didn't know exactly what to say. I didn't want to dwell on his illness."

"The amazing thing about all of it was the fact that Mike has never even met Marcus," Mrs. Tracy said. "It just goes to show that you don't have to know someone in order to have a friend. Mike is a very special person."

Augustyniak also followed up his letter a few weeks later by paying the Tracys and their neighbors a personal visit.

Another person who found out about Marcus Tracy and decided to do something for the boy was Edward O'Reilly, from nearby Fort Wayne. O'Reilly, 87, was featured in a segment of "Unsung Hobby Heroes" in this column a while back. He has been a tremendous friend to the Tracys.

"Marcus and Mr. O'Reilly are good friends," Mrs. Tracy said. "They share each other's enthusiam for baseball. Mr. O'Reilly has shared many of his treasured moments with sports figures he has personally met and corresponded with."

O'Reilly also began to furnish Marcus with some sports collectibles, especially those relating to the Cubs — Marcus' favorite team.

Undoubtedly, the hobby has now gained another die-hard in the person of Marcus. He may never become that famous ballplayer that all boys dream of, but how many people actually do anyway?

With the help of family, friends, and truly special people like Augustyniak and O'Reilly, Marcus continues to strive for a normal, happy life, and as his mother said, "He's well on his way."

Sometimes with the hustle and bustle of rookie cards, error cards, price guides, and the like, we lose sight of what the hobby is all about — people sharing their love through sports. Even though Marcus Tracy doesn't boast a collection to rival Barry Halper's, there's no question that he loves sports just as much, and that truly qualifies him as a special kind of hobby hero. — Paul Richman, Around the Horn, Feb. 3, 1984

* * *

Kids Get No Respect!

I am 12 years old and I would like to say us kids can't deal with the prices of baseball cards. I can't see paying 30 cents for a card and having to pay $1.50 for postage and handling. Or having ads that say "minimum order $10." It just does not make sense. I hope some advertisers realize that kids are people too and like to spend money on cards just as long as the prices are low. Thank you for letting me speak out. — Kevin Richards, Metairie, La., Reader Reaction, Jan. 18, 1985

* * *

Say It Ain't So, Tony

By Rich Marazzi

I guess every kid had a favorite corner store that served as a supply depot for buying baseball cards and other goodies, like wax false teeth, licorice sticks and Bonomos Turkish Taffey. My store was called the Hill Street Market, appropriately named since it was on Hill Street in Ansonia, Conn., which is where I was raised. For the last 35 years, though, the establishment was usually just called "Tony's," because the proprietor was a second generation Italian named Anthony Russo.

Recently, I stopped by Tony's to pick up a few odds and ends, when he surprised me with the news that he was closing shop. The announcement nearly knocked my socks off. I swallowed hard and just gazed at Tony for a moment. I was hoping that it wasn't true, that he was just kidding like he used to do when I was a kid. The finality of it hit me worse than the days the wrecking ball wasted away Ebbets Field and then the Polo Grounds.

My roots with that corner store go back a long way. Prior to Tony's ownership, a Polish immigrant named Stanley Fedorowicz owned it. Stanley was a portly man who always wore a white apron (as did Tony). His wife Sophie was usually in the store. She had a warm smile, and normally wore a babushka and a sweater which covered her puffy arms.

It was during this time that I collected 1950 Bowman baseball cards, that colorful little 252-card set with the "five star" logo on the back. My favorite card was Yogi Berra (#46) posed in his catcher's squatting position. It seemed like such a friendly set, because many of the players were pictured with a smile — like Dom DiMaggio, Walt Droppo, Dick Kryhoski, Hank Majeski, Alex Kellner, Paul Lehner, Gil Coan, Willie "Puddin Head" Jones, Johnny Lindell, Bill Werle, plus many more. They seemed like such happy guys. This was impressive to a 7-year-old. One day I made five or six trips to the store to buy cards before Stanley finally cut me off. It hurt me at the time, but in retrospect, I know he did the correct thing. My greed threatened Stanley's card supply. I guess I broke the unwritten rule of sharing.

My time spent in the store increased between the ages of 11 and 13, the height of my collecting years. I really loaded up on cards from 1954-56. Names like Bob Talbot, Ray Crone and Rip Repulski seemed more important to me than Dwight D. Eisenhower or Sam Rayburn.

Then came Tony. He was a devout Yankee fan, and that served as a common bond for us. We loved talking Yankee baseball and lived and died with every pitch. It was an era of daytime baseball, and Tony never missed a beat with his little radio blaring near the meat counter. Mel Allen and Red Barber's broadcasts were as much a part of the store as Ivory Soap and Gabby Hayes' Quaker Puffed Rice. It was almost like Yankee Stadium-North, with its homespun personality not found in the huge sterile chain stores of today.

Red Sox fans were friendly enemies. I think some of the greatest verbal wars east of the Mississippi took place in Tony's when my friend Don (a diehard Bosox fan) walked in. I always thought Red Sox fans should take a course in logic. Imagine arguing over the merits of Elston Howard versus Sammy White.

During the first 12 years of my life I suffered two traumatic experiences. The first was when I failed to make the Little League as an 8-year-old. The second was the 1955 World Series when the Dodgers beat the Yankees.

That autumn I was in the seventh grade and was fortunate enough to have an extended summer vacation until late October because Lincoln School (named after a former president) was undergoing renovation.

Since some of my friends went to school elsewhere, the streets were dull and empty. The noisy summer sounds of children were replaced by the quiet, calm of back-to-school September mornings.

Tony helped ease my boredom by allowing me to do some odd jobs around the store in exchange for an ice cream or soda later in the day. With the upcoming Yankees-Dodgers Subway Series, I was gearing up by making small wagers with anybody that would walk in the store and bet with me. When the Yankees lost I was in shock. I'll never forgive Sandy Amoros and Johnny Podres. Born in 1943, I had never seen the Yankees lose a World Series. Didn't think they ever would. How could this happen, I thought? Tony and I were in mourning for several days. I'm not sure that I ever got over it.

The Hill Street Market was not just a sports kennel for me. I remember collecting Howdy Doody stickers from loaves of Wonder Bread. You remember Phineas T. Bluster, Clarabell, Chief Thunderthud, Princess Summer-Fall-Winter-Spring and Buffalo Bob?

And each year I would cast my vote in the Rheingold Beer Beauty Contest. Tony's store would be decorated with large-sized pictures of beautiful girls. I always fell in love with one and stuffed the ballot box.

Tony's homemade smoked Kielbasa at Easter was known for miles around. I'll never forget the wonderful aroma that would fill the store.

Creamsicles, Popsicles, sticky fly-catching strips hanging from the ceiling (ugh) and, yes, baseball cards. Wonderful memories.

'Say it ain't so, Tony! — Rich Marazzi, Batting the Breeze, July 10, 1987

* * *

Unopened Rack Packs

Please, I need some help to explain an ad I saw recently. Someone had labeled this special rack pack "extremely rare" because it — a 1983 Topps rack pack — had Boggs and Gwynn on top. The price: a simple $350!! Now, I figure I could own about six complete sets of '83 Topps cards for that price, and therefore own six Boggs and six Gwynns.

I guess if someone is enticed into purchasing this item, he had better not leave it lying around because some "kid" may open it.

Are these items worth this much because there are people actually willing to buy them? I collect unopened material, but I can't believe one rack pack could be worth the same as several or more complete sets from the same year, depending on who's showing on top. — Dean Leiby, Brecksville, Ohio, Reader Reaction, Aug. 7, 1987

* * *

What Do We Like About The Hobby?

By Ted Taylor

In a recent reader poll I posed numerous questions about what you, as hobbyists, like and what you don't like about current baseball cards. The results were interesting and we've aired them in a previous column. Perhaps one or more of the "big three" companies will pick up on your suggestions.

As a spinoff of that survey, I asked readers to let me know what it was they like best about the hobby and the answers were diverse and many are worth sharing with each of you.

Richard Borgerson of Bellingham, Minn., says a whole lot, "baseball cards keep me young...just ask my wife...I'm 33-years-old and still act like a little kid." And isn't that what a hobby is supposed to do? Anybody can act like an adult. Mike Gillen of East Grand Fords, Minn., takes it a step further, "I have a very pressure-intensive job and my cards allow me pure relaxation and short periods of pure freedom."

"Baseball cards relax me and the time I spend with them takes my mind off of everything else," says Jim Smith of Woonsocket, R.I. Bob Lekostaj of Elmwood Park, Ill., likes baseball cards because "they make me feel closer to the players and the game I love!"

Mike Boyd, of Milford, Del., associates "the memories of the players I've seen in the past" with collecting, while Mike Honeyman, of Westlake Village, Calif., sees the hobby "as great fun and a challenge."

"I like the opportunity of reliving the players' careers over and over again," says Chuck Berndt of McHenry, Ill. John Farkas, of Melbourne, Fla., collects cards because he sees it as "a chance for the average fan to feel more a part of the game."

Joe Linder, of Opa Locka, Fla., says that "cards bring me fond memories and the action shots are so interesting that they never get boring."

"What I like most about baseball cards is the nostalgia value of the older cards...even four or five years old. I enjoy comparing a veteran player's cards with his new cards to see how he has changed in appearance and how he has developed his stats," says Bill Phifer, of Merrick, N.Y.

Pete Mitchell, of Mission Viejo, Calif., gets right to the point when he says, "with every pack I open I become a little younger."

Steve Birmingham says that "no matter how many cards you get there is always something unusual around that you haven't seen before...cards can always be compared to earlier issues, for example, the 1958 Topps and the 1941 Goudey."

Mike Sisti says that cards provide an escape for him, "when I go through my cards I'm in a different world...away from the sadness brought about by such things as the passing of Jackie Gleason. When I heard that 'The Great One' had died I had to escape into the world of cards."

And so the theme went through over 100 letters. Collectors like the cards as a vehicle of enjoyment. Only one letter, out of the entire bunch, refereed to the idea of making a profit. That letter came from Christopher Beck of Clymr, N.Y., who said, "I collect them because they are there...that they're worth a little something, too, is nice."

This slant on the hobby is, admittedly, different than the one that is normally heard. Where promoters push $10 autographs at card shows and "the word" is put out about a recently-signed postcard going for $1,700. The idea, of course, is to plant that seed about inflated values.

I'm convinced that, if tomorrow, all the high rollers checked out of our hobby that we'd still proceed, thank you, with the enjoyment factor intact. I realize, of course, that I'm out of sync here with a lot of hobbyists, but there are certain levels of participation in the hobby and it's up to each of us to pick the one we want to play in.

"Level One" would be the "big bucks operator." He's the guy who trades in $600 Babe Ruth cards and buys and sells collections in the five- and six-figure arena. It's likely he wouldn't know a drag bunt from a drag queen. But he's there and he's influencing everything that the other levels of collecting touch. My guess is that this level encompasses about 15 percent of the hobby players.

"Level Two" would include most of the people who responded to this column. They're the people who collect cards for the pure enjoyment of it. It's not unusual for them to shell out money on a regular basis to acquire what they'd like. It would be unusual, however, for them to skip a mortgage payment to buy a signed Paul Waner card. I'd guess that 65 percent in the hobby fall in here.

"Level Three" is made up of the future of the hobby — the kids. While the high rollers overlook them and many show dealers can't be bothered with them, let's remember that we all started out at this level and there was something about the hobby that hooked us, for keeps, as youngsters. They make up, probably, 20 percent of the purchasers of baseball cards and related hobby materials. Though, in dollars spent, they don't make a significant dent.

One letter, of all that I've received in recent months, struck a real chord with me and it summarizes what I see this column as being all about.

Richard West of San Antonio writes, "keep up the good work on the column...it's refreshing to read one where the word 'investment' isn't mentioned every third sentence." Ted Taylor, Off the Cuff, Aug. 14, 1987

* * *

Eye Of The Turkey

Just who does Jim Hawkins think he is by saying that Boston superstar Jim Rice hasn't produced good enough statistics to be elected to the Hall of Fame? Rice has been one of the most consistent ballplayers since 1975 in all of baseball.

He is a lifetime .300 hitter with over 350 home runs, 1,300 runs batted in, and 2,200 hits. During his MVP 1978 season, Rice had one of the best years in the history of modern baseball. Yet Hawkins thinks that Reggie Jackson belongs in Cooperstown. Jackson is a one-dimensional player who can't hit for average or field to save his life.

Hawkins shouldn't call his column Eye of the Hawk, but Eye of the Turkey. — Eric Miller, Yardley, Pa., Reader Reaction, Aug. 28, 1987

* * *

Collecting Conversations

I recently attended a card show in King of Prussia, Pa., and overheard a father-son conversation that got my attention.

The father leaned down to his 6- or 7-year-old son and tried to explain to him how the single card — a 1968 All-Star card, I believe — was someday going to be much more valuable than the price they had just paid. The son didn't seem to buy the explanation. Instead, he had his own opinion.

"I didn't want to buy that card. I wanted to buy some packs to open. It's more fun to open the packs and look." It seems like the boy wanted to collect, but dad wanted him to invest.

Perhaps this conversation indicates the hobby's current direction. I hope not. I hope there are still many card buyers, both young and old, who enter the hobby for the fun of collecting. Maybe this is one time dad should listen to his young son. — C. Robert Hofheinz, Glen Riddle, Pa., Reader Reaction, March 18, 1988

* * *

Get Ready To Be Blasted!

During my five years as ad manager of SCD, I made it my policy to never write a letter when I was angry. It's too easy to be irrational when angry and write something you'll regret. Once it's in the mail, you can't get it back. Whenever I wrote a letter that was negative in nature, I waited 24 hours before I sent it out. I re-read it one more time before mailing and many times I made corrections.

I'm in a bad mood today as I write this. My truck blew a rear main seal that cost $375 to fix. I also had to have a new muffler put on and that ran me $80. Plus, I got a fishing citation for $60 that I'm fighting in court. And I owe money on my federal and state income tax.

So I felt good about getting out of town for a couple of days (March 4-6) to attend the EPSCC Willow Grove show. But then I missed my departing flight and was assessed a penalty fee of $109 by the airline. There were no more flights out of Appleton, so I had to drive two hours to Milwaukee to catch a plane to Philadelphia.

I finally made it to Philly. The Philly show is one of the best, but the George Washington Motor Lodge, which is adjacent to the Convention Center, is one of the worst. There was no hot water for a Saturday morning shower. But at least I had room heat. The person who stayed there last time must not have. It looked as if someone had built a campfire on the rug in my room to stay warm.

Upon my return to Milwaukee, I discovered I had lost the keys to my vehicle. A locksmith charged $42 to make a new key. I was too tired to make the three-hour drive home, so I had to dish out $36 for a motel room for the night.

So today I'm going to show a side of me most have not seen. I'm going to blast all of you dealers and collectors who think a 1988 Gregg Jefferies card is worth $8. I'm going to rip you dumbbells who charge more for a 1988 Donruss Joey Meyer than his 1987 rookie card.

What? I'm out of room! Boy, are you lucky! — Dan Albaugh, The Price Guide Report, March 25, 1988

* * *

A Fan's Dream Evaporates
Hawk (Almost) Knew A HOFer

By Jim Hawkins

The following story is true. As best as I can remember. Some of the details are by now a bit foggy because, as you will discover, I wasn't paying too close attention at the time. I was too busy being cool.

Today, I could kick myself.

Certainly, my tale is not unique. Or original. Not by a long shot.

If you own a store, if you've been a dealer for very long, or if you're a dedicated collector, I guarantee you've heard similar refrain. At least a hundred times. Probably, if you've examined your conscience, you even have a comparable tale or two to tell yourself.

I like to call this story, "If Only..." It falls into the category of "The Cards Your Mother Threw Away."

Once upon a time, shortly after I had outgrown baseball cards, when I finally came to my senses and realized it was immensely more significant — not to mention more profitable — to sink 8-balls than it was to play second base or try to throw strikes — which I didn't do particularly well anyway — I began to inhabit the principal pool hall in my hometown.

To this day, when I drive by the joint, which has long since been demolished, I get a little nostalgic. Which tells you how many excuses there are to get nostalgic in Superior, Wis. Let's see, there's our old house...and Sammy's Pizza...Ed and Joe's Pool Hall...and our house...well, you get the picture. It was that kind of town.

But, back to the story.

In the beginning, of course, none of us were actually old enough to legally set foot in a pool hall. I guess the legislators thought unless you were 16 years old you couldn't spit straight. Aside from spitting, I honestly can't think of anything else of any real significance that ever went on down there.

Aside, that is, from "The Big Games." We weren't allowed to participate, of course. We didn't dare ask — not that we were anywhere near good enough, or that we would have been accepted, even if we had been sufficiently talented.

But if you were a regular at Ed and Joe's — and, God, that was what we wanted to be, "regulars" — you always knew when there was a "Big Game" coming up. The Big Shooters, the pool room's superstars, all stopped by once in a while to practice. But when two or three suddenly showed up together, you knew "The Game" was on.

They were truly a Runyan-esque cast of characters. There was "The Dude," who I swear could cut a ball backwards; and "Back-A-Pocket," a guy so good he had a whole game named after him, or vice-versa; and a stately, silverhaired gentleman, who never seemed to say much but who always was automatically admitted to The Game.

According to the grapevine, the old guy had once been a big league ballplayer or something, although I honestly cannot recall anyone ever bragging about his stats or even mentioning his name.

To those of us who sat on the bench along the far wall, in relative darkness, watching the men play, his identity was no big deal, either. I mean, the old guy was good, but he didn't win often enough to merit a whole lot of respect or attention. Besides, Morrie Arnovich, who owned the sporting goods store down in the lower end of town, had been a big league ballplayer, too. And he never came in the pool hall.

Never once can I remember anyone ever asking the silver-haired gent for his autograph, or imploring him to tell all about his baseball career.

Eventually, I learned his name and happened to mention it, quite casually, to my grandmother, who was in her day quite a baseball fan. Yes, she said, she had heard of the man — in fact, she and his wife were good friends. Big deal, I thought.

As I said, the pool hall where I "grew up" is long gone. So, unfortunately, is the grey-haired former ballplayer who used to shoot pool there. His name: Hall of Famer Dave Bancroft.

I only wish I knew then what I know now. I saw him shoot pool dozens of times, but I never even shook the man's hand or said hello. — Jim Hawkins, Eye of the Hawk, April 22, 1988

* * *

Locating The Proper Evidence
Brett Homer Ball Is Identified

By Jim Hawkins

George Brett stood at home plate and watched the ball go. Like an artist admiring his latest effort on canvas, or a body builder marveling at his reflection in a mirror, Brett watched in wonderment as the baseball soared upward and onward.

The rules insist that a batter striking a ball must proceed immediately to first base, lest the ball be retrieved before he arrives, thereby negating the blow. However, in this instance, Brett was in no hurry. He knew there was no reason to rush.

"You hit one that far," he explained afterwards, "You've got to watch."

Brett's mammoth blast, against a fast ball from Detroit Tiger pitcher Jeff Robinson, cleared the triple-tiered right field stands, 94 feet high and 370 feet from home plate, bounced on the back edge of the roof and landed on Trumbull Avenue below, then ricocheted off the texi cab barn across the street.

It traveled between 450 and 475 feet — only the 22nd home run ever hit completely out of ancient Tiger Stadium, and the 20th to right field. The fact that the flight of the ball was undoubtedly aided by a 24 mph wind blowing out failed to diminish the significance of the feat.

"I don't think I've ever hit a ball that far," admitted Brett, as he was ushered into a most exclusive club that includes the likes of Ted Williams, Mickey Mantle, Norm Cash and Harmon Killebrew. "It's a great feeling. I didn't feel a darn thing. I just heard a loud crack. You don't feel any resistance. It's an amazing thing.

"Very seldom do I watch my home runs," continued the Kansas City Royals superstar first baseman. "But I couldn't help it. I knew the wind was blowing out. I just wanted to see how far it would go. This is one home run I'll never forget."

I was hosting a card show in nearby Dearborn, Mich., when Brett connected. George had been our special guest, signing autographs the night before and now we had the Tigers-Royals game on the radio, coming over the public address system in the arena.

As they heard Brett's blast described on the radio, the crowd at the show, dealers and collectors alike, came alive.

My first thought, naturally, was to raise the price of the extra baseballs Brett had signed the night before. But a collector walking by had a better idea. "How would you like to get your hands on that ball he just hit?" he inquired.

"Yup," I replied, nodding my head, all the while knowing that would be impossible.

The following day, a young man, baseball in hand, knocked on the door of the visitors' clubhouse at Tiger Stadium, offering to sell "the ball Brett hit out of the park."

"Thanks, but no thanks," said Rip Collins, the veteran clubhouse attendant, noting that the ball was not even smudged.

Late in the day, another kid showed up, spouting the same story and sporting a similar near-mint condition ball. Needless to say, Rip's response was the same.

Nor was he fooled by a third fellow, who at least had the good sense to display a scuffed ball to support his song and dance.

You see, the baseball Brett actually hit had been captured by a parking lot attendant across the street, who had made a habit of catching such collectibles. In fact, he already has the ball that rocketed over the roof off the bat of Reggie Jackson and former Tiger Ruppert Jones — each signed by the slugger who sent it into orbit.

This time, he brought the ball to the Royals' clubhouse and returned it to Brett, who rewarded him with a couple of autographed bats.

Brett plans to display his home run ball in his restaurant near Los Angeles. "I'll probably put it next to the pine tar bat," he said with a smile.

Meanwhile, the parking lot attendant across the street from Tiger Stadium is now wondering how much his other two over-the-roof balls may be worth.

The problem, as I explained to him and these three would-be "entrepreneurs" who knocked on the clubhouse door discovered — is proving after the fact that these particular baseballs are really the ones that flew over the roof.

Some things, I guess, are worth more in memories than in money. Some things were never meant to be sold. — Jim Hawkins, Eye of the Hawk, May 13, 1988

* * *

Card Grading Flunks

Recently, I have noticed the start of what I believe will be a serious negative to this hobby. I am specifically referring to card grading services.

On the surface, these services sound good. They supposedly eliminate difference of opinion, provide information guidelines and end price disputes. Do they work in practice? I do not beleive so.

The very reason they do not work is that the service's opinion is just that — an opinion, no better, certainly no worse and most certainly no more important than any other informed person's opinion.

Simply because this hobby has exploded in popularity do not feel like we need "experts" to tell us a card's condition. This hobby has given years of enjoyment, profits and losses to children and adults alike without this service and I believe we do not need it now.

If you would like to view a hobby that has eagerly accepted these expert grading services and see how good they have done, talk to a serious coin collector. That hobby has lots of experts with opinions you can pay a lot of money to receive.

They also supply fancy holders and certificates for your money and when you go to another dealer to sell your coin, reputable dealers still disagree with the service and offer you a price based upon their opinion.

Those services have done nothing but generate revenue for the service and confusion for the collector of coins. Card collectors should say "no thanks." — Tom Reed, Bryan, Ohio, Reader Reaction, May 27, 1988

* * *

Old-Timers Thrill Adoring Fans Again

By Tom Mortenson

The way we were: It was a Milwaukee baseball fan's ultimate delight. No, it wasn't the Braves against the Yankees or the Brewers against the Cardinals in the World Series...But it was just about the next best thing.

Spahn, Burdette, Mathews, Aaron, Logan, Pafko, Torre, Scott, Bando, Thomas, Fingers, Moore, Vuckovich and many other popular players were all in uniform again.

Sure, there may be a few more lines and wrinkles these days. Nothing stays the same forever. But for a few hours on Saturday June 4, the kid in us returned.

It was the third appearance at Milwaukee County Stadium of the Equitable Old-Timers Series. More than 43,000 fans came to see old-timers from the time Eisenhower was in the White House, to relatively young old-timers who retired as recently as 1987. The five-inning old-timers contest was played between the Equitable All-Stars, composed mostly of former Milwaukee Braves players, against a group of former Milwaukee Brewers. Obviously, Equitable tries to get as many familiar players and hometown favorites as possible for each game.

Equitable old-timers games are held each summer at all of the Major League stadiums. For each old-timers game Equitable donates $10,000 to BAT (Baseball Alumni Team), a financial assistance program formed in 1986 for needy former players and umpires.

Seeing those familiar baseball faces in the clubhouse prior to the game was a real treat. The casual atmosphere and the clowning around was a little bit unexpected. Here were Hall of Fame greats and others whose familiar names and faces have graced countless baseball cards, yearbooks, magazines and newspapers.

Here was my boyhood idol Eddie Mathews, just a few feet away, laughing and joking with Burdette, Spahn and Logan. I remembered for a brief moment that all the baseball cards I had saved of Mathews were the most dogeared of all the cards I owned because I handled them the most. No doubt about it, baseball and baseball cards were an obsession then, and still are. The only baseball statue I ever owned (and still have) is a Hartland Eddie Mathews.

Mathews was so popular in Milwaukee and the state of Wisconsin in the 1950s that just about every young male in the state wanted to grow up batting left-handed and playing third base for the rest of his life.

Hank Aaron arrived in the clubhouse a little later than most of the others. The airline had lost his luggage. Amid a chorus of "Here's Hank" and "Hi Henry," he greeted everyone with a smile and a hand-shake. Imagine, here I was, shaking hands with a baseball legend, "The Hammer" himself.

A table in the clubhouse contained several cases of official Rawlings baseballs to be signed by the former players. The men would sign a few while dressing, all the while joking with and ribbing each other.

Warren Spahn, who has signed countless autographs in his life, kidded a clubhouse attendant that he (the attendant) should sign Spahn's name for him on the balls because he was tired of it. Spahn just smiled and continued signing though.

Here too was former Braves shortstop Johnny Logan kidding his former teammate Frank Torre by saying, "Hey Frank. I just told him (Andy Pafko) that I thought you were a lot better first baseman than Adcock." Then, adding with a laugh, "of course, Joe's not here tonight to hear that." Torre countered Logan's barb with, "just don't be giving me any of those throws in the dirt tonight."

Current Milwaukee Brewer outfielder Jim Adduci, a Chicago native, brought a baseball over to former Cubs and White Sox star Ron Santo and politely asked him to sign it for him. Santo told Adduci that Fergie Jenkins was there and he (Adduci) got him to sign the ball as well.

George "Boomer" Scott, looking as though he had not missed too many meals lately, made his appearance with a radio headset and earphones on. He was listening to an NBA game. "I don't really care if the Lakers win again," he said.

Rick Manning, age 33 and recently retired, made this comment on the field, "I had to get out of that old-timers room. They kept saying, 'Son, get me a Coke.'"

During batting practice before the game, "Mr. Baseball," Bob Uecker, made his appearance, dressed in a Braves jersey, with a Cardinals cap facing forward and a Phillies cap facing backward.

Gorman Thomas, looking tanned and fit from playing golf, ripped a few shots from the batting cage over the left field fence.

Mathews, while complaining that he didn't have his glasses on and couldn't see, pounded a line drive that took one hop and went over the right field wall.

Aaron, from his familiar batting stance, swung and missed several pitches and laughed heartily at his inability to hit batting practice pitches from Andy Etchebarren and Rollie Fingers.

Charlie Moore, hardly a real old-timer, took candid photos of the goings-on.

Some of the old-timers (most noticeably Luke Appling and Pete Vuckovich) made the rounds along the box seats, signing autographs and chatting with admiring fans.

Fittingly, the master of ceremonies for the old-timers contest was former Milwaukee Braves, Marquette Warriors and Wisconsin Badgers sportscaster Earl Gillespie. Now retired and living in Florida,

Gillespie is remembered by Wisconsin fans (who had never heard of Harry Caray) for his familiar descriptions of home runs with his version of "Holy Cow."

Familiar tunes from the '50s and '60s and '70s put fans in even more of a nostalgic mood.

Almost unnoticed by everyone were "Ducky" and Dick Schofield Jr. talking together. Dick Sr. was a member of the Brewer old-timers (finishing his career with the team in 1971) and Dick Jr. was in town with the California Angels, who were playing the current Brewers in the regularly-scheduled game.

The clowning and the camaraderie continued on through the game. Hall of Famer Spahn, along with his old buddy Lou Burdette, each pitched a perfect inning for the All-Stars. Burdette, who was often accused of throwing a spitball during his career, proceeded to "load one up."

The rules for the old-timers games are a little flexible. Sal Bando singled to drive in Pete Vuckovich with the tying run. That's right, Pete Vuckovich, the 1982 Cy Young Award Winner.

Rollie Fingers was called for a balk with a runner on third, just to bring the game up-to-date.

Willie Horton had a double and single for the All-Stars. Joe Torre nearly had a home run, doubling off the left-field fence.

The score ended tied at four. That didn't really matter, though. We got to see our childhood heroes again. Nothing else really mattered. The players seemed to love it as much as the fans did. — Tom Mortenson, The Coach's Box, June 24, 1988

* * *

A Slugger?
Pass The Smelling Salts

I enjoyed the article you guys did on Jerry McNertney in your 400th issue. I always like to read anything on the heroes of Jim Bouton's Ball Four.

However, one paragraph in the story really made me chuckle. The article claimed McNertney had little chance of making the White Sox as a first baseman because "such slugging first sackers as Roy Sievers and Joe Cunningham were ahead of him."

Well, to me, someone like Willie McCovey was a slugging first baseman. So was Joe Adcock. But Joe Cunningham??? No way!

Joe Cunningham a slugger? Pass me the smelling salts.

Joe Cunningham played 12 years in the majors, mostly with St. Louis. During his career, he averaged .291 and hit a total of 64 homers.

In other words, "slugging Joe" averaged about five home runs a season.

In 1964, Joe played about 40 games for the White Sox and was held homerless. Maybe the wind was blowing in during those games.

Frankly, I'd say my sister was more of a "slugger" than Joe Cunningham. If J.C. was a slugger, then Bob Uecker was the second coming of Babe Ruth. — Tim "Shoe" Sullivan, Stevens Point, Wis., Reader Reaction, July 22, 1988

* * *

One Step Above Counterfeiting

A recent issue of SCD included two ads related to the restoration of paper collectibles, including baseball cards.

I was surprised and intrigued by this, but even more surprised when one of the advertisements was from a company from my small home-town of 2,500 in California.

I decided to drop in on the advertiser to find out more information. He told me that he had been involved in restoration of comic books for several years, and that baseball cards was a field that he and several others were getting into.

The restoration included the removal of creases or stains, and the sharpening of corners.

I went away from the conversation enthused, thinking that for a nominal fee I could remove the crease from my '56 Mantle or my '51 Williams, and that it would be worth my while to sharpen the corners of just about all my less-than-mint superstar cards from the 1950s.

The charge quoted was $30 per hour, with the average time spent restoring a card with a crease and/or rounded corners a little less than an hour.

After thinking about the idea of restoring baseball cards in the week since that conversation, I have become more and more against it.

I was told that most dealers using this service for the resale of their cards do not represent the cards as restored. It seems to me that this practice is just one step above counterfeiting.

Some kind of identifying mark must be put on the card signifying that it has been restored. The intent of restoring, without this distinguishing mark, is the same as counterfeiting — that is, trying to establish value where there was none.

With an excellent 1952 Topps Mantle going around for $2,000, and a mint one in the $8,000 range, and an experienced restoration artist able to upgrade the excellent one in a matter of minutes, we have a very dangerous situation to the collector of premium baseball cards.

If the practice of restoring baseball cards becomes widespread, one or two things would happen:

— Collectors will be forced to carry sophisticated microscopes with them at all times, so they can distinguish an authentic premium collectible from a restored one, or

— The price of excellent and mint cards will become very close to each other. Why would a collector pay any significant premium for a mint card when his neighborhood restoration artist can upgrade the vg-ex one for a relative pittance?

The supply of mint and near mint cards would greatly increase, and as a result, prices for those conditions would fall dramatically.

While I kind of like the idea of a closer relationship between excellent and mint prices, I strongly believe that we should discourage any entry of the field of paper restoration into baseball cards and sports collectibles.

I urge SCD to discontinue any advertisements relating to the restoration of sports collectibles and for readers to consider the ramifications of being trained in or using these restoration services unless a governing body of the hobby could establish some regulations to effectively monitor the practice of restoration. — John Sipma, Nevada City, Calif., Reader Reaction, July 22, 1988

* * *

Publisher Admits Guilt In Autograph Forgery

By Bob Lemke

Sure, I faked an autograph. What are you going to do? Hang me?

Besides, the statute of limitations has expired.

Besides, I was eight years old.

If you're a real baseball card collector, as opposed to an investor or speculator, I don't have to explain to you how a baseball card from your childhood years can function as a time machine.

One glimpse of a card you may not have seen for 25 years can instantly transport you back through the years to a time and place when that card first made an impression on you.

I caught a glimpse of a 1956 Topps Phil Rizzuto card in a dealer's case at a recent show and it was 1959 again.

As I recall, I was playing strikeout with myself against the wall of the shanty across the street. Unless you grew up on the west side of the tracks in Fond du Lac, Wis., 30 years ago, you'll need a break here for some definitions:

Strikeout: A baseball game for up to four or so players. The pitcher tries to hit with a tennis ball a fairly generous strike zone painted on a wall. The batter tries to drive the ball past the pitcher and other fielders, if any.

Strikeouts and walks were called on the basis of where the ball hit the wall on each pitch. There was no baserunning; runs were scored by forcing ghost runners around the bags with walks and hits. A ball hit on the ground past the pitcher was a single. A bouncing ball past the pitcher was a double. A line drive less than head-high past the pitcher was a triple, unless caught.

And, a ball that went over the head of the pitcher and any extra fielders was a home run. Outs were counted if the pitcher fielded any of the balls before they rolled dead, or if a line drive or fly ball was caught by any fielder. We used the corners of the shanty for foul lines.

When you didn't have enough guys for regular baseball (and we could make a pretty good game of regular baseball with only five players on a team, if the batting team provided the catcher), strikeout — as opposed to Indian ball, infield baseball of left-field only baseball — was a good game in that it allowed for real pitching and hitting.

Across the street: An unnamed municipal recreational facility that consisted of one square city block. In spring and summer, it offered two softball fields and a hardball diamond. In the fall, the nearby junior high used it for a football pactice field. In the winter, it was flooded for ice skating.

The kids just called it "across the street," because it was. The four blocks that faced the park accounted for a good 30 kids (not the same as 30 good kids), not counting girls.

Shanty: Except for the chain-link backstops on the ballfields, and a row of trees on the north side of the park, the shanty was the only obstruction to the wide open space. A 15x30' concrete block bunker, its primary purpose was to serve as a warming house during ice skating season. During the summer, it provided a bubbler (water fountain in the idiom of non-Cheeseheads) on the south wall and open bathrooms during Little League and softball games. The rest of the time we just whizzed on its wall as nature called.

That's the stage. Here's the drama.

I was across the street playing strikeout with myself when I noticed an unusual amount of activity in Smet's side yard. There were a lot of comings and goings from the playhouse-workshop-woodshed complex that served a certain segment of the neighborhood as a place to retreat from parents or rival gangs or to sneak a cigarette.

I hollered over for permission to enter the yard. Like naval vessels, it was a breach of protocol to enter another kid's yard without permission — unless you were chasing him and he was running for his house.

Both Gary (my age) and Larry (a couple of years younger) met me on the curb. I asked what was going on and was told they had constructed a house of horrors — admission 10 cents.

At that age, like any other normal kid, I thought it was great fun to be led blindfolded through a cardboard maze, fondling peeled-grape "eyeballs" and cold-spaghetti gut piles while somebody snuck up and screamed in my ear every few seconds — but I didn't have a dime.

As usual, my allowance was blown the day it was received on baseball cards. Not being especially close to the Smets (in later years we would become members of different young men's social clubs), I was told there was no chance of a freebie.

I went home to scrounge up something of value to pay the cost of admission.

Bob Lemke once forged Phil Rizzuto's signature to use as admission to get into a haunted house.

I don't know where, at the age of 8, I got the idea that a ballplayer's autograph had any intrinsic value, but I hit on the idea of trading one for a free pass to the house of horrors. The thing was, I didn't have any autographs to trade. Undaunted, I decided to fake one.

I got out a sheet of white notepaper, a pencil and a stack of my 1956 Topps cards. The '57s and '58s didn't have autographs on the cards, and the facsimilie signatures were too small to trace on the '59s.

Out of reverence for the home team, I immediately rejected any notion of faking a Milwaukee Brave's signature. Going through the rest of my stack of '56s, I settled on Phil Rizzuto. Being knobs, I figured the Smet brothers would also be Yankee fans. Since Rizzuto was retired by then, there was no chance they could corner him at County Stadium during the next World Series — didn't the Braves and the Yankees always play in the World Series in the late 1950s? — and have him unmask the signature as a phony.

It seemed the perfect scheme. I traced the signature over a few times until I got one that looked good and then went to consummate the crime.

I rapped on the door of the haunted house and Gary answered. I offered him the deal, one "for real" Phil Rizzuto autograph for admission. He looked at the paper in my hand, then pointed at a sign on the door and said scornfully, "The sign says 'Admission 10 cents,' not 'Admission one Phil Rizzuto autograph.'" He slammed the door.

I called him the F-word, gobbed on his sign and went home. I don't know what happened to the autograph.

I never got into that haunted house — and haven't been to one since.

* * *

Looking at the '56 Phil Rizzuto card I remembered the tableau as if it were yesterday. If you don't understand how a flood of childhood memories can be locked in a baseball card, and released a half a lifetime later — you're reading the wrong magazine. — Bob Lemke, The Bleacher Bum, July 22, 1988

* * *

Mirror, Mirror, On The Wall

I would like to share an experience I had on a new way of collecting.

At the recent Houston Astrodome show, two young girls approached my table and wanted to know if I had any Steve Sax or Danny Jackson cards. I politely said no and then the fun began.

One of the two started reading off names from a list. I stopped them after several names and told them these are really some very unique requests.

They both started to giggle and one answered "well, these are the best looking guys in the game."

At first I thought these girls were putting me on and then I asked to see their list. I could not believe what I was reading. It was their Top 60 Best Looking Major League Players.

I would like to give you a list of their top 10:

1) Steve Sax, 2) Danny Jackson, 3) Roger McDowell, 4) Ryne Sandberg, 5) Kevin Elster, 6) Dave Righetti, 7) Nick Esasky, 8) Dave Anderson, 9) Bobby Welch, 10) Dave Magadan

Others included #29 Ron Darling, #35 Will Clark, #45 Bob Brower and #56 Paul Molitor.

I wonder if your company would dare run a beauty contest with female fans voting. — Larry Cernoch, Sugarland, Texas, Reader Reaction, July 22, 1988

* * *

Take Two And Call Me In The Morn

After reading your magazine, other hobby publications and watching television coverage of the National, I have come to the conclusion that we have all taken ourselves too seriously.

To help alleviate this situation, I have enclosed two cards. When I take baseball cards too seriously, I just look at these two cards and remember that they are only cards and yes, you can still have fun with them.

The two cards are titled "Opening Day at Denver Stadium" and "Night Game at Wrigley" (pre Aug. 8, 1988). — Kasey Ignarski, Chicago, Ill., Reader Reaction, Aug. 12, 1988

* * *

91

He Doesn't Want The Reprint

Recently, I was at a local retail store and saw on a rack several packs of cards distributed by Collectors Marketing Corp. On the front of each pack it read "100 Baseball Cards, Contains Topps and Others, Stars and Superstars. The Cards You Need for Your Collection."

I bought a pack and, much to my dismay, when I opened it there was the Tom Filer reprint card that I read about in SCD (p. 30, July 22). These are definitely not the cards I want in my collection.

If that company chooses to distribute these phony cards they should at least tell people that the cards are not the real thing, instead of collectors having to find out themselves.

In my book, there is no difference in value between that Tom Filer and this one. (See illustration) — Brian Feezor, Winston-Salem, N.C., Reader Reaction, Aug. 12, 1988

* * *

Hold The National In Iola

Unlike your various columnists, the wife and I, as collectors and attendees, had a near perfect experience at the Atlantic City National.

We stayed in nearby Philadelphia to enjoy some of what it has to offer and simply drove to Atlantic City on Thursday and then again on Friday for the convention.

At the opening of the convention we walked in with our Ticketron tickets without a moment's hesitation (very much unlike Dallas), enjoyed the wide aisles and found enough interesting memorabilia to part with a significant amount of money.

We bought, sold, traded and headed home Friday evening.

All-day parking was close at hand for $3. These are important issues from a collector's point of view.

Admittedly, we are not considering a move to Atlantic City, but the convention took us to a city we probably would not have otherwise visited.

We strolled the boardwalk, noticing the wide variety of people and businesses, ate some fast food and tossed a few quarters in the slots.

The mess from a bombarding sea gull came quickly out of my shirt.

Why must we be so opinionated and negative, pontificating about inconveniences that any traveler or convention attendee can encounter anywhere?

Perhaps a future convention should be held at the Hyatt Regency Iola Wisconsin so that we can enjoy the highest possible level of cuisine and ambiance. — Dean Kinzer, Chicago, Ill., Reader Reaction, Aug. 19, 1988

* * *

Are We Really Making Money?

By Jim Hawkins

Thinking out loud: It occurred to me the other day, as I patiently listened to yet another dealer lament the lack of sales at yet another show, that there may not be as much money in this hobby as we like to think, or sometimes lead ourselves to believe. Maybe, in fact, there never was.

I'm oversimplifying things a great deal, I admit, but if you'll bear with me a moment and pay close attention to the following scenario, I believe you'll see my point:

Week One — Dealer A buys a small collection for $2,000 and brings it to a show in say, Chicago, where he proceeds to sell the entire collection to Dealer B for $2,200. Both dealers go home happy, convinced that this transaction, coupled with all their others, made it a successful show.

Week Two — Dealer A takes the $2,200 he received in Chicago from Dealer B to a show in St. Louis, where he buys $2,200 worth of cards from Dealer C.

Meanwhile, at that same St. Louis show, Dealer B decides to sell the collection he purchased a week earlier from Dealer A to Dealer D for $2,400.

Dealer A, Dealer B, Dealer C and Dealer D all depart the St. Louis show, never doubting that the weekend had been worthwhile.

Week Three — Dealer A decides he doesn't really need the cards he bought in St. Louis for $2,200, carries them to a show in New York, where he sells them to his old friend, Dealer B, for $2,300.

Meanwhile, Dealer D is momentarily short of cash so he decides to dump the cards he bought from Dealer B to Dealer C for $2,300.

Again, all four men leave the show smug and smiling.

Yet let's look at the net results:

Dealer A, who started the ball rolling by spending $2,000, has $2,300 in his cash box — a $300 profit to show for three weeks worth of work.

Dealer B, who has also been busy three weekends in a row, is out $2,100 — although he does now have additional inventory which he believes is worth at least $2,300. Net profit, assuming he sells those cards at that price, is $200.

Dealer C sold some cards and bought some cards. He still has some cards and, after two shows, a $100 net loss.

Dealer D bought some cards and sold those same cards. After two weeks, he, too, is out $100.

As I said before, I'm oversimplifying things a great deal. But, as every dealer can attest, such transactions go on all the time.

Often, for some dealers, they constitute the highlights of an otherwise slow show.

And far too many dealers, I fear, lose sight of the bottom line, of their actual net profit or loss, when they look at the pile of bills in their cash box or the new inventory in their showcase.

You hear dealer after dealer, at show after show, boasting "I did $5,000." Or "I did $8,500." Or, "I topped $10,000 again."

How many of those guys, I wonder, ever stop crowing long enough to systematically figure out how much money they actually made? Or lost?

And how many dealers go out of business, bad-mouthing and blaming the hobby for their failure, when in truth it was their own stupidity that turned them belly-up?

I don't know about you, but I'm getting awfully tired of listening to those lame-brained, self annointed, holier-than-thou ninnies who continually insist upon attacking our hobby and the people in it because of the high prices of baseball cards and athletes' autographs.

"Gee whiz, those cards only cost a penny when I was a kid," goes the unfortunately all-too-familiar refrain. "And I never had to pay for autographs."

Well, I can remember when cards cost a penny, too. Because that was all they were worth.

I can remember when a nickel bought a good-sized candy bar and it cost a quarter to go to a first-run movie. And I'm not that old.

An incredible increase in demand, coupled with the same inflation that has ravaged the rest of our society — NOT greedy dealers or athletes — have driven up the prices of everything connected with this hobby.

To those who whine that high prices have taken all the fun out of this hobby, I say: Do us all a favor next time there's a show near you, stay home!

Better yet, go to a movie. And be sure to let the ticket seller know you are only going to pay him a quarter and not a penny more! — Jim Hawkins, Eye of the Hawk, Sept. 2, 1988

* * *

Are They Really "Working?"

An open letter to the baseball players chosen to do shows:

First of all, you are very fortunate to have been chosen because the money is great to fantastic!

The working (?) hours are great, the benefits are good and the work isn't that hard!

Realize we the people that attend these shows help to pay that big money. So don't start in by saying "I don't sign bats," "I don't sign that card," "No pictures please," or "Only one item."

If I spend $10 to $20 for an autograph, I don't expect any negative attitude; for that money I'll do whatever I want to do with that autograph.

If they would have the friendliness of a Banks, Gomez, Snider, Spahn, Ford or Newcombe, it would help their image.

Also, if they would not give the cold, unfriendly looks (if they do look up) or the scribbled, hurried-up autograph and get-out-of-here attitude.

If they don't want to bend a little bit, get them out! And get a player who would really enjoy doing a show, one that wouldn't mind signing bats, or that card, or say sure to a picture.

So, next time, be ready to bend or give a little or else you might have to go out and get a job and go to work. — Paul Stein, Pasadena, Calif., Reader Reaction, Sept. 23, 1988

* * *

Starting Lineup Figurines Prompt Identity Crisis

By Ted Taylor

"Let me guess," said the cashier, "you're having a birthday party for your little boy and these are going to be the favors. Right?"

That, to her, seemed like the perfectly logical explanation for why a grownup would be walking up to the checkout line at a K-Mart with a dozen little baseball player statues. But, before I could agree with her, my wife Cindy quickly chimed in with the explanation, "Oh, no. Our son is 19. These are for him." And she pointed directly at me.

And so it was, that I bought my first dozen Kenner "Starting Lineup" baseball statues.

I had spent the entire summer seeking out this little item, having read about it in SCD, but I had never seen any of them for sale anywhere. And, then on the last day of August, there I was in our local K-Mart killing time waiting for my wife to pick up some odds and ends, when, lo and behold, there the little critters were on a shelf in the middle of the toy section.

What first caught my eye was the $2.97 price tag. I mean I had heard that the Mattingly was already selling for upwards of $16 and even the commons were bringing five and six bucks each. And now I had a shot at a bunch of them at $2.97-a-toss.

While I was carefully picking out players of my choice — Mike Schmidt, Dave Winfield, Rickey Henderson, Gary Carter, Von Hayes — a young guy swooped down on me and scooped up 30 of the little suckers, tossed them in his cart, and made a bee-line for the checkout counter. I'm sure I'll catch his act at some future date at a Philadelphia area card show and he'll be getting 10 bucks or more for them.

Somehow he left me a few and I gathered my booty and headed toward the checkout counter showdown. I hadn't felt such trepidation since I was a teen-ager buying baseball cards. Now cards were acceptable, but I wasn't so sure about little toy baseball players.

After my wife had revealed all my deep secrets to the cashier another store employee came over and told us that the Kenner toy had just been put on the counter that day and that they had been selling like "hot cakes." The lady smiled and said, "I guess we underpriced them."

Upon leaving K-Mart my wife suggested we try "Toys R Us" for more. Maybe even some guys that I didn't get at K-Mart. And, sure enough, the folks at "Toys" had tons of them. The problem, though, was two-fold. First, all that they had were Phillies players and I had already gotten them four stores down. The second problem was that they were charging a dollar more — $3.98 — for their "Starting Lineup" offerings.

I must admit that when I first read about the little guys in SCD this spring I kind of wrote the idea off. But now that I've gotten ahold of some of them I have a sneaking suspicion that they may well have become a long-term icon of the hobby.

I'm not so sure how many collectors will go for the whole set — even at three bucks that's a pretty hefty outlay — but as the years go by I'm certain that even the common players will be in demand. Team collectors, especially, will want to, at least, get a couple from their home club.

Canadians, I note, get the short end of the stick. Only Tim Raines of the Expos and George Bell of the Blue Jays have made it into Kenner's Hall of Fame. While not all the players really look all that much like the person they're supposed to represent, the figures are pretty nice and uniforms are true to big league style. Even though a nitpicker will point out that the player names they've put on the back of the Yankee road uniforms don't belong there and many of the batters are the exact same guy from waist down, I still think they're kind of nice and I intend to buy some more — if I can get them at $2.97. — Ted Taylor, Off the Cuff, Sept. 30, 1988

* * *

High Ticket Prices — It's A Vicious Circle

By Jim Hawkins

Bad checks...Broken contracts...Cancelled shows...

Like it or not, those are among the new facts of life in this burgeoning-but-no-longer-quite-so-friendly hobby.

And, whether you realize it, or whether you have ever written a bum check, broken a contract or cancelled a show, such sleazy conduct nevertheless affects you and the prices you are called upon to pay for admission and autograph tickets at shows you attend.

The No. 1 complaint in the hobby right now, I believe, is that autograph prices are too damn high! I don't disagree.

Twenty dollars, $15, $10, sometimes even five bucks can be too much to have to pay for a particular signature.

But that certainly does not mean things are about to change.

Frankly, I have a hunch autograph prices are going to continue to climb even higher — further choking and, I fear, even threatening the future well-being of this hobby.

Who is to blame? We all are — promoters and dealers and collectors and certainly the athletes, too. We have all, in our own way, contributed to the problem.

"This industry," in the words of sports agent Ric Bachrach, "has created a monster. The whole thing has gotten warped. It's out of whack right now."

Bachrach, by his own admission, has contributed to the problem, too. He has helped create the monster that now threatens to devour a good portion of this hobby.

Bachrach owns Sports Marketing Service Ltd., of Chicago, an agency that, for a fee, will couple together a promoter wishing to stage an event with an athlete anxious to capitalize on his name and fame.

He knows some athletes, a whole lot of athletes, ask for a whole lot of money to simply sit and sign their names — a whole lot more money than they have any right or reason to demand.

"You have a lot of athletes walking around with a very warped opinion of themselves," he says.

But Bachrach also knows that no matter how outrageous an athlete's asking price may seem, chances are there will be a promoter — and probably a whole lot of promoters — willing, indeed even eager, to pay that price.

"If I think it's a bad deal, I'll tell people it's a bad deal," says Bachrach. "I'll tell them, 'I think you're nuts. But if you want him, you've got him.' Because that's my job.

"If people are dumb enough to give somebody three times what he's worth, well, it's their money. But in that respect I'm part of the problem, too."

Meanwhile, the promoter keeps increasing autograph prices in a never-ending struggle to make ends meet, and collectors continue to pay those inflated prices, convincing the promoter that maybe he wasn't such a fool for promising the athlete five figures in the first place.

And so long as the athlete keeps getting paid, so long as promoters keep clamoring for his services, he sees no reason not to continue jacking up his price.

It is, you see, a simple, yet vicious, circle. But when that rosy chain of success is suddenly broken — as seems to be happening more and more often lately as the stakes have soared — watch out!

"I'm frustrated and I'm disgusted," declares Bachrach. "I deal with corporate America, with public relations people and ad agencies and promotional entities all the time.

"And I like the baseball card show business. I like a lot of the promoters in it. And I want to service the baseball card show business as a legitimate industry, too.

"But I've gotten to the point where I don't even want to talk to some people in your industry any more. I'm fed up with the seedy nature of certain people in the card show business.

"It bothers me a great deal. It just eats my heart out. I'm so sick of bad checks and bad people in this business that I don't know what to say.

"I've set up players at shows, with signed contracts, only to have the players get stiffed by the promoter with bad checks. Of course, the athletes come back to me looking for their money.

"I've got one guy threatening to sue me because he's out $5,000 and another guy who's out $7,000. I don't blame them for being upset. They showed up. They did their jobs. They deserved to get paid.

"One promoter owes me roughly $4,500 in fees," continues Bachrach. "I guess I'm going to have to sue him to try to get it. I don't have any other choice.

"And that $4,500 doesn't even take into account the damage to my credibility and my business, or all of my aggravation and phone calls.

"Don't misunderstand. I'm not talking about legitimate major show promoters here. We're all in business to make money.

"But sometimes you lose. That happens.

"When a reputable promoter has a bad show, he eats it, he absorbs the loss, everybody gets paid and he goes on about his business. That's what being in business is all about.

"But in the last two years, it seems like everybody and his brother has decided to become a card show promoter. They think every guy who has ever run a show is just rolling in dough and they want to get their slice of the pie.

"And every one of those guys figures he's got to have the best talent that there has ever been and he's going to pay the most to get it.

"They're not capitalized. They think being in business is a free ride. Well, it's not.

"So what you have are these fly-by-night promoters going out of business, going broke, owing bills all over the place.

"Like the guy in upstate New York who promised Gary Carter $10,000 to do a show. Gary walked in the door, there were about five tables there and maybe 30 people, and the promoter said: 'I've got $150 in my pocket. Take it or leave it.'

"Gary walked out. He never even got reimbursed for his air fare. And people wonder why players want more money or won't do shows.

"Card shows are nice," contines Bachrach. "They provide a great opportunity for a lot of players to make a lot of money.

"And they've given a lot of people a chance to come in close personal touch with an athlete who, while he's certainly not better than any of the rest of us, has accomplished great things in his lifetime. And we all aspire to greatness.

"But all of us in this business have prostituted ourselves. We have blown this thing totally out of proportion. To some degree, we are all guilty. Because we have all contributed to this problem. And we have all walked away from it," Bachrach says.

You wonder, where will it all lead? And where will it all end? And when? And how? — Jim Hawkins, Eye of the Hawk, Oct. 14, 1988

* * *

You're Getting Old When... 'No Neck' Gets Traded For Reggie

By Dave Miedema

You know you're getting old when...

You recall not caring if your favorite player signed your baseball "on the sweet spot."

You gazed in disgust at a pack full of hapless players after having just purchased some 1969 Topps cards at the local five and ten.

You, as a Boston resident, found yourself cheering for a guy named Nixon without having to clarify that you meant the home team's catcher, not the presidential candidate.

You saw the name "Esposito" in the Chicago Tribune sports pages and it had nothing to do with hockey.

You told your card-saving rival on the next block that he was a liar when he said he had a 1969 football card of O.J. Simpson (O.J.'s first card was 1970).

You couldn't figure out what the blazes Kenny Holtzman was doing pictured on the fifth series checklist in 1968. (It was a perfect 9-0 record earned through pitching on weekend furloughs from the Illinois National Guard).

You were stumped as to why the sky was green on Sammy Drake's card while his undershirt was purple — there were no SCD price guides to tell you about photo and color variations in 1962.

You read "Letters to the Editor" pages that contained gripes about real problems like autograph forging, auction reneging and mail order fraud, not inane whining about too many dealers writing columns or why everyone else is a shmoe because they don't collect the same things the letter writer does.

You saw Pete Burnside's card and wondered when the Orioles started putting "Ws" on their caps.

You tacked yet another group of foldout posters from Topps on your bedroom wall.

You wondered why the first two series of the 1968 set were crammed with guys like Mays, Aaron, Gibson, Brooks Robinson, and Clemente, but the seventh series was dominated by the likes of Clete Boyer, Ken Harrelson, and Tommy Harper.

You wanted to meet the big names of the hobby — Lionel Carter, Frank Nagy, Dick Reuss, and other devoted collectors. The big names weren't all guys who took out five-page ads, waved money at you in photos or claimed to be number one without really specifically saying just what they were number one at.

You tried to figure out just who Donn Clendenon was snarling at on his 1968 card. The pitcher? The umpire? His manager? A muttonhead sportswriter?

Your pen pal in Houston got Nellie Fox's autograph at the Astrodome and you didn't chastise him for getting it in his school autograph book instead of on a 1964 Topps Giant card, or any card, for that matter.

You pitched that funny-looking 1967 card with Roger Maris as a Yankee, when everyone, even the sissy kid across the street, knew that Maris had been traded to the Cardinals, and besides, there was nothing on the back of the card, anyway.

You couldn't figure out why the 1958 set had no card #145, or why Stan Musial had an All-Star card, but no regular card.

You actually saw Wrigley Field on TV with people sitting in the center field bleachers, and no wire mesh baskets to keep drunken bleacher bums from jumping (or falling) out onto the field.

You beamed with pride when, perusing a stack of 1962 cards, you knew who Ken Halin was and your college-age, know-it-all older brother didn't.

You had friends in school who told you how dumb you were for trading your 1969 card of No Neck Williams for a '69 of some guy named Reggie Jackson, because Williams was the most popular (and funny looking) White Sox player.

The only way you got away with a second autograph was to tell the player it was for your little brother.

You were telling the truth when you said that.

You actually saw Norm Cash and Johnny Callison on the field wearing White Sox uniforms.

You laughed at your 1973 card of Bill Hands, with the hurler on the mound in a poorly airbrushed Twins uniform at Wrigley Field.

You likewise chortled at the box score that evening that showed the pitchers of record at that day's Twins-A's game as WP-Hands, LP-Fingers.

You didn't have to worry that your best friends would skip your wedding to set up at a card show with the same dealers and the same material they see 40 other weekends out of the year.

You came home with a broken Tony Perez bat, and it was because Perez had given it to you during batting practice, not because you had shelled out $50 for it at the monthly baseball card show.

You were left hung out to dry with an incomplete biography on Gordon Richardson's card in 1966.

You couldn't understand why Cookie Rojas looked so happy wearing such goofy-looking glasses.

You were the envy of your friends at school because your mom actually wrote a note fibbing that you were home sick so that you could go see the season opener.

You remember the hobby's Big Three as being SCD, Sports Collectors News and the Trader Speaks.

You actually subscribed to Sports Scoop.

You wanted to know what Little Leaguer Ty Cline stole his uniform from for his 1962 Topps card.

You considered it a good day because five players signed an autograph on your scorecard, rather than a waste of time because only one player signed all five cards you needed for that year's sets.

You were hissed at by the other fans if you wanted more than one autograph.

You pondered why the card for Reds' shortsop Cardenas called him "Leo" some years and "Chico" other years.

You stayed around after the game, not for autographs, but for volunteer cleanup detail, with free grandstand passes for the next game as your reward. After all, you could always get Ken Hubb's autograph on your Little Leaguer's mitt some other time, right? — Dave Miedema, Up Autograph Alley, Oct. 21, 1988

* * *

Signing Session With Terry Was A Delight

By Jim Hawkins

I knew Bill Terry was ill. I also knew he would overcome his latest hurdle, just as he had surmounted every other obstacle that had been placed in his path.

Besides, he still had so much to do. He was planning to write a book, to tell all about his bitter battles with the legendary John McGraw and his contempt for the current state of much of what is major league baseball. He maintained an office at the automobile dealership that bears his name and one or two days a week he was at work behind his desk there. Then there were the autograph sessions, which he truly seemed to enjoy. Even at age 90 — or 92 if you believe baseball's official encyclopedia — Bill Terry was a busy man.

That is why I was sadly surprised when I heard he had passed away. He was so feisty, so sure of himself and firm in his convictions to the point of being hard-headed, I got the feeling he would somehow last forever. Or at least until he himself decided it was time to go.

My son, Mark, and I spent a day with him last summer, meeting him at his home in Jacksonville, Fla., for a private autograph session. Actually we had planned to stay much longer.

I had heard Terry was an extremely slow signer. And the first time we spoke on the phone to set the date, he acknowledged that fact.

"Better get here early on Friday," the Hall of Famer admonished me. "And plan on staying through Sunday. I'm pretty old, you know."

Right away, I knew I was going to like the man.

Later, Bill notified me that he wanted to change the date of the get together so that he could attend Willie Stargell's induction ceremonies at Cooperstown.

"I understand you want to go to Cooperstown," I said, when I contacted him by phone.

"No, I have to go," he replied. "The Hall of Fame wants me up there."

That was Bill. All business.

Our signing session was a sheer delight. He greeted my son and I at the door and quickly made it clear he knew as much about me and my sportswriting career as I knew about him. (He knew Denny McLain once dumped a bucket of water over my head, and I knew he once batted .401. I fear my "claim to fame" was far more overrated than his was.)

He regaled us with tales of his running feud with John McGraw and his encounters with other of the game's greats, now names from some remote and distant past.

And for six hours he sat there at his dining room table and signed his name to the bats and balls and photos and cards that we put in front of him.

Sure, by today's assembly-line show standards he was slow. But he obviously took great pride in what he was doing.

In an effort to help him along and expedite things, I started to take each baseball out of its box and hand it to him.

"I can do that," he reprimanded me.

Then he would pick up each ball and turn it over and over slowly in his hand until he came to the precise spot where he preferred to sign.

Sometimes, he would begin, "B...i...l...l..." The he would stop and sit, staring at the ball for several seconds.

Finally, he would say, "Let me see that last one."

I would show him the last ball he had autographed. "Yeah, that's it," he would say. Then he would resume his signture. For a moment or so, he had forgotten how to sign his name.

Occasionally, he would impress himself with his signature.

"How about this one?" Terry would exclaim, holding the ball to show off his autograph. I found myself hoping the collector who eventually received that ball would appreciate it as much as Bill enjoyed signing it.

I asked him to sign a few baseballs with the added notation ".401" to commemorate his status as the last .400 hitter in the National League. He graciously obliged.

But after a few balls he looked up with a somewhat sheepish smile.

"I just gave myself an extra point," he confessed.

On the ball, he had written: "Bill Terry, .402."

He openly questioned the sanity of one collector who sent a couple dozen copies of the same non-descript black-and-white photo to be signed and repeatedly marveled that so many people would be so willing to pay so much money for something so simple as his signature.

Yet he clearly enjoyed his task.

He signed in a variety of different ways, depending upon his whim and whether or not a particular item happened to catch his eye.

Sometimes it was, "Bill Terry." Other items received a "Wm. Terry," or a "W.H. Terry." Most of the time he signed the more familiar "W.H. (Bill) Terry."

He told of one collector who, by prior arrangement, had sent him a couple hundred items to be signed, with an appropriate check, of course. For one reason or another, Terry put off signing the stuff and the collector began to bug him.

"I woke up in the middle of the night," Bill recalled, "and I decided it was time to get that stuff done. So I got up, sat down here at the table and started signing. By breakfast, I was finished."

After all, business is business.

As I said earlier, the day we were there, Terry sat and signed for six hours. Non-stop. Several times I suggested he might take a break, to visit the bathroom or get a drink of water or whatever. But there was no stopping him.

This was business. This was work. And Terry attacked it with the same focus and determination that made him so successful as a baseball player and later in his business ventures.

In one day, he virtually completed the task that we expected to take three. When we left his home, Terry seemed almost disappointed that the autograph session was over and there was no more work to be done.

"You've got to be tired," I said, as he showed us to the door.

"Yeah, I've been sitting in that chair all day," he replied. "Now I guess I'll go sit in that chair over there for a while." — Jim Hawkins, Eye of the Hawk, Feb. 3, 1989

* * *

What If It Said "Hi Mom" Instead?

What has the hobby of card collecting come to?

I used to buy cards in the '60s and early '70s to get a Johnny Bench or Willie Mays, not because they were worth X amount of dollars, but because they were two of my favorite players.

I got back into "collecting" in 1985 because I remembered the fun of it as a youth. I will admit I too got caught up in the rookie card mania.

Sure, it didn't make much sense for an '86 Topps Darren Daulton to be worth as much as the same year Carlton Fisk, but hey, it was his rookie card.

I even set up at a card show and did quite well, before things had gotten out of hand with the rookie, pre-rookie and now, of all things, high school players on cards.

These things were still not enough to completely sour me on recent cards until this weekend. I attended a show and dealers and customers were almost begging me to pay $40 for an '89 Fleer card #616, just because what was written on the bat.

I wonder if they would pay even a dime if the knob of the bat said "Hi Mom" instead of the obscenity?

I realize it will be corrected and is supposed to be in short supply in the future, but $40 for a card fresh out of a 45 cent pack?

As for me, I'll stick to my Bench, Mays and pre-80s cards, thank you.

The other tragedy to this mess is the fine player this trick was played on. The Ripken family was, and still is, one of the class acts in baseball. — John Westover, Brownsville, Ind., Reader Reaction, Feb. 17, 1989

* * *

Hobby's Future Loses Nostalgia

As a baseball fan and memorabilia collector, I saw something the other day that really turned my stomach.

A local television station ran a short piece, pertinent to the hobby, that I would like to relate.

Call me naive, a bleeding heart, or just out of step with the real world. But to myself (and I'm sure some others), it kind of signifies a great loss to fans, especially young fans, of baseball.

A local card shop is holding seminars of "classes" for young card collectors — er, excuse me, make that young dealers — on the art or business of pricing, trading, and the general wheeling and dealing of baseball cards.

Attentively fixed in their seats, the youngsters, who looked to be in the 10-13 year old age group, listened as the individual (the card shop owner? somebody's father? Elvis?) went over the nuances of making it big in baseball cards.

This older individual is quoted as describing these kids as the future "stockbrokers" of the "hobby" — or should I write, of the business — as this bears little resemblance to any hobby.

He also notes that, oddly, it is the 30-50 year olds that "look longingly at the cards" and "buy for nostalgia," while the youngsters are buying for investment. (I wonder what they're getting for allowances nowadays?)

The question is finally put to one of the little s--ts," Would you trade a more valuable card for your favorite player?"

In his best television voice (the kid must be watching his share of television interviews; he's got it down pat!) he says, "No, I would not."

Give the kid an A plus, teach...! Also, mark it down as an "L" in the loss column.

Gone are the days when even a common player's card was considered "neat," just because it looked good. (I guess today, one would say, it had "great graphics, and bold colors.")

Gone are the days of just hoping that the old Mick was in that five-cent pack. (And when, one glorious day in the summer of '60, after attaining a pile of cards that stacked nine or 10 inches high, I reached the promised land, and opened up a solitary pack, to find Mickey Mantle. I let the whole store know it! I GOT MICKEY MANTLE!)

Gone are the those days. Just like there will never be anther Brooklyn Dodger, the uniqueness of the baseball card has just passed from the scene.

I feel a loss for those kids — for a nostalgia that they will never experience... — J.R. Smith, Redmond, Wash. P.S. That word isn't what you might think. I meant to write "snots." Reader Reaction, Aug. 18, 1989

* * *

It All Started With A Bus Trip With Mom...

By Dave Miedema

In sports collectors' eyes, she wears the white hat or the dark cowl.

To some, she was the unknowing, uncaring interloper who unwittingly discarded some of the most precious moments of their youth, using spring cleaning, or "you didn't get your room picked up," as the most viable excuses for dumping your shoebox full of 1963 Fleers or '59 Topps or '54 Bowmans down the garbage disposal.

Some saw her as the miserly fussbudget who wouldn't give them a shiny nickel for an after school trip to the corner five-and-dime for a pack of cherished pasteboards with the colorful wax wrapper.

What a joy it was tearing off the coated paper, and seeing that all-powerful (in playground trading) Mays, Banks or Mantle card — which you had duplicates of, so you could coerce the snot-nosed rich kid to part with 50 of his doubles for the cherished card.

Or maybe you dragged home to dinner a drooping jaw after tearing the cover off and seeing that you now owned 18 Mike Baxes cards, or your 13th Don Dillard.

One of those guys is OK, but 13? Heck, even the snot-nosed rich kid's dumb sister wouldn't want more than one!

Sometimes, the woman tried to understand what those boxes of gum-scented cardboard were really all about.

Perhaps she couldn't figure out why the numbers on the back of a 1967 Jim Maloney card fascinated you so much more than the numbers in your 4th grade math textbook.

She may have grimaced when the talk, at your school's PTA meeting with cranky old Mrs. Del Campo, centered around why you were carting those waste-of-time-and-money baseball cards to your desk, and, ultimately, to Mrs. Del Campo's trash bin, from which you pulled them out during the day's spelling test to show to your buddy seated in front of you, never mind that you were pulling down a B average.

She may have grimaced, but she didn't cross the line and take your childhood to the big metal trash drum out back.

If you were really lucky, though, I mean soooooo lucky as to have one who was "cool," and not one who didn't understand, the highlights of your youth could travel further and further with encouragement tendered towards it.

In my case, the woman did more than just stand back and watch my hoard of cardboard overrun the house.

When I first wrote at age 15 for a hobby magazine, the long defunct Sports Scoop, she was the proofreader and advisor. Although she had no formal training or any professional experience in the field, her abilities with words and lyrics were among the best that I have ever encountered.

Not only was she a guide in the early days of my writing career, which has now spanned more than 15 years in seven different journals, but she was my very exposure to the hobby I warmly embrace today.

Things would be far different, perhaps nonexistant, had it not been for her presence in 1973. When I saw an advertisement in Baseball Digest for the first-ever Chicago area baseball card convention, my desire to attend what seemed to be heaven became reality.

She never liked to travel, particularly on public transportation. Yet, with my father in the hospital at the time, and with her overprotective, but caring concerns for my traveling to 95th Street and Cicero Avenue on four different busses from our home, she sacrificed a leisurely, restful Sunday to make sure I could attend that show.

My life, and the hobby, were never the same again, although, hopefully, changed for the better, on both counts.

Often, during my late teens, she was my sounding board for ideas I considered radical or controversial, but worthy of space in my columns.

She wasn't 100 percent in her judgement calls, but overall her record in advising me was far better than I would have done on my own.

I also possessed a large jersey collection before changing from solely a collector to a saver and seller who sought to make an honest, profitable sideline income in sports collectibles.

But I'm still attached enough and nostalgic enough to be concerned about the items and the people who were dealing in them with me.

One of mom's greatest gifts to me was a simple one — an education in machine washing my collection. Until my midsection became a bit too ample, I was known for wearing my uniform shirts everywhere — to shows, my office, church functions (including worship services), ball games, and more.

All that exposure as "the jersey man," as then-Pirates trainer Tony Bartirome used to call me, wouldn't have been possible without mom's teaching me laundry basics, such as don't use the hot cycle, avoid bleach, Whisk is acceptable, etc.

It sounds rather mundane, but the results — not seeing my Reds jersey materialize with pink lettering, or having my Veeck-era Sox navy blues become sky blue — bore testament to yet another of her many skills, albeit ones that don't net million-dollar contracts or card show appearances.

She was a guide in my writings, and encouragement in my transactions, a supportive person of my marriage, a fine sounding board for my hobby (and other) problems in my youth, and she introduced me to the pastime I have enjoyed longer than any other — the organized baseball card collecting hobby — by giving up her day of rest to hop on the 80A bus with me for a two-hour trek to Burbank, Ill.

She was my mother.

My mom died Aug. 17 of natural causes. Her death was a great loss.

Still, though, she was a part of my life for nearly 31 years, most of during which I've had some form of constant contact with the items and people you see on the pages before and after this column.

As much as I feel a part of my life is gone forever as a result of her passing, I also realize that the positives — the help, support, encouragement, and backing she gave me in my pursuit of finding a niche of success and fame in the sports collecting hobby, outweigh the negatives of her departure.

In the many years, God willing, that I continue to live, work, play and enjoy my life, family, and hobby, I will remember a Sunday bus ride, a selfless woman, and a primitive card show in a tiny southern suburb of Chicago as three forces that shaped the rest of my life.

Card shows, even then, were not one-of-a-kind events, as 1989 hobbyists would surely attest to; just peek at this issue's Convention Calendar.

I've ridden the bus hundreds of times on Sundays, be it a jaunt to a card show, a journey to church, or a trip to the old ball yard.

When it comes to my mother, though, no person I have ever known, or will ever know, will duplicate her. There could be no substitute, and no improvement, in a woman who raised me. She's definitely one-of-a-kind.

We love you, Mom. Goodbye...for now. — Dave Miedema, Shirt Off My Back, Sept. 22, 1989

* * *

How Fast Is Canseco's Car? Dial 1-900-234-JOSE

By Jim Hawkins

Holy Hotline, Batman! Hold the phone! Have you heard the news?

Now even us Caped Crusaders can call Jose Canseco himself for his latest word on last night's sacrifice fly or the acceleration potential of his automobile.

For a nominal fee, of course.

But shucks, at $2 for the first minute and one buck for each additional 60 seconds, that sure beats the heck out of standing in line for two hours for the privilege of paying $15 for his signature.

Uh-huh. I can hardly wait.

Let's see: We can now enjoy the exorbitant prices of the Home Shopping Channel that Pete Rose made famous on cable TV, or shop by phone from your living room with the aid of the most recent edition of SCD.

But it is this latest brainstorm, Pay-To-Listen-To-Jose, that really intrigues me. This just may be the greatest money-making scheme since somebody got up enough nerve to charge 30 cents to slap a slice of cheese on a hamburger.

Think of the potential.

If Babe Ruth was still alive, we could call 1-900-PETE to hear the Bambino call his next home run. Or 1-900-COBB to hear Ty Cobb chat about his most recent fist fight or feud.

Or how about 1-900-PETE for Pete Rose's views on next Sunday's football games? Pigskin Pete predicts! You bet!

You've got to hand it to Jose. The Oakland A's prolific slugger has come up with quite an idea. Jim and Tammy Bakker must, indeed, be proud.

Under the circumstances, I figured I ought to give the cat a call — courtesy of Krause Publications' lucrative expense account, of course.

Maybe I could convince Canseco to appear at one of my upcoming shows. At least I'd get the chance to say hello.

In fact, I called a couple of times, on two different days. As a public service, I proudly present the "highlights" of those conversations here.

"Hi, I'm Jose Canseco," announced the voice on the other end of the telephone line. "Thank you for calling my hotline."

You can imagine my excitement.

"Yo, Jose," I blurted out, "How's it going, big guy?"

But, alas, Jose was no longer on the line.

Instead, another voice instructed me to "Press one" on my touchtone phone "to hear Jose talk about yesterday's game and about his personal life."

"To hear Jose discuss the topics of steroids," the sales pitch continued, "his ownership of guns or about speeding, press two."

Hey, now we're getting somewhere. That wasn't what I had called about, but at least it sounded interesting.

I glanced at my watch — after all, meter was running — and dutifully pressed number two.

"Hi," said Jose again, "this is Jose Canseco covering the hot topics about guns, steroids and speeding."

I pulled up my chair and sat down, ready to hear Jose reveal all.

"First of all, the topic about guns. I will explain in depth what happened to me the day when I was arrested with the gun, the truth from Jose Canseco."

The truth, the whole truth, and nothing but the truth. Wow!

"I was driving to San Francisco, with my wife Ester in my red Jaguar, which most people have seen or have heard of — it's probably more popular than I am nowadays.

"We came to the Children's Hospital and we stopped. There was no one there. And there was no indication also that that was government property.

"I was upstairs, having my wrist X-rayed. My wife was waiting for me down in the lobby. As soon as my wrist was X-rayed, we learned that it was fractured. We came back down, we got inside the car, and all of a sudden I was asked to step out of the car by a police officer.

"I was told that I was carrying an illegal weapon inside my car. After, I found out the laws in California are a lot different from the ones in Florida, considering the registration.

"I was arrested, I was given my rights, I was taken to jail, where I was fingerprinted. This was the first time it has ever happened to me, so it was a very scary event.

"I was fingerprinted and asked a whole bunch of questions by an FBI agent that they had to bring in. I explained to them that I had acquired the gun for my own protection and my wife's protection.

"In Florida that is perfectly legal and I do have a registration for it. Then I found out the laws in California are totally different.

"After that happened, I was asked by the police officers to take mug shots with them and sign autographs."

For free, Jose? Come on. What were you trying to do, ruin your reputation?

At least, I hope you didn't personalize.

"Now covering the other hot topic, steroids. The steroid incident started when a gentleman named Thomas Boswell started rumors on national TV that I, Jose Canseco, was taking steriods.

"This gentleman said this about me when it was totally untrue. A guy who is 6-3 1/2, 230 pounds and I work extremely hard.

"The last three or four years I've been working out during the off-season probably 2 1/2 to 3 hours a day, always looking for some type of way to better myself, such as weight-lifting or diet.

"I'm the type of person who wants to become the best player in the game. I'm also trying to wear off the stereotype that big guys who are heavy cannot run.

"I did that last year with the 40-40 record, the 40 home runs and the 40 stolen bases.

"I also built a gym in my house that cost me approximately $850,000. The gym is probably 33-feet-by-25-feet; it's a very large professional gym.

"And I'm in there probably 2 1/2 to 3 hours a day, trying to better myself in the game of baseball to become the best player possible. And that will cover steroids."

"Wait," the reporter in me interjected. "I have a couple of questions."

But Jose wasn't listening.

"Next, I'd like to say to all my fans that see me in my Porsche and in my Jaguar that I do enjoy, I love driving exotic cars.

"Obviously, when you buy an exotic car, they're extremely fast. So sometimes they tend to get away from you. You accelerate a little bit and boom, you're up to 70 or 80 miles an hour."

There was more. Much more. At two bucks a minute, Canseco can afford to be generous with his words.

Frankly, I was bored. If you'd care to hear more, feel free to call.

The number is: 1-900-234-JOSE. You're on your own.

Oh, by the way. For reading this column you owe me two bucks. I know, I know. The check is in the mail. — Jim Hawkins, Eye of the Hawk, Oct. 27, 1989.

* * *

Where Have All The Heroes Gone?

By Ric Apter

Baseball has been an important part of our language and culture — a microcosm of our people.

Today, seemingly more than ever, the sport pervades our national awareness. Baseball is the symbol for much of what we consider to be American.

In his collection of essays called "Fathers playing catch with sons," Donald Hall writes "baseball is continuous, like nothing else among American things, an endless game of repeated summers, joining the long generations of all the fathers and all the sons."

Other fine writers like Roger Angell write loving, poetic prose about the beauty of the game and the skills of its heroes.

New baseball statisticians seek out its hidden truths in numbers. Books on baseball are numerous and popular — whether they be of photographs or statistics, essays or analysis, biography or autobiography, historical retrospectives or personal reminiscences, exposes or hero pieces.

The theatre and the cinema have also discovered baseball — from the family drama Fences to the gritty minor league reality of Bull Durham, from the pathos of Bang the Drum Slowly to Eight Men Out.

Even slapstick humor finds a baseball source in Major League.

The arts are utilizing the familiar framework of the sport not just to entertain, but to probe serious universal subjects which may include friendship, honor, commitment, and love.

Two films have used baseball as a representative of bigger themes with great effectiveness: The Natural has a mythical baseball hero in its metaphorical battle of good versus evil; Field of Dreams uses the love of playing baseball as a metaphor for contrasting those who believe in dreams and pursue them with those who are cynical and scoff at dreamers.

The more recent Field of Dreams is an eloquent and moving picture. More effective than The Natural, it is not really a baseball movie but rather a movie with baseball in it (if you watch anticipating a mere sports movie you may be disappointed).

Field of Dreams is about those who dare to dream. No ideal of an American dream pursued is as effective or as believable as baseball.

However, if baseball truly personifies America, then it must portray our glory and our disgrace.

Unfortunately, The Natural is probably more timely in its theme than Field of Dreams.

Baseball today is not so much about the pursuit of a dream as it is about the battle between good and evil. And more and more, baseball not representing what we aspire to, but what we look down upon.

And more and more, in a distinctly American phenomenon, we not only encourage the demise of our baseball heroes, we even act as the catalysts for their very downfall.

For the '67 movie The Graduate, Simon and Garfunkel wrote a song wistfully asking "where have you gone Joe DiMaggio? A nation turns its lonely eyes to you?"

Paul Simon's poignant lyrics used the image of the star Yankee outfielder to evoke nostalgic memories of simpler days gone by — days when men could be clearly and unequivocally cheered as heroes.

And who but Joe DiMaggio better symbolized our lost conceit of the noble, heroic American male?

The "Yankee Clipper" was grace and power in pinstripes. His presence lit up a ball field.

On and off the diamond he exuded a quiet confidence, an air of modest dignity. His many worshippers revered his skill, admired his pose, and cherished his very aura.

Today, excellent authors such as Christopher Lehmann-Haupt ("Me and DiMaggio") and David Halberstam ("Summer of '49") write their way back into the memories and the fantasies represented by Joe DiMaggio.

Everything "Joltin Joe" did was done with class. He was a Jimmy Stewart in a baseball uniform, the famous public figure who could still retain an air of private mystery.

He was ever the personification of the ideal American hero.

Paul Simon's song foreshadowed a change in our society; it anticipated the vanishing hero.

Simon had a feeling that the 1960s was a time of transition in our values. He, and many of you, sadly understand that today's generation has no basis for comprehending the subtle reference to Joe DiMaggio in the lyrics of "Mrs. Robinson."

The professional ballplayer as a symbol for public ideals has sadly become an oxymoron — a contradiction in terms.

Many current fans know Joe D. only as someone who plugs coffee makers and espouses certificates of deposit on television.

Others also know that he signs autographs — for a fee: $15-$20 for flat items, $25 for baseballs, and please don't bother to request his signature on a bat.

This is hardly the stuff of which heroes are made.

But where have all the heroes gone?

This is not to suggest that sports stars are legitimate heroes, or that they must accept or embrace the responsibility of being "role models" — though it would certainly be nice if they did.

They are in the public eye for sure. They are emulated and imitated by young boys.

But, just maybe, boys ought to be taught that players are human and often not worthy of their reverence.

My son, Tim, was 11 when he went to a card show with me. He brought a color photo of Darryl Strawberry with him, and I paid $8 (even back three years ago) for a ticket entitling him to a Strawberry autograph.

It was late afternoon, quite quiet, with no autograph line.

Tim asked Strawberry if he would write "To Tim" on the picture. He was curtly told there were no personalizations.

There was no one waiting behind him. To preface his signature with "To Tim" would have taken Strawberry all of 10 seconds. He would not!

Freed from this onerous task of writing his name, Strawberry turned rudely away from Tim and sent back to laughing and joking with some "hangers-on."

Tim was crushed, but he had learned a valuable — if painful — lesson.

"He may be a good ball player, Dad," he said, "but he sure isn't a good guy — he's a jerk!"

This is not to suggest that the heroes from the past were paragons of virtue. Legends have assured us that this is not true.

It is also not to suggest that any parent would not be proud to have children who display the character of an Orel Hershiser or a Dale Murphy.

But things are certainly different today. What generation has lusted for negative reports about their sports heroes the way ours has?

And what generation has had more negative news to ponder, more gossip and rumor to digest, than ours?

Infidelity was certginly not invented in the 1980s. But the flaunting of it, the writing of column after column about it, the interviewing of the participants on television and in magazines, and the calm acceptance that it is now a natural part of a preseason analysis about a team's pennant chances, is certainly unique to today's society.

Paternity suits and palimony suits are almost an accepted part of the daily sports page. One almost expects it to be included in the box summarizing transactions.

The old-time ballplayers were known as pretty hard drinkers. Some even had careers destroyed by alcohol.

But people who are drunk drivers endanger the lives of others. We deserve better from our stars, just as we demand more from our fellow citizens.

Players today periodically march off to substance abuse re-hab. Players from the past were not regularly suspended or banned from professional sports for using or selling drugs.

And players never used to kill themselves with illegal stimulants.

Yes, where have all the heroes gone?

If DiMaggio's retirement in 1951 was the end of an era of "pure" heroes, what would Paul Simon write — and lament — about today as a logical sequel?

Would he note with sorrow player strikes and players disdainfully trying to break multi-million dollar contracts?

Would he weep over players who exhibit low morals?

Would he lament players who milk their fame for every cent they can?

Would Simon sing "Say it isn't so" when a player is confronted by rumors that he illegally bet on games?

Where have all the heroes gone?

Perhaps the saddest aspect of the demise of the sports hero is the role the fan is playing.

There is a solid argument for asserting that the absence of heroes is just what the fans want since their behavior often seems predicated on bringing out the dark side of people, and accentuating the negative.

The fan today decries foul public behavior of many players he roots for, then goes to the ballpark, drinks to excess, and chants obscenities.

The player is criticized as being a poor example for our kids, but the fan takes no responsibility for being a negative model.

Newspapers print betting lines for games, ads for betting services, and betting recommendations. Then they write sanctimonious columns about people who bet illegally with bookies.

Television commentators will decry fighting in professional sports, but then show the film clips of a batter charging the pitcher's mound for days after it occurred.

The fan today scorns players who get $5, $10, now even $20 for one autograph. But the same fan keeps meeting the price.

The person who complains the loudest about greed is usually the one who schemes the hardest to get extra items autographed for resale, or who resorts to any means to obtain a player's equipment.

We are no longer pursuing a piece of the dream, or a part of a hobby collection, we are part of the crass materialism; we are working in cynical concert with the very same anti-heroes we criticize.

We do not seek a piece of the dream as much as we seek a piece of the very player we are demeaning.

Promoters sneer at the money players demand for appearing at shows; they tell horror stories of broken or unfulfilled contracts.

And yet they keep paying the outrageous prices and putting up with the temperamental and inconsiderate signers.

The other side of the coin is that the promoters have not always acted in good faith themselves. Apparently, according to recent articles, some promoters have even consented to pay players in cash to help them avoid paying tax on this income.

Where have all the heroes gone?

Maybe we get only what we deserve!

Maybe the sad but true fact — as we look around at many of our political figures and our business leaders and our college coaches — is that there are precious few heroes within our society for the professional athletes to model themselves after.

There can be no commercialization of the American professional athlete unless the public wishes to commercialize them.

There should be no holding up to judgement of today's flawed athletes until the damners are worthy of being judged themselves.

If our values are so drastically misplaced, how can we demand that the players be any better?

A player goes into drug re-hab and people do not ask what society can do about this terrible problem; they worry instead how the price of the players rookie card will be effected, or if his team can hold up in the pennant race until he returns.

A player is accused of illegally betting on games and next to no one is concerned about the integrity of our national sport or the message that is being conveyed to our children.

Rather, people are more focused on whether this all-time star will be denied his Hall of Fame niche, or whether they can buy one of his rings or uniforms since it is rumored that he is selling memorabilia to cope with money problems.

Many players today exhibit promiscuous, insensitive, and irresponsible sexual morals. They are not met with censure; instead, grown men smile and treat it as a perk of the player's fame — a perk to be envied.

It used to be different.

We have chased away our own heroes. That is where our heroes have gone.

Baseball card collecting as a love, as a hobby, clearly represents a longing for the simpler times of the past. Some of us hold onto our yesterdays and our heroes via these cardboard emblems.

The baseball card once symbolized a owning a piece of the player's dream — not a piece of the player. And that was enough! How very simple it once was!

If the fan, as hero seeker, wanted more information about his favorite player he did not consult the tabloids, the gossip columns or the front page. He read the sports pages.

Or he simply turned over his favorite player's baseball card and there was all he really wanted to know: the player's home and birthday, his hobbies and schooling, his height and weight, and his record as a baseball player.

Once upon a time a baseball field was where a boy lived his most wonderful dream.

The dream was not for a multi-year contract, a lucrative commercial, or even great glory.

The dream was the opportunity to play the game at its highest level — just to play the game, to have people cheer you as you hit and threw a ball, and ran on that wonderous green grass (and probably, if you looked deep enough into each dreamer, to have his own baseball card.)

Field of Dreams speaks to those of us who still remember those dreams, those of us who miss them, those of us who still dream them. — Ric Apter, Collecting as an Investor, Oct. 27, 1989

* * *

Cable's Offers Make Him Cringe

Flicking through the cable channels at night I cringe as I see "The greatest investment opportunity ever" being sold.

Baseball cards?

I cringe as I see the numbers on the screen showing all of the people calling to buy these "sets" of cards. How I wish I could tell them that they haven't bought a set, but rather 100 or so mostly common cards.

I cringe as I hear how a mom or dad has called in to buy junior the "set" and that they couldn't get this cheap anywhere.

And they are just ecstatic as to how much in value their investment is going to be worth.

I cringe as these announcements rant and rave of the "great investment" that these cards are, always calling to mind the great values of early Topps cards and never letting the public know that just like the great investment of stocks, not all go up.

But some do actually and, god forbid, don't dare tell the public that some investments actually go down!

Is this bad for the hobby? (What hobby? According to the announcers, this is investing!)

I again cringe when I think what's going to happen in a year or two when all those hundreds and thousands of people line up at their local hobby stores to cash in their "great investment" of baseball sets.

These people are only then going to learn what they really bought and probably find out it's not even worth what they paid for it. And then what?

Well, all those thousands of people are going to scream loudly to the media, blasting the baseball card people for getting them into this investment scam.

And then everyone will come running out with their cards trying to sell and only then will they find out what "investments" they really have.

I am not against anyone making large amounts, or small amounts, and I realize and accept baseball cards as a business. However, I find it hard to watch (yes, I cringe) as these shopping clubs and television ads continue to knowingly and willingly deceive the uneducated public.

I recently had the strange misfortune to have a fellow coworker stop by my office and ask if I thought his 100 classic (common) cards he bought off television were worth more than $100 yet like they said they would be.

Is there anyone else upset or am I "cringing" over nothing? — Joe Uhlarik, Roselle, Ill., Reader Reaction, Nov. 10, 1989

* * *

$89? How About $44.75?

On Dec. 7 at approximately 7:30 p.m. a certain cable shopping network advertised a "handsome Bo Jackson autograph on an official American League baseball" with a ridiculous retail price tag of $89. $89!

Do you believe that?! This network thinks a Bo Jackson baseball retails for $89.

Where in the world do they get this price tag? Who died and made a Bo Jackson baseball worth $89?

Anyway, as a special "reduced" price, you can grab the official Bo Jackson signature for "only" $44.75!!!!!

Even Wade Boggs (who is making big bucks doing a live appearance on the network) believes the ball is a steal at that price.

Everybody better dial in to order before it's too late! Hurry! Quantities are limited!

I feel terribly sorry for the many people who bought this ball for holiday gifts, for their own collections, or for investments.

I really wish these cable shopping networks would stop airing hobby-related memorabilia items for ridiculous prices. They should leave the hobby (excuse me, it is not safe to call it a business now) alone. — Todd Pugatch, North Andover, Mass., Reader Reaction, Jan. 5, 1990

* * *

Taking A Look Back At The Decade

By Ted Taylor

Ten years ago those involved in the hobby were having serious doubts about how much bigger the baseball memorabilia pastime could become.

Little did I suspect, late in 1979, that the next 10 years would spark stunning growth and development, turning baseball cards and sports memorabilia from a leisure occupation into a multi-billion dollar major industry.

The hobby, in 1979, was great fun. There was a buck to be made. Hobby shows were thriving, hobby publications had loyal readerships, people were making lifelong friendships in person, via mail and over the phone, and Topps was making millions.

Back in 1979 Philadelphian Donald Peck knew, deep down, that the baseball card hobby was just scraping the tip of the iceberg.

Peck, I believe, more than anyone else, can stand back today and take credit for as much of what has happened the past 10 years.

Peck, then the president of a small Philadelphia bubble gum company named after its founder, Frank H. Fleer, knew Topps was making good dollars selling baseball cards.

Peck knew Topps had a monopoly on the current roster of big league baseball players and be wanted a piece of that action for his Fleer company.

When Peck successfully challenged Topps in U.S. District Court, he broke Topps' stranglehold on baseball cards.

Thanks to a ruling by Judge Clarence Newcomer, the era of multiple card companies was ushered in in 1981. That Topps lost the verdict, but kept its place as the dominant card company throughout the 1980s, is a tribute to its marketing skills and understanding of the marketplace.

But Peck was only one of a handful of people and events that shaped the bobby in the 1980s, as it became bigtime and national for everyone to see and participate in.

Let's face it. Today baseball cards are big business.

They are sold on network television and are traded and manipulated like stock certificates. In fact, many people will tell you baseball cards are better investments than stocks.

If Peck opened the door for Donruss, Score and Upper Deck, it was a March 1980 auction in Willow Grove, Pa., that opened the eyes of America and sent them running to their long-forgotten attic stashes of baseball cards in search of a financial bonanza.

Ironically, prior to the Philly show auction that year, I and show co-chairman Bob Schmierer had been getting terrible reports out of the Midwest regarding a down turn in prices realized for older baseball cards.

A show in Indianapolis a few weeks before had been a near tragedy concerning auction winnings.

We hoped the word hadn't made its way East when we opened the doors to a show that made history, as three 1952 Topps Mickey Mantle cards went for $3,000 each in the auction.

Absolutely incredible, said the news media. The story played from coast-to-coast.

Ironically, the young men who bought the three Mantle cards later actually sold them at a loss, but no one ever reported that story.

The deed had been done. It was official. Baseball cards translated into big bucks, while would-be dealers and collectors flocked to the hobby. Money changed hands with reckless abandon.

Sure, things turned back down again that same year, but the spark was ignited. When the 1981 Fleer and Donruss cards appeared on the shelves next to the oldline Topps cards, the race was on.

Three players also shaped the destiny of the hobby. One was dead, one was retired and one was very much active as the decade began.

The trio consisted of Honus Wagner, Mickey Mantle and Pete Rose.

Wagner's T-206 card is the hobby's holy grail. How many exist? Who cares? If you find a mint one, I'll find you $100,000.

The tale about Wagner not smoking, thus demanding the recall of his cigarette card, is probably so much hockus. But it plays well and has been told so many times that most of us believe it.

Mantle was the logical successor to Babe Ruth, Lou Gehrig and Jo DiMaggio. He was a mystic ex-Yankee, a handsome blond Oklahoma farm boy who could hit the ball a ton. His card sold for three grand.

Mantle was and has been the consummate superstar show guest and coveted autograph for the whole decade.

Rose showed us how to market. He marketed himself in every form imaginable. If any serious collector does not have at least one autographed Rose item in his collection he just isn't trying.

Even as Rose's reputation and career was sinking into the sunset, you could flip on the QVC TV network and catch him selling memorabilia. Now he's selling his book.

The 1980s also produced two superstars of its own on the playing field— Don Mattingly and Jose Canseco.

They, not Doc Gooden, Roger Clemens, Mark McGwire or Eric Davis, are the dominant superstars. Their cards and autographs are the most valuable and most coveted of the new things.

It's arguable whether the Mattingly and Canseco rookie cards ever get to the $500 plateau achieved during the '80s by the 1963 Topps Rose rookie. But they'll both pass the $100 mark.

If those guys were selling, somebody had to be doing the buying.

There's one man who stands head and shoulders above all others. The hobby either loves him or hates him, but they all know him as "Mr. Mint," Alan Rosen.

When I first met Alan in the early part of the decade, he didn't know Steve Carlton from Carlton the Doorman on the Rhoda television show. But he did his homework and he learned.

Rosen's flamboyance has had a lot to do with the hobby's national recognition.

A longtime hobbyist once said to me that many guys who don't like Rosen in public privately acknowledge that he's made a lot of money for them and the rest of the hobby over the years.

Sure, there are probably people who would pay more for your collection. There are guys you'd rather have stop by your house.

But for sheer bravado and sheer public relations value for the hobby, when you talk about people who buy cards and memorabilia, everybody talks about Mr. Mint.

Another man who moved into the hobby and then made it sit up and take notice was Frank Steele of the Perez-Steele duo.

Back in the mid-1970s Steele was a neophyte collector who was mostly interested in cards and memorabilia regarding his beloved Pittsburgh Pirates.

Among his earliest deals, he says, was when he paid "much, too much" for a 1954 Topps of the O'Brien twins.

But that was probably the last time Steele came out second in any hobby transactions.

That Steele and artist Dick Perez produced a collector-issued post-card set, the most expensive set of the decade, tells you all you need to know about Steele's marketing and business skills and Perez's talent as an artist.

Steele also parlayed Perez's talents into an agreement with Donruss to produce the "Diamond Kings" subsets and other related issues.

There's no doubt Steele, during the 1980s, cast a long shadow over the hobby, which benefited greatly from his participation.

Another individual whose role in the hobby's growth, a proprietor of a small print shop in Collegeville and the cousin of a former pitcher, also had vision and imagination.

Jeff Rogovin was a baseball fan, but not a card collector, when he decided to produce a set of Reading Phillies cards in the middle of the decade.

Within two years he had revolutionized an aspect of the hobby — minor league card collecting — that had been hovering on the brink of "happening" since the idea was first nurtured by New Yorker Mike Aronstein.

Rogovin took Aronstein's idea to the next level, mass production, and showed that not only could cards be produced on time and in season, but that you could also make money doing it.

When Rogovin's company, ProCards, produced more than 100 teams in one season, getting them all out on time, a new standard had been set. New companies jumped into the marketplace.

The hobby not only recognized the significance of minor league cards, but made a place for them in the mainstream of collecting.

I'd be remiss if I didn't also toss a bouquet in the direction of Krause Publications. They, too, have played a leading part in the fantastic growth of the hobby in the 1980s.

When Sports Collectors Digest went weekly and Baseball Cards Magazine went monthly, a loud and clear message was sent to the rest of the world that there was plenty going on and plenty to report about in the hobby of baseball card collecting.

Sure, other publications exist, but there's only ever been one number one, SCD. And Krause, there when the decade began, is there today, bigger and better than ever.

The final accolade for the success of the hobby goes to you, the hobbyist. Your interest, your discovery of the fun of collecting, has made this growth and prosperity possible.

Sure, we sometimes get some flack about the bad actors in the hobby. But I believe this hobby carries with it such an element of pure fun and relaxation that even if the values of every item dropped through the floor there would still be a large number of collectors who would keep right on collecting into the 21st century.

There are others who have influenced the hobby who are also worthy mention. They include:

Paul Mullan — He began the decade as the brains behind the baseball card operation at Donruss and ended it as C.E.O. and chairman of the Fleer Co. He'll exert new influences in the hobby into the 1990s.

Kit Young — One of the largest, if not the largest, mail-order baseball card dealers in the country. Young left his family's banking business to pursue his dream. His latest innovation is the annual Hawaii Trade Show, the closest thing to an actual convention that exists in today's hobby.

Howard "Smitty" Smith — The Texas liquidator showed the hobby that you can literally buy or sell anything. Smitty, from San Antonio, has bought and sold entire sports leagues and created markets for things that we didn't even think we wanted to buy.

Gavin Riley — One of the driving forces behind the creation of the national show concept. That the show has endured throughout the decade is a tribute to Riley's tenacity and his belief that our hobby needed such a thing.

Richard Gelman — A New York banker, and the son of hobby pioneer Woody Gelman, he used his business acumen to make his dad's "Card Collector's Co." one of the longest-running successful hobby stores in the land. Gelman's latest venture into television should pioneer yet another fertile field for the hobby.

Bob Feller is a regular at card shows.

Bob Feller — He's one of most personable and accessible superstars who ever lived. Feller has been targeted by critics for his willingness to sign autographs at the drop of a hat.

Some say Feller's as bad as Pete Rose. Feller recognized the potential of the hobby long before it ever occurred to most others. Plus, he was one hell of a pitcher.

Bob Schmierer — He took the Eastern Pennsylvania Sports Collectors Club and the Willow Grove show light years beyond what anyone thought possible. Yes, other promoters are now approaching his standard of excellence. But he showed the way and maintained the class of the "Philly Show" for an entire decade.

I also think of the many quality hobby dealers who carried the ball into and out of the 1980s, such as Walter Hall, Bill Henderson, Tony Galovich, Bill Bossert, Joe Dugan, Jerry Blank, Irv Lerner, Lou Avon, Gary Sawatski, Audre Gold, Tony Carrafiell, Ernie Montella, Steve Freedman, Dave Miedema, Max Solomon, Phil Specter, Lew Lipset and Tom Reid.

The 1980s have been a great decade. We've seen unprecedented growth in our hobby.

I just can't help thinking that 1990 will bring more of the same with it, and I can hardly wait to sit down at my typewriter, 10 years hence, to write that decade wrapup. — Ted Taylor, Off the Cuff, Jan. 5, 1990

* * *

Billy Martin — A Feisty Fighter Since Day One

By Jim Hawkins

"If they praise you as a hustler, there's always going to be somebody who calls you a troublemaker." — Billy Martin

It was Christmas evening and I was debating whether to plunge my fork into yet another plate of holiday ham when the news first flashed across the bottom of the TV screen.

"...Billy Martin Killed in Car Crash..."

I suppose I should say I was shocked. The truth is, I was not.

Saddened? Of course. But shocked?

To those of us who knew Billy Martin well, nothing the man ever did, said, or ever had happen to him came as a great surprise.

When Billy Martin was involved, you soon learned to expect the unexpected. He lived life on the edge, constantly tempting fate, courting disaster, challenging all comers.

My first impression to the tragic Christmas night news was that Billy had finally bucked the odds once too often.

I certainly mean no disrespect. I covered the Tigers day after day during the three seasons he labored in Detroit. We spent countless hours together, at the ballpark and away.

I liked the man. I truly did. Most of the time.

Yet every once in a while all I could do was shake my head at his self-destructive antics.

Billy Martin was many things to many people — a feisty fighter who swung first and let other people sort things out later...champion of the underdog...baseball genius...umpire baiter...loyal friend.

Whatever team he managed, fans loved him. Billy always went out of his way to make sure of that.

He made it clear he was on their side by attacking, with all of his fury, everyone and everything that threatened to deprive their favorite baseball team of victory.

Yet I saw that same Billy Martin erupt and rough up a skinny supermarket stockboy, whose only crime was to aggressively seek an autograph at the entrance to the Tigers team bus after a tough loss.

Of course, the Tigers were on the road at the time and, as Martin explained later, he naturally assumed the young man was an enemy.

Many of his players loved him, too. At least for a while.

As a manager, Billy Martin was a winner. There was no doubt about that.

He demonstrated that everywhere he went, from Minnesota to Detroit to Texas to Oakland and finally to New York.

Yet he walked out on the Tigers in a huff, quitting for a day during spring training. He also once fell sound asleep in the manager's office between games of a Sunday afternoon doubleheader — two acts which hardly inspired the troops.

If a player was producing for him, winning ball games with his bat, arm, or glove, there was nothing in this world Martin wouldn't do for the guy.

But if a player faltered, failed to hit, throw strikes or catch a few fly balls, well, watch out!

Martin frequently feuded and even occasionally fought with his own players and the front office staff, all the way up to the top — not only with George Steinbrenner in New York, but everywhere he went.

When his teams won, which was often, Martin never hesitated to claim credit. And, quite frankly, that credit was frequently due.

He was a superb strategist and a master at coaxing the most out of his players. In that respect, Billy was one of the very best who has ever managed the game.

The problem was, Martin's teams — like all baseball teams — were not invincible. And in his mind, Billy Martin never lost a game.

It was always his players who let him down, or the umpires who conspired to cheat him on a close call, or the front office that failed to give him the athletes he needed, or the insidious press that provoked the other side.

And, in the wake of defeat, he didn't hesitate to make those feelings known. Perhaps that was because he truly believed if there were nine Billy Martins on the field, a team would never lose a game.

After all, Billy Martin was, first and foremost, almost from the day he was born, a fighter.

The thing I will remember about Billy, above all else, is that he was always at war — yet he was, at the same time, always his worst enemy.

That day the Tigers unceremoniously dumped him in 1973 — less than one year after he had coaxed the over-the-hill, makeshift Tigers to within one hit of the World Series — I remember writing:

"The Tigers hired Billy Martin because they liked the way he handled men. They fired him because they didn't like the way he handled himself."

Billy refused to speak to me for more than a year after that, claiming I was one of the reasons why he had been fired in Detroit. I often wondered where he imagined I got so much power.

Then, without warning, Martin walked up to me one day in Florida, shook my hand and said, "Let's be friends again." Vintage Billy.

Martin's father walked out on the family when Billy was only eight months old. Billy spent the rest of his life battling the world and anyone else who got in his way.

If his undersized frame didn't get him into trouble, his oversized nose or his every-ready mouth usually did. Being from the wrong side of the tracks didn't help any either.

"A lot of guys in our neighborhood carried knives," Martin recalled many years ago. "When you'd walk home from school there'd be 50 or 60 guys laying on the grass just waiting.

"And, unless you walked right through the middle of them to show them you weren't afraid, one of them would get up and challenge you."

And one thing Billy Martin never did until the day he died was back down.

It was precisely that attitude that prompted Martin's high school principal to summon the then 4-foot-11, 90-pound Billy to his office one afternoon.

"How come," the obviously upset principal wanted to know, "you're always around when a fight breaks out?"

To which, according to the legend, Billy replied with undisguised pride: "I'm just lucky, I guess." — Jim Hawkins, Eye of the Hawk, Jan. 19, 1990

* * *

Holy Cow! What's Happening?

By Dick Gilkeson

I don't know what you are experiencing, but variation madness has descended upon Portland, Ore.

I went to a show on Jan. 6, armed with information that others had given me "off the network" regarding the 1990 error and variation cards. I'd heard that the Upper Deck McDonald card was already selling for $120, which was pretty amazing since many of the major dealers in this area hadn't even seen the Upper Deck cards yet, and that a Baines Donruss card was going for $45.

As I generally do, I quickly scouted all the tables in the room and noticed that most had red 1990 Donruss Nolan Ryan cards prominently displayed. "$25 each or $45 for the pair" read most of their signs. Where most recently Pro Set football cards had been big sellers at card shows, suddenly it was clear that it was error season.

After making my rounds I drifted over to a table with a McDonald card with the "rookie" logo displayed just in time to hear the dealer tell an older woman that, "It's $140 dollars and going up. Remember the Murphy card last year? Well there's only 6,000 of these printed." I wondered how he knew that, particulary when I noticed he had five of them for sale.

I spotted another friend of mine who often sits behind his own table at shows. He told me that he was strictly shopping that day. I noticed an Upper Deck box under his arm. "What did you pay for it?" I asked.

He answered that he'd paid $145 because he wanted to get a McDonald. Obviously, he too believed it was in short supply and that the Portland dealers who'd found it were particularly blessed.

I drifted over to another table. The dealer there had an error "set" of the 20 Donruss All-Star cards for $100. In addition, he had a complete set of Donruss cards including all the errors except the Baines "line through the star" version. "How much for the set?" I inquired.

"Two hundred," be replied. "Don't you think it's worth it?" I remember just kind of shaking my head and drifting away to another table.

There I found the Score Ryne Sandberg "3B" error with a $60 price tag. Error boxes were going for "only" $45, and moving quickly, I might add. I bought a few wax packs priced at $3 apiece as the vendor told me, "If you get a Sandberg that isn't the error card I'll give you the error card I've got displayed."

Obviously, since the top of the box was dated "DECO41989" on the inside, he wasn't sure whether the card had been corrected by them or not. (Incidentally, one dealer I talked to was incredulous that Score had gotten its product out that early. He still hasn't seen any of his order.)

I started wondering about all the card companies who were able to catch their errors so early, and wondering if just a little more scrutiny prior to issue could have saved us all this escalating error frenzy.

At any rate as I opened my sixth pack (I'd talked him into selling me his packs at $2 and actually felt good), I spotted the Sandberg, card number 561. And it had no position listed on it. I told the dealer I hadn't gotten the "3B error" version so he gave me the one he had displayed in addition as promised.

I paid him and smugly moved on hoping that I now had two Sandberg error cards for the price of one, and that a third corrected "2B" version would be easy to find.

Everywhere I went for the next hour or so, people were asking about the new errors, and dealers were selling lots of cards by the boxes. The halls outside the card show room were full of kids and their folks tearing through wax packs as quickly as they could. Sharks couldn't have moved more quickly toward their prey.

I wondered if card shows all over the country were experiencing the same phenomenon — where, as the day wore on, prices of the error cards got higher and higher. Given that the Upper Deck "error" boxes all sold in the first hour at about $145 to $180 each, I wondered how many more could have been sold that first Sunday in January, particularly if they'd been priced under $30 each as dealers has advertised them prior to actually receiving them, and hearing "on the net" of the errrors.

So what's happening? Is the greed we saw so prevalent in the '80s trickling over into the '90s? Are dealers to blame for inflated prices? Are consumers? Are the card companies? Is a computer network that tracks price increases by the minute?

I wish I could know for sure. Until last year I'd enjoyed collecting variations because generally they were a challenge to find, and priced within my means. Suddenly, almost overnight the Murphy card was $200, and the Perry football card $150. More than a few veteran variation collectors I've talked to were considering dropping out of the race.

If addictions weren't so hard to part with, I'm sure many of us would already have passed on the more expensive cards before now.

So what's responsible for driving many old-time collectors away from a part of the hobby we enjoy? Maybe Donruss is onto something when they encourage us to gamble by having us peer at the inside of their wrappers to see if we've won a prize.

The spinning wheel dealers, too. Are we developing a lottery mentality, where we increasingly buy products for the added chance to get something for next to nothing?

And who can blame dealers who sold their Murphy cards last January under $1 only to see prices march up to the current level? Why not price them high and force consumers to a exercise their option to not buy to bring the prices down? After all, spring training hasn't even started yet, and it will be easier to lower the price as the year goes on, than to kick oneself for selling too cheaply.

Who really controls the market? Who "needs" to have the cards? I remember a column I read a few years ago regarding collecting. The author stated that he never "needed" a card, but there were several he "wanted." Wise advice for all of us.

As this is written, 35 Donruss 1990 cards have been identified with errors and 29 have been corrected, not including the puzzle variations. Is it Donruss' poor quality control that is to blame?

Apparently Upper Deck was able to catch their well-known error well before the cards got into the hobby, creating suspicion. Are the card companies the villains?

Hard to blame them since Upper Deck, for example, actually told their dealers who had ordered more than 10 cases that their orders would be halved. Funny strategy if its motivation was short-term greed, I'd say.

No, as we used to say when others would point their fingers at us, "Look and see how many are pointing at you."

I'm not pleased at what is happening, since I view the cards I collect as a fun-filled hobby, and not as an investment. My ability to build "master sets," to find all the different varieties and inserts, is being regularly eroded.

But I think I know who is to blame. It's that same person who paid $2 for a Score wax pack just as surely as it's the person who paid $180 for a wax box. It's those of us who got caught up in the madness that the '80s will be remembered for.

When the McDonald card goes over $300, we all need to ask ourselves if this hobby isn't heading too far off track, and what we personally can do about it.

Naturally, I welcome dissenting opinions and will publish some of the best thoughts any of you have on this matter in future columns. — Dick Gilkeson, The Variation Collector, Feb. 2, 1990

* * *

Maybe He Should Have Been On A Card

By Mark K. Larson

One of my heroes died last month...

No, he wasn't a professional athlete, immortalized on a card. Nor was he a dealer, or a collector.

He really didn't have a whole lot to do with this hobby. And he wasn't really an avid sports fan.

Oh, sure, he knew the teams and the prime-time players. But he had to. He had to know the facts, had to keep informed on the events of this world, including sports, which is a big part of many of our lives.

He'd be tickled that I'm writing this as I sit in a teen-ager-filled Hardees restaurant on a Friday night, eating two mushroom and swiss burgers, laughing at the pudgy kid next to me as he stuffs french fries into his cheeks as a chipmunk would do.

My hero is a teacher — a journalism professor, one who encouraged me to be me, but to do the best I could do in doing it.

He's the same man who, though he wasn't an athlete, made me nervous as he — still dressed in his work clothes, a suit — sat in the bleachers, yelling words of encouragement to the guys on our college newspaper staff softball team.

I didn't want to drop a fly ball, or take a called second strike; I couldn't screw up in front of him. I had to do my best.

He instilled that fear in me in the classroom, too, by publicly embarrassing students, without revealing names, when they didn't work up to potential.

I'd walk away from the humiliation with the conviction that "Damn it, I'll show him I can do it better; I'll get an 'A' next time on something I'd be proud to hang on my refrigerator."

And, do you know what? I usually rose to his challenge.

I'll remember the time he told our class our writing should "make others realize in the gizzard what otherwise is an abstraction in the mind. Does it move you? Transport you? Make you cry or laugh?"

And I'll remember him telling me poor writing means I should owe the world a tree.

He's the same teacher who, after several classmates teased me about a sentimental column about my grandmother, wrote me a note, complimenting me on the piece and the style in which I'd written it.

He recalled another student who, unbeknownst to me, was also criticized by her peers and teachers for writing a "dumb" piece not related at all to the university.

But, he said, that former student is the only one from our school to ever win a Pulitzer Prize.

My story "shows you can write," he'd written, and "so, you see, writing about Granny puts you in very good company, sir. Keep up the good work."

I'd lost track of my professor since he left the University of Wisconsin-Eau Claire a few years back to rub shoulders with the likes of Danny Manning and Larry Brown at the University of Kansas.

But I'll never forget how proud he made me feel when he gave me an "A" on the feature page I designed for a class project.

My layout package was about baseball card collecting, and included a column on my hero, Robin Yount, a story about the history of card collecting, an interview with the local card shop owner, and a price list.

This man (who'd told me his eldest son, the journalist, once wanted to be a major league pitcher, only to have his arm "wrecked by a dumb coach who kept him in too long and just plain harmed his arm"), said in his review of my project, "Let's go to press with this...or, batter up!"

My "design and copy work well and make me long for the days when I had three little guys running around here trading baseball cards...and I've been accused, of course, of losing some of them over the years in late moves," he wrote.

He ended his critique with a question about whether I knew what was on the door of his study, which used to be his eldest son's room.

"A door-sized poster or Yaz; that's what!"

Every day I have the chance to "work" with some of my heroes, such as Carl Yastrzemski or Robin Yount, because they're depicted on baseball cards.

But I guess one of my most important heroes was never on a card...

Mr. Polk, I'll probably never win a Pulitzer Prize. And I'll probably never write a book which I can dedicate to you. But this one's for you...

In the Hobby March 1975

35,000 and counting...Ruth Russell's story, reprinted in the March 15, 1975, SCD, estimates there are 30,000 to 35,000 collectors nationwide.

Sieve, sieve, sieve...Willopus, in Rochester, N.Y., offers T-shirts for the "hockey freak." The $3.50 shirt says "Hockey is my game," and shows a picture of a gap-toothed smiley face.

Is this club still around?...Topps Chewing Gum Inc. has formed a "Topps Sports Club." A $2.50 annual fee garners such items as a newsletter, posters, autographed pictures, patches and preseason samples.

Home field advantage...At the Indiana Sports Collectors Association's second annual card flipping contest, defending champion Tom Koppa, of Houston, loses his title to Dan Aron, from Indianapolis.

A pair of Twin killers...Ray Fulton, Windsor, Pa., is auctioning off an autographed Twins baseball which contains 18 signatures, including Rod Carew, Tony Oliva, Harmon Killebrew and Bert Blyleven.

In the Hobby March 1980

Will the real Reggie please stand up?...Reggie Jackson appears in the 1979 World Series program in a Seattle Mariners uniform; his Yankee uniform didn't arrive until after a photo session before the All-Star game in Seattle. Jackson could have borrowed well-known imposter Barry Bremer's Yankee uniform; he tried to be in the team picture.

The puck stops here... Since 1967, John Qualls, Mich., has accumulated more than 600 hockey pucks.

Yikes!...R. Bartosz, Pennsauken, Pa., offers official Philadelphia Phillies usherette uniforms, hot pants, capes and jump suits.

In the Hobby March 1985

These guys make nice role models...In his March 1, 1981 "Up Autograph Alley," Dave Miedema picks his "All-Nice Guy" team, which includes Dale Murphy, Gary Carter, Al Bumbry, Alan Trammell, Lou Whitaker, and Ron Guidry.

Look at the price now...Gene Curtis, East Rockaway, N.Y., is selling his 1973 Topps set, in very good condition, for $75.

Kentucky pride...Chuck Finster, Bunker Hill, Ind., wants Kyle Macy cards.

Props for a slasher movie?...James Kwilos, Dearborn, Mich, will trade jerseys for authentic, game-worn fiberglass pro goalie masks.

They screwed up in reverse...In the March "Reader Reaction," Keith Olberman, Hastings-on-Hudson, N.Y., says he bought a Fleer wax box which had no doubles out of the 540 cards. That's bad business, he says.

Now you can have the whole set...Topps has issued its book showing pictures of 35 years of cards. — Mark K. Larson, Marking Time, March 23, 1990

* * *

Money Grubbing Error Seekers

I'm concerned. And I think we should stop and ask ourselves why we like certain cards more than orders and why we choose to buy certain cards over others.

Probably we can all agree that we like cards of rookies, stars, and favorite players.

And the photography, card design and color coordination make some cards more nifty than others, right?

So then why is there so much interest in these so-called "error" cards?

These days people are shelling out mega-bucks for cards that manufacturers inadvertently (well, hopefully inadvertently) goofed on.

We seem to like cards with wrong player positions or birthdates. Apparently, a Ryne Sandberg third base is better than a Ryne Sandberg at his true second base position.

So, in essence, we're willing to pay extra money for second-hand material.

If we keep happily demanding "error" cards, the card manufacturer sees little incentive to make error-free sets.

I'm ashamed to admit that even I found myself coveting the 1990 Donruss Nolan Ryan error cards — not because they're Nolan Ryan cards, but because the error pair sells for $30 to $40.

My, how we've become money grubbing creatures!

The avalanche of popularity seems to have started with the Fleer Billy Ripken obscentity card. This diseased our brains and left the focus of true card collecting joy blurred.

Hopefully, a cure for this plague is near. — Jeffrey Iwami, Los Angeles, Calif., Reader Reaction, April 13, 1990

* * *

What's The Attraction Of New Promo Cards?

By Bob Lemke

Promo cards: One of the current fads among dealers (I'm not sure the average collector has been caught up by it quite yet), is exorbitant prices for card companies' recent promotional cards.

It started with the so-called 1988 Upper Deck promo pair of Wally Joyner and DeWayne Buice. Three different types of prototype cards were produced as samples. All prototype cards use the same photos.

The photos on the Joyner prototype cards are different from those used on Joyner's regular-issue 1989 UD card, while the Buice photos are the same on the samples and the issued cards. The three types of promo cards differ in the placement of the hologram on the back of the cards.

Type I has the hologram at the top of the card. Type 2 has the hologram at the very bottom of the card, flush with the bottom edge. On Type 3 cards, the hologram is about the same place it is on issued 1989 cards, but is rectangular, rather than diamond-shaped.

There have been ads in the publications recently quoting prices in the range of $500-700 for Type I pairs, $300-600 for Type 2, and $90-150 for Type 3.

Some sellers have bandied about production figures in the neighborhood of fewer than 1,000 for Type 1, 2,000-5,000 for Type 2 and 18,000 for Type 3.

My own inquiries of the folks at Upper Deck indicated a different scale of scarcity. I was told by a spokesman that production of the Type I promos was in the area of 10,000-12,000; that the real rarity was the Type 2 cards, at about 6,000-8,000, and that Type 3 pairs were produced to the tune of 30,000.

Regardless of the actual numbers, the scramble for the UD promos spawned a feeding frenzy when Donruss, in soliciting orders for its 1990 cards, sent each of its dealer network members a pair of promo cards from a set of 12.

Single promo cards quickly hit $25 on the wholesale level, with Bo and Nolan Ryan promos going even higher. These are, no doubt, scarce by modern card production standards, but $25 for a brand-new card that has to have been printed in quantities of tens of thousands?

The latest, and least understandable, manifestation of this phenomenon is the demand for Upper Deck's samples of its proposed Looney Tunes baseball series.

Nine-card sets with a full-size hologram card were produced to test the waters for this issue. At last glance, they were being offered at $100 per set.

Can it really be possible that slapping a label that says "promo card" on a pasteboard that depicts Bugs Bunny in a baseball uniform makes it a $10 card?

That would lend new weight to the old truism, "You can't grow broke underestimating the taste of the American (card collecting) public."

I can't see Looney Tune cards selling for 59 cents a pack, let alone $10 a card. — Bob Lemke, The Bleacher Bum, May 4, 1990

* * *

People In Glass Houses Shouldn't Throw Stones

By Jim Hawkins

It's time to put on your batting helmet, once more, card show mavens, hounds and aficionados.

Our hobby is under attack — again. This week's barrage comes from my old colleague Steve Wulf, baseball oracle for no less of a national institution than Sports Illustrated.

"Be kind to the kid seeking your autograph," Wulf admonishes today's multi-millionaire fly chasers in SI's otherwise remarkably readable baseball issue. Nothing wrong there.

I truly wish a few of my past show guests, who, in self-defense I will not identify, would have heeded that advice.

But wait, there's more from SI:

"...And," Wulf continues, "don't do card shows for money unless the money goes to a worthy cause (other than yourself)."

Gee, thanks, Steve. Hey, folks, please don't buy Sports Illustrated either, unless the money goes to a worthy cause (other than the publisher — who, in turn, pays Steve Wulf's salary.)

Nothing personal, Steve. What goes around comes around, right?

Later, in the same column, Wulf quotes — and I quote "one baseball player who appropriately enough asks to remain nameless," as follows:

"I don't see how guys can make a little kid pay five dollars to stand in line at a card show and not even talk to him when the child comes up. Signing for charity is one thing. Signing to make money is totally reprehensible."

No wonder the player preferred to hide his name.

Someone far more sarcastic than myself might suggest that playing baseball — a game we all mastered, at least to some degree, soon after we learned how to ride a two-wheel bike — for money, indeed, for millions of dollars per year, might also be deemed slightly sinful.

Certainly no more meritorious than selling signatures to a never ending line, of eager, smiling autograph seekers.

Of course, this is only SCD — Not SI. What do we know?

(And, before you make that smart remark: Yes, I have had my prose published in Sports Illustrated. Ten pages worth. And, egotistically enough, I must admit, I have the back copies to prove it.)

Hey, if a ballplayer wants to sign autographs at one of my card shows and donate his portion of the proceeds to charity, I have no problem with that.

In fact, the man should — and would — be applauded.

If, after we agree upon an appearance fee, an athlete wants to pick a charity to receive his check, that's fine with me.

And I'll be happy to let collectors know that is where the money they pay for their autograph tickets is going. I'll even notify the press. Consider this an open invitation to all who are so inclined.

But, based upon my experience, most players — past and present — aren't the least bit interested in doing that. To date, not a single player has ever suggested any such thing. And, quite frankly, I don't blame them.

Furthermore, if an athlete wants to chat with every collector who comes through the line, pat every kid on the head and answer every inane question that inevitably comes up, I'm all for it.

I think that's great — as long as that athlete doesn't get up at the end of two or three hours, demand his money, and leave hundreds of people standing in line, holding their autograph tickets.

So, Sports Illustrated, if you want to intrude upon the conscience of today's seven figure superstars, that's your prerogative. Just don't do it at the expense of this hobby. You know the old saying, "People in glass houses..."

At least we don't expect every athlete we deal with to cooperate and enrich us for free. We're more than willing to pay the players who help us to prosper — whether it be by appearing on baseball cards, or signing autographs at shows. — Jim Hawkins, Eye of the Hawk, May 25, 1990

* * *

1973-74: Red Wheels And Deals In Detroit

By Red Wimmer

At the continual urgings of my wife I recently spent time cleaning and straightening the storage areas in our closets and basement.

While toiling on this venture, I came across a box labeled 1973-74 — my hoard of 1974 Topps baseball sets from Sears, for which I had paid $2 a set.

As I looked through the box, other treasures from that era surfaced. And then the memories of those two years started to flash back in my mind.

The summer of 1973 was my first card show. It all started innocently enough.

My wife Diana told me that my golf partner, best man, and fellow hockey player, Ingolf Bach, had called earlier and invited me to go with him to the Midwest Sports Collectors Show being held at the Troy (Mich.) Hilton.

My wife wanted me to go because I had been working too hard on my summer job as a country club photographer, going to each club to take pictures at all the celebrity tournaments. I said OK.

Ingolf picked me up later that evening and we were off to my first card show. Little did I or my wife realize what this show would do to our future lives together.

After paying our admission, we walked around. Wow, was this place huge. There had to be 70 or 80 tables here.

Ingolf introduced me to John Rumierez, who I found out lived near me in Dearborn. (He now resides in King of Prussa, Pa.) We scanned the rows and rows of tables with stacks of cards on them.

This was in the days before dealers had everything in plastic, and covering cards in cases was unheard of.

And get this — no price guides. You needed a card, fine — how about 5 cents, or whatever.

As I wandered around, I noticed a tall handsome gentleman with a cute wife and piles of tabloid newspapers on their table. Their ions and a cute little girl named Mary Jo were handing out the papers.

So, I took one from her. What the heck, it was free (one of my favorite terms).

I glanced at the masthead and it read Sports Collectors Digest, Vol. #1, Number #1. I rolled it up, stuck it in my back pocket and wandered on.

Soon I came to Bill Carrolls' table, where I first saw them in a neat stack — a pile of beautiful white-faced cards with hockey players on them.

They beckoned me to pick them up. As I looked through the stack, I saw the names of all the stars of the 1950s, such as Bathgate, Howe, Lindsay and Flamman.

Later I found out these gems were 1954-55 Topps hockey cards, marked at about 25 cents each except the Howe; he wanted 50 cents for him.

After paying for the cards I went looking for any other hockey cards I could find. I spent $20 that evening on hockey cards.

At about 9 p.m. I found Ingolf. We decided to stay a while for the auction being run by Lloyd Toerpe and Frank Nagy.

I watched in amazement while the items were auctioned off, such as a set of child's size Babe Ruth underwear with a picture of the Babe on the box. Who would ever want something like that? I wondered.

The highlight of the evening was a card called a T206 or something of a guy named Wagner. It went for about $2,000. This amazed me to no end.

After it was over Ingolf remarked "that may be a super investment for the future."

"Sure," I answered, "but I'll stay in the stock market. No way are baseball cards ever going to be big money collectibles like stamps and coins."

After the auction I took my bag of hockey cards and we went home. When my wife saw the cards she wondered what sane adult male would ever buy hockey cards.

But by going to this show I learned there were others out there who collected sports items.

I had a collection of programs, sticks, and pucks from covering games in Montreal, Toronto, Detroit, and Chicago.

I was so intrigued with the show that night I went back again the next day to further satisfy my appetite for hockey cards.

I also started buying cards via the mail from the Card Collectors Store in New York, run by Woody Gelman, and subscribed to Sports Collectors Digest, run out of Milan, Mich.

In the fall I was back at my teaching job when pal Ingolf called, asking if I wanted to go to a mini-show being held at Chuck Brooks' store, a place called the Sports Hobbyist, in a seedy area of Detroit.

A mini show was a gathering of about a dozen dealers at his store. The tables were six footers, or a slab of plywood on top of the garbage can, or a door set up on a couple of saw horses.

The tables went for $2, unless you donated some beer to the icebox in the back room.

One of the dealers there was Jack Wallen, from Chicago, who was selling used Chicago Cougars jerseys for $65 each.

Come on now, who would shell out that kind of money for a used shirt?

On another table was a stack of programs, guides, and magazines for sale. Can you imagine anyone paying money for used reading material?

As I looked around the room I saw a couple dealers from the Troy show set up and other dealers, including Tom Tuschak, John Rumeriz, and Jim Beckett, from Bowling Green, Ohio. (He would later go on to fame and fortune in Texas, publishing price guides.)

I met others, too, such as Lambros Milonas, Ed Budnick, Flea-market Jack, and Bill Tuttle.

I also noticed two youngsters, being followed by their dad, making buys around the room. At that time they were too young to drive.

Today the pair, Mark and Jim Dehem, own Jac's Detour, a popular watering hole on Detroit's East side. This is where the boys got their start and now they set up at all the top shows in the country, such as the National, in Cleveland, and St. Martha's.

At one of Brooks' mini shows, Bill Reed, from Hamilton, Ontario, came in with a load of OPC hockey and baseball. Reed was a wholesaler running his stuff across the border.

A few dealers made buys off him. Even Brooks picked up some sets for his store.

But the guy really making the buys was Wilf Jonake, who was always buying unopened boxes, cases and sets and putting them away.

For years I watched him in operation buying. He very seldom ever set up at a show, instead preferring to cruise the show, making deals and buys for his customers.

Even today at major shows, such as Cincinnati or the National, he still cruises the aisles.

As to my $2 sets of '74 Topps baseball cards, that came in December. Topps and Sears teamed up to market the 1974 set, including two traded sets in a special box for the Christmas sale. It was advertised at $9.95.

After Christmas, there was a blowout sale for $3.98 a set. I went down to our local Sears and saw a whole load of them. The department manager couldn't get rid of them.

After talking to him I said, half joking, "I'll take them all for $2 a set."

He agreed and I was now en route to becoming a dealer. I gave him my Sears credit card and now was the proud owner of about 200 sets and a $400 bill.

(Note: One of the reasons the 1974 Topps baseball sets are cheaper than others in the 1970s was because Sears was selling them to everyone.)

At the next mini show I sold some of the sets for $4 each and recouped most of my expenses.

Another interesting turning point in my collecting also occurred in the summer of 1974, when a hustler named Gary Davidson invented the World Football League.

He conned a lot of millionaires to put up money for a franchise. In Detroit, the team was called the Wheels.

Sonny Grandelius was hired on as the general manager, since he couldn't get a National Football League management job. The coach was former Eastern Michigan Coach Danny Boisture.

The team wanted to play at Tiger Stadium but the Detroit Lions didn't want them there. They looked at Wayne University's stadium but that was too small, so they ended up at Rynearson Stadium at Eastern Michigan University in Ypsilanti (about 30 miles west of Detroit).

One of the hangups with the Wheels, besides money, was a lack of players. They even scheduled walk-on tryouts at Belle Isle Park, which turned into a real gong show.

Finally they got it together for the opening game in Ypsilanti. Being a free-lance photographer, I had called the Wheel's PR man, Ray Hozer, for a pass and a parking pass.

Being that they were hard up for ink, I was given a pass, with hardly any questions asked.

Before the opening game on July 17, 1974, I attended another mini show at Brooks' store. Here I saw them — Wheels' press guides and some opening game programs.

They hadn't even played a game yet and someone was selling their stuff. And what really got me was the price — almost twice the cover price.

Finally, the big opening game day came. Ingolf and I took off in his MG, down the highway with the top down.

We arrived at the game, and we did what every sportswriter does in the press box — chow down and have a couple beers on the house.

As I walked around the press box looking for a few extra programs, I saw him again — the guy from the Troy Hilton show who was giving away those Sports Collectors Digests.

He had some programs in his hand and was walking over to the back door. He gave them to that little girl from the show and her brother.

Down the stairs they ran to the employees' parking lot to deposit them into a car. Moments later I saw him go into the coaches' box with a beer and a hot dog. Gosh, was he a coach or millionaire owner?

Then I saw them, a great collecting find — a box of Wheels media guides which I needed for my collection.

I edged closer to the case and put in my hand to get a few. Just then another hand was next to mine.

I looked up and there he was again, looking at me. Now what? I wondered.

Was the guy going to ask me what I was doing? Ask me to leave? Would he create a scene? Was my press pass in jeopardy?

But just then my buddy, Ingolf, appeared with another hot dog and beer in tow. "Oh Red," he said. "This is John Stommen, the guy you wanted to meet. He's a collector, too."

I asked him what he was doing here and he informed me he was a spotter for the games. We both let out a sigh of relief and proceeded to help ourselves to build up our respective collections.

And that is how I was formally introduced to John Stommen, the founder and godfather of SCD.

We used to go down to the dressing rooms after the game to see the sideline officials who were also full-time school teachers in the area.

After the third game, one of the officials asked us if the team was having financial difficulties. I asked him why, and he said that after the first game they had a whole pile of towels and a case of cold beer in the room.

After the second game they had two bottles for each official and one towel each. Today we had a towel and a Coke.

Then it hit me; the freebies in the press box were now limited to a beer and a hot dog before the game and nothing after that.

Then everyone wanted to be paid and eventually they didn't have programs for some of the games. Hotels, printer, etc., were not getting paid.

For the nationally televised game we were sitting on the press box roof on a nice warm evening when we saw a sight I'll never forget. Busload after busload started coming down the road.

People by the thousands were coming into the stadium to sit on the other side so when the TV cameras showed crowd shots there would be people in the stands.

We later found out that the Wheels went into the inner city of Detroit, picked up all these people, and gave them a free ride and ticket out to the game.

One of the humorous events of the season happened one night when assistant trainer Tom Shaw was standing behind the bench. The fans were tossing a frisbee around.

One fan let it go near the bench. Shaw picked it up and kept it. The fans started to boo.

Naturally, the players and fans thought the catcalls were for them. Then Shaw threw the frisbee back to the fans. Everyone started cheering loudly.

The coaches all looked out on the field. Did we score or intercept the ball? To this day I don't believe they ever knew what happened.

Things really got bad for the Wheels. Tom Shaw (now the Red Wings old-timers trainer) related a story of how bad things were.

Rip Collins, the head trainer (now with the Detroit Tigers), called Shaw late one night, wanting Shaw to come and help him load the equipment in the team van.

Shaw was also told to pack a bag. The Wheels had a charter to fly to Hawaii for a game. But Shaw was told not to say anything because the creditors were trying to attack the equipment for non-payment of bills.

Finally, in the middle of the season, the Wheels folded their operation. I wondered what happened to all the guides, programs, and stuff.

I called a few people I knew. They said they cleared out all their personal stuff and everyone was fired.

He suggested I call the building manager at the Lafayette Building in Detroit. I called my manager and explained my position to him. His answer was "come on over and take what you want."

I couldn't wait for the 3 p.m. bell to ring that day. A.J. Foyt would have won more races if he would have driven like I did to get to the offices.

After parking my car and feeding the meter, I rode the elevator to their offices. My heart pounded with excitement as I got to the door.

I turned the handle and it was locked. I pounded on the door and no answer.

Dejected, I started back to the elevator to leave. Just then the elevator door opened and out came two janitors with two big garbage cans on a cart.

I followed them into the offices. They asked me what I was doing since all the employees and coaches had come in the morning and cleaned out their personal belongings.

I explained my situation and they agreed to let me expand my dealer inventory. I looked around like a kid in a toy shop and found a couple cases of programs.

The guys said, "Take them." Then they emptied out the desks and file cabinets.

I took my cases down to the car, fed the meter, and raced back upstairs. When I got there, they were locking up for the evening.

They had placed the two large garbage cans outside the doors and told me to come back tomorrow morning if I wanted more stuff. Darn, I had to work tomorrow.

Well, I thought, I could take a personal business day, and this was business, wasn't it?

As I started to leave with my two empty boxes I looked at the two garbage cans. There on top were two big packs of GO WHEELS bumper stickers. I picked them up and put them into the box.

Well, there was no one around to see me going through the cans. If anyone did see me, I could tell them I was a bag lady in training or a government agent looking for evidence.

Almost immediately my digging-in provided results. A stack of about 200 media guides were in there, not just Wheels, but from all the teams in the league. Wow, what a find.

I spent the next hour coming and going feeding the meter. By the time I finished both cans were about empty. I really saved those janitors a lot of work, too.

When I got home I put the treasures in the garage. Mama's car would have to stay out tonight.

The next day I made several trips downtown to fill my dealers stock. Boy, I couldn't wait for Brooks' next mini show or the Troy Hilton show.

My wife couldn't wait either, as she informed me that my car, not hers, would stay out tonight and that I had better not mess up her half of the garage with all that junk.

Then she mumbled something about my good buddy Ingolf, who got me started in all these wacky adventures, something about where he could stick something. I didn't catch the whole sentence.

Ingolf was always coming up with great ideas, like getting me to go play golf with him in his company car.

That doesn't seem like much, but the course was in Banff Springs, 60 miles west of Calgary, Alberta, about three days drive each way, and he didn't even tell the boss he was going. Just told his secretary he was going on the road for a few days.

He was also the guy who gave another friend a stack of Glendale Meats Tiger cards, to get him interested in card collecting.

I continued to sort through the boxes. Some of the stuff I found included schedules, tickets, loads of guides, programs, business letters, meeting minutes, and my all-time classic find — an album full of letters from players and lawyers wanting to play for the Wheels.

My favorite letter was from a lawyer extolling the athletic prowess of his client. The last paragraph alluded to the fact that, if given a tryout with the Wheels, the prison where he was staying would grant him an early parole.

After the Wheels came the Stags of the World Hockey League and the Detroit Loves of World Team Tennis League and my first attempt at promoting a show.

But that's another story for another issue. By the way, does anyone know whatever became of Gary Davidson? Let me know. I have some bills he may want to pay. — Robert "Red" Wimmer, Point Shot, June 29, 1990

* * *

If You Could Only Keep One Card, Which One Would It Be?

By Ted Taylor

Occasionally my wife Cindy reaches a point where she's ready to bundle me and my baseball card/memorabilia collection up and toss us out the door.

She's not mad at me; it's because, like most longtime collectors, I have stuff spread all over the house, on shelves, in closets, under things, inside of things, on top of things.

Our collections, I'm afraid, grow at an out-of-control speed as we run around getting some of these, one of those and a couple of the others.

With five or six major sets now out, minor league sets in the hundreds and several special sets, cards alone consume incredible space.

The other night Cindy and I were discussing the choices I'd have to make if, someday, I had to cut my collection down to just a few cherished items. If you think such choices are easy, I challenge you to think about it.

Suppose, for example, that you could only keep one favorite card, one favorite set, one favorite autographed ball, one favorite program, etc. — just one favorite thing from the vast hoard of things you've lumped together in your collection.

At first I thought it would be easy. But believe me, it isn't.

I'll share with you some of my thought process and, perhaps, you'll think about it and share your ideas with me.

First, my favorite card.

This was a real problem. I've been collecting baseball cards since I was seven years old (1948), so I've logged a load of them over the years.

My first thought was that my favorite was a 1948 Bowman of Emil "The Antelope" Verban; I think it was the first card I ever bought.

But the Verban card is black-and-white, and it really isn't a very good picture. OK, so chuck that idea.

Next, I considered the 1950 Bowman card of Del Ennis. I once traded this card (of my favorite player) to a kid named Robert Westerman for 40 cards that I didn't have.

Then I walked down to the local Five-and-Ten and, in the very next pack I bought, I got another. But, nope, that card wasn't it.

I thought about the 1952 Topps card of Gus Zernial, the one with all the balls nailed to the bat, but that was so silly it really shouldn't be a saver, even though I really liked big "Ozark Ike" an awful lot.

When all was said and done, I settled on a card that I just always liked for the way it looked — card #278 of the 1951 Bowman set.

It's of an obscure pitcher named Norman Roy, who pitched one season in the big leagues. Roy was 4-3 for the 1950 Boston Braves and was sent out to Triple A Milwaukee in May 1955, never to return.

Why do I like that card enough to make it my saver? The reality of it is that I like the art.

I like the look of the player, I like the green of the trees and I love the blue fast-back auto (probably a Chevy or a Buick) parked behind a tree over Roy's left shoulder.

It's just a great picture.

Remember, I'm not saving for investment purposes. I'm saving because I like what I can keep in this scenario.

Next, we'd come to the one set I'd keep, if I could only keep one. Here comes another tough call.

I thought about the 1967 Topps set, a real beauty with lots of great players in it. I thought long and hard about the 1953 Topps, because of its artwork, and the 1951 Bowman for the same reason.

But the set I settled on was, again, for personal reasons — the 1950 Bowman. The 1950 Bowman set was issued when I was nine, during a year that the hometown Phillies ended a 35-year hiatus from first place and a National League pennant.

The set contains all my favorite Phillies in their brand new candy-striped uniforms. Most of their World Series rivals, the dreaded New York Yankees, are in their blue pinstriped splendor.

Dealers will tell you the 1950 set didn't have enough stars to be a real heavyweight set. But it does contain people such as Jackie Robinson, Rich Ashburn, Phil Rizzuto, Yogi Berra, Ted Williams and Warren Spahn, who, for my money, were pretty significant in their day.

My favorite autographed baseball, heck, that was easy. I picked a 1976 Phillies ball, with signatures from Steve Carlton and Mike Schmidt on it.

Why? It was the first team since 1950 to finish first. Even though it didn't make it out of the playoffs, it was a darn good club.

The only challenger was a 1949 A's ball I acquired when my Uncle Ernie took me to Shibe Park back in June 1949, to see an A's-Red Sox game.

Uncle Ernie knew some of the ballplayers (he called a few of them his "drinking buddies," whatever that meant), so he got me a bunch of signatures on a real American League ball.

Still, that 1976 ball was signed by a better club, with better players. And by then I was a real Phillies fan.

Favorite book? Heck, that's easy too. What kind of a baseball fan would be caught dead without his Baseball Encyclopedia?

Biography? If I had two books to choose, my second would be Robert Cramer's Babe.

Favorite program? Again, that's an easy one — the one I kept from Game Six of the 1980 World Series when the Phillies, finally, won a World Championship.

My second choice would be a 1950 Phillies World Series program, just because that team meant so much to me.

My favorite yearbook would be the 1949 A's yearbook, which I bought at the very first game I ever attended. The nostalgic value is super.

Whenever I look at it and think about how Connie Mack traded away a kid included in that book — Nelson Fox — I see the stage being set for the sale of the club to Arnold Johnson a scant six years later.

Favorite baseball movie or video tape?

That would be a tough one. A couple of years back Pride of the Yankees would have won hands down. Now it's a tough call between Field of Dreams, The Natural, and the Gary Cooper/Lou Gehrig flick.

If I could only chose one, though, I suspect I might save Field of Dreams. As an aside, I note that John Goodman (of Roseanne) will be cast as Babe Ruth in an upcoming television movie.

I wonder why somebody doesn't make a big screen Babe Ruth movie that would put the awful William Bendix flick out of circulation forever.

I collect uniforms, too, so I'd have to save only one. I guess my Art Mahaffey jersey (done in the 1950s style) would get the nod here.

It was a great style, one that I understand Bill Giles is considering bringing back. He's got my vote, by the way.

Hats? I guess I'd keep my 1950 A's hat. It is plain and all that, but sentiment plays a big part in my selections.

My second choice would be one of those pre-1950 red, white and blue Phillies caps.

Autographed picture? A tough call, between my personalized Ted Williams and my personalized Reggie Jackson.

Since Reggie and I share the same alma mater, I'll keep his.

And, if I could only keep one hobby memory, it would be from the March 1980 Willow Grove (Philly) show, when I realized our hobby was about to go national, about to become something bigger than any of us ever suspected.

That was the show when, as the auctioneer, I got to sell three 1952 Topps Mickey Mantle cards for an incredible $9,000!

It seems so long ago, and yet it was just 10 years ago. So much of what happened in this hobby spun out of that moment, when it occurred to a few visionary people that there was more to the baseball hobby than flipping and trading.

In a way, though, it is also a bit of a sad memory because the little private hobby that we all loved then and shared as a personal kind of thing moved away from us. It will never return. — Ted Taylor, Off the Cuff, Aug. 10, 1990

* * *

It's Time To More Clearly Define The National Convention's Role

By Jim Hawkins

Nobody asked me, but...

It's time, I do believe, for this industry to more clearly define our now out-of-control National Convention and get our priorities straight.

What, exactly, do we think our annual National should be?

What do we want to get out of the show?

What do we need to get out of the show?

What we actually have now, in my opinion, are two shows.

Two shows with two different purposes, two different philosophies, and two different sets of goals, all compressed into one.

And in our misguided effort to do two things at once, we end up not doing either of them as well as we could, or should.

What we need to consider is having two National Conventions each year. One would be strictly a trade show, a business meeting if you will, open to dealers and promoters, anyone who makes his living, or a major portion of it, from this hobby.

Manufacturers and suppliers, the so-called corporate sponsors, could man elaborate booths, displaying and explaining their latest product lines.

There could be seminars and lectures, with serious sessions focusing on the serious subjects, ranging from bad checks to forged signatures, that confront this industry.

The trade show could be run by the fledgling dealer association, if it gets off the ground — yes, with help from Smith Bucklin, if need be — and funded by dues, registration fees, and most of all by the manufacturers and suppliers who would pay for the privilege of spending several days in close contact with the people who buy their product in quantity.

And, most important of all, the show would send everyone home filled with new ideas on how to improve their businesses.

The second "convention," of course, would be as the national is supposed to be now: "The Baseball Card and Sports Memorabilia Show of the Year."

The biggest and best dealers in this industry buying and selling the widest array of world class sports memorabilia to be found in this land. A collector's dream come true!

Naturally, the show would be open to the public, with blockbuster autograph guests, and the main focus on making money — which, after all, is precisely how most of us envision the National right now.

* * *

111

Why, when we in this hobby vote on something as significant as the site of our next National, or the members of the National Convention Committee, are we not required to sign our ballots?

When I vote each year for the Hall of Fame, I have to sign my ballot. Without that signature, the ballot is simply null and void.

The same thing held true when I voted for Most Valuable Player or the Cy Young Award or Rookie of the Year. And I certainly didn't object.

I think we should also be required to sign our ballots when voting on hobby business. And, in the event of question or controversy, the results ought to be made public.

Anyone who isn't willing to have his vote published, provided it serves a purpose, does not deserve a vote.

* * *

Here's a sobering thought for you: Now that the well-heeled corporate sponsors have usurped center stage at our National Convention, pushing their products, passing out free samples, and most important of all, compiling extensive mailing lists, what do they need dealers for anyway?

Armed with the names and addresses of their potential customers — the same customers who used to patronize the dealers — why shouldn't those producers eliminate the middleman and deal directly with the buying public?

I have a theory I would like to share with you.

I believe there are between 6,000 and 10,000 collectors in this country who would like to attend the National every year.

When the show is held in an easily-accessible location, such as Chicago, all 10,000, give or take a few, are likely to turn out. When it is held in a more out-of-the-way city, maybe only 5,000 of those hardcore collectors will make it.

There is also a collector base in each major metropolitan area, which can be counted on to patronize a National in that area. It varies in size from city to city, of course.

Those are the folks that make the annual shows in Willow Grove, Strongsville, St. Louis, Cincinnati and Plymouth, to name five, so consistently successful.

Together, those two groups give us a guaranteed attendance of 10,000 to 20,000 collectors at each and every National, depending upon where it is held.

The rest of the crowd, whether that number be 10,000 or 100,000 more, lured to the show by massive advertising but with no real interest, is all fluff!

The curious and the bored. The same crowd that can be counted upon to fill every major shopping mall on a rainy Saturday afternoon.

You may question my numbers. They certainly are not based on any scientific survey. But I don't believe you can dispute the basic premise.

It's something we all ought to keep in mind next time we are tempted to get excited when a promoter predicts mind-boggling attendance at his show.

* * *

Idle thought: would it be better to have 100 tables costing $1,000 each, or 1,000 tables costing $100 each?

The bottom line, the money in the promoter's pocket, in each case would be the same.

But which formula would create a better show?

* * *

It would have required a lot of work and research, I realize, but I would have been a heckuva lot more impressed with Smith Bucklin if it had come to the Friday night Wham-Bam-Thank-You-Ma'am meeting in Arlington, prepared to tell us some things we don't know.

For example, which metropolitan areas lead the nation in:

a.) Subscriptions to the various hobby publications, which can reasonably be translated into interest and potential sales;

b.) Attendance and spending habits at area shows;

c.) Support of area baseball card shops.

Who knows? If Smith Bucklin had stepped forward and dazzled us with significant statistics like that, combined with information on the availability of the now-needed-mega-halls in those particular areas, I might even have voted for the proposal! — Jim Hawkins, Eye of the Hawk, Aug. 24, 1990

Ryan's Quest Poses Dilemma For Brewer Fans

By Mark K. Larson

"You're not the only one with mixed emotions. You're not the only ship adrift on this ocean." — From the Rolling Stones' song "Mixed Emotions"

Milwaukee Brewer pitcher Jaime Navarro did his part to prep the fans prior to the game, calling for more and more applause before he tossed a batting practice baseball to the cheering fans in the right field bleachers in Milwaukee County Stadium.

Nolan Ryan did the rest.

The Brewer fans were facing a dilemma, for rarely do the home team fans root for the opposition to win. But this night was special.

Brewer Manager Tom Trebelborn, also aware of the dilemma facing the fans, told a reporter before the game, "They want to see history being made. They're not necessarily rooting against us, but they do want to see history."

Nolan Ryan was seeking win #300.

I'd never, ever, rooted against the Brewers. What to do?

Brewer General Manager Harry Dalton, who had traded the ever-popular Jim Fregosi in a deal to bring Ryan to California in 1972, admitted to a reporter that he had mixed emotions:

"I hope he pitches well and doesn't get a decision and we win. There will be an emotional split.

"In a summer when all the baseball personality news has not been outstanding, it's nice to have a Nolan Ryan to talk about.

"He's been that kind of credit to the game ever since he got into it. He's a real bright light for baseball."

Those of the 55,097 (51,533 paid, the ninth largest crowd to see a major league game this year) fans who arrived early cheered as Ryan walked to the bullpen, and as he returned to the dugout to wait for the bottom of the first inning, to pursue a milestone.

Ryan received a standing ovation when he took the mound. All eyes were locked on him. Said Milwaukee Brewer starter Chris Bosio to a reporter before the game: "My eyes will definitely be on Mr. Ryan (tonight). He's amazing to watch. I'd give anything to have his leg drive.

"He's one of those players that everybody in the ballpark turns their head to watch. With every pitch he makes there's going to be a lot of oohs and aahs. I really don't expect to hear a lot when I'm out there."

Ryan told reporters he expected the fans to root for the Brewers first, but their priorities might shift if he were still around in the later innings.

My ultimate dilemma occurred when, in the third inning of a scoreless game, my favorite, Robin Yount, stepped in against Ryan with a runner on first.

Yount responded with what I believe is the most beautiful, exciting play in baseball — a Robin Yount triple, where he goes flying around second and barely beats the throw to third. I was pumped up, standing and clapping for my hero.

Brewers 1, Texas 0. Would it be insurmountable?

Nope.

The Rangers gave Ryan a 5-1 lead to work with entering the eighth. But the Brewers, with the aid of two Julio Franco errors, including one on a possible inning-ending double play, rallied for two runs.

5-3. Now how should I feel?

Bobby Valentine's actions squashed my indecisiveness when he strolled to the mound to pull Ryan. I joined the fans, voicing my disapproval. Valentine was showered with boos.

Our priorities had shifted. We wanted Ryan to stay in, to win.

Flashbulbs popped. And, as if the National Anthem were about to be sung, the fans stood up together, and clapped. And clapped. And clapped. And cheered. And cheered. And cheered.

The crescendo built, peaking when Ryan doffed his cap and raised his right arm to acknowledge the fans. Euphoria.

It was electric. I had goosebumps.

I didn't care if I ever got back. I didn't want it to end.

Ryan had said he had wanted to win #300 in Texas, but the Milwaukee County Stadium fans had really made him seem at home.

About the ovation, Ryan told reporters: "That's a special feeling that's hard to explain. The only other time I really experienced that was last year when I came back to Anaheim for the first time after being gone for nine years.

"That was a little different because I had pitched there for eight years and had a special relationship with the fans in Anaheim.

"The fans in Milwaukee, I think it reflected on them as baseball fans and the way I perceived it is it was their way of saying that they appreciate my efforts and my career and they were supportive of me tonight. It was very special."

Very special. Something I'll never forget.

"My attitude," Ryan told a reporter before the game, "is I want people to have a positive experience when they come to the ballpark. I know when I take my own kids to a game, I don't want it to be a negative experience.

"I want it to be something they can remember. As a parent and as a ballplayer, that's the way I want people to perceive me."

I will. Thanks, Nolan.

In the Hobby August 1975

Hope to see you next year: Attendance at the 7th Annual West Coast Convention, Aug. 16-17, in Anaheim, Calif., has increased from 13 the first year to 700, a record.

Yahoo for Wahoo: Jonathan Feldman, Silver Spring, Md., wants cards of Sam "Wahoo" Crawford in a Reds uniform, Noodles Hahn, Bubbles Hargrave, Heinie Groh and Eppa Rixey.

His bubble will burst: On the Aug. 31, 1975, SCD cover, Joe Garagiola is measuring a bubble blown by Johnny Bench for the Bazooka Big League Bubble Gum blowing championship. The winner gets $1,000 to give to his favorite charity for children.

In the Hobby August 1980

The door is open for new companies: U.S. District Judge Clarence C. Newcomer rules Topps Chewing Gum Co. is guilty of monopolizing the baseball card business, violating federal antitrust laws.

How much do you want for this Gary Carter rookie card?: The New York Times recently printed a story about Montreal Expos catcher Gary Carter's card collection. "I don't even know how much they're worth because I don't plan to sell any. The value is that I enjoy them," he said.

In the Hobby August 1985

I confess: Joe Garagiola, the guest speaker at the National Convention in Anaheim, admits he collects. "I'm a collector and I'm proud to be a collector. Collecting let's the little boy in you jump out."

RIP: In his Aug. 2, 1985, "On the Baseball Beat," Irwin Coben reports that Toronto reliever Bill Caudill buried his pet mouse, IAN II, which he'd kept in the clubhouse, under the Toronto bullpen in Exhibition Stadium.

Sweetness: A 1983 Bears/Bucs program signed "Walter Payton, Sweetness #34," is for sale by John Squires, Palo Alto, Calif.

Without the expressed written consent: A collector in Alburg, Vt., offers for $21 two cassettes containing the entire first game ever for the Toronto Blue Jays, April 7, 1977.

On the rise: SCD Publisher Bob Lemke, attending a show in Plymouth, Mich., the weekend Tom Seaver notched his 300th career victory, reports in the Aug. 30, 1985, issue that Seaver rookies, listed at $85, were selling for more than $100 in Plymouth. — Mark K. Larson, Marking Time, Aug. 31, 1990

* * *

History In The Making
Here's What We'll Remember
About Nolan Ryan's 300th Win

By Mark K. Larson

"I'm just not one to reflect back on my career yet. I'm sure that at some point in time I will. But tomorrow I'll be up early getting ready for my next start." — Nolan Ryan, after he'd won his 300th game in Milwaukee.

But to the fans who had seen him win that night, Ryan's comment contradicted everything they were feeling. The night had been a festive one, a historic milestone, a moment to be cherished. An experience that will always be remembered.

Several people from Krause Publication's sports division were participants in the standing ovations Ryan received at County Stadium July 31, 1990, when Ryan won #300, 11-3 against the Milwaukee Brewers.

Each holds memories which will last forever. Their memories and players' quotes taken from several newspapers are captured here:

Steve Ellingboe, Sports Collectors Digest's executive editor, remembers:

"The circus-like atmosphere before the game, the dozens of news people, live TV remotes, photographers, etc., similar to a World Series or All-Star game.

"The mixed emotions of the fans, cheering simultaneously for their hometown Brewers and for Nolan Ryan, reluctantly hoping the hometown favorites would lose so they could see baseball history.

"The warm outpouring of adulation and emotion that greeted Ryan when he first took the mound, when he was removed in the eighth inning, and, of course, when he came back out after the victory. An ovation that seemed to continue forever.

"Even after the Rangers and the media left the field, the fans remained standing, frozen in time, savoring the history they had witnessed. It was a special night.

Nolan Ryan captured win #300 in Milwaukee.

"Reporters were asking us about memorabilia from the game. What should they save?

"My answer: 'The memory of being there.'"

Kit Kiefer, the editor of Baseball Cards Magazine, remembers:

"The hair jobs on the TV people. I've never seen so much perfect hair that wasn't attached to mannekins. Then again, maybe it was..."

More than 300 media type were on hand, including representatives from ESPN and the Rangers television network, both which broadcast the game.

Kiefer, during a brief, live interview for the Channel 6's 6 p.m. sports report in Milwaukee, was asked what collectibles fans should save from the game.

He suggested ticket stubs, programs and any commemorative certificates which might be distributed after the game.

Ryan, who autographed lineup cards for each of the umpires after the game, kept the ball hit for the final out, and said he'd give each teammate a game ball. The Baseball Hall of Fame will get a ball, too, and Ryan's cap.

Rick Hines, an SCD editorial assistant, remembers:

"The fact that I was actually witnessing a historic event. It was my first trip to County Stadium, and it was my son's 13th birthday present.

"I also thought back to last fall, when I sold my 1968 Topps set with a Near Mint Nolan Ryan rookie card. I went home and cried."

According to Jeff Kurowski, SCD's price guide coordinator, the Ryan rookie card is valued at $1,500.

Rick's son, Wyeth Hines, said:

"What I remember about Nolan Ryan's 300th win is it was my birthday present and not many birthday presents go down in history.

"Not only did I see Ryan get #300, but I saw a grand slam by Julio Franco, a solo shot by Pete Incaviglia, and three triples in one game (Robin Yount, Jeff Huson and Rafael Palmeiro)."

Said Ryan, after the game, about Franco's homer, which gave Texas an 11-3 lead in the ninth: "It was a tough game up to that point. Julio's homer was the key hit. That gave us a cushion because two runs is nothing against Milwaukee."

Ryan later signed a baseball for Incaviglia, whose homer preceded Franco's.

Duke Tuomi, an ad salesman for SCD, remembers:

"The special moment when all 55,000 fans clapped their hands and gave a standing ovation to Nolan Ryan."

"I have great respect for the man. When they took him out of the game, I gave him my own standing ovation...It was inevitable that he was going to win his 300th," said Milwaukee Brewer designated hitter Dave Parker.

Said Ryan about the ovation: "It was real rewarding to see the Milwaukee fans react the way they did. That really speaks well for them. It was a unique situation."

Duke remembers: "Texas Rangers rookie shortstop Jeff Huson brought the lineup card to home plate. Why?"

We never found out why, but Huson, who's fifth-inning two-run triple gave Ryan a 4-1 lead, said after the game, "I think going into the game everybody wanted to make the big hit or the big play to win it for Nolan. To come through and get that hit, that's something I'll remember forever."

Huson had Ryan sign a sheet of paper that had the team's pregame batting schedule. He wrote: "I appreciate your help, Nolan Ryan."

Duke remembers: "Julio Franco's errors probably kept Nolan from pitching a complete game victory."

"To this locker room, Nolan is a leader, a legend, a respectable man," said Franco, who received a hug and words of encouragement from Ryan after the game.

Said Parker, "I thought we battled the heck out of him. I thought we had him on the ropes. I have great respect for the man. It's a great achievement for Nolan. I just wish he could've done it someplace else."

Said Ryan about the eighth: "The eighth inning was really tough on me physically. I knew it would be my last inning. I never thought I'd pitch a complete game."

A resounding shower of boos greeted Bobby Valentine as he strolled to the mound to take out Ryan, leading 5-3, in the eighth. As Ryan walked off the field, flashbulbs popped all around the stadium, and the boos changed to cheers.

Ryan doffed his cap and waved his arm to acknowledge the fans, who didn't want to stop cheering.

Duke remembers: "Most of the crowd stayed until the end and even after."

The applause started again in the bottom of the ninth, with two out and two strikes on Robin Yount. When Yount flied to Gary Pettis to end the game, the fans erupted into a five-minute ovation.

Duke remembers: "Why didn't the Brewers have a special program made up?"

The Brewers did distribute a commemorative certificate to fans after the game was over.

Duke remembers: "Nolan giving Gary Sheffield a little 'chin music.'"

Sheffield, who wasn't even born when Ryan won his first game, walked four times against Ryan in a game last year.

He told reporters the day before Ryan's 300th win: "All I know is I'm scared. Last time he knocked me down four times. I didn't even want to go back up there. I'm a little shaky right now. I know he's going to come in on you, way in. One time he almost hit me in the face. I'll always remember that."

Sheffield, with his team trailing 5-1, popped out with two men on, and no out in the eighth. A pumped up Ryan threw him a 96 mph fastball during the inning.

Sheffield finished the game 0-4, with a strikeout, but said, "I'm glad to have played the game against Nolan, when he got his accomplishment. I don't even feel like we lost tonight."

But teammate Greg Vaughn disagreed, saying, "I'm not going to brag that I played in the game and punched out twice (struck out) the day Nolan won No. 300."

Scott Kelnhofer, an editorial assistant for Baseball Card News, said:

"What I'll remember most from Nolan Ryan's 300th victory is the tremendous pro-Ryan feeling exhibited by the 55,000 fans at the game, especially the standing ovation he received when he left the game in the eighth inning.

"The crowd wanted Ryan to win because he deserves a milestone like 300 victories. He's a modern-day superstar who doesn't walk out of spring training to have contracts renegotiated, who doesn't knock down opposing hitters and then challenge them to a fight, who never bad mouths an opponent, a teammate, an umpire, the fans, or anyone.

"He accepts the limelight, but doesn't covet it. All he does is train very hard to be what he is: the best pitcher in the game.

"He gets paid the big money, but not because he feels he should get it.

"They say good guys finish last, but Nolan Ryan is a great guy who will never be anything but a winner." — Mark K. Larson, Aug. 31, 1990

* * *

Reedy May Have Been Billy Martin's Best Friend

By Jim Hawkins

This was going o be a "good news" column about my friend, Bill Reedy.

Well, Reedy is still my good friend, but unfortunately the news is not good.

In case you are unfamiliar with the name, Bill Reedy is the 54-year-old Detroit sports bar owner and influential political operative who, with the possible exception of Mickey Mantle, happened to be Billy Martin's best friend.

Such a close friend, in fact, that Martin invited Reedy and his wife, Carol, to upstate New York last winter to spend Christmas with Billy and his wife.

Such a close friend, in fact, that Reedy passed up the opportunity to spend the holiday at home with his own family and went.

"Billy," Reedy explained so many times, "was like a brother to me."

The rest, tragically, is history. On Christmas afternoon, the two men left Martin's 150-acre farm to run a few errands. They also stopped at one of Billy's favorite hangouts for some holiday cheer.

On the way home, Martin's 1989 Ford pickup truck slid off the icy road, skidded more than 100 feet down a gully and crashed into a culvert running under his own driveway, killing the 61-year-old Martin and leaving Reedy with a broken hip and pelvis.

When help arrived, unaware that Billy was dead, Reedy declared he had been driving. As Reedy explained later, he was lying to protect his buddy, who throughout his life had a penchant for getting himself into trouble.

"I've been lying for Billy Martin for years," said Reedy. "People who knew us knew that Bill Reedy lied to protect his friend." Only later did Reedy realize how much trouble he was getting himself into.

To make a long — and for Reedy, agonizing — story short, Reedy was charged and convicted of driving under the influence of liquor. The jury simply did not believe him when he said Billy, not he, was driving.

Reedy was fined $350 plus $25 court costs and his New York driving privileges were suspended for six months — the minimum sentence he could have received.

But that was far from the worst part.

In addition to the tens of thousands of dollars he has already been forced to spend, defending himself against a misdemeanor, Reedy now faces a civil lawsuit by Martin's widow, and fourth wife, Jilluann, 34.

And, of course, there remains the memory of the death of his best friend.

"That," admits Reedy, "will hurt for a long time. I just want to forget the rest of this. All I want to remember is Billy."

I will long remember that fateful Christmas evening, too. Shortly after the news of Martin's untimely death had flashed across the bottom of my TV screen, I received a call from the Associated Press, asking if I could help establish the identity of the man who had been in the vehicle with Billy when he was killed.

"We need to know who the man is and what his relationship with Billy Martin was" the AP reporter explained.

"The other man's name is William Reedy."

Immediately, my heart sunk. Just a few weeks earlier, I had spent several hours with Reedy while Ted Williams was in the Detroit area for a private signing and card show that I sponsored in conjunction with Don and Bill Stein of the On Deck Circle.

Jim Hawkins, Bill Reedy, Ted Williams and Don Stein at a private signing for the Jimmy Fund.

Without any fanfare or publicity, Reedy closed his saloon one Friday evening, turning away his own customers, to host a "by-invitation-only" fund raiser for Williams' favorite charity, The Jimmy Fund.

Reedy invited 75 to 100 of his closest friends, asked them each to make out a check to the charity, then gave them all they cared to eat or drink, and turned over every penny of the evening's proceeds — more than $7,000 — to The Jimmy Fund.

The evening cost Reedy plenty, yet all he asked was: "Do you think Ted had a good time?"

And when the representative from The Jimmy Fund, who had flown in for the affair, forgot to take the donation checks with him when he returned to Boston, Reedy drove 60 miles to Toledo on a bitter cold Saturday night to personally deliver the contributions to Ted and me.

In the wake of his conviction, Reedy continues to maintain his innocence. "Billy and I know that he was driving that truck," says Reedy. "That's all that matters." Meanwhile, Martin's children have rallied behind their dad's friend.

Martin's son, 25-year-old Billy Joe, flew to Detroit to attend a fund raiser staged by friends to help Reedy defray some of his legal expenses.

"I know that my dad wouldn't want Bill (Reedy) to have to go through all of this," Billy Joe Martin told the preas while he was in town.

"I believe Bill when he says he was covering up for my father when he told the police at first that he (Reedy) was driving. They were true friends.

"He didn't know my dad was dead when he said that. He wanted to save him more bad press, that's all."

Martin's 37-year-old daughter, Kelly Martin-Knight, flew to upstate New York and sat behind Reedy during the trial and, according to the Detroit News report, "glared at her stepmother."

In the weeks and months leading up to his trial, Reedy and I spoke several times as he contacted Mickey Mantle, Ted Williams and others, attempting to put together a combination celebrity golf tournament/baseball card show to raise money to establish a college fund for Martin's granddaughter.

Finally, with his trial and all of its ramifications staring him in the face, Reedy reluctantly was forced to put that project on the back burner.

But from the day I first spoke to him about the accident, shortly after he was released from the hospital, when he was still walking gingerly with a cane, Reedy has professed his innocence.

"You know Billy," he said, with tears in his eyes. "There was no way, in his town, he was going to let anyone drive his truck."

Yes, I did know Billy. We occasionally even yelled at one another during Martin's days as a manager of the Tigers.

I also know Bill Reedy. And I believe him when he says he was not driving.

For some reason, Martin seemed to thrive on turmoil. Many times I marvelled at the fact that he was frequently his own worse enemy, often lying when the truth was clearly on his side.

Billy Martin died as he lived. Suddenly. Unexpectedly. And even in death his memory is shrouded in turmoil.

For once, though, I suspect Billy would like all of the controvesy to disappear. Because, for all of his faults, Billy Martin was loyal to his friends.

And Billy Reedy just may have been the best friend Billy Martin ever had. — Jim Hawkins, Eye of the Hawk, Oct. 19, 1990

* * *

Is The Goose That Lays The Golden Egg Being Killed?

By Dick Gilkeson

Now that the Pro Set hockey card error count is well over 100, and may exceed 200 before the final tally is in, it's time to ask the card companies what happened to quality considerations?

Sure, I have appreciated the enhanced photography on the newer cards, and look forward to the new Topps baseball photographs, (did I really write that?), but photography alone does not make a quality product.

Most recently, the Upper Deck oversight, which occurred when baseball card numbers 1 to 199 in the early high number packs were printed without the copyright line, added 99 new flawed cards to the swelling ranks.

Fleer, using two printers, apparently printed all its basketball cards with and without the line below the 48 minute statistics.

Score accidently let some cards from a renumbered 100-card football set get packaged in its "Hot Card" blisters.

Pro Set accidently let some #75 Cody Risien football cards sneak out in its final Series I football packaging, which still contained many of the other error cards with incorrect or missing data.

NBA Hoops printed its 1990 #13 basketball card without #13 on the card. Fleer did the same with its #84 football card. And on and on.

As one card executive explained to me recently, "We're all just going too fast."

With the high rewards associated with being the first cards in a sport on the market in any given season, it's relatively easy to understand why the attention to quality is given a back seat.

But when we consumers can't trust the pictures, data, or integrity of the sealed product, I wonder if the goose that laid the golden egg is gradually being killed.

The borderless Pro Set design is impressive, but far less impressive has been the number of cards I've bought that have had top/bottom overlaps with other cards or strange indentations that don't smooth out.

In fairness to Pro Set, I can appreciate the problems in simultaneously getting more than 500 new plant people up to speed. I am very forgiving right now, but will be less so as the company's production people gain experience.

The hockey card text and picture errors are much tougher to forgive. It's hard to believe Pro Set packaged so many Brett Hull prototype cards as the #1 card in the regular hockey issue.

The set hadn't been on the street a week before people started calling me, asking if Pro Set had printed another #1 card since the Hull card was also issued in a slightly different form as #263.

The two boxes I initially bought contained three #1 Hulls and no #1 Ray "Borque's".

When a fellow called and said he had gotten two football cards per hockey pack in a box he bought, I didn't question his story.

If the company was making automobiles, imagine how consumers would react...

Although Topps makes far fewer text errors, (those computers ought to be full of good data after 40 years in the business), I still can't believe how poor the glossy process is.

I have had trouble finding Big Baseball cards, (yes, I actually bought some of this dying product), with anything resembling a uniform glossing.

At times, the cards appear to have been sprayed by an art student who just learned how to use a mist sprayer.

Most recently, the 1990 glossy insert football set I assembled is so spotty I have given up thinking I can sell or trade my doubles as anything more than VG.

Dealers advertising their glossy sets as "Tiffany" are degrading what once was a name meaning true quality.

Topps continues to use gray cardboard, presumably because the Food and Drug Administration or somebody says it can't use the white cardboard stock others are using because Topps packages bubble gum with its cards.

Seems to me Topps could separate the gum from the cards by wrapping it separately, or separating it from the other cards with the insert cards we are flooded with.

At the least, it's time for new packaging that doesn't leave one card per pack with wax stains. How about it, Topps?

With all the money you are making, can't we expect a few improvements in packaging? I presume that the main issue is money.

Most of us would appreciate it if the Fleer people would check the artwork both its printers use when more than one us used.

The "error" and "corrected" basketball cards might better be labelled "cards from printer A" and "cards from printer B."

Do we really need to deal with card differences based on using multiple printers? Is uniformity that difficult to establish?

Hopefully this problem will disappear when Fleer expands its internal capacity in 1991.

Back to Upper Deck. Thank God the company has introduced holograms in a hobby increasingly dealing with counterfeiting.

I shudder to imagine the forging that might have occurred on the Reggie Jackson cards if the real autographed versions hadn't been produced with their own holograms; however, I wonder if it is possible to do some work on the hologram affixing apparatus?

My apologies to those who wrote me about Upper Deck cards with missing, misplaced, or multiple holograms; there were too many letters from all of you to be able to respond.

I appreciate Upper Deck's willingness to listen and superb attitude regarding quality despite these lapses. Not putting stars in your sets as #1 cards (that get dinged in storage more than others), and double packaging are just two of the little ways that assure me Upper Deck is concerned about our ability to get and keep high quality cards.

I hope Score does not get in over its head with too many products. The Score folks have been among the best at returning my calls and tracking down errors to the source.

I worry that as the company rushes from baseball to football to hockey it'll be paying less attention to any one set. It is hoped the company will not become totally numbers-driven. Time will tell.

Actually, for a relative newcomer, Score has done very well so far regarding quality. I very, very rarely find a grossly miscut card.

In fact, I assembled my football set from packs this year by looking at the backs only while I was collating.

Because I worked in a high technology manufacturing plant producing microchips, I know cutting cards uniformly is not a goal that is impossible to attain.

Manufacturers other than Score might learn something from how Score/Optigraphics manages their process.

Earlier this year I mentioned the problems Donruss has printing cards with any color consistency. My 1990 baseball set has seemingly all shades of red, from orange to dark red.

In addition, the Donruss folks seem to be the leader in producing cards with small, strange, blotches. The front designs in 1990, where lines and letters often were mismatched, gave that set a rather cheaply-produced feel.

It is hoped that as Donruss gets wealthier, it'll upgrade its printing process and produce cards more akin to its Leaf set.

Yes, I know, it's just cards aimed at kids, so what's the big deal? Topps is making cards so kids who can't afford to buy Upper Deck can still buy, and that's helping the hobby in the long run, presumably.

Maybe I really shouldn't be so concerned. As in any market, the buyer will decide whose product continues to sell and whose gets left behind.

What I see currently is a very recent cooling off, with more focus on where hobby dollars are being spent.

I believe companies that do not make strong efforts to improve their quality in all phases of their operations may well be perceived as less than serious players and bypassed by both dealers and collectors.

The special insert card craze is in full swing, but that will also pass as a gimmick for selling cards. Ultimately, quality will win out, even though quality sometimes mean taking a little more time and care.

Card manufacturers, take note. The day may come when consumers start returning defective cards, (and not just those creased and off-center), to you in droves.

Other manufacturers have learned that quality means doing things right the first time. Their yields have continually increased and many industries have as their goal zero defects, particularly as consumers have become willing to take the time and put up the expense of returning substandard products.

This industry is likely already on a path of over-saturation, particularly in areas such as hockey cards. Some kind of a shake out is likely to occur soon.

Quality and value are the hallmarks of companies that have survived the longest in this country.

And to you little companies trying to break into this game without the proper licenses and so forth, when you produce strange little sets with orange borders and Wayne Gretzky's name misspelled "Gretsky," don't expect buyers, even dedicated Gretzky collectors like me, to buy your products.

These inferior products are on the way out, if they ever really found the way in. We're looking at some tough times ahead, but "buyable" will not likely equate to cheap. Just a word to the wise... — Dick Gilkeson, The Variation Collector, Nov. 23, 1990

* * *

Recession Kicks Memorabilia Back Into The Hobby Market

By Joshua Leland Evans

The state of the hobby market is quite interesting right now.

The economic recession that exists across America has caused many people to sell, generating a tremendous amount of material into the marketplace.

This always seems to have a positive effect; it spurs activity and interest, as is the case here.

The card market is soft overall, but some areas are stronger than others.

The weakest areas (for all cards, from tobaccos to Topps) lie between the grades of Very Good to EX-MT.

One of the reasons for the weakness of EX-MT material is that the price guides do not reflect this softening.

While a Babe Ruth Goudey would easily sell for $4,000 in the Near Mint/Mint grade, the EX-MT card which catalogues at $3,000 is realistically saleable at $1,500 to $2,000.

And dealers or collectors may hold out, not out of stubbornness or greed, but ignorance.

Prices of high quality cards in Near Mint or better condition remains strong. As always, the stuff sells when priced reasonably.

Dealers with inflated prices looking for "investors" boast heavy inventories, low turnover and no cash flow.

However, finds of truly rare and exotic material, as usual, will move faster than Rickey Henderson on the basepaths.

As for the pantheon material such as the T206 Honus Wagner, 1933 Goudey Nap Lajoie and the 1952 Topps Mickey Mantle, these cards sell in any grade, on any day of the year. If priced fairly.

As for lesser grade material (less than VG), the core collector is looking for "types," and this area will always be strong. Just ask Phil Spector.

As for the new stuff, there is such a perverse proliferation of brand new material coming out on a seemingly daily basis. The market can't and will not absorb it all.

Companies such as Upper Deck, who monitor and limit quantity and make quality an obsession, will be here to stay. Topps is such a giant — with a distribution system to match — that it has about as much a chance of getting pushed out as McDonald's.

As for the rest, time will only tell.

Overall, the memorabilia market is twice as strong as cards. Some areas are weaker than six to 12 months ago, but still sell when buyer meets seller without a large club with a nail sticking out of the end of it.

However, certain fields are red hot.

Press pins are still cold, but are making a bit of a comeback (a slight twitch).

I wish the person who writes the Tuff Stuff Price Guide was one of my customers. Pins are selling for one-half to two-thirds of that guide.

Autographed baseballs have enjoyed one of the greatest runs since Jesse Owens in 1932 Berlin. However, they have slowed down quite a bit, and in the previous few months were selling for about half of their previous levels.

The fat of the market — Jackie Robinson Brooklyn Dodger team baseballs, rare single signature and Babe Ruth baseballs — were the hardest hit.

All have since rebounded, as the educated dealers have lowered their prices. This is the best thing that could have happened.

Areas that show tremendous interest include stadium artifacts such as seats and signs (Comiskey Park's headlines didn't hurt), signed photographs of Hall of Famers, championship rings and trophies, and anything that's truly beautiful or historically important.

But the area of the 1990s will be flannel uniforms. Several collectors and dealers have prepared for this eventuality.

A few have entered into my $100,000 Club with the purchase or trade of Babe Ruth and Lou Gehrig jerseys in the $100,000 range and Joe DiMaggio, Mickey Mantle and Ty Cobb flannels in the $50,00-75,000 range.

But almost all are dealers (with collectors hearts) speculating, not collecting. This may prove interesting, if not rewarding.

Bats, especially those signed, were the place to be in 1990, the Studio 54 of sports memorabilia. The 500 Home Run Club is the one to join; signed bats are king.

Because Mantle and DiMaggio refuse to sign and many other Hall of Famers are threatening not to, asking more to sign, and sometimes not signing at all, hobbyists speculate that their bats will be the next banned rarity.

I don't know about the "new" collectibles, such as lithographs limited to one million, ugly statues that don't look anything like who they're supposed to be, signed bats from the reunion of the 1952 Pirates (possibly the worst team ever), and overpriced limited-edition

photographs of Van Lingo Mungo (where the negative has been sealed in a mayonnaise jar and #1 was sent directly to Cooperstown's basement). I don't care, either.

Overall, the better memorabilia is on fire. After a disastrous summer, collectors have returned to their senses and have again realized that this stuff is truly rare.

I don't mean rare like old baseball cards of which there are thousands. I mean rare like there are only two, or three!

The investor market is nearly dead. Like scared rabbits, investors have left at the first sign of softening. As always, the core collector is here to stay; those who truly love the stuff will always be here.

But a word of advice — these are the best times to collect. The worst investment is what your neighbor calls a "good investment." The best investment is what everyone else says is a "bad investment."

Ty Cobb may have not only bought Coca-Cola if he were around today; he may have been buying his own autograph. — Joshua Leland Evans, Balls in the Attic, Dec. 28, 1990,

* * *

Rose Book Is Fascinating, But Didn't Make Me Feel Proud

By Jim Hawkins

I've read a few sports books in my life. A few hundred would be more accurate.

I've also authored a couple. So I think I know most of the tricks of the trade.

But frankly, at the risk of sounding jaundiced, I find most sports books bor-r-r-ring.

More often than not, unfortunately, sports books represent the hasty efforts of sports writers who happen to also own tape recorders and have their share of bills to pay.

At the risk of revealing a precious trade secret, the "wannabe" author collects all of the old newspaper clippings he can find on a particular subject and spreads them out, end-to-end, across the nearest bed.

To update his story, he sits down with his subject and records as many clever quotes and as much additional information as he can coax in a single session.

Put the bedspread information together with the insight gleaned from those cassettes, and presto: you have a sports book!

That, I'm happy to report, was definitely not the technique used by Michael Sokolove when he produced "HUSTLE, The Myth, Life and Lies of Pete Rose" (Simon & Schuster Inc., $19.95).

It is undoubtedly the best thing written to date about the whole, sorry, sordid Pete Rose affair. It's a must read for anyone who cares at all about baseball, Pete Rose — or this hobby.

However, as a public service to those dealers and collectors who steadfastly refuse to read anything more informative than a price guide, I would like to tell you what Sokolove has to say about Rose, as well as our chosen profession.

A word of warning: You're not going to like it.

On his personal impression of this industry, Sokolove writes:

"Even outside of Rose's involvement in it, 'the hobby,' as memorabilia dealers sometimes refer to their industry, is rife with counterfeiting, fraud, forged autographs, and theft. Without overstating the case, it is a cesspool."

That's us he's talking about, you know — you and me. I don't know about you, but I don't particularly appreciate it.

And yet, while Sokolove may certainly be guilty of overstating his case, there definitely is no denying what he says is, at least to some degree, true.

Sokolove goes into great detail about Rose's life and lifestyle, in an effort to illustrate where — and hopefully explain why — Rose went wrong.

It is all interesting reading — especially when he elaborates on Rose's relationship with this industry. Without giving away the plot, let me tell you Sokolove affixes much of the blame for Rose's fall from grace on our business.

"With its low standards for honesty and fair dealing, and its cast of shady characters," writes Sokolove, "the memorabilia business was a natural for Rose, and he dove into it headfirst.

"He was one of the most frequent signers at autograph shows. Blessed with a first and last name that stretched only eight letters, he could scribble better than six-hundred 'Pete Roses' in an hour (never pausing to look at, let alone talk to, the autograph-seekers) and for a couple of hours' work it wasn't unusual for him to be paid $20,000 by the promoter.

"He also sold, as has been widely reported, many of the items connected with his record-breaking hits. Whatever sentiment he had for them was washed over by his thirst to raise money to pay debts and keep gambling.

"Rose, in pleading guilty to federal tax charges on April 20, 1990, admitted to failing to report $348,720 in earnings from baseball card shows and memorabilia sales in the four year period between 1984 and 1987.

"That was not the total of his memorabilia-related income; there were hundreds of thousands of dollars more that he did report and pay taxes on — as well as the possiblity that there was more unreported cash the government did not discover."

I realize, to those who have kept abreast of the Rose scandal, none of the above is particularly new or terribly shocking — although it certainly does make this hobby, at best, look like an unwitting accomplice.

"Rose's main connection to the memorabilia industry," Sokolove continues, "was Mike Bertolini, whom he first met in 1985 when Bertolini was sent to Florida by his employer at a Brooklyn card shop to line Rose up for an autograph show.

"Bertolini was nineteen at the time: he succeeded in signing Rose for a show at a Brooklyn grammar school, which he had attended on the morning before a Reds-Mets game.

"Within a year, Rose had taken him into his entourage, Bertolini became a merchandiser of autographed Pete Rose baseballs, bats, uniform jerseys, and photographs, and, with Rose's name behind him, a major promoter of autograph shows featuring such big names as Joe DiMaggio, Ted Williams, Willie Mays, and Mickey Mantle.

"Baseball's investigators tacked an extraordinary flow of money from Rose to Bertolini. In 1986, Rose wrote twenty-one separate $8,000 checks, for a total of $168,000.

"Government regulations require banks to file currency reports on transactions of $10,000 or more. The checks were made out to ficticious names, but Bertolini was able to get them cashed at a newsstand in the garment district in Manhattan.

(Rose seemed to have written any name that came into his head. One of the checks was made out to "Herbie Lee," which was Rose's nickname for Mike Schmidt.)

"In addition, between 1987 and 1989, Rose either cosigned or took out loans for Bertolini totaling $218,000. He also regularly sent him undetermined amounts of cash, usually via Federal Express.

"The Dowd Report concluded that Rose was using Bertolini as a conduit to place bets through New York bookmakers, and that the money funneled to him went toward Rose's gambling debts.

"Rose denied this. He said the cash was to finance Bertolini's card shows, to pay players and explayers up front for their appearances, and to rent halls."

I have no desire, nor do I feel qualified, to pass judgment on the veracity of Sokolove's research or his conclusions. Suffice to say, however, it is obvious throughout the book that Sokolove did his homework.

As I said, I found the book fascinating, and I highly recommend it.

It did not, however, make me feel particularly proud. — Jim Hawkins, Eye of the Hawk, April 12, 1991

* * *

It's Not As Easy Being Congenial When Big Money Is On The Line

By Ted Taylor

One of the major selling points of the Professional Golfers' Association's senior tour has always been the opportunity to mix nostalgia with some pretty good stuff.

Over the years the lure of the tour has generated considerable spectator and sponsor interest. As a result of all that interest, the so-called old-timers are now playing for some pretty healthy dollars.

Philadelphia, without a regular PGA Tour stop since 1981, has taken the annual Bell Atlantic Classic Senior Tour event to heart over the past seven years.

An estimated crowd of close to 90,000 people jammed the sprawling White Manor Country Club Grounds in Malvern, Pa., the last weekend in May.

Arnold Palmer as usual charmed the socks off the populace. He had his regular army of followers despite a distant finish from the top of the money heap.

Chi Chi Rodriguez, another Senior Tour favorite, conducted his usual kids clinic before the event. He spent the weekend being gracious and friendly to the paying customers.

And then there was Lee Trevino.

Trevino has made a lot of money on the Senior Tour. He is a very popular player among golf's followers.

He's found new life playing with the over-50 set. But during the weekend of the Bell Atlantic Classic a new darker side of Trevino's personality came into focus.

Trevino candidly turned nasty. He ripped his longtime caddie "Herman" in the national media for giving him the wrong club.

He also spent the entire time on the practice greens and on the fairways in a total funk.

A longtime also-ran in his last years on the PGA Tour, Trevino has been a dominant player on the Senior track. But it seems like he's only happy now if he's in first place. And he was never there at White Manor.

Trevino was in the hunt the whole way but never got any closer than two strokes of the eventual winner, the classy Jim Ferree.

When the tournament was over, Trevino, who played with Ferree on the final day, was not evident at the press tent or anywhere else the press was likely to encounter him.

I've been around professional golf for the past five years. This is a new side of Lee Trevino; it isn't the product the Senior Tour is trying to sell.

Everyone is entitled to an off-day or two. It is hoped that that's what was happening to Trevino.

However, the seniors are now playing for big dollars — the Bell Atlantic was worth $88,000 to the winner. It's not quite as easy to be congenial when big money is on the line.

In direct contrast to "Super Mex" Trevino, most of the seniors were congenial and willing to sign autographs at a specially-prepared booth near the 18th hole. A popular vehicle for the autographs was the new Pro Set golf cards which were selling for $10 per set of 100 cards.

In addition, smaller sets of 25 Senior Tour players were also available to fans entering the grounds.

When I saw a woman get Arnold Palmer's autograph on a Pro Set card I thought she was going to faint dead away.

Arnold is the consummate superstar. It really doesn't matter that his game is not what it once was; if he's in your tournament you're going to be successful.

A professional golf event is unlike any other spectator sport because to get the feel of the action you have to move around the course with the players.

If you've never been to a tournament you really owe it to yourself to do so. There's no other pro sport where you can be so close to the action that you're almost a part of it.

Mary Ann Saleski, the executive director of the event, and her staff (including 1,100 volunteers) go out of their way to make the fans' enjoyment a top priority, so it's even more of a tragedy when a pro such as Lee Trevino gives the event and the game of golf a black eye.
— Ted Taylor, Off the Cuff, June 21, 1991

* * *

Why Are The Lines So Long?, The Alien Asked

By Dick Gilkeson

As our saucer passed over the Anaheim Convention Center on the evening of July 2 we noticed a couple of very long lines of human beings waiting to enter.

We decided to see what was going on, so we put on our best human being disguises and headed toward the lines.

As we approached, a young fellow came over and asked if we needed some identification. Naturally, we said "yes" so he offered to sell us a photocopy of a document called a "business license" for $20.

He told us we would need it to get in.

We quickly bought it and went to the back of about a 6,000 person-long line which extended back into the parking garage and then wound back on itself again.

As we stood in line, we asked why all the people were there. Someone answered that this was the National Baseball Card Convention Trade Show Night.

We had flown over baseball parks before, so we knew a little about what baseball was. But we didn't know exactly what these cards were.

"Could you show us a few cards?" we asked. But the young fellow told us that people were there to get them; it was unlikely that anyone had brought any.

When we asked why the line was so long, he said it was because the people inside were giving away free cards which a newspaper ad said might be worth $100.

He wondered why we didn't know. We said that we were new in town and didn't know much about baseball.

He shook his head at us in amazement.

Why are the lines so long?, the alien asked.

When we heard that the doors opened at 4 p.m. we wondered why the line wasn't moving much. Others told us they were only letting a few people in at a time.

By 6 p.m. we were close enough to the main door so we could see that they were not letting anyone in. Shortly thereafter, we were told that they were trying to get everyone who was inside to come out; but few people came out.

About a half hour later, one guy came by us and said it was a "zoo" inside. The people in charge were pushing people toward the exits because they wouldn't leave.

We figured there must be something awfully valuable inside, but no one had mentioned wild animals.

After another half hour, some people from a company called Upper Deck came outside and started distributing little photographs to the steady droves of people who were finally leaving.

We asked to look at the photos to see why they were apparently so valuable and were told that they were Montana and Sanders promo cards worth $50.

We had taken plenty of photographs from our saucer — even some of Montana as we flew over the state — and began to wonder if we had something really valuable on the ship.

When asked why they were so valuable, a young woman said it was because there weren't many of them made, compared to the millions of cards printed with each baseball player's face on them.

We started feeling really good at this point. After all, we only had one copy of each photo card of Earth that we had taken in the saucer.

"What else are people here for?" we asked.

Several people began to look at us strangely, but told us we could meet the people who ran the various companies sponsoring the show.

But most of the people were there strictly to "load up on the promos."

At about 7 p.m. the line started moving toward the doors. We were thankful because nature was calling (yes, aliens need to go, too), and no porta-potties had been set up outside.

However, just as we got close to the main doors, several police officers quickly closed them, announcing that the fire marshall would not allow running in the building.

We asked why people were running and were told that it was to avoid being in the back of the long lines.

"You mean there are more lines like this inside?" we asked.

"Of course. What do you think?" was the answer.

120

By now the line we were in had become a mob, all pressing against the doors. Several people who had exited had simply turned around and were now trying to get back in.

Finally, after several threats, from people with official looking badges, about the fire marshall being upset, we got in. The story we got was accurate.

There were more long lines inside.

"Which line is Upper Deck?" "Which line is for Pro Set? And are they giving away anything good?"

"Where'd you get that card?"

"Isn't Fleer giving any cards away?"

"Have you seen the Score border design?"

Everyone wanted answers to these questions and other similar ones.

We stood in line, and about 25 minutes later we had a "Sanders" and a "Montana." Clearly, both were not of the states we visited.

We wondered if they would have any value back on Ork. We doubted that they would, since they seemed to be made strictly of cardboard.

One card was supposed to have gold in it, but ours were paper only. At any rate, we just followed the people who were ahead of us to another line, and then another.

By 7:50 p.m. when they told us we had to leave we had a small stack of "promos." Just as we got outside a fellow approached us and asked us what we had.

When we showed him, he said he'd give us $50 for all of it. When we said "no" he said he'd make it $100.

He seemed to want them so badly that we decided to part with them. After all, they had no gold in them.

He quickly peeled off a $100 bill, grabbed the cards, and sped off to another couple nearby.

"So that's what a trade show is all about," we mused. "All this fuss over a few pieces of worthless cardboard.

"These Earth people are much stranger than we ever predicted. With these kind of strange value systems we don't have to worry about being challenged in space for a long, long time."

(Our alien friends also went to the show. If we can interpret their next message regarding the show itself, we'll print it in a future article.) — Dick Gilkeson, Aug. 2, 1991

* * *

Confessions Of A Baseball Show Brat Packer

By Suzanne Wimmer

Editor's note: Robert "Red" Wimmer is on vacation. His daughter, Suzanne, replaces him this week as she reflects on her days as a "show brat."

Years ago, you hated me.

I was the kid who pushed all the elevator buttons at the 1984 National in Chicago.

I also was involved in the infamous ice machine riot of 1983 — along with Kim and Amber Ockomon, Angela Hubbel, Jeff and Scott Maxwell, and my sister, Amy — at the annual Cincinnati show.

And I was the one who rollerskated down the aisles of the first and second annual Dearborn, Mich., Sports Collectors Convention.

Yes, it's true. I am a member of the original baseball card brat pack.

My name is Suzanne Wimmer. You might remember me as Suzy or Sue or, as Jim Hawkins called me — "madam queen."

And, boy, was I annoying.

I extorted money from my father, Robert "Red" Wimmer (of hockey fights video cassettes and Olympia Brick plaques fame), by pocketing half of the money I received working at his table. I conned Ed Budnick into giving me free baseball cards, and I often could be found with fellow brat packer Jill Wallace singing showtunes over the loudspeaker at a plethora of sports collecting events.

Remember me now?

But please forgive me — I knew not what I was doing. In fact, I was probably having a better time than you were.

When Al Kaline was inducted into the Baseball Hall of Fame, in Cooperstown, N.Y., you were sitting in on countless ceremonies, autograph sessions and looking at pictures of "Shoeless" Joe Jackson.

I was cruising the main drag, eating ice cream and switching the signs at our hotel from "No Vacancy" to "Vacancy." To a 10-year-old, that's utopia.

But my adventures became more daring. At the 1982 Plymouth Show, I perfected my shampoo-swiping skills (I still have quite a stash of Hilton memorabilia). And at the 1986 Texas National, I learned how to sneak into the hotel bar.

Granted, it was just dad and me at the event, making every wrongdoing not only fun, but easy.

Rob Lipset and I could be found any night of that show at approximately 10 p.m. in the bar dancing or drinking margaritas.

We could be seen at 10:45 p.m. being kicked out of the establishment (I was only 15 and he was 18), and then at 11:15 p.m. back in the place, this time in different shirts and drinking pina coladas instead.

We were such rebels.

There was a whole gang of baseball card show groupies who terrorized the circuit from 1982 to our retirement in about 1988.

We came from all over the country, including Michigan (the "wild Wallaces," Angela "hellraiser" Hubbel, my sister and me, the "wacky" Wimmers), Indiana (the "out-of-control" Ockomons), and New York (Rob "the rebel" Lipset), just to name a few. And nobody could escape us.

Those were the days when kids did more than just hang out at the "free gum" table. Today's sports collecting offspring just can't compare. They have no guts.

Here I am, 21 years old, yet rarely do any little convention rugrats annoy me. They're calm. They sit behind their parents' table, obediently arranging cards or giving change.

It's been years since I was pegged with an ice cube because I was caught in the crossfire of a boys vs. girls battle.

I can't remember the last time I had to stop on 15 floors to get to my room because the buttons were all pressed.

And I couldn't tell you the last time some kid tried to talk me into giving away "really cool" Mork and Mindy cards because they didn't have any money.

I feel a little sorry that I was the subject of so much scorn during my youth, but I don't regret it. It was my job as a baseball card brat packer.

The sad thing is, nobody continued the tradition.

This is my call to all the little ones who really believe they have to work their parents' tables — you're too young to conform.

Come talk to me sometime. I'll teach you the ropes, and then I'll hide you when hotel security tries to hunt you down.

Sorry parents, I may be too old to be a juvenile delinquent, but I'm too young to enjoy a quiet card show. — Suzanne Wimmer, Point Shot, March 20, 1992

* * *

Brightening A Child's Day
Schulkes Donates Cards
To Leukemia-Stricken Patients

By Tom Hultman

James Schulkes never thought a spring training baseball game would change his life.

But, somehow, someway it did.

In 1989, Schulkes, who lived in New York at the time, was thinking about moving to Florida.

He visited Port St. Lucie, Fla., to check out the area for possible homes. While he was catching a few rays, he decided to take in a New York Mets exhibition game.

The rest is history.

At the game, veteran catcher and the Leukemia Society's National Sports Chairman Gary Carter was receiving a check from a local television station on behalf of the charity.

Impressed with Carter's dedication to helping victims of leukemia and related diseases, Schulkes was determined to find a way to help the Society.

The solution was easy. He was a collector of baseball cards since 1986 and had thousands of baseball cards in his closet at home.

"I was inspired with all the work Gary Carter does for the Leukemia Society," Schulkes said. "When I got back to New York and I thought there was something I could do to help the Society."

Since that day in 1989, Schulkes has donated more than 150,000 cards — cards he purchased out of his own pocket — as gifts for leukemia patients across the United States.

"What I do is I have been prospecting on certain new releases, and I break down the boxes and sell the expensive cards to come close to breaking even on what I laid out," he said. "I donate the rest of the cards.

"Every year I have donated at least 25,000 cards."

Schulkes' efforts did not go without notice.

Last November, the Leukemia Society of America honored Schulkes with a Special Recognition Award, which was created to honor individuals or organizations who have significantly supported the Society's national programs.

"That was the epitome of everything," he said. "It really didn't sink in how much of an effect this is having on the kids until I got that award.

"It made me realize what good this is really doing. I would like to see other dealers and other collectors get involved with this too.

"I always see all these letters (in magazines) saying collectors have all these extra commons that they don't know what to do with. I want to get other people involved and see if they can donate the cards as well."

In addition, the Mets organized a presentation before a 1989 game where the 25-year-old would present Carter and the Leukemia Society with a collection of cards.

"We did the presentation on the field. I met Gary Carter and got some autographs from him," he said. "Ever since, I see Gary at least once a year. He does a charity golf tournament here in southeast Florida.

"I volunteer and help them out so I get to see him every year."

According to Schulkes, Carter is one of the nicest men around.

"He is the most genuine person that I have ever met in my life," he said. "He is an absolutely wonderful person. He always has a smile on his face no matter what is going on in his personal life or in his career.

"No matter what type of mood you are in, he brightens up the entire room."

And the idea of helping out children has brightened up Schulkes' life.

"I think it is great," he said. "I put one set of each away for my kids one day. I think the kids in the hospital need something to get their minds off of things. I think this is a good way to start.

"Baseball cards is an engulfing hobby, as most people know. Once you get involved it takes up much of your spare time."

Schulkes, who is an EKG technician at a local hospital, said the cards are distributed by the Leukemia Society. He boxes the cards, sends them to the Society's National office in New York, which in turn ships them to hospitals around the nation.

"I personally have never been able to hear from anyone, but there have been numerous letters sent to the office in New York," he said.

"The children and parents think this is fantastic because the kids have nothing but time on their hands when they are in the hospital. They need something to keep them occupied."

Before 1991, Schulkes let the Leukemia Society decide how many cards each child would receive.

Last year he packaged the cards in boxes of 100, and they kept the cards in the New York area at Mount Sinai Hospital.

This year he boxed the cards in 25-card team set bags, which allows the cards (1,000 packages) to be easily distributed across the country.

"The cards are usually sent around the country to the larger cancer hospitals," he said. "In 1990, when I moved to Florida, I got a couple of people involved — a dealer and a friend — and we came up with 100,000 cards for that one donation. Those definitely went all over the country."

Schulkes also has been randomly inserting autographed cards of 1991 No. 1 draft picks, including Aaron Sele, Brent Gales and other players.

"I've got 10 cards each autographed that I'm randomly going to stick in with the cards," he said. "The players were great. They are still in Single-A, and they are not hounded for autographs yet."

But don't get the idea that he has given all his cards away. Schulkes said he has set aside plenty of cards for his children — when he and his wife, Ann, decide it's time.

"Now that I'm a collector, I think it would be great to give my kids cards 10 or 15 years from now," he said. "Unfortunately, my parents didn't save any of their cards. Down the road, getting older cards is more of an addiction than the newer cards.

"I'm saving the cards for my kids. Hopefully, they'll be collectors one day, too."

As for the future, Schulkes said he will continue to donate cards each year.

"Every year is guaranteed that I'm going to donate at least 25,000 cards," he said. "This year there will be less cards, but they will be Topps Stadium Club and Fleer Ultra, all the good stuff.

"The Leukemia Society has been fantastic," he said. "I just wanted to donate the cards and get a couple of autographs from Gary Carter. That was the only intent."

"(Assistant Director of Public Relations for the Leukemia Society) Marty Siederer called me and asked if I would mind a little publicity. I said, 'No problem.' WFAN radio in New York called me that night and did an interview with me on the phone. I was a nervous wreck.

"I had no idea there would be any publicity like this. I thought I'd be in a small picture in the Leukemia Society newsletter. Then, WWOR-TV in New York called me for an interview. I was also interviewed in a feature article in the New York Daily News and the New York Post."

You could say this whole recognition thing caught him by surprise...big time.

"They made such a big thing out of it," he said. "It was absolutely amazing. Since I have been to the Gary Carter golf tournament every year. I have been to the Foot Locker SlamFest. Ken Griffey Jr. was there two years ago and I met him, and Dave Justice and Barry Sanders. It was unbelievable.

"When you work with the charities you get an awful lot in return without even asking for it. I had no idea this was in store for me. It has been wonderful." — Tom Hultman, Two-Minute Warning, Oct. 2, 1992

* * *

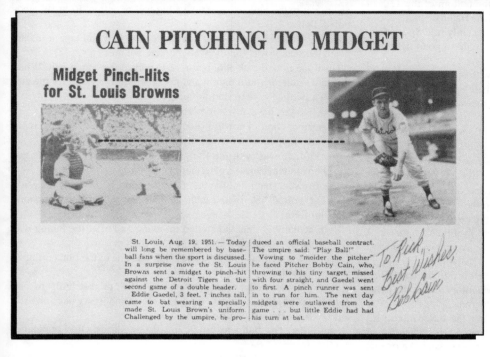

CAIN PITCHING TO MIDGET

Midget Pinch-Hits for St. Louis Browns

St. Louis, Aug. 19, 1951. — Today will long be remembered by baseball fans when the sport is discussed. In a surprise move the St. Louis Browns sent a midget to pinch-hit against the Detroit Tigers in the second game of a double header.

Eddie Gaedel, 3 feet, 7 inches tall, came to bat wearing a specially made St. Louis Brown's uniform. Challenged by the umpire, he produced an official baseball contract. The umpire said: "Play Ball!"

Vowing to "moider the pitcher" he faced Pitcher Bobby Cain, who, throwing to his tiny target, missed with four straight, and Gaedel went to first. A pinch runner was sent in to run for him. The next day midgets were outlawed from the game . . . but little Eddie had had his turn at bat.

To Rick, Best Wishes, Bob Cain

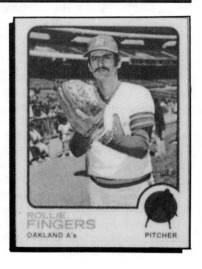

ROLLIE FINGERS
OAKLAND A's   PITCHER

Bob Cain was noted for pitching to midget Eddie Gaedel, while Rollie Fingers was noted for his handlebar mustache.

What's missing on these Topps cards: 1969, #597; 1970, #502; 1971, #384; and 1972, #241? Don't they look a little bare?

Although he was pictured on these four cards, his trademark didn't appear on a card until 1973. Rollie Fingers, in Rich Marazzi's Nov. 12, 1992, Batting the Breeze column, explains how his famous handlebar mustache came about:

"I grew it in spring training in 1972. Reggie (Jackson) came to spring training with a mustache and wouldn't shave it off. So myself, Catfish (Hunter), Darold Knowles and Bob Locker decided to start growing mustaches. We figured if we grew them, Dick Williams, the manager, would tell us to cut them off and Reggie would have to cut his off.

"Then they (management) got wind of what we were doing and decided to have a promotional mustache day on Opening Day. Finley told all the players that if they wear mustaches on Opening Day, we'll each get $300. So for $300 I would have grown one on my hind end considering I was making about $10,000 a year then."

Every player has an anecdote or two such as Fingers does about doing something we've all dreamed about — starring in the big leagues. But if Academy Award nominee Ray Kinsella could create another ball field on a farm in Iowa, who would be the players' choices for that Field of Dreams?

In his Oct. 18, 1991, Batting the Breeze, column, Marazzi provided a variety of players' responses to the question "Who would you like to see walk out of that corn patch if you were standing on Kinsella's farm field?"

Chicago Cubs' first baseman Mark Grace wanted to see Babe Ruth return and take a few cuts. "He's the guy that ever since you're young you hear he was the greatest player to ever play the game," Grace told Marazzi.

Did all-time strikeout king Nolan Ryan select another pitching great, such as Walter Johnson, or maybe Bob Feller? Nope. "Ted Williams," he emphatically answered.

How about pitcher Jim Kaat? Who would he pick? A horse. Secretariat, the gallant Kentucky Derby winner. "I think he was a great athlete, and if I wasn't a ballplayer I would want to ride him," Kaat told Marazzi.

Outfielder Ron Kittle chose Raquel Welch. "Our property looks just like that farm (Kinsella's). I look every day but she never comes out," he said.

Several players, including Kent Hrbek, Alvaro Espinoza, Brett Butler and Dave Gallagher, all answered "My Dad," as tributes to their deceased fathers.

Like any other poll, some people weren't serious with their answers. Chapter 5 offers a bit of the jocular, wry humor ballplayers exude, such as several tongue-in-cheek responses Marazzi received to his question.

Said baseball comedian Bob Uecker, "If I saw somebody come walk out of a corn patch, I'd probably run away."

Joked Giants announcer Hank Greenwalk, "I guess the guy you'd most expect to see come out of the cornfield is Cobb."

And, added Mickey McDermott, the eccentric southpaw of the 1950s, "My mother-in-law with my money."

Chapter 5 also recaps some of baseball's historic moments, in the words of the players who were there, such Bob Cain's thoughts on facing a midget, Eddie Gaedel; to Johnny Callison's reaction when the Phillies lost 10 in a row down the stretch to lose the National League pennant to the St. Louis Cardinals in 1964; to who's shoes Hank Aaron was wearing when he hit either home run #714 or #715.

Joe Adcock

A cursory glance of Joe Adcock's season totals from 1959 will show that he knocked in 76 runs for the Milwaukee Braves.

But that's the trouble with cursory glances of figures on a page — they tell little about the human drama behind those numbers.

For in Joe Adcock's case, one of those 76 runs batted in, one that came early in the season for the Braves' slugging first baseman-outfielder, beat the Pirates' Harvey Haddix in the bottom of the 13th of what for 12 innings had been a perfect game for Haddix.

"I was determined to break it up," Adcock recently told Sports Collectors Digest. "I said to my teammates, 'I'm fixin' to go to right field and break up this ball game.'

"Haddix had stayed on that outside corner with me all night long. He struck me out twice and I hadn't hit the ball out of the infield. I thought to myself that one of the first two pitches would be away from me. Sure enough, the second pitch he threw I hit, and hit hard to the opposite field, and it went over. I was just goin' for a single, really."

Ironically, that's about all that Adcock was credited with by National League President Warren Giles the next day, even though the ball fell just beyond the outfield fence for what looked like a home run.

There was one out with Felix Mantilla on second and Hank Aaron on first when Adcock stepped to the plate in the bottom of the 13th. (Mantilla, who had reached base on a throwing error by Pirates' third baseman Don Hoak, was sacrificed to second by Eddie Mathews. A double play was in order, and Haddix gave Aaron an intentional walk.)

Aaron, apparently thinking Adcock's liner fell inside the fence for a base hit and that the game was over when Mantilla crossed the plate, touched second and headed for the Braves' dugout.

With his head down, Adcock was travelling the basepaths in his home run trot. He passed second base and neared third when it was made apparent to him what had happened. Moments later, Aaron and Adcock tried to retrace their steps, but it was too late.

Giles therefore ruled that Adcock was entitled only to a double and that the extra-inning drama ended when Mantilla touched the plate. The final score would stand at 1-0.

So, when you look at Joe Adcock's season totals for 1959, know that but for a baserunning mix-up, he might have had 26 homers, not 25. But know too, that one of those 76 ribbies of his broke up what is considered to be one of the greatest pitching performances to grace the National Pastime. — David Craft, July 1, 1988

* * *

Johnny Antonelli

Having Willie Mays as a center fielder was a definite asset, Antonelli says. "When Willie Mays would tap his glove you knew he was going to catch the ball and if you see the highlights (of Mays' catch of Vic Wertz's 460-foot drive at the Polo Grounds in the '54 Series), you can see that when Willie is running back, he is tapping his glove with the ball squarely in sight." — Fluffy Saccucci, Oct. 13, 1989

* * *

Jerry Augustine

SCD: Who were the tricksters out in the bullpen?

Augustine: Charlie Moore was a classic. Charlie was in the bullpen before he became an outfielder.

Ned Yost. Pete Ladd. Bobby Galasso. Billy Castro. Eddie Rodriguez. I could go on and on. Rollie Fingers. Pete Broberg. Eddie Sprague.

SCD: All of those guys were characters.

Augustine: Well, at some time or another, everybody pulls a prank. I think the biggest trickster was Charlie Moore.

We had a lot of fun with Charlie. He was always doing something.

SCD: Could you give us an example?

Augustine: Well, in baseball, you always talk about the hotfoot. Charlie was well-known as a hotfoot expert.

But we tried to do what is known as the hot seat. We had the folding chairs out in the bullpen. You take a big ball of cotton. Rubbing alcohol. A lighter.

During batting practice, you take the cotton ball and tape it underneath the seat. It was Charlie who did that, not me!

Then you took the alcohol bottle and sprayed the cotton ball. When the game started, you'd light it and just sit around and wait for the guy who was sitting there to start jumping (laughs).

SCD: Do you have any stories about the opposing bullpens?

Augustine: I don't know if I should even tell it...but we were playing the Texas Rangers on a Sunday afternoon.

Sparky Lyle was with the Rangers, along with...Jim Kern. We got the phone number for the other bullpen.

The Brewers started a little bit of a rally, and Charlie said, "Hey, it's time for action!" He dialed their number and yelled into the phone "Get up Kern!"

Kern actually got up and started throwing and after the inning was over, Charlie dialed again and mumbled "Sit him down."

We had a good time with that one. That was one of the funnier things that happened.

SCD: We remember from reading in Ball Four that bullpens can sometimes be strange places. We heard Moe Drabowsky once ordered a pizza from Hong Kong from a bullpen.

Augustine: Yes, bullpens can be interesting places. Oh, I remember another one!

One time, we're playing on national television, and there was a beach ball going crazy out there in the outfield. The phone rang in our bullpen, and the caller was Ray Sadecki, our former teammate.

He was at home watching us on TV! He called the bullpen and we answered and said, "Ray, how are you? Where are you? Are you in the clubhouse?"

It was really funny. He said, "No, I'm at home. Get that beach ball off the field. I'm watching you guys on TV!"

He called County Stadium and somehow was able to get through to the bullpen phone. That was pretty neat.

SCD: Speaking of County Stadium, what do you think of their bratwurst?

Augustine: Best in the world!

SCD: Did you guys ever eat brats in the bullpen?

Augustine: I'd be a liar if I said we didn't (laughs).

SCD: Do you have any stories about "Mr. Baseball" — Bob Uecker?

Augustine: Bob Uecker? Only that he's probably one of the funniest men I've ever known. I just have to see Bob Uecker personally and I start laughing.

There are stories upon stories about the guy. The man is just...to me...I laugh when I just see him. I see him driving by in the car and I start laughing.

He hits a funny note with me. And I like the guy, too. I really do. He is really a great guy.

SCD: Did you see the movie "Major League?" Bob Uecker had a big role in that.

(Uecker portrayed Cleveland Indians announcer Harry Doyle. Even though the film was about the Indians, many of the baseball scenes were shot at Milwaukee County Stadium which, technically speaking, played the role of Cleveland's Municipal Stadium.)

Augustine: Yes, I did. I went down to the stadium for one day's filming in the Yankee dugout. I'm in the movie three times. A lot of people don't know where the spots are, but I do.

SCD: We recall one scene where Pete Vuckovich almost charges out of the New York dugout after a beanball incident with Indian reliever/ex-con "Wild Thing" Vaughn (played by Charlie Sheen).

Augustine: Right! I'm standing there right next to Vukie in the dugout! Vukie had a great role, and Ueck was fantastic. Vukie was the Yankee first baseman.

SCD: Right, and Uecker had a hilarious line on Vuke's character (Yankee slugger Clu Haywood). He said he leads the league in nasal hair.

Then, Vuke puts one into orbit off "Wild Thing" and Ueck moans "That one's headed for South America. They'll need a visa to catch it. Wow, all that's left is a vapor trail."

Augustine: (Laughing) Yeah, Vuke had a great time. He's one of a kind. So's Ueck. — Tim Sullivan and Randy Wievel, May 17, 1991

* * *

Jack Baldschun

Jack Baldschun retired in 1971 with a lifetime log of 48-41, 60 saves, and a 3.70 ERA. Additionally, he established the National League record for most games pitched in relief with no starts, 457, which has since been broken by Kent Tekulve...

...SCD: Then tell us about your famous double.

Baldschun: Off of Barney Schultz! St. Louis knuckleballer. This was at Connie Mack Stadium in Philadelphia. (Note: throughout the interview, Baldschun equally referred to the Phillies' ballpark as either Connie Mack Stadium or Shibe Park.) Barney threw me a knuckler up in my eyes. I closed my eyes and swung as hard as I could and actually hit it! I think it was in '64. 1963 or 1964. I must've closed my eyes since I actually hit it. The ball hit off the left-center field wall. Not left! Left-center. Missed a homer by a foot!

SCD: Speaking of towering blasts, Hank Aaron ended up with 755 major league home runs. How many of those were yours?

Baldschun: One. I feel pretty proud of that. Actually it was his 257th home run, on May 2, 1962, in Connie Mack Stadium in Philadelphia. Some fan caught it in the grandstands...

...SCD: Who hit the longest home run off of you?

Baldschun: Gil Hodges. It was out at the L.A. coliseum. I made a mistake and threw him a high fastball just like I did with Aaron and he hit it a ton. That ball barely cleared the screen, a line drive, but it took out two rows of seats above the second exit! It was still climbing way the heck up there...

...SCD: Tell us about the '61 Phillies 23 game losing streak.

Baldschun: Oh, this is beautiful. Last year, a guy from the Baltimore Sun called me up in Green Bay. He said the Orioles were coming into Milwaukee with a chance to beat or tie the record for most consecutive losses from Opening Day. He said he looked in the record books for teams that had losing streaks like that and wanted to find out what it was like. He tried calling some of the guys from the Tigers and Washington Senators but couldn't get through since they were all dead.

So, the guy said he looked in the record books and found out that I was on the team that lost 23 in a row. Even though we didn't do it from the beginning of the season, we did do it in July and August and he wanted to know what it felt like.

SCD: What did it feel like? What did you tell him?

Baldschun: Well, this wasn't something I thought a lot about. I said I didn't feel very good about it or something like that. But a short time later, I suddenly had over two weeks of solid phone calls. Sports Illustrated called. Television stations. People came to the house. Every night when I'd come home I'd have five or six more calls.

SCD: Why was everybody just calling you?

Baldschun: Oh, they weren't. One guy called and said he just got done talking to my roommate Johnny Buzhardt. Another said he talked to my teammate Clay Dalrymple. I woke up one morning and decided I had to come up with an answer for these people. Finally, I told one guy: "Well, it's kind of like you come home from work and see your house burning. It's terrible, but what can you do about it? How would you feel?"

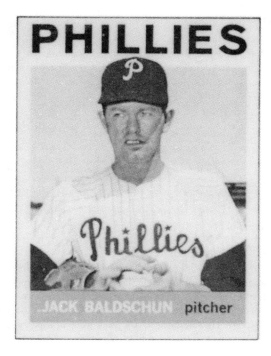

Jack Baldschun

SCD: OK, that handled the Orioles' losing streak last year, but what about the Phillies' streak when you were there? Wasn't there something about Mauch and his reverse curfew?

Baldschun: Yes. During the time we had this losing streak, Mauch tried everything possible to get it over with. We had early curfews. All kinds of things going on. Extra batting practice. No batting practice. Extra infield practice.

Well, we'd just got done playing in Chicago. We lost again and were coming into Milwaukee to play the Braves. We came in by bus at about 7 in the evening. Before we got off the bus, Mauch stood up and said, "OK guys, about the game tomorrow, the first thing is we'll have no batting practice. No infield, either. Just show up for the game. Put your uniforms on and come out to play."

SCD: That didn't sound too tough.

Baldschun: There's more. Then Mauch said, "Tonight, curfew will be 4:30 in the morning. If I catch anybody in their room before that time it's a $100 fine!"

Well, we couldn't believe this because everybody was so darn tired and all we wanted to do was grab a bite to eat and go to bed.

SCD: Did some of the players come in early?

Baldschun: Heck, no! We didn't know what to do all night so the whole team went across the street from the hotel to a little bar on the corner. A country and western bar. We all sat there in the booths drinking beer and waiting for two o'clock to come. Once two o'clock came, we walked back to the hotel and then saw an unbelievable sight! Ballplayers were laying all over the lobby! They were laying over chairs, tables, on the floor...everywhere! Nobody went to their room. Nobody could go to their room without getting fined! We went out and lost the game the next day anyhow.

SCD: So the streak continued?

Baldschun: Yup, and you know, I found out something else about that streak. Somebody else looked it up later. The only game I lost during that streak was the 20th game. Right after the 4:30 reverse curfew. We had the darn thing won but I lost it by letting Al Spangler hit a goldarn single up the middle.

SCD: You only lost one game during that streak? How many games did you win during that time?

Baldschun: How many did I win? Well, let me think...ah, you almost had me there! Pretty tricky, guys. Next question...it's your dime.

SCD: But the Phillies did snap the losing streak in Milwaukee.

Baldschun: (laughing) Yes. We flew back to Philadelphia and Frank Sullivan (a veteran pitcher who once claimed he was "in twilight of a mediocre career") started to get off the plane and said, "Let's not all get off at the same time so the fans can't get us all with one shot!" In other words, let's not walk in a single line...

...SCD: You mentioned Gene Mauch earlier. Tell us about the famous spareribs incident.

Baldschun: That was in '64. It was in Houston. We were winning the pennant and it was like, all of a sudden, everybody wanted to get into the visiting clubhouse to eat. We knew there was a spread there that was unbelievable. Houston's clubhouse man put out the best food in the league. It was like gourmet dining.

At any rate, we lost the ball game and everybody rushed into the clubhouse to eat. We got to the clubhouse and, sure enough, there was this fantastic spread out on the table. Mauch came storming in and took his arm and pushed everything off the table onto the floor and into the lockers. He screamed, "You jerks were in a hurry to get the game over with just to eat?? I'll teach you that you guys aren't going to eat tonight!"

Spareribs. Barbecued chicken. You name it, that food went flying everywhere. Afterwards, he calmed down and offered anybody whose suit was ruined $200. And, back then, it was $45 a suit. Wes Covington and Tony Gonzalez got new suits out of it...

...SCD: You faced so many great hitters in the National League. Did you ever get drilled on the mound?

Baldschun: Oh, too many times to count. I got hit so many times it's ridiculous. I'll tell you, when those balls come back at you, they're coming hard. You have everything you can do just to defend yourself. I had balls take my cap off, hit my ear...heck, I had one that hit me right in the chin. I was knocked out and stumbled towards third base. When I woke up, I was standing on first base! I said, "How in the world did I get here?"

I thought I had a broken jaw, but when I opened my mouth to see if it was broken, shoot, there was nothing wrong with it so I went back to the mound and pitched some more.

SCD: That seemed pretty scary. What was the strangest thing that ever happened to you on the mound?

Baldschun: I remember something that happened my last year in Philly. Mauch came up one day and said he wanted me to start throwing more fastballs. You know, save the screwball for my out pitch. Well, that was fine with me, but we both knew I didn't have a fastball. So, one time we're in Chicago and Ron Santo's up there. Mauch comes out and tells me to throw him all fastballs.

The count went 3 and 2. All fastballs. I was working him inside and out trying to strike him out. If I could've thrown my screwball I'd have had him long ago. The sixth one was a fastball on the outside corner. He was surprised. Probably looking for a screwball. He took it out of the catcher's glove and lined a triple into right field. See, it just wasn't fast enough to get it by him.

Right after that, Mauch came out to the mound to take me out. I said fine and I told him that was the last time he'd ever come out and tell me how to pitch. Send me to the minors, anything, but don't tell me what to throw.

I got traded to Baltimore not long after that...

...SCD: We covered the pitching aspect of your career but we also heard rumors that you had an unusual stolen base during your career. What happened?

Baldschun: OK. This wasn't the same game that I hit my double. Got that. A different game. Well, I was on second base against the Giants. You've got to remember that I didn't get that far very often. Anyway, I'm on second base, and there's two outs and Cookie Rojas is the batter. Cookie has a full count on him. Nobody's on first...I'm just out there on second. Full count on Rojas.

Now, all I remembered from my younger days about baserunning was that if there's a full count on the batter and two out, you're going on the next pitch.

So, the pitch came in and Cookie took a half swing. Tom Haller was the catcher, and he caught the ball and started heading for his dugout thinking Cookie had struck out when in reality it was ball four. At the same time, I put my head down and started racing for third, conveniently forgetting first base was open.

I was halfway to third base and everybody was yelling "What in the hell is happening?" George Myatt was our coach at third and he threw his arms up and screamed, "Hit the deck! For Chrissakes, hit it!" The Giants were yelling to Haller "You dummy, the guy's stealing third. Throw it!"

Well, Haller finally threw the ball and Myatt's still screaming "Get down!" Heck, I was already to third so I simply sat on the base. Anyhow, that was my stolen base in the majors. I never scored from there, either. Got stranded.

SCD: Did they stop the game and give you the base?

Baldschun: Heck no. — Tim Sullivan, Randy Wievel and Archie Hansen, May 5, 1989

* * *

Yogi Berra

One Yankee official claims that he telephoned Yogi early one morning: "Yogi, did I get you out of bed?" he asked.

"No, I had to get up to answer the phone anyway," Yogi said. — Mark McDowell, June 19, 1987

* * *

Jim Bouton

An important day in those formative years for the youngster unfolded when he was playing out in the yard while his dad was digging in the garden.

"Hey, Dad — what's your favorite team?"

"Well, I like the Giants."

"OK, the Giants are my favorite team, too."

And from that point on, Jim Bouton pulled for the New York Giants as only a baseball-mad kid could in the late 1940s and early 1950s, when New York City boasted three Major League teams. He listened to Giants games on the radio, memorized the names and positions of all the players (even today he can recite the starting lineup and most of the part-timers), collected baseball cards, and of course, took in a few games at the Polo Grounds, with Bob (brother, a year and a half his junior) and their little brother Pete (four years younger than Bob) in tow. Sometimes, Jim and Bob went with a couple of their friends.

Using a scientific approach, they once tried to catch foul balls hit into the upper deck of the left field bleachers.

"We invented this thing to help us snare a few balls," Bouton explained. "We took a fishing net and tied it to a bamboo pole. We practiced using it out in front of our house, throwing long fly balls to the guy holding the net. Only trouble was, we actually tried to fire the ball into the net, which as we found out later, of course, did not accurately reflect a game situation, where the batter is doing everything he can to not hit the ball into the fish net held by a boy darting in and out of rows of seats often occupied by other fans.

"On the bus ride into the ballpark, a lady sitting across from us spied our net and asked, 'Are you boys going crabbing?', and we broke into fits of laughter.

"When we got to the Polo Grounds the lady at the ticket gate stopped us and told us we couldn't go in with 'that thing' as she called it. So we went to another gate. But this time we had our jackets draped over it and carried it upright, waist-high. We marched right in, single file, and once inside, the ushers for some reason let us keep it. We really felt we were on to something when we heard one of them say, 'Well, now I've seen everything.'

"We never caught a ball in the net, but the possibility of catching a ball in the net was almost as much fun..."

...Bouton claims he never got into any games until his senior year at Bloom Township.

"All I did was warm up," he said. "In fact, my nickname in high school was 'Warm up Bouton.'

"High school was a miserable time for me. I had pimples on my face, I wore braces on my teeth, I was still skinny, and I sat on the bench. I was a real squirrel. I wasn't smart enough to be a nerd. Nerds knew that amps times volts equals neurons, and I didn't even know that at the time." — David Craft, Jan. 18, 1991

* * *

Jim Bouton

As a pitcher, Bouton had style on the mound. Not exactly chic. More like "cheeck."

He was a master of mimicry, that boy. One of his classic manuevers came in Boston, in a game in which he was mowing down the Red Sox and irritating the hell out of their Yankee-hating fans. It was during the Dick (as in, "the Monster") Radatz era, when the 6-foot-6-inch relief ace, after busting a third-strike fastball past a weak-kneed batter, would walk off the mound, briskly and confidently, with his arms raised above his head. It never failed to stir the Fenway Faithful to glee.

"I pitched something like a two-hit shutout that day," Bouton said. "I had really good stuff. I came marching off the mound and gave the Boston fans my impression of the Radatz triumphant march, and they were furious with me. They threw stuff at me, booed me, heaped scorn down on me, and all because I had dared to use the patented Radatz strut. I so enjoyed doing that. It was great fun."

It was vintage Bouton, but perhaps Bulldog's finest moment occurred during a game against the Indians.

Rocky Colavito, a fine, all-around ballplayer who terrorized opposing pitchers with his power, was at the plate when Bouton's alter ego, "Mimic Man," took over.

"Rocky had this ritual just before he would get set in the batter's box," Bouton explained. "He would take half a practice swing and bring the bat around slowly and point at the pitcher, sort of in slow motion, and stare at you. He'd do this about four or five times, and then step in.

"I was pitching a really good game that day, and feeling a little bit cocky out there on the mound, so just when he brought his bat forward and pointed it at me, I brought my arm forward, and pointed the ball at him. And he did his bat thing again, and I brought my pitching arm forward again, and pretty soon he started laughing, and then I started laughing, and it just plain looked strange.

"Of course, he could afford to laugh. He was fairly confident that when I did pitch the ball he would knock it right through my chest cavity for a double. Actually, I almost walked him because I was laughing so hard I'd lost my concentration..."

...Even fans who don't go after his actual signature are likely to have experienced any one of several items with Jim Bouton's unmistakable inprint on it.

For starters there is Big League Chew, shredded bubble gum in a pouch that (sort of) resembles chewing tobacco. Bouton and Rob Nelson thought that one up while spittin' the real thing in the bullpen of the Portland Mavericks back in the late '70s. And their bubble hasn't burst yet. Millions of dollars of Big League Chew, as Bouton proudly notes in press releases, have been chewed up, wadded up and left in the backs of station wagons by the nation's kids.

Another popular confectionery with the young at heart is Big League Ice Cream, with sticks that are shaped like baseball bats, branded with the autographs of 26 Major League players. They became a top seller for its manufacturer, Good Humor.

The hobby world is also the place for Collect-A-Books, another Bouton idea that has rapidly become a favorite among collectors, as have Big League Cards, authentic trading cards that serve as business cards. They are customized by printing the photo of one's choice in full color on the front, with whatever information one desires on the back.

Not all of Bulldog's ideas have been profitable, however. Let's see...there were the statistical slide rules (one featuring the Mets and their opponents and one with the Yankees and theirs). When they debuted a few years ago Bouton sold 20,000 of them in just a month's time...which left him with only 80,000 to sell before the end of the season a few weeks later.

And who can forget — make that remember — Rodney's Cube, a takeoff on the Rubik's Cube fad that got no more respect than a man who endorsed it: Rodney Dangerfield.

"Yeah, we've had some things that didn't work out the way we had hoped," Bouton admitted. "In fact, what people may not realize is that years ago we wanted to provide a sugarless version of Big League Chew.

"This was before Nutrasweet, you know, and the sweetner being used during testing resulted in some unusual findings. Researchers discovered that the sugarless bubble gum, when consumed in large enough quantities by kids, gave the kids diarrhea. Not exactly the kind of marketing ploy we were looking for." — David Craft, Jan. 25, 1991

* * *

Rocky Bridges

Where was Bridges when Bobby Thomson lined an 0-1 pitch into the stands to give the Giants the National League pennant and send Rocky and the rest of the Dodgers home for the winter?

"Oh, I was at my accustomed spot, sitting on my butt in the Dodger's dugout," Bridges deadpanned. — David Craft, Nov. 18, 1988

* * *

Lou Brock

Brock resorted to the Uecker story early in his talk, recounting for those assembled about how the .200-hitting catcher and Milwaukee native was signed by his hometown Braves.

According to Brock, and this is one of those entertaining stories where the degree of truth is irrelevant, the Braves made a decision to sign Uecker and dispatched a scout to the young backstop's home to sign the contract. Seated at the kitchen table, the scout told the family of the Braves' interest in their son, adding that they were talking about a bonus in the area of $4,000.

"This family can't come up with that kind of money," responded Uecker's father." — T.S. O'Connell, Jan. 3, 1992

* * *

Bob Cain

He's the answer to one of the most oft asked baseball trivia questions. Who was the pitcher when Eddie Gaedel pinch hit for the St. Louis Browns on Aug. 19, 1953?

If you're up on your baseball you'll know it was Bob "Sugar" Cain, left-hander for the Detroit Tigers during that historic moment in baseball history. Cain later pitched for Bill Veeck and the Browns and had a six-year career mark of 37-44...

...Cain said there were no racial problems when Manchester played Nashua as far as he knew, but he did remember a Campanella story. "When he was on the Nashua club he was getting 100 baby chickens for every home run he hit and I think he had around 43 home runs that year, or something like that. It was a tremendous amount, anyway."

According to Bob Broeg's 1971 book, Super Stars of Baseball, this was in 1946, but Campanella might have played in Nashua more than one season and the baby chicken offer might have been good in more than one year. Anyway, according to Broeg, Campanella hit 13 home runs for Nashua, which had no outfield fence. "A local farmer offered 100 chickens for every home run. Campy sent his 1,300 prizes to his father, who raised them as a sideline to his vegetable business..."

...Cain, who has recounted the Eddie Gaedel story hundreds of times, said he never tires of it. "It stays fresh on my mind. I can remember it just like it happened yesterday.

"None of our players, as far as I know, knew a thing about it. That was one secret Bill Veeck did keep. The only ones, as far as we know, that knew about it, was Bill Durney, the traveling secretary, and publicity director Bob Fischel. Outside of that I don't know who knew about it."

Gaedel had actually made an earlier appearance on the field in between games of a doubleheader. Celebrating the 50th anniversary of his radio sponsor, the Falstaff Brewing Co., and also that of the 50th anniversary of the foundation of the American League, Veeck had a huge birthday cake drawn onto the field between games. (St. Louis and Ned Garver lost the opener 5-2).

What should pop out of the cake but 3-foot-7 inch Eddie Gaedel in a Browns' uniform. Public address announcer Bernie Ebert told the crowd of 18,369 that Gaedel was a birthday present to manager Zack Taylor. The 65-pound Gaedel was forgotten until the game was underway. Cain explains:

"This was in the first inning. They had Frank Saucier starting in center field and he was their leadoff hitter. At that time he had a real bad arm. He couldn't throw. When they came to bat they put Eddie Gaedel in to pinch hit for Saucier. Nobody knew anything about it. Matter of fact, we thought it was a big joke to begin with.

"Ed Hurley (home plate umpire), he walked over towards the Browns' dugout, and Taylor walked out and had a contract in his hip pocket. Hurley asked Zack Taylor what was going on and he said he had a signed contract. Hurley wanted to see the contract and Taylor pulled it out of his pocket and showed it to him. You could see his neck (Hurley's) was getting red, but he headed back towards home plate and yelled out, 'Play ball!'

"Our catcher, Bob Swift, thought it was such a joke that he laid down on the ground to try to give me a target low enough. Hurley got after him and made him get up on his haunches in a squat position. He tried to give me a low target because Bob was serious about the whole situation. He tried to give me the low target but I couldn't get the ball low enough. I was kind of halfway afraid of throwing hard. I might get a wild pitch inside and hit him and he couldn't get out of the way of it. The four pitches that I did throw I don't think they were too much that high. They were up by his head, but for an ordinary batter they wouldn't have been so bad."

After four straight pitches out of the strike zone, Gaedel trotted down to first base, and according to Cain, he was tipping his hat to the crowd with every step. "He stood on first base and the Browns sent Jim Delsing in to run for him. As Jim got on first base Eddie Gaedel patted him on the rear and then he ran across the field back over to the dugout, tipping his hat all the way. I had to start bearing down on the next batter, but pitching to Gaedel got me out of my rhythm. I walked another man, another one got a base hit and before I knew it I was in real trouble that first inning. But I got out of the inning and we won the ball game 6-2. I went all the way.

"We would have loved to have gotten at least one strike on him," continued Cain. "The saying is Bill Veeck was up on the roof of the stadium with a shotgun in his hand and he said he was going to shoot Gaedel if he even swung at a pitch. We were hoping we could get one down there low enough.

"Bill Veeck played this thing so smooth," added Cain. "He signed Eddie to a $100 contract and he waived the 30-day waiting period. He didn't send it to the commissioner's office until the night before the game, knowing darn good and well the commissioner (A.B. "Happy" Chandler) wouldn't have time to handle that before game time. After the commissioner found out about it that night midgets were barred from baseball." — Rick Hines, May 3, 1991

* * *

Johnny Callison

Who can forget the infamous El Foldo by the Phillies in 1964? On Sept. 21, of that year, the Phils were 6-and-one-half games ahead in first place with only 12 to play, but somehow they still lost the N.L. pennant to the St. Louis Cardinals on the last day of the season. When asked what happened, Callison responded, "I don't know, nobody really knows the answer. It's just that everything that could go wrong went wrong. We (The Phils) never had a losing streak all year and it just happened to be at that time."

Callison recalls that everybody on the team played hard but it was just that the Phils ran into some hot teams down the stretch. Laments Callison, "To think that we were going to lose 10 in a row and the Cardinals were going to win 10 in a row, it just doesn't happen. But it did. I puked a little bit and cried." — Fluffy Saccucci, July 19, 1991

* * *

Bernie Carbo

Paul Green: You got involved in a rather interesting dispute in a play at the plate in that series. (1970 World Series)

Bernie Carbo: Right, that was with Elrod Hendricks. Ken Burkhart was the umpire and I was at third base and there was a man on first. It was the eighth inning and we were a run down. Ty Cline was the hitter. Alex Grammas told me to keep them from getting a double play if I could and to go home on anything hit on the ground. Ty Cline topped the ball, and Burkhart jumped out to see if it was fair or foul. I was going down the line and I saw Burkhart step in front of the baseline, I slowed down to almost a walk. Then I realized I could do one of two things — either try to make it back to third or try to score. I tried to score and went around Burkhart.

Elrod tagged me with the glove, but he had the ball in the other hand. I missed home plate and Burkhart called me out. Then when I was arguing about the play, I stepped on home plate, so I should have been safe. The funny thing about it was Sparky (Anderson) came out and said "If you get kicked out of the game it's going to cost you $500," so I just shut up and walked back to the dugout while he continued to argue.

I saw Elrod Hendricks in spring training the following year and he asked me what Sports Illustrated gave me for the picture of the play. I told him they gave me a check for $100 and he said, "They sent me one for $100 too." I think Sports Illustrated used that picture for about the next five years. You could walk through airports, sports book stores or whatever and there would be pictures of that play, but we got a grand total of $100. — Paul Green, Aug. 1, 1986

* * *

Roger Clemens

Clemens, who also is known as the Rocket, said he wouldn't trade his nickname for anything.

"I enjoy it. I think everyone should have one," he said. "(Bruce) Hurst gave me that in '86 when I struck out those 20 guys (April 29, vs. Seattle). It kind of stuck and Hursty is looking for some royalties off that nickname right now." — Tom Hultman, Dec. 20, 1991

* * *

Rocky Colavito

George Brett says he was offered $10,000 for his famous pine tar bat. However, Brett says he wants to stick with it all season and would consider selling only if the money went to charity.

"About 95 percent of the players today put pine tar on their bats," claims Royals batting coach Rocky Colavito. "I've only seen maybe Al Rosen, Minnie Minoso and Norm Cash in my time" who didn't.

Did Colavito ever put any kind of goo on his bats?

"I never put anything on my bats," Colavito said proudly. "All I ever did was bounce them on the end down on the concrete. The ones that had the sharpest ring, those I made my game bats. The ones that sounded duller were my batting practice bats." — Irwin Cohen, On the Baseball Beat, Sept. 2, 1983

* * *

Gene Conley

With his baseball career somewhat in question because of the arm problems, basketball seemed like a chance for Gene Conley to refurbish a career in sports.

After the 1958 World Series, Conley had taken his $4,500 losers-share check and used it as a down payment on a new home. Then he called Red Auerbach, his old coach with the Boston Celtics (Conley played the 1952-53 season with the Celtics) and asked if he needed another good basketball player. After seeing that Gene was in good shape, that he still had good hands and good quickness and mobility for a big man, he agreed to allow Conley to return to the Celtics.

The Celtics needed a backup for their great center, Bill Russell, and Gene fit the bill.

"We had some good players on those teams — Russell, Cousy, Sharman, Heinsohn," says Conley. "I would fill in as a center for Russell on defense and play forward on offense. They'd send me in to mix it up with Wilt Chamberlain and Wayne Embry, people like that. They were BIG! I'm 6'8", and Wilt used to call me 'Shorty.' He could eat soup off my head."

"Did you see the other day where Jabbar only had one rebound in a game?" he asks. "Wilt would say that if he didn't get 30 rebounds a game, they'd boo him. He was mean!" — Tom Mortenson, July 15, 1988

* * *

Chuck Connors

As a professional baseball player, Chuck Connors had the justly-deserved reputation of being a "character." One of his patented routines, for example, was his home run soiree, which he regularly performed in the Pacific Coast League.

"It'd take me five minutes to round the bases if I hit a home run," Connors recalled in 1962. "I'd stop majestically at first, slide to second, cartwheel to third — and crawl home."

Like many other ballplayers, Connors also enjoyed taunting umpires. "I used to memorize passages from Shakespeare," says Connors, and pull 'em on the umps, like, 'The slings and arrows of outrageous fortune I can take, but your blindness is ridiculous.'" One day, an umpire with more than a passing interest in Shakespeare finished one of Connors' passages and then threw the lanky, 6'5" first baseman out of the game.

One of Connors' fondest memories in his continuing war with the umpires occurred when one of the boys in blue made a bad call against him. For two weeks Connors sulked about the injustice of the call and then hit upon an idea — one which would avenge the "crime" without getting him kicked out of the ball game.

"I waited until he (the umpire) made a bad call in favor of a guy on the other team," recalls Connors. "We were in the field. I came charging in from first base, arms waving and jaw wagging. I wiggled my finger under his nose, and all that wild gesticulating with my hambone hands made it look to the crowd as though I was about to kill him.

"What I was actually saying, though, was 'Ump, that was a great call and I'm backing you up on it. It took guts to make a call like that. If they start a fight I'm on your side.' He was dumbfounded — he couldn't possibly throw me out of the game for being on his side, and all the while the crowd thought I was really laying it on him."

Because he was a self-admitted ham and clown, Connors wasn't particularly popular among the fans in opposition ball parks. In fact, the crowd would sometimes start booing the minute Connors took the field. Connors, however, didn't take this abuse lying down and often retaliated in his own special way.

"One day I had a miserable day at the plate and went 0 for 5," Connors relates. "So next day the crowd was laying for me. But I was ready for 'em. Instead of running onto the field from the clubhouse, I ran right up into the stands. I had both hands full of raw hamburger and just chucked it at 'em in pieces, hollering, 'Here, you lions, eat this!'" — William J. Felchner, Sept. 15, 1989

* * *

Moe Drabowsky

Paul Green: You developed a reputation as one of the game's premier practical jokers. Did you work at it or did it just come naturally?

Moe Drabowsky: I called myself the MVP (Most Valuable Prankster) for about three years at Baltimore. It's amazing. I've been out of the game 13 years and just got a two-page story from San Diego on characters in the bullpen. I got a lot of ink about it.

Moe Drabowsky

Green: Did you ever hit Chief Nokahoma in Atlanta with a cherry bomb?

Drabowsky: No, that's when I knew my career was over. I couldn't get the cherry bomb over the fence. When it landed in fair territory I knew the end was in sight.

Green: That particular cherry bomb almost ended Lou Brock's career or life depending on the strength of his heart, didn't it?

Drawbosky: Yes, I was concerned about Brock. What I had done was to put a cherry bomb in a cigarette. I don't know if you're familiar with the technique, but I had 12 minutes before it went off. It happened to go off near Brock, but when I didn't clear the fence with it my immediate concern was that someone would hit a ball near the thing and Brock would go over for it and have the thing go off in his face. Being a gambling type of individual I figured I'd take my chances with it. Heck, in 12 minutes I might even be in the game so I wouldn't be anywhere near the scene of the crime. Of course, I watched the clock closely and fortunately no one hit a ball there, but there was a huge explosion 12 minutes later. In those years the Atlanta Braves weren't drawing too many people so the upper deck was closed, but as soon as that cherry bomb went off, I jumped off the bullpen bench and started pointing to the upper deck yelling, "There he is, there he is."

Green: Did you just enjoy doing these things or was life in the bullpen too boring?

Drabowsky: You can't sit for eight or nine innings waiting to get in the game. You could get all tied up in knots, so having a fairly fertile mind, it was really a defense mechanism against the pressure of the day. It would take your mind off the seriousness of what you might be confronting later. It was my method of relaxation.

Green: Were there great jokes you wanted to pull but never had a chance?

Drabowsky: Of course you're somewhat limited because some bullpens are in view of 30,000 people. Now in Yankee Stadium or Shea Stadium you can get behind the stands and pretty much out of sight. We had a tremendous rivalry between Baltimore and Kansas City. I went to the Kansas City Royals in the 1969 expansion draft and when we would do things to them they would come to our bullpen and paint home plate black and the pitching rubber orange along with putting Baltimore Orioles colors in our bullpen.

Green: Coming to the bullpen finding that sort of damage you'd have to retaliate, I suspect.

Drabowsky: You can't just sit there. You have to do something. I would initiate commando attacks. We'd put mud on our faces and about the third or fourth inning load up our pockets with rocks and dirt balls. Then behind the cover of the center field fence and the trees in center field from a hill overlooking their bullpen, we'd open fire on them, we'd just blow them away. I guess they felt that was a neat thing so the next afternoon in broad daylight they retaliated in kind. In the press box or the general manager's seat, I guess you can see what's going on back there and their general manager wanted to know why in the world they were all furtively sneaking around through the trees out in center field.

Green: To a general manager I suppose such conduct would be disconcerting.

Drabowsky: Apparently, but it was all good-natured fun.

Green: Did anyone ever get upset? You had to rub someone the wrong way?

Drabowsky: Some of the Latin Americans didn't appreciate my snake and things of that nature. Those guys are petrified of anything that moves. I know I drove poor Luis Aparicio crazy.

Green: Do you still bring him such presents?

Drabowsky: I promised not to do it any more, at least to Luis and some of the others. I'm afraid they might have a coronary. When you're younger you can withstand the shock, but later on in life I'm not so sure.

Green: Certainly, there were highlights. Giving Kuhn a hot foot had to be right up there.

Drabowsky: Yes, it was. If a guy was a marked man, we got him. One of our favorite targets was Jim Elliot, the sportswriter for the Baltimore Sun. I actually started to feel sorry for him. We just got him day after day after day. It got to the point where it just wasn't any fun. Instead of sticking two matches in his shoes, I'd take out the book of 20 and just put 10 in each shoe and get all 20 flaming. He looked like a battleship during World War II that had taken about 15 direct hits and was going down in the Pacific. Ruined a number of pairs of his shoes.

Green: But your creativity wasn't limited to the routine. You apparently worked at hitting Charlie Finley's sheep with fungoes as well.

Drabowsky: Oh, sure. I know one Kansas City writer said we had a bunch of donkeys in the outfield that couldn't catch anything. Maybe that was why they didn't have much practice before the game because I was always taking aim at the sheep up there.

Green: Did you ever get the shepherd?

Drabowsky: No, but you could scare the sheep. When you get nine or 10 scared sheep, who run up the side of a hill and huddle in a corner, they make a much bigger target than one lonely shepherd. — Paul Green, Oct. 25, 1985

* * *

Moe Drabowsky

Drabowsky said he realized his career was coming to an end one day at Fenway Park.

"The bases were loaded and Tommy Harper was up. I threw a fastball and I watched the ball go to the plate and I said, 'when in the world is that ball gonna get to the plate?' I said, 'Hey, my career is over.'"

It really wasn't that bad of a career, although Drabowsky's wit helped keep him and his teammates loose, making him even more valuable than his record may have indicated.

Two of Drabowsky's "most famous" pranks involved switching opposing teams listed on the Green Monster when he was playing at Fenway Park and making a call to the Kansas City bullpen — when he was a member of the Orioles.

As he tells it, Drabowsky had been the player rep with the Royals before he was traded for Bobby Floyd. On his first trip back into Kansas City, Drabowsky said Jim Nash was in the process of throwing a three-hitter at the Orioles, "just cruising along."

Drabowsky was familiar with the telephone system used at the Kansas City ballpark and dialed the K.C. bullpen. "When their coach answered I just yelled 'Get (Lew) Krausse hot in a hurry!' and hung up the phone. All of a sudden two bodies came charging out of the little dugout area down in the bullpen and Krausse began to heat up feverishly.

"I let him warm up 3-4 minutes, then called again and said, 'That's enough — sit him down.'"

After the game, an Oriole loss, Drabowsky's teammates wondered why the bullpen pitchers were smiling so much. When the team found out about Drabowsky's prank, the media learned about it and publicized the incident. — Gary Herron, March 9, 1990

* * *

Ryne Duren

For those of you out there who have been publically scrutinized over the years for wearing glasses, former major league starting pitcher/ace reliever Ryne Duren should be your hero. Duren, who wore marble-thick spectacles during his entire big-league career, and who was reputed to be the perpetrator of many an errant pitch, managed to overcome his somewhat debilitating impaired vision problem and see it through to a successful pro baseball career in the majors...

...Throughout his big-league career, Duren was tabbed by baseball people as being a wild pitcher who had trouble picking up the plate because of his poor eyesight. That, coupled with his 90-plus mile-an-hour fastball intimidated many an alarmed batter. Did Duren personally think that he was that wild as a pitcher? Says Duren, "I was (at first) but then after a while with a little goading from some of the guys on the team (the Yankees), I did scatter one once in a while (but intentionally)."

Duren points out in particular one guy on that Yankee team, third base coach Frank Crosetti, as being the one who chided him into throwing pitches every which way. Relates Duren of Crosetti's urgings, "He always thought that it was good thinking if I'd miss the catcher completely during my warm-up throws." Duren also adds that his show of wildness was demonstrated for the sake of the fans because they got a big kick out of it. "It was more for the fans later (in my career) than it was for the opposition," jokes Duren. — Fluffy Saccucci, Oct. 19, 1990

* * *

Mark Fidrych

But what got more attention from the news hounds who dogged his heels that summer was his talking to the ball.

While everybody asked feverishly about what he was saying to the ball, the rookie would try to dismiss his mannerisms as part of his game. "It (talking to the ball, etc.) was just something I did in high school."

And what was he saying to that traditionally uncommunicative horsehide? According to Fidrych, it was just a way of keeping his concentration, and the specific words carry less importance. He told Sports Illustrated's Ron Fimrite that year that the attention to that particular quirk was overblown.

"A batter tips his hat and hits his spikes and nobody pays attention. My pitching coach says that I can go out there and stand on my head if it'll help me. What I'm really doing, I'm talking out loud to myself, not the ball. I'll tell myself to bring my arm down, things like that. Haven't you ever talked to yourself walking down the street? Yeah, but if I went 9-19 instead of 19-9, they'd be saying, 'Put this kid in the loony bin.'" — T.S. O'Connell, May 15, 1992

* * *

Al Gionfriddo

How many times have you seen it? Almost every year, before the start of a World Series game on TV in the pregame warmups, there's an old film clip aired of a scurrying little guy crashing into the fence with the cap flying off his head, making a leaping, over-the-shoulder catch of a long fly ball. And immediately the next scene shifts to a disgruntled Joe DiMaggio kicking the dirt near second base in frustration.

The guy that snared that drive was 5-foot-6, 165-pound outfielder Al Gionfriddo of the old Brooklyn Dodgers.

That catch, one of the greatest in Series history, occurred on Oct. 5, 1947, in deep left-center field at old Yankee Stadium in Game 6 of the series. There were two outs in the bottom of the sixth inning.

What made Gionfriddo's catch even more significant was the fact that at the time, with the Dodgers leading 8-5, the Yankees had two men aboard and the potential three-run homer by DiMaggio would have knotted the score at 8-8.

The Dodgers beat the Yankees 8-6 in that game. But the Yankees nudged a run in the bottom of the ninth that would've, had it not been for Gionfriddo's acrobatic defensive heroics, resulted in a 9-8 Yankee victory.

So, in essence, Gionfriddo's brilliant catch was a game-saver that day. The Yanks came back the next day to salvage the Series in Game 7 with a 5-2 win.

But, regardless, Gionfriddo's grab of Joe D's shot will forever be etched in the minds of all those fortunate enough to have seen it.

Retracing his steps, Gionfriddo recently turned back the clock 44 years and gave his account of how "The Catch" evolved.

In Gionfriddo's words, this is how he remembers it: "First of all, I looked into the dugout and they're (the Dodger coaches) movin' me close to the left-field line (at Yankee Stadium), figurin' that DiMaggio may try to pull the ball, so I played him pretty close to the line. Well, when he hit the ball I didn't know whether or not I had a chance to catch it. I knew that it was hit into deep left-center field, so I put my head down and ran with my back toward home plate, toward where I thought the ball was gonna be, and that was in left-center field by the bullpen gate.

"I just kept running and then I turned and looked up at the ball. I just knew that I didn't have a chance to get it right there. So I turned my head and ran for the spot that I thought the ball would be, the bullpen gate, and I looked up over my left shoulder with my back toward home plate and reached up with my right hand, 'cause I'm a left-handed thrower, and caught the ball in the webbing of my glove as it was about to go over the bullpen gate.

"I really didn't think that I made such a great catch and I didn't make too much ado about it," he adds. "All I know is that I saved a home run from scoring against our pitcher and our team, and three runs were saved.

"It really makes a man feel great when he finds out that he saved the ball game," says Gionfriddo proudly. — Fluffy Saccucci, March 6, 1992

* * *

Vernon "Lefty" Gomez

All Hall of Famers are automatically invited to attend the annual induction ceremonies...some never trouble to attend after their own election, but Lefty Gomez was always on hand to welcome the new inductees and to take part in the various ceremonies surrounding the event. And he loved to sit in an easy chair in the spacious lobby of Cooperstown's Hotel Otesaga where he would talk baseball by the hour with his fellow Hall of Famers, reporters and fans...and I never saw him turn down a request for an autograph.

Gomez particularly enjoyed talking about the All-Star Game. He was the starting and winning pitcher in the inaugural All-Star Game played in 1933 at Chicago's Comiskey Park and even drove in the first run ever in the mid-summer classic when his single in the second inning drove in Jimmy Dykes from first base.

"That base hit gave me as much satisfaction as anything I've done in baseball" Gomez said during one of those Otesaga sessions. "Nobody expected me to deliver in that situation and I was as much surprised as anybody in the ball park..."

...No matter how critical the situation became on the baseball field, Lefty retained both his wit and his poise. When asked at the Otesaga one day as to which incident he remembered with the most relish, he replied — almost without a pause — that it came during the second game of the 1936 World Series against the hard-hitting New York Giants at the Polo Grounds.

A half-century after the episode Gomez remembered it well as he replied:

"It was early in the game, I was a little wild and before I knew it there were two runners on base. Suddenly I heard a plane flying over the ballpark — it was a big airliner — and I just stepped off the mound, forgot about the runners, the batter, the game and everything else. I stood there watching calmly, until the plane completely disappeared from sight.

"Sure, I kept 45,000 fans (as well as the players) waiting and everyone wondered why I stopped the game this way...some people thought I was just plain crazy. Well, I was a little tense and I wanted to ease the tension a bit. As I recall, I came out of the inning pretty well unscathed."

The Yankees went on to whip the Giants 18-4 as Gomez went the distance, walking seven and striking out eight.

This mists of antiquity may have settled a bit on the game's details, but Lefty Gomez will always be remembered as the player who stopped the World Series dead in its tracks to watch an airplane in flight. — Robert Obojski, March 17, 1989

* * *

Don Grate

The professional baseball career of Don Grate has some of the elements, if not the magic, embodied in the box office smash The Natural.

Grate was a young pitching prospect whose major league career was cut short by an arm injury. He made a comeback — nearly all the way — as an outfielder and in the process set and re-set an unofficial record that may still be intact today.

I recently had the opportunity to talk baseball with Don Grate. If you're a fan of minor league baseball in the 1950s, I think you'll enjoy listening in...

...Don Grate's major league career consisted of two short stints on the mound with the Philadelphia Phillies in the player-lean years just after World War II.

The right-hander's lifetime major league record is an even 1-1, with a 9.37 ERA, but that's not where the story begins — or ends...

...And there's no doubt that Don Grate had one of the strongest throwing arms in professional baseball.

In 1952, Grate set a distance record for throwing a baseball.

The Lookouts were visiting the New Orleans Pelicans, a Pittsburgh Pirates farm club, late in the 1952 season. Grate recalls, "They had the field day exercises to bring in more people — egg tossing, fungo hitting and so forth."

After watching a couple of future Pirates outfielders who were themselves known for having strong throwing arms, Dale Long and Frank Thomas, throw for distance, Chattanooga manager Cal Ermer encouraged Grate to throw.

According to Grate, "Ermer said, 'Why don't you throw? You can throw a ball farther than they can. You can win a pair of trousers and a shirt.'"

Grate replied, "I don't want to throw, I'm liable to hurt my arm or something. Ermer said, 'Just go out and throw anyway — and try not to hurt your arm.'

"So, I threw a ball from center field in the old Pelican ballpark, and the darn ball went over the press box; they couldn't measure it.

"Ermer got the idea I could throw for a world's record. When we got back to Chattanooga he said, '(team president) Joe Engel will give you a fabulous prize if you break the old record Shel LeJeune had in 1924 or 1927 or something like that. I think he threw a ball like 424 feet.'" (Grate's recollection was close on the throw, but off on the year. In 1910, LeJeune threw for a world's record 426' 9 1/2".)

On Sept. 7, prior to the final game of the 1952 season, Grate broke the 42-year-old record. "I threw one that afternoon they couldn't measure," Grate said. "It hit the top of the dugout from center field. They measured to the dugout and it was 440-some feet. The 'fabulous prize' was a couple hundred dollars. I said, 'Gee, wow, thanks.'"

According to an account in The Sporting News Baseball Guide, that throw was recorded at 434'1".

The following year Grate broke his own record during a field meet preceding the Lookouts Aug. 23 game in Chattanooga. His new mark was set at 443'3". The ball was duly inscribed, autographed and sent to the Hall of Fame in Cooperstown, N.Y.

Grate made another long throw in that period that didn't get into the record books but it did get him out of prison.

He explained, "One occasion Cal Ermer asked me to pitch against the prisoners at Atlanta Federal Prison. I pitched that ball game, and I think we won something like 6-2. I don't think I shut them out.

"They had all the prisoners that were on good behavior roped off around the outfield and the rest of them were up in the main prison building looking out the windows. That prison was something like 10 stories high, I guess."

After the game, a guard approached Chattanooga manager Cal Ermer and told him the team couldn't leave just yet.

According to Grate, the guard said, "The prisoners are all riled up and they're going to have some kind of disturbance. They understand you have some fellow that threw the baseball for a world's record. They're up there betting cigarettes on whether he can throw a baseball from the baseball diamond and break one of those windows up in the prison. If your player doesn't make an attempt we're going to have a riot because everybody's betting."

Grate continued, "So Ermer says to me, 'Grate, can you throw a baseball from the pitcher's mound up to that prison?' I said, 'Yes, I think so. How far is it?' He said it was 300-and-some feet over there for sure, and I said, 'I don't want to. I'm kind of tired from pitching.' He said, 'Well, give it a shot.' The guard said, 'You'd better or you're not getting out of here.' So I said to Ermer, 'Do I have to?' He said, 'You want to go home?' I said, 'Yeah, sure.' He said, 'Throw.'

"So I threw one, and of all of the windows they have in that prison it hit one with the bars on the outside. It hit the dividing bar that separates the window panes. The guard said, 'You're going to have to throw another one.' I threw that on top of the prison," Grate laughed, "and they let us all go home..."

...Grate also ended the 1956 season with a new record for throwing the baseball. Before a crowd of 10,620 on the Millers Fan Appreciation Night, Grate added a couple of feet to the world's record, with a heave of 445'1".

"I had to get outside the old Bloomington ballpark," Grate said. The center field gate was opened to give Grate a running start on his throw.

"That thing hit eight or ten feet up on the backstop," Grate said. "They only measured it to the bottom of the backstop and that was 445 feet. You should probably add another 10 or 15 feet to it."

Though he received a $100 prize for the throw, Grate said, "I was just doing it for fun. If I'd been doing it today, maybe I could be on a Wheaties package or something." (Not impossible, when you consider that in the late 1950s, Wheaties' world headquarters was in Minneapolis and they were a prolific issuer of minor league memorabilia there.) — Bob Lemke, The Bleacher Bum, Feb. 24, 1989

* * *

Reggie Jackson

The atmosphere was completely different in New York than it was in Oakland or Baltimore for Reggie. The New York media, always looking to expose controversy, suggested that Jackson's cockiness and ego would make it difficult for him to get along with his new teammates. An article in Sport magazine quoted Jackson as saying, "I'm the straw that stirs the drink." Jackson says that the meaning of that statement was misinterpreted and hurt him in his relationship with his teammates. "We had Catfish Hunter, (Graig) Nettles, (Ron) Guidry, (Thurman) Munson, Chris Chambliss, Willie Randolph. But I did believe that I was the missing link, the catalyst that the team needed to win. But I just didn't say it properly," he says...

...One of the most memorable moments Jackson gave the Angel fans was his 500th career home run in 1984. He says that the milestone home run represented his entrance into an exclusive club. "After I hit the 500th home run I felt that, at that point, I was branded as a great player. I wasn't a Babe Ruth or a Hank Aaron or a Willie Mays, but I felt that that home run allowed me into the corral. I feel that it (500 home run club) is the most prestigious group in all of baseball," he says. — Tom Mortenson, Oct. 11, 1991

* * *

Fergie Jenkins

"When I talk to Little Leaguers, I tell them that you're going to learn the game from day to day — don't try to learn it in one day, one week, or one month or one summer because as you grow, you're going to learn more about the game. And don't get impatient, just because you strike out, don't get a defeated attitude.

"A lot of kids cry at 11- and 12-years-old when they don't do well, and that's not a good sign. When you get defeated, hold your head up high because you're going to get an opportunity to play in a couple of days and to display your talent. The thing that you want to do is learn every time you play the game." — Ross Forman, Nov. 8, 1991

* * *

Si Johnson

In recalling his big league career, Si Johnson naturally mentions some of the game's shining stars. Here are some of his anecdotes:

"The very first pitcher I ever hit against was Grover Cleveland Alexander. I'd read so much about him, of course, that I was scared to death to face him. But I was fortunate. I got a hit off him. I very seldom hit my weight, and the next day the newspaper has something about me being a good-hitting pitcher. I thought, yes, they got that wrong. And those opposing pitchers went gunnin' for me after that. They made sure I failed at bat.

"Ernie Lombardi was my catcher most of the time at Cincinnati, and Cincinnati is a hot place to play ball during the summer. Once in a while, Schnozz would come out to the mound, soaking wet with all that gear on, and tell me, 'For Chrissakes, Si, get 'em out so we can go get a beer!' People often wonder what the pitcher and catcher talk about out there on the mound. Well, I can tell you: it's just about anything but baseball." — David Craft, Jan. 19, 1990

* * *

Vernal "Nippy" Jones:

Some players are remembered for just one solitary incident in their career.

Bobby Thomson is remembered for his dramatic home run in the 1951 playoff game between the New York Giants and the Brooklyn Dodgers. Ralph Branca is remembered as the pitcher who gave up the "shot heard 'round the world."

Mickey Owen will always be remembered for the third strike that got away in the '41 World Series.

Bill Buckner, despite closing in on 3,000 lifetime hits, will always be saddled with that grounder that skipped between his legs in the '86 Series.

But Vernal "Nippy" Jones is remembered for putting his best foot forward.

Jones made baseball history with some quick thinking and some fancy footwork. While pinch-hitting for Warren Spahn in the 1957 World Series between the Milwaukee Braves and the New York Yankees, he started a rally by getting nicked in the foot by a pitch.

Although umpire Augie Donatelli didn't believe Jones initially when he said he'd been hit by a pitch, Jones produced the physical evidence — the baseball with a black shoe polish mark on it — and Donatelli, over the Yankees strident protests, had to agree.

A similar incident occurred with Cleon Jones in the 1969 World Series between the New York Mets and Baltimore Orioles. But Nippy Jones will always be remembered as the first player to make shoe polish a deciding part of the game.

Vernal Jones was born in Los Angeles in 1925. When asked how he got the nickname "Nippy," he smiles as he says, "Well, I could tell you a couple of different stories, but I guess I'll tell you the truth. The truth is my father was nicknamed 'Nip.' He liked to take a nip of the bottle now and then. When I'd tag along with him they used to say, 'there goes Nip and Little Nipper.' From then on, 'Nippy' just stuck. With a name like Vernal, I guess you have to have a nickname."...

...After bouncing around with several minor league teams from '53 to '56, Jones got another call to the majors midway through the '57 season. This time it was with the Milwaukee Braves, who were in the middle of a pennant race.

When Braves slugger Joe Adcock broke his leg, Nippy Jones got the call. The Braves needed a right-handed-hitting first baseman to platoon with Frank Torre, and Jones fit the bill.

"One thing I remember that I'm proud of is that between Frank Torre and myself, we played almost flawless defense at first base," recalls Jones.

When Milwaukee ended up in the World Series and with the Braves down 5-4 in the fourth game against a powerful Yankee team, Jones stepped up to the plate for his most famous at-bat.

"It was the bottom of the ninth and Fred Haney told me to get a bat," Jones says. "He wanted me to hit for Spahn. Now you've got to remember that Spahn was a real good hitting pitcher. Tommy Byrne was pitching for New York and he was a left-hander, so I guess Fred wanted to play the percentages and go with a right-handed batter.

"It was either the first or the second pitch, and the ball was coming in low and inside. I felt it hit my foot. I started to trot down toward first base. Well, Augie Donatelli was the home plate umpire and he says, 'Get back; it was a ball.' I said, 'It hit my foot.' Then I saw the ball on the ground. Yogi Berra was trying to get to it, but I beat him to it. I noticed a black spot on it and showed it to Augie. He took one look at it and pointed down to first base. Then Felix Mantilla went in to run for me. Schoendienst bunted him to second. Then Johnny Logan hit a double and tied the game. Then in the 10th, Eddie Mathews hit the home run off Bob Grim to win the game. Most people remember that I got hit on the foot but nobody remembers that it was Eddie that hit the home run to win the game." — Tom Mortenson, March 24, 1989

* * *

Ralph Kiner

Ralph Kiner's brief radio stint in Chicago with Bob Elson also included doing A.L. day game recreations in the studio whenever the Sox were at home for a night game. Like other announcers who did recreations, Kiner provided the play-by-play details to a game being played many miles away, unseen by the studio announcer.

"It goes back to the days of the old (telegraph) ticker tape," Kiner reminisced. "It was the best experience I ever had in broadcasting as far as honing my skills.

"A fly ball to left would come over the ticker simply as '7.' That was it. So, you could make it a line drive and a great catch, or routine out, or whatever. We always started about 15 minutes late, because invariably the tape would break down, or the operator at the other end would leave the room for a cup of coffee or something, and then you really had to improvise.

"Even by starting late we could run into problems, though. For example, over the tape it would say, 'base hit to left field,' and I'd make it a line drive or a bloop single, or whatever, and the runner was on first. But then I'd get a correction — 'flyout to left' — and so now I'd have to get that runner off first base. I could have him picked off, or maybe caught stealing, and it was really something, because it allowed your imagination to run wild.

"You could have a lot of fun with it if the ticker broke down or the operator wasn't sending. You'd have 'rain delays' even though in reality the game was being played in bright sunshine somewhere, or bench-clearing fights, or a guy lying in a heap on the ground after

making an incredible catch when he really caught the ball just back of short. That's why those games sounded so great, because in many ways they were fictitious." — David Craft, April 27, 1990

* * *

Mike Krukow

Another "memorable" moment in Krukow's career occurred in his rookie season. "I'll never forget the time I was getting loose before my first pitching start at Wrigley Field. I'm out running wind sprints back and forth with pitching teammates Bruce Sutter and Bill Bonham and this kid leans out from the bleacher section and he goes 'Hey you! Number 40! (my uniform number) What's your name, man?' And I ignore him, I mean, I'm in the big leagues. This guy should know who I am.

"So, I come back the next wind sprint and the same guy yells, 'Hey 40! What's your name, man?' And now I've got the red ass, I say to myself, this son-of-a-gun has got to know who I am. I'm in the big leagues for Christ's sake! Then Bill Bonham says to me, 'Listen kid, if he (the kid in the bleachers) tells you that again, just tell him to go buy a program.' And I said OK. Sure enough, just like clockwork, I'm waiting for this hemorrhoid (the kid in the bleachers) now and I'm going by him and he leans out again and yells, 'Hey 40! What's your name?' I look up and I say to him, 'Go buy a program, meat!' and he says to me, 'I did, and you ain't in it.'" — Fluffy Saccucci, Dec. 20, 1991

* * *

Don Larsen

Show promoter Bob Pressley, his wife, Jackie, and I had sat down in the hotel lounge when a customer from a nearby table approached our companion.

"Mr. Larsen," asked the customer. "Could you tell me who was in the starting lineup the day you pitched your perfect game?"

"You tell me," said the surly, yet smiling, former hurler, the only pitcher to toss a perfect game in World Series competition.

"Bauer, Collins, Mantle, Berra, Howard, Martin, McDougald, Carey," proudly answered the man.

Larsen took a sip of his fresh double brandy manhattan, then said, "Nope, Slaughter. Not Howard, Enos Slaughter." After the customer thanked Larsen for his time, the big right-hander turned around and said, "Not a day goes by that someone doesn't ask me something about that game."

Don't misunderstand Don Larsen's feelings about the recognition. His pitching performance 34 years ago on Oct. 8, 1956, made a legend out of an otherwise .500 pitcher. He's eternally grateful for the distinction, admitting that this one accomplishment has provided him with benefits in other facets of life that he might not otherwise have had. — Bill Ballew, Nov. 16, 1990

* * *

Bill Lee

SCD: You have called Boston's Fenway Park a religious shrine. What does that make domed stadiums?

Bill Lee: Sacrilegious. To play ball in those stadiums is sacrilegious. I was forced to play in one because I got traded to Montreal, but I didn't like it and I purposely didn't think about it. The only way I could pitch in those places was to get into a hitter-pitcher relationship where I never even thought that I was on Astroturf. I blocked out everything while I was on the field, and I think I had that ability. I had tunnel vision. The Houston Astrodome smells bad; a lot of the domed stadiums smell like dirty sneakers. How would you like to play your whole life inside an old Adidas tennis shoe?...

...SCD: You were an above-average major league pitcher and a no-nonsense on-field performer. Does it bother you that people remember you more for being a superflake?

Lee: Someone once said, "It's better to have bad press than no press at all." The squeaky wheel gets the grease, and I believe I'm squeaking in the right direction for the planet and for the people on the planet and for the true meaning of baseball. True baseball fans are statisticians at heart: they collect baseball cards, they play Strat-O-Matic baseball, and therefore they'll realize that I was a good hitting pitcher, I was a good fielding pitcher, and I did everything according to Hoyle; that was consistent with my philosophy of the game.

SCD: You mentioned baseball cards. Do you collect them?

Lee: I don't believe in collecting anything, basically because I'm a nomad. It would be like maintaining your old excess baggage. My theory is if you can't get it all in the trunk of a '62 Chevy you don't need need it."

SCD: Some baseball fans seem to place baseball cards alongside the Rosella Stone or Dead Sea Scrolls in terms of historical and social significance. I take it you don't agree?

Lee: That's a good analogy. I don't quite place it with those two, but I believe if you are looking through a box of dusty old cards and you come across Mickey Mantle's rookie card, that's the same thing as finding the Andrea Doria sunk off the coast of Nantucket. You know it's a find. But when kids send me my baseball card, I autograph them and send them back. My son collects them; he collects everything about baseball. I don't discourage it; it allows him to read and helps him with statistics, which will help him with economics. And he'll learn the game.

My oldest son doesn't collect baseball cards. He's a lot like me, kind of mysterious in some ways.

SCD: If you were the commissioner of baseball, what would be your first edicts.

Lee: My first edict as Commissioner of Baseball would be to get rid of the designated hitter, to bring back the 25-man roster, to get rid of Astroturf, maintain smaller ballparks, and revamp quality old ballparks. I'd bring back Crosley Field in Cincinnati. I'd try to revamp the minor leagues. I'd outlaw video instant replays. I'd outlaw mascots. I'd put organic foods in the stands. I would make cold, pasteurized beer mandatory from small breweries located near the ballparks — no giant multinational breweries. I would bring back warm, roasted peanuts. Just the smell of grass and those warm, roasted peanuts should be enough to make people come to the park. I would just try to reduce it to an organic game, the way it used to be...

...SCD: How would you characterize the New York fan?

Lee: The New York fan is a blood-thirsty, carniverous fan who slinks out of the subways. What you've gotta do with them is face them and show them no quarter and stick up for your beliefs, and then they'll put their arms around you and take you downtown to a bar, and you'll have a good time...

...SCD: Are you saying that you got along well with Don Zimmer, the man you called a gerbil?

Lee: I got along well with Don Zimmer when he was a third base coach, but when he was elevated to manager he went through a bad spell. He's a great baseball man. He's given his life to baseball. His fatal flaw was that he was a manager in a city where he, as a player, had a very difficult time with pitchers. Pitching is 90 percent of the game of baseball, and pitching happened to be the stuff that got him out 80 percent of the time. Poor Don; I hate to say this, but you were a .200 hitter, and that basically is the philosophy that dictates how you think. I feel sorry for him, because I never criticized Zimmer except in his treatment of Bernie Carbo. I actually praised him when I called him a gerbil, because I had said that Billy Martin was a no-good, dirty rat and Zimmer was not that way. Zimmer doesn't know this, but it's a great story. He collapsed one day on the field and everybody on our club laughed except me, and I was one of the few people who helped him back off the field. He does not realize it to this day because he was unconscious. You cannot fault Don for his tenacity as a manager. But it shows that he's a man of emotion more than reason. My theory is you have to develop on three levels simultaneously in order to achieve perfection; the psychological, the physical and the emotional. If any one of these outweighs the others, then you're destined to be spit on the Astroturf of life. — Kit Kiefer, April 21, 1989

* * *

Buck Leonard

"I roomed with Cool Papa Bell for five years. He was very fast. We were very close friends right up to his recent death." Bell was the master of the bunt and run. Could he really score from first on a bunt? "Well, I'll tell you how he did that. We only had two colored umpires in the Negro Leagues. So on a bunt, sometimes Bell, when the umpires were looking at the ball and at first base, would skip second base altogether. He would cut across behind the pitcher's mound and keep on going to third and then home. But he was very fast." — Rick Van Blair, Aug. 2, 1991

* * *

Don Liddle

SCD: You were on the mound in game one for a moment that has been played and played, the famous catch. What sort of a pitch was it that Wertz hit off you?

Bill Lee

Don Liddle: Well, they took my best pitch away from me. I had relieved a considerable amount for Leo (Durocher) and any time he brought me in to face a left-hander we tried to make them hit the curve or the low sinker. We had gone over the hitters before the first game and they said Wertz was a low ball hitter, that he was fairly muscle-bound and that he swung up at the high fastball, but that he was a better low ball hitter. When I went to the mound, Leo said, "Make him hit the high fastball." Even Westrum questioned Leo. He said, "Leo, with Don's curve?" But Leo said, "Make him hit the high fastball," so that's what we did and that's what he hit.

SCD: He hit it a long way.

Liddle: Yes he did, he hit it a long, long way.

SCD: When he made contact, did you think it would be trouble?

Liddle: I didn't know exactly the height, but I didn't think Willie could catch it. I knew it was really hit well. I broke, I didn't exactly see Willie catch it. There were two men on and I didn't know whether to back up home or third base. When I got turned around, I saw the man who had been on second high-tailing it back to second base. Lord God, Willie caught it.

SCD: Did you say anything to Willie?

Liddle: Well, they pulled the next hitter, Glynn, and brought in a right-handed hitter. Then Leo came out and took me out. In the Polo Grounds, our clubhouse was in center field so I went to the clubhouse. So I walked by Willie then. I didn't stop, I didn't think that would look right, but I did talk to him as I was going by. I told him how great a catch it was. — Paul Green, Aug. 5, 1988

* * *

Dale Long

Dale Long recently reminisced about his historic eighth home run he bashed that night in 1956.

"It was a curve ball — Carl Erskine had a good one — but I don't remember the count or anything," he said. "I know I hit it good and I hit it just by the 375 mark.

"If it had been over a foot to the right of it (the 375-marker), it wouldn't have made it because there was a large screen on top of the fence there."

Despite the scrutiny of a nation, Long felt no pressure that night. "I was 28 years old (actually 30) and I had been around the horn a couple of times," he said. "If you do it, you're a hero. If you don't you're a goat.

"I felt pretty good about it (the record) and when I hit the eighth one the people just wouldn't sit down and stop applauding. They had to stop the game and Mr. Branch Rickey said that that was the first time he had ever seen a curtain call. Back in those days you didn't dare show up the opposition because you'd eat the next one."

What does Long remember the most about that streak? "I remember that I was also hitting for average, up around the .350 mark," he said. "I was getting a lot of base hits and I just felt like I could hit anybody. I didn't care who threw it or what they threw. I was pretty confident."

Because of his incredible streak, much notoriety was heaped upon Long, climaxing with an appearance on the Ed Sullivan Show right after he homered in his seventh straight game.

"Being a boy from a small town in Massachusetts and being able to appear on the Ed Sullivan Show was a big thrill," Long said.

Even Pirate General Manager Joe L. Brown got caught up in the fanfare. He awarded Long a $2,500 reward for his accomplishment. Part of the reason was the Pirates were in first place — a situation unheard of at the time.

What were Long's thoughts on Don Mattingly's run at the streak?

"I was kind of pulling for him and yet I wasn't. He didn't break it, he just tied it, so I'm working on it 33 years now." — Fluffy Saccucci, Dec. 1, 1989

* * *

Frank Malzone

SCD: You were the first Gold Glove third baseman ever, back when there was only one selected from both leagues. And you won it the first three years of the award. You led five straight years in double plays, right?

FM: I couldn't tell you. In '57 I set a major league record in fielding for leading every category, even errors. (Laughs) I had the highest fielding percentage so that means I got to a lot more balls than other guys did. It was a strange state, because usually the guy with the highest average doesn't have the most errors, also. I didn't even know it until I saw it on the back of one of the bubble gum cards. It said it was the first time in history a third baseman did that. I think it was the first time in history an infielder did it. I never realized it until I saw it on the back of the card and then I looked it up in the (Baseball) Encyclopedia. I looked all through the third basemen and it was right.

I always kid Brooks Robinson about the first Gold Glove. I say, "You might have more than I have, but I've got one you'll never get!" It says "Major League" on it; it doesn't say "American League." Like you said, there were only nine players (selected) that year.

SCD: With the first three Gold Gloves, you were the top third baseman in the majors at that time and you had some tough competition.

FM: Brooksie got there in '58 (to stay) so there were two years that he was playing that I still won the Gold Glove but he hadn't got that World Series recognition yet, which meant a lot to him. National television makes a lot of difference.

You can name players, like Clete Boyer. Before he got to the Yankees he was just another player. Graig Nettles, when he was with Cleveland nobody ever mentioned him. They get to the Yankees and they become great players because they got in a World Series and got the recognition.

It happens to a lot of players. Unfortunately, I never got to play in a World Series. The only thing I regret in baseball is not being in a World Series. — Brent Kelley, Nov. 16, 1990

* * *

Mickey Mantle

Born in 1931, Mickey was raised during the Great Depression, a period the Mantles struggled to survive. His dearly loved father, Mutt Mantle, was a farmer and later a lead miner. Mickey was named after Mickey Cochrane, the Hall of Fame catcher who was deeply admired by Mutt. But Mickey's first idol played in St. Louis.

"My first hero was Stan Musial. I grew up in northeastern Oklahoma about 200 miles from St. Louis. We didn't have TV so we listened to the radio all of the time. Harry Caray used to broadcast the games.

"When I saw Joe DiMaggio he became my idol. Then I saw Ted Williams hit. I think he's the greatest hitter that ever lived so he became my idol," said Mickey....

...In 1951, the Yankees and Giants switched spring training camps with the Yankees going to Phoenix, Ariz., and the Giants to St. Petersburg, Fla. Mantle was an amalgam of Ruth and Cobb hitting home runs and batting .402. It proved to be his ticket to the big leagues.

The Yankee's scheduled opener in Washington was rained out so the team returned to New York to open against the Red Sox. The Yankee lineup read: Jackie Jensen (LF), Phil Rizzuto (SS), Mantle (RF),

DiMaggio (CF), Yogi Berra (C), Johnny Mize (1B), Gil McDougald (3B), Jerry Coleman (2B), and Vic Raschi (P). Before the game, Berra walked up to Mantle and said, "Hey kid, are you nervous?"

Mickey looked at him and said, "No."

Yogi joked, "Well how come you're wearing your jockstrap on the outside of your uniform?" — Rich Marazzi, Batting the Breeze, Feb. 13, 1987

* * *

Eddie Mathews

Most teams seem to have that one special individual the fans idolize. In Milwaukee it was Eddie Mathews.

Every Brave player was an automatic hero in the state of Wisconsin the moment the Boston Braves moved to Milwaukee in April 1953. Throughout the '50s and early '60s, Henry Aaron, Warren Spahn, Joe Adcock, Lew Burdette, Andy Pafko, Johnny Logan, Del Crandall, Billy Bruton, Bob Buhl, Bobby Thomson and all the others were adored by Milwaukee's baseball-hungry fans.

The biggest fan favorite of them all was the handsome and powerful Eddie Mathews — the guy radio announcer Earl Gillespie nicknamed "The Brookfield Bomber..."

...In 1952, in what was to become the Braves' final year in Boston, team management made a commitment to give its young players in the organization some needed experience.

"Early in the year, they (team management) made up their minds to go with us (younger players)," Mathews said of his first year in the big leagues. "They just decided to stick some of us in there and see what happens.

"Some of the Boston sportswriters even flew out to Santa Barbara to talk to me. We had (Johnny) Logan, (Bob) Buhl, (Warren) Spahn, Earl Torgeson, Walker Cooper on that team, and they called us the 'Rocket Rockies.' But we were very young and we didn't have a good team. That's being mild. We had a lousy team!"

Mathews' most vivid memory of playing for Boston occurred on the next to last day of the 1952 season: "We were far out of it, and I ended up hitting three home runs at Ebbets Field against the Dodgers. And I tied up the game the last day of the season in the seventh inning, and everybody got mad at me for tying it up!"

Mathews finished the season with 25 home runs and the promise of a brilliant future. With the Braves losing on the field to National League opponents, and at the gate in competition with the popular Red Sox, the team moved to Milwaukee just prior to the 1953 season.

"We didn't have any attendance (in Boston)," Mathews said with a laugh. "We had a bunch of pigeons and a bunch of gamblers, and that's about the extent of it..."

...In 1953 and 1954 Mathews began to get national media exposure for his very powerful swing. The cover of the very first issue of Sports Illustrated (Aug. 16, 1954) features a Mark Kauffman photo, taken at a night baseball game in Milwaukee, of Eddie's classic swing. While the first issue has become a valuable collectible, Mathews said he didn't realize that being on the cover of the first issue would be such a distinction.

"I didn't know that making the cover would be such a big deal," he said. "It doesn't really show my face. It's become a collector's item and a trivia question."

With his success, Mathews quickly became the darling of Milwaukee fans. Beseiged by autograph seekers, bobby-soxers and well-wishers everywhere, it became difficult to live a normal life.

"I was too young to even understand what was going on," Mathews said about being idolized by Milwaukee fans. "I couldn't begin to tell you what it was like." — Tom Mortenson, Oct. 6, 1989

* * *

Johnny Mize

Like many ballplayers of his time, Johnny Mize served his country in World War II, and in the process missed several key seasons in his career. His three-year stint with Navy included a stay on the Pacific island of Tinian in 1945 in the closing weeks of the war.

Johnny Mize

"There were a few Sundays when we were off duty, my buddies and I, and we would get us one of those big canned hams, two or three loaves of bread, some mayonnaise and pickles, and a case of beer, and go for a drive up on a hill and spend the day relaxing," Mize recalled.

"One time we noticed some Marines sittin' on top of a hill overlooking the whole area below. Man, they watched everything like hawks. Heck, we'd just sit there, eatin' sandwiches and drinkin' a few beers and havin' a good time, never really asking ourselves what those Marines over there were guarding."

Part of what those Marines were guarding on Tinian arrived on July 26, aboard the U.S. cruiser Indianapolis — the basic components of the atomic bomb that would be dropped on Hiroshima, Japan, within two weeks. On the night of July 28, transport planes landed at Tinian with the last of the uranium isotope U-235 needed to assemble the bomb.

"We found out later that's why they were sittin' up there," Mize said of the Marine sentries. "We were told later it wasn't really armed until they got it on the plane, but if I'd have known we were picnicking a few yards away from that thing I would've asked for a transfer." — David Craft, Sept. 25, 1987

* * *

Johnny Mize

"If you go to see a ball game, you'll see what I mean," says Mize about the quality of play of today's players.

"I was watchin' an Atlanta game the other night and everybody walked off the field when there was only two outs. It shows you where their head's at," he says with a smooth drawl.

"Luke Appling was tryin' to help this guy who was playin' third base for the Atlanta Braves a few years ago. He told me you can't tell 'em nothin'. The hit .220 and they think they're a superstar. They all try to put the ball in orbit. They don't try to get the run in. I guess that's just the way it is today. They know everything. It's like the old sayin', hire a kid who's just out of high school while they still know everything," he jokes.

"I saw a Cubs game on television the other day and the outfielder misses the relay man. I don't know what they're teachin' 'em. They don't seem to be able to anticipate the situation," he adds.

Enos Slaughter agrees. "We had pride in ourselves — pride in our uniforms, not like these prima donnas playin' today," he says.

"When they threw the reserve clause out of baseball they killed the game. The players today have too much power," says Slaughter.

"When I broke in with St. Louis in 1938, we each got a cap and a uniform. We had to pay for everything else," he says. "We had to pay to have it laundered, pay for our soda, sandwiches, everything. You go in a clubhouse today and it's an air-conditioned, carpeted lounge. It's like a darn beauty parlor with hair dryers. It's really something," he says.

With only eight teams in a league, competition was fierce for employment in the major leagues when Slaughter and Mize played. Many talented athletes spent their entire careers in the minors, never getting a chance at the "big time." "If you didn't hit .300, you'd go back to the minors to learn how," says Mize.

Did younger players ever seek advice from Mize when he was an established star? "No, not really," he answers. "Sometimes veteran players like Rizzuto would come up and ask what they were doin' wrong, but not the younger players."

"In those days, you played with broken fingers, broken toes," says Slaughter. "Nowadays if they have a hangnail, they're out for two weeks."

"I was on first base one time and I looked up and got hit with a line drive off the bat of Nippy Jones. It broke my nose. It really cleared out my sinuses. I sat out one game and was back in the lineup the next day," he says...

...Mize says that players today don't seem to have fun playing baseball. "We had a lot of fun around the clubhouse," he says. "We had Pepper Martin and Dizzy Dean on that team in St. Louis. One time they bought some white overalls and pretended to be guys installing an air-conditioner in the barber shop in St. Louis. They were banging on chairs, cutting holes in the wall and everything," he laughs. "Pepper was always doing something crazy, high jumping over a pot-bellied stove in Boston, giving somebody a hot foot, or putting gum on your arm so it'd stick to the hair. He had Pepper Martin's Mudcat Band and every song sounded the same."

Mize elaborated on more of Martin's character. "He'd go to the trick shop (novelty) and buy sneezing powder and spread it around," he says. "He'd ride the rails every year to spring training. He'd get a ride on a freight train to save money." — Tom Mortenson, Sept. 9, 1988

* * *

Bobo Newsom

The Bible of Baseball says that a line drive off the bat of Oscar Judd hit pitcher Bobo Newsom in the head one afternoon. The ball ricocheted a couple of hundred feet into center field and fell in safely for a hit.

The blow staggered Newsom, but Bobo refused to be taken out of the game. Celestial music floated gently through Newsom's head and an enormous lump grew on his broad brow as the innings progressed. In an angelic daze, Bobo mowed down one batter after another. Newsom disclosed later that "old Bobo didn't know nothing for a few innings afterward," but the temporary amnesia didn't prevent the hurler from leaving the field with a complete game victory.

"It just goes to show ya," drawled the right-handed Newsom, "old Bobo's a better pitcher when he's unconscious than most guys are when they're wide awake."...

...Arriving at the Greenville Park during batting practice, Newsom dropped his bags by the dugout and surveyed the field. The club's manager, Hal Weafer, greeted his new acquisition by asking if Newsom had a fastball.

"Mister," Newsom replied, "Bobo's so fast he's got the umpires complaining they can't call what they can't see."

Weafer asked if Newsom had a curve. "Bobo's curve," said Bobo, "hooked around the third base bag a couple of times on the way to the plate."

"I don't care how much stuff you've got," Weafer told Newsom, "unless you've got control."

"Then you've got no worries," Newsom said. "I can pick the whiskers off a fly at 100 feet."

"If you've got a tenth of the stuff you claim," Weafer said, "we won't have enough dough to pay you for one day's work."

"That's right," Newsom answered, "but a guy's got to start somewhere."

Weafer nodded and told Newsom to take the mound. The Greenville manager strolled to the sidelines to get a good look at his new pitcher. Newsom wound up and fired a strike — to the third base coach's box. The wild pitch missed Weafer's head by a fly's whisker, but caromed off the unsuspecting skull of the team's best pitcher. The Greenville ace crumpled to the ground and Weafer grabbed the nearest bat. The fleet-footed Newsom managed to stay one step ahead of Weafer as the two men sped again and again around the basepaths. The pair scored several runs before order was restored...

...Newsom appeared as a starter, a reliever and as a pinch-runner for the Angels in 1933. In his spare time, he provided commentary for the club's radio broadcasts. The work behind the microphone paid off when Newsom talked an opposing runner out of scoring a run in the late innings of a game that season.

"I entered the game as a relief pitcher," Newsom said. "Our starter had filled the bases while I was warming up in front of our dugout. He had three balls on the next batter and I started to the mound before he made his last pitch. The pitcher throws a fourth wide one, walking the batter.

"The guy on third starts to lumber home like all them guys lumber when they score a forced run. I pass the fellow on my way to the mound. 'You lucky stiff,' I tell him, 'scoring a cheap run like that.' He stops to argue. So I say he's lucky being forced home because if he had to run, he couldn't score from third on a double.

"That makes the big lug sore and he starts to the plate again. I headed out to the mound and we're still hollering insults at each other. The guy is so mad he misses the plate. By some miracle, the umpire notices he misses the plate. I call for the ball and then run after the fellow in the dugout.

"He thinks I'm going to take a swing at him, but I just tag him with the ball. The umpire calls him out. Then I fan the next two batters and we win the game."

Newsom told the tale for 20 years, but the story never received the appreciation he thought it deserved. In 1952, after a teammate gave the plot a less than enthusiastic review, a disappointed Newsom wondered whether the story needed some spice. "Maybe," said Newsom, "I should work up something about a blonde." — Russell Streur, Feb. 7, 1992

* * *

Willard Nixon

But 1956 did provide Nixon with his most memorable game of his career, a contest that took place on Aug. 7 against the Yankees in Fenway Park. Nixon was pitching against Don Larsen, and the game was scoreless going into the 11th inning.

138

"I had two men out and (Mickey) Mantle was up," recalled Nixon. "I threw him a slider, and he hit a high fly ball to left field, but I knew it wasn't out. Williams went back and pounded his glove. But the ball hit his glove and bounced out and Mantle got a double.

"Well, the fans just tore that place apart," continued Nixon. "They booed Williams, like they liked to, and Ted was stomping around out there and pitching a fit. Yogi (Berra) was up and on the first pitch, he hit a blue dart to left. You knew it was off the wall and Mantle was going to score. But Williams jumped up there and hit the wall and caught the ball.

"When he caught the ball, the people out in left just start giving him an ovation. But Williams started spitting at them. Then he ran in and got to second base and spit up towards the press box. Then he came in the dugout and came back out on the first step and he spit over the dugout. People were absolutely going crazy."

In the bottom of the 11th, Nixon began a rally by reaching first on an Andy Carey error. That was followed by a Moose Skowron error on an attempted sacrifice by Billy Goodman, leaving runners on first and second with nobody out. Nixon was lifted for a pinch runner, Billy Consolo. The inning's third batter, Billy Klaus, walked, loading the bases with no one out and Williams at bat.

"The fans started again. They were booing him something awful," said Nixon. "The Yankees brought in Tommy Byrne to pitch to Williams, who was still burning about the incident earlier. Well, they walked Williams on four pitches and we won the game. But Williams took that bat and he threw it just as high in the air as he possibly could and ran into the dugout. And of course, the fans started again.

"I couldn't wait until the papers came out because I just knew I was going to get a big write-up," admitted the winning pitcher. "But the only way that you could tell that I had pitched, beating the Yankees 1-0 in 11 innings, was by my name in the box score. Everything else was Williams did this and Williams did that. All this spitting and he was fined $5,000 by (Tom) Yawkey, who said it was the greatest game he ever saw." — Bill Ballew, Feb. 2, 1990

* * *

Johnny Oates

The "tools of ignorance" were part of his gear, but former major league catcher Johnny Oates has always understood the moment at hand.

For instance, there was the time when he was a schoolboy...

"My older sister is 10 years older than I am, and I can remember guys would come to the house to date her," Oates explained to Sports Collectors Digest. "I often wanted to go out with 'em to the movies or for ice cream, and they didn't want me taggin' along.

"One time, a guy came to our home and said, 'I'll tell you what, John. I'll play some catch with you in the front yard if you stay home.' I said, 'Deal.' So we went out and played catch for a while and then my sister and her date would go off to the movies and I'd be happy as a lark.

"My mom and dad saw that, and decided the arrangement was fair, so from then on, they decided my sister's dates had to first play catch with me."

When Oates thinks back to his childhood days, he proudly notes that his older sister and older brother were involved in softball, baseball and basketball in high school, that his younger brother also played baseball, and that their father played semipro baseball in his younger days, taking the mound for several cotton mill teams in the south.

Oates himself can recall putting on his older brother's tennis shoes and tossing balls around the house. As he grew up, Oates says, he played baseball all summer long and between it, basketball and other high school sports. "I came home right after school maybe 10 times in four years," he adds laughingly.

"By that time, a number of my friends were out looking for jobs so they could have their own automobile, or extra spending money," Oates pointed out.

"Fortunately, I didn't have to work during the summertime. Not that we had money — 'cause we were a very poor family. But when I went into high school my father got a construction job, and that helped. By that time, we were living just outside of Richmond, Va., and I had more opportunities to play baseball than my older brother had, living in the country all his life..." — David Craft, Aug. 19, 1988

* * *

Tony Oliva

Some people find it fun to speculate about what "might have been" for a player under different circumstances. I asked Tony Oliva what he thought his stats might look like if he had played his career in the Metrodome (also known as the "Homerdome") as opposed to roomy, windy Metropolitan Stadium...the home of the Twins during Oliva's playing days. "It's hard to say, because today the balls carry all over...no matter where you play. But I believe if you took our '64 ball club, and put it in the Metrodome, we might have hit 90 more home runs (as a team). Because Killebrew probably would have hit 60 home runs, Mincher maybe 40 or 50, and I know, personally, if I had played in the Dome, I'd have hit 40 home runs, average. Center field (in old Metropolitan Stadium) was 430 feet, the alleys were 380, and the lines were 358. The Dome is a lot smaller." — Dave Sabini, Oct. 21, 1988

* * *

Jim Palmer

In addition to Rick Dempsey, a character noted for his jaunts around the bases during rain delays, Tommy Davis and Moe Drabowsky kept things loose on the team.

"When we won our first World Series (1966), we won it in Kansas City and immediately got on the plane to L.A. The next thing you know, Moe had wrapped this snake around Luis Aparicio's neck and put little garter snakes in Paul Blair's uniform. Blair ended up dressing in the dugout. He wouldn't go back in. He just hated snakes," said Palmer.

Davis, who ended his career as a designated hitter, would often spend time playing Palmer one-on-one in a game of Nerf basketball in the clubhouse or eating in between at-bats.

"Earl Weaver would say 'Go in and get Davis.' Tommy'd come running out with mustard on his mouth because he'd been eating hot dogs," Palmer said, noting Davis, who hit a league leading .346 and had 27 home runs and 153 RBI in 1962 with Los Angeles, could wake up from a nap and go get a hit.

Sometimes, there would be no one on the bench.

"Earl used to look down the bench and there'd be no one there. McNally'd be working on his golf swing in the locker room."

Palmer and Weaver often did not agree with each other. The relationship the two had is the question he is asked about the most.

"Most people ask me about Earl. Did we hate each other as much as people thought we did? I just thought that Earl needed somebody to tell him what the real truth was.

"Boris Pasternak, in one of his excerpts, said 'Once in every generation comes along a fool who tells the truth as he perceives it.' Well, Earl wasn't a fool, but he did preceive the truth the way he perceived it.

"So somebody needed to be there to be his arch-personality to let him know that. I don't mean this really critically, because Earl was a great manager.

"Once we won 109, 108, and 101 games Earl lost a little bit of introspection. So somebody had to be there to let him know."

Palmer wasn't the only player who questioned Weaver about his actions, though.

"We had a lot of players. John Lowenstein always used to kid him. He'd ask him why he did something. But I did it because I wanted to know what he was thinking.

"Some might construe that as being critical, or whatever, but it also depends on the tone of how you ask it." — Mark K. Larson, Sept. 2, 1988

* * *

Joe Pepitone

Pepitone played in only three games for the Braves before he decided to hang up his cleats for good.

"I remember Hank Aaron coming up to me and trying to convince me to stay," he said, "but I just wasn't up to it at that point in my life. The travel, trying to produce for the team when I was playing only part time...it just wasn't going right. So, I retired at the age of 32.

"Hank asked me if he could have my pair of spikes, which I gave him. I think he hit his 714th or 715th home run wearing my old pair of baseball shoes. I'm very proud of that." — David Craft, Nov. 29, 1991

* * *

J.W. Porter

Cleveland was an interesting year. I had been traded for (Jim) Hegan and, believe it or not, with all the great ballplayers to have come through Cleveland in their history, they had a newspaper poll that winter (1957) and Hegan was a write-in candidate for the most popular player in Cleveland Indian history. And two weeks after the poll they traded him for me.

So I go over as probably the most unpopular player in their history. Even though what little I played that year I did well, they hated me. I hit a home run in the bottom of the ninth to win a game and got standing boos. — Brent Kelley, Nov. 24, 1989

* * *

Boog Powell

While Boog Powell had a 17-year career, which included four World Series appearances, his post-baseball life might be how he is most remembered.

You know, Powell and former umpire Jim Honochick sitting together at a bar discussing the merits of Lite Beer from Miller when Honochick, whose eyesight had always been in question due to his profession, abruptly asks another bar partron, "Hey, aren't you Boog Powell?"

"Lite (Beer) commercials have been a great experience," said Powell, who has appeared in 16 different commercials. "I don't think any of us ever expected (the commercial's appeal) would turn out the way

it has. We thought the commercials would be a one-shot deal, which had pretty good money. Then all of a sudden it started rolling and every year I was doing two commercials.

"One of the neat things about the Lite Beer commercials is the friendship between all the guys. Most of us had been on a team sport, be it baseball, football, hockey or whatever, and when you walk on to the set, it is almost as if you were walking into a clubhouse. We're always joking around." — Ross Forman, Aug. 2, 1991

* * *

Vic Power

SCD: You were great friends with Jimmy Piersall.

Power: It didn't start out that way. When I was on Kansas City and he was on Boston, he got mad when I caught his line drive to first and he shouted, "You black son of a bitch!" from the dugout. The next time he got on first, I told Bobby Shantz to throw over. Shantz didn't want to do it because we were way ahead and Piersall wasn't going to run, but I insisted. So he threw to first and I gave Piersall a hard tag on the back of the neck. He got mad and yelled at me for hitting him so hard, and I told him I was going to kill him and dropped my glove, and the umpires ran up and it looked like we were going to fight. Then he took a deep breath and said, "You don't want to kill me. I've got a big family." And everyone started laughing.

When we played together in Cleveland, he gave me his book Fear Strikes Out to read and it was a very sad story. He wasn't crazy anymore, he said, but he was still sick and I tried to protect him. Joe Cronin, the American League president, kept sending him telegrams to behave. I'll never forget when Jimmy got into an argument with an umpire and took a water pistol from his pocket and shot water into the umpire's face — that was awful.

He once asked for time when batting against Detroit and ran into the clubhouse. He came back with something hidden in his hand. It turned out to be a mosquito spray. When the ball was pitched, he whipped it out and sprayed the ball. There was smoke all over and everyone was laughing.

Then there was the time he took a home run ball that bounced back on the field and threw it at Bill Veeck's expensive new scoreboard, which was blaring music and explosive noises — and it broke. I remember that he hit a home run against Jim Bunning in a key game in front of 40,000 people. He bowed to all the people, but wouldn't run. Suddenly took off as if he was beating out an inside-the-park homer and he slid into home plate. And then he just lay there sleeping. That caused a big fight. We had to run out there and save him. One day, they let about 8,000 kids into the ballpark free and they sat in the stands together. When Jimmy was in the outfield, they yelled for him to come over and sign autographs. Well, he waved them to come onto the field and they climbed over the fence and ran over to him — and during the middle of the game, he started signing autographs. But it was dangerous in Yankee Stadium when some tough young guys started calling him names and he challenged them to a fight and a bunch of them went onto the field after him. They started kicking him. Temple, who was a tough guy, really really hit those guys. Jimmy wasn't a fighter. He would just throw tantrums like a little boy.

We used to love to drive him crazy. He didn't smoke and every time he got on the bus, Barry Latman and the others would light up cigars and blow smoke at him, and he'd go wild and make the driver stop so he could take a taxi. I think I enjoyed playing with him more than anyone because he would do something different every day — and that kept me relaxed. — Danny Peary, March, 9, 1990

* * *

Jerry Reuss

Oh yes — those Reuss stories told by Jay Johnstone in his three books are true, Reuss said. Reuss is on Johnstone's roster of the "All-Crazy Team" as a starting pitcher; check out the photo in Temporary Insanity of Reuss posing shirtless — with a cigarette hanging out of each nostril — between Don Stanhouse and Johnstone, who have cigarettes hanging from their mouths.

"I know it's accurate because Jay called when he wrote the book and asked if he had the story straight and so it's pretty much out of my mouth the way it was.

"So many of the things I did were spur of the moment, things I thought would be funny situations and I went ahead and did it and as a result the antics have become somewhat legendary. I'm not a legend but the antics are.

"Every time I walk into a clubhouse there's somebody there that says, 'Hey, I remember when you...' and the just go ahead and fill in the blank," Reuss continued.

"I have to think, 'Yeah, I did do that, didn't I?'" Gary Herron, May 10, 1991

* * *

Brooks Robinson

In 1970 and '71, as the Orioles completed a three-year stint in the Fall Classic, Robinson would get 16 hits in 43 at bats, but it was his glove work in 1970 that set the baseball world, and a lot of the rest of the world, too, on its ear.

"I knew it was special...I realized it after three games," said Robinson, who recalled that he had had two- or three-game stretches when he could seem to do no wrong, but never for five games. But really, that's not quite accurate, because the 1970 Series actually started on something of a sour note for Robinson.

Brooks Robinson

Though it isn't the sort of thing that immediately springs to mind for the average fan, Robinson flubbed the first chance hit his way in that Series. "In the first inning of the first game I made an error. I couldn't

believe it, the first ball hit to me. I started to think 'you just can't handle the pressure,'" recalled Robinson with a wink. — T.S. O'Connell, Sept. 6, 1991

* * *

Eddie Robinson

Robinson called former teammate Yogi Berra "genuine." "A lot of that stuff that's written is true and not put on. It just happened. That doesn't mean that Yogi's not a smart guy, because I think he is. He just says and does some funny things. He and (A.L. President) Bobby Brown, who's a friend of mine, were rooming together. Yogi was reading a comic book and Bobby Brown was reading a medical journal (he later became a doctor). They turned the lights out and Yogi says, 'How'd your's turn out, Bobby?'" — Rick Hines, March 1, 1991

* * *

Babe Ruth

June 13, 1948, has become a memorable day in Dave's (Blumenthal) life. It was the day he took two still photographs at a special Old-Timers Day honoring the legendary Babe Ruth. They are most likely the last photographs of the Babe in uniform, because he died just two months later. One photograph depicts an aging Ruth at the microphone addressing the crowd in his farewell to the fans. The other picture shows Ruth seated in the locker room after the event.

Blumenthal recalls vividly the situation that day: "I was using a 4x5 Graflex Speed Graphic camera. I had my knee on the ground for the photo. I always had one knee on the ground. I remember the look of admiration Mel Allen had in his eyes for the Babe. Later in the locker room, after taking the picture there, I told him, 'Babe, these pictures will perpetuate you forever.' He took my hand and asked me not to publish the pictures for at least 20 years. He wasn't well. Two months later, on Aug. 16, he died."

Blumenthal remembers Babe Ruth as a true humanitarian.

"He was getting criticized by some of the New York press for doing certain things just for publicity," Blumenthal says. "I remember one incident when he went to see a young boy in the hospital who was dying of leukemia. He brought the kid a ball. He made sure that no one from the press would know he went to see the boy." — Tom Mortenson, Sept. 2, 1988

* * *

Red Schoendienst

SCD: Speaking of All-Star games, was your homer in the 1950 game the highlight of your 15 games?

RS: Well, I think so. That particular game, I didn't think I was going to get into the game. Kiddingly, I said I was going to hit a home run, you know, but I wasn't a home run hitter. That was the first extra-inning All-Star game there was, and then I hit the home run. It was quite an honor that didn't really sink in until the game was over. I also finished that game by making a double play.

SCD: It was quite an inning for you.

RS: Yes, and you know, after the game, a clubhouse guy comes to me and says, "Red, a guy in the upper deck in left field (of Comiskey Park) caught your ball, and he wants to know if you'd like to have it." I says, "Absolutely. Now what does he want?" He says, "Well, he'd like to have an autographed ball of the (N.L. All-Star) team." The guy probably knew that everyone who played got an autographed team ball, so I says I'll be happy to give him this autographed ball for the ball that I hit. And I did. And about three minutes later, there was another knock on the door, and this other guy says "I caught Red Schoendienst's ball!" So I don't know if I got the right one or not. Everyone's got a trick, I guess. — Dave Sabaini, Oct. 27, 1989

* * *

Dick Schofield

Paul Green: Did you ever get thrown out of a game before you ever got to play in one?

Dick Schofield: Yes, of course that was (Eddie) Stanky's fault. He made me thow a towel out on the field.

Green: So you were under orders.

Schofield: Yes, I was under orders. We had had some trouble and the umpire came over to the dugout and asked Stanky who threw the towel out. Stanky just looked down at me and said, "Schofield threw that towel out." I wasn't going to play anyhow so that got me kicked out.

Green: That must have felt a little odd.

Schofield: Yes, I thought that it might be all over, that I'd never get to play. It's kind of funny as you look back on it though.

Green: I imagine a couple of the guys gave you a pretty good ribbing about it at the time.

Schofield: A lot of people still remember it. They'll say, "You got kicked out of a game before you ever got in a game," and things like that. I have one record anyhow. — Paul Green, July 10, 1987

* * *

Tom Seaver

Late in the 1985 season, Seaver's 19th in the major leagues, he practically guaranteed his induction into the Hall of Fame when he won his 300th game. He was a member of the Chicago White Sox, but the win came over the Yankees in New York City.

"It was a great day," recalled Seaver. "From a personal standpoint, it was the best day I ever had in the big leagues. It was my most enjoyable day. I loved every minute of it."

But was Seaver, who spent all but the last three seasons of his career as a National Leaguer, disappointed that win number 300 came in the American League?

"No, not at all," said Seaver. "You get to 300, there are no disappointments at all." — Dave Sabaini, Sept. 8, 1989

* * *

Rip Sewell

Paul Green: Did you have any trouble with the umpires with it?

Sewell: At first I did, but the dean of umpires, Catfish Klem, was sent to Pittsburgh. He said, "Rip, I want you to go out on that mound and I want four or five hitters up here and a catcher. I'm going to be behind the plate. I want you to throw that do-do ball or blooper ball or whatever they call it, and I'm going to be the judge." We had two or three batters up there and Al Lopez was the catcher and I demonstrated it. He told his umpires that if the ball came over for a strike, they were supposed to call it a strike.

The rule book said that any ball which goes over for a strike other than rolling it, from the letters to the knees, has to be called a strike. I showed Klem I could throw just as many strikes with it and he got his umpires together and told them it was a strike and they had better call it. So it made history and the fans loved that pitch. They ate it up.

Green: Didn't LaRoche of the Yankees try it a few years back?

Sewell: He threw two or three of them but they weren't the real blooper. He did strike one guy out on it. I saw that.

Green: Could you throw it at any time?

Sewell: Any time. I had about five pitches, two or three change of paces, fastball, curve, slider, and a sinker, but I could throw the blooper for a strike as easy as I could throw any other pitch. Dominic Dallessandro with Chicago was a little fellow and I had three men on

base, three balls and two strikes on him in the ninth inning, and I threw him a blooper ball. He started to swing and stopped, started again and stopped, and the umpire called him out because it was right over the middle of the plate.

Dominic Dallessandro took that bat and pointed it toward me like a gun and said, "You SOB, if this was a shot gun, I'd shoot you right between the eyes." Charlie Grimm was the third base coach and he fell over backwards and laid on his back for five minutes.

Green: That had to be quite a game ending. Did any other people do unusual things when you threw it?

Sewell: Whitey Kurowski on the Cardinals wouldn't swing at it. When I threw it to him he wouldn't swing at it. He'd spit at it. He'd spit tobacco juice at it. He hated that thing. I threw Debs Garms one in St. Louis and he jumped right straight up in the air and swung at it like he was chopping cotton. It was a funny thing to see.

Green: Could anyone hit it well?

Sewell: No one hit it good. No one ever hit it good. A lot of people say why didn't they bunt it, but they had to wait and turn around to bunt it. A good bunter loves the fastball because he doesn't give it away until the last second. They had to give it away when I threw them the blooper.

Green: Didn't Dizzy Trout try and throw you one in an exhibition game?

Sewell: See, I started that pitch against Detroit. The paper had big headlines that I would pitch against Trout. It was cold but we had about 45,000 people there for an exhibition game. He was pitching for them. We only pitched three innings but I got their hitters to pop it up and came up to bat and Trout just tossed one up there and I hit the hell out of it down third base, but the guy caught the ball. I hit it pretty good. It was a show and the people love it.

Green: Did you ever figure out how to hit it?

Sewell: No.

Green: Williams got you in the All-Star Game.

Sewell: I'll tell you about that. He and I know, and the umpire, who was Larry Goetz, know what happened. See we were beat 8-0 and I wasn't supposed to pitch because my elbow was swollen. Before the game I was hitting fungos and Ted Williams was warming up. He had never seen the blooper and he hollered down to me, "Hey Rip, you wouldn't throw that damn ball in a game like this would you?" I hollered back, "Yes, I would boy. You're going to get it," knowing that I wasn't going in. So sure enough I had the cahnce to throw it to him. He came up to the plate and was shaking his head "no" and I was nodding "yes."

I threw him one on the first pitch and he swung at it from Port Arthur about as hard as he could and fouled it back over the National League dugout. I threw him another which was about an inch and a half outside. Of course, if Ted Williams didn't swing it was a ball.

Green: That's true.

Sewell: So he kept shaking his head "no" and I nodded "yes" and threw him a fast ball right over the plate and he took it for a strike. He looked out at me to say "no" but I said, "Yeah, you're going to get it." So I threw him my Sunday blooper ball. He walked up on it about five feet, he was out of the batter's box, and hit the ball over the right field fence in the bullpen for a home run. He trotted around the bases and I walked inside the bases talking to him. He was laughing.

Green: What were you saying?

Sewell: I was saying, "Hey turkey, you were out of the batter's box," and he said, "Hell, I know it." The 45,000 people there that night stood up and applauded Ted Williams for 10 minutes.

Green: The next batter was Keller wasn't it?

Sewell: Right, King Kong Keller. I threw him one on the first pitch and he swung about as hard as he could and it went straight up in the air about 10 feet over the catcher. Phil Masi was the catcher and he was laughing so hard he damn near dropped the ball. That was the third out. — Paul Green, Oct. 26, 1984

* * *

Roy Sievers

Tragedies were not the only plays the Browns performed, however, as owner Bill Veeck's introduction of midget Eddie Gaedel to the baseball world was high comedy in its most entertaining form — live and in living color.

"At first, nobody knew what the heck was goin' on, you know. Gaedel comes out of the cake wearing a Browns uniform, and everybody thought it was a funny stunt and everything.

"Then, when it began to dawn on us that the midget was walkin' toward the plate with a bat in his hand, oh man! The Detroit manager, Red Rolfe, was hollerin' and moanin' that the midget was gonna bat, and the place was going wild with laughter and we had the p.a. announcer say we're all to meet the newest member of the St. Louis Browns.

"Rolfe was yellin' 'He can't hit! He can't hit!' and Mr. Veeck's up in the press box waving Gaedel's contract and sayin' 'I got the contract right here!' Oh man, it was funny. Four pitches later, Gaedel walks and Delsing went in to run for him.

"But Mr. Veeck was good for baseball. He cared about people, especially the fans. He created excitement and anticipation at the ballpark. The fireworks, the gag prizes, the nice gifts, even prizes of money. He was a good man." — David Craft, July 15, 1988

* * *

Ted Simmons

Irwin Cohen: You've played in three decades. What has been your biggest thrill?

Simmons: The seventh game of the World Series (1982, Brewers vs. St. Louis). Although we lost in a seven game World Series with St. Louis, in the bottom of the sixth inning of that game we were ahead 3-1. I thought we were going to win. Although we lost I still have that personal experience of being in the seventh game of the World Series and being ahead 3-1, as every boy that loves baseball dreams of being in the World Series. I was in many wiffle ball games as a kid and created that situation in my fantasy at least a thousand times. I dreamed that as a kid and to find myself in that situation as an adult is pretty special stuff. — Irwin Cohen, On the Baseball Beat, Jan. 3, 1986

* * *

Sibby Sisti

Sisti remembers catcher Walker Cooper as one of the team's main pranksters. One story in particular he enjoys telling about Cooper makes him chuckle: "We'd go to spring training in Florida and Walker would spot some kid, a rookie that could run like a deer. He'd go up and tell the kid 'I'll race you 50 yards for $100.' The kid would take one look at him and agree right away. Then Cooper would have somebody start them and they'd take off. The kid would go past him like a shot and pass the finish line and Walker would come trotting along way behind. Then when the kid would say, 'where's my $100?' Walker would say, 'I didn't say I'd beat you. I just said I'd race you for $100.'"...

...Astute fans of baseball movies may remember that Sibby Sisti appeared in the motion picture The Natural, which starred Robert Redford as Roy Hobbs. Sisti's role in the movie was that of the Pittsburgh manager, the team that opposed Hobbs' team, the ficticious New York Knights.

Sisti describes the events leading up to his appearance in the movie as something of a fluke. "Sal Maglie called me one day and asked if I'd like to come down for a stadium dedication they were having," recalls Sisti. "I went down there and the mayor and some local politicians were there.

"Afterward, some lady came up and introduced herself and said they were looking for people to be in a baseball movie. I told her that I didn't know anything about acting and she said, 'that's OK.' She asked for my name and phone number and said someone would give me a call. I really didn't expect to hear from anyone and then one day, about a month later, they called and asked if I'd like to come down to appear in the movie."

Sisti says his work in the movie involved a lot of waiting around. "It seemed like I did absolutely nothing for three weeks. I'd go out there at 6 p.m. and play pinochle," he says. When the film crew's technical adviser was unable to come to work, Sisti was asked to be a consultant for two days and he even gave a few pointers to leading man Redford.

"He handled himself very well," says Sisti of movie star Redford. "He's a left-handed hitter and it seemed like he was hitting up in the air with an uppercut swing. I asked him if he played golf and showed him that he could grip the bat like a golf club. Paul Waner had shown me how to take a golf grip on a bat and I explained it to him (Redford). Whether he ever used it (advice) or not, I don't know," says Sisti.

Sisti adds that Redford is a great fan of Ted Williams. "That's why he wanted uniform #9."

Redford and Sisti had their picture taken together on the set during the filming of The Natural, and the former major leaguer had some 8-by-10-inch color prints made up for friends.

He says he's seen The Natural about 100 times and thinks it's a good wholesome family movie. "I didn't see that other one (Bull Durham), but I don't think I'd enjoy it. If you can't take your family to it, I don't think I'd enjoy it very much," he reasons. — Tom Mortenson, Nov. 16, 1990

* * *

Enos Slaughter

Q: We all know you want very much to get into the Hall of Fame. How important is it to you?

A: It would make my baseball career complete. I really feel I have the statistics to get in. It's the thing I want the most.

Q: Is there anything you wished you could have accomplished?

A: Yes. I really wanted to play in the 1960 season so I could have played in four decades — the '30s, '40s, '50s and '60s. I think Williams was the only player to do that.

Q: Is there anything else you would like to add?

A: Well, Bob, I had a good career and loved every minute of it. I hope my fans will support me and write to the baseball writers and ask to get me elected to the Hall of Fame. — Bob Mason, The Sport Scene, June 15, 1977

* * *

Warren Spahn

Q: Does being in the Hall of Fame mean much to you?

A: Yes, very much so. I take a lot of pride in being one of a handful of players to be so honored. It's nice to know that of the thousands of players who have been in the game, I have been chosen to be among the greatest.

Q: What would you say was the top thrill of your baseball career?

A: That's a really tough question. I suppose winning the World Series in 1957. This is something that every player tries for. It is really satisfying to be a champion after a long, hard season. My one personal thrill would be winning my 300th game.

Q: It must have been exciting pitching all those no-hitters.

A: No, not at all. Pitching a no-hit game is really a grind. The pressure is really on you. The players in the dugout don't talk to you, fearing that they might jinx your game. It is constantly on your mind and you can't wait for the game to be over. I suppose it's nice to have done it, but I never really enjoyed it. — Bob Mason, The Sport Scene, June 30, 1977

* * *

Warren Spahn

It was Warren Spahn who made the perceptive observation: "The secret of hitting is timing, while the secret of pitching is upsetting a batter's timing." Insofar as the spitter is concerned, Spahn commented: "I threw a spitter only one time in my career and on that occasion the batter connected and hit the ball out of the park. I never tried it again. Perfecting a good spitter takes a lot of concentration and practice, and I really didn't need it in my repertoire." — Robert Obojski, May 31, 1991

* * *

Warren Spahn

When asked if he has any advice for youngsters hoping for a successful career as a professional pitcher, the 363-game winner offers the following words, "Get an education first. There are no shortcuts. The way to success is hard work. I think that the problem in baseball is that too many pitchers don't throw enough. There are not too many people that are going to agree with me, but I feel that today's pitchers never get in shape.

"I was forunate. I never had a weight problem. I could go to spring training and start throwing hard right away. All these goofy, trick pitches eventually hurt a guy's arm.

"Secondly, steroids and drugs are not going to do the job for you. There's something good about being tired after a day's work. There's a nice feeling. You can never push that fatigue barrier back until you've reached the limit and go a little further. Then all of a sudden, you're going further than you've ever dreamed." — Tom Mortenson and Kevin Huard, Feb. 28. 1992

* * *

Tracy Stallard

With one pitch and one swing of the bat, Red Sox hurler Tracy Stallard and Yankee slugger Roger Maris carved their way into the major league record books on Oct. 1, 1961.

It was a bright, sunny afternoon at Yankee Stadium with more than 23,000 anxious fans in attendance. It was the last day of the regular season that Maris dug in at the plate, facing Stallard in the fourth inning with none on.

Maris worked the count to two balls and no strikes, and on the next pitch he pulled a fastball out over the plate on a high arc over the right-field fence, just to the left of the 344-foot marker and into the outstretched hands of a frenzied mob of spectators. It was his 61st homer of the season and the game's only run.

The historic ball was grabbed by a Brooklyn native Sal Durante, who received $5,000 for his prize catch.

On choosing to pitch to Maris in that record-breaking situation, Stallard recalls, "I had two balls and no strikes on Maris and I didn't want to walk him because the Yankees had some pretty good hitters on that club, and so I just had to get a strike on him."

At the instant Maris connected, did Stallard think the ball was gone for a homer? "I didn't think so, even though Maris hit it hard and high. Lou Clinton, the right fielder, was looking up and he acted like he might have a chance to catch it, but it went well into the seats," recalls Stallard...

...More than 30 years after giving up Roger Maris' dramatic 61st home run, Stallard lends his thoughts to the subject in retrospect. "I'm glad Maris did it and he did it fair and square. I've read and had people tell me that they've seen places where somebody had said that I just let him do it. I don't know how in the hell you let somebody hit a home run unless you just carry the ball up to the plate. I did my best and that was all I could do," said Stallard. — Fluffy Saccucci, June 19, 1992

* * *

Rennie Stennett

Rennie Stennett was the best hitter in baseball.

At least for one day.

On Sept. 16, 1975, Stennett chalked up seven hits in seven at bats, leading the Pittsburgh Pirates to a 22-0 shellacking of the Chicago Cubs.

No other player in modern baseball history has matched that feat.

Wilbert Robinson, playing before the turn of the century (1892), is the only other person to ever get seven hits in a nine-inning game.

Topps recognized Stennett's achievement with a Record Breakers card in their 1976 set (#6).

Rennie, however, would remember the day regardless.

"It was one of those days when I was full of confidence," Stennett said. "I knew I could hit the ball well, and I was confident it would fall in.

"After the third hit, one of the umpires said, 'Rennie, the way you're batting, you just might have a 4-for-4 day.' He didn't realize I was just getting started."

Stennett was fortunate to even be in the starting lineup.

"I had a swollen ankle, and after the first inning, the trainer said I should come out of the game. But the manager (Danny Murtaugh) said, 'We'll take him out as soon as he makes an out.'

"I never did make that out. Finally, in the eighth, I got the seventh hit, and Willie Randolph came in to run for me."

When he left the game, Stennett had faced four pitchers, getting four singles, two doubles and a triple.

He scored five times, got two hits in both the first inning and the fifth inning, and set a record that may never be broken.

"What makes the record difficult is that you rarely get seven at bats in a game," he said. "It's a rarity to get even six chances. But we just pounded them that day, and I kept getting to the plate again and again." — Larry Powell, Aug. 7, 1992

* * *

Don Sutton

Don Sutton vividly remembers June 18, 1986. Pitching for California in Anaheim Stadium against the Texas Rangers, Sutton was attempting for the second time to notch his 300th major league victory.

"Gary Ward check-swing called strike three," said Sutton, reminiscing about the final out of his 5-1, three-hit complete game victory. "I can replay that last inning slo-mo."

For Sutton, that win is the most memorable moment of his 23-year career, and the one that put him in a elite class of hurlers. He is one of only 20 pitchers to reach the 300-win plateau...

..."I don't mind trades," said Sutton. As long as they keep the game 90 feet down the baselines and 60 feet, six inches to the mound, and you have eight guys that will dive for the ball for you, it doesn't matter.

"This is a statement that has ticked off some people that I have worked for: I never was in love with the name on the uniform," continued Sutton. "I was in love with being a ballplayer. And even more than that, I was in love with the art of pitching. If you had said, 'You're going to Leningrad and starting in four days,' that's great. It's still pitching.

"All I ever wanted to be was a pitcher growing up. I really didn't want to be a Dodger or an Astro or a Spokane Indian or a Toledo Mud Hen. I wanted to be a pitcher. The name might change and the hat and all that kind of stuff, but what I wanted to do was pitch. If you asked me where I wanted to play, I'd have said in the middle of the diamond. Whose diamond, I don't care. I just didn't want to be abused, and I didn't want to be someplace where everybody didn't want to win. But as far as being traded and all of that and have it affect me, no, it just meant you had to move."...

...The former pitcher admits he thinks of being elected into the Hall.

"Usually only when I'm awake," said Sutton with a laugh. "You're darn right I think about it (the Hall of Fame). That's one of my big reasons for wanting to play and be good at it. Once I found out there was one, I wanted to be there. And I wanted to play well enough to be considered for it. That was one of the big motivating factors in my life." — Bill Ballew, Feb. 1, 1991

* * *

Gorman Thomas

Gorman Thomas: A lady wrote me a letter one time. She said she really enjoys the little mannerisms I go through prior to hitting a baseball. I never really thought about it until she wrote me a letter. One day I said I'm going to see what she meant and I went through all of my regimentation. It was kind of weird. I realize there were a lot of things I didn't know that I did.

When I tape my wrists, I like to tape my left wrist first. There's a favorite T-shirt that I wear that I save only for the second half of the season. It says, "Stormin' Gorman" and "Bambi's No. 1 Bomber." I've had it since '78 and it's in threads. It has been resewed 15 or 20 times. If I had a good day at bat or in the field I always took the same route to the park when I was in Milwaukee. It's just little things like

that. I really don't plan things. It's basically reflex action. If someone would follow me around for a couple of days, they'll probably come up with a lot. — Irwin Cohen, On the Baseball Beat, July 18, 1986

* * *

Marv Throneberry

It's been almost 30 years since Marv Throneberry last swung a bat professionally. But the man affectionately known as Marvelous Marv still swings around the country appearing at card shows and promoting Miller Lite beer.

He stopped at a show in Chicago March 16 and his 13th Lite beer commercial premiered the following day during the NBA Game of the Week.

Throneberry, who had a .237 lifetime batting average during his seven seasons in the major leagues, has been a spokesman for Miller Lite since its creation in 1975.

"All of the commericals have been fun," Throneberry said. "When you're (filming) with a group (of former athletes) like the ones we've got, for four days, you just get tired of laughing because somebody's coming up with something all of the time."

Throneberry said his favorite commerical was a Christmas special six years ago "because we told everybody that we weren't going to pull any jokes, that we were all serious. And it took two years for people to believe us. They kept saying, 'I don't get the punchline on that (commercial).'"

Throneberry added: "A lot of people think we are trying to get kids to drink, but we aren't. What we're trying to say is...if you're going to drink, please try ours, or, if you're drinking another brand, would you try ours? No commercial we've ever made said we'd like you to drink this beer. The commericals always relate to...if you're going to drink, would you try ours?"

Throneberry, who is joined on Lite's illustrious roster by such notables as Bob Uecker and John Madden, said Lite Beer "picks its spokesman by trying to get guys who the average person would be comfortable going into a bar, sitting down and having a beer with." — Ross Forman, April 26, 1991

* * *

Bob Uecker

Irwin Cohen: Looking back on your playing days, what do you consider your most memorable moment?

Bob Uecker: Seeing someone fall out of the upper deck in Philadelphia. That was my greatest thrill in baseball.

Cohen: What happened to the fan?

Uecker: He got up and walked away and they booed him. I think the World Series in 1964 with the Cardinals — the championship season — was really a thrill. At that time there were no divisions. You had to beat all the clubs in your league and went against the club in the other league without any playoffs. It was the Cardinals against the Yankees. I didn't get a chance to play in the Series, which was neither here nor there to me, but I was still on the club and I'll never forget it. The next year we finished seventh but I played more so that alleviated some of it for me.

Bob Uecker

Cohen: What was your biggest disappointment?

Uecker: My biggest disappointment? It happens each and every year when they have the Hall of Fame voting. I sit around every year waiting for a call and nothing happens. It really gets aggravating. I even stood in there wearing a uniform. I wanted to know what it felt like being in there. I stood there like a mannequin but some kid squealed on me and they ran me out of there. — Irwin Cohen, On the Baseball Beat, March 2, 1984

* * *

Gary Varsho

SCD: We're just going to jump around on subjects here. Did you play anything like wiffleball when you were growing up as a kid in Marshfield?

Gary Varsho: Not wiffleball. My brother Jimmy and I liked to play a game with a tennis ball and a wall. All we had was a pitcher and batter and the ball would bounce back to you off the wall after you struck the guy out. We made up our own rules. Any ground ball would be an out. Line drives would be hits...you know, things like that. We had a fence for homers.

SCD: Did you win a lot of those games?

Varsho: Oh, I was usually the oldest player. I think I won my share...

...SCD: Did you play in the first night game at Wrigley Field?

Varsho: I was there, but I didn't get into the game. Didn't get into the second one either.

SCD: Damn!

Varsho: That's all right. It was a privilege just being there.

SCD: Was it tough at all seeing the ball?

Varsho: It was tough at first. The lights weren't adjusted real well. It's getting better, though. Hey, it's a first time. They'll keep improving. — Tim Sullivan, March 10, 1989

* * *

Armando Vazquez

Over the years, every person affiliated with the Negro Leagues, from the players to the owners to the club secretaries, have related stories of dealing with "Jim Crow" America on either side of the Mason-Dixon line. Vazquez is no exception.

"I remember one time we played in Nashville, Tenn.," Vazquez began, "and after the game we went downtown to a restaurant about 12 o'clock at night to get something to eat. I went into the restaurant first and they threw me out.

"They told me, 'You gotta go to the back door to buy what you want. You can't come in here.' I got so mad when they told me that...this was my second year, now, and I was just a kid...that when I saw a little guy with a small truck filled with watermelon I went over and bought one watermelon from him. I ate the whole thing, I was so hungry. But I got so sick after that that I couldn't sleep that night. I remember that (episode) because it happened so early in my career." — David Craft, June 21, 1991

* * *

Coot Veal

It's well-known that for any team to be successful, it must have a smooth and steady shortstop to anchor its infield. And unless his name is Ernie Banks or Cal Ripken, this sure-handed shortstop is usually not well-known among the masses, especially if he doesn't carry a big stick.

Such is the case of Orville Inman Veal, better known as "Coot" around Macon, Ga., where he is best known. Except for some long-time, die-hard Detroit Tiger fans, Veal is not a household name, even though he played shortstop in the majors for parts of six years during the late 1950s and early 1960s.

A self-described "good field, no hit" infielder, Veal accomplished a life-long dream by playing in the majors, regardless of his relative obscurity. And today, as vice president of Macon Mine and Mill, Veal fondly remembers his time in professional baseball.

Born on July 9, 1932, in Sandersville, Ga., Veal grew up in Macon playing baseball and basketball through high school. It was in high school that Veal picked up the nickname "Coot," a name that has stuck with him to this day.

"I was playing third base in high school ball in Macon, and they used to have black barnstorming teams come through," recalled Veal. "And one of the teams had a third baseman named Coot, and my coach picked it up from that. If you know my name, you know I needed a nickname." — Bill Ballew, Jan. 5, 1990

* * *

Harry Walker

When he was a youngster, Harry said he didn't get a lot of baseball advice from his brother, who was being groomed as Earle Combs' replacement with the New York Yankees.

"He was 8 years older than me, and wasn't around that much when I was growing up," Walker told SCD. "Oh, we'd play catch and talk sometimes when he came home after the baseball season was over, but I pretty much learned how to play by just going and doing it on my own.

"I wasn't really a fan," Walker added. "I never read the papers or followed the game in those days. All I wanted to do was play ball.

"I didn't weigh more than 100 pounds and people thought I was sickly," drawled Walker. "That's because I just loved to play. I just ran from daylight to dark, and ran it (weight) off. I'd get together with a bunch of neighborhood kids for a morning game, a different bunch for an afternoon game, come home for supper and find another game in the evening to get in..."

..."One of the most frequently-asked questions posed to Walker is, "How did you get your nickname — 'the Hat?'"

"That nickname came from the habit I had of adjusting my cap when I came up to the plate," he answered. "In those days caps were made with horsehair in there and it would sometimes stick to your head. It was just a habit I had."

Another trademark that originated with and became associated with Harry Walker is the two-tone bat.

"In 1941 when I was with Columbus I was in Louisville, and I went down to the Hillerich and Bradsby bat factory," he said. "Everyone was gone except for Mr. Hillerich, one of the owners. He said they didn't have any new bats in the model I liked. Just as I was about to leave he said the only bat close to what I wanted was a two-toned bat they were using to stir stain. I took it anyway and hit a home run in the Little World Series the first time I used it. I went 4-for-4. And that's what they now call the Walker Finish. I've still got it. It's a 35-ounce, 35-inch model. Man, it's got wood in it!" — Tom Mortenson, Nov. 3, 1989

* * *

Herb Washington

He also holds one of the most intriguing (and stangest) career stat sheets of any player in the history of baseball:

G 104, AB 0, R 33, H 0, RBI 0, Avg. .000, SB 30

Today, a World Championship ring sits atop his right ring finger. He can look back and fondly recall holding two world speed records. He was the product of a man's "progressive vision," (who also turned dull uniforms into bold expressions of Kelly green, gold and white.)

Herb Washington was all that and more...

...Designated runner! Designated runner? The American League was barely getting hold of the previous season's new wrinkle: the designated hitter. But in Charlie Finley's uncanny ability to merge baseball with box office, it had some internal logic. One man with speed to burn. One man who, every time he takes over a base, has but one goal: To run, to steal, to make things happen. To explode from second and turn a base hit into a run. Not a pitcher running for a flat-footed slugger. A surface-to-air missle. The fans would love it. So did Washington.

"It struck me as this was going to be some easy work!" he says with a laugh. "It shows how naive I was about how difficult it really was going to be. I thought with my speed that the catchers just didn't stand a chance, quite frankly. However, your fate is still with the pitchers," he continues, "and it became a matter of learning to read them."

The man who had earlier dueled the likes of John Carlos and Mel Pender step for step, now had to learn to watch the feet of Jim Palmer and challenge the arm of Thurman Munson.

With a one year, no-cut contract in hand, Washington headed late to the A's spring training camp in Mesa, Ariz. He would be a special case, working out with his own private mentor.

"When I was in his office," Washington says, "Finley called up the Dodgers and said, 'Hey, I need Maury Wills.' They said, 'No way! He's under contract to the Dodgers.' Finley said, 'Look, I just hired a guy — a track man — to steal bases, and I need Maury for 10 days.' They worked out a deal, and I showed up to work with one of the most prolific base stealers prior to Henderson...to teach me how to slide, get big leads, things like that."...

...If Washington's arrival caused a stir with fans and the media, what did his teammates think? After all, he was joining the league's base stealing champ Bill North and some other players, like Bert Campaneris, who weren't just a one-dimensional asset. Washington was not there to throw strikes, bunt for base hits, go in for late-inning defense. He was merely hired to run. The reaction? "Lukewarm, at best," Washington recalls. "The first day...maybe Vida Blue and Bill North did it...they took a piece of adhesive tape and ran it across the locker room like a finish line. It was a cool reception. The Athletics weren't a slow ballclub by any stretch of the imagination."...

..."But let's look at what the 24th and 25th players contribute to every team in the league. Normally," he continues, "it is an individual who is back and forth from the minors to the majors. How much of a contribution does this individual normally make? You usually can't even measure it. Therefore, if you could take an individual who's job is only to steal bases, and he can win ball games and it can be distinctly pointed to — there were 10 such ball games in 1974. I argue that my value is much greater than the average 25th man.

"For example," he continues, "it's the eighth inning — Sal Bando gets a single. Herb Washington goes in to run for him, steals second and then scores on a ball that Bando couldn't possibly score on — even in his dreams! It ties or wins the game. I had a direct hand in the outcome of that game. It happened 10 times that year."...

..."When I was in Oakland," he says, "I'd get a signal from the bench or the third base coach — and people didn't know this — but when I got the signal to steal, I had to go on the very next pitch! Pitchout, fastball, whatever, it didn't matter. If I got a poor jump, it didn't matter."...

...Herb says he can't honestly remember his first steal. (Sports Illustrated reported it was against the White Sox. As first baseman Dick Allen taunted, "Gonna go? Gonna go?" Washington darted off, saying "Bye" to Allen as he took off.) He says things bottomed out in the season's first half — a one-for-six stretch cooled even his jets but a post All-Star break 10 steals in a row only served to jump start that engine and kick in the afterburners...

..."I'll tell you why he (Dick Allen) sticks out a lot, as far as other teams," says Washington. "He was the first individual to make me feel comfortable. He went out of his way, just to say some kind words. A guy of that stature, helping to settle me. I'm on first base and Allen reaches over and he grabs my ankle! And I'm like, 'What's wrong with you?!?' And he says, 'Well, I raise race horses and you can always tell a great race horse by his ankles. You know, we just played California and Mickey Rivers can fly!' I said, 'What? You think he can fly?' Well, everybody's entitled to his opinion.' So, I steal a base and my hat comes off. Dick Allen picks up my hat, brings it down and gives it to me. He says, 'Hell, Mickey can fly — but you can low fly!'

"From that time on, he always made a point to find me whenever we played against him...to come on over and talk with me. He didn't have to do that." — Pete Dobrovitz, Oct. 14, 1988

* * *

Bill "Bugs" Werle

SCD: Your nickname was "Bugs." How did you get that?

Bill Werle: I went to the University of California. My uncle was an agriculture inspector for the county down in Stockton. I had a chance to go to Cal on a scholarship and he asked what I was going to take. I said I didn't know and he suggested I take entomology. He said it was a hell of a field.

So I ended up taking entomology but I didn't realize I was going to be involved so much with science courses. (Laughs) It was a tough course!

That's where the name came from — studying bugs in school. — Brent Kelley, July 5, 1991

* * *

Bob Will

One thing that isn't different is the game's ability to surprise participants and spectators alike. Even when people think they have seen it all, something that opens a few eyes — opens them wide enough, in fact, to let a few teardrops fall, as was the case with Casey Stengel and his 1962 Mets. Will was on hand for one of the year's more notorious blunders.

The action unfolded at the Polo Grounds on June 17, 1962. Will remembers it as the first game of a Sunday doubleheader with the hapless Mets, and Don Elston was pitching for the visiting Cubbies.

"Marvelous" Marv Throneberry, the Mets' first baseman, socked a pitch into the gap in right-center field. George Altman hurriedly chased after the ball, which was rolling along the base of the wall as "the Marvelous One" chugged around the bases for an apparent triple.

"The fans were going crazy. The Mets bench is whooping it up, and Marv is standing on the bag at third, winded but happy," Bob recalled.

"George gets the ball back to the infield, time is called, and either Ken Hubbs at second, or Ernie Banks at first, called for the ball and when Elston tossed it to him, umpire Dusty Boggess gives the 'out' signal.

"Well, the fans explode, and Casey pops out of the Mets dugout, walking in that funny gait of his, waving his arms at Boggess and saying, 'What the heck's going on here? Whaddya mean by calling him out?!'

"And Boggess says, 'Casey, just calm down. The guy missed first base.' Then Stengel said, 'How would you know? You were standin in the outfield watchin' where the ball was goin'!' And Boggess just looked at him and said, 'Casey, the big lummox missed second, too.'

"Well, the Mets went on to lose the game by a run or two, and afterward, Casey is walking across center field toward the clubhouse. Some of us Cub players were walking behind him — at a safe distance — but we couldn't help but hear him talking to himself, saying, 'What have I gotta do to win a game? What else can happen to me?' And he's waving his arms around and gesturing while talking to himself. We were laughing so hard that it hurt." — David Craft, July 12, 1991

* * *

Billy Williams

To Billy Williams, the World Series, or as Milwaukee Brewer Gorman Thomas called it, "The Grand Ol' Opry of Baseball," was a dream...a hope to be recognized as a part of the greatest team in the world.

Unfortunately, Williams never saw that dream materialize, but did have another fulfilled Jan. 14 when the Baseball Writers Association of America voted the Chicago Cub and Oakland Athletic great into the Hall of Fame.

"That (making the Hall of Fame) means a lot to me," Williams said while anticipating the vote at a Jan. 11 sports memorabilia show hosted by Grand Slam U.S.A. and the Elgin (Ill.) Baseball Card and Comic Book Store.

"When you're in the hall, you're recognized as one of the best that ever was. You're rated up there with the greats, like Aaron, Mays and Musial."

Unlike many of the greats of his era, however, Williams' election took a considerably longer time. Although his statistics — 426 homers, 1,475 RBI and a .290 batting average — are superior to a number of his constituents, Williams was not elected until his sixth year of eligibility.

Exposure was the reason for the delay, or actually, a lack of it.

"I never played in a World Series, and that hurt in the balloting," sighed Williams, who is currently a hitting instructor in the Cub organization. "The Series gives a player a good deal of exposure. The country's top writers are there, and the television coverage is incredible."...

...Williams has many fond memories of his 18-year playing career that began in 1959. His favorite occurred when the outfielder was center stage on "Billy Williams Day." On June 29, 1969, Williams tied and surpassed Stan Musial's then record 895 consecutive game streak in a doubleheader with the defending National League champion St. Louis Cardinals. Billy received a number of awards between games, but what he remembers most was what he gave in return — four hits, including a double and two triples in the nightcap. The Cubs won the game 12-1 to complete a doubleheader sweep.

"That was a very emotional day for me," said the sweet swinger as he autographed a souvenir button from that game. "The timing was terrific," he said with a smile.

Timing was important for another of Williams' fondest memories. In a 1971 series with Pittsburgh, Billy recalls a personal contest with Roberto Clemente, Willie Stargell and himself.

"I don't remember the scores from the three-game series, or who even won," he said. "But the three of us kept leading our teams back when it seemed the game was lost. The competitiveness was tremendous. It seemed like the three of us rose above everyone else on the field."

Seeing youngsters buying and trading cards brought back memories of Billy collecting Duke Snider cards as a youth in Alabama.

"Duke Snider was my favorite player because I liked the Dodgers and Duke batted left-handed and played outfield," he said. — Mike Jaros, April 10, 1987

* * *

Billy Williams

Billy Williams credits Rogers Hornsby, a Cubs coach when Billy first joined the club in 1959, with helping him refine his swing.

"I think he had only five friends, and I was one of 'em," Williams jokingly said. "There were times when I spent hours in the batting cage trying to master the strike zone. I was in there swinging one day when he saw me and started talking about the strike zone.

"As batting practice ended, he said, 'OK, you're gonna hit 10 balls in a row — hard.' I might hit seven good ones but then foul one off. He'd have me start from scratch, trying again to hit 10 balls in a row — hard. Rogers Hornsby brought out the best in me as a hitter."...

...Williams also found it a challenge to bat against some of the game's toughest hurlers, names like Koufax, Drysdale, Gibson, Sadecki.

Sadecki? Ray Sadecki?

"Ray Sadecki," Williams said, sighing. "When he first came to the big leagues, he came over the top, and I hit him pretty good. Then he started dropping down sidearm and throwing me junk. You see, I was an agressive hitter, and when he started throwing this junk to me, well...

"I remember a game when I was with Oakland, late in my career. We were playing in Kansas City. Chuck Tanner was managing our ballclub then, and we needed badly to win this particular game. And wouldn't you know it, when I come to bat they bring in Ray Sadecki? I told Chuck that if he wanted to pinch hit for me, he could, because I couldn't hit that son of a gun.

"Chuck just said, 'Nahhh, you can do it, Billy. You're gonna hit him today. I can feel it.' Well, I coaxed a walk out of Sadecki, and for me, that was a moral victory." — David Craft, Jan. 20, 1989

* * *

Ted Williams

The year was 1941. FDR was in the White House. The world was at war, without us. Joe DiMaggio was carefully collecting base hits in 56 consecutive games. And, up in Boston, "The Kid" was busy batting .406.

For that formidable feat, Ted Williams was paid the far-from-formidable fee of $18,000. Yup. That's what the guy got. For batting .406, for winning the mid-summer All-Star Game with a dramatic ninth-inning homer, for playing major league baseball for the entire season. Eighteen thousand dollars.

Translated into today's inflated terms, that is about as much money as Jim Rice, who presently patrols Ted's old position, left field, for the Boston Red Sox, receives for playing one game!

That comparison was brought up to Williams during the weekend we recently spent together while he was in Detroit to sign autographs at one of my sports collectors shows. And he readily admitted the incredible incongruity of it all has crossed his mind a time or two.

"I'm not jealous about it, but I do envy today's ballplayers a little bit," he conceded. "I think they're very lucky to be playing baseball in this day and age when the clubs apparently can afford to pay them that kind of dough. They're very lucky guys in great circumstances.

"Oh, there are some outstanding players today. I'm sure there are some who could play in any era. But there are some guys making $400,000, $500,000, $600,000 and their names come up for salary arbitration and I say, 'Well, who does he play for?' I don't even know. I never heard of them."

And how much would a younger Ted Williams, say fresh from a .406 season, be worth on today's market?

"DiMaggio once was asked that same question and he made a terrific remark," replied Williams. "He said, 'If I were in those circumstances today, I'd simply sit down with the owner and say, 'Now what percentage of the club are you going to give me.' That's a pretty good answer, I thought." — Jim Hawkins, Eye of the Hawk, June 26, 1987

* * *

Al "Apples" Wilmore

The nickname "Apples" came about when Wilmore was a youngster. "When I was a kid, every so often my mother would give us kids a penny or two and we'd run to the store. Everyone else used to buy candy, but I'd buy apples. I used to eat the whole apple, everything but the stem, so they started calling me Apples. I've had that nickname ever since I was about 5 or 6 years old. If I die tomorrow in Philadelphia, and they put my name right down, not many people would know me, but if they put Apples in there, they would know me." Wilmore said he still loves apples, everything but apple cider. — Rick Hines, Nov. 20, 1992

* * *

Dooley Womack

Dooley Womack: I was loose, the sinker was working. I was putting the ball where I wanted it.

This is where Houk was such an effective manager. I don't know if this (streak) was in the first of the year or later. I just remember halfway in the season, I came in. Baltimore's beating us, 1-0, in the Stadium, Houk brings me in to sort of hold them down in the top of the ninth to give us a chance at it in the bottom of the ninth.

Before the smoke is all over, we're losing 5-0. Houk comes to the mound and says, "Man, you're like a coiled spring. If I cut the rope, you'd spring your ass right out of this stadium." (Laughs) People wonder what the manager says. He laid it on me. "I want you to throw that ball right down the middle of the plate and let him hit the ball out of this park."

I said, "OK." And I did. I threw the ball down the middle of the plate to Curt Blefary and he hit a dunker over short and it was a double. And I threw Frank Robinson down the middle and he hit a home run in the elevator shaft — it went straight up. He threw his bat and almost threw it into the stands. Ellie pulled that bat in.

Before the inning was over they had scored four. After the game, Houk came up to me and he said, "Dooley, you having any personal problems?"

I said, "No, sir."

"Well, something's bothering you and I want you to tell me."

I said, "Skipper, the only thing that's bothering me, and it's in the back of my mind today, is I want to have a second half like the first." I think I had saved nine, won four, earned average was down in the low twos. I mean, I was really cruising.

He said, "If that's all your problem is, I want you to go home tonight, have a couple of Bloody Marys, eat a big steak," and the way he put it, "take a good s--- and come out and play baseball tomorrow night." (Laughs)

I loved it! I went home and did exactly what he said. The next day I went out and threw one pitch, got the team out, and we won the ball game. — Brent Kelley, Nov. 29, 1991

* * *

Carl Yastrzemski

Meanwhile, the Red Sox were a team on bad times. They were consistent losers until the memorable '67 season, when the Red Sox and Carl Yastrzemski gave Boston its first pennant in 21 years. Nineteen sixty-seven was also Yaz's best year statistically, as he clubbed 44 homers, knocked in 121 RBI and posted a .326 average to win the Triple Crown. It was Boston's dramatic turnabout from the ninth-place season of '66 that helped Yaz reach such great heights.

"I've always said the only reason I won the Triple Crown that year is because the pennant race came down to the last day and the last out," Yastrzemski said. "You weren't thinking about winning a Triple Crown, you were thinking whatever situation came up in the game that you could help the ballclub to win the pennant. Two individual goals I went for when we weren't involved in the pennant race were going for 400 home runs, that took me 18 days, 17 days. Then of course the 3,000 hits took me 12 at bats...So, individually going for something was not my strong suit.

"I would have never won it (the Triple Crown) if we were out of the race or if we weren't involved in it the last four or five days. Being in the pennant race, your concentration, your intensity is there, where if you're going for something individually I think you press a little too much." — Doug Letch, June 30, 1989

* * *

Chapter 6
Feelings

When George Brett reached his milestone 3,000th career hit during the 1992 season, collectors were given the chance to own balls from hits #2,975 to #2,998.

As Dave Miedema reported in his Oct. 2, 1992, Shirt off My Back column, "if you collect baseballs, have some dollars to kick into a good cause, and would like to own a piece of history related to a sure Hall of Famer when his eligibility comes up, George Brett has a deal for you."

A $300, or more, donation toward the ALS Association, which is seeking a cure for Lou Gehrig's Disease, constituted a bid toward one of those 23 baseballs. The higher the bid, the closer toward ball #2,998 the bidder would receive.

The bidding process would only cover "retrievable" baseballs, meaning if a fan caught a ball fair and square, ALS wouldn't make the fan relinquish it, Miedema reported.

"In the meantime, on behalf of ALS, I'm hoping for a big run of singles, conventional doubles and triples by the younger major league Brett brother," he added.

That's one example of how a major leaguer returns something to the fans who support him throughout his career. Others, such as Joe DiMaggio, meticulously sign their names for those seeking autographs, as Robert Obojski reported in the March 15, 1991, SCD, in his Madison Avenue 26 show report.

Margo Howard, an office manager for The National Pastime, which sponsored the show in New York Feb. 2-3, 1991, told Miedema, "Above all, we must note that Joe DiMaggio takes pains in signing every single autograph carefully. He makes it a point to keep his signature on every item bold and neat. And that's exactly the kind of ballplayer he was...he did everything with style and professionalism."

DiMaggio signed 1,800 items — 1,700 flat items and 100 baseballs. It's not uncommon for a player to avoid signing certain things, as Miedema reported in his Sept. 17, 1982, Up Autograph Alley column regarding the nice guys on the Kansas City Royals.

"Some of the nice guys on the team, both in person and in the mail, include Frank White, Dan Quisenberry, Larry Gura, Dennis Leonard, John Wathan and Paul Splittorff. Gura, however, will not sign his 1981 Topps cards. When asked why he won't sign that card at Comiskey Park, Gura smiled and said, 'I've gotta have one card I won't sign.'"

Other players simply refused to sign anything, as Tot Holmes reported in an Aug. 5, 1988, story about the mail signing habits of former Los Angeles Dodgers stars. Said pitcher Mike Marshall:

"I never did sign and I still don't. The reason is really very simple. I'm not important enough for anyone to want my signature. I'm not going to pretend I am. I'm not going to act like I am.

George Brett

"I have nothing against the people who are asking for the autograph. I'm glad to say 'hi' and shake their hands. Later in my career I started handing out photo postcards. I just can't stand there like someone they should be fawning over. I don't feel like I am that important to them.

"Now I think I was to my daughters and I think I am to the people I teach — to these people I am generating something; I am someone important. But I'm not going to promote a myth that major league baseball players have some value in this society other than entertainment."

Marshall wasn't the front-runner in Bill Dod's April 16, 1982, No Dod About It column list of the toughest players to get autographs from. Heading his list was pitcher Ron Reed, followed by Rod Carew, Steve Carlton, George Hendrick and Reggie Jackson. Then came Johnny Bench, George Brett, Marshall, Bake McBride, Graig Nettles, Dave Parker and Willie Stargell.

The next bunch included John Denny, Fred Lynn, Pete Rose, Dick Ruthven, Mike Schmidt, Reggie Smith and Carl Yastrzemski, followed by Vida Blue, Cesar Cedeno, Joe Ferguson, Cliff Johnson, Dave Kingman, Joe Morgan, Jim Rice, Frank Robinson, and Gary Templeton.

The last group included Bob Boone, Cecil Cooper, Ivan DeJesus, Dennis Eckersley, Jerry Grote, Oscar Gamble, Mike LaCoss, Hal McRae, Jim Palmer, Darrell Porter, Rusty Staub, Ted Simmons, Manny Trillo and Willie Wilson.

Nice guys, according to Dave Miedema in his March 1, 1985, Up Autograph Alley column, included National Leaguers Steve Garvey, Bill Doran, Ron Cey, Larry Bowa, Andre Dawson, Dale Murphy, Gary Matthews, Gary Carter, Craig McMurtry, Eric Show, Mark Thurmond, Steve Trout, Kent Tekulve, Craig Lefferts, Dave Dravecky, George Frazier, Tug McGraw and Joe Sambito.

American Leaguers included Jim Sundberg, Dave Bergman, Lou Whitaker, Alan Trammell, Toby Harrah, Al Bumbry, Rudy Law, Brett Butler, Ron Guidry, Storm Davis, Britt Burns, Frank Viola, Dennis Lamp, Tippy Martinez, Auerilo Rodriguez, Ray Burris and Matt Young.

And some players are even collectors, too, be it when they were kids, or as active players, as Rich Marazzi noted in his Oct. 2, 1992, Batting the Breeze column about California Angels' star pitcher Mark Langston, who spent a fortune on 7-Eleven Slurpee cups featuring big league ballplayers.

Langston also had a little bit of that early-age mentality towards cards that many of us had, too. "If I had two or three of a certain card I used to put them on my bicycle spokes," he said.

Today, Langston collects baseballs signed by rock 'n rollers, such as Bruce Hornsby and the group Yes. But he doesn't collect anything from the players he competes against.

Chapter 6 offers insight into players' thoughts on the memorabilia and card collecting hobby, what things they may have kept from their careers, and their views on signing autographs.

Hank Aaron

Aaron believes he became one of the first autograph guests at a card show. "Let me tell you, I think I can be referred to as a pioneer on the card show circuit," he said. "When I was playing for the Milwaukee Brewers in 1976, I was invited to a card show in Detroit to sign autographs. Not many people at the time even knew what a card show was because the Detroit event was the first of its kind. I was paid something like $2,000 for my appearance there, and that was considered big money for a personal appearance at the time."

At card shows Henry Aaron has been seen signing everything from objects like Babe Ruth's mandolin of the 1920s to copies of Sports Collectors Digest. — Robert Obojski, July 3, 1992

* * *

Shawn Abner

Shawn who?

I noted the scheduled appearance of the "great" Shawn Abner at a baseball card and memorabilia convention. I don't know about other autograph collectors, but I'm disappointed I couldn't be there in person to pay $3 for the autograph of the MVP of the Carolina League.

You don't know how great my relief was to see that I could get his autograph by mail. Only $8 for an eight-by-ten color photo! What a deal. Just $12 for an official N.L. ball. What a bummer. I was hoping for an official Carolina League ball. The best steal of all, though, was the $65 for a signed Mint bat. I imagine this guy has accumulated one or two over his illustrious career by now.

For those individuals who took advantage of this questionable opportunity, I'd like to give you all a great deal on a "scarce" K-Mart set or valuable rookie card of Joe Charboneau. Let me get my bait on the line first. I only hope my line is strong enough. I just know I'm going to reel in some big fish.

Let's be realistic. This guy hasn't accomplished a thing. I'm not saying he won't, but at this point in his career he should be on his knees begging us to take his autograph. — Jim Wright, Ogden, Utah, Reader Reaction, Jan. 3, 1986

* * *

Hank Arft

Arft said he gets two or three autograph requests per week and he quickly responds. One of the main requests from fans is that he sign his nickname, "Bow Wow."

"Yes, a lot of times they ask me to sign 'Bow Wow,'" he said. "I kind of picked that up in Philadelphia. One of the fans in Philadelphia gave me that 'Bow Wow' name. He kept riding me and I don't know why, but he kind of picked on me. My last name is Arft, A-R-F-T. It's kind of like a dog barking. He's the one that set 'Bow Wow' on me and it stuck with me. Every now and then I read an article in the St. Louis paper where they run names of ballplayers and mine will be in there with Hank Arft 'Bow Wow,' with nicknames you know."

Arft's 1949 Bowman card contains his nickname on the front of the card. "I was kind of surprised when I saw it on there 'cause I didn't realize it was coming out on that," he said. "I still didn't mind, though." — Rick Hines, Aug. 16, 1991

* * *

Jerry Augustine

SCD: What do you think about the card collecting hobby?

Augustine: It's amazing. Baseball is the epitome of collecting right now, but football, basketball and hockey are all coming on strong. Gee, they're coming out now with fishing cards! Did you know that?

It's incredible. How does a guy?...I think the next big sport to take off in cards will be football.

SCD: We know you collected cards as a kid before they met their dreaded fate in the bike spokes. Do you collect anything now?

Augustine: Not really. I hate to say that, but I'm not a big collector. My kids are the collectors of the house.

If I'm out to something like an old-timers game, I'll collect some autographs. But when I get home, I don't see them anymore. My kids get them.

But if I happened to get, oh, let's say a Paul Molitor ball or a Robin Yount ball, guys I'm good friends with, I'd be more willing to keep those to give to somebody in a hospital or a needy child or something like that.

SCD: Did you keep any memorabilia from your playing days?

Augustine: I have the '82 uniform at home and the Brewer uniform from my first year. But it's not like I keep them in a precious spot. Sometimes my kids wear them while they're playing outside.

SCD: Did you keep any other memorabilia? How about your first "K?"

Augustine: I probably have that baseball at home. I have the ball from my first win. It was against the Yankees in September of 1975.

I have a tape of my first win at home. That was announced by Merle Harmon and Bob Uecker.

Yes, I have some of that stuff at home but I can't really tell you where it is because I don't know. My wife puts it in a good spot, I guess. — Tim Sullivan and Randy Wievel, May 17, 1991

* * *

Dusty Baker

Credit to Dusty Baker of the Dodgers. I spotted this letter in The Sporting News:

"My wife and I were in St. Louis recently to see the Dodgers play the Cardinals. As early arrivals, we noticed many young fans attempting to get autographs from Dodger players. Many of the Dodgers ignored the requests, except Dusty Baker. Not only did he sign baseball cards for children, he also engaged in conversation with people in the stands. I always regarded Baker as a fine player, but now I also regard him as a fine gentleman. I only wish that more major league baseball players would follow Baker's example." Carl Bainbridge Jr., Louisville, Ky. — Wirt Gammon, Wirt's Words, Jan. 15, 1980

* * *

Jack Baldschun

SCD: Did you keep any memorabilia from your playing days?

Jack Baldschun: Well, nobody ever really thought much about that. I do have two Cincinnati Reds uniforms, one home and one away — the sleeveless ones with the black bands on because of Fred Hutchinson dying.

SCD: Let's go back to the baseball cards for a minute. Do you have any baseball cards of yourself?

Baldschun: I certainly do! Some years ago, I asked a friend if he could possibly pick me up a few cards of myself as a player. Lo and behold, it was the Christmas of '87 and he sent me a package.

I got this huge package in the mail and my wife Charlotte said I couldn't open it until Christmas. So, I waited and waited and that was the first thing I opened in Green Bay at Christmas. I opened the package and inside was a bunch of newspaper stuffing. Then, somewhere in the middle was a beautiful frame with all eight of my baseball cards over the years. I was elated!

I tell you, there were tears in my eyes. It was the best present I ever got in my entire life. They're hanging up in my recreation room right now.

SCD: Do you do many card shows?

Baldschun: No, I've only been asked to do one. That was in Philadelphia. I'd like to do more, though. Who knows?

SCD: Do you have any idea what your cards are worth?

Baldschun: (laughing): Six cents? 20 cents? Hah!!! I understand they're giving them away!

SCD: What is your policy about signing autographs?

Baldschun: OK, I'd say I get three to five letters a week. I try to respond to everybody if they send a self-addressed stamped envelope. I try to get it done the same day. In fact, I'll sign whatever they send. I figure if anyone wants to take the time to send something to me, well, I'll return the favor. The only photos I've ever kept were the ones that didn't come with a return address. I didn't have any place to send them. — Tim Sullivan, May 5, 1989

* * *

Ernie Banks

Ernie Banks, one of the most popular players in Chicago Cubs history, will be an "honorary host" of this year's National Convention — an appropriate choice, since Banks is one of the best spokesmen for baseball and the sports memorabilia hobby. Earlier this year Ernie found the time to chat with SCD.

SCD: Any comments on your role in the National Convention here in Chicago?

Banks: I'm looking forward to it and I think there's no better place to have the National Card Collectors Show than in Chicago. A lot of people, a lot of collectors...baseball interest is extremely high in Chicago and I know all the players come through here to play from all the respective teams. They enjoy it and I'm looking forward to being a big part of the National Card Collectors Show this year.

SCD: How do you feel about the fans in general? Do you still get lots of mail? Do you still autograph through the mail?

Banks: Yes, I do. I get quite a bit of mail, as all the retired players do. We respond to the mail and we want to make sure that we keep in contact with our fans. As far as all the shows, as you know DiMaggio, Mays, Aaron, all of us enjoy doing the shows because we have a chance to be around people that love us and love baseball. They're really a good audience and fun to be around and have a lot of good nostalgia. Most of all, it's good for the kids too that collect baseball cards. They learn a lot about business and they can have a chance to meet each other and develop good friendships.

SCD: What did you think about that Atlantic City show?

Banks: I like it. In the East it's a little bit different. Everybody gets excited and things were a little bit disorganized. Overall, for the players who were part of it, we enjoyed it, we enjoyed being with the people and talking to them and signing autographs. Monte Irvin was there, Willie Mays...we enjoy it. It's a lot of fun to be around people who follow the game of baseball.

SCD: What kinds of mementos and memorabilia have you saved over the years?

Banks: Well, I'm starting a collection now. I've got a puzzle that was done of me 25 years ago. A friend of mine from Syracuse, N.Y., has given me several baseball cards from when I began my career, in the middle of my career and toward the end, so I've started my own collection for my grandkids. It's a lot of fun.

SCD: Do people send you stuff unsolicited and just say, "Keep it?" I imagine you get some of that.

Banks: I do. Especially with the card shows. I get quite a bit of stuff that I haven't seen in quite a few years. For instance, I made the Sports Magazine book cover, my own book "Mr. Cub"...so people do keep me informed and they give me certain things that they have in excess. I'm trying to collect all that now.

SCD: What would you say is your biggest highlight since you retired as a player?

Banks: The highlight was the card show this past year in Atlantic City when we had 11 500-plus home run hitters there. To see all the guys there together — Mike Schmidt, Aaron, Mays, Ted Williams...It gave us a chance to chat and visit, socialize and most of all sign autographs for the fans. It was a great joy to renew old acquaintances and meet a lot of fans who followed our careers. — Greg Sholes, June 30, 1989

* * *

Jesse Barfield

Personal memorabilia adorns the Barfield household. Barfield says that quite a bit of it is from his playing days with the Toronto Blue Jays. He says that most of the memorabilia was given to him by the Blue Jay fans and that one fan, in particular, gave him a scrapbook with newspaper clippings, photos, and baseball cards that chronicled his career up until he was traded to the Yankees.

Other personal memorabilia saved by Barfield include his home run crown trophy and his numerous Gold Glove awards which are all displayed in his trophy case at home.

Barfield's arsenal of other players' memorabilia gathered reads like a Who's Who of Baseball Collectibles, such as autographed baseballs of Hall of Famers Mickey Mantle, Ernie Banks and Billy Williams. Also included in this majestic array of items are autographed bats from Mike Schmidt, Mickey Mantle, Dick Allen, George Brett, and of all people, a pitcher, Nolan Ryan.

Barfield relates a very interesting incident concerning how he acquired the bat of boyhood idol Dick Allen. Remembers Barfield of the strange but fortunate encounter: "When I was with Toronto, I met Dick Allen at an Old-Timers Game that he had been invited to. At first, I didn't know if he was there (at the game) so I walked out on the field and asked if Dick Allen was there and was told that he was on the bench. I then went to my dugout and took one of the bats that I used and sandpapered my signature off of it. I also grabbed a baseball. I then ran across the field like a little kid and asked and got Dick Allen to sign the bat in the area formerly occupied by my signature, along with the baseball."

A very-highly priced bit of nostalgia memorabilia is also a part of Barfield's collection. It's an autographed photo of Satchel Paige which was given to him by his uncle, Albert Overton, before he passed away a few years ago. According to Barfield, Overton, who played baseball for many years in the old Negro Leagues, acquired the personally-inscribed photo directly from the great pitching legend. — Fluffy Saccucci, Oct. 5, 1990

* * *

Johnny Bench

Thanks, Johnny...

I have read and heard so much lately about the high price the players are demanding for autographs, the players' unfriendly demeanor, their policy of not signing balls, bats, etc., that I felt it was time the readers read about a truly class act.

I attended a show recently in Toledo, Ohio, where Johnny Bench was signing autographs. I arrived early and was among the first 20 people in line.

As we were waiting for Johnny to arrive, I must say I was rather skeptical about whether or not this was going to be a positive experience. I had heard rumors that Mr. Bench was not the most friendly signer and when I heard he was going to be there for five hours and that 1,500 tickets had been sold, I figured I was going to be just another number in the assembly line of autograph seekers.

Well, from the moment Mr. Bench walked into the room smiling, waving and chatting with everyone, I knew my suspicions were wrong.

Mr. Bench was the friendliest and most gracious signer I have ever met. He smiled, shook hands and said hello to everyone.

He also took the time to chat with and pose for pictures for anyone who asked. He signed anything put in front of him — from cards, balls and bats, to gloves, jerseys and hats.

Despite the announcement from the promoter beforehand that there would be no personalization, I saw Mr. Bench sneak in a few "Best Wishes" and "Catch Ya Laters."

I was still around when Mr. Bench was finishing up and I was pleased to see that even after five hours and 1,500 autographs later he was still as cheerful and personable as when he started.

It was a wonderful day for all the fans and another great performance by the best catcher of all time. Thanks, Johnny. — Rick Kahle, Columbus, Ohio, Reader Reaction, Dec. 2, 1988

* * *

Johnny Bench

I read with great interest an article about signing autographs in the New York Times by Johnny Bench. It is taken from his book, Catch You Later, The Autobiography of Johnny Bench. He has a message for autograph hunters. Let's try to understand. His fear is to be surrounded by them. It is as follows:

"I get more than 15,000 letters a year. Some are addressed to Johnny Bench, Cincinnati Reds; others are sent to my home, complete with the address and zip code. Some are scrawled in third-grade penmanship, some are in crayon. Others are typed, doused in perfume, smeared with lipstick, even stocked with unmentionables. But all the letters, on expensive stationery or paper that looks as if it barely made it through recycling, want something from me.

"They come from fans. Any athlete, no matter how famous or how obscure, knows the blessing and the curse of the fans. I have had my joys and frustrations, times when I think my fans are the greatest, times when I think they are animals.

"No matter where I am or what time of the year it is, not a day goes by when I do not somehow make some allowances for the public and what it does to me.

"In Cincinnati, I try to avoid walking down the street during the day. I go into movies after the picture has started and leave before the lights go up. The same goes for concerts and athletic events. I try to eat in my restaurants, or in those where I can sit in a corner and enjoy the meal. I hang around a few bars where the people know me and nod and let me drink with my friends. I say none of this immodestly, simply as a matter of fact.

"I have read all the stories about what an s.o.b. I am, or can be, when it comes to signing autographs and meeting the public. I know all the charges, the bit about signing only when the camera is on, and so forth. I know better than anyone, because as a kid I used to grade big-league players on their attitudes, on who signed and who did not, and then I went home and practiced my autograph in preparation for that 'SOME DAY.'

"Now I know why a lot of players did not sign or kept it to a minimum. As far as kids are concerned, especially those who haunt ball parks, they are wise and fast and brassy as hell. Everyone thinks he is the only kid asking for the autograph, and as long as you sign his it is O.K. It is his world.

"But if you sign one, you have to sign them all or pace it so you can make it to your car or the bus. Most people who have never been crowded for their autograph do not realize the crush.

"I used to sit outside the park for 20 minutes to an hour. I was young, and I loved those kids for wanting my signature. I did not mind that there was never a 'please' or a 'thank you,' or that the same kid hit me 10 times and only so he could sell them to his friends.

"Before long it was not an isolated thing, but an everyday phenomenon. Every day, I started to change my attitude toward autographs. Now I have to be in control of the scene, and that usually means a barrier between me and the fans. I will sign along the fence or whatever, but not where I can be surrounded. I run from the locker room to my car and make an obvious escape." — Wirt Gammon, Wirt's Words, Sept. 15, 1979

* * *

Paul Blair

Blair said he has "no problem" signing autographs for anyone who asks.

"Thankfully," he says, "people do still remember me, even after 11 years. And it makes you feel good! It's nice to know people appreciate your ability and the way you played baseball during your career."

"I know I was very fortunate and privileged to be a major league baseball player — and everything that goes along with it, which includes the autographs, is fun for me. I'm just glad to have the opportunity."

Blair is not a collector — "never have been a memorabilia freak and probably never will be," he says.

"I know what I did, so I have no desire to go out and collect cards or get 'em signed — I'd rather play golf." Ross Forman, Oct. 25, 1991

* * *

Steve Blass

SCD: What do you think about the sports memorabilia business?

Blass: I'm amazed. I think it's great to go to a show and see a Stan Musial card, or a jersey or a bat of DiMaggio or someone of that caliber. It's amazing to see what people have saved.

When the last game at Forbes Field was played, I joined the herd of people that ran to the big scoreboard in left field. I was able to get a "2" and an "8" since my number was 28.

Some people came to the last game with tools to remove seats, signs, etc. One guy even got a toilet! — Chuck Greenwood, May 1, 1992

* * *

Wade Boggs

The current Sport Americana Baseball Card Alphabetical Checklist needs more than three columns to list all the cards he's been on; it seems he's in every card set issued since 1983.

But five-time American League batting champion Wade Boggs is familiar with all those baseball cards on which he's pictured.

Although he doesn't collect them all or have a particular favorite one, the third baseman admits it's a thrill to be pictured on cards, especially that first one.

He feels good knowing he might be pictured on a card which some kid puts into his bicycle spokes, something Boggs, too, did as a youngster.

The lifetime .346 hitter (entering the 1991 season) also hasn't saved much memorabilia from his career, but does have a trophy room in his home to display the awards he's won.

Boggs doesn't charge for autographs or seek charitable donations and signs for the fans if he has time at the ballpark. He says he tries to answer all of the mail he receives — which sometimes reaches 600 letters a day — because it comes with the territory of being a successful athlete.

During Boston's April swing through Cleveland, Boggs, entering the 1991 season 216 hits shy of 2,000, answered a few questions about the hobby before a game on a rainy Saturday afternoon.

Then he went out and added two more hits...

...SCD: As far as the fan mail that you receive, there again you are a popular player, and your statistics are a part of that. Do you acknowledge fan mail? Do you sign fan mail requests?

WB: I try to sign as much of it as I can. I get anywhere from 500 to 600 letters a day. So it's kind of tough to acknowledge every bit of fan mail that I do get. But I try to do the majority of it...

...SCD: I'm going to skip back one more time to baseball cards. I guess that's sort of a symbolic moment for a player in a sense that he's finally made it, that he's on a big league baseball card. Do you remember your reactions when you saw the first time you were on a card? How did that make you feel?

WB: Well, it's a big thrill because when you're growing up you put them in your bicycle tires and that kind of thing. And now you're on one and you know that you're in somebody's bicycle spokes, so that makes you feel good.

SCD: Do you think that baseball card collecting is too much of a business now in a sense that — you know, you've done shows before — you've got people who are making money off of your name as opposed to collectors who are just collecting.

It's sort of geared more now, it's focusing more on the monetary aspect in a sense? People aren't necessarily collecting memories anymore. Do you have a reaction to that?

WB: It's entrepreneurship; there's a lot of money to be made. But the thing about it is there's so much counterfeit stuff that goes around that somebody says "OK, here's a Wade Boggs game-used bat" and it's totally fake and somebody's paying $600 for a game-used bat and they're getting ripped off.

That's the thing that upsets me about the industry, because it's not regulated enough, and a lot of people are getting ripped off out there.

SCD: Is there anything that you could do about it...is there any way that you could think of that we could police this a little bit better?

WB: Well, you could go to a show and arrest probably three-quarters of the people that run it because the majority of that stuff is stolen. Either that or it's counterfeit jerseys.

I've gone to card shows; I've had people come up and hand me jerseys to sign and they're not my jerseys.

You know, there's money to be made when you steal stuff and I don't think that it's any different than stealing a radio or stealing a TV or anything like that. But when you steal a bat or you steal a glove, you can't really put a price on it as a player. But collectors sure put a price on it.

SCD: That would be a negative aspect of it (the hobby). What would you see as a positive aspect of the hobby? What I'm getting at is is it fair to make ballplayers role models and idols — have kids idolize guys who are on cards? Is that something fair for people to do?

WB: Well, the thing about role models is it's a stereotype that comes with being an athlete or something like that. And whenever you're under the spotlight and stuff like that then people expect you to be role models to their kids.

I think parents should be role models. That's the perfect role model. But parents want to put the blame on athletes. — Mark K. Larson, July 5, 1991

* * *

Bob Boone

"I've got the baseballs from my first hit, my first home run, and my 1,000th hit. I have a book from Harvey Kuenn that's important to me." — Rich Marazzi, Batting the Breeze, July 8, 1988

* * *

George Brett

There has been an abundance of memorabilia George Brett could have picked up along the way of his major league career. But bachelor Brett let most of it pass him by.

"I really don't have anything of importance," he said. "I have some autographed balls, a couple of bats and stuff like that. But I'm not a collector.

"I don't try to get autographed balls from them (other players). I think if I had kids it would be different. I know Bret Saberhagen gets autographed balls from a lot of the great players in the league, and in spring training from the other league, but they're for his son. I don't have any sons or any daughters, so as far as collecting it for myself, I don't do that."

Getting a George Brett autograph is pretty tough these days. Brett, who signed freely in his early playing days, has been turned off by the greed shown by many collectors.

"I don't sign in hotels, I don't sign anything that's sent to my house, and it's impossible to answer them all at the stadium," he said.

"You get so many (requests) nowadays, it's a business. It (autographing) used to be fun when you first came up...you'd take time and actually write a (return) envelope, and write something on the card or whatever they sent you. But now you do it and people turn around and sell it. So I don't do it (autograph).

"It's not fun signing autographs like it used to be," Brett said. "You wake up in the morning, go outside of the hotel, and there's 20 kids out there. You come back at 11:30, 12 at night, and there's still 20 kids out there...the same 20 kids! You could sign one for every kid there the first day, and the kids will be there the next day and night with another one. Now what do they need so many of them (autographs) for? That's what I don't understand.

"It's frustrating. It takes a lot of fun out of playing the game because everywhere you go, people want to sign stuff. I try to pick out cute little kids in the stands with their mothers who come to the park and aren't going to sell it. The kids at the hotels just get them to sell them, and I don't think that's right." — Dave Sabaini, Sept. 1, 1989

* * *

George Brett

SCD: What is your most prized baseball memento?

Brett: I'm wearing it. My 1985 World Series victory ring. And, you know, several fans at this show have given me souvenirs. One fan gave me a New York Yankees banner for winning the American League Eastern Division in 1980. But since we (the Royals) beat them three straight in the playoffs, he gave me the banner for my trophy room. I like coming to New York...when I travel here during the season, it's all work, but by visiting here for an autograph show I have more of a chance to go out and really see the town.

SCD: What are your memories of that famous "pine tar" game of July 25, 1983, at Yankee Stadium?

Brett: I laugh at that incident now, but I never became so angry on the ballfield in my life when the home plate umpire disallowed my two-run homer in the ninth inning and called me out because I had too much pine tar on the bat. Our manager, Dick Howser, really got sore at me for charging at the umpire like a wild bull. I signed lots of stuff at this show connected with that game.

Brett gave the bat to collector Barry Halper, who also got the home run ball and the can of pine tar Brett used. Halper eventually gave the bat to Brett, who displayed it in his Kansas City restaurant for a few years. Then he loaned the bat to the Hall of Fame. — Robert Obojski, Feb. 21, 1992

* * *

Lou Brock

Lou Brock

It was almost the end of warmups. Soon, I'd be herded into a photog pen along the field foul line. As I headed that way, I spotted Lou Brock. From TV appearances, I knew him to be an articulate guy. Why not steal a few moments from the "stealingest" player (938) of all time?

Brock: My legs are OK, I still walk around. If I can't get to where I want to go, I call a cab! I haven't prepared for this game. The preparation is to put on a uniform, walk out here and see if you can still stand up. I just want to last the night. Five innings — two hours, whichever comes first.

SCD: You've had a baseball to sign thrown at you already tonight. How do you deal with the requests?

Brock: I think you have to understand what it is. Nowadays, there's a collector's market. There's a difference between the autograph seeker and the collector. I think for most players it's hard to decipher which is which. I have grown to know now — there is a difference. Autograph

seekers will ask for you to personalize something. All collectors (dealers) will say, "Give me your autograph." They'll charge, the others will not.

SCD: What about answering mail requests?

Brock: I don't answer mail. The fact is, I can't tell who it is. Is somebody going to profiteer on it? Then, certainly I'd like to know who they are. Therefore, some of the fans probably do get hurt sending things through the mail because of that. We didn't create that situation. The marketeers created that situation.

For a player to try to decipher which is which, I think he's gonna go crazy trying. And I think if the collectors were up front, it would solve part of the problem that exists. When they say, "This player is no good because he won't sign autographs." I think somewhere along the line — even the public — this industry is so new, people really don't see it. Five years ago, somebody told me there was gonna be a collectors market and you could sell an autograph — I'd say, "You gotta be kidding." But it's there. It's big money. It's greed and the players have a difficult time with it. — Pete Dobrovitz, July 29, 1988

* * *

Ernie Broglio

Chicagoland Sports Collectors Association President Jeff Blatt has brought some of baseball's greatest players to the Windy City for shows during his three years as the club's No. 1 man.

DiMaggio and Durocher. Mantle and Mays. Spahn and Stargell. Robinson and Robinson. Appling and Aparicio. Mize and McCovey. The list goes on.

During the first weekend in June, the CSCA sponsored a two-day, seven guest show at the O'Hare Marriott, highlighted by Willie Mays, Monte Irvin, Leo Durocher, future Hall of Famer Rollie Fingers, Lou Brock and Ernie Broglio.

"Ernie who?" you ask?

Well, 26 years ago, he was 18-8 with a 2.99 ERA for the St. Louis Cardinals. And on June 15, 1964, the Cardinals traded the right-handed pitcher to the Chicago Cubs for a young outfielder by the name of Lou Brock.

That's right. Broglio is The Guy The Cubs Traded Brock For.

"This is really pretty exciting. I really enjoyed myself," said the 53-year-old Broglio, who was making his first-ever show appearance as an autograph guest. "I never knew there were so many baseball books. I've never seen this many in my life."

Broglio played in the big leagues from 1959 until his retirement in 1966. He had a 77-74 lifetime mark with a 3.74 ERA. His best season was in 1960 when he was 21-9 with a 2.75 ERA.

Currently he makes his home in San Jose, Calif. Broglio said he still receives autograph requests via the mail, usually averaging seven to 10 a week.

The strangest request he ever received, he said, was a couple of years ago when a fan wrote and asked him to endorse a check for one cent. The writer explained he was collecting checks of former St. Louis Cardinals. For proof, the fan sent a photocopy of a check signed by Stan Musial.

"I don't have any complaints with (signing autographs)," Broglio said. "If the person is buying something and you're autographing it, it's their money...if they want to keep it, fine. If they want to sell it, fine.

"We (major leaguers) are all real fortunate to be able to play the game of baseball. Look at the kids that don't get this opportunity, the ones that play years and years in the minor leagues. They don't have the opportunity to come to these things (baseball card shows). That's why I say, 'I don't understand why (some former players) would consider how much is made off a signature (when a collector sells it).'"

Now in his sixth year in the beer distributing business, Broglio, who admitted he is rarely recognized in public, said he never collected things while a player, but admits now he wishes he would have.

Broglio, though, did leave the show with a couple of autographed Lou Brock pictures. He also signed a photo to Brock: "To Lou, the guy who made me famous."

Outside of work, Broglio said he leads a "very dull life." He said he plays golf two or three times a month with a 15 handicap.

Broglio has apppeared in two old-timers games, one in the Eastern League and one in Chicago three years ago.

"It was kind of funny (at the Chicago Old-Timers Game)," he said. "Even 25 years later, they (fans) still remember. Lou walked out and got a standing ovation. I walked out and got a standing boo." — Ross Forman, July 21, 1989

* * *

Al Bumbry

In court on a speeding ticket, Oriole outfielder Al Bumbry was "sentenced" to 20 minutes of autograph signing as a community service. Judge Darrow Glaser of Washington County, Md., said he couldn't order Bumbry to win another World Series, and he said a fine would be negligible.

Bumbry went to his car and returned with a stack of color photos. Judge Glaser also just happened to have a photo of Bumbry in his possession, too. — Wirt Gammon, Wirt's Words, May 11, 1984

* * *

Roy Campanella

Special signing session: California show promoter Harlan Werner has announced that he has contacted former Brooklyn Dodgers star catcher and Hall of Famer Roy Campanella to a special one-time signing session to autograph a total of 750 items.

Campanella, who became paralyzed as a result of an automobile accident in 1958, has agreed to sign 250 Perez-Steele Great Moments cards, 250 Sports Collectors Warehouse lithographs and 250 Gateway envelopes. These will be the only items which will be autographed, reports Werner.

According to Werner, Campanella will be able to autograph the items with the help of a special device which holds his hand steady. "All the autographs Roy signs will be legible and look similar to his signature prior to the accident," says Werner. "In 1984, he signed seven cards with the help of the device," adds Werner.

"In many ways this is like having Babe Ruth come back today to sign autographs. I'm delighted and honored that Roy has decided to accept my offer," says Werner.

According to the contract, which Werner reports was three years in the making, Campanella can not sign any other autographs for a minimum of two years. "He's indicated that once he's done this, he has no desire to ever sign anything else again."

Werner went on to mention that a longtime family friend was instrumental in getting Campanella to agree to the session. "He (Campanella) lives close to me and I've done some work with other Dodgers. Plus, the deal was aided by a longtime family friend," says Werner. "We're doing everything in a very professional manner," he says.

Werner expects the signing of the 750 items to take place over an eight to 10 day period.

Of the 750 items to be autographed, Werner says those collectors who already own Perez-Steele Great Moments cards can have their own cards signed and returned.

Collectors purchasing a Campanella-signed item will have their item recorded by Werner's Sports Placement Service and also receive a notorized document verifying that Campanella actually signed the item. — Tom Mortenson, The Coach's Box, Feb. 10, 1989

* * *

Jose Canseco

Mike Pitzer, a nice-looking 15-year-old from the Seattle area, had one of those Wally Joyner-Jose Canseco rookie all-stars cards, and asked the Oakland slugger to autograph it.

Canseco responded by drawing a mustache and beard on Joyner, pictured next to Canseco on the card.

Needless to say, Pitzer was disappointed in Canseco's behavior and disappointed that the card was defaced. He took out his frustration by penning a letter to the Seattle Times.

The Times forwarded copies of the letter to the Oakland Athletics and the commissioner's office. Peter Ueberroth sent Pitzer an autographed baseball and a letter.

"In reading your letter to the editor in the Seattle Times," wrote the baseball commissioner, "I was sorry to learn of your mishap. I hope your experience does not dampen your enthusiasm and love for baseball. I know I cannot replace your damaged baseball card, but I hope you enjoy the enclosed autographed baseball. Best regards, Peter Ueberroth."

Pitzer later received a package from Canseco containing a baseball. There was writing on the ball, no drawing. It said, "To Mike, Best Wishes, Jose Canseco."

I wonder what a Fleer bearded Joyner-Canseco all-star rookie card is worth? — Irwin Cohen, On the Baseball Beat, Nov. 20, 1987

* * *

Harry Caray, Jack Buck

Hey! Hey! Made His Day!

I am one of those autograph collectors who sends items to the ballparks to be signed. I get lucky more often than not.

I want to relate an autograph story to you, for all those who are hesitant about sending cards or pictures in to be autographed.

Recently, I obtained an 8-by-10 inch picture of Harry Caray and Jack Buck at a St. Louis card show. My intentions were to have both eventually autograph it.

The Cardinals opened a three game homestand on Sept. 9 with the Cubs. On Sept. 8, I sent this 8-by-10 to Jack Buck with intentions of having him autograph it.

On the evening of Sept. 9, I'm watching the Cubs broadcast on their cable station. I was reading my SCD and watching the game.

In the third inning of the game I heard Harry make a statement, "Look what Jack Buck brought over."

I looked up and to my surprise there was my 8-by-10 on the Cubs broadcast. Harry was showing the television audience the old picture of he and Jack Buck.

I knew it was mine because Jack Buck had personalized it and my name was on the 8-by-10. I was even more elated when I saw that Mr. Buck had Harry autograph it also. This I hadn't counted on.

I just want to say that of all the autographs I have gotten in the past, or will in the future, these autographs will be, by far, the best.

Autograph collectors, remember, take a chance; it might be worth your while.

Send an item that you don't mind not getting back, write a nice letter, be sincere and send along a self-addressed stamped envelope. You too might be lucky. — Roger Jones, Sesser, Ill., Reader Reaction, Oct. 7, 1988

* * *

Chico Cardenas

In an era when a Hall of Famer's autograph can command as much as $25, Leo Cardenas autographs are typically free of charge at three or four small shows in the Cincinnati area each year. Investors are paying $8 for Ken Griffey Jr.'s signature at the larger Cincinnati shows. Cardenas isn't concerned about the resale value of his autograph; there probably isn't any. (According to the monthly price guides, even Cardenas' 1960 rookie is a common.) He enjoys seeing the kids putting his autographed cards and pieces of paper into their notebooks. The smile so evident on most of his baseball cards remains intact. Cardenas still marvels that kids will pay $3 for his countenance in an 8 x 10 color glossy.

"It don't matter to me how many autographs I sign, because I enjoy being around people," Cardenas explains. "That last time, they say, 'Leo, you can get ready to go when you want to,' but I tell them, no, it's all right. I enjoy watching the kids buy cards and trade cards. You know, they get fanatic."

At a pre-Christmas show, Cardenas brightened noticeably when a proud owner unrolled a Sports Illustrated poster of Cardenas, airborn in midpivot. "That was taken in Pittsburgh, you know, the old park (Forbes Field). It's been so long since I've seen a poster like that. That was taken in 1962," Cardenas recalls quickly.

Reminded of a 1968 card (Topps #480) featuring him and fellow All-Stars Tony Oliva and Roberto Clemente, Leo nods immediately: "At the All-Star Game (1967 in Anaheim), they have so many Latin players. And the sportswriters are going to see a lot of Latins together and take a picture. You know, to give money more publicity. If you can keep that card, it's going to be worth a lot of money." — Wade Swormstedt, April 20, 1990

* * *

Rod Carew

Dear Fellow Sports Collectors:

I'm sure many of you do not realize that I, too, am a serious collector of sports memorabilia.

My home is filled with many treasured items of childhood baseball heroes as well as wonderful awards presented to me. I'd like you to know that it gives me a tremendous feeling of pride over the years, so many of you have requested a piece of memorabilia about me.

Because of this it disappoints me that most memorabilia concerning me is obtained from one collector to another instead of from me to you.

Therefore, I would like to make a limited offering during the off season of the items listed below.

Please keep in mind that each item listed is not pre-signed and will be autographed to you personally and in a manner which is more rewarding to you.

In this way I feel this would truly be a piece of memorabilia that would offer a personal touch between myself and you the collector. All requests for memorabilia and correspondence should be sent to me personally, Rod Carew.

My sincere thanks for being a fan of baseball and the support so many of you have shown me over the years, Rod Carew

8"x10" color photo of me in aciton, personally autographed to you: $9.95

Autographed baseball with personal inscription: $12.95

My autobiography, "Carew," by Ira Berkow, signed, with my personal inscription and numbered: $15.95

My personal authentic Rod Carew Adirondack bat, personally autographed to you: $99.50

Please note, all items will be accompanied by a letter of authenticity from me. — Rod Carew, Yorba Linda, Calif., an ad in the Jan. 15, 1982 issue

* * *

Rod Carew

SCD: How long have you been collecting, and what got you started?

Carew: I started collecting about 10 years ago. I didn't really begin with the idea in mind to be a collector, I just wanted my own cards. Then I wanted a few of my teammates. The next thing I knew, I had several hundred thousand baseball cards.

SCD: Do you have any particular favorites?

Carew: From an art standpoint, I really like the older cards for players like Aaron, Snider, Clemente, that era. The cards were simpler then, cleaner. They were about the player and I think that understatement appeals to me...

...SCD: Do you have a favorite Rod Carew card?

Carew: I'd have to say that my favorite Rod Carew card is my Topps rookie card. And, I don't think that just on sentiment. Even though it was my first card, I really think that photo captured me.

SCD: Has Hank Allen ever called you to thank you for making his rookie card so valuable?

Carew: (Laughs) No...

...SCD: Do you have any favorite career mementos?

Carew: Yes, in 1978 I was awarded the Roberto Clemente Award by Major League Baseball in recognition for contributions made to the community off the field. I think that has the most meaning to me. Roberto was a very special player, and a very special person.

I also enjoy showing off my 1,000th hit and 3,000th hit totals. I cracked both bats in the exact same place...

...SCD: How do you feel about card shows?

Carew: I don't mind doing shows, but I think sometimes the players get a bad rap. We don't charge people for our autographs. We get a flat appearance fee, no different than we would get at a speaking appearance to a corporation. It's up to the promoters to decide if and how much they want to charge for autographs.

The problem I have with shows is two-fold. It's the players who are not courteous to the fans, and promoters who are likewise rude to people. I can't do anything about other players, but I can avoid promoters rushing people through autograph lines like they are cattle.

As far as I am concerned, if a person wants an autograph personalized, or a picture taken, that's what I am there for and that's what I am going to do. To avoid a promoter getting beat, we'll always guarantee a show promoter a minimum number of autographs per show. That way I can take my time and make sure the process is an enjoyable one for everyone. Even so, I'm still considered a fast signer. — March 8, 1991

* * *

Steve Carlton, Gaylord Perry

Super Steve

It was my privilege and pleasure to have had a small part in the promotion of the highly successful Steve Carlton/Gaylord Perry Baseball Card Show held at the Stouffer's Valley Forge Hotel Oct. 30-31.

Whitey Willenborg, his lovely wife, Jean, and the whole team who worked so hard are to be congratulated. A crowd in excess of 5,300 attended the two-day event. A banquet was held Saturday night for dealers and their wives. The food was fantastic and enjoyed by all (especially yours truly).

Steve Carlton, who signed 3,400 autographs, was warm, cheerful, personable and a real joy to everyone from beginning to end. Steve personalized any item requested, posed for pictures with fans, shook thousands of hands, and laughed and joked with many collectors.

So, let the rumor die that Steve Carlton is anything but a warm, friendly guy, when treated in a like manner.

Gaylord Perry, too, was fabulous and endeared himself to thousands of Phillie people. He also signed thousands of autographs, posed for pictures (even with yours truly) and delighted the crowd. He also brought little burlap bags of peanuts, grown on his farm, which were quickly purchased by those who like unusual collectibles. A very nice surprise came on Sunday when Phillie catcher Bob Boone came and stayed for an autograph session.

We in the Delaware Valley are truly blessed to have a great team like our Phillies. To Super Steve, I say: A super try will get #5 Cy! — Jim Hastings, Wilmington, Del., Reader Reaction, Dec. 24, 1982

* * *

Gary Carter

Pete Henrici, Baseball Nostalgia, Doubleday Plaza, Coopertown, N.Y., writes that he's found another athlete-collector — "or rather found me." Gary Carter of the Expos and his wife stopped in the store. Gary said he had saved all the cards he had collected while he was growing up in the 1960s and had a good number of complete sets. He showed interest in the conventions and was also amazed to hear how sophisticated the card collecting hobby had become, with checklists, publications, etc. Pete gave him a copy of SCD to begin his "education." — Wirt Gammon, Wirt's Words, Dec. 12, 1976

* * *

Gary Carter

George Vecsey recently authored a fine story on Montreal Expos catcher Gary Carter in the prestigious New York Times.

The story dealt with the fact that Carter is a baseball card collector.

Vecsey's story should warm the hearts of true collectors everywhere because, while mentioning that baseball card collecting has become at least as profitable as buying stock, with shops, conventions and publications quoting the value of cards the way Dow Jones quotes closing stock prices, Vecsey quoted Gary Carter as follows:

"I don't even know how much they're worth because I don't plan to sell any. The value is that I enjoy them."

The story states that Carter started collecting cards when he was five years old. He says, "It started when I was 5. I'd go to Nick's Liquor or the Alpha Beta store and buy the packs. Later I bought them at the Little League's concession stand."

Gary isn't much on having his cards autographed. He said, "I was always a meticulous person. I still am. I never got autographs on them or signed my own name, the way some kids do. I wanted to have a complete set in mint condition."

As he was growing up in Fullerton, Calif., Carter stated "I'd see myself playing in the major leagues. I'd imagine myself on a baseball card." Carter added that collecting cards is like having a scrapbook of baseball.

Vecsey's story on Carter went on to relate that the Expos catcher has amassed cards covering several periods. His older brother, Gordon, who played two years in the minors, gave him his early 1950s Topps and Bowman cards. Carter's "own" collection covers the years from 1959 through 1967, at which point he entered high school and like so many of us at that stage, "stopped collecting completely." But when he joined the Expos in 1974 and was signed by Topps for his own card, he remembered the dream and now has complete sets from 1975 through 1980.

Carter says, "Every spring I get a whole box of new cards from somebody. I put them in order, and usually I'm missing around 75, so I trade with other guys. Once I get a full set, that's it."

As luck would have it, Gary Carter is featured on the cover of the first annual Sports Collectors Yearbook, the John Stommen-Dan Even production detailed in the Our Hobby column on page three of this issue. We featured Gary after getting a photo of him from Bob Bartosz, along with a note from Bob saying that Gary had told him during a Veterans Stadium visit that he needed a few cards to fill out various sets and would pay a visit to Bob's store the next time the Expos were in town. — Aug. 15, 1980

* * *

Orlando Cepeda

Here's one for Orlando Cepeda

I had the opportunity to meet Orlando Cepeda on two occasions this year, and both times he impressed me as a fine gentleman.

The first time was at the San Francisco Giants fantasy camp in April when Orlando was one of the former stars who spent the week with middle-aged men pretending to be 12-year-old boys.

He spent considerable time teaching many of us the fundamentals of baseball in a fatherly way.

I have a picture of Orlando holding my 1 1/2-year-old son, with both of them laughing at a private joke.

In October, Orlando was in town to participate in the media kickoff for a World Series Dream Game sponsored by a local hospital foundation.

When his turn came to speak to the press and dignitaries, he was humorous, professional and sincere.

The real Orlando emerged when the children came into the room.

They crawled all over Orlando, and he smothered every one of them with kisses, love and personal attention.

It was obvious that he was enjoying himself as much as the children.

Orlando Cepeda represents the finest of Major League Baseball, and he has my vote for the Hall of Fame. — Geoffrey E. Gonsher, Phoenix, Ariz., Reader Reaction, Jan. 6, 1989

* * *

Chris Chambliss

"I've got the bat and ball from the home run I hit in the 1976 playoffs (against Mark Littell of the Royals). A security guard got the ball for me.

"I have my Gold Glove and the first home run ball I hit. It was against Tom Hall of the Twins." — Rich Marazzi, Batting the Breeze, July 8, 1988

* * *

Roger Clemens

"I had baseball cards (when I was growing up), but back then, you weren't into collecting, you just had them," he said. "You went out and got them, and just had a bunch of cards around."

"I would trade the cards for favorite players who I liked at that time. You know, the 'Big Red Machine' guys and things like that. I had cards of that nature, but nothing to the effect of what it is now."

Believe it or not, Clemens still has those cards. His mother has been keeping tabs on the collection.

"I have a few cards yet. That is something my mother has collected for me," he said. "She's collecting my cards now and doing it for my boys. She's into that and enjoys doing it. I just don't have the time right now to do that. She keeps it up to date."...

...According to Clemens, he doesn't mind signing cards, as long as he keeps it under control.

"You want to keep it simple," he said. "Don't get too crazy with it. I think it's neat. When my first card came out, I was really happy. I thought it was neat to have one. To be an athlete and have your picture on a baseball card is a pretty neat thing."...

...Clemens said he loves to sign autographs. However, he said he can tell when someone is sending children in with many cards, and looking to make a fast buck.

"You can read between between the lines. And I don't like that," he said. "If you keep it under control and go with the flow, and just keep the kids happy by doing as many as you can. There will be a day when you're running late and you don't have time to sign, then you're a jerk.

"When I hear somone say, 'Oh, he's no good (because he didn't sign an autograph),' I say, 'Haven't you ever had a bad day? Give the guy another chance.' Don't judge him on one time. Sometimes a guy can't sign for a half-hour every day. You try to pick off a few of the kids because they really enjoy it. And I was one of those kids at one time. I think you remember it. And I think these days most of the guys remember it." — Tom Hultman, Dec. 20, 1991

* * *

Rocky Colavito

Irwin Cohen: Did you collect baseball cards?

Rocky Colavito: Of course. Of course. The shame of it is that I gave 'em to my kid cousin when I thought that I outgrew 'em. It was a big mistake, I guess.

Cohen: Did you ask players for autographs when you were hanging around Yankee Stadium?

Colavito: Oh, yes. I used to do that, too.

Cohen: Ever get turned down?

Colavito: Oh sure.

Cohen: Did that make an impression upon you and shape your attitude to the fans when you were a player?

Colavito: It was more or less the manner you were asked or approached. I could see both sides. I'm glad to do it as long as people are polite and realize that we have connections to make and sometimes we don't have time to stand there and give autographs. I understand it much more today and always promised myself that when I was a player I would oblige whenever possible...

...Cohen: Could you tell us something about your family and where you make your home during the off-season?

Colavito: I make my home in Pennsylvania — I'm not going to give you the exact town. For one thing, I'm not crazy about that book that gives your address out. I'll tell you what — I've got to find out who puts out that book. I've got to stop them. I feel very strongly about that. This guy is making a living off of our addresses. I don't think

that's really right. That kind of stuff annoys the hell out of me! It's just like that company that puts out 8-by-10s and companies that put out cards — there's one in Detroit — that I've got to call. The Detroit News is putting out a card with my picture on it without my permission. Do you know the card?

Cohen: Sure. It's from the Detroit News' 'Boys of Summer' set depicting the history of baseball in Detroit.

Colavito: Right. That's it. I never signed them. So nobody's going to have an autographed Detroit card of mine. Ever! Unless I come to some kind of agreement with them. I just don't understand how people have the nerve to do that kind of thing! I just don't understand that! They don't even ask you! Put your picture on a cardboard and sell it. Make money off it and they don't think anything of it! They don't think anything about sharing the profits with anyone else! It's not just me, it's a lot of players that I know that feel that way.

Cohen: How do you feel about signing blank index cards that someone may possibly sell?

Colavito: I don't know for sure that they're going to sell it so I sign it. But if someone sends me eight or 10 then I won't sign it. If they send two or three then I'll sign it. I sign all of the Topps cards. I'm just not saying this as a brag...but it's a fact, I'm one of the best there is at signing the stuff. When people send me stuff I usually oblige 'em. — Irwin Cohen, On the Baseball Beat, June 11, 1982

* * *

Rocky Colavito

BUFFALO, June 20 — There's a few autograph seekers milling about the entrance to the Hyatt Hotel's banquet room. About a half hour earlier, three or four had rushed up to Rocky Colavito, legendary outfielder who once hit four home runs in a game (June 10, 1959, vs. Baltimore). At 55, Colavito, now grey, but still trim and athletic, moves quickly past. "I'd like to get some lunch, please."

As he was about to return, no one knew what to expect. "Treat him like gold," said one man, shuffling about his day's autographed bounty. "Yeah, he's really touchy," chimed in another I watched for a few minutes. Rocky signed a ball, a few cards, then questioned an autograph seeker. "Did I get you already?" "No, remember you said we should wait until you were done eating."

Colavito pauses, then signs, "I got a memory like an elephant." Now, it's my turn; not for an autograph, but for a few minutes of time. I say I'm writing free-lance for Sports Collectors Digest. The former Indian and Tiger nods knowingly, ("SCD?" he asks.) then suggests we head off down the hall for a quieter place to talk.

As I turned my tape recorder on, it was really apparent that the man who hit 40 homers three times and once played 234 games without an error in the outfield now wanted to take a couple of swings at the problems with the baseball collecting hobby and wanted to clear up a few errors he believes fans may have about the way he and other former big leaguers now approach autograph requests.

SCD: What's your attitude about people coming up for your autograph? Obviously there are dealers, multiple autograph requests.

RC: Well, it's not really a problem. It's just that I know some of these guys are dealers and they get your autograph and they sell it. And I don't think that's right. I've always been a stickler for doing the right thing. And I ask, like if I come to a thing like this, I try to sign one, you know, for whoever asks. I try to hold it to that.

I've always been very lenient about it, but some people just take advantage and they bring 10-15 things to sign and I don't think that's really fair. It's not fair to the other people there. It's not fair to me.

SCD: Do you think it is getting out of hand? This whole idea, the money that's changing hands — $15 for an autograph, $45 for a ball. We see the ads all the time.

RC: I can't say it's out of hand, you know, you gotta remember one thing; the only thing that we can do today is make an appearance. I mean, you can't play anymore and you can't command the kind of money that you made before, which was not really a lot of money as opposed to what they're making today.

But the thing is — the ballplayer, himself, isn't getting $10 an autograph or whatever it is. That's (for) the guy that runs the show. The ballplayer commits to a certain amount of money that he gets for doing the show. Then, the guy that's running the show, he's the one that sets the price as to how much it is to get in the thing because he's paying for the room that you get it in.

And, you know, you don't want to work for nothing. Nobody wants to do that. All you're trying to do is make a living and raise your family, that's all it really is.

So, if we get asked to go to a place, and it draws a lot of people — everybody's happy. Nobody is saying to anyone, "Hey! We're forcing you to go and pay the $5, $10, $15, whatever it is!"

For the different calibre of player, they change the different price. If a guy's a big name star, a Hall of Famer, they know it'll command more money to get into the place. At one time, I didn't feel that way; you know you shouldn't (charge for signing), but you know what? It's the way that we can make a living — make a few bucks — I can't say that you can make a living out of it. You can only do so many.

But I don't think there's anything wrong with that. I heard where (radio commentator) Paul Harvey — I heard it myself, I had the station on — into Willie Mays. Willie really has no control over that, as far as deals go. Again, I come back to the guy that runs the show. He's the one who sets the price of the autograph.

SCD: What do you do as far as mail requests go?

RC: It depends. There's a guy out in, I think it's Iowa, who's made up a book with our addresses in it. (Editor's note: The Sport Americana Baseball Address List is published by Edgewater Book Co. of Cleveland and written by R.J. Smalling and Dennis W. Eckes.)

Now, here's a guy that makes a living selling these books and he puts your name and address in, which I think is wrong. I don't think anybody should have that liberty to invade your privacy and put your name and address in the book. Then, he sends you a postcard and says to you, "Would you like to buy the book?"

I mean, we're the ballplayers and if it wasn't for us, he wouldn't be making a living! He wouldn't have a book! And then, he comes up and says "Do you wanna buy a book?" If he wanted to create some good feeling among the players, he'd say, "Hey, I'm gonna send you a book — there are addresses of all your old friends. That's my way of making a living." You know, come up front with it. And, I've threatened him with a lawsuit.

SCD: So, when people use that address and send you stuff, what do you do?

RC: There's a key here. There's a key to the address that I know and nobody else knows. So I know if it comes from that book.

SCD: So if it comes out of that book, you don't sign?

RC: I, mostly, return those. And I try to do it nicely. I put on the envelope "REFUSED." This way, they don't have to pay the extra.

See, I could open the thing, take what's in it, put it in the envelope that's in it — they usually send you a stamped, self-addressed envelope — now they're paying double postage.

So, I try to save them that because I know these people are only trying to get your autograph. It's not a malicious thing — not with them, not with me. But I have to try to do what I think is right and put a stop to some of these guys who are making a living at our expense.

There are so many people, also, who are printing pictures and cards and stuff and they're making a living from us. And they give us nothing! I mean, that's not right. We gotta make a living, also.

(I called Jack Smalling, researcher for the address book in Ames, Iowa. He's been compiling player addresses since 1964. It began as a mimeographed publication, sold by mail order. In 1975, he switched to the computer-generated storage and printing still used today. The first book publication was issued in 1984. There are updates every two years. Number 4, currently on the stands, sells for $9.95. When I relayed Colavito's comments about his work, he first offered a quick "no comment." But, as I detailed some of Colavito's criticisms, he said, "His address is public information. Write to the Post Office (in the city) where he lives and they'll give it to you." So I asked, "Is his problem really with the Post Office?" He answered, "Could be." "Have you heard from his lawyer; he says he's going to sue you?" "Not yet. But it's public information.")

SCD: What are you doing now?

RC: Well, I do a few personal appearances and I have a couple of other things in the fire. I don't do a whole lot of them (shows). I don't want to prostitute myself. I do what I want to do. And, I love to hunt and I love to fish...

...SCD: Can't this boom in the autograph business help some of those guys? Obviously, the fans are crazy about EVERYBODY of that era. (1950s-1960s)

RC: That's right. The nostalgia's there. A lot of these fans are from way back. Even those in their 30s and 40s, it's unbelievable how they remember you.

Cause you know, it's one thing — when you're the best fan is when you're a kid. Your mind is not cluttered with trying to make a living, trying to do something in the business world.

I used to read a box score and absorb everything in it. Of course, in those days, you didn't have many box scores! You had eight for both leagues. You knocked them out.

I know my pal Andy Fallone (gestures to a man across from us) — he was in Brooklyn, I was in the Bronx, and we picked up the Daily News, looked in the back, right away) — who hit the home runs?

The line scores used to be there nice and fat. You knew who pitched, how many innings, but the home runs, boy, I couldn't wait to get that night edition.

You know, we used to get it on the corner, 10:00-10:30. You never could beat those days. That was the greatest time. — Pete Dobrovitz, July 29, 1988

* * *

David Cone

For Cone, who recently turned 26, his attraction to baseball cards started back in the mid-70s. "I was definitely into it," Cone said. "It was big! We even had a little baseball card game with dice. According to the statistics on the cards, you'd get the better odds with the dice. We invented a game like that." And who were the hot cards to have, for gaming purposes?

"Johnny Bench was the big one. He was probably the most popular one." Remember, this was the "pre-mint" era, where no one was counting every little nick. "With the game, they weren't in the best of condition, but we weren't really worried about that."...

...Enough about baseball — the game. Let's get back to baseball — the cards. Clearly, Cone's nowhere near the collector Carter or Hershiser is. In fact, he says it's his parents who have been collecting all the cards he's been on.

That doesn't mean he is without opinions on the subject. Of all the cards he's on now, he says his favorite is the new Fleer issue which features him posed with ex-Royal Danny Jackson, "N.L. Pitching Power."

"It's interesting, probably the best I've seen to date. I like the action shots," he said, motioning to a Score card that's caught him midway through his delivery. "They're just better than a mug shot. More attractive to me."

For just how good a pitcher David Cone was in '88, he's that much better a card show guest in '89. I've been carting a tape recorder and camera around to these things for a while now, relating experiences of stars in action. I don't know if I'll ever see better from a young hot star with every reason to be arrogant or cocky.

Cone is none of that; his style and modest approach took me back 20 years when a player might have even done a double-take when you called his name for a signing. ("Aw shucks — who, me?")

Cone is a piece of work, a class act all the way. Here's a guy who politely asks the fan if he'd want an item personalized. He'll check the spelling of a name, "Is that Sandy with a 'y' or an 'i'?" Kids coming up with items are always given a strong handshake.

Beaming dads eat it up when those kids are invited right up on stage to sit on David's lap or stand right next to him arm-in-arm while the flash fires away.

He's not a card show junkie, filling his offseason with show after show in an unabashed money grab. "The demand has been there," Cone said. "I just didn't want to go on the road. I do that all season. I made a decision to stay in the upstate area and have done just a select few shows. I think there's a lot of Mets fans up here that don't get a chance to get to Flushing."

On this day, Cone would sign more than 700 items. There was a kind word for every fan; particularly the children. He'd hold up a baby clad in Met garb while "Mother Met" was beside herself and Dad took the pictures while handling the stroller at the same time.

He'd take a few moments to tell a fan how he'd best go about sending an item to be mail signed. "You could send it down to Florida, but it might get lost in the mix. By the time it gets there, we might be already heading north. I'd hate to see you lose something. You're better off waiting and sending it to me this summer." How many players you know give two licks if a fan loses anything at all?

"With the mail, I try to get to it all," Cone said. "It's tough, it really is. You go on the road and you get back and there's a pile waiting for you. It takes time. I'm not gonna say I'm an angel that gets to them all, but I try to read them and definitely sign the ones from the kids."

And if you should catch Dave at a show, be ready to bring anything for signing. More than once on this day, his hand glided over a case of baseballs presented to him by a fan or maybe, it was a dealer — he didn't care. Many times, he'd be handed a stack of beautiful 8 x 10 authorized color prints. The blue Sharpie would make a strong, bold signature on each.

As the show drew to a close, more than one dealer made his way up with stacks of items, a sight that would drive some ballplayers crazy. Cone didn't mind at all. In fact, he found it hard to believe that one dealer would want to come back for several return visits with items. "Aren't you tired of me yet?" he asked. "I feel like I'm here and obviously there's some money being made. Most of these people are Mets fans and I'm willing to accommodate them any way they need me here. I'm here — I'm not gonna sit down with a calculator and scrutinize every single guy that comes by. I'm here to have a good time, meet Met fans and hopefully, it'll be a positive experience."

Two more quick snapshots of Cone in action to give you an idea of the kind of guy he is at a show. Man walks up with two pictures for signing, but he's purchased only one autograph ticket. Cone signs the first and is about to go ahead and sign the second when officials with the show note the ticket shortage and explain the one ticket per signing policy to the man. "Hey, I'm sorry," Cone heartily apologized. "If it were up to me, I'd do it."

Or, the little kid who mustered up every bit of courage he could to hand over his cards to be signed. Wide-eyed it was clear, baseball was now a big deal in his life and this guy before him was a hero. Cone shook his hand, got up and leaned across the table so the boy's dad could get a real close-up shot with David at eye-level.

As the boy walked away, he quickly shoved a napkin in Cone's direction. In it, scrawled in pencil, was the message: "Dear Dave, I think you're the best pitcher in baseball. I like the Mets. I hope you do good this year. I'm your biggest fan."

It stayed by Cone's side all afternoon. I'm sure the kid's encounter with his hero will stay with him, just maybe, forever. — Pete Dobrovitz, March 10, 1989

* * *

Pat Corrales

Pat Corrales is a collector. Not cards, bats.

"I've got the bats of Stan Musial, Ted Williams, Roger Maris, Hank Aaron, Reggie Jackson and a bunch of others," the Indians manager said. "I've got a whole laundry bag full in storage at home."

Corrales started his collection in the Reds spring training camp in 1963 when Mickey Mantle gave the rookie catcher a bat. Corrales, who appears on his first Topps card in 1965 sharing space on a Phillies rookie card with Costen Shockley, kept asking famous players for bats. Corrales tries to get bats of Hall of Famers and those he thinks will be enshrined. He wants to add the bats of Don Mattingly, Wade Boggs and Dave Winfield to his growing collection.

The oldest bat in the Corrales collection belonged to Napolean Lajoie of the Indians some 80 years ago. Corrales corraled that when he managed the Texas Rangers and Paul Richards was the general manager.

"I told Paul about my collection and he said he had a couple of bats he'd let me have," Corrales recalled. "One was Lajoie's and the other was Rudy York's, who set the record for most home runs in one month." — Irwin Cohen, July 17, 1987

* * *

Stan Coveleski

I was greeted at the door by an elderly man who looked like, and reminded me amazingly, of my own grandfather. He was wearing a flannel shirt and a pair of grey pants. He said, "Hello, please come in."

This man was baseball Hall of Fame pitcher and former Cleveland Indian great Stanley Coveleski.

After receiving a baseball star address list a couple of weeks earlier and noticing that a former baseball star lived where I was planning to go, I thought that possibly I could meet this legendary figure in person.

The day previously I had looked Mr. Coveleski's name up in the South Bend phone directory and to my surprise, there it was, along with all of the other numbers and addresses.

I called his home to see if it was possible for me to come and visit and talk with him for a while. I talked to both him and his wife of over 50 years on the phone for about five minutes.

They both assured me that it would be no problem at all for me to come to their home and talk with them the next day, which was a Saturday.

As I entered their home, I finally realized that he was a human being just as you and I. Most people like myself think of people like Coveleski, Ruth, Aaron, etc., as immortals, but as you must all realize, this is very far from the truth.

These sports stars are as much human as we are. They have feelings, and they feel the need to be accepted even after their playing careers are over. Many players such as Stan Coveleski are long forgotten by many. Therefore, I feel he was glad to have me visit and talk with him for this time.

I walked into what was the single most fantastic room I had ever been in. Mr. Coveleski offered my father and I a seat, and Stan sat in what was probably "his chair," just as Archie Bunker has his.

When we had been seated for a moment his wife came in and introduced herself and I in turn introduced myself and my dad to her.

As we were sitting and talking I was just looking around in pure amazement. When Mrs. Coveleski noticed my obvious interests, she said, "Go ahead, get up and look around."

I couldn't believe this, just like a wolf in a hen house, here I was, an avid baseball nut and a sports collector, in a room that probably belongs in Cooperstown.

The first thing I noticed was a large picture on the wall in a gorgeous wood frame of the great Babe Ruth. Probably two-feet-by-three-feet in size, and beautifully inscribed, "to Stanley, Best Wishes Always, Mrs. Babe Ruth."

When I brought this picture to my dad's attention he asked Mr. Coveleski if the Babe ever hit one off him. Stan just chuckled and said, "Oh, yes! The Babe hit them off everyone." He continued to tell us that the Babe had hit only three off him, insinuating that he felt fortunate to be taken advantage of only three times by the great Babe Ruth.

As I continued around the room I saw about five or six autographed baseballs in protective covers on the top of the television set. These baseballs, Mr. Coveleski explained, are given to each of the Hall of Famers each year at the Cooperstown Induction ceremonies. Each player in attendance signs each ball and they all receive one to take home with them.

Stan Coveleski was inducted in 1969 along with Roy Campanella, Stan Musial an Waite Hoyt; therefore, the first ball he had was the one from that year. The signatures included Zack Wheat, Pie Traynor, Frank Frisch, Ray Schalk, Heinie Manush, Dizzy Dean, Casey Stengel and many others. In all there were about 30 autographs.

At that point, I remembered my own autograph collection and talked to them about the letters I write to baseball's Hall of Famers and past stars. I explained to them that some Hall of Famers will not usually honor mail requests with their own signatures. Players like Roy Campanella obviously can't answer autograph requests, but there are other Hall of Famers such as Mantle, Paige, Williams and sometimes Berra and Wynn, who, as far as I know, are physically capable but don't usually honor requests for their autographs through the mails.

Mrs. Coveleski stated, "I don't like those players not granting requests for their autographs like that." She continued, "Covey never denies anyone his autograph." Which all autograph collectors know, as Stan Coveleski answers all autograph requests sent.

Before coming to their home I had so many questions to ask, but when I got there, I could think of none. Finally, I recalled a question which stuck out vividly, and I asked Covey, "About how many autograph requests do you get per day?" He replied, "Oh, I usually get three or four a day, sometimes more, sometimes less." I continued, "Do you mind these requests?" He was quick to answer, "No, not at all."

At this point, Mrs. Coveleski disappeared from the room saying, "I must show you these." When she returned to the room a minute or so later she had two small boxes in her hand. I had no idea what these boxes contained. She motioned for me to come over and see them.

In the first box was a 1920 World Series ring. Stan Coveleski had been the star in this series, winning three games for the Indians and having a remarkable 0.67 ERA in the three games he pitched. The ring was truly as beautiful as Liz Taylor's diamond (at least in my eyes), and was in excellent shape, regardless of its age.

In the second box was Stan's Hall of Fame ring from his 1969 induction at Cooperstown. The entire time I was admiring these masterpieces, both Mr. and Mrs. Coveleski's faces were glowing with delight and happiness as I'm sure the rings bring many fond memories back to them.

I questioned Covey as to why he didn't wear them, and he replied, "They are just too heavy to wear everyday."

As I wandered around the room further I saw a picture of Coveleski in a car apparently on a baseball diamond somewhere. I asked about this picture and he told me this was in Cleveland on Stan Coveleski Day in 1969. He continued to tell all of us of all the wonderful gifts he had received on that day.

When wondering what Stan did today, I asked him what he did in his spare time. "Well," he said, "I really like to fish, and I go just about every day when the weather is nice."

After visiting with them for about an hour we thought we had taken enough of these kind peoples time and said that we'd better leave. I thanked them gratefully for allowing us to come into their home and for sharing their part of baseball history wth us. Mrs. Coveleski assured us that it was their pleasure and invited us to come back again.

Just think, I shook the hand that served three home runs up to Babe Ruth, and the hand that almost single-handedly won the 1920 World Series for the Cleveland Indians.

On that day, I finally realized that Stan Coveleski and all other sports heroes were not immortal gods, but humans just as you or I.

Along with the 1920 World Series credits, Covey won 20 or more games five straight seasons and had 214 lifetime victories.

Oh, what a day!!! — Ken Burlington, March 31, 1977

* * *

Del Crandall

"My 1957 World Series ring is the most significant thing. I also have my uniform from the '57 Braves team if the moths haven't eaten it.

"I have the first home run ball I hit. It was off Blix Donnelly of the Phillies in 1949 at Braves Field in Boston." — Rich Marazzi, Batting the Breeze, July 8, 1988

* * *

Jimmie Crutchfield

Crutchfield then excused himself, walked to the closet and took out a tote bag. The bag's weight pulled the 5-foot-6, 150-pound Crutchfield over to the side, but he managed, saying he could handle it.

"I don't look at these often," he said. "In fact, I'll sometimes go five years without looking at them. And up until a couple of years ago, I never, ever looked at them."

Inside the bag, Crutchfield clutched a key to Negro League baseball history. In fact, there were eight keys — eight thick photo albums filled with Negro League newspaper articles, photos, souvenirs and the like. The newspapers have yellowed with time, but the articles are clear.

"When I left my home in Moberly, Mo., for the Birmingham Black Barons (in 1929), everyone basically just laughed at me and said I didn't have a chance in the world to make it (as a professional baseball player)," Crutchfield said. "I weighed about 140 pounds, so they said things like, 'Hey, Crutch, see you next week,' and 'Hey, Crutch, you did buy your bus fare back, didn't you?'

"I knew my family and friends wouldn't get a chance to read about me, so I just started saving clippings. I'd play in one city, then have fans (from that city) send me the newspaper clipping at the (next) city I was going to."

A priceless memorabilia collection was born.

"It never occurred to me why (the other players) weren't doing the same thing (saving clips), because they had to know they weren't going to be playing baseball their whole life," said Crutchfield, an outfielder, who played for several teams from 1930-46.

"With so many people, if you don't have something to show them (to prove that you played), they'll say, 'No you didn't.' Especially in my case."

That's because of Crutchfield's size. Or, lack thereof, as the case may be.

"When I left baseball, I went to work in the Chicago post office and no one ever talked to me about baseball, basically because no one knew I played," Crutchfield said. "Then one day, back in 1946, someone said, 'Hey, I heard you were a baseball player.'

"I told the guy I did and he couldn't believe it...and he just walked away.

"So, my wife, Julia, told me to carry one of my clippings with me...that way, they'll believe me."

And with Julia's comment, a tradition began.

Crutchfield photocopied three newspaper clippings, folded them carefully and placed them in his wallet. To this day, they still remain there.

The first clip is from Crutchfield's 1930 Opening Day game. The headline reads: 'Black Barons Shutout Stars Behind Paige: Crutchfield Drives in Three Runs With a Homer and a Single.' He had three hits that day as Birmingham beat the St. Louis Stars team 3-0 that featured James "Cool Papa" Bell, Willie Wells and George Giles.

"I was young and the smallest man on the field, so I almost had to hit," Crutchfield said. "Pitchers often thought they could just throw the ball by me because of my size. But I could pick that ball up...I had good eyes. Plus, I was pretty lucky."

Crutchfield also carries a clip from an All-Star game. On it, the headline proclaims, 'Most Colorful Game in History of Series Won by West: Crowd in Frenzy of Excitement over Thrilling Plays. Jones Brilliant on Mound and also gets homer. Crutchfield's barehanded catch is fielding highlight.'...

...In addition to the clips, Crutchfield also has three albums filled with fan mail letters.

"You should see the letters I've received from people asking for my autograph, especially the ones from kids all over the country," he said.

Crutchfield answers all of his mail, with some exceptions, though.

"There are some guys who have the nerve to say, 'Would you sign these five or six cards for me?'" he said. "I found out they then were selling (the signatures) and I don't like that."

Crutchfield still receives six to 10 letters per week. "It's nice to be recognized and I don't mind signing at all." — Ross Forman, Sept. 4, 1992

* * *

Bob Davidson

National League umpire Bob Davidson says he thinks back to a time a few years ago, and could kick himself for what he said.

Davidson recalls: "My mom called me from Duluth, and said, 'Bobby, I've got these shoeboxes full of old baseball cards. What do you want me to do with 'em?' I said, 'Oh, go ahead and throw 'em out, or give 'em away.'

"At that time, I had no idea that they might be worth something in the future. I had a lot of Topps cards, some good ones, as I remember, and I'd carefully cut out the cards from the backs of the Post cereals boxes. I had some football cards, too. Well, whatever my mom did with 'em, they're all gone now."

These days, however, Davidson has what few people can say they possess.

"I save lineup cards of each game I work behind the plate," Davidson said. "After each game, when I get back to the hotel, I'll turn the card over and on its back write down the names of the guys I worked with — you know, the umpire at first base, second base, third base — the score of the game, and I note whether I threw somebody out of the game or if there was some big hoopla.

"I have four years' worth of 'em. I think a lot of guys are doing that now. I've noticed some other umpires are always saving their lineup cards after the game."

Davidson also has a few special autographed baseballs.

"I have a couple from the 1987 All-Star Game that I worked," he said, "with the names of all the guys I worked with. That's special to me, because Dick Stello's name is on there. He worked that game with me, and he was a close friend of mine. He passed away in 1987.

"I also have a baseball from the 1988 National League playoffs, which I worked, including the fifth game behind the plate. I have all the guys' signatures on that ball, plus the signatures of (Bart) Giamatti and (Peter) Ueberroth, the incoming and outgoing commissioners." — David Craft, March 24, 1989

* * *

Glenn Davis

And, of course, there was his long-running disagreement with Topps over the controversial Garbage Pail Kids card set.

"A number of players refused to sign Topps cards beginning back in 1986 beacause of Garbage Pail Kids," Davis said. "It was a protest, the only kind we could do, because we didn't want to have anything to do with, or seem to endorse, a product that polluted kids' minds.

"The best part of the protest was that it was successful. Topps met with us, listened to our complaints, and assured us that they valued our opinions. Topps quit making the cards."

Davis added, "I sign Topps cards again. I'm glad they listened to us."

Bring your Topps cards to Davis, but don't bother with Broder cards.

"I don't want anything to do with bootleg pictures. Companies sign up and pay big money for the right to use our pictures. It's not fair for some to pay and for others not to pay.

"This affects more than just me. Rob Broder is making business off us. He was asked to pay the rights fee like everyone else and he said he didn't care. That's not right," Davis said...

...Half the kids who approached Davis during a January autograph session at a Columbus card show approached him in awe.

Davis spent time with every kid, chatting with each, trying to put the nervous kids at ease.

"The main thing is the kids," Davis said. "This makes a lasting impression on them. They'll remember talking with a famous person, getting an autograph from a famous athlete, the rest of their lives.

Glenn Davis

"They'll talk about it for months, especially the ones who were too shy to talk to me when they were here on the stage. If that's important to them, it should be that important to me, too.

"It's another way to minister to kids. Give them your time. Besides, it's a lot of fun." — Dave Platta, April 13, 1990

* * *

Andre Dawson

He's made millions of dollars playing baseball the past 16 years.

He'll be making at least $2 million next season.

So, why does Andre Dawson spend a few weekends each year signing autographs at sports card shows?

"I like meeting new fans around the country," says Dawson, a featured guest at the Midwest Sports Collectors Convention in St. Louis last month. "I've been doing it the last four years. I try to do about three shows a year. I enjoy it more when it's somewhere I haven't done a show before."

All shows are different, says Dawson. Some are good, others aren't.

"The audience is the key," he says. "If they have fun, you have fun."

Dawson enjoys signing for everyone, but finds the most pleasure in those autographs he signs for youngsters.

"I like to see the expressions on their faces," he says. "I've always felt the kids are the backbone of the business. The kids are the ones that get the biggest thrill out of it. They make it enjoyable for me." — Tony Prudom, Dec. 25, 1992

* * *

Don Denkinger

Rows of autographed baseballs rest neatly on a shelf in the game room. Framed photographs — some taken with celebrities such as Mr. T — fill up an adjoining wall. Other mementos, such as mounted baseball bats, gag gifts from family and friends, and boxes of fan letters and notes of support, are here, too.

There's no reason to think anything sinister is in the room, but there is. Mixed in with the well-wishes are several anonymous notes written by some very sick people. The host's smiles quickly turned to a frown as he slowly shook his head in disbelief.

"I just got another death threat last week," said Denkinger, a 20-year veteran of American League umpiring. "As soon as I saw what it was I contacted the league office, and they contacted the FBI, which has been handling the matter."

He left it at that. No reason to dwell on negative matters, especially since Christmas was only weeks away and there was much to be done. The Denkinger children are all grown now and moved away, and the holidays are a time for reuniting the family and getting back in touch with old friends.

Ironically, the thing that has helped Don Denkinger be a good provider for his family over the years is also responsible for the death threats and poison-pen letters: baseball. Or, more specifically, being a Major League umpire in the glare of the public spotlight.

The vindictive correspondence is lingering evidence that some people still blame Denkinger for the Cardinals losing the 1985 World Series to the cross-state Royals. His controversial call in Game Six and his "presence" behind the plate in Game Seven, the accusations go, caused the Cardinals' downfall after they led in the Series, three games to two, and led in Game Six, 1-0, going into the bottom of the ninth.

Many other baseball fans — Cardinal rooters included — point to a poor toss to first base and a subsequent passed ball, both committed by St. Louis in that wild ninth inning, as keys to the Royals' comeback in Game Six, and the Cardinals' anemic .185 batting average in the Series as the real reason why St. Louis couldn't nail down that championship...

...Collecting: I never collected a baseball card in my life. It's a big entity now, though, and I probably get three or four of my own cards to autograph every day. In the course of a year, I probably get 15 or 20 people from all walks of life who call or write to find out if I've got a uniform for sale or some other paraphernalia that's associated with a major league umpire on the field. I have collected a number of autographed baseballs over the years, some from Hall of Famers, some from people I think will make the Hall of Fame someday. I've got some pictures and so forth. I've got a ball and the lineup card from the game that broke the Baltimore Orioles' losing streak in 1988. I worked the plate that game, and after the game one of the other umpires in my crew offered me $200 for the lineup card. I get a few requests from people who want me to get 'em autographs of some of the big-name players in the American League, but I mean, sheesh, let's face it, everybody wants a baseball with Jose Canseco's or Roger Clemens' autograph on it. — David Craft, March 17, 1989

* * *

Bucky Dent

Baseball instructional school. Piloting the Yankees' Triple A farm club in the International League. Always on the go. Does Dent ever have time to sign autographs or mingle with the fans?

"When I get stuff in the mail now...I try to get to our ballpark in Columbus early," Dent said. "I try to sit down and sign as much of it as I can and send it right back.

"Usually, at the various ballparks, home and away, when there are so many people around and I'm busy trying to prepare for the game, I try to sign as many things as I can. Usually what happens, though, is if somebody gives me a stack of cards, I'll sign one or two of 'em and I just give 'em right back.

"I'm in the same boat as other people in baseball. We don't always have time to sign every card or picture. I hope fans understand our situation. I don't like to turn people away, or cause hurt feelings, but many times I've got so much to do I can't possibly sign everything that's being waved at me or always send stuff back right away."

As a youngster Dent never collected baseball cards or player autographs. A few years ago, however, he began to collect autographed baseballs, notably from Hall of Famers and likely candidates for the Hall of Fame, such as Gaylord Perry and Phil Niekro.

"That's how it started, really, by getting autographs of pitchers I faced, like Gaylord, who'd won 300 games in their career," Dent said. "And playing in New York, you know, has given me the opportunity to acquire signatures of some great players appearing at old-timers games.

"I love to meet these guys, and sit around and talk to them about their playing days. Allie Reynolds, Bill Dickey, Enos Slaughter. I've gotten to see Mickey Mantle. And, Roger Maris, back when he was alive. Whitey Ford's one of my favorites. I get to see him quite a bit."
— David Craft, Aug. 26, 1988

* * *

Joe DiMaggio

Recently my wife and I were in the San Francisco area visiting my folks and doing some sightseeing. One morning we were walking along the wharf and I decided to stop in at DiMaggio's restaurant. Who knows, I thought, perhaps Joe would be there.

Well, we walked in shortly after opening time and my eyeballs nearly fell out — there was the Jolter on the phone behind the reception desk. The hostess started to show us to a table when I interjected with why I had come.

You see, I just happened to have about 35 different DiMaggio cards ranging from the Goudey-Play Ball type issue to the 1976 DQ issue.

After showing these to her and some curious waiters, I was introduced to DiMag. I then explained that I was a great fan of his and was wondering if he had a minute to sign some of my cards.

"You want me to sign all of these?" he asked.

I said "No, I couldn't ask that of you, sir. There are many here I received signatures on in the mail from you. Could you tell me if you really signed them? The ones that aren't signed I'd be most grateful if you could."

We talked some more and I told him of my suspicion that most were signed by his sister Marie. As he was signing a few he remarked, "Yes, I do see many here that Marie signed. What do you expect, though. You see, I travel nine months out of the year. I get back and there are stacks of letters, balls, you name it. I surely couldn't sign all my mail, could I?"

What do you say to Joe DiMaggio when he asks you that?

"Oh, definitely, Mr. DiMaggio, that is a lot," I stuttered out.

We did some more talking about his travel for the Bowery Bank, the coffee people and various other endorsements and old-timers games.

"Yes," he said, "I'll go to some of the games, but I won't play any more. My back gives me trouble."

Soon again, the talk turned back to the cards. "I never did care for these companies," DiMag said. "The modern players in particular aren't getting a pittance of what they should."

It was at this time my wife asked him if he saved his own cards. "No, I don't care about them too much," he replied.

I might add here that there were a number that he couldn't recall signing agreements for.

As the conversation wound down, he told me he was going out of town the next day and had to run. My wife got a couple of pictures of us together and as he left he said, "Say hi to your folks in Martinez for me. You know I was born there." I said I sure would and we parted as I told him I would try to get in touch if he was ever in Houston. On our way out of the restaurant with about eight of my items signed, the hostess gave me some matchbooks and a souvenir menu. I expressed my gratitude and promised I'd be down soon for dinner.

Some observations:

DiMag himself — At first, Joe DiMaggio seemed cold and rather 'stand-offish' to being approached by a fan. (I guess the phone call had let his almost finished breakfast get cold). It was only after I assured him that I didn't want all my items signed and could carry on a fairly knowledgeable conversation about what he was doing today that he warmed up, even to the point of putting his arm around me for one of the pictures.

The signature — Naturally, I was very excited to get some DiMaggio signatures in person. After carefully studying the ones I got in the mail, I've decided that 90 or so signatures I received that way are all fakes, save four of them I got last summer. Back when I was getting them regularly, I thought these four were fakes. It took me a while to come to grips with this as to me three Goudey Heads Up, two 1939 Play Balls, a Leaf, and many other DiMaggio issues were shattered in value. Certainly, I'm not qualified to judge anyone else's signatures, but for my personal collection I used this criteria for establishing fakes.

On all the real ones, the M in DiMaggio has a downward loop when you first start to write it. Practically all of my mail signtures had an upward loop. Also, the o at the end of DiMaggipo in the ones I got in person stopped abruptly, where all the mail ones, except four, had a loop on it. I'm not really into autographs and again, am no expert, so do not think of sending me any signatures for evaluation.

Hindsight — Would it have been proper for me to ask DiMag that if he couldn't sign personally to have Marie return his mail unsigned???
— Ron Gordon, July 31, 1976

* * *

Doug Drabek

Todd Murray: Did you collect baseball cards when you were younger?

Doug Drabek: I did but I stopped when I was 11.

Murray: Do you keep any memorabilia pertaining to your career?

Drabek: I have all of my uniforms and I save all of the cards of the players and coaches that I'm associated with and I get them to sign their cards. For instance, I have all the cards of Jim Rooker (former Pirates pitcher and current Pirate broadcaster) signed. I have a book, The Pictorial History of Baseball, that I get autographs in and I'm also a hat fanatic. I collect hats dating all the way back to Little League.

Murray: Do you enjoy signing autographs?

Drabek: Yes, when I was younger I dreamed about being down on the field and being able to sign autographs for the kids. That dream has come true and I enjoy doing it. — Todd Murray, June 10, 1988

* * *

Don Drysdale

Drysdale, who regularly appears at card shows, said he receives a steady stream of fan mail, at least 50 letters a week.

And do you answer autograph requests, Don?

"Oh yeah," he said. "I try to be as receptive as I can in terms of signing autographs, and then just hope people understand when I don't have time to do it.

"Pee Wee Reese always had a saying: 'Don't worry about (signing autographs). The time to start worrying is when they stop asking you.'" — Ross Forman, June 28, 1991

* * *

Bob Feller

It only took a few minutes until I spotted the man I had hoped to see, five-time All-Star and Hall of Famer Bob Feller. I had heard reports he was the epitome of class at card shows; always quick with a smile and some pleasant conversation. I knew he had walked an amazing 194 men in 1941 and still won 25 games. But I didn't know Bob was the self-proclaimed King of the Autograph. He had a lot to say about the hobby and after telling his wife he'd be joining her for lunch in a bit, he started saying it.

Feller: I go to a lot of these shows, probably as many as anyone. But I have to admit that I've signed more autographs than anybody in history, by far, because I travel all over the minor leagues all summer and have for many, many years. I'll be doing it again on the West Coast next year.

I'm eliminating East Coast minor league ballpark appearances this year. I'll do the old-timers, the card shows, then I'll do the work for the Indians in spring training, coaching and I run their public speakers bureau. But I'm collecting some antique tractors, and my wife likes to collect antiques. We're gonna travel to Europe. We were there this year twice already.

SCD: I know there's a problem with the pros who get autographs merely to sell, but what about the true fan who approaches you?

Feller: I try to use good judement in it. I'm sure I make some mistakes. I hope my percentage is fairly decent. I know when you get letters from little kids, you have to make a judgement; is it really from a little kid?

My wife reads most of the stuff and she's pretty good at remembering zip codes and addresses. If you get too many of them, you can bet somebody's got a dozen little kids writing in to get autographed balls. You send the stuff along and they're selling it.

If there's any decision to be made, I always go in favor of signing the autograph. If they write a personal letter. If they don't write a personal letter, or if it just says "Dear ----, Sign this." (He shakes his head). If they send a stamped, self-addressed envelope. A lot of them don't send a stamped envelope. Some of them are pretty dumb.

SCD: Is it getting out of hand? The prices?

Feller: Well, I'm not DiMaggio or Aaron, but I try to shake hands with everybody and smile at 'em. I may miss a few. Depending on, of course, the card show promoter. He may try to run 'em through as fast as possible.

Since I've traveled so much and made so many shows, a lot of people have my autograph. I've done more of this than anyone in history!

SCD: What's the toughest part of being on the receiving end?

Feller: There's no problems around a hotel, really. The real problem is at the ballpark, coming and going. Not only for old-timers but for the present-day players. The clubs don't protect them in the parking lot. They make them accessible either consciously or subconsciously. There's no way you can stop and sign a hundred autographs. Or a thousand on big days.

The best thing to do is to sign none. Just go to your car, because you've probably got your wife and a couple of screaming kids waiting for you — the present-day players (have).

Once you stop, you've got the bus there waiting for you and you've got all the other guys yelling for you to get on. If you really want autographs, the best way to do it is to go to autograph shows. Or write in and ask for an autograph.

SCD: The autograph, at one time, seemed to represent a memory — the moment you met a player you admired, in person. Now, it's just a commodity, available to anyone who wants to buy — no contact, no memory at all. Does that bother you?

Feller: Actually, your autograph is your property. It's like anything else; you can either give it away or sell it, depending on the occasion. Now, I don't give autographs away through the mail. I did at one time; I don't anymore because it was overdone.

I will give them a nice autograph on a card, or if they don't send anything, (I'll sign) on a nice piece of paper and return it to them. I charge $3 for them.

But around the hotels, or an airport, I'll sign at the ballpark over the rails tonight. At all the old-timers games, I sign as fast as I can, as many as I can. But there's no way you can please them all. — Pete Dobrovitz, July 29, 1988

* * *

Mark Fidrych

Mike Andler, Mukwonago, Wis., says to add another feather to Mark Fidrych's cap for being courteous to autograph collectors. He says that in the last series in Milwaukee he asked Mark to sign his program, which he did. Then, says Mike, "he noticed two baseballs in my jacket pocket and asked me if he could sign them. I didn't object." — Andy Waldman, Sport Talk, Nov. 30, 1976

* * *

Mark Fidrych

Mark Fidrych

He was known simply as "The Bird."

A minor league manager thought Mark Fidrych really looked and acted like the Sesame Street character. Others said it was the way he talked, or 'chirped,' to the ball before throwing it.

Some were just amused by the way he'd get down on one knee, like a kid playing in a sandbox, and manicure the pitcher's mound.

In one magical summer way back in 1976, the Detroit Tiger pitcher became the best known personality in baseball.

Blessed with a slick slider and blazing fastball, he finished with a 19-9 record, started the All-Star Game and was the American League Rookie of the Year.

When he got his first major league start in May, he nearly tossed a no-hitter. In June, the lanky Fidrych hosted three sold-out dates in a row. None of the Tiger greats had ever done that before. Not Al Kaline, not Charlie Gehringer, not even Ty Cobb.

Win or lose, his following, sometimes 50,000 strong, would wait in the stands for him, chanting "We Want The Bird," refusing to leave until he answered their curtain call.

In all, nearly a million flocked to the ancient Tiger Stadium to see the 21-year-old sensation.

But a series of injuries spoiled his encore in 1977 and eventually forced him out of baseball...

...Fidrych doesn't get back to Detroit much anymore, but when he does he's still mobbed by autograph hunters and well wishers. Though young Tiger fans could never appreciate what he did or who he was, Fidrych remains one of the motor city's loved sports heroes.

"People come up to me and ask how I'm doing. Or they say I remember that game when you did this and that. It's nice to know they remember the little things — the details. It was a long time ago and I don't even remember a lot of it."

Neil Heffernan, manager of Sportsland USA, a souvenir store near Tiger Stadium, says his "Bird" collectibles sold well even after Fidrych fell from glory. While most of his original 'Bird' stock is no longer available, Heffernan says Fidrych baseball cards and posters are still consistent sellers.

"There aren't many of his artifacts left, but we still get a lot of requests that we just can't satisfy. We still sell his Tiger cards and for a while we sold his minor league card from Pawtucket. His Topps rookie card is something we still get on a regular basis. It goes for around $2.50 in these parts, but that's about four times the national price."

Sportsland USA was just starting out when Fidrych was in his heyday, so the store didn't have a huge inventory. But Heffernan remembers "anything that had anything to do with 'The Bird' was gone in a hurry.

"With all the guys selling stuff on the streets, there were hundreds of gimmicks going. The slogan was 'The Bird Is The Word.' They had it on T-shirts, bumper stickers and a record. There was even a 'Bird' whistle. You'd put water in it and it would warble like a bird.

"When you're as close to the stadium as I am it's tough to get excited about ball players. But he was one that we'll never see the likes of again. He was a phenomenon."

Though Fidrych says he never collected baseball cards or autographs as a youngster, he did assemble quite a collection of memories during his playing days.

Tucked away at his ranch are his old jerseys, a collection of bats and an autographed pair of New York Yankee shorts from the late Bronx catcher Thurman Munson.

During his rookie season, Fidrych managed to score one of George Scott's huge, black bats in the heat of the battle.

"I told (Detroit catcher) to ask George if I could have a bat," Fidrych said. "I said if he's gonna give me one, tell him to look over and tip his hat."

When Scott returned to the Milwaukee dugout, fresh from grounding out, he looked out to the mound, smiled at "The Bird" and tipped his hat. "The next thing I knew I had a bat sent over." — Vernon W. Smith, Oct. 28, 1988

* * *

Mark Fidrych

Ah, yes, the fans. The throngs who witnessed that amazing summer are almost as much a part of the story as the antics of "The Bird." Even now at card shows, which he does judiciously and only in situations where the autographs are free, people come up to him and recount how much that amazing season meant to them. "Now I understand the significance of what happened but when I played you didn't know what it was," says Fidrych. "Now, people talk about it and it makes you feel good." — T.S. O'Connell, May 15, 1992

* * *

Rollie Fingers

Irwin Cohen: Were you into collecting baseball cards and trying to get autographs when you went to Dodger Stadium?

Rollie Fingers: I had thousands of baseball cards and most of them were all of the Dodgers. I tried to get autographs just like any other kid.

Cohen: Of course, you appear on many cards and other types of memorabilia. What does your collection consist of today?

Fingers: I've got some stuff from the World Series I've been in with Oakland (1972, '73 and '74) and some odds and ends that I've accumulated over the years. Also, I have some baseballs with some of the records that I've set but nothing more than that. — Irwin Cohen, On the Baseball Beat, Jan. 31, 1986

* * *

Rollie Fingers

Here's One For Rollie

In June my family and I made our visit to the Baseball Hall of Fame in Cooperstown, N.Y. It was the weekend of the 50th Anniversary Celebration of the Hall's opening.

Because I'm an old baseball fan (the Brooklyn Dodgers are still in my genes!), and as a stamp collector, the visit satisfied two of my important interests: visiting and enjoying the museum and also attending the first day of issuance of the new Lou Gehrig stamp on June 10.

We thoroughly enjoyed the weekend, the Hall, the old-timers' game, the weather, and also the opportunity to schmooz with other fans and philatelists.

Of all the experiences, there's one in particular that I would like to share with your readers. I, like other fans, have in the past experienced some indifferent, and even rude, players at shows and at ballparks. From my own observations, these incidents are in the minority.

On Friday, June 9, the day before the anniversary celebration, my family and I were in the Hall. We were pleasantly surprised to notice Rollie Fingers and his wife meandering through the museum, carefully scrutinizing each display case. (He was hard to miss with his trademark mustache).

We were hesitant to approach him for his autograph, as he seemed to be absorbed in the fascinating items on display, and he and his wife were exchanging comments on each one.

In the course of the next 20-30 minutes, he was constantly recognized and approached by at least 12-15 fans for autographs, pictures and conversation. After each interruption, he calmly returned to viewing the displays.

All through his time, he was extremely cordial and cooperative, never once showing any sign of upset. He politely and happily continued to sign everything that was handled to him without hesitation.

He joked and made small conversation with anyone who seemed to request it. He was also most gracious even when asked to pose with fans for photographs.

When kiddingly asked by someone in our family whether he was to charge us for all these autographs, he responded, in kind, simply, "It doesn't cost me anything to move my fingers."

Rollie thanked everyone who approached him, even though it seemed that he was being constantly interrupted. He remained patient and courteous.

At the old-timers' game, he was one of the very few players who stood signing autographs for an extended period of time prior to the game.

In the museum, I didn't have a flash on my camera, and asked Rollie if I could take his picture outside in the sunlight when he was ready to leave the Hall. Sure enough, he remembered and obliged. I took my picture of a real classy guy!

Throughout, he was a gentleman, in spite of what certainly must have been, at best, an annoyance to him and his wife, and, at worst, an insensitive intrusion into a private time in his life.

If the Hall's committee should ever call me, Rollie has my vote! — Sam Berkowitz, Columbia, Md., Reader Reaction, Aug. 11, 1989

* * *

Whitey Ford

Debit to autograph collectors of a profiteering type, as brought out by Greg Evanella, Harrington Park, N.J., in a letter. "I attended the New York convention and must confess that Whitey Ford's appearance to sign autographs was a drawing factor for me, as he had never responded to my mail requests. I no longer wonder why. As a friend and I were about to enter the room to join a line of about 10 for Ford's autograph, some fellow, about 20, stopped us and asked if we'd each get Ford to sign an obviously mass-produced 8x10 glossy. If we would do that, we could keep the spare ourselves. I had 1956 and 1957 cards for Ford to sign, but my friend had nothing, so he accepted the offer. We saw in front of us that others had accepted the glossies request, and that Ford was quite annoyed. Apparently it had been going on all morning. I got my friend to forget the request and get Ford's autograph on a sheet of paper. I also noticed that we were the only ones at hand who asked him to please sign and then thanked him. What is collecting coming to? No wonder Ford is sour on autographing in general. Some do for profit the things that ruin collectding for us all." — Wirt Gammon, Wirt's Words, Jan. 15, 1980

* * *

Joe Garagiola

Joe Garagiola says thanks

I had a great exsperience that I'd like to share with you about the "hobby." I phrase it that way because it involved dealers, collectors and just people.

Rich and Marie Gimino and Bob Wilkie had a card show Saturday and Sunday, Oct. 8-9. I thought it would be a good opportunity to sell the Surf books for the Baseball Alumni Team, so I talked to them about a table, which they graciously let me have, free.

I was there a short time on Saturday with Willie Stargell (the autograph personality) and we did well with the crowd and selling books. I wasn't there during the Stargell autograph session.

Since Rich, Marie and Bob bought a good quantity of books, I agreed to come back on Sunday and sign autographs. I didn't know what to expect, so I went alone.

I thought I'd sit at the book table and, in between sales, sign autographs. What a surprise I had.

I started at the table, but had to move to the stage for autographs. I didn't know who would sell the books, but Rich Gimino and Will Davis took care of manning the table.

The business came in spurts, and every time the line thinned out, a dealer came forward with some incentive like the next 10 people who buy a $10 book will get an uncut sheet with Canseco and McGwire.

Or, the next five will get a wax pack. Or, if you sell 10 books in the next 10 minutes, I'll donate $50.

It went like that all day, and it was unbelievable. The dealers really kept it alive.

And the collectors not only bought the books, but made donations, or gave me money and didn't take books, simply saying "We want to help."

Also, Stan Marks held an auction for B.A.T. I bought some items I'd collected from my Game of the Week travels, but the dealers also chipped in with enough items to really make it a big league auction.

Thanks to them, we had everything from Mattingly shoes to football jerseys to Canseco rookie cards.

I only wish that the next time a TV network does a show about the hobby, they'll show this caring side. It isn't just "how much is this card worth?" or "how much can I get for this?"

This was a case of "I can help, and I will."

The dealers and collectors didn't know who they were helping, only that they were helping baseball people.

Those guys who have come up against a bad hop will be happy to know a lot of good people still remember them.

I wish I could tell you the names of everyone who made it such a great day, but to all of them I say thanks. We left with more than $6,000 for B.A.T., and it seemed like at least six million friends. — Joe Garagiola, Baseball Alumni Team, New York, N.Y., Reader Reaction, Nov. 11, 1988

* * *

Ron Gardenhire

Mets' shortstop Ron Gardenhire has been collecting autographs of some of his heroes, having them scrawl their signatures across their career records in the Baseball Encyclopedia. He had the book in his van during spring training. During the season he either ships it in the equipment truck or lugs it aboard airliners. He particularly likes to have it on hand for old-timers games. — Wirt Gammon, Wirt's Words, May 11, 1984

* * *

Steve Garvey

One item which he doesn't sign is his 1982 Donruss card (#84). In 1992, Garvey will sign one card for Multiple Sclerosis, which will then auction off the card. Once again, it's just his way of giving something back to the fans.

Garvey says his last Topps card, (#100 in 1987) picturing him as a Padre, and his rookie card, a 1971 Topps (#341), are his two favorites.

The rookie card, especially, means a lot to him. He was quite thrilled when he saw himself pictured on a card.

"I think it's a boyhood dream come true and you get a big kick out of it. You try to get as many as you can because you don't know if there's going to be another one," he said.

Garvey's least favorite card is one he calls the "Wes Parker Memorial," a 1973 Topps card (#213) which pictures him heading to home plate after a home run. But Parker, waiting to greet him, fills up most of the card space.

Garvey also doesn't like his 1979 Topps card (#50). He and the catcher are at home plate, looking toward the dugout. Garvey's tongue is hanging out.

His rhetorical question, posed to Topps with a laugh, is "Did you try to pick out the worst shot? Is it something I said?" — Mark K. Larson, Aug. 10, 1990

* * *

Bob Gibson

Bob Gibson, St. Louis pitcher: Sometimes I sign autographs, sometimes I don't. Personally I think anyone who saves autographs is crazy." OK, Bob, but all of us have a crazy streak somewhere. — Wirt Gammon, Wirt's Words, Oct. 15, 1975

* * *

Al Gionfriddo

One might assume that the ball involved in "The Catch" (against Joe DiMaggio in the 1947 World Series) would have been kept by someone and possibly donated to the Baseball Hall of Fame. Not so, says Gionfriddo. "You know, I was so excited when I came in from the outfield after making the catch, I threw the ball onto the pitcher's mound. The ball stayed in the game and, would you believe it? I'm the first guy up in the next inning, the top of the seventh, and I fouled the first pitch off up into the stands. Somebody there got it and probably didn't even know the value of the ball." — Fluffy Saccucci, March 6, 1992

* * *

Tom Glavine

SCD: What is your attitude about the current state of the trading card and sports memorabilia hobby?

Glavine: It has gotten to the point where it is really a big business. Most of the players are in between on it. It is OK for the kids. It keeps them off the streets in the sense that it gives them something to be interested in that isn't violent or dangerous. It gives them heroes and people to look up to as role models. The players enjoy the interaction with the kids. On the other hand, when you get the same people coming back time and again for autographs or whatever, that's a problem. It gets a bit old as far as the players are concerned. You don't like to be signing five cards for everyone. One or two per person is fine. That's all they really need. I don't have any strict rules myself about signing, but it can get tough in a crowd. I just try to get everybody I can. My feeling is that autographs are OK as a personal thing, where the kids or the people want to be able to say they met you or they follow your career. But when money gets involved, that's tiresome. It takes away from the real collectors...

...SCD: Are there any particular things that you refuse to sign? Are there any special nicknames or other things that people ask you to add to your signature?

Glavine: I don't have any nicknames, so generally people just ask me to sign my name. There are some requests for me to add "Cy Young Award" under my signature, which I am happy to do if I have the time and the crowd isn't too big. I try to sign for everyone when asked. Also, at the ballpark, I try to get over to the stands once or

twice a week, before the games, to sign autographs. At other times it is tough to do that because I may be taking a treatment in the trainer's room or lifting weights. — Rick Firfer, Aug. 14, 1992

* * *

Ken Griffey Jr.

A Waste Of Time
An Open Letter To Ken Griffey Jr:

I am writing this to hopefully get a question answered.

I took a picture of you while you were batting during the home run hitting contest at this past year's All-Star game workout. I had an 8-by-10-inch photo made up and sent it to be signed at a recent card show you were at.

I received a phone call and was told that you refused to sign my photo because it was not licensed. What's the deal? Is this because you want everyone to have the same picture of you?

Let me tell you something. You have been around for a couple of years. I don't know where you get off doing this.

I have had some players much greater than you thrilled to sign pictures I have taken of them — Carlton Fisk, Hank Aaron, Jerry Rice, Carl Yastrzemski, Tom Seaver, Brooks Robinson, Willie Mays, and that's to only mention a few.

So, the next time you do a show, make sure the promoters tell people about this silly rule of yours. Maybe then some people will save their money.

I realize $4.89 is not much to you, even though I did enjoy ripping it up. I wish I hadn't wasted my time in the first place. — Brenda Pringle, Grabill, Ind., Reader Reaction, March 1, 1991

* * *

Ozzie Guillen

Another reason for the lack of previous shows attended is the fact he annually returns home to Venezuela during the winter.

"And there are not really (too many shows there)," Guillen said. "But, the number of shows is starting to pick up and (it's) getting bigger now. I think in a couple more years they're almost going to be as big as they are here (in the USA)."

Plus, he added, "If you do shows every day, people will get tired of seeing you."

However, Guillen is still among the most sought-after players. Especially because he's amicable.

"I like signing," Guillen said. "People want your autograph because they like you. The bad thing will be when they don't want your autograph anymore; that's what you have to worry about." — Ross Forman, Aug. 28, 1992

* * *

Tony Gwynn

Tony Gwynn, decked out in sunglasses similar to those that Arnold Schwarzenegger made famous in The Terminator, stepped out of the visitor's dugout at Wrigley Field and walked toward the batting cage.

Then it began.

The autograph crunch, that is.

Countless autograph seekers sporting cards, programs and other items bearing Gwynn's likeness rushed toward the field to get a signature from the San Diego outfielder. Gwynn obliged, then moved toward the cage.

But not before he was asked again — this time by a member of the Wrigley Field grounds crew. He wanted a ball signed. And again, Gwynn obliged.

In case it's not obvious by now, Tony Gwynn is a pretty humble, not to mention generous, guy. To him, signing autographs are just part of the job.

And it's a good thing Gwynn feels that way, because he's in demand. Four batting titles, six all-star game appearances and four Gold Glove Awards will do that to a guy's popularity.

But even the good-natured Gwynn feels pressed from time to time. Sometimes the autograph hounds are just too much.

"There are people out there who try to get you to sign the same card four times so they can sell three and keep one for themselves," the personable Gwynn said after displaying his picture-perfect batting stroke.

"There's no way around it," he said, "and guys have their own ways of dealing with it. What I like to do is sign a couple on my way out, a couple on my way in, and sign some cards and stuff at the ballpark... but you're not going to please everybody."...

..."If people want an autograph and they're willing to pay the kind of money they're being asked to pay to get a (Jose) Canseco, they should have that opportunity," he said. "If they don't want to come, they don't have to come. And obviously, people want the opportunity to get an autograph because they're still flocking to these things.

"In today's business, that might be the only way that you're going to be able to tell that that's really his autograph — because you sat there and you saw him sign it. When you send stuff in the mail, there's no guarantee that the player's signing it. It could be somebody else." — Sean McDevitt, July 12, 1991

* * *

Tony Gwynn

In fact, the first time that this four-time batting champion saw himself on a card he couldn't believe his eyes.

"I was shocked," he said with a laugh. "I collected cards when I was a kid until I was a sophomore in high school. Then I stopped collecting, but like most families, my mom ended up throwing the box of cards in the garbage. Now, I think to myself, those would be worth a fortune if I could get those cards back.

"You go through high school and college and then you sign your first professional contract, and, all of a sudden, kids come up to you with your own card and what a shock. What a shock to see your own card.

"It didn't turn out to be a very good card. And now I'm stuck with this rookie card for the rest of my life. It's nice to sit down and look at your cards and see the stats. It's quite a feeling."

Gwynn said he is looking forward to seeing the reaction of his second-year teammates, who will be seeing themselves on a card for the first time this year.

"It's funny to go through the clubhouse. Last year we had a lot of rookies and this year it will be interesting to see what type of faces they have when they look at themselves on a card for the first time," Gwynn said. "It's a lot nicer (than it used to be) because there are a lot of nice cards out there." — Tom Hultman, March 20, 1992

* * *

Pete Harnisch

SCD: What is your opinion of the hobby?

Harnisch: I did it when I was young. I had a lot of fun with it, flipping, throwing them against the wall, playing match, unmatch with my buddies and stuff and trying to take everybody else's cards and things like that. I think it's a little bit different now. There's so much money in it now. Even back when I was younger there wasn't, and that wasn't that long ago. It wasn't nearly as much money as there is in it now, so it creates a different attitude about the whole thing, overall. — Rick Hines, Sept. 6, 1991

* * *

Toby Harrah

When asked his feelings toward autograph seekers and memorabilia collectors, Harrah doesn't mince words. People, regardless of age or gender, who ask him to sign a number of items at once, try his patience, he said.

On the other hand, people who approach him with a request for a single autograph are more likely to get a positive response.

"All I ever wanted to do was be a ballplayer," Harrah said. "Even now that I'm retired from playing, I still have very strong feelings about the game and what it means to people everywhere.

"Every time somebody comes up and asks me for my autograph, I feel like they're paying me a compliment. The least I can do is sign my name on a card or a program or a piece of paper. It's really a privilege. One of these days they may never ask me to sign another autograph.

"Especially if it's a little girl or a little boy or an older person, and they say, 'Can I have your autograph?' — it's a nice feeling. Hey, I can't wait to sign. And hopefully, that person'll be a fan for life. But the ones who are pushy or demand you sign a bunch of items, I don't have time for them." — David Craft, Sept. 9, 1988

* * *

Rickey Henderson

Irwin Cohen: I'm sure you didn't collect baseball cards in your youth, but what about other things related to sports?

Rickey Henderson: Oh no. That's one thing I didn't do, collect baseball cards. A few times I went to a baseball game and, you know, at that time Oakland had the great teams and my idol was Reggie Jackson. I got the guy's autograph but I really didn't go after guys to get autographs. I was too embarrassed to ask for autographs...

...Cohen: You appear on a card from all three major sets — Topps, Fleer and Donruss. Which card do you like best?

Henderson: (Looking at the cards carefully) My favorite card, mainly I prefer this one (Topps). But this is also a great card right here (Fleer). This other one (Donruss) ain't that bad, and they have great cards this year but this one isn't one of my favorite pictures of me.

Cohen: Do you save the cards that you appear on?

Henderson: I try to save most of the baseball cards that I appear on. But mainly I think that my mother is mostly a great baseball fan of mine, so all that I get I show to her and she'll take 'em and keep 'em. She won't let me keep 'em so mainly she collects most of 'em. — Irwin Cohen, On the Baseball Beat, Oct. 15, 1982

* * *

Billy Hitchcock

SCD: How much fan mail do you get today?

Hitchcock: Oh, gosh. This new Topps thing that came out with the '53 cards — I'm with the A's — I get an awful lot of them. I'd say I get maybe 10 a week, 30 or 40 a month. I always sign.

But I guess some of the present-day ballplayers won't sign unless some money's involved. — Brent Kelley, Sept. 18, 1992

* * *

Frank Howard

It's a quiet but powerful memory of baseball, made even more vivid by its solitude (unlike those noisy World Series reminiscences everyone remembers). A mid-June heat wave has sent sweaty fans to County Stadium in T-shirts and shorts. A wave of charcoal-and-brats perfume, courtesy of thousands of parking lot tailgaters, sneaks over the right-field wall.

My brother and I are sitting in front row box seats just to the left of the Brewer dugout (the kind of tickets where a friend of a friend of a friend knew some company VIP), craning our heads to catch a glimpse of Bob Uecker in the broadcast booth.

On the field is Brewer catcher Charlie Moore, armored in his pock-marked and scarred battle gear. At home plate is Brewer coach Frank Howard, wielding his favorite weapon — a Louisville slugger. The man's size alone is a source of amazement. Howard looks like Mighty Joe Young compared to the well-built Moore.

Howard stands at home plate, tosses a ball a couple of feet in the air with his left hand, and almost in the same motion cocks the bat and swings. A gun-shot crack echoes across the red and green plastic seats of the sleepy stadium; the ball is sent skyward — straight up — like a satellite, disappearing from the glare of the soft neon lights and into the twilight, appearing seemingly minutes later as a white blur. Moore, following the ball's flight all the way, snares it near the visitors' on-deck circle.

The popup clinic is repeated with Moore 10 or 11 more times; Howard's muscles ripple under his short sleeves as the toss-and-swing program is repeated with machine-like perfection. The ball is never missed; it's never even mis-hit. It's a stunning sight to watch Howard consistently hit popups that high and that accurate, as the ball always falls inside roughly a 30-foot area around home plate. That kind of power and accuracy is frightening, my brother and I agree. This guy has to be in the Hall of Fame...

...At a recent card show in Chicago, the Capital Punisher finished his stint in the autographing seat and wandered around the floor, shaking hands with fans and laughing with memorabilia dealers.

"I usually do about two shows a year," he says. "I would like to do more, because I think these shows do a super job of enhancing the game of major league baseball. I think they're great for the fans. It gives them a chance to interact and to meet with some of the present players, and it gives them a chance to get together with some of the Hall of Famers.

"I think they're a fun thing. I know I've had fun at the few I've done every year."

The hobby's boom has greatly helped the U.S. Postal Service. Howard, to nobody's surprise but his own, has found his mailbox stuffed with autograph requests.

"I probably get more requests for autographs now than when I played," he says. On the other hand, he's not taken aback when it comes to the increased interest in baseball-related shows and the advantages they offer fans and players.

"Baseball's kind of a nostalgic game, anyway," he says. "We live in kind of an age of nostalgia right now, so I think these shows bring back a lot of former great players and gives them a chance to supplement their income. Everybody wants recognition. And so many times in sports, you're like yesterday's news. Once you're released as a player or get out of the game — sometimes you're very quickly forgotten. But these shows bring back the point that no, you're not forgotten. There are a lot of people who remember you and some of the thrills you gave them, and like I said, it's a fun package."...

...Howard, who now lives in the Washington, D.C., area, has established an off-season career with Jim Beam distillers. On the side he works some card shows and fantasy camps.

When reminded of those little things from which heroes are built — autograph sessions, shaking hands, and mile-high popups in front of teen-age fans — Howard chuckles.

"We try to put a little levity and a little fun into it," he says. "We try to make it entertaining for the fans. Without the fans, we're out of business, so whatever we can do to sell our game in a positive way, we try to do." — Don Butler, April 7, 1989

* * *

Catfish Hunter

When it comes to nice guys, none rank higher than Jim "Catfish" Hunter, the Hall of Famer who attends about eight shows annually — and answers each fan mail letter "personally."

But things didn't start out so smoothly.

"I went to my first show in '86 or '87 in New York," Hunter said, "and I didn't like it."

"This little boy came up (for an autograph), yet didn't have a ticket, so the promoter screamed at him. Finally, I just grabbed the young man's picture and signed it. The promoter then said, 'You can't do that.' But I still did.

"For a long time after that, I didn't go to any shows."

Hunter, who appeared July 18 at a show in Rosemont, Ill., makes most of his appearances on the East Coast.

"The young kids sure are into the hobby...I know my kids are," said Hunter, the father of three (sons Paul and Todd, and daughter Kim). "In fact, my kids tell me how much each of my bubble gum cards is worth."

"They've got most of my bubble gum cards, and they go off trying to talk people out of them. But people are smart."

Hunter has appeared on more than 30 cards. His rookie card is a '65 Topps (No. 526), which sells for about $175. Hunter, though, isn't a collector. Instead, he used to "put them in the spokes of a bicycle, so they'd make a noise."

"I can tell you when each one (of the pictures for my cards) was taken, as well as most of the (8x10) pictures that I sign," he said.

"There's a guy in Detroit who took most of the pictures, along with the only two people who took pictures (for cards)...and their ancestors are probably richer than everyone else because they probably have rookie cards of everyone who was in baseball during the '40s, '50s and '60s. And they even have authentic pictures.

"I never collected anything — cards, autographs, anything. In fact, I went to a ball game in old Griffith Stadium in Washington and once got seven foul balls. Everyone said, 'Are you going to get them signed?' and I responded, 'No, I'm going to play with them.' And that's what I did."

Does he regret that move?

"No," he said, "because I think I did more by playing with them than getting them signed."...

...The A's also featured a colorful character in the front office — owner Charlie Finley.

"Mr. Finley probably was the smartest owner in baseball, even though he's often remembered for what didn't work, (such as) the flourescent orange baseballs," said Hunter, who still has a pair of the infamous white shoes that Finley created.

"I don't remember who we were playing in the first game (with those white shoes), but the (opposing) hitter fell down on the first pitch, saying he couldn't see the baseball because of the white shoes. But they went on to beat us 17-2, so I don't think the white shoes made any difference." — Ross Forman, Sept. 11, 1992

* * *

171

Monte Irvin

I saw Monte Irvin there on Saturday. I didn't bring anything with me for him to sign, so I had him sign my issue of SCD on the page with the announcement of his appearance there and he seemed surprised when he saw that with his name in it. — Andy Waldman, Sport Talk, Dec. 15, 1977

* * *

Monte Irvin

The Feb. 24-25 autographing appearance by Negro League players in Rosemont, Ill., had special meaning for Monte Irvin.

"This gives me a chance to help (Negro League players earn a little money because they never made any and they need it," said Irvin, the most noted of the 16 former Negro League players who appeared.

"When you get older, you get sick and you need the money; and most of these guys are living off social security. They really need the money.

"Plus, these other fellas are getting some recognition, credit and fanfare here, which they never got (during their playing days). And it makes me happy seeing them happy."...

..."The Negro League Baseball Players Association set will be nice. It's a Perez-Steele-type of set and will be something up-to-date of these (former players) for the baseball card collectors to get signed," Irvin said.

The non-profit NLBPA was established last year to aide former Negro League players who are elderly, indigent and in poor health.

"Anything that's being done to help these former players is appreciated," Irvin said.

"There has been some interest expressed in (the Negro League players) because the story they have to tell is very, very interesting. They're telling it and people are listening.

"I just hope (interest in the Negro League players) will catch on and the thing to do will be to get the autographs and learn more about these former great stars." — Ross Forman, March 22, 1991

* * *

Randy Jackson

SCD: You have a distinction shared with no one. You hit the last home run by a Brooklyn Dodger, Sept. 28, 1957. Do you remember it?

RJ: That's what they tell me. (Laughs) I don't know who it was against or who it was off of. I don't remember it at all.

Why do you remember those things? Who would even go back and search to find who the last Dodger was to hit a home run? Somebody did, I guess.

You don't think of it at the time. If I'd thought of it, I'd have stolen a bunch of uniforms. (Laughs) And I'd bought hundreds of 1952 Topps. I think the last time I checked on mine, it was $150 to $160. I bought one for $40 back years ago and I've got it framed.

SCD: Do you have all of your cards?

RJ: I've got a bunch of 'em, yeah. I've got as many as I can find. I've got 'em framed and put up on the wall.

And I've got a lot of pictures of things that happened. You know, grand slams and called out on strikes in the World Series.

I sent one (picture) off to President Eisenhower when we were meeting him on the pitcher's mound during the World Series. He and I were just fixing to be introduced and they took it (the picture). I sent it to the White House and he sent it back autographed with a nice note from secretary.

I've got things like that that nobody else in the world has. I've got a pretty nice wall. — Brent Kelley, Jan. 4, 1991

* * *

Reggie Jackson

Retiring as an active player certainly hasn't meant that Reggie Jackson isn't busy. He has a multitude of business and personal interests including being a spokesman for the Upper Deck Co. "I went out to Upper Deck's plant one day to buy some cards for myself, and they talked to me," says Jackson of how he became involved with the California-based card company. "I met their president, Richard McWilliam, and their vice president, Don Bodow. We talked and they asked me to come back. I'm pleased to be associated with Upper Deck. They're a first-class company."...

...Reggie says that unlike many pro players, he was a card collector himself as a kid, and still is today. And fortunately for him, he was able to save some of his cards from his early days. He can also be seen occasionally at card shows these days buying star cards, including his own 1969 Topps rookie card. He says he has a special fondness for that card. "It was my first card and I was excited about it," he explains. — Tom Mortenson, Oct. 11, 1991

* * *

Gregg Jefferies

DENVER — "I wouldn't pay $3.50 for a Gregg Jefferies' card."

That familiar refrain has echoed in card shops, at shows and wherever dealers and collectors congregate since the '88s appeared in February. Since then, Jefferies had commanded the highest price ever for a player with only six major league at bats, truly the epitome of rookie card mania.

On Memorial Day in Denver, the disclaiming statement carried more heft than normal card chatter as the speaker was Gregg Jefferies.

"It's a joke," Jefferies said, "I wouldn't pay $3.50 for my card. I'm overrated."

Gregg Jefferies

His blunt self-assessment stems from a realistic approach to his current standing as a player compared to the inflated value of his card. "Who am I?" Jefferies questioned.

"I am a minor league player who has proven that he can play, hit well at the AA and A level. Minor league. That's the point, I am a minor league player."

When reminded that Tim Wallach (26 homers, 123 RBI, .298 for the '87 Expos) is selling for a dime or less and his card is escalating to the $5 mark in the metropolitan New York area, Jefferies replied, "Wallach is a great major league ballplayer, underrated, and I am just a minor leaguer."

Since the beginning of the year, Jefferies has been caught in a whirlwind of publicity, photo sessions, unrealistic expectations and outright mob scenes, trophies and irritants of his newly acquired fame.

"It has been blown out of proportion," Jefferies said. "In Omaha last week, I needed a police escort to get out of the ballpark.

"People were shoving pens in my face, they were just caving in on me. A police officer asked me if I needed some help and I took it."

God-like expectations have followed the massive publicity received by the 20-year-old Met farmhand. "People are saying that I'm going to be the next Mickey Mantle, the next Pete Rose. Those are great players, Hall of Fame players.

"All I'm ever going to be is Gregg Jefferies."

Defining who Gregg Jefferies is, what he expects of himself and how he wants to be remembered is easy for the Met infielder.

"I'm a hard worker who works hard at his job just like anyone else. I want to be consistent, that's the most important thing for me.

"I'm aware that because of my size (Jefferies is considerably smaller than he appears in the Donruss and Fleer cards, where he admits to being somewhat overweight. He's listed at 5'7", 175 pounds), I'm not going to hit 40 homers every year. I'm just going to work and do what I can within my limits."...

...Jefferies' modern-day hero is New York Yankees first baseman Don Mattingly. "I really like the way he hits and the ballplayer he is," Jefferies said. "I was thinking of writing to him and asking for a signed picture. It would really be a big thrill for me to meet him and just sit down and talk hitting with him."

Realizing that he has been a Diamond matinee idol at 20 has been difficult for Jefferies. "I'm only 20 and still can't believe that kids look up to me," Jefferies said. "I have my dad to thank for helping me with that. He has never let me forget why I'm here and how important the fans are. I really try to sign everything and get to the mail...but sometimes I just don't have the time." — Bob Drzewiczewski, July 1, 1988

* * *

Gregg Jefferies

"If this was a year ago," the dealer said, "there'd be 1,000 people here. The place would have been packed."

The dealer was referring to a recent card show crowd in Rochester, N.Y. The draw was Gregg Jefferies.

A year ago, Jefferies was still a hot property. In March of '88, Sports Illustrated made him the focal point of its coverage of major league rookies. There was no "cover jinx" at work, but after he had been likened to Mantle, Rose, Mays and Boggs in one paragraph, the 21-year-old two-time Minor League Rookie of the Year found himself not on the high seas of stardom but back instead in Tidewater, adrift in the game of baseball; floating (some would say drowning) amid rumors of his impending position switches.

Where would he carve out his niche in New York? Third base, replacing Johnson? Left field? Shortstop, with slick fielding but light hitting Kevin Elster dealt off to another club? Met VP Joe McIlvaine was quoted: "When Gregg's ready, we'll create a position for him." As Darryl Strawberry would prophetically tell Esquire magazine, "You can't compare a 20-year-old kid to a Hall of Famer, 'cause he'll only disappoint."

"It was just something I went through, putting too much pressure on myself," Jefferies says while he plows through at least a three-inch pile of 8-by-10 glossies awaiting his sharp signature.

Still, by the end of 1988, Jefferies had been called up and ignited the Mets in the final stretch drive. There were costly fielding mistakes, errors of judgement — rookie errors. But in January of 1989, there was still enough fan/collector interest to justify the dealer's observation. The rookie cards were not escalating at meteoric rates anymore, but they were holding steady. There was the "Met Magic." Plus, there was the promise of bigger and better things in the upcoming season.

No one was ready to anticipate what would come next. "Last year, I didn't even know I was going to play second," he says. "I was working on third the whole time. When they told me, it was a surprise." If Gregg was surprised, fans started to look elsewhere. Maybe he wasn't the second coming of Ty Cobb. Maybe the money was better spent on those Bo Jackson cards, or Ruben Sierra, or even the Ken Griffey Jr. rookies. By mid-summer it was easier to buy Jefferies cards than it was for him to buy hits.

Batting average/expectations/card prices. It's one of those cold, inescapable equations of this hobby/industry...

...This year on off days Jefferies won't be on the card show circuit. "I try to stay away from card shows," he says. "I don't do too many, and don't plan to do many. When I'm home, I like to be home with my family and my friends. I like working out. It just takes away from my workout. I do like meeting the people and talking with them. But it's just not really easy to do during the season."

What about answering fan autograph requests? "The mail requests are still crazy," he says. "When I'm home, I get about 20 pieces a day. I try to keep up as best I can. For the most part, I'll get them all done. But when I get back to New York, it's more like 100 — it's a lot."

The whole autograph craze is a source of amusement to Jefferies. "I was never an autograph collector at all. I've got baseballs from my first big league hit and my first RBI, my first two home run game, the baseballs I hit out and the bat. For Christmas, I gave my parents my rookie jersey."

He talks fondly of his card collection, still sitting in a binder back in the Millbrae, Calif., Jefferies homestead.

"I've still got the cards from when I was real young," he says. "Back into the '70s, way back!

"Ron Cey, Steve Garvey — the Dodgers were my team. I loved them when I was younger. My big thrill in the playoffs in '88 was getting to meet Cey."

The right hand bears a ring that catches a flash of light. It's a gold horseshoe encrusted in diamond sparkles. "It's something I always wanted," Jefferies says. "My American Legion coach had one. I've always loved horseshoe rings. Soon as my 21st birthday came, my parents got it for me."

Now he wants another ring for the other hand. "A World Series ring'd be real nice." — Pete Dobrovitz, Feb. 9, 1990

* * *

Fergie Jenkins

But with Jenkins, it isn't just a signature that the fan receives. "I think you have to be personable when you sign, especially with kids," he says. "I'll always shake their hands, take a picture with them or just ask them how they're doing."

"A lot of times the kids will come up there (for an autograph), and they're just terrified. They look at me and don't know what to think, but I just try to be as friendly as possible and make the person welcome." — Ross Forman, Nov. 8, 1991

* * *

Tommy John

"I collected a bunch of bats that I made into bar stools. Some of them include Willie Stargell and Hank Aaron.

"I had a baseball signed by Thurman Munson the night before he was killed. I gave it to a friend but he gave it back.

"I have a signed ball from each team that I played on." — Rich Marazzi, Batting the Breeze, July 8, 1988

* * *

Tommy John

SCD: What about your hobbies? What do you do on your own time?

Tommy John: I'm starting to mess around doing some golf repair work. In fact, if we ever get settled someplace where I have a large work room, I would go into it full-time. One of the other things I do on road trips is I read a lot. Three guys on our ballclub, Tim Stoddard, Richard Dotson and myself, we'll go through two or three books a road trip.

SCD: Do you collect any memorabilia from baseball?

TJ: I collected baseball cards as a kid, but I have no idea where they are now, they may have been thrown out a long time ago. I get balls from certain people. A friend of mine here in Chicago, I got him a ball the night before Thurman Munson was killed. About a year later, he gave the ball back to me. He said he thought I could use it more and appreciate it more. It's one of my most treasured items. I got baseball bats one year. It must have been about 75 or 80 bats from different ballplayers, and I had some bar stools made out of them. I'm thinking I might do that same thing again. And I have pictures of every team I've played on. But as far as autographs, I've never gotten into that. Maybe I should have. I was reading in the paper the other day, baseball cards in the last 10 years or so is the best investment you can put your dollars into.

SCD: You don't collect autographs, but you're known to freely give them to kids who catch you around the ballpark. What's your philosophy on signing autographs?

TJ: Well, if I'm outside like at the hotel, at the ballpark, or whatever, I'll sign autographs, as many as I can. But the thing that a lot of people don't understand is when you get to the ballpark, and you're out on the field, you're not supposed to sign autographs. Maybe they should have one night a week when they have a couple of players go sign autographs in a corner someplace for fans. Fans pay their money to come to these games to get autographs and there's no way to get to the players to get autographs and that's what's tough.

SCD: What about appearing at baseball card shows?

TJ: Sometimes people are a little resentful of ballplayers going to these autograph shows, but the ones that I've seen and I've been involved in, everything is done up front, people know what's involved, they know what the price is going to be. Many of them don't save them (autographs) anyway; they're going to pay the $6 and have Tommy John sign it and then go out and sell it for $25. It's a big business and if the people (fans) can make a dollar on it off the ballplayers like that, that's the ballplayers way of giving back to the fan for paying his money to watch us play. — Dave Sabaini, Aug. 19, 1988

* * *

Nippy Jones

Asked if he still gets fan mail these days, he responds, "I get about 15-20 autograph requests a month. My wife lays everything out on the table for me to sign. She loves to do it."

When asked if he still possesses any memorabilia besides his '57 World Series ring from his playing days, he answers, "Oh, yes. I've got all kinds of baseballs. I've still got a sweat jacket and two first baseman's mitts."

In June of 1988, (along with pictures, cards and shoe brushes) Jones autographed the famous baseball that hit him in the foot in '57. Chad Blossfield, a former ballboy with the Braves, brought the ball to a card show in Milwaukee where Jones appeared as an autograph guest. Blossfield had kept the historic ball that had been given to him by an umpire. — Tom Mortenson, March 24, 1989

* * *

Jim Kaat

SCD: Sixteen Gold Gloves. You have them all down in your basement somewhere?

Kaat: No; I've got them spread all over. Some I've given away, and I've kept a certain amount of them, and I'm auctioning off one this month at the card show we're having for the Ataxia Foundation, for Bob Allison.

SCD: Anything else from your career you've saved?

Kaat: I've got some baseballs and bats, and the one thing I've saved that's more important than anything is the glove that I used. I think that glove's about 20-some years old; I mean, if you saw it in the street you wouldn't pick it up. That's my one link with the game; it's like keeping an old pair of jeans, my old glove from about 1965.

SCD: What do you think of this whole hobby and how it's grown?

Kaat: Well, the fact that there are that many people interested in baseball I like. I don't like doing a lot of the shows. The only way I do a show anymore is for a cause like the Ataxia Foundation. I've done a couple in the past and I wish that I hadn't. As a player, the memorabilia is fine. The autographs? Unless they're going for a cause, I don't want to be a part of signing my name for profit. But I think it's neat. I mean, I'm a baseball-history lover myself, so if I could get my hands on, say, a Philadelphia Athletics jersey of 1952 that would thrill me to no end, because that was Bobby Shantz's MVP year.

The memorabilia part I like. I like to talk about the history of the game, and to see the displays at Cooperstown and some of the old uniforms I like. The selling of autographs I don't, and yet I don't pass judgment because I know there are a lot of guys that played years ago that are not in the position I'm in today doing it because they're making a living doing it, because they never made a lot of money playing baseball. I understand that, and I certainly don't criticize them for doing it. But me, personally, that part of it I will probably never be a part of. — Kit Kiefer, Oct. 19, 1990

* * *

Harmon Killebrew

SCD: Do you or anybody in your family collect baseball cards or any other kinds of cards?

Killebrew: I suppose my oldest son does most of the collecting. Both of my sons are into collecting right now and trying particularly to get a lot of my stuff which I never kept. If I had known what was going to happen I would have kept it, like everybody else. They're (my sons) putting together collections. As far as their favorites, I guess everybody's is their rookie cards.

SCD: What is your favorite baseball card of you?

Killebrew: I guess the rookie card, the 1955 Topps would have to be...it's not a very pretty picture.

SCD: Do you collect autographs of other players and what are some of the big names that you have?

Killebrew: You know, I never have except for Ted Williams. I got an autographed picture from Ted when I was very young and that's among my very treasured things. In 1959 President Eisenhower came out to the ballpark in Washington and asked me for an autographed ball for his grandson David and I told him, "Mr. President, I'll give you one if you give me one," which he did, and I still have it. That's one of my treasured autographs. I've collected a few here in the last few years but not very many for myself, mostly for my kids and grandkids. — Fluffy Saccucci, June 8, 1989

* * *

Ralph Kiner

Kiner, like most Hall of Famers, is a popular draw at card shows and conventions around the country these days. He seems to enjoy the attention afforded him as one of baseball's great sluggers.

He is a gracious signer. And although he charges $5 an autograph for requests by mail (more for bats and balls), all of the money is turned over to a Christian organization. Kiner's wife handles the postage and trips to the post office.

Ralph says he has no favorite card or 8x10 of himself that he signs for people. In fact, while he generally sees the same cards and glossies every year, he occasionally gets something to sign that he's never seen before or has long since forgotten existed.

"What's interesting to me is that the only 8x10 color photo of me as a player is from 1955, when I was with Cleveland," Kiner said. "And I see that one almost as much as any of the black-and-white stuff done while I was in a Pittsburgh Pirate uniform." — David Craft, April 27, 1990

* * *

Cal Koonce

In addition to being involved in baseball as a scout for the Texas Rangers, Cal Koonce, along with his son, Chris, is a weekend baseball card dealer in North Carolina. SCD talked with Koonce about the hobby, both as a former player and as a dealer...

...SCD: What's it like selling a card of yourself?

Koonce: It's a little unusual to be marketing something that has your picture on it. People ask me, "What is your card worth?" They're looking around the table and they see the Mattinglys and the Strawberrys and the Cansecos and the Rickey Hendersons. And I say, "How about a buck?" They say, "A buck?" And I say, "Yeah, are you afraid to pay a dollar for a 1963 card?" They go thumbing through their price guides real quick to see what the price is. I say, "Don't waste your time because it's not even listed." It's really funny now to talk about it in a sense like that, but I don't feel like I need to charge $10 or $15 just because I'm getting a name on something. Kids get a lot of fun out of it.

I've had parents come back three or four months later and say, "Cal, they may have other cards at a higher price, but just because you were here and they talked to you, your card is the number one card of these kids." And you know when they say that you feel like you've done something and made the kids enjoy the hobby they're involved in. — Rick Hines, April 12, 1992

* * *

Mike Krukow

Krukow says that as a kid he had a reverence for card collecting but that he did it in an unusual manner, like sort of Las Vegas-style. "What I would do is I would start off every year with a pack of cards and we'd play at school every day a game, just like pitching pennies, only we used to pitch baseball cards the same way instead.

"We'd throw 'em (the cards) up against the wall and the guy who landed the card closest to the wall would win. We had five or six guys pitchin' cards and you could win five or six cards on one throw. Well, I was king (of that game) and I would come home with a handful of baseball cards, and by the end of the season I'd have about four boxfuls."

Krukow's favorite card out of the whole bunch is one of Don "Popeye" Zimmer. That's because Krukow's uncle, Tim Ryan, knew and played against Zimmer while in the minors back in the 1940s, and his uncle thought that Zimmer was a pretty neat guy. — Fluffy Saccucci, Dec. 20, 1991

* * *

Tony Kubek

Irwin Cohen: Did you collect autographs or cards?

Tony Kubek: Never did. In fact, there was no such thing as baseball cards that I knew of when I was a kid. There were the great old cards but I didn't know of it. I do honestly remember collecting cards — but those were war cards like during the second World War when I was very small — cards with battleships on them and airplanes on them. We used to flip them on the streets all the time. I never traded them or bought them. I just won them in flipping contests.

SCD: What about the baseball cards that you appeared on? Do you still have those?

Kubek: I've never really been a saver of them. My kids have them because Sy Berger from Topps every year sends a collection to my sons and daughters and they've got them stacked up. It's not really an organized kind of collecting that they do, though, but I've seen them and I think it's an interesting and fascinating hobby. — Irwin Cohen, On the Baseball Beat, March 4, 1983

* * *

Harvey Kuenn

Irwin Cohen: You were a hero to many youngsters and appeared on many Topps baseball cards. Do you still have them?

Harvey Kuenn: Yes, I do. I was very fortunate in that I kept almost all the cards and I do have them in a frame now and I'm very proud of it.

Cohen: In your long career you've had a chance to amass a large collection of memorabilia. Besides All-Star rings and trophies, what other items do you have?

Kuenn: The thing I cherish most is the silver bat from when I won the batting title in 1959. I also have the first glove I used and my first uniform from Detroit and also the uniform from the Giants when we won the pennant in 1962. — Irwin Cohen, On the Baseball Beat, Aug. 6, 1982

* * *

Rusty Kuntz

Rusty Kuntz: I get to know the players on a personal basis. Last year for the first time, the very first time, and I've been playing for eight years now, I actually got Reggie Jackson's autograph. Reggie Jackson actually gave me an autograph on my baseball!! He turned me down for years and then he found out I was a player and signed it. That was a big thrill just like it is for everybody else.

Irwin Cohen: Do you have a special display area for your baseball and things?

Kuntz: Oh yes. I've got one room in my house back in Paso Robles. It's just a collectors room. I've got pictures and I've got bats and I've got old gloves. I also got Carlton Fisk's old shoes that he autographed for me and I've got one of his old catching gloves that he autographed. He was one of my favorite catchers besides Marc Hill.

I've also got the bat that Ron Kittle used to hit his 50th home run in Edmonton a couple of years ago. And I don't care what level you're at, when you hit 50 home runs that's 50 home runs and that's quite an accomplishment.

He didn't realize what the value of that baseball bat would be and I asked him if I could have it and he OK'd it. And now he's just begging me for it and I've got it on my wall. But one of these days I'll just give it to him. I'll just wait 'til it goes up in value a little bit more. — Irwin Cohen, On the Baseball Beat, June 8, 1984

* * *

Carney Lansford

If you want to make Carney Lansford mad, show him his 1981 Topps, Fleer and Donruss cards.

"Where do they get those pictures?" raged the American League's leading hitter. "Couldn't they use better pictures on my cards?"

Lansford, who hit .336 for the Red Sox, grew a beard after the sets were issued.

Beard or not, pitchers aren't happy to see Lansford step to the plate.

Lansford was the first American League batting champ to swing from the right side since Alex Johnson of the California Angels in 1970. — Irwin Cohen, On the Baseball Beat, Nov. 20, 1981

* * *

Dave LaPoint

What a shot in the arm it would be for our shows if all of the autograph guests shared the attitude of pitcher Dave LaPoint. When the former Tiger left-hander appeared at one of my shows last May, he spent every penny of the money I paid him buying complete sets of cards from various dealers to complete his personal collection. — Jim Hawkins, Eye of the Hawk, Aug. 7, 1987

* * *

Don Larsen

The next day at the card show, Larsen signed for the Atlanta crowd, responding politely with short answers when show attendees asked their questions. In addition to seemingly endless baseballs and posed photographs, Larsen signed numerous copies of the photograph picturing him delivering the final pitch of that historic World Series game with second baseman Billy Martin and the Yankee Stadium scoreboard in the background. The biggest request among the customers was for Larsen to sign the date of his perfect game in addition to his name.

"That crap just started recently," said Larsen. "It seems like if one person does it, then everybody has to do it. I was at a show in Houston with Yogi (Berra). I ask them why didn't they make Yogi sign the date, too. He did just as much as I did..."

...From a collector's standpoint, Larsen appeared on more than 19 cards, including 10 of Topps' regular issues and two Bowman cards. His 1954 Bowman issue, No. 101, is his rookie card. He says he never collected his own cards, but has all of them now.

Card shows and occasional alumni player events are about the only way he stays in touch with the major leagues. When asked about the differences in the game in 1990 and the time he played, Larsen simply said, "I wouldn't be qualified to say that. I'll leave that up to the guys playing today."

As for appearing at shows, Larsen said, "I don't mind them. I don't like to travel too much. The long traveling to shows can get old, but I don't mind them." — Bill Ballew, Nov. 16, 1990

* * *

Tommy Lasorda

Wherever he goes he draws a crowd. Whether it's holding court with a group of senior citizens or kissing and coddling a baby, Tommy Lasorda is a showman's showman.

Still high from the Los Angeles Dodgers' World Series victory over the Oakland Athletics, Lasorda recently took a break from his hectic speaking schedule to return to the place where it all started.

Lasorda was at Dodgertown, the Dodgers' spring training complex in this south Florida community of Vero Beach, to make an appearance at a Dodgers fantasy camp for a little motivating, hobnobbing, instructing, autograph signing and, of course, showing off.

His repertoire of stories is seemingly endless and Lasorda is a master at charming everyone he comes into contact with — and that's a lot of people. Still, Lasorda claims to never tire of the constant attention his celebrity status brings.

"That's the good part," Lasorda said. "That's what I enjoy. I like to make people happy and if I make people happy, then I'm happy.

"I just autographed a bat for a guy to give to his kid. It made him happy, it made his kid happy, and that makes me happy. Now I go home to my wife and if I'm happy, it makes her happy and if she's happy it makes my kids happy. Now just look at how many happy people there are by me autographing that bat." — Bill Boeding, Jan. 27, 1989

* * *

Vance Law

The Laws of Vance: One of baseball's top autograph signers is Cubs third baseman Vance Law.

A former Expo, White Sox, and Pirate, Law returned to the Windy City as a free agent. His 1988 numbers earned him his first National League All-Star berth.

The Utah resident reflects his dad, ex-Pirate pitching star Vernon Law, in good will and kindness towards his fans.

However, that good will and patience can be stretched to the limits by autograph seekers, Law related in an interview with the Chicago Tribune.

"The only thing I don't like is when someone sends me five of the same card and expects me to sign five," he said.

"I'll sign one of them...not all of them...for their personal collection and that's it. I don't think I have to help him make a living."

Law, who signs fan mail (mostly cards) before most games in the clubhouse, also mentioned a pet peeve for him and many teammates — excessive multiples.

"Don't ask (a player) to sign 15 cards at the same time. We don't have time to stand there and sign 15 for one person and 10 for the next guy. Ask (us) to sign one or two and be satisfied with that," he said.

The Cub star also has one other tip that seldom gets mentioned in any autograph column, probably because most of us assume it to be too elementary and basic to merit special instruction. But Law finds it to be a recurring pain in autograph signing.

"Have a pen that works. Sometimes they hand you a card and don't have a pen. Or, they hand you a card and they have a pen and you start to write and it doesn't work, and you turn the card over and try to get it to work — that bugs the heck out of us," said Law.

For those who feel compelled to hand a player a stack of 10 cards, or can't be bothered to bring a writing implement with you that works, read those words and learn from them. — Dave Miedema, Up Autograph Alley, Aug. 11, 1989

* * *

Mark Lemke

Had Atlanta won the (1991) Series, Lemke would have been the consensus Most Valuable Player...

...Nearly every weekend (in the off-season), Lemke was asked to appear at a card show, a retail store's grand opening, an awards banquet or some other similar event. No Atlanta player was in more demand, and considering that his teammates included National League MVP Terry Pendleton and Cy Young Award winner Tom Glavine, that was no small feat.

"I signed autographs at quite a few card shows," Lemke said. "I don't mind the shows, even though I never have been big on them. But I felt last year was a great year for the Braves. The city of Atlanta was real excited about the team, and I took the signing opportunity more from that aspect, to try to see and thank the fans and not try to make as much money as I could from it. I made good money during the winter, but I restricted my card show appearances to the Southeast. I did do one near my hometown in New York, but that was it." — Bill Ballew, Oct. 2, 1992

* * *

Buck Leonard

Hofer's Mailman Writes

I thought I would offer this information on Hall of Fame autographs. One of the readers suggested that we send our requests directly to Cooperstown and they would forward them to the player.

Here in Rocky Mount, N.C., I happen to be Buck Leonard's mailman. He receives about 15 requests a week, of which about five have been forwarded from the Hall of Fame.

I don't know if the Hall forwards all such mail, but they seem to do a good job with Buck's mail. — Joe Hardy, Rocky Mount, N.C., Reader Reaction, Sept. 25, 1981

* * *

Mickey Lolich

With the millions of dollars being doled out by card collectors for valuable cardboard portraits nowadays, does Lolich collect at all? "No, I don't," says Lolich. "Even as a kid I never collected cards...I was not a baseball fan."

Lolich adds that when he was young, the kids in Portland that he used to play baseball with used to collect cards and argue issues such as who the best third baseman was and so forth, but says that he would always tell them "let's get our gloves and let's go play."...

...Although Lolich has not collected cards, he has managed to keep some personal memorabilia from his career. Included are his MVP trophies, the last baseballs of the three World Series games that he won in '68, along with the uniform that he donned in that epic Fall Classic, baseballs he used in All-Star game appearances, and the balls he used to set the Tiger career Strikeout record and the American League career strikeout record for lefties.

Memorabilia from other big-league players are also a part of Lolich's forte. If you go into his doughnut shop, the Mickey Lolich Donut and Pastry Shop in Lake Orion, Mich., you'll encounter the following precious commodities. In the shop is a coat rack, which is actually a bat rack, which is constructed from autographed baseball bats of Reggie Jackson, Pete Rose, Ted Williams, Al Kaline, Stan Musial, and other notables.

Also on display are uniforms of pitchers that Lolich thinks will make it to the Hall of Fame someday, such as Gaylord Perry, Steve Carlton, Nolan Ryan, and recent Hall of Fame inductee Jim Palmer. — Fluffy Saccucci, Nov. 30, 1990

* * *

Greg Luzinski, Mike Marshall

Greg Luzinski is among the most cheerful, possibly because he has youngsters of his own. Greg suggests to signature seekers these rules: Never approach an athlete in a restaurant. Be prepared with pen and paper (no scrap paper or scrapbook)...In a crowd stand quietly and hold your paper high in the air to catch the attention and remember that your good manners can catch his attention in an unruly crowd...If you fail, write to the athlete in care of the club. Athletes prefer that.

I might add: Never ask Mike Marshall. He will tell you to ask your teacher for one, as he is more deserving. But I did hear that in his last playing days Mike softened up somewhat for autographers. — Wirt Gammon, Wirt's Words, Nov. 15, 1977

* * *

Mickey Mantle

SCD: Did you save any important memorabilia from your career?

Mantle: I've got a 500 home run ball, three MVP trophies, the triple crown, the Hickock Belt, the Silver Bat. I've got a tape measure that they gave me when I hit the 565-foot home run in Washington. Somebody gave me a tape measure. I've got a lot of baseballs, like the one I hit when I went past (Jimmie) Foxx.

SCD: Isn't one of your proudest pieces of memorabilia something you got from Roger Maris?

Mantle: Yes, it's in the (Mickey Mantle's in New York City) restaurant. Roger gave me a baseball just before he died with his picture on one side. He signed it for me. It says, "To Mickey, the greatest of them all." I have some stuff in the restaurant. There's a painting of Roger and me and a painting of Billy and me. We have a Roger Maris booth and a Billy Martin booth...

...SCD: You mentioneed that you never really collected baseball cards of yourself, but you would sometimes bring them home for your boys.

Mantle: They (Topps) used to send us boxes of gum cards and my boys would take the gum out and throw the cards away...

...SCD: On your autograph, it seems like almost every time you sign, whether it's a photo or a ball, you never see a smudged Mickey Mantle autograph. Is there a reason why you take a lot of time to sign?

Mantle: Well, if a kid's paying $30 for me to sign something for him, I feel like he's got a right to get a good one. I see some kids come through the lines that don't look like they can afford it anyway. And not just because of that, I just feel that I should do as good as I can. I don't like to pick up a ball where there's five autographs on it and I can't tell who signed it. I like to see who else is on the ball. Sometimes you can't even see who's on the ball.

SCD: Certainly the Mantle autograph is probably one of the most legible in the hobby, and in this day and age a lot of players sign autographs real quick to get through the line, and the autographs, of course, change over 20-30 years. But your's probably got better over the years from when you first played. You obviously take your time to give somebody a signature.

Mantle: Well, actually, it really p----- me off when it doesn't come out good. If I sign an autograph and it doesn't look good, it makes me mad. I just got through signing copies of my book, My Favorite Summer. We had 1,956 hardback books, and we just sold Score Board 1,656 books. It's a leatherbound book, and I had to sign it in gold on the cover.

We're just sending them back to Score Board now, so it will probably be a couple of weeks before they're out. But you talk about hard to sign, that might be the hardest thing I've ever gotten into. That gold stuff is hard to write with anyway, and then on leather.

SCD: How about signing caps in silver pen?

Mantle: This was worse. The ones that I didn't think came out very good — I took out and we're going to get some more.

SCD: People have seen you do that. Sometimes when collectors have gone through the autograph line with a picture and you didn't think your autograph came out that good, you sent the kid up to get another photo.

Mantle: I'll do that several times if it doesn't look very good. Because I do try, and sometimes it just doesn't come out.

SCD: Your signature has changed somewhat over the years.

Mantle: It's changed a heck of a lot since my first years. It hasn't changed that much since collecting has become big. Ever since I've been signing things at cards shows it's been about the same.

SCD: How does it make you feel, at a card show, when fans say "We think you're the greatest?" Do you ever get sick of hearing that?

Mantle: That's half the fun of doing the show, to have guys compliment you. I've had a lot of people ask me that question, "Don't you get tired of doing this?" And the answer is no, because it's flattering as hell. I haven't played for 22-23 years. For people to still remember you and come up and have tears in their eyes and say that I was their boyhood idol and everything, it's pretty flattering. And then they bring their kids with them, and say, "There he is, son. That's the greatest ballplayer that ever lived."

SCD: And they really mean it, too?

Mantle: Oh yeah, a lot of guys have tears in their eyes, and it makes you get goosebumps sometimes...

...SCD: Is there any reason you don't sign bats anymore?

Mantle: It's just that when I go to a card show, it takes like an hour and a half longer to sign bats. You know what I mean? It takes me three hours to sign 700 autographs, and if I'm not going to sign bats in a card show for kids that are paying money to get them signed, then I'm not going to sign.

Hey, I don't sign for my own kids, my mom or anybody. It comes down to the thing that I don't want to sign them at card shows, and if I'm not going to sign them for kids who are paying money to get them signed, then I'm not going to sign them for anybody.

SCD: Mickey Mantle does not sign bats for anybody. Even ballplayers who have played with him can't get a bat signed by Mickey Mantle?

Mantle: I'll tell you, it's really embarrassing. Every once in a while, you'll see somebody coming up with a bat, or you'll get a bat in the mail. Peter Jennings, he has a bat, and he called the restaurant to get it signed and I told him I can't sign it. It's harder than hell to turn somebody down once in a while, but you've got to. You can't just sign one every once in a while. If I'm going to sign one, I'm going to sign one for everybody. — Kevin Huard, Nov. 29, 1991

* * *

Mickey Mantle

"What was your reaction after you learned that one of your old Yankee uniforms sold for $111,100 at auction this past January?" Mickey Mantle was asked when he was appearing at the "Madison Avenue 33 baseball card, collectibles and memorabilia show staged on Feb. 1-2 (Saturday and Sunday) at New York City's Armenian Church Ballroom and sponsored by the National Pastime.

"That's really unbelievable," said Mantle. "I never made more than $100,000 playing for the Yankees, and now someone pays more than that for my sweats. I wish I had saved my underwear from that uniform...then it would have been worth even more," quipped Mantle...

..."I realize that a small percentage of guys who get invited to card shows don't much care what their signature looks like," Mantle told SCD, "but I'm here to please the fans, and the least I can do is to make the autograph look presentable."

Moreover, he never refuses a request to have his photo taken, and is generally more than happy to exchange a few words with fans who pass through his autograph line. — Robert Obojski, March 13, 1992

* * *

Billy Martin

Let's begin with the Yankees that were polite. Manager Billy Martin was by far the kindest of all the Yankees. He stood and signed autographs until the last person was satisfied. Other Yanks that presented no problems were Bucky Dent, Paul Blair, Rich Gossage, Catfish Hunter, Sparky Lyle, Ed Figueroa, Rawly Eastwick, Jim Spencer, Roy White, Fred Stanley, Lou Piniella, Dick Tidrow, and, believe it or not, Chris Chambliss. — Ken Burlington, June 15, 1978

* * *

Edgar Martinez

SCD: What about memorabilia — do you trade bats and autographs with your teammates or other players?

Martinez: I hope to some day get into that. I don't really feel I should do that yet because I'm still kind of new at this. But, yes, there are some guys who I would like to trade with so I will have the memories. It has nothing to do with the value of the stuff. — Rick Firfer, June 12, 1992

* * *

Eddie Mathews

Hooray for Eddie Mathews.

At a recent show in Arlington, Texas, Eddie Mathews was there as a guest. He was most gracious and was taking time to visit with the fans and to take an occasional picture.

As I was getting close to the signing table, the promoter told Mr. Mathews he would have to "cut out all the personalization and the picture taking."

Mr. Mathews replied, "We'll do what I want to. These people are paying for this."

After many shows of ungrateful stars and promoters, this was a breath of fresh air in the hobby. I sure would like to thank Mr. Mathews for this experience. — Kevin Street, Grapevine, Texas, Reader Reaction, Aug. 12, 1988

* * *

Eddie Mathews

What does Eddie Mathews think about the booming baseball card and memorabilia business that is sweeping the country?

"I never dreamed in my wildest dreams it would be like this," he said. "I'm amazed! I'm tickled to death to see this. I think it's really healthy. I get a kick out of seeing the kids (as an autograph guest at shows). It's a way for some of us (former players) to pick up a few bucks and see the fans again."

Mathews' 1952 Topps rookie card #407 is currently valued at $1,800 in near mint condition.

Another popular collectible is the Eddie Mathews Hartland statue. Since the three Braves figures (Mathews, Aaron and Spahn) were produced in higher quantities than some of the other players, they don't command as much as Harmon Killebrew, Rocky Colavito or Dick Groat Hartlands. "We didn't think much about it at the time," he says of being one of the stars selected for the series. "They're coming back with a commemorative series of them again. We probably only got a couple hundred dollars apiece for it (rights to produce the original figures)."

How many autographs does he think he's signed through the years?

"I have no idea how many I've signed," he said. "This is my 40th year of signing — I started in 1949. We always signed in the parking lot for kids."

Did he save any items of memorabilia from his career?

"I never saved any uniforms. I gave my '57 Braves championship ring to my oldest son (Ed Mathews III) and my '68 Tigers championship ring to my youngest son," he said. — Tom Mortenson, Oct. 6, 1989

* * *

Don Mattingly

Mattingly — a positive impression

My son Jeff, an avid Don Mattingly fan, and I recently made a trip to Evansville, Ind., to Mattingly's 23 for my son's birthday.

Upon our arrival, we were given a tour of the restaurant and the tremendous memorabilia housed on its walls by the host, Dennis Sexton.

We later returned that evening, met Mattingly at the souvenir shop, ate dinner and found Donny still signing autographs for the kids about two hours later.

He was extremely courteous at all times, conversing with everyone, and asked personal questions of his fans as well as answering any and all questions put to him.

Mattingly certainly made a positive impression on my 9-year-old son, which he will not soon forget, when he posed with Jeff for a photo.

Anyone traveling in Indiana should, in my opinion, make an effort to visit Mattingly's 23.

I'm sure you will enjoy your visit as much as we did and, if you're real lucky, you might even get to meet the "real" Don Mattingly. — Gary and Jeff Metza, Schuykill Haven, Pa., Reader Reaction, Jan. 13, 1989

* * *

Willie Mays

But on this muggy Saturday afternoon, more than 1,500 fans would parade through an abandoned store in one of those outlet malls just to meet this man. The name is magic. People would spend $14 for every autograph. Some fans would plunk down fistfuls of autograph tickets and not bat an eyelash. I knew Willie would earn $10,000 to sit from 11:30 a.m. to 3:30 p.m. and sign an endless stream of bats, balls, books, glossies and much more.

But as people walked away, I also knew that there were unsatisfied customers. Many who came with no expectations seemed resigned to the fate of this autograph industry. They got what they came for, but not much else. Willie shook an occasional hand, but seemed uncomfortable with any attempts at conversation. Those working the show who'd been with him the night before called him a genuinely nice man, talkative, quick with a story, genuinely happy to be there.

Promoter Alan George said, "I had heard about his reputation beforehand, too. I decided to bring a friend with me to pick him up at the airport rather than go alone. I just didn't feel comfortable. But I was surprised. He seemed like such a gentleman. We sat and talked. It got late. It was tough to leave. He just sat there with us talking about baseball and the hobby."

But to a man, they all could only shake their heads in wonder at the overnight transformation. "It's weird," said one. "He comes in today and it's like a different guy."

It wasn't just the demeanor. Around the floors, there were complaints about the signings themselves. Some said Willie wouldn't use the pens they brought up. Signing a ball on the sweet spot was a request that wasn't always honored. Bats were signed with a totally random site selection, often on the backside of the bat head. Try to display that one.

One collector has a set of 500 hitter bats he's working on — all signings in black Sharpie. Despite a request for the same, Willie started signing in blue.

And forget personalization. That was quite a blow to one man who displayed a bat signed by living Hall of Fame great stars, each signature also bearing the date of the signing underneath — all but Willie's. Some autographs would even be smeared in his handling as they were lifted away.

Willie started the day using the standard Accountant fine point pen, but early on complained that it "makes my fingers swell." He switched to a different black pen that distributed ink through a fine felt tip point. Many with signed baseballs were afraid bleeding was inevitable.

But maybe these people were just being a little too demanding. I mean, does it really matter if it's black or blue ink? Does it make much difference if Willie signs above or below Mantle on the ball? How much can fans really expect of a guy who's sitting in a hot room, cranking out one signature every six seconds because there were sold tickets to be honored, a promoter to be satisfied?

I saw Willie sign baseballs, then roll them away, across the table like rejects on an assembly line. His eyes were nearly always cast downward, there was hardly ever the hint of a smile at all. But I'd also seen him put his left hand to his right shoulder and stretch out his still massive muscular right arm. I saw the swelling in his wrist. I saw his fingers so cramped, he could barely grip the pen between his thumb and index finger. And it was oppressively hot. The line never seemed to end and when it almost did, wound up plop another stack of couple dozen 8x10s.

Rather than complain, he'd just dig in. Never a word about multiple signings or large orders clearly from dealers at the show...

...SCD: What should someone expect...

Mays: Nothing.

SCD: For paying for an autograph?

Mays: I don't know. I don't get involved in that...I work for the dealer and I think the dealer is responsible for me. As far as I'm concerned, he's running the show. I have nothing to do with the show.

SCD: But as far as their interaction with you? Obviously, you know, some people want to talk to you, they want to meet you more than the autograph. It's kind of like meeting the Pope.

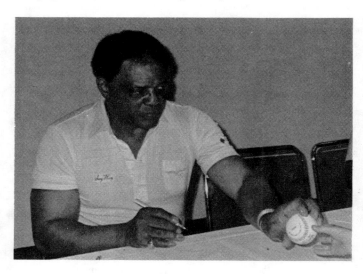

Willie Mays

Mays: No, I disagree. You can't do that. I think when they come here, it's a job that I go to. And I think, you're talking about the Pope, you can't compare me with the Pope.

SCD: But some people...

Mays: No, no, that's not the right word. You got to pick another subject. I'm in sports. I appreciate when they come and line up. But you don't get to the Pope — you can get to me.

SCD: But you're a hero...

Mays: Yes.

SCD: For some people, it's not even the fact that there's ink on a piece of paper. They want to know that they met you, shook your hand, maybe talked to you and they'd be able to think that they can do that.

Mays: Oh yeah. I haven't had any privacy since I was 12 years old. So I understand all that. But I don't want to be put in a category with the religious types, which I think is not right. I'm into the sports world and like I say, I appreciate people coming over to have me sign whatever you want to bring. It's a wonderful feeling.

SCD: Is there any way this could be done differently? The hobby, getting the autographs?

Mays: What more do you want to do? For three hours, you've got twelve, fourteen hundred people. What more could you want to do?...

...SCD: How does it make you feel — you've been out of the game for now, what 15 years?

Mays: Since '73.

SCD: And yet, people pay $14 for your autograph.

Mays: That's what I was trying to explain to him...it's not the money. It's the people that come to stay for three hours and say hello to you. You know, you can't measure that by the dollars you get out of things. Hell, I probably could make more money doing something else. But to me, making the money and doing the things with the people is a great feeling. I'm talking about anywhere I go, not just these little places ...anywhere I go. That's a wonderful feeling. There's not that many people that have that. I'm talking about drawing well, all kinds...the people that came today, there was all kinds. Old...you know, to me that's a wonderful feeling. — Pete Dobrovitz, June 23, 1989

* * *

Tug McGraw

SCD: How do you handle all the requests — people coming up to you?

McGraw: I think it's fantastic! The idea that people have an interest in celebrities and the curiosity is fun — it's exciting. To be a part of that is fun for me, too.

SCD: Take mail requests?

McGraw: Yeah, whenever I have time. If I'm not doing anything. I'll write it down and send it back. I'm about two years behind! You gotta be real patient with me (laughter). But I get to it eventually. I don't go to the memorabilia shows or that kind of stuff because they're always on weekends. And I like to have my private time on the weekends.

SCD: How do you find the fans? For the most part — gracious? Obnoxious?

McGraw: They're just people. Some people are real nice and some people are pretty nervy sometimes. That's just human nature. Everybody's different, so you just deal with it. There's no general stereotype. You handle everything as it happens. — Pete Dobrovitz, July 29, 1988

* * *

Fred McGriff

But if McGriff is having an identity crisis, the numerous autograph seekers who keep his mailbox full at San Diego Jack Murphy Stadium sure don't know about it. It seems the 27-year-old McGriff has an easier time giving opposing National League pitchers headaches than he does keeping up with the mail.

"It's kind of difficult, really," he said before a small Padres-Cardinals game at St. Louis. "You get all kinds of mail, all kinds of letters. It's almost impossible to sign all the cards that you get because a lot of people put five or six cards in the letters. Before you know it, they're all stacking up on you."

McGriff said that the flood of mail hasn't discouraged him from signing, although it's tough to keep up.

"I try to (sign) when I get some free time," the soft-spoken slugger said, "but you get to a point where you get so many letters it's tough to find some time where you can get to all of them." — Sean McDevitt, Aug. 23, 1991

* * *

Mark McGwire

Pass through the door of this hospitality suite, and you may as well have set foot on location of a Fellini shoot.

Umpire Kenny Kaiser's All-Star Charity Dinner has all the casting call for a documentary on a slice of the 1988 American Apple Pie. The "Chevy to the Levee" is now a white ultra-stretch limo. The "good ole boys" are no longer drinking "whiskey on rye:" now it's diet Pepsi or Absolut with a twist on ice...

...I was making my way toward Oakland slugger Mark McGwire, but first had to take in one more scene that Frederico would have surely thrown into "Americord." Big John Studd, all 6'9", and God only knows how many pounds, was telling young Mark a thing or two about the virtues of "bulking up."

Now remember, at 6'5", 225 pounds, McGwire's no slouch. But here's Studd cradling a cereal bowl in one hand and a dinner plate in the other. The bowl is filled with poached eggs. I mean, filled.

The plate is piled high with toast and bacon. McGwire can't resist the urge to just sit there and watch the wrestler start down eggs by the gulpful. The cholesterol count had to be giving Mark's career batting average a run for it's money.

It was at that moment that I approached Mark for an interview, recorder in hand. Weirdness was swirling all around and maybe, at first, Mark was wondering if this was going to be just another episode. "What do you want to talk about?" "Oh, I don't know — this past season...the next one."

McGwire looked at Studd, who snorted one of those "oh, not another one of those interviews" snorts between gulps. "Well, I'm writing for SCD and I'd really like to talk a little about the hobby industry, your autographing policies..."

Before I could even finish the thought, McGwire was off and running. It was like he'd been sitting back, waiting on just that pitch and he was ready for it — ready to really tee off and sound off about everything that's wrong with the hobby. It was his turn at bat. And you get to read his best cuts.

On dealers-turned-autograph seekers: I won't sign in hotels anymore because of these guys. I know they pay kids to stand there and get them. I just won't do it. It just gets too hard to judge.

As far as somebody's trying to make a living, it'll hurt these young kids who just want your autograph because it's you. I like it when kids want your autograph for what it is — for yourself. And that's how it used to be. "I got Mickey Mantle's autograph!"

Instead of today, kids or whoever are getting a Jose Canseco autograph — but it's worth this much money now. I mean, that discourages me; it really upsets me when somebody says, "Now it's worth x amount of dollars," when somebody's putting a dollar sign ahead of the autograph. I think it upsets every ballplayer.

On unauthorized cards and reproductions: Forget it. I just won't sign any of them. This guy Broder — now here's a guy who takes pictures of pictures and turns them into baseball cards...I won't sign any of them sent to me or handed to me. It's hard with the 8 x 10s because you just don't know where they're coming from.

On his at-the-ballpark signing policy: I try and get out three out of four or five days during a homestand. I'll do what I can. But here again, it's hard because you hear every story in the book. A guy will say "Come on! I drove a hundred miles to get here to get your autograph." And I'm thinking, "Right! I just heard that one yesterday!" You know, people say — they pay their money for tickets, they pay my salary. I don't see THEIR names on my paycheck!

On mail requests: I'll tell you — our clubhouse guy, now there's a lot of great ballplayers gone through Oakland — Reggie Jackson, Rollie Fingers, Sal Bando, Gene Tenace — right on down the line. That just gives you a little sign of what happens. I'm sure Jose gets a little bit more than myself right now, just because of what he's done. But up to last year, it was four to one. That's a lot of mail!

A lot of people say, "I never got it back." That's another thing I'd like to get...if you people can write this...when people send mail to me, please send a self-addressed envelope! If they don't send a self-addressed envelope, they don't get their stuff back. My feeling is, if they take the time to write my name on it and put a stamp on it, they can take the time to write their name on it and stamp it for a return address.

Ballplayers just don't have time to go to the post office and get stamps. It's hilarious. Some people will actually send a baseball in a box, then inside the box there's five dollars for me to return it. I don't have the time.

On autographing bats: I have a friend named Walt Harris out of Newport Beach who's the only guy in the country that sells my bats right now. If anybody has an unsigned bat out there, I won't sign it at a card show or anything. He's the only guy in the country that has my bats and I'll sign my bats for him only. There's an abundance of baseballs and cards out there, but bats are hard to come by. I want to make it hard to come by. There's no more than, I would say, 300 or 400 bats out there, which is not that much for how many people there are that want them.

On the McGwire Alaskan team card: The people up there, from what I understand, it was strictly that the proceeds go to the Alaskan League. They called me and asked me if they could have my approval of doing it and I said, "Yes." I played up there — it was a big stepping stone in my career. I was a pitcher before I went up there. When I came back from there, I was a hitter. To me, that's no big deal. I'm more than happy to do that. That league helped me in my career. — Pete Dobrovitz, Jan. 6, 1989

* * *

Gene Michael

"My glove. I also have the second base from the old Yankee Stadium." — Rich Marazzi, Batting the Breeze, July 8, 1988

* * *

Minnie Minoso

In 1980 the White Sox brought Minnie back for two plate appearances, making his playing career span five decades. As a player, he was an exciting talent; as a personality, he is still adored by fans.

As the guest celebrity April 23 at the Strongsville, Ohio, show, it was easy to see why fans of all ages love the outgoing Minoso. They shower him with affection, and he returns it tenfold. Unlike many other former or current stars who look at signing autographs as a boring chore, Minnie seems to enjoy every minute of the attention.

Greeting everyone lined up for his autograph, he looks them in the eye, smiles, asks "how are you?", or shakes hands. He personalizes photos, cards or any item the person requests.

He seems to really enjoy signing for children, giving a wink and asking, "How's school?"

Brian Boston, an Akron, Ohio, collector at the Strongsville show, recalled for SCD how Minnie treated fans at Chicago's Comiskey Park in the early '50s.

"I'd visit relatives in Chicago every year during the summer," Boston said. "I remember after the games how Minnie would stay and sign autographs for fans. He'd still be in his uniform, signing long after the other players left the park. Then, after about an hour or so of signing, he'd excuse himself to go take a shower and change clothes. He'd tell anyone who hadn't gotten an autograph or who wanted to ask questions to meet him outside the park by his car. He'd tell them where his car was and stay there until everyone who wanted a Minnie Minoso autograph got one."...

...Paul Reis (manager of community relations for the White Sox and Minoso's boss in his public relations capacity with the team) also recalled the time Minnie and a sales representative were scheduled to make another appearance somewhere in the Chicago metropolitan area. "They were taking separate cars, and since the sales rep knew where they were headed, he asked Minnie to follow him in his car," Reis said.

"They take off down the freeway and all of a sudden, Minnie passes the guy like a shot. He's chasing another car ahead of him at 75 mph. All the time, the sales rep is wondering what's going on. Well, the car Minnie's chasing pulls over and Minnie pulls over and leaps out of his car and opens the trunk.

"He takes out a couple of White Sox caps and gives them to the people in the car. It seems that all this happened because those people recognized him in his car and waved to him. He probably didn't realize that the reason they recognized him was because his license plate reads MINOSO." — Tom Mortenson, May 27, 1988

* * *

Greg Minton

"I have a unique bat at home. I hit one home run in my big league career. I hit it with a Duane Kuiper bat. I have it mounted on my wall. Duane's bat has two home runs in it, one for him, and one for me." — Rich Marazzi, Batting the Breeze, July 8, 1988

* * *

Don Money

Several turns down country roads lead to a small farm in Vineland, N.J. A modest sign introduces the premises as "Third Sacker Farms."

The door is answered by a man well over six feet in height. Dressed in blue overalls, he gives the impression of someone about to get down to some hard work. His smile is wise and handshake firm.

"Come on in, son," he greets. "Oh, that's my woodpile for the fireplace," he says, referring to the obstacle near the doorway.

Once seated in his kitchen, he spots a squirrel on the back patio.

"Hey Sharon," he says to his wife, "your buddy is back looking for food again."

Stirring his coffee, he makes a comment about the weather. Moving two recently-painted picture frames out of his way, he nods and smiles.

"Fire away," he commands.

Meet Don Money, husband, father, farmer, man of the earth. And former major league player for the Philadelphia Phillies and Milwaukee Brewers.

Although Money has been retired for almost seven years now, it seems some things haven't changed. Money reacts to questions in the same fashion as he reacted to the crack of a bat, the speeding line drive.

It was his fielding excellence that made him one of the finer performers at third base. He would hear the question, bob his head, and then dive right into it, just as he did to a bounding ball down the third base line. His timing is still there in many respects. And so are the memories...

...Money had very few problems with fans, and considers himself to have been fairly popular. "I think I was liked most of the time. The only bad publicity was if I didn't sign an autograph. It's part of the job. There was always that 1 percent that didn't get one. And some-

body's father would call the paper and say, 'So and so didn't sign my son's autograph.' People don't realize that they come to a game once or twice a year and it happens to be the game that you go 0-4 at the plate and just don't feel like signing." — Erik S. Cagle, Sept. 22, 1989

* * *

Joe Morgan

One For Joe Morgan

It is about time we hear of some good people that are a part of our hobby. The people from Mostly Baseball, located in California, recently ran a show with Joe Morgan as their guest.

Mail orders were being taken, so I thought I would send a couple of commemorative envelopes out to get signed.

The ad that ran in SCD said nothing about "no personalizations," so I thought I would take a chance and ask to have them signed to my son, Alexander Morgan Wyllie (he was named after my favorite ballplayer — Joe Morgan), which I explained in a letter to Mostly Baseball.

I received my order back on July 1 and I really didn't know what to expect when I opened the envelope.

There are many stories of people getting the wrong thing back in the mail, not getting the same thing back, or getting nothing at all returned.

No words could describe how I felt when I opened the envelope. I received my two items back and they were personalized to my son.

Also included was a note from Joe Morgan. It read, "I hope your son grows up and becomes a Cincinnati Red. Thanks, Joe Morgan."

Fellow hobbyists, I have just added three more items to my collection of Joe Morgan memorabilia. These three items probably wouldn't have any meaning or value to anyone else in the hobby, but they are priceless to me.

Is this the true meaning of collecting? — Jeff Wyllie, Quakertown, Pa., Reader Reaction, July 22, 1988

* * *

Bobby Murcer

"My rocking chair. They gave me a rocking chair in 1975 when the Yankees played at Shea Stadium. When I got traded to San Francisco somebody sent it out there. Then when I got traded to the Cubs it was sent there and it followed me back to New York.

"I have the ball I hit for my 100th and 200th home runs and 1,000th RBI." — Rich Marazzi, Batting the Breeze, July 8, 1988

* * *

Dale Murphy

Irwin Cohen: Did you collect baseball cards or try to get autographs when you attended games at Candlestick Park?

Dale Murphy: I saved some cards but I didn't keep them. I don't know where they are now.

Cohen: What about the cards that you appear on? Do you save them?

Murphy: I have some. I try to save them but I'm not sure where they are.

Cohen: What about the cards that you are on this year from Topps, Fleer and Donruss? Which one do you like best?

Murphy: (Examining the cards) I think Topps always does a good job. I kind of look like that I have a pot belly in this one (Fleer). I like the Donruss pose, though.

Cohen: Do you save any type of memorabilia that you may come in contact with or things that you are a part of?

Murphy: I got some newspapers from when certain things have happened. Like when we won our first 13 games in a row earlier in the season. And, of course, I have the All-Star memorabilia. — Irwin Cohen, On the Baseball Beat, Nov. 26, 1982

* * *

Stan Musial

When SCD asked Musial at Madison Avenue 26 why he signed with his right hand, he answered: "Way back in my elementary school days in Donora, Pa., my teacher saw me writing left-handed, grabbed a ruler, whacked me across the knuckles with it, and demanded that I write only with my right hand. She said that 'southpaw writing' was too awkward since all our school desks were right-handed and I've never written with my left hand since." — Robert Obojski, March 15, 1991

* * *

Graig Nettles

Bill Madden's recent column in the New York Daily News says that the number one baseball card of 1981, value wise, is the Fleer "error card" of Graig Nettles. Madden quotes collectors as saying they are scarce enough to be worth $10 to $20 already. Nettles is quoted in the column as saying, "I'm saving 'em myself in hopes of putting my kids through college." — John Stommen, Phil Stommen, Our Hobby, June 30, 1981

* * *

Graig Nettles

Graig Nettles tells me he has four or five of his Fleer error cards now..."By the way, did you see that picture of the guy burning a Mantle card worth $1,300?" Nettles asked me.

The picture the Yankees third baseman was referring to was, of course, the photo of David Cartier, the card dealer from New Britain, Conn., lighting a '52 Topps Mantle.

Cartier, 43, was burning mad about the baseball strike and the lack of feeling toward the fan and decided to show his displeasure by torching what he claimed was an expensive card.

"Who did he (Cartier) think he's hurting?" asked Nettles.

"Certainly not us (the players)," he said answering his own question. Why burn the Mantle card?

Mantle is a great guest on the card show circuit and had nothing to do with the strike. Cartier should have burned the cards of the player rep on each club. — Irwin Cohen, On the Baseball Beat, Oct. 9, 1981

* * *

Hal Newhouser

Hal Newhouser realized things would change once he became a Hall of Famer — he just didn't expect it to be so dramatic.

"I used to get 100-150 (fan mail) letters per month prior to the Hall of Fame (announcement)," Newhouser said. "But now, the mailman brings it in in these crates that are like laundry baskets. And he brings in three or four (crates) a day.

"I thought the amount of annual requests might change 100 percent. But in reality, it's changed 500 percent."

In addition to the mail, the former Detroit Tiger pitcher is swamped for banquet appearances, not to mention Little League games, and even the July 14 Major League Baseball All-Star game in San Diego. Plus, he said, people regularly call on the telephone and neighbors even stop by his Michigan home.

"There are so many, many things that have changed since the Hall of Fame announcement," he said. "I get cards from all over the world congratulating me. And not knowing these people, I think it's such a great honor. I just hope I can represent them."

And yes, Newhouser does indeed answer his mail. At least he tries to.

"I've set up a base where I have a girl who separates the mail from the bills," Newhouser explained. "She sets aside all of the autograph requests and I set up time daily to sign.

"I spend about two hours a day when I'm at home signing autographs, trying to reply to all of the letters. But, it's almost impossible."

He added, "I try to get to the kids' (letters) quickly, as well as the senior citizens. I'm 71, yet get letters from someone say, who's 82 and says, 'I remember watching you pitch.' Those are the ones I always try to answer quickly because they're the great fans. I just do the best I can. I have only one body and it can only be spread one way. So, I try to satisfy everyone." — Ross Forman, Oct. 30, 1992

* * *

Phil Niekro

Irwin Cohen: Since I'm not too much younger than you, we probably grew up following the same Tigers clubs. My favorite player while growing up was Hoot Evers. Which player was your favorite?

Phil Niekro: Mine was Hoot Evers, too. I can remember everybody hooting, going Hoot, Hoot, Hoot at the ballpark. That really stuck in my mind when I was small. Also, when we would be in the car we could also pick up the Cleveland games and I heard names like Al Rosen and Bob Feller and they became favorites, too.

Cohen: Did you collect baseball cards? Or autographs?

Phil Niekro

183

Niekro: Those weren't out in my area, I think. At least I didn't know about it. And if there was I didn't have the money to spend on bubble gum cards at that time. I didn't get autographs when we went to the ballpark, either. I don't think I got an autograph until I became a major league pitcher.

Cohen: Since you became a major leaguer, have you saved any type of memorabilia?

Niekro: I got a collection of bats. Every time I go someplace I carry a baseball with me and get celebrities to autograph it. I've got a chest-full of singers, dancers, movie stars, baseball players. Everybody. — Irwin Cohen, On the Baseball Beat, Aug. 19, 1983

* * *

Phil Niekro

Superstar, Super Guy

As a subscriber to Sports Collectors Digest, I enjoy reading about which players sign autographs and which do not.

This past June 17, the Empire Baseball for Youth from Modesto, Calif., had a unique experience.

As part of a fundraiser, we asked Phil Niekro if he would consider being part of a raffle in which the winning Little Leaguer would go to San Francisco to see the Giants play Atlanta. Prior to the game, the winner would have lunch with Niekro. All we could offer him for his services was the meal and transportation to and from his hotel. He graciously consented to do this.

Nine-year-old Douglas Hamilton won the raffle and had a day he will probably never forget.

Niekro not only had lunch with us, but he spent the whole afternoon talking with us about everything from baseball to fishing, telling jokes, discussing education and signing autograph after autograph after autograph.

When we left the restaurant, we dropped him off at Candlestick Park. He took our group on a little tour through the locker room, and he gave Douglas his personal bat and cap.

For this whole day, Niekro did not request an honorarium.

He has been playing this game for many years and is definitely a superstar and a super guy. — Rod Oldfield, Modesto, Calif., Reader Reaction, Sept. 16, 1983

* * *

Phil Niekro

Will Cooperstown get the ball used in Phil Niekro's 300th career victory?

"If Cooperstown wants the ball, they'll have to get it from my dad," Phil said. "He's the one who put the ball in my hand in the first place, and he's the one I want to have it."

Phil Sr. has coal miner's lung problems and can't get to see his son pitch in person anymore. Phil's dad hurt his arm while pitching for the coal mining team and the injury forced him to learn a new pitch — the knuckleball.

He also taught it to his sons. Ten-year-old Phil Jr. would often play catch with his dad. They'd throw the knuckler to each other and the rest is history. — Irwin Cohen, On the Baseball Beat, Oct. 25, 1985

* * *

Matt Nokes

Matt Nokes was simply too busy to collect baseball cards as a youngster. "I tended to throw away the cards and eat the gum," he chuckles now. "Just because I didn't see the significance (in collecting) because it wasn't really big then."

He has gained a new appreciation for the hobby these days, however, as his busy show appearance schedule indicates. He enjoys meeting the fans at the shows, primarily because he has more time to sign autographs.

Although he is a willing mail-signer, Nokes confesses he, like many active players, gets behind during the playing season.

"Right now, I think I have one box (of autograph requests) that I haven't done," he notes. But he wasn't always able to be that current with the requests.

"My first year, I got seven large U-Haul boxes jam-packed with letters. There were close to 20,000 pieces of mail there! But it's all under control now. It makes you feel like Santa Claus!" — Dave Sabaini, Jan. 11, 1991

* * *

Johnny Oates

When asked about baseball cards featuring Johnny Oates, the native North Carolinian mentions the 1972 Topps "Orioles Rookies" card.

"Some kid came up to me and said, 'I paid about a buck for your card the other day, but that's only because Don Baylor's on it.' That's OK, I think Roric Harrison and I both know that having Don on there is a big plus."

Although Oates collected cards as a youngster (he recalls laying them out on a table in a diamond configuration according to each player's position), it is his son who is an avid collector these days. — David Craft, Aug. 19, 1988

* * *

Blue Moon Odom

Always In A Blue Moon

On June 4 and 5 a group of old-timers was in town for a benefit game and John "Blue Moon" Odom and his wife were present.

I know they have advertised his availability to do card shows in SCD. Therefore, I thought I would pass on these comments.

Blue Moon is a fun person, personable, and not at all shy about signing autographs. I think he would be a wonderful guest at a show, as he enjoys discussing his years in baseball and he enjoys personalizing autographs. He also has a nice signature which is readable.

I know nothing about fees or costs but can only speak from this experience with him and his wife Gayle. Show promoters would do well to consider having Blue Moon as their guest. — Barrie G. Sullivan II, Denver, Colo., Reader Reaction, July 15, 1988

* * *

Tony Oliva

On this particular afternoon in Chicago, the fans begin filing into old Comiskey Park. You can still get close to the field before a game at Comiskey, and fans begin calling out to Oliva. A middle-aged man tells Tony he was "the greatest" and that Tony was always his favorite.

Tony asks a writer for a pen, then bends over near the batting cage to pick up a ball. He writes something on the ball, then signs it and tosses it to the fan. Class. When the writer comments that that would be a great souvenir, Tony tells him to pick up a ball, and does the same for the writer.

Still a fan favorite, Tony has a number of mementoes from his playing days. "I have saved many, many little things. I have a Golden Glove at home, I worked very hard for that...I'll never forget it. There's my World Series ring and all the All-Star Games (he was named to eight consecutive games, then a record)."

If the fans still love Tony, you get the impression that the feeling is mutual. Tony talks to them, and is accommodating with autographs. "Almost every day I sign a few autographs. Also, they send a lot of them to me at home. I don't know how, but they (fans) got my home address and every day I receive at least three or four letters. I answer those letters, too. It's nice to see that the fans still remember you and ask for your autograph." — Dave Sabaini, Oct. 21, 1988

* * *

Donn Pall

SCD: Can you share some of your favorite letters with us?

DP: Well, the letters I like best are the ones that tell me I made somebody's day. Or the letters from people who tell me their kids slept with the baseball I gave them for two weeks. Then you know you are really having an impact on someone.

One letter came from a father who had brought his daughter to Comiskey Park for a game, and they came down to the railing and I talked to the little girl for a minute or so and then I signed a baseball and gave it to her.

When the letter came from her father thanking me for being so nice to the daughter, there was a key chain in it that the little girl had bought for me by saving up her allowance. I was really touched. I still use that key chain to this day, and I still correspond from time to time with the people in that family.

SCD: Any others that stick out in your memory?

DP: There was one other that I am really proud of. I got a copy of a letter that one season ticket holder sent to Jerry Reinsdorf, the White Sox owner. He told Mr. Reinsdorf how he had been thinking about giving up his season tickets because the price had gone up and the team wasn't doing so well and it really wasn't a lot of fun coming to the park.

But then he brought his kids to the park one day and I was chatting with a group that his kids were in and signing autographs for them. And he wrote this letter to Mr. Reinsdorf that because of me, he decided to keep his season tickets. I love that kind of response from the fans and I tell my teammates that's why I spend so much time with the fans before a game. — Rick Firfer, Aug. 9, 1991

* * *

Rafael Palmeiro

The good-looking young collector blended in nicely with the crowd at a recent card show, then he walked up to the autograph table and took a seat.

Rafael Palmeiro spent last season with the Texas Rangers, after coming up through the Chicago Cubs system and establishing himself as one of the best young hitters in the game.

"I don't get to do many shows," said the friendly Palmeiro, "I'd really like to do the more of them."

Since this show was fairly close to Chicago, many fans throughout the day told "Raffy" how much they wished he was still with the Cubs.

"That (the trade) wasn't my decision," he says. "I really loved Chicago and the fans, not that Texas isn't nice."...

...Palmeiro smiles easily and often as he signs hundreds of autographs. Several times he invited fans around the table for photos when they asked. There is little wonder he is emerging as a fan favorite. He's a willing autograph signer away from shows, too.

"I always try to sign at the park," said Palmeiro. He had some good advice for fans who want to get home-town hero's autographs.

"It's best if (fans) wait until the visiting team is taking batting practice to hit the home team for autographs," hinted Raffy. "Another good time is after we've gotten through with infield practice."

Palmeiro is a reliable mail signer, too.

"I get probably 200 requests or more each week," says the outfielder. "I'll sign two or three for one person, but if they send more than that, I'll send them back."

While someone as close to the hobby as Palmeiro is well aware that some people are getting his autograph to sell, that doesn't particularly bother him.

"Selling this stuff doesn't bother me," says Palmeiro. "They bought it, they can do what they want. But what does bother me is when I see some parents encouraging their kids to sell them."

Palmeiro may wish he at least had the option to sell some of his childhood collection. He, like so many adults, has a "horror story" to tell.

"I had about 10,000 cards," he recalled wistfully. "They were in the 1967 to 1975 range. But when I was in high school, and had left them alone for a while, my mom cleaned up one day and threw them out."

But even that traumatic experience has not changed his attitude toward collecting. In fact, he is more active now than ever before.

"I've replaced some of my favorite cards," he notes, "my Seaver rookie and cards of Hank Aaron, Yaz and Steve Garvey." — Dave Sabaini, April 27, 1990

* * *

Jim Palmer

Palmer usually attends five or six shows annually.

"Personally, I go (to shows) to meet the people," Palmer said. "People tell me that Brooks (Robinson) and I are the two friendliest guys. But I feel that if someone wants to pay for my autograph, I at least ought to be nice to them.

"I learned at a young age that the most important part of the game is the fans. And although baseball in general doesn't always treat the fan very well — with strikes, lockouts and whatever — the longer you're around the game, the more you realize how important fans are." — Ross Forman, May 8, 1992

* * *

Dave Parker

"My two silver bats, MVP trophy (1978), and the ball from the first grand slam I hit. My World Series ring was important but it had fake diamonds." — Rich Marazzi, July 8, 1988

* * *

Larry Parrish

Irwin Cohen: Tell us where you were brought up and who your childhood heroes were.

Larry Parrish: I was brought up in a little town in Florida — Haines City. My heroes were the New York Yankees, especially Mickey Mantle.

Cohen: Did you collect baseball cards like most kids?

Parrish: I had shoeboxes full and some cards that are worth a lot of money today. I burned them up using them in the spokes of my bicycle. I wish I had them now. Some of them might be worth $500 apiece. I remember one — it was a Zack Wheat. It must have been from 1910, but I'd just keep putting cards in the spokes to hear the "brrrr" sound as I drove around on my bicycle. — Irwin Cohen, On the Baseball Beat, March 13, 1987

* * *

Red Patterson

SCD: Did you keep a lot of mementoes and special items through the years?

Patterson: You know, I am probably an example of the world's worst collector. I should have a long string of World Series rings and a tremendous collection of press pins. I don't have hardly any of that now. Through the years, I've given some of it away. Some things were taken when my home was robbed here in California. One of the things I still have is a silver-plated set of plates and little cups that the Yankees gave me when they won five straight World Championships.

SCD: What do you think of this collecting craze that is going on today?

Patterson: I go into mourning when I think what I could have. Just recently, I gave an original Willard Mullins cartoon away to charity. Wes Parker said it was worth about $200,000. I was going to give it to the Hall of Fame but I decided to give it to a group that is fighting Cystic Fibrosis.

We call it the 65 Roses Club. That's because the kids couldn't say Cystic Fibrosis. When they tried to say Cystic Fibrosis, it sounded more like "65 Roses." The cartoon was of Mickey Mantle. It showed Mickey coming to the plate and a couple of surveyors getting ready with the tape measure.

Anyway, I turned it over to charity and it raised a quite a bit of money at an auction. When you start to measure things you've done, things you've enjoyed doing, the things that stand out in my mind are the money we've been able to raise for charity.

Orel Hershiser is the Dodgers team representative for the 65 Roses Club and Wally Joyner is the representative here with the Angels. I really want baseball to recognize this terrible disease (Cystic Fibrosis). — David Blumenthal, May 26, 1989

* * *

Terry Pendleton

On a more positive note, Terry Pendleton, getting caught in the spirit of Donruss' mistake madness, has signed his error card "Jeff" Pendleton, as the error on the card indicates. — Dave Miedema, Up Autograph Alley, June 7, 1985

* * *

Gaylord Perry

Paul Green: Let's spend a minute on your business. When did it come to mind that maybe you had some things to sell that collectors might want?

Gaylord Perry: Well, playing over the years you learn we've got just avid baseball fans out there, and they like to keep items of some of their favorite ballplayers. I was very fortunate, in that stuff that I used — you know, shoes, baseballs — I just never threw anything away. I kept the things and I tried to take care of them.

When I moved out to the farm here in 1975 and built my house I had a special place for all my stuff. A lot of it — like shoes and hats and baseballs — I just had so many that I didn't need them all, so I thought I would give collectors an opportunity to have a part of that. I could throw it away, but this gives them a chance and makes it worth my time in keeping it all these years and storing it and taking care of it.

Green: Had you ever collected baseball cards when growing up?

Perry: Not a whole lot.

Green: Are there things you are offering which you think collectors might find particularly interesting?

Perry: Well, one special thing is that I got Topps to make up a special set of six baseball cards. I purchased the rights to them all. There's a rookie card, a picture from the year I pitched the no-hitter, Cy Young in Cleveland, 2,500 strike outs, the Cy Young in San Diego, and the 300th win with Seattle.

Gaylord Perry

They are really six of the highlights of my career, and I had them made up myself. I use them in my peanuts, and if a collector wants a set of six of them they can get them from me.

Green: The most expensive items are the jerseys. Are they all from Seattle?

Perry: Most of them are Mariner jerseys. I just had some extras made up, don't have a whole bunch of them left.

Green: You actually have had a table at at least one show, haven't you?

Perry: Yes. Most of the time I have somebody run it for me, and I just sit and talk with the fans. I have pictures I've saved over the years and had some nice ones made up from negatives for the different parts of my career, and people like to remember those years whether they are Giants fans or Cleveland fans, San Diego or Seattle. I don't have a lot of them but the people seem to like them.

Green: Do you enjoy the shows?

Perry: Oh yes. I enjoy the kids coming by. You know, they always have something to ask you or tell you, so we have some good times at those shows. — Paul Green, Jan. 6, 1984

* * *

Gaylord Perry

Gaylord Perry sold the uniform shirt he wore while pitching his 300th victory game to a collector for a goodly sum. The collector told another collector of his recent purchase and collector No. 2 told collector No. 1 that he also purchased a uniform shirt that Perry said he wore while pitching his 300th win game. The collector went to Perry for an explanation. "Simple," Perry said, "I changed shirts in the fifth inning." They always said Gaylord was a smart pitcher. — Irwin Cohen, On the Baseball Beat, April 27, 1984

* * *

Gaylord Perry

Along with ranching, Perry is a favorite on the national card show circuit, signing autographs for fans. And he will sign anything, including Vaseline and other containers.

"This is a fun job, I have fun doing it. I had a fun day," he said after signing at the St. Louis card show in June. "I don't have a problem signing Vaseline or KY Jelly containers. In fact, I signed a few today." — Shawn Reilly, Sept. 4, 1992

* * *

Boog Powell

Powell added: "I've signed a lot of weird things, everything from golf balls to jock straps. I've also signed in some weird places, such as body parts.

"I think (the public) gives ballplayers and the people who are (promoting) autographing (card) shows a bad rap. But I think people who come to autograph shows expect to pay for an autograph, and I don't see a thing wrong with that. There is nothing wrong with that at all.

"Now if someone was to come up to me and say, 'I can't afford your autograph,' I will tell them, 'This show doesn't last forever and if you catch me afterwards, I'll be glad to sign something for free, within reason. But I just cannot sign (for free) inside the show.'"

And how, you ask, did John Wesley Powell get the nickname Boog?

"My father used to call me a little booger, and it's just gotten shortened," he explained. "Dizzy Dean did an interview with me the first year I was in the big leagues and said, 'Son, that's the worst name I've ever heard. You've got to change it.'

"Now here's a guy named Dizzy, whose got a brother named Daffy, saying I've got a bad name..." — Ross Forman, Aug. 2, 1991

* * *

Kirby Puckett

I don't know about you, but I shake my head in disgust and disbelief everytime I read comments like those which were recently attributed to Minnesota Twins star Kirby Puckett, who, after admittedly earning $40,000 to $50,000 on the baseball card show circuit last year, now says he is fed up and finished with the pay-by-the-autograph plan.

"One of the things I hated," Puckett was quoted as saying, "was little kids coming up with a bunch of cards and I could only sign one. It's hard to tell kids when they pay their $7 that you can only sign one thing. I have a heart and I feel bad about doing that."

If it truly bothers Mr. Puckett that much, why in the world doesn't he — and every other athlete who feels the same way — simply agree to appear at shows for FREE, with the understanding that the promoter will also give the autographs away?

I can't imagine any promoter in his right mind turning down an offer like that.

How about it, guys? If you are willing to give away your autograph, I certainly am, too! — Jim Hawkins, Eye of the Hawk, June 2, 1989

* * *

Dennis Rasmussen

Dennis Rasmussen keeps a Curtis Wilkerson baseball card above his locker. "It's to remind me never to take any hitter for granted," the Yankee lefty said. With George Steinbrenner in attendance during spring training in 1986, Wilkerson hit a damaging home run off Rasmussen. Wilkerson's stats on the back of his card reveal that he only has one big league home run in 1,115 at-bats. — Irwin Cohen, On the Baseball Beat, May 22, 1987

* * *

Jerry Reuss

Former pitcher Jerry Reuss hopes some of Sports Collectors Digest's readers can help him in his search for photos of him in the early '70s.

"It's something fans could help me with," he said. "I need photos of when I played with the Cardinals and Houston in the early '70s, action pictures or things I posed for. We'll work something out in trade."

He said he has "raided some files" in the organizations he's played for, "but I don't have as much as I'd like."

Reuss said he still has some things from his career, including the balls from his no-hitter and All-Star game victory.

"It's somewhere at home," he said. "I wrote no-hitter on it. When Sutter saved the All-Star game in '80, he signed it and I saved it."

"Primarily what I have is just me."

"I've saved my stuff," he continued. "I'm not interested in collecting the cards and re-selling them. That hasn't excited me."

Someday he hopes to write a book.

"Then we'll sit down with a tape recorder. I'll be on Costas or Carson, promoting my book or movie or whatever it'll be." — Gary Herron, May 10, 1991

* * *

Bobby Richardson

SCD: What baseball cards do you like best of yourself?

Bobby Richardson: Well, I'm amazed at the price of the rookie cards of the older guys and certainly in my own case now; I guess it depends on where you are and what the book value might be, but it's certainly going up, so I like my rookie card (1957 Topps) the best. It was one when I was younger, of course, and there aren't too many of them around.

I have, on occasion, been to a card show and I've had two of them given to me. In fact, at one of the card shows that I went to the folks, who knew that I didn't have anything, were really nice and gave to me a full set of my cards which I in turn gave to my six-year-old grandson who lives in New Jersey.

SCD: Have you saved your baseball mementos and which ones do you have and which are your favorites?

Richardson: Well, the only things I would have are either watches or World Series rings and Gold Glove awards. I have five children and I've just given each one of my children either a ring, glove or whatever it might be.

The only thing that I have is in '62 when we played the Giants (in the Series). Instead of a ring, I got a watch. It's a Rolex watch and I have been wearing that for 27 years. I don't wear rings.

SCD: Do you have any memorabilia from other players?

Richardson: No, not really. The only thing that I've got is a picture of Babe Ruth and Lou Gehrig that was hanging in Yankee Stadium. When Maris and Mantle hit the home runs (1961), it was taken down and Big Pete (Yankee employee) gave it to me and they (Yankee Stadium personnel) gave it to me and they put up one of Mantle and Maris and it's got the original frame on it.

Gaylord Perry came down to see me (in South Carolina) several years ago and he saw the picture (of Ruth and Gehrig) and told me that he thought I should have it and he gave me a Babe Ruth bat and a Lou Gehrig bat that he had had. So, I've got them but those are about the only things I have of other players. — Fluffy Saccucci, June 16, 1989

either Associated Catholic Charities or Baltimore Goodwill. They (autograph seekers) can make the checks out to either of those charities and send it to me," says Robinson.

"I really didn't know if it was the right thing to do, but the response I've had has just been fantastic. The money goes to help the homeless and the poor, and to feed the poor. It's been a good way to raise $15,000 a year." — Dave Sabaini, Sept. 8, 1989

* * *

Brooks Robinson

Hall of Famer off the field, too

Each week it is routine to read about another ill-mannered performance by a so-called star at an autograph show.

It is a real pleasure to write about a recent show in East Fishkill, N.Y., featuring Brooks Robinson. The autographs were free, one per person, and controlled by a numbered ticket.

Everyone received a firm handshake in addition to Robinson's autograph.

He had his picture taken with anyone who requested it and answered any question or remark put to him.

It is hard to measure the pleasure and good will generated by Robinson's appearance.

Brooks Robinson gets my vote for his Hall of Fame performance off the ball field. — Robert Gumbings, Poughkeepsie, N.Y., Nov. 17, 1989

* * *

Frank Robinson

SCD: How long have you been doing card shows, Frank?

Robinson: Well, I don't know. I guess maybe off and on for about seven, eight years.

SCD: How do you compare the hobby then to what it is now?

Robinson: I think it's just like everything else. Like baseball itself, many things have gotten better. Salaries have gotten better.

It's become more of a business. More people have gotten into it. More quality people have gotten into it, things like that. More people come out to get the autographs.

Sometimes shows turn out great and sometimes they don't turn out so good. So I look at it as, the public is willing to do this because they have an article signed now that's not just an autograph for the autograph's sake.

Also, people are doing it now for investment purposes. It isn't just a hobby. I think the public understands that it's become much more of a business and it's the wave of the future...

...SCD: Do you collect anything? Any items of yourself such as cards or statues?

Robinson: No. I don't collect anything.

SCD: Does anyone in your family?

Robinson: No, believe it or not, they don't, neither myself or my family. Once in a while, if I see a special piece, a special photograph or autograph, or something, I'll pick it up — not for myself — more or less for my daughter. I don't get that much stuff. I'm not really into it. I haven't ever been into it.

SCD: You signed your name for free, as many ballplayers did, for many years in the '50s, '60s and '70s. A lot of these items have surfaced for sale and in auctions. Some players who played in those days are now going to shows and other engagements and are now making a little money themselves.

Do you think that some of these items you may have signed several years ago are now being sold? How do you feel about that?

Robinson: That was fine then, but it really does bother me today to see someone selling that autograph or article of clothing — a hat or something like that — for big bucks. That does bother me.

But again, it's their property. There's nothing I can do about it. So I don't get real upset about it — but it does bother me.

SCD: Do you get asked for your autograph a lot in Baltimore, or when you're on the road?

Robinson: I probably get asked for my autograph much more now since I've been out of baseball as a player. I think that's because this has become a real big business and more people collect autographs now. Some even want autograph-after-autograph on the same article.

SCD: Does it upset you when you see one person with half-a-dozen balls that he wants you to sign and not all those balls are going to stay in his collection?

Robinson: Well, I know that for a fact they're not. I don't care what he tells me (laughs). I know if you get a dozen balls autographed by me, you're not going to keep all those balls for yourself.

It's the same with photographs. If someone comes up to you to sign 10, 12, 15, 20 of the same photograph, and they're going to sit there and look you in the eye and say "Oh no, I'm going to keep all these," come on, how stupid do you think I am? That's what turns me off. What I would usually do there is only sign one.

SCD: Warren Spahn mentioned that he had been signing at home and has asked "What should I do? I keep getting boxes of this stuff to sign. I just can't sign any more. I have to just stay around the house all day and sign this stuff."

Has this sort of thing happened to you too, with everything piling up so much that you have to refuse mail?

Robinson: Well, you're right. And what even turned me off before — and I did it on my own — when I was signing autographs in the mail, when I started getting 10 or 12 of the same thing to sign, I felt I had to refuse.

And now, I think the word has gotten out that Frank Robinson doesn't sign through the mail. I get very few autograph requests through the mail. Maybe I'm wrong, but I don't even send it back. I just keep it and give it to somebody. I don't even send it back.

And what also turned me off was when someone would write for an autograph and wouldn't even send a return envelope for me to send it back. People would send me balls and things like that and I would have to pack it up and go down to the post office and send it back.

SCD: There's no reason for anyone to send anything to Frank Robinson to sign, thinking he might sign it at a weak moment?

Robinson: Yes. Please don't send anything through the mail for Frank Robinson to sign. He's not signing. He does not return the articles.

SCD: There seems to be a lot of interest in the players from the '50s and '60s now. One of the big interests is in the members of the 500 home run club. Why do you think there is so much interest in guys like yourself, Killebrew, Mantle, Williams, Aaron, Mays, McCovey?

Robinson: I think the youngsters are just learning about some of us, and the people that are a little bit older, they were around at the time — at that age — when we were coming along, they want to reminisce a little bit.

They remember it. They want to be a part of it. They say, "Hey, I remember you."

When I hit the ball out of the ballpark in Baltimore, there were maybe 20 or 30 thousand people there. But now, over the course of years, everybody I see says they saw that. I said, "I don't know of any park that holds 500,000 people." (laughs) — Kevin Huard, Jan. 12, 1990

* * *

Pete Rose

SCD: Your popularity among collectors at card shows seems to be good — both in the East and across the country.

Rose: Well, first of all, it's always been a pleasure to come to the East because of the dedication the fans have for the sport. It seems like a lot of people are familiar with me ever since the '75 World Series. Being at shows is like going to the ballpark because I can talk to the people and talk about baseball and enjoy doing something like being around the game of baseball.

The card shows are like going to the ballpark to me, and that's why I enjoy it so much. That's why we're doing a lot of them around the country because we found out that the people were there. The people were very coordial. People were autograph collecting and we're gratified by the turnouts that we get in all the shows that we do.

SCD: Even though the economy isn't the greatest, some card shows have still done well lately.

Rose: I think people realize that this stuff is a business and the value of the stuff continues to rise. But, I think the economy's on the rebound and I look for this card show and memorabilia business to really continue to grow and grow and grow. It's grown mountains in the last 10 years.

I've seen it and I've been a part of it. I'm very enthusiastic when I go out and see the people. I try to shake hands with as many as I can. I try to talk to as many as I can and it's just a lot of fun...

SCD: In terms of the hobby, do you still collect, or have you collected anything over the years?

Rose: No, I wish I did. I started buying some rookie cards here the last couple weeks. I missed out, because I wish I'd kept all the cards that I had when I was a kid. I didn't have the foresight to look ahead like some people did.

SCD: So are all your uniforms like from the '60s and game bats gone?

Rose: Oh no. I've got all my All-Star bats, every All-Star bat I used, and all my World Series bats, that kind of stuff that I actually used on the field. I have a 4,256 bat and ball. The 4,192 uniform I loaned to the Hall of Fame. I have a lot of memorabilia. I thought you were talking about card collecting. — Kevin Huard, Feb. 21, 1992

* * *

Mike Schmidt

SCD: Will Mike Schmidt be doing any type of signings or card shows?

Schmidt: Well, that's tough. On the record that's very tough. No, I am not. I've chosen to take the stance for myself personally, against public signing of memorabilia for profit. The key word there is public.

SCD: Such as the 500 Home Run Show?

Schmidt: Right. Now I could be put in the position someday where if the 500 home run hitters do something together, somebody sponsors something, and they need me to make it happen, it would be hard for me to create a situation where an Eddie Mathews or Harmon Killebrew couldn't be involved in something because it had to be all of them or none of them.

The one guy missing is me and I refuse to do it, if it were something that was for the 500 Home Run Club, I might be forced to come out. But, I will not do any public autograph signing for profit. I don't know if I could put it any better than that.

SCD: It seems like several of the 500 home run hitters aren't signing bats anymore.

Schmidt: You all have created a real — I don't know if soap opera is the right word — but you've created an industry here that puts the professional athlete in a very precarious situation. Those that played in an era where there wasn't big money, want, and I guess if I were in their position would, want to take advantage of this industry and the profits that there are for all of the people involved.

For those that played in an era of big money, myself included, think we have to have a different perspective on the whole thing. However, that doesn't discount the fact that the collectors that are out there, they could care less whether Willie Mays made $100,000 a year and Mike Schmidt played for $2 million. They want the item autographed, and they know the value of that item, and they'll pursue and persist in order to get that item.

I don't know what the answer is. We have someone whose life is ruined, who we all know, because of the spinoffs of the memorabilia collecting industry. And you all know what I mean by spinoffs. The man's life has been ruined by the industry.

Can it ever be controlled to the point where it's legit? I don't know. I don't know how the federal government is going to intervene in order for it to ever be controlled, I really don't know. Eventually they will. I have chosen, for my own sake, for my own personal well being, to eliminate any public signing for profit.

SCD: Will you sign at times.

Schmidt: Tonight at my radio show I know there were a lot of guys after the radio show that layed items in front of me, that will be in those gentlemen's stock of collectibles, whatever they collect, whether for business reasons or for private reasons.

SCD: When someone places a dozen baseballs in front of you to sign, they're obviously going to sell them on the streets.

Schmidt: I can recognize that. The autographs that I sign here at our establishment are people with the right intentions.

SCD: Well, the thing is, you never know where it ends up. Mickey Mantle once said that he's seen items that he's signed in good faith, apparently back in the '50s, being sold for up to $10,000.

Schmidt: Those things are the most valuable items, something he signed on good faith as a young player. It has a hell of a lot more value than something he's signed at a card show.

SCD: What about the sale of jerseys?

Schmidt: I've supplemented my income over the years because of the memorabilia industry. I'd be lying if I told you I didn't. I don't think there's anybody in baseball nowadays that hasn't somewhere, somehow. It would be hypocritical if I didn't admit to that.

However, experience tells me that it can become an addiction to a professional athlete, and it can get out of hand, it can get out of control. Some collectors themselves can allow it to get out of control because they're very selfish and hoard, and they don't care.

They'll pay for anything just to get something, and it can lead to problems, they create Pete Roses. And I am not going to allow that to happen to me. That's basically my stance.

SCD: It sounds like you have it pretty much in control.

Schmidt: It sounds kind of like a guy who says I have my drinking problem in control. There's a truth to it, I have my memorabilia problem in control. I'm in control of the temptation that people put out there for athletes, and as long as they keep putting it out there they're nothing more than suppliers.

You have a drug, and the drug is the ability to be paid for your autographs. As long as you have that, you're going to have guys that are addicted to that. And I am doing my best to wean myself off of that addiction.

There were a lot of guys who never will, and there are a lot of guys who feel that they were slighted in their career in terms of income and this is their way to get back. This is their way to make up what they lost.

SCD: A lot of guys that played in the '50s were probably making $30,000 a year. And they feel now where, if they can make $90,000 over the course of 52 weeks doing shows, they're going to do it.

Schmidt: Right, and they don't care. They're not aware, they don't know.

SCD: You're not upset at individual collectors who are looking for Mike Schmidt items? If somebody came in your restaurant and walked up to you with a bat, you'd sign it?

Schmidt: Absolutely. — Kevin Huard, Sept. 21, 1990

* * *

Tom Seaver

With his many accomplishments and personal highlights, one might speculate that Seaver has a roomful of memorabilia at home. But that is not the case.

"Well, I have a couple of things at home from when I won my 300th game," said Seaver. "That meant a lot to me...to be able to do it in New York, and it was a packed house in front of a lot of friends of mine there at the stadium. It was a great day. It was a day I'll always remember, and there's rarely a day that goes by that I don't think about it."

When asked what else he is up to these days besides broadcasting, Seaver grinned and said, "Well, I look at a lot of the memorabilia I have from my 300th win." He broke into extended laughter, and explained.

"The reason I'm doing this is because the Scooter (Phil Rizzuto) is right behind us, and I kid him every day that it was Phil Rizzuto Day at Yankee Stadium when I won my 300th. And a day doesn't go by that I don't remind him."

Seaver, not a big collector, is not an easy autograph, and doesn't do many shows. He has, however, observed the growth within the hobby.

"It's gone crazy!" he said. "Some people collect antiques, some collect cars, some people collect glassware, some people collect art, and some people collect baseball memorabilia. That's what it really comes down to."

But the Seaver autograph will continue to be a relatively tough one to get, as Seaver rarely signs through the mail, and doesn't accept many show appearance requests.

"I do maybe one or two shows a year," Seaver said. "I don't particularly like them, but I'll do one or two a year." — Dave Sabaini, Sept. 8, 1989

* * *

Ruben Sierra

In 1987, the interest only intensified. Just eight major leaguers hit 30 or more homers before their 22nd birthday. That list includes Jimmie Foxx, Ted Williams, Mel Ott, Frank Robinson, and now Sierra. Only 16 had 100 or more RBI at that age. Again, add Sierra to a roster that included Ty Cobb, Joe DiMaggio, Al Kaline and Hank Aaron.

The card prices began to rise above a dollar, then two and maybe more.

But in 1988, Ruben Sierra rookie cards tailed off in direct relationship to his on-field performance. He hit just .254, pumping just 23 homers and a "mere" 91 RBI. The switch-hitter opened the season with a .202 average through the first 29 games and critics said, "We told you so. Not consistent. Clemente?! Hah!"

His problems were particularly acute from the left side. He hit .239 for the year, with 76 whiffs in 422 trips. Scouts said he was a sucker for outside pitches, pulling off the ball.

As the year begins, Sierra rookies go for $1.50 to $1.75 and there are reasons to believe if you can find any out there, it may be the biggest bargain of all. Here's another one of those stats: only 13 players had more homers than Sierra's 69 before their 23rd birthdays. That's 15 less than Mark McGwire's career total. It's 20 more than Bo Jackson's. All three have played three seasons, but remember, Sierra is a full two years younger than Mark, three years younger than Bo.

And don't start quoting card prices or trends to Ruben's skipper, Bobby Valentine.

"If I start looking at guys based on what his baseball card is worth, I'm going to be in trouble," Valentine says. "I think he is doing a great job. He is probably a better player now than anybody in this league at his age." — Pete Dobrovitz, May 12, 1989

* * *

Ted Simmons

Irwin Cohen: Did you come to the stadium often and hang around and try for autographs like most youngsters?

Ted Simmons: Well, I was never big on autographs as much as getting down to the ballpark to watch the games. I liked to get there early to watch batting practice so I could possibly get my greasy little paws on a baseball hit into the stands.

Before I had money enough to get in, I used to sit out in the street behind the home plate area and wait for them to hit high foul balls during the game that hopefully would go over the roof and out and get a ball.

Cohen: You broke into the big leagues in 1968 with the Cardinals and appeared on many photos and cards and other types of memorabilia. Have you saved much of it?

Simmons: I've never done much of it myself. I've got a full set for my mom from back then to the present day. She likes that sort of thing and it's for her personal satisfaction. You know you play 15 years and you see so many cards and autograph so many cards that you sort of wonder to yourself what would you ever do with all of them all over the house. I've never been a collector of baseball memorabilia, personally.

Cohen: What about the All-Star and World Series rings?

Simmons: Those are very special to me, of course. What I've done is put them all together, tend to display them together. Those things are nice mementoes of my career. But that's a little different than say, four, five or six thousand baseball cards. — Irwin Cohen, On the Baseball Beat, Jan. 3, 1986

* * *

Ted Simmons

During the season I spent a number of hours in hotel lobbies autograph hunting. I wonder if other collectors have also noticed that more and more ballplayers are refusing to sign gum cards. This season the following players, to name a few, told me they'd sign photos, but not cards: Ted Simmons, Bake McBride, Mike Schmidt, Dick Ruthven, Greg Luzinski.

I did ask Ted Simmons his reason and he replied, "Next year you'll be here with a handful of those things and expect me to sign them all." The most I ever ask for in person is two items, and then, they are always two different items. I must admit I recently saw one collector giving players 10-15 cards, with as many as five from the same year. Come on, autograph collectors, please help us all by being resonable. — Foxy Gagnon, Where Are They Now, Nov. 30, 1980

* * *

Enos Slaughter

SCD: What do you make of this sudden explosion of interest in the older players? (I said "sudden" — I figured a decade is sudden in the bigger scheme of things.)

Slaughter: I think it's great. I think it's kind of like these golf players. You take Sam Snead and those guys. Win all those tournaments and they got peanuts. Meal money. And now, since they got these senior citizens playing golf, they make more money in a week now than they made in their whole career. Course, we don't get that kind of money playing these old-timer games, but $25,000 was the most I ever made, you know — so every few dollars comes along, you know, helps you buy a cold biscuit!

SCD: You get out to a lot of the card shows?

Slaughter: I'm booked from now til November! Card shows and these games. Play a lot of celebrity golf tournaments. Help the needy. March of Dimes. Girl Scouts. Mentally Retarded. Perry Como puts one on. Fifteen years ago, we raised 25 bucks. Now it's half a million dollars! Crippled kids. This year it went toward AIDS.

SCD: Now, you're not warming up in the field, just stick work tonight?

Slaughter: If I have to, I could field, I've got a spur in my ankle. Anyway, we got young players like Virdon and Brock and Billy Williams. Those guys, they, they're still in the peak! But I'm going to swing...I don't think they're going to call me out on strikes!

SCD: When people send you things in the mail, do you sign? How do you handle it?

Slaughter: Well, I'm glad you asked that question. I probably average 15 to 25 letters a day. I don't mind signing three (per person). If they'd cut 'em down to three, it would give me a lot more time, because I get a lot with five or six in it. And, you know, when you get a lot of mail like that it really takes a lot of my time. I very seldom let mail stay in my house three days. (Enos, can you talk to Tug and Cat-fish about that?) I do most of my signing at five o'clock in the morning.

SCD: Why?

Slaughter: Well, I get up that time. You're in the country, you know when it's daylight. You go out and work the field while it's cool. You're going to come in about noontime and get a little siesta. Go back at 3 or 4 a.m. That's the privilege of working on a farm, runnin' your own business. — Pete Dobrovitz, July 29, 1988

* * *

Enos Slaughter

Slaughter is continuously asked at card shows to put the date of his "Mad Dash" under his autograph on various pieces of memorabilia. When asked to sign the Perez-Steele card depicting the play at the plate, he likes to point at the drawing's error.

"They got it a--backwards," said Slaughter with a smile. "You look at the photograph and then look at the card. The umpire and everything are all reversed." — Bill Ballew, May 31, 1991

* * *

Duke Snider

"Do I get writer's cramp signing all these baseballs?

"Yes, a little, maybe, but I'd much rather autograph a baseball rather than trying to hit one thrown by a pitcher like Juan Marichal," says Edwin Donald "Duke" Snider...

...On the subject of baseball card collecting, Snider answered, "Did I collect baseball cards as a youngster? Not much.

"I don't recall too many card sets being sold in our area of California...maybe I wasn't paying attention, but nowadays all kinds of series are being poured out, even minor league sets. This has got to be the 'Golden Age' of collecting." — Robert Obojski, Dec. 30, 1988

* * *

Warren Spahn

Event rings clearly in his mind

I recently attended a card show in Marshalltown, Iowa. The guest signer was Warren Spahn and his autograph was free with your paid admission.

Because this was my first show that I have attended where someone was signing autographs, I wasn't sure what to expect.

Well, my expectations were put to ease very quickly. I only had to stand in line for 30 minutes (I expected it to be longer) and when I got up to Mr. Spahn he was very friendly.

I was with my sister and her son and Spahn signed all three items for us. He looked, smiled and even talked to us.

But the biggest thrill was when I commented on his rings. He then took off his Hall of Fame ring and World Championship ring and handed them over to me.

We talked as I held the rings and looked at them. What a great time.

So, I just wish to say thanks to Mr. Spahn and recommend him to anyone looking for a great player to sign autographs.

Also, keep up the great work, SCD. — Tim Pillack, Waterloo, Iowa, Reader Reaction, Oct. 21, 1988

* * *

Warren Spahn

When asked how he feels about today's interest in sports collecting, baseball's winningest lefty answers, "I love it. The dummies that are out there playing today have made heroes out of us again. People want our autograph."

Warren Spahn

He says he enjoys going around the country to card shows meeting people. "If I didn't enjoy it, I wouldn't do it. Most of the people that come to card shows are there just to make you feel good. I enjoy talking with them. I enjoy talking with kids. By and large, those people are baseball nuts and thank God, and thank the world for them."

Spahn says he saved some personal memorabilia items himself, including his 1957 Cy Young Award and his World Series uniforms and rings. "I gave my son (Greg) my 1948 World Series ring, that's the year he was born," he reports.

"I've got my World Series uniforms. We had to turn in our (regular season) uniforms at the end of the year. The World Series uniforms we were able to keep. I never really wanted to buy one. Furthermore, I can't get in 'em anymore."

The great southpaw told SCD that he also saved a baseball from the last out of each one of his 363 major league victories. "I have no idea why I started doing it," he says. "The further I got into it, the more eager I became. The funny part of it was that the last out of my 300th victory was a fly ball to Hank Aaron. I think it was Joe Torre or (Del) Crandall that came out to congratulate me and I took off running to right field (to retrieve the ball). I was afraid Hank was going to throw it in the stands. That's a true story."

He adds that he's collected things that really aren't in the norm. "I have a baseball signed in Japanese by the Hiroshima team when they won the championship when I was over there," he says. "I have a baseball that's signed by all the astronauts that were in Houston when I happened to be there."

On the matter of autograph fees, Spahn has these comments, "Of course, you always run into somebody who resents the fact that they have to pay for an autograph. I would never want to charge an individual for my autograph.

"I did an interview with a guy from a local television station in San Jose (Calif.) He asked me if it was OK if he interviewed me while I was signing. His first question was, 'Don't you feel guilty about taking money from kids for your autograph?' I said, 'Wait a minute, I

don't charge the kids. The promoter sets up the card shows and he has overhead — like the motel and putting on the show. So they're paying an entrance fee as well as an autograph fee.'"

"I said, 'I'll tell you what. I think kids today have more money than their parents do.' We're developing young entrepreneurs because those kids are taking good care of those cards. Mint condition is the password. Hell, they think so much of those cards that they might even make their beds in the morning. They might even take out the trash.

"When they get to be about 15 or 16 they might even think about buying something they want with that money they made from cards instead of stealing it. I'm tickled to death that they are interested in collecting baseball cards. Hey, there's been stamp collectors and automobile collectors around forever. I'm glad to see baseball is a part of it.

"I just don't want to see people ripping other people off with phony stuff and phony autographs. Those things are out there. I'm delighted when a kid comes up to me and he beams and he wants to have his picture taken with me. Hey, I'm pleased with that." — Tom Mortenson, Feb. 28, 1992

* * *

Terry Steinbach

Here's one for Terry Steinbach

I'd like to take this opportunity to share with your readers a couple of positive experiences associated with our sports card and memorabilia collecting club and SCD.

In July, I wrote a letter to you to solicit donations for our newly-formed club at Bald Eagle-Nittany High School. The response from collectors and dealers was a pleasant and welcomed surprise.

No less than 12 different individuals or companies responded to the letter by donating items from supplies to cards to stickers. Without question, the donator's actions were welcomed and appreciated.

In early August, I received an envelope from Charles Sutton, an agent for Oakland A's star Terry Steinbach. The envelope contained numerous autographed cards by Steinbach.

Sutton indicated that Terry had been reading SCD, saw my letter, and was compelled to help the students in our club. He took the time to contact Sutton and instruct him to send the cards.

This gesture by a star like Terry Steinbach was in my opinion above and beyond the call of duty. To say the least B.E.N. High School's students are more of A's and Steinbach's fans as a result of his generosity.

As a matter of fact, our students are reading box scores and pennant races for the Oakland A's, thanks to Terry Steinbach.

If more stars showed compassion to the fans, baseball would have trouble finding space in the stadiums.

In a day and age where selfish and unethical actions are commonplace, it is heartwarming to see the generosity shown by the dealers and Mr. Steinbach.

I want to extend my sincere thanks for helping our kids get started in the hobby — Norm Palovcsik, assistant principal, B.E.N. High School, Mill Hall, Pa., Reader Reaction, Oct. 13, 1989.

* * *

George Steinbrenner

Though often criticized, Yankee owner George Steinbrenner rates credit. For instance, he brought the Yankees to Tuscaloosa for a game with the University of Alabama and sat through the cold, rainy exhibition contest signing hundreds of autographs.

Also, Steinbrenner has given the net proceeds from his opening game to the U.S. Olympic team. Fine gestures, indeed. — Wirt Gammon, Wirt's Words, May 11, 1984

* * *

Steve Stone

"I find the idea of a player charging for his autograph disgusting. It makes me want to throw up. You have $3 million players charging kids $7 for an autograph. I think (they) ought to be hit in the head with a two-by-four. So I never do (shows), I never charge for an autograph. I never will." — Sean McDevitt, July 19, 1991

* * *

Rick Sutcliffe

Since 1984, Rick Sutcliffe has been a fixture on the North Side of Chicago. The Cubs' right-handed pitcher has a 76-60 record in that time, including an amazing 16-1 mark in the team's N.L. East Championship season of 1984 and a league-leading 18-10 slate in 1987. And remember, he only pitched in five games last season due to shoulder surgery.

Also standing tall has been the Sutcliffe foundation, which contributes to numerous charities and social agencies in the Chicagoland area.

"The foundation officially began in December 1984, when I signed the five-year contract with the Cubs; I donated $100,000," said the 34-year-old Sutcliffe, who spent time with Los Angeles and Cleveland before being traded to the Cubs. "I have pledged $100,000 to the foundation each year since, along with any endorsements, commericals or appearances I make. All of that money goes to the foundation.

"The money is distributed each year according to how the board of directors feels appropriate; the board being my agent/friend Barry Axlerod, actor Mark Harmon and Randy Owen, who is the lead singer for the music group Alabama."

Sutcliffe's wife, Robin, and Cubs' Public Relations Director Ned Colletti are also actively involved in the Foundation, which annually gives away 20 college scholarships, and 50 tickets to every Cubs home game.

"The only criteria we have (for the tickets) is that (the people) normally wouldn't be able to come to the game," Sutcliffe explained. "It can be because of finances, handicap, or just about any (reason).

"All someone has to do is write us and we try to accommodate."

Sutcliffe's charitable work also includes monthly visits to Children's Memorial Hospital in Chicago. "When I go, I take gifts (stuffed animals, T-shirts, helmets, autographed baseballs, pictures) for each kid and I also take an IOU program.

"I give my phone number (to the kids in the IOU program) and tell them that when they get well and get out of the hospital, all they have to do is call me and I'll have tickets for them to come and watch the Cubs play.

"I used to have a lot of trouble getting guys to come with me when I went (in '84)," Sutcliffe said. "Today if I asked someone, there isn't a guy who wouldn't come with me."

Sutcliffe said former teammate/current Yankees' pitcher Scott Sanderson was actively involved, as is All-Star Andre Dawson.

"Andre is great," Sutcliffe said. "You'd think a guy like Andre, with his schedule and (the number of) appearances he's required to make (wouldn't want to do more). But, I could walk up to him today and ask him to go with me tonight and he'd cancel whatever he had planned and he'd be there with me."

Sutcliffe, whose charity work dates back to the late-1970s while still a member of the Dodgers, said the foundation's goal is to build a Christian oriented kids camp, which will include nature trails, fishing, boating and a petting zoo. Then, he could spend plenty of time with the kids.

In the meantime, though, Sutcliffe corresponds with the youngsters he has touched by mail. His locker at Wrigley Field is flooded with fan mail, many from the Los Angeles, Cleveland and Chicago kids Sutcliffe has come in contact with, as well as the natural fan mail of a three-time All-Star.

"(The mail) is incredible; it's unbelievable. I was with the Dodgers when (they had) (Steve) Garvey, (Ron) Cey and all those guys (from that era), yet I'd say the Cubs receive more (fan) mail than any other club I've been associated with, or have even heard of," said Sutcliffe, who received about 400 birthday cards this past summer.

"It takes me an awful long time (to respond), but I do. I try to read each letter, but it takes a while. I answer a lot of my mail on the road, simply because I have the time on the road. I probably answer 30 (letters) a day."

Sutcliffe does not, and will not, appear at card shows.

"I couldn't handle having a child come through and know he paid $10, just to get my autograph," he explained. "There are times when I will sign for a company or a store, if they make a large donation to the foundation, but only with the stipulation that they will not charge." — Ross Forman, March 29, 1991

* * *

Bruce Sutter

What does Bruce Sutter think of his high ERA of 4.48 in 1985? "I just hope they don't put this season on the back of my baseball card," the Atlanta bullpenner said. — Irwin Cohen, On the Baseball Beat, Nov. 22, 1985

* * *

Don Sutton

SCD: You were in Houston signing autographs on one day and in Massachusetts the next. Your hand must get pretty tired?

Sutton: I've figured out where to put the Band-Aids now so that the blisters don't get there. A question we keep getting asked, and I guess people who come through the lines are concerned, is "do you have writer's cramp?"

Well, I've never had that, but the blisters do get there. Pitch 23 years and never get a blister, and sign autographs for two days and get them...

...SCD: In terms of collecting, have you ever collected anything during your life?

Sutton: Like everybody else, I wish I'd only kept the shoeboxes that I had as a youngster. And I used to keep everything of Mantle's. I was a Mickey Mantle freak so I kept Mickey Mantle and all the Yankee stuff in the middle '50s, early '60s, anything that had to do with the Yankees. I even kept the ice cream lids, I kept all of that stuff.

I think most recently just my stuff because I have a 20-year-old son who's interested, so I pretty much help him collect things. But I also have in my career things from some of the guys I've played against that I've admired, I've gotten things from them. Not so much because it would be valuable later, just because I admired Roberto Clemente and it meant a lot to me when he would sign a picture to say "to a great competitor."

That meant something to me. So I got it for the message conveyed to me, more than hoping that it would go up in value. The things that are important to me are going to be important to me because they're mine, not because somebody else wants them. — Kevin Huard, Feb. 1, 1991

* * *

Don Sutton

When he's not in the booth or on the golf course, Sutton can also be found at speaking engagements and related benefits for the Make-A-Wish Foundation and United Cerebral Palsy. He also attends card shows when time permits and he has been working with hobbyists Greg Baxter and Eric Curry in arranging show appearances.

"I really don't do that many shows," said Sutton. "Maybe five a year. I really enjoy them as long as they're set up nice and orderly and there's some time allowed to visit with the people. I don't like being pushed. If I see somebody I know or they have a question, I want to talk to them. I don't want to just sit there and push them through. The people deserve more than just a name on the paper unless they're jerks and in that case it doesn't last that long any way."

Jerks are something Sutton feels he has avoided when it comes to autograph requests. Instead, he appreciates most of the people who ask him for his signature.

"I'm not as well-known and as visible as a lot of guys," said Sutton, "so I probably don't get as many (requests) as a lot of people. But the one thing which I'm very grateful for is that I seem to attract the nice people. It's not the guys who come and slap down a bunch of stuff and say, 'Here, sign this!' Instead, they seem to be pretty nice people. It's amazing because it seems like a lot of them fall in the under 10 and over 50 age groups."

Sutton also says he didn't save a large amount of memorabilia from his career, but did accumulate a few balls and bats.

"It really didn't seem that important to me until everybody else started asking me for it," Sutton said. "I have the game balls from most of my significant wins. I have two dozen balls from my 300th win because my son was ballboy that night and every time one was thrown out of the game, he stuck it in a bag." — Bill Ballew, Feb. 1, 1991

* * *

Frank Tanana

Tanana's faith is not just a Sunday morning slice of his life, but a reference point which affects all corners of it. Even his approach to autograph collecting is shaped by his Christian commitment.

"Honestly, if I weren't a Christian I would have chucked signing autographs a long time ago, a long time ago! It's become such a business, I get no kick out of it anymore. But it's a great opportunity for me to share Christ, to share my faith with somebody who needs Jesus in their life.

"I make a point to put a scripture verse on every autograph I sign because personally my name means nothing, but God's name means everything. So I take what I consider something rather silly, which is signing my name to something and being thought of as something, OK, beyond the average guy.

"To be actually idolized, hero worshipped and all that stuff is rather silly. I'm just like the guy who works in the factory. I'm just a human being. So if through signing an autograph I can give glory to the one who is worthy of that devotion, of that honor, then I'll do it."

However, there are limits on Tanana's patience with autograph collectors. He has been soured by those who send him large batches of items to sign, with multiples of the same item. And by those whose names he recognizes from writing him time and again.

"I still enjoy signing for kids, preferably at the ballpark or at the hotel if there's not too many around. But the guys who just keep sending them, year after year, you know it's for business. If there's anyone reading this article who sends things over and over again, let me warn them, I'll just throw their stuff away." — Dave Moriah, Oct. 12, 1990

* * *

Frank Thomas

All the notoriety has meant the big first baseman has had a busy, busy off-season. His baseball cards are shooting up in value, a sure sign he's in demand on the baseball card show circuit.

"I really like doing card shows," Thomas said. "They're really a great experience. Some folks don't know who you are, which can make things interesting.

"You have to do the shows if you're a ballplayer, and you really ought to do the smaller cities. That's where the fans are, and a lot of players don't appreciate it, but the fans have a lot to do with what happens in your career.

"There's another side — I like working with kids and talking to them. They're funny, and a lot of fun. I'm pretty good with kids, so that makes it easier."

Thomas did a show in Atlanta in late November, the same show that featured Mickey Mantle and several other Hall of Famers.

While Thomas sat discussing the past and the future, a man came out of the crowd, walked up to Thomas and shook his hand.

The man told him he had a great career ahead of him in Chicago, that he would accomplish great things, and that the people of Chicago would love him.

The man knew what he was talking about. After all, who knows more about the baseball fans of the Windy City, and what they are like, than Ernie Banks? — Dave Platta, April 26, 1991

* * *

Andre Thornton

Irwin Cohen: Since you weren't a fan, it's safe to assume that you didn't collect cards or baseball memorabilia. But what about the cards and memorabilia that you appear on? Do you save those?

Andre Thornton: You're right, I never collected cards or sought autographs. I'm not that big on memorabilia. Trophies and things, some I put up and some I don't. That's not a big issue with me. Maybe later on. I'm not going to clutter up the house with them.

Cohen: What's your attitude toward the autograph seeker?

Thornton: If it's done in an orderly way, I don't mind it. I'm not a real good autograph giver in the sense that I won't stand out there for an hour and just sign autographs. I know many people will disagree with that, but for me I just feel that I'd rather have them write me and include a self-addressed stamped envelope and I'll autograph it and write back. To stand for a long time and give autographs, no, I'm not too keen on that. — Irwin Cohen, On the Baseball Beat, Dec. 4, 1987

* * *

Mike Torrez

The Yankees went on to defeat the Los Angeles Dodgers in the 1978 World Series 4 games to 2...and that was the team's last world championship.

The championship ring features the intertwined "NY" letters Yankees logo made up of 20-odd diamonds set upon a blue sapphire field, with the band being executed in 14K gold.

When asked if he'd ever be interested in selling his ring, Torrez replied, "No way would I sell the ring at any price."

Torrez went on to say quite emphatically that a World Series victory ring stands as the epitome of a major league player's career. — Robert Obojski, Nov. 29, 1991

* * *

Alan Trammell

Irwin Cohen: Did you collect cards in your younger days?

Alan Trammell: Yes, I did. I collected them from about 1967 through 1973 and through those years I think I collected just about every one.

Cohen: Do you still have them?

Trammell: Yes, I do. I haven't brought them out of the closet as yet. They're still in my closet.

Cohen: What about autographs? Did you collect those?

Trammell: Yes. At the old-timers game in San Diego or when some good players would be around I'd go get their autographs. Hank Aaron was one I got. In fact, I once got Hank Aaron's autograph three times in one day.

Cohen: Do you like giving autographs?

Trammell: Oh yes. Definitely. Now that I'm a ballplayer I can look back and realize when I was turned down and I understand that there are times when you just can't go over and sign. But I try to sign as much as possible.

Alan Trammell

Cohen: Do you keep a scrapbook of your career?

Trammell: My mother does that and a couple of buddies back home. They get the Detroit papers and they collect that sort of stuff for me.

Cohen: What about the baseball cards that you appear on? Do you have them in any special display area?

Trammell: No, not as yet. I have a trophy room but it's not complete. Once I get it all together and set up then I'll have it for my collection.

Cohen: You appear on all three card companies this year — Topps, Fleer and Donruss. Plus, you appear on a Donruss Diamond Kings. Which card is your favorite?

Trammell: I like the Donruss action photo of me fielding. I think they're all pretty decent and all the companies did a pretty good job.

Cohen: As far as design, which card company appeals to you?

Trammell: Again, I like the action shots and that's what appeals to me. I think kids like those best, too. The drawing by Donruss is nice also but I'll go with the action photo. — Irwin Cohen, On the Baseball Beat, July 9, 1982

* * *

Alan Trammell

Among my guests at a recent show were 1987 Tiger of the Year Alan Trammell and former heavyweight boxing champ Muhammad Ali. Trammell, the man who should have been the American League MVP, didn't know Ali would be appearing with him until he arrived in town, three days before the show.

Trammell's first request? "Hey, you gotta let me meet him. I gotta get his autograph."

He did. — Jim Hawkins, Eye of the Hawk, Feb. 12, 1988

* * *

Bob Uecker

Irwin Cohen: You were born in 1935 and Bowmans and Topps came out when you were in your teens. Did you buy them in the late '40s and early '50s?

Bob Uecker: I don't think kids were any different then than they are now. If anything was collectible they grabbed it. I sometimes wish that I had kept all that stuff because I gave it away. I had a card collection just like everybody else. Who would have thought that cards would be as big a business as it is now. Some of those cards that I had — the value they reached is just unbelievable. My card is up to a buck now, I think.

Cohen: Do you have the Topps cards of yourself?

Uecker: No. I don't keep any of that stuff. I gave it all away. I gave some to my mother. She seems to cherish that stuff. It's funny when you get that stuff to sign in the mail. People still send me that stuff to sign and it's a lot of fun when I see those things.

Cohen: You mean you really didn't save anything? With all the celebrities like Johnny Carson and all other television shows you've been on?

Uecker: I'm not a celebrity seeker. The shows and stuff I do — those people are just people to me. I would never ask them for an autograph. I mean I've got a picture of Frank Sinatra because Sinatra is like the president of the United States.

Some of the entertainers I've become friends with but, it's more like a friendly-type thing and not a hero-type thing. It's really funny because people in show business get as big a kick hanging around baseball or football and basketball people as the other way around. It's very evident out in California when you see entertainers at sporting events there. But to get back to collecting, I'm not really a collector of anything. I know, though, about cards and Sports Collectors Digest and I've read your articles.

Cohen: You never kept a scrapbook of your playing career?

Uecker: The scrapbook was one page. I used to keep stuff when I was an amateur player. You know the Sunday writings and that stuff. That was a big deal at that time. Things like that and about my first years in the minor leagues I kept. I think my mother kept something, though. If I had to fill a scrapbook on my playing career I'd still be waiting. — Irwin Cohen, On the Baseball Beat, March 2, 1984

* * *

Gary Varsho

SCD: When you were growing up in Marshfield (Wis.), did you collect baseball cards?

Varsho: You bet! Football cards, too.

SCD: What is or was your favorite set?

Varsho: Well, I don't know about sets. See, my hero was Willie Mays. I tried to collect as many Willie Mays cards as I could afford.

SCD: So, Mays was the number one guy when you were a kid?

Varsho: Definitely. In fact, when I joined the Cubs at Candlestick Park last year, I didn't know what uniform number I was going to get and I ended up getting #24. That was the only time I ever wore #24, and I was really thrilled to get Willie's number once I hit the big leagues.

SCD: Did you collect any other cards besides Mays?

Varsho: As a kid, it was mostly Mays, but I did have a few others like Frank Robinson, Hank Aaron, and some of those guys. After Mays retired, I ended up following George Brett a lot.

SCD: Speaking of Aaron, were you a big Braves fan?

Varsho: Oh, yeah!

SCD: The Milwaukee Braves?

Varsho: Well, I was born in '61 and, they moved out in, I believe '66. The Milwaukee Braves were a little before my time. I was mostly a big Brewer fan.

SCD: Did you ever get anyone's autograph?

Varsho: You bet! I got Mays' autograph on a ball in '86 in spring training. We (the Cubs) were down there playing the Giants and Mays was there as a hitting instructor watching Joel Youngblood and some of those guys.

SCD: So that had to be a thrill.

Varsho: Hey, it was something I just had to do! Meeting Mays, getting his autograph...it was a must for me!

SCD: Do you still collect baseball cards now?

Varsho: Sure. I still try to get Mays and Brett. I even collect some of the cards that come along now, like Clemens, Canseco...

SCD: What about guys like Grace, Dawson and Varsho?

Varsho: I guess I collect some of the Cubs. I mean, my wife Kay will go out and get cards of the guys that I play with. That goes for the guys I was in the minors with, too. Someone like Wade Rowdon. Wade plays third base and he was with the Cubs. He's on an '87 Fleer update. I believe he's going to play in Japan this year.

SCD: So, if someone wanted to start a Gary Varsho fan club and give you a nice present, you'd be happy to get Mays, Brett and Wade Rowdon?

Varsho (laughing): Oh, you bet. That would be great!

SCD: Would you pay $50 for a 1986 Donruss Canseco card? That's what it's going for these days.

Varsho: No, but I might pay $50 for a Willie Mays card.

SCD: $50 for a Willie Mays rookie card?

Varsho (laugh): Oh, no no no!! I mean just in general!! If I was to invest in $50 in a card, I'd probably choose someone like Mays...

...SCD: Gary, what's your philosophy about signing autographs?

Varsho: Heck, to me signing autographs is a pleasure. I mean, you've got to understand there's certain times and places when it's best to do that, but if I have the opportunity, I'll sign as many autographs as I can. I thought last year in Chicago I took time out signing but you also have to understand we're out to do a job also. Geez, as for autographs, you should remember that I'm an autograph seeker myself.

I mean, I was in the Hall of Fame game against the Indians last year. Geez, everywhere you looked there were Hall of Famers. Ted Williams, Stan Musial, Willie Stargell. I had my pen and baseballs and was running around all over the place getting autographs. Heck, it was the chance in a lifetime! If I'm going to go out to get autographs, I sure don't mind if any boy, girl, man, lady whoever wants mine. Like I said, it's a pleasure for me to sign.

SCD: Would you sign if a fan sends you something in the mail?

Varsho: Sure, I think most guys do. From what I can see, I'm sure all my Cub teammates do. You bet. Guys come in early in the morning... like Mark Grace, Dawson, Sandberg...they have tons and tons of mail sitting there. They go through 25 to 50 letters a day. I've watched it every day. They sign what they can if the fan included a self-addressed stamped envelope and our clubhouse man Yosh Kiwano takes care of it.

SCD: Have you ever seen a teammate get out the rubber stamp and go to it?

Varsho: Never. These guys sign everything themselves...

...SCD: Do any of your teammates collect baseball cards?

Varsho: That I don't know.

SCD: Is there a league policy against players flipping baseballs into the stands?

Varsho: I don't know if it's a league policy, but we're told not to do it. If you do it for one, then everyone would want a ball. This starts in the minor leagues. You could throw a ball up there, but if a kid misses it and it hits someone in the eye, you got a lawsuit against yourself. It's very riskful on your part. You want to be nice, but you have to watch out, too. I guess there are some guys who'll flip them in there, however. — Tim Sullivan, March 10, 1989

* * *

Robin Ventura

The first time "#1 Draft Pick" Robin Ventura walked up to the plate wearing a Chicago White Sox uniform, he was getting ready to face "Rated Rookie" Pete Harnisch — a pitcher for the Baltimore Orioles. The premiere confrontation between these two young baseball talents resulted in nothing more than a walk. Although it was considered an unofficial at-bat, the beginning of Robin Ventura's baseball career was officially underway.

Ventura did manage, though, to collect his first major league hit later that Sept. 12, 1989, night against the Baltimore Orioles. He singled to right off former "Team USA" teammate Ben McDonald.

The White Sox made the Oklahoma State slugger the 10th overall pick in the June 1988 draft. Soon after the draft, the Topps Chewing Gum Co. produced the first nationally-available Ventura card.

Ventura said his 1989 Topps card is his favorite card of himself.

"It's special because I am a professional, but I was pictured in my college uniform," Ventura said. "I like that because it shows where I am from."

Ventura said he was shocked when he first saw the card.

"My little brother first showed it to me," Ventura said. "I have always seen other peoples' and have collected them. It was kind of a shock to actually have one with your name on it."

Out of the subset, #1 Draft Picks, Oklahoma State was represented by two players — Monty Fariss and Robin Ventura. Ventura said he would make a trade.

"If I could get away with it, I would trade two of my cards for one of Monty's," Ventura said. "I like Monty's better because he has a better look to him."

Baseball collectibles aren't the only Ventura collectibles. A 17-by-24-inch color poster of Ventura is available from the Oklahoma State baseball office. The poster depicts Ventura in an OSU uniform as well as an Olympic inset.

Another collectible is the 1989 Stillwater Telephone Directory, which depicts the three Oklahoma State gold medal medalists in the Seoul Olympics. On the cover with Ventura is John Smith and Kenny Monday — both former Oklahoma State wrestlers who won the gold in their respective 136- and 163-pound classes. — Jeff Shelton, Feb. 9, 1990

* * *

Bob Watson

"I have a Pete Rose bat and a Willie Stargell bat autographed.

"I have a Seiko platinum watch commemorating baseball's one millionth run that I scored. The only others to have such a watch are the president of Seiko and former Commissioner Bowie Kuhn.

"I don't have my spikes that I wore when I scored the run. They were taken from the clubhouse during the second game of a doubleheader and sent to the Hall of Fame without my approval." Rich Marazzi, July 8, 1988

* * *

Bill Werle

When I got to the big leagues I thought I'd like to have autographed pictures of all these players. I started to collect these pictures.

When I lived in San Francisco right after the war I knew this guy casually who lived just below us. One time I'm in Brooklyn and this photographer comes up to me and says, "Did you ever live in San Francisco on South Avenue?" I said yes and he said he was the neighbor right below me. We struck up a friendship and he was a head AP photographer and he was right on the field all the time. In those days, they used to be almost underneath the hitter.

I said, "How about saving me some of those real great shots?" So every time I came to Brooklyn he gave me a big armful of these things. I'd lug 'em back to Pittsburgh and I'd keep 'em in my locker and as every club would come around I'd get the pictures out — Mize or Brazle or Pollet or whoever it might be — and I'd have 'em autograph 'em.

So here I am collecting these things and thinking somewhere along the line I'm going to have a use for these. Finally, when I built the house I'm living in now I finally made a collage of all these pictures. I've got 17 frames and each frame is probably two-and-a-half-feet by almost three feet and maybe each one has 20-25 pictures in it.

I'm sure a lot of 'em are worth a lot of money. I've got one with Ted Williams, Walt Droppo, Wally Westlake and Kiner all standing there together, all autographed. — Brent Kelley, July 5, 1991

* * *

Frank White

Irwin Cohen: You've been with the Royals since 1973 and have been in the World Series and have had the opportunity to accumulate a lot of personal memorabilia. Have you done so?

Frank White: My wife has accumulated articles for many years but she's never been able to sit down and put it into a book or things like that. The thing that I like to do is occasionally I'll ask a player for a bat or to autograph a baseball for me personally. I've played with many people over the years that are not playing anymore so I want to remember them.

Earlier this season, I asked Vada Pinson (now the batting coach of the Tigers) to autograph a ball for me as he played with the Royals. He's one of the nicest people I've ever met and I felt it would be nice to have his name in my collection.

Cohen: How many balls do you have in your collection?

White: I haven't counted, but somewhere around 30. — Irwin Cohen, On the Baseball Beat, Nov. 8, 1985

* * *

Bob Will

Bob Will didn't know it at the time, but as he collected base hits in the big leagues he was collecting memorabilia from the big leaguers.

Will was an outfielder for the Chicago Cubs for his entire major league career. As one who frequently changed bats and batting stances to deal with various game situations and various pitching styles he faced, Will would ask to borrow teammates' bats. There even were occasions, standing around the batting cage, when he asked opponents if he could keep one of their extra bats. Often they said "yes."

At season's end Will emptied his locker and lugged all his equipment back home for winter storage. Some of the stuff made the return trip with him to spring training the following year; some of the stuff did not.

When he retired from professional baseball in 1964, Will discovered he had accumulated nearly 50 different bats, which is either a testament to his bat handling, or proof that he could see their value 30 years down the road. ("I'm very careful with how I handle them now," Will says.)

Will also collected baseballs, and in the process had them autographed by such greats as Charlie Grimm, Lefty Grove, Monte Irvin and many others. After he left baseball and entered the banking profession, however, Will often gave his top customers these signed mementos, which is either a testament to his generosity or proof that he was unable to see their value 30 years down the road. ("I've got two left," he says. "Wish I had the others.")...

...Specifically, Will's collection includes two game bats once owned by Musial, a bat given to Will by Clemente ("someone I admired both as a player and because he was such a nice fella," Will points out), photographs of Will with Stengel or Robinson or Williams or other baseball legends, and a few autographed baseballs. — David Craft, July 12, 1991

* * *

Billy Williams

Irwin Cohen: You began your big league career in 1959 with the Cubs and ended it in 1976 with Oakland. You appeared, of course, on numerous baseball cards. Do you have one of each?

Billy Williams: I have a lot of cards around in a box that I have at home. I started several years ago to make a photo album or to make a book from and my wife is taking care of it and hasn't finished the project as yet.

Cohen: Do you have any other memorabilia related to your career?

Williams: From teams I played with in Chicago I saved some balls. Of course, Leo (Durocher) is on many of the balls. Of course Ernie Banks was a Cubs player and is on some balls but I also have autographed balls with Willie Mays, Hank Aaron and other Hall of Fame people. When I play in old-timer games I always take some balls to get autographed. — Irwin Cohen, On the Baseball Beat, July 6, 1984

* * *

Dick Williams

"I think these (card) shows are all right," Williams said.

"You sure see a lot of people, so you know baseball is not a dying sport." Williams' youngest son, Marc, 27, is an avid collector, primarily cards from the 1950s to the mid-70s, "and some of them are in pretty good condition. I know that if he wanted to go to college (with the money from the cards), he could...and yet he already has graduated from Seattle University."

Williams still receives numerous autograph requests annually. And he does respond.

"Even if you move, and I've moved quite a bit over the past few years, (collectors) can still find you," Williams said. "But (signing autographs) is enjoyable; it really is.

"In the past, I've signed everything, including skin...but just the nice parts.

"If someone's got a decent piece of paper and a pen, I'll be glad to sign something." — Ross Forman, Dec. 18, 1992

* * *

Ted Williams

Like a lot of ballplayers from his day, Williams wasn't a big collector of memorabilia. "I don't have any old bats or uniforms," he said. "Nobody collected back then. If you needed one, you'd get a new one."

Williams says that he was fortunate to hang on to his two A.L. MVP Awards. "Luckily, I have my two Most Valuable Player Awards," he told SCD. "The only reason I have them is that in 1960, my last year, we had a terrific hurricane in the (Florida) Keys. That's where I lived. I lost all my good pictures, everything I ever had memorabilia-wise.

"The only reason I have the MVP Awards is that I kept them in Fenway Park so they were safe. The other thing I have that I've very proud of is the Medal of Freedom that I just got. That's quite a distinguished recognition and I'm happy about that. But I really don't have much memorabilia."

Williams revealed that he is a reader of SCD himself. "I know how important the magazine is to the whole industry and baseball," he said.

Williams added that he's only asked one player for an autograph. "The only guy I ever asked for an autograph was Babe Ruth," said Williams. "The first time I met him in Yankee Stadium in 1939 he signed a ball. He wrote 'To Ted Williams, your pal, Babe Ruth.' I was really kind of touched by that and I thought that was a great way to sign something.

"Now I've signed a lot of balls that very same way. I think it's a nice little touch for kids. Somebody stole the ball out of my house. I don't know where it is. I'd like to alert the world that it was stolen. If you see it, contact me in care of Major League Baseball — $1,000 reward." — Kevin Huard, July 17, 1992

* * *

Early Wynn

The odds are about 11-to-1 that if you send something to Hall of Famer Early Wynn you'll wind up with a mimeographed form letter telling you why you didn't get his autograph in return.

The big right-hander has created a list of 11 reasons why he won't be sending back most anything you send him to be autographed. But he does tell you that you may "buy" an envelope from Gateway Stamp Co. (and he gives the address) or a signed baseball from Star Cube (again, he tells you how to do it).

His first two reasons are valid. One tells you that you failed to include a self-addressed envelope, and the other tells you that you failed to enclose a stamp. What I'm not clear on here, though, is if you failed to do both of those, how does he get the rejection letter back to you? Does he provide a stamp to reject your request?

The next nine reasons are a little bit more in the "gray" area.

Reason number three tells you that the pictures you sent him were taken without authority. Does that mean if you, the fan, took a snapshot of Early sometime in his career he won't sign it because you didn't ask him if you could?

Reason number four says that what you sent him was an illegally-printed picture. He mentions TCMA and Renata Galasso by name, here. It's a point for him, though an arguable one.

Rolling right along, like H & R Block and their 17 reasons for doing your income taxes, Wynn tells you in item five that you have no authorization to sell printed matter, whatever that means. I'd guess if someone sends him a book or something he won't sign it. He's a little fuzzy there.

Item six smacks at a growing segment of our hobby, the sale or trade of home addresses. Early lists it as "private address (which is wrong) sold illegally in an unauthorized magazine." Many in the hobby feel that this era may soon be coming to an end and that sooner or later one or more of the players will claim "invasion of privacy" and seek an injunction to end the sale of home addresses.

In item seven Wynn rejects the request because "you are a professional collector." And this is one where a segment of our hobby has to accept the blame and has to live with the fact that greed, or whatever, has made life difficult for the pure collector. Of course I'm not sure what yardstick Mr. Wynn uses to determine who is a "pro" and who isn't.

Item eight tells you that he didn't sign your item because they were "early picture cards taken from files from past years and made into postcards," whatever that means.

Item nine tells you that you sent too many items. Valid and a legitimate complaint by many players. This branches into item 10 where he declines your request because you've written to him before. Again there are collectors who make pigs out of themselves and we all suffer.

His final item tells you not to write to a Bayview Parkway address because he doesn't live there. He adds that it is the home of his daughter and she just doesn't want to be bothered. And who can blame her?

Wynn does tell you in his letter that he honors all Hall of Fame cards and items from Cooperstown, and he does sign them personally. I would suspect, then, that this includes the Perez-Steele postcards, since they carry the endorsement and approval of the Hall.

As a parting shot the big ex-hurler says, "If the items you bought are not legal, don't blame me. I did not sell them to you." That about says it. — Ted Taylor, Off the Cuff, March 4, 1983

* * *

198

Chapter 7
Other Sports

Walter Payton cards were a hot collectible in the 1980s; other cards provided collectors with a lot of laughs.

What were the top 10 football card developments of the 1980s?

In his Jan. 5, 1990, Gridiron Gossip column, Chuck Bennett concluded: 1) The baseball card boom in the last decade had a run-off effect, creating significant interest in football cards, which were moderately increasing in value compared to baseball. 2) More football card price guides existed now, too, and 3) Score and Pro Set provided competition for Topps. 4) Football is America's sport, the king of the hill for television viewers; you have to be fan of the game before you're a collector. 5) McDonald's sets were a boost to the hobby, giving it national exposure.

6) As Walter Payton's rushing yards rose, so did the prices of his cards, becoming the hottest collectible on the market. 7) Sports Collectors Digest provided editorial coverage and advertising outlets, creating a surge in interest in football cards. 8) Investors saw the mad rush toward baseball cards in the decade, so they put their money towards football cards, which were far cheaper and less abundant. 9) The rookie card craze offered great potential in demand and value for football cards. 10) The 1984 Topps and USFL sets are potentially two of the best investments.

Tom Hultman, in his July 24, 1992, Two-Minute Warning column, provided a few laughs with his choices of the television-movie star lookalikes, the bad airbrushes, the bad hair styles and the miscellaneous silly Topps football cards from the 1970s.

TV-movie star lookalikes included Diron Talbert, who, on his 1973 Topps card is a hands down winner as a Burt Reynolds lookalike, and Pat Toomay, who, on his 1974 card, is a spitting image of "Gentle Ben's" Clint Howard.

Poorly airbrushed cards resulted because Topps wasn't granted a license with National Football League Properties during the 1970s. MacArthur Lane has, along with his green airbrushed jersey, a green left ear, while the football C.L. Whittington is holding on his 1976 card was airbrushed to say "WPD" instead of "NFL." Craig Morton's 1977 card has him with the right team, the Broncos, but since he'd been traded from the Giants, Topps "painted" his jersey bright orange, and changed his number from 15 to 5, but you can still see the No. 1 on his jersey.

Two New York Jets in the 1973 set, John Riggins and Chris Farasopoulos, sport two of the biggest heads of hair, while Larry Grantham features the Elvis look.

Miscellaneous choices included Dave Grayson's 1970 card, where he looks like he's singing "I'm a Little Teacup;" kicker Don Cockroft's 1977 card, which gives the illusion of him kicking a teammate in the butt; and Jim Tyrer's 1974 card, where he appears to be taking off a helmet which had been superglued onto his head.

Goofy cards weren't limited just to football, though. When readers were asked for opinions on what prestigious company Warren Jabali's 1973-74 Topps basketball card has as one of the worst cards ever made, Don Butler set up their responses in the Jan. 5, 1990, SCD by saying: "Like Godzilla movies, there's enough stupidity preserved on film for everybody to choose something different."

Among the nominations were, with corresponding reader's remarks: Basketball — 1970-71 Topps John Block #58 (For those of us really into arms and hands is a rare underwater shot of John Block.); 1971-72 Topps Emmett Bryant #48 (Emmett Bryant performing his disappearing forehead and wrists trick.); 1973-74 Topps Garfield Heard #99 (Garfield Heard shooting for two from the showers); and 1974-75 Don Watts #142.

Hockey — 1970-71 Topps Phil Esposito #11 (Phil Esposito sporting every center's choice for slacks in 1970.); 1971-72 Topps Ken Hodge #20 and #115 (Ken Hodge shows that the fashion statement is spreading.); 1975-76 Topps Darryl Sittler #328 (One haircut and three different shades still don't hide the fact that Darryl Sittler was the only excitement to the 1974-75 Leafs.); 1976-77 Topps Al Smith #152 (Al Smith sporting the Shemp Howard look.); 1978-79 Topps Jim Watson (Signs are now relayed in the NHL as Jim Watson tells Orest Kindrachuck which way the opposing goal is through sophisticated signals.); 1978-79 Topps Pierre Plant #177 (1978. The year punk rock captured the hearts of New York. Or was it puck rock?); and 1979-80 Morris Lukowich #202 (Morris Lukowich during his prize-winning appearance on "Wheel of Fortune.")

Football — 1963 Topps Andy Cverko #78 (Curly Howard as a wacky Dallas Cowboy. "Hey Moe! Hey Larry! I'm a guahd."); 1963 Topps Bernie Casey #137 (49ers camp seemed to be a nice place for this tea party until Bernie Casey crashed it.); 1964 Fleer Vince Costello #32 (Vince Costello feels it is imperative to defend a 1963 Thunderbird.); 1970 Topps Joe Namath #150 (Joe should have never picked at it in the first place.); 1974 Topps Wally Chambers #474; 1975 Topps John Leypoldt #273 (John Leypoldt attempting to kick a field goal with both legs.); 1978 Topps Tom Banks #140; 1981 Topps Randy Gradishar #116 (Randy Gradishar swears you can hear the ocean inside his helmet.); 1984 Topps Darrol Ray #155 (Darrol Ray didn't want a game ball as a souvenir. He opted for the arm of an unknown Tampa Bay Buccaneer.); and 1988 Topps Stan Talley #332 (He is shown following through on a punt. The only problem is that the football is still in his hand!).

NFL Souvenirs Are Big Business

By Tom Gregg

Wide receiver Bob Hayes figured that he'd heard the last from the NFL when he retired in 1976 and started a clothing business.

He figured wrong. A league representative was there when the store opened.

"Hey, my man, what can I do for you?" Hayes asked, probably sensing that the well-tailored white fellow hadn't come to look at African dashikis.

"Um, it's about your sign outside, Mr. Hayes."

The one-time Olympic sprinter brightened a little. "Yeah, that baby's all right. Friend of mine did it for me. You can see it a long way off."

"Yes, it showed up very well in the photo they ran in the Herald yesterday...and it definitely is a shot-in-the-arm for your business. I hope we can work something out so you can keep right on using it."

Having the Dallas Cowboys helmet on his storefront sign, Hayes had unknowingly run afoul of one of the league copyrights, held and policed by a subsidiary called NFL Properties Inc. Continuing to display it would cost him near five figures minimum. Assuming he could pass the other tests first.

Hayes was entitled to be, as the saying goes, shocked but not surprised. Shocked that the NFL found out so quick, but not surprised that they came down on him once they did. As a recent insider, Bullet Bob knew that the league is, and has long been, the safest sports business around. "Everyone in professional sports looks up to the NFL," the Wall Street Journal recently reported.

It almost had to be that good to survive. The league started with just $5,000 of a sponsoring grain company's money in 1921, had to battle firmly-entrenched competition from baseball and college football. But by some time in the late 1960s — various polls continually differ — it ultimately overthrew baseball as America's favorite sport. Asking price for an NFL franchise has gone from $40,000 or less in the 1930s to $30 million or more today.

All this has been due in no small measure to NFL Properties, which has cultivated and capitalized on the league image since 1966. There are subsidiaries in the other major pro sports doing the same thing. But the others, from all indications, aren't doing quite as well.

How well is the NFLP doing? Impossible to measure precisely. An educated guess has them cashing checks totaling $10 million yearly, compared with basketball's $2 million and hockey's $3.4 million. Properties President Bob Carey declines to give any revenue figures because they tend to mislead.

"Money isn't a critical factor here," he says from his New York office. "Promotion and service are." Meaning that his division is doing things that are reflective in game attendance increases, money which the NFLP never sees. Their intangible contribution has been extravagantly valued as high as $100 million. Somewhere well between 10 and 100 mill extremes seems safe.

One thing is definite. Contrary to what Bob Hayes might think, few of the hundred Props employees in two offices spend much time just scanning the skylines for unauthorized use of NFL logos. The telephones won't let them. One knowledgeable league sales rep has likened the New York headquarters to a patent office, bombarded with ideas. Carey readily agrees.

"Seventy-five percent of our business approaches us," he says. "We were getting about 150 inquiries a day at one point, and we just couldn't handle it. We ended up putting together a one-minute recorded message to separate the serious ones."

The jokers and dreamers are discouraged by the talk of minimum licensing guarantees (often $10,000) and royalties against wholesale value (usually 7 percent). They seldom make out the requested written application.

Those serious enough to write are divided again in two. The smaller group, "companies like Canon, Kodak, and Pepsi-Cola, want to know 'How can I sell more?' They're more of a problem. They have no established channels of distribution, so we sit down and work with them," Carey says.

When they stand up again, the self-billed professional consulting firm invariably has worked out a program for its new client which includes one or more sales boosters. These include: magazine advertising; the point of purchase premium, such as the popular Shell portrait giveaway; the mail-in premium, like Kellogg's NFL belt buckle offer; and/or the sales incentive, typically game tickets, trips, or big-ticket merchandise like team jackets and wall plaques for successful company salesmen.

The second and larger group of applicants to NFLP are the bright-idea people, or in some cases the not-so-bright idea. Ninety-nine percent of them are doomed to rejection.

"People (usually manufacturers) have wanted to put our name on toilet seat covers, fruitcakes, jockstraps, even a hot-air balloon," Carey deadpans. He and the league are serious about not hitching their wagon to anything cornball. Beyond that, the item needs to be priced within the ordinary person's budget, and the prospect needs to show a sound financial footing. The league doesn't want any limos or losers either.

What the two groups of applicants basically want (with a respectful nod to the separate line of excellent publications produced by Properties' L.A. office) is into or out of the bountiful NFL merchandise catalog. All the premiums and incentives call it home, and each of the marketing plans that Props blocks out for clients is only as good as the catalog lineup.

NFL retailers like Sears and J.C. Penny likewise expect good stuff. But of course all the screening pays off in quality. Carey estimates a decent year's gross on all officially-licensed products at $100 million. That's a lot of...well, if not fruitcakes, then what?

Try these from among nearly 500 items, not counting team variations, from roughly a hundred manufacturers: clothing of every description, blankets, cushions, and craft kits, license plates, lighters, and lunch bags. Only two go much over $15.

None of the team items pictured is a Cowboys item, which isn't too realistic; rumor has it that 25 percent of all licensed sales is Cowboys material. President Carey, however, claims that it's closer to half, even though the club has been away from the Super Bowl five years. But, yes, "America's Team" is still ahead of the rest of a pack headed by the Dolphins, Steelers and Redskins.

Cowboy Bob Hayes will probably appreciate that. And with additional business experience and the passage of time, he's probably come to appreciate the NFLP's humming little operation, too. — Tom Gregg, Off the Top of My Head, March 16, 1984

* * *

Ouch: Last week's news item in Sports Illustrated on people using metal detectors to determine which cases contained Pro Set's Lombardi Trophy card results in yet another black eye for the hobby in general and a major one for football card collectors.

We'd heard of at least three incidents — all involving dealers — in which metal detectors were successfully used to find Lombardi cards in early cases. Word got out, though, that Pro Set had inserted a strip of foil in each case to effectively discourage cheats.

I don't know if metal detectors are still being used, but I sincerely hope these dealers stop ruining the sport of collecting for the rest of us. Pro Set had basically a good idea which since has been abused. — Don Butler, Football Card Price Guide Report, Sept. 14, 1990.

* * *

Was Hulkster on a football card? Nobody knows where it started, but some dealers apparently believe that former Charger Terry Owens turned out to be Hulk Hogan. Can this be true? Should dealers charge $15 for Owens' 1973 rookie card and $5 each for his 1974 and 1975 cards?

No way. According to Owens' 1973 Topps card, he stood 6-6 and weighed 268. He'd be 46 years old right now. Wrestling publications list Hulk's true name as Terry Bolleo, not Terry Owens. Hogan/Bolleo graduated from high school in 1971, meaning he would have had to start an NFL career at around age 20 — impossible because of the NFL's then-stringent draft laws. The San Diego Chargers verify Owens is not Hulk Hogan.

Owens' cards should be at common price, where they belong. — Don Butler, Football Card Price Guide Report, April 5, 1991

* * *

Troy Aikman

Dallas Cowboys quarterback Troy Aikman is on the verge of waging his own battle on multiple-request autograph seekers which, he hopes, will wean out the people looking to make a profit from a free signature.

Unlike most other players, Aikman has a strategy for dealing with multiple requests.

"Right now we're in the process of putting those names in a computer and keeping track of who sends in requests for autographs," Aikman says. "Usually you can get a pretty good idea of who the people that have shops are who send in cards to get signed or sell for a profit."

Like most other players, Aikman will sign only one or two items to be signed.

"I think (getting cards signed for a profit) is wrong," Aikman says. "It's wrong if they're going to get my autograph and then turn around and sell it for a profit to kids.

"I would love to personalize every one, but because of the numbers, I can't do that. Sometimes they'll put in two or three football cards, covers of magazines or posters. But I want those kids to be able to have them."

Aikman estimates he receives 1,000-1,100 requests per week during the season.

"After the season it slows down some. After my first couple of years in the league it slowed down quite a bit in the off-season. After this past season, it hasn't slowed down all that much." — Don Butler, Aug. 21, 1992

* * *

Brian Baschnagel

Baschnagel said two fan letters "really stand out in my mind."

"The first (letter) came from a physician who I didn't even know," Baschnagel explained. "After I played one year with a broken arm and had to play five or six games with a cast, the physician wrote, 'You'll remember your heroics when you lose the use of your arm.'

"I had cleared my playing with our medical staff beforehand, but still, the letter was very interesting.

"The other letter that I'm very proud of is from a local judge whom I had never met. Shortly after I got released from the Bears, I received a letter from this Supreme Court justice thanking me. He went on to tell me of the joy he got out of watching me play. I thought that was extremely rewarding, especially from someone in his position, because I never thought he'd take the time to write a letter like that."

Baschnagel also has received his share of...well, let's just say odd-ball mail.

First, there was the unsigned letter with $5.

"I had caught a touchdown pass against Minnesota to win a game," Baschnagel recalled, "and the letter just said, 'Brian, this is part of my winnings, thanks to your catch. Thank you.'" — Ross Forman, Aug. 21, 1992

* * *

Sammy Baugh

SCD: What do you think about all the new interest on the football Hall of Fame players? I suppose you've noticed by an increase in your mail the last few years or so?

Baugh: I don't like an athlete selling his autograph. I used to sit and sign for an hour after a game. Nowadays, some of them don't even want to give an autograph unless they're paid for it. I don't like that. I receive money in the mail — $10, $5 or something. Hell, I don't keep the check. I just send it back. — Todd Patterson, Nov. 27, 1992

* * *

Bobby Bell

Bell isn't a collector, but "I try to keep anything that's odd. I try to get one of everything."

And for collectors, the odd certainly includes Bell's infamous high-top shoes.

"I had a great big box full of the shoes, but nobody would wear them or wanted them, so I was going to pitch them in the garbage," Bell recalls. "But then, a guy said, 'I'll give $250 for a pair of those high-tops.' So I sold the shoes and now I've gotten into selling them to collectors."

At one time, Bell had 36 pairs, shoes dating back to his college days.

"I had gotten used to carrying them around and I didn't want to get rid of them," he said. — Ross Forman, May 8, 1992

* * *

Ken Bowman

SCD: Did you collect anything when you were growing up?

Bowman: I used to collect coins when I was a kid. My dad had a gas station and I used to go through the change box all the time. I collected Indianhead pennies. Buffalo nickels. I guess I got involved with football around the ninth grade and kind of let the coin collection go. Since then, I can't say I collected anything except Packer memorabilia from my playing days.

SCD: What Packer memorabilia did you collect?

Bowman: I have a plaque at home from the Ice Bowl. It has a piece of the goal post on it. A picture of the team. I have an etching that was done of the Ice Bowl game and the block. Jerry (Kramer), Bart (Starr), and several of the others signed it.

SCD: Did you get a plaque after making it into the Packer Hall of Fame?

Bowman: Yes, I have that too.

SCD: How did you get a plaque that has a piece of the Lambeau Field goalpost?

Bowman: Well, the fans tore down the goalpost. I picked up the plaque in a card shop. Apparently, someone sold the guy about a two-foot piece of the goalpost and he made a nice plaque out of it. It's really kind of nice. It's an authentic piece of the goalpost along with a photo on the plaque of the fans tearing it down after the Ice Bowl game.

SCD: That etching of your Ice Bowl block must be really special. And Bart and Jerry signed it?

Bowman: Yes, they did, and it is special to me...

...SCD: Just one final question. It's tough thinking of something that you've never been asked before, but let's try this: How come the Cleveland Browns don't have anything on their helmets?

Bowman (Big laugh): The Cleveland Browns have nothing on their helmets because they have nothing in their helmets. — Tim Sullivan and Randy Wievel, April 12, 1991

* * *

Tony Canadeo

SCD: What about the playing memorabilia?

Canadeo: Well, most of the things I had as a player are either in Canton, Ohio, or in the Green Bay Packer Hall of Fame. I do remember that Bob Noel, our equipment manager, once made me a jersey to keep. I still have that, but everything else is in the Packer Hall or in Canton.

SCD: So that jersey makes up just about your entire collection?

Canadeo: That's about it. I do have a few game balls at home. The one I treasure most is a ball from my last game. We beat the Bears. You'll never believe how I got that one!

SCD: What happened?

Canadeo: My mother was sitting with my brothers in the end zone at Wrigley Field. We kicked a field goal, or maybe it was an extra point, and the football landed right in her lap! I have that ball at home right now.

SCD: As long as we're talking about collecting, would it be right to say you don't collect anything at all?

Canadeo: Just money. Now that I think about it, that's true. I collect money. I save those silver half-dollars. And it's true about my mother catching that ball against the Bears.

SCD: In general, what is your personal attitude or policy towards signing autographs? Do you get cards or photos to sign through the mail?

Canadeo: I enjoy signing those. That's no problem if the person includes a stamped envelope. However, every once in a while someone will send me a dozen 8x10s to sign. I don't really go for that because it's obvious the guy just wants me to sign so he can resell them.

SCD: So you get about 30 requests each week?

Canadeo: That's about right. Thirty or so requests to sign things a week. And like I said, I'll sign anything else unless it looks suspicious. If somebody says he has a collection and sends one or two cards, I sign. But if a person sends me eight or 10 cards, you know something's wrong.

SCD: Do you charge anything to sign through the mail?

Canadeo: Never. I never have. But again, if someone sends a bunch of things...if it's suspicious, we'd probably charge the guy something. — Tim Sullivan and Randy Wievel, Oct. 26, 1990

* * *

Tony Dorsett

Personal awards hung onto by Dorsett include a Super Bowl ring from the 1987 Dallas-Denver game, the Rookie of the Year trophy from 1977, and the Heisman Trophy that he won while at Pitt in '76.

"Awards are awards to me and I pretty much just set them down and cuff them all together," said Dorsett, "but the Heisman Trophy stands out amongst them all." — Fluffy Saccucci, Nov. 21, 1991

* * *

Vince Ferragamo

"I think it's good for the fans to be able to come up and get your autograph, but I'd never attend a show that I'd have to charge for my autograph because I don't believe it's right," he said.

"I'm not a collector, but I did buy a Super Bowl poster during the show and will get all of the guys to sign it because I think it's a treasure." — Ross Forman, Feb. 28, 1992

* * *

Forrest Gregg

SCD: Have you noticed a big increase in autograph requests?

Gregg: Yes, and if you want to know what my greatest complaint is, it is people sending me multiple items to sign. I know what they want to do with them. They are doing it for a monetary reason.

I will not sign five cards. I personalize all requests. It got pretty bad there for a while, but I guess the word got around when I started signing only one item. Every day I get some. I have a stack now that I need to sign. — Todd Patterson, Dec. 6, 1991

* * *

Elroy Hirsch

What does Hirsch think about football players charging for autographs at card shows? "I think it's ridiculous," Hirsch says. "I think that we football players have an obligation to the public to sign for free and I think that it's the least we can do in return for their support."

Hirsch has hung onto many mementos from his brilliant career. He says he has everything connected with anything that he ever did. He has his Wisconsin jersey, Michigan jersey, Ram jersey, Chicago Tribune All-Star game jersey, helmets from all the aforementioned teams, and pictures of clippings of his whole career. He adds that these items are scattered in disarray all over his basement, but says that this winter he's going to take time aside to organize it all.

As for the favorite memento of the lot that he possesses, Hirsch thinks it's the trophy he received from the Chicago Tribune All-Star game in 1946 for being named the Most Valuable Player. "It's a nice big trophy, and the fact that it came against my future pro team, the Rams, gave it special meaning for me." — Fluffy Saccucci, Feb. 2, 1990

* * *

E.J. Holub

As far as signing autographs, Holub is happy to comply. He is always honored that somebody remembers him.

"You never know the influence you might have on the kids," Holub said. "I lived in Lubbock and I went to a Texas Tech football game and I asked one of the guys to give me an autograph after a game when I was just real small.

"He just pushed me aside and said, 'Don't bother me, little boy, I'm tired.' And I don't know why that's always stuck with me in my mind. It really hurt my feelings because I went up to him to ask him for his autograph and I was very sincere about it.

"And as long as they keep asking I'll comply because I don't want to hurt their feelings," he added. "I've seen some boys that come get my autograph and while I'm still signing others I see them walking off and they look at it and they just throw it away. That's OK because there's a lot of them who kept them." — Jeff Shelton, Sept. 6, 1991

* * *

Paul Hornung

SCD: Paul, you couldn't help noticing all this sports memorabilia around here. Did you collect sports memorabilia and, if so, do you still have any of it?

Hornung: I never collected things like that when I was a kid. I don't even remember ever asking for an autograph when I was a kid. Maybe that's because of where I grew up. See, we had no "stars" in Louisville, Ky. There were no professional sports in the city. I think I remember asking a couple of U of L basketball players for an autograph because they were in town. That was when I was 12 or 13, but I don't ever remember actually collecting anything.

SCD: Do you still have anything from the Packers, such as uniforms or trophies?

Hornung: No, I gave all my trophies away and gave the Heisman Trophy back to Notre Dame. There's only one trophy in my house, and that's my wife's golf trophy. That's it. I just don't believe in trophies. I never have been much for that. I went in some athletes' homes when I was young and I thought their trophies were a little gaudy. I've known some athletes who built their whole homes around a trophy room, but I thought that was kind of superfluous.

SCD: Isn't there a funny story about the wife of some Heisman winner who kept seeing the trophy just about every where she went?

Hornung: That's the old Heisman Trophy story. The wife was Terry Moore, the actress who married Glenn Davis. Glenn was Army's Heisman winner in 1946. Now, Terry Moore didn't know the Heisman Trophy from Heinz soup. She asked Davis what the trophy was, and he told her it was the Heisman.

She asked, "What's a Heisman Trophy?" Davis told her it's given to the outstanding college football player in America each year and it's very rare. There's only one given out each year.

Well, they got married and a week later went over to Tom Harmon's house. Terry Moore looked up on the mantel and there's that trophy again. (Harmon, a Michigan halfback, won the Heisman in 1940.)

This gets even better. Glenn Davis, of course, was great friends of Doc Blanchard. So, they took a trip to see Doc. They went to dinner at Doc's and there's that trophy! (Blanchard, a fullback for Army, won the Heisman in 1945, one year before Davis won it.)

Then, there was Les Horvath, a dentist from Ohio State who'd moved to Los Angeles and was a good friend of Glenn's. They got back off the trip to Doc's and went over to Horvath's house...and there's the Heisman Trophy again! (Horvath was the Heisman winner in 1944, one year before Doc Blanchard.)

Terry Moore looked at Glenn Davis and said, "I thought you said that trophy was special! Everybody in the bleeping world's got one!"

That's a true story...

...SCD: There are probably some Babe Parilli football cards at this show. Is this the first card show you've ever appeared at?

Hornung: Yes, this is the first one I worked. I've had a couple of offers before but I could never make it. Willie Mays plays in my golf tournament and he told me there's a lot of work in it if you really want

to work. Of course, they pay those baseball players a pretty good figure to sit around. There are a lot of these card shows and now they're getting into the football end of it. I think you'll see an explosion in football cards in the next five or 10 years.

SCD: Did you get paid anything to be on a football card when you were a player?

Hornung: No, sir. The football cards weren't very popular in my day.

SCD: Do you have any of your own football cards?

Hornung: No, but I get about a hundred a month in the mail for me to sign.

SCD: How do you respond to your mail?

Hornung: I answer or sign everything as long as the people send a self-addressed stamped envelope. When I return it in their envelope, I also stick a card in there that says I'll also send them an 8x10 signed glossy if they send $10. That money goes to charity. I give it over to the Sisters Visitor program in Louisville.

Paul Hornung

SCD: What happens if someone sends you 20 things to sign?

Hornung: As long as there's an SASE, I sign them and send them back. Normally, about three out of 10 people who receive my signed things and card will write back for a photo to help out charity.

SCD: So it seems like you're a good signer. We understand that Bill Russell, the ex-Celtic great, isn't much for autographs.

Hornung: I sign them all. Russell has a fixation. He won't sign anything. But if people diligently send me pictures or cards they've saved, I'll sign. I feel that all athletes have a responsibility to sign and return them. I believe most of these photos and things that are sent to me to sign come from the Hall of Fame. People go to Canton, Ohio, and they buy paraphernalia at the Hall of Fame. Then they get the address from the Hall and send it on.

The Hall of Fame is in business to sell these cards and paraphernalia. If they don't give out my address, it's going to hurt their sales a little bit. It's a slight invasion of privacy, but it's an invasion where I feel an athlete has a responsibility...to the kids, especially. How can anybody turn down a kid? I don't understand that thinking...

...SCD: You had one of your greatest days ever with five touchdowns against the Baltimore Colts in 1965. If memory serves us right, that game at Memorial Stadium was played in a dense fog. What was it like that day?

Hornung: It was great that day. (Hearty laughter.) Lombardi would've had a heart attack if he knew what I did the night before that game. I wasn't going to play. I was hurt. I was hurt as far as I was concerned and as far as the trainer was concerned. But I wasn't hurt as far as Lombardi was concerned. He never felt anybody was injured unless there was a bone sticking out of your leg.

Well, because of the injury, I went out the night before and fell in love. Dick Szymanski was the center for the Colts. He and I went to Notre Dame together. Dick picked me up about midnight and we went out. I still remember the rock and roll group. Freddie Bell and the Bell Boys. It was a hell of a rock and roll group. We stayed in there all night until about 4:30 in the morning. I finally got back around 6:30.

So, I knew I wasn't going to play. But before the game Lombardi asked me how I felt and I almost swallowed my olive. I knew what he was leading up to. He said he was going to start me and I said "Oh yeah, that's great!" My reflexes weren't as diminished as I thought they would be. I had a hell of a day. I always wanted to tell Vince that, but I think that would've really hurt his credibility.

SCD: Was that the same way Max McGee felt before the first Super Bowl?

Hornung: Absolutely! He didn't have one wink's rest, because I was his roommate. I was getting married on Wednesday, so I wasn't going to sneak out. Max and I, usually, both played better after we snuck out. But see what happens after you get to be about 28, that stuff starts catching up to you.

SCD: Were all those stories about you breaking curfew true?

Hornung: The times when I actually broke curfew were rare. People would report a story, and everybody seemed to think this went on game after game after game. It got blown out of proportion. In all my career, spanning over 100 games over 10 years, I probably snuck out three times the night before a game.

Now, it is a little different during the exhibition season. I snuck out every time we were in Milwaukee. I knew my way around the Astor Hotel better than the janitor. Max and I knew the exits from all the hotels in Milwaukee...

...SCD: You mentioned Dick Butkus. Did he ever bite you?

Hornung: No. I'd remember it.

SCD: Did you ever bite Butkus?

Hornung: Hell, no! (Laughter.)

SCD: Let's get serious, Paul. Do you know who the Masked Marauder in the Miller Lite commercial is?

Hornung: (Leaning back and chuckling) Well, if it's not our boy from Milwaukee, you've got a scoop.

SCD: Do you get together with the Lite Beer guys at all?

Hornung: No, I haven't done the Lite Beer ads in seven, eight years now. Asked for too much money years ago.

SCD: Were those commercials as fun to make as they are to watch?

Hornung: Sure. Those guys were great. Bubba (Smith) and Deacon (Jones) took care of everything and kept things light. Now Bubba's a teetotaler. — Tim Sullivan, Randy Wievel, Archie Hansen and Jim Krueger, July 7, 1989

* * *

Raghib Ismail

Rocket, who really didn't collect cards when he was younger, said the hobby has plenty of positives.

"I think it's pretty cool," he said. "It's a healthy thing and it's turning into a big business now. But I think (card collecting) can be a dirty business because companies can make cards of certain individuals, with their permission, and then say they did it by mistake, knowing that the card would be worth more — like a bootleg card.

"I think (bootleg cards) can be an underhanded thing. That's a small percentage. Other than that, I think it's a good hobby for everyone." — Tom Hultman, Oct. 4, 1991

* * *

Joe Kapp

"I think the way the QB Legends show was run, where no one was paying for an autograph, is terrific. I'm just glad my name is not Darryle Lamonica — K-A-P-P is nice and easy." — Ross Forman, Feb. 28, 1992

* * *

Dick Lane

SCD: What is your attitude toward the hobby of collecting cards and memorabilia?

Lane: I think it's all right if it's not done to the extreme, (if it doesn't) get out of hand. I think I've had a good name over the years since 1952 (rookie year); that's a long time.

Just recently, the name (Lane's autograph) has been of some value to the people that are in the business. I've been to about three or four shows that really went all out to make the show a success. I have no qualms with it unless it gets oversaturated.

SCD: Do you enjoy the shows?

Lane: I enjoy them. I meet a lot of interesting people. This is what a football player, or an athlete for that matter, thrives on. We all can't be a Michael Jordan, even though we play our hearts out like he does. We enjoy knowing we have fans that still care, that they think a lot of us, what we did. — Rick Hines, Sept. 6, 1991

* * *

Don Maynard

"Why, you ask, did I retire from football?" Maynard says with a grin. "Well, one day I came home and my wife had used my helmet as a planter." — Ross Forman, July 24, 1992

* * *

Dave Meggett

Dave Meggett, the New York Giants super young back, had a few comments about Action Packed and cards in general during the photo shoot which resulted in this week's Sports Collectors Digest cover.

"Two of the greatest thrills of my rookie season with the Giants was making the Pro Bowl and becoming a hot card in the Action Packed set," he said.

Meggett's first card appeared in the Action Packed 1989 test set.

Finding out his card was worth more than those of Phil Simms and Lawrence Taylor was also exciting, he said.

"The talk in minicamp between myself, O.J. Anderson, Lawrence Taylor and Mark Bavaro was who would be the 10 players to make the set this year," he said. (For the record, it was Anderson, Meggett, Taylor, Odessa Turner, Carl Banks, Bavaro, Mark Collins, Leonard Marshall, Gary Reasons and Simms.)

"People on other teams have been calling me to see if I could find out if they were one of the 10 selected from their team this year," he said. "It has been the talk of the locker rooms.

"I made the big rookie mistake," Meggett says. "I gave away all my rookie cards."

Hi-Pro marketing gave him some more cards, which Meggett said he'd "put away and save." — July 13, 1990, SCD Football Card Price Guide

* * *

Chris Miller

Miller said the first thing he does when he receives some of his cards is look at his mugshot.

"First, I check out the pictures and say, 'OK, this one doesn't look too bad,'" he said. "It's funny, last year I had a beard for a week or two. And most of my cards in this year's card sets picture me with a beard. It's weird how that gets around.

"A poster of me just came out recently and I have a beard on that and on a lot of cards from this year I have a beard. I think those photos may have been taken at the same game." — Tom Hultman, Nov. 27, 1992

* * *

Art Monk

According to Monk, the football card hobby is something children need in today's society.

"I think it is a neat deal. I think it is something for the kids," Monk said. "As crazy as the world is nowadays with kids and the problems that kids have, I think it is good for them to have a hobby and interest — something that can keep them out of trouble.

"Something that they can afford to buy, get into and keep track of and follow certain people." — Tom Hultman, Dec. 11, 1992

* * *

Emmitt Smith

In just two seasons, Smith has become very aware of the hobby and what it means in terms of dollars. For many, this hobby is a business. Smith has learned that first-hand as he and his father have opened a hobby store in Pensacola, Fla.

"It is a business. It's turning from a collectible item to a business deal," said Smith. "People are receiving the cards, getting them signed, trading them and making a profit. The general public is also making a profit. It's almost like the stock market."...

...Listening to Smith talk about football cards is listening to someone who is well informed on the hobby. He knows cards. He likes cards. But what about the other NFL players?

"If they are not aware of it (the growth and power in the hobby), they are quickly learning about it. I believe now that after talking to some of the older veterans in the league they wish they had kept their cards. Many of them wish they had kept the memorabilia from their playing days because today it is worth a lot of money," Smith said.

Still, according to Smith, the players don't spend a lot of time talking about the cards. "We don't talk a lot about the cards. The only time we talk about the cards is when we are looking through a card magazine. I talk to the guys about the values of the cards. A lot of the guys still don't realize the value in the cards."...

...Finally, Smith seems to let his father do most of the collecting. "My father does the collecting. I just provide him with all my cards. Whatever my father collects is really my collection too — it's all in the family. Some of my personal stuff is for sale, but some of it is not for sale. My rookie helmet is my most prized collection, along with this year's helmet," Smith said. — Chuck Bennett, May 8, 1992

* * *

Bob St. Clair

"I was at a White House dinner last year with Gayle Sayers and Mrs. Bush," St. Clair explained. "The waiter brought my steak, which was raw. I started cutting it, adding salt and pepper, and getting it ready to eat. I see Mrs. Bush looking at my plate and she says, 'Mr. St. Clair, if that's not done quite enough for you, I'll have the waiter bring it back.'

"Then I had to explain to her that I eat it this way and she just shook her head and said, 'I'll bet that's a first in the White House.'"

St. Clair's eating habits are...unique, to say the least.

St. Clair, who now works as a national marketing coordinator for Rani, a mandarin orange juice company, eats all red meat raw.

"I never cook it," he said, "because I prefer it raw."

"Ever since I was a little kid, my grandmother, who was part Indian, used to feed me scraps of raw meat when she was preparing dinner. And I just acquired a taste for the taste of raw meat. And that's the way I prefer it. Some people like it medium; some people like it well done; but I like it uncooked.

"That (red meat) doesn't get too many people looking at you strangely, but when you order raw liver, like I do, then they start looking at you strangely."...

...San Francisco slipped to 7-4-1 in '54 and St. Clair had — understandably — one of his most memorable games ever.

"I blocked a punt against Norm Van Brocklin in the L.A. Coliseum," St. Clair recalled. "I got in there so quickly that I knocked the ball away from his foot before he even had a chance to hit it and, instead, he hit me right in the teeth and knocked out five teeth.

"The funny thing about that story — if anything can be amusing about losing teeth — was the fact that we got a delay of game penalty because I was on my hands and knees, confused, looking for my teeth. Then, I came out of the game and the coach was mad as hell at me." — Ross Forman, Aug. 21, 1992

* * *

Jan Stenerud

Stenerud's reputation for long-distance kicks often intimidated opponents. A visiting coach once asked Kansas City groundskeeper George Toma about the dozens of white "X" marks painted on the stadium wall 10 full yards beyond the end zone. "Those are the spots where Stenerud's kickoff have hit the fence," Toma explained to the astonished coach. — Aug. 16, 1991

* * *

Derrick Thomas

"It's something that is very flattering to me," Thomas said of signing autographs. "It seems like they usually want me to sign football cards, and I think it's neat to see all the various cards I've been on. To me, it's fun because I like people, especially the kids.

"It doesn't bother me to get caught up in a crowd of kids for a half an hour signing autographs," Thomas added. "Some players seem to be bothered by it, but to me it's a part of the business. If I wasn't playing well, they wouldn't want me to sign something. So it all goes hand in hand." — Scott Kelnhofer, Dec. 25, 1992

* * *

Thurman Thomas

He definitely is organized when it comes to knowing the price of his 1989 Score rookie card, which is $40.

"I know the value of one card — my rookie card," he said. "That's the one everyone is looking for. The guys in the locker room always ask me, when my card goes up, if I have any extra rookie cards I can give them."

According to Thomas, his rookie card caught his eye when he saw it for the first time.

"You always want to play in the NFL, now you see a card of yourself," he said. "It is quite a thrill and it is something special." — Tom Hultman, Feb. 14, 1992

* * *

Clyde "Bulldog" Turner

SCD: I have heard that some players in your day partied pretty hard.

Turner: We always had a party Sunday night after the game. And there were rumors that one or two guys might be taking "wide-awake" pills, but I don't know.

Coach Halas always told us to never have more than two drinks in the same bar at a time. You were supposed to move on to another establishment. That way the public wouldn't think that a player drank too much.

Everywhere you go, everyone you meet wants to know the difference between pro football today and when I was playing. Of course, the number one difference is salaries. And secondly, not many of us knew how to dance once we scored a touchdown. Finally, the misuse of illegal drugs today.

George McAfee tells a story that one year, when the Bears had a great team, the team would go out and score 35 points in the first half. Sometimes we'd kind of loaf in the second half.

So Halas decided that we were getting stale. Some guy talked him into feeding us vitamins. Each player got a bottle. A few players took them to a chemist to have them analyzed. It was saltpeter tablets. — Todd Patterson, Oct. 25, 1991

* * *

Johnny Unitas

Was Raymond Berry, or Jimmy Orr, or anyone else his favorite receiver? "My favorite receiver was anybody who could get open," laughed Unitas. "I didn't want the football, I'd rather him have it." — Rick Hines, Sept. 18, 1992

* * *

Randy White

A good feeling was what White felt when he was Dallas' No. 1 pick in 1974. He won the Outland Trophy and the Vince Lombardi Award as college football's top lineman.

After he entered the NFL, he took his idol Ray Nitschke's advice.

"He told me not to make any friends. He said to knock the crap out of them and I'll make all the friends I need," White said. — Tom Hultman, Feb. 28, 1992

* * *

Doug Williams

Williams says that he never collected cards. He did, however, save most of his memorabilia from his pro playing days. Included are the football shoes he wore in Super Bowl XXII — "I had those bronzed" — along with helmets and jerseys from the Buccaneers, the Redskins and the two USFL teams that he played for (Outlaws and Wranglers). And, of course, his Super Bowl ring and MVP award. — Fluffy Saccucci, Jan. 24, 1992

* * *

Collecting Hockey Brawls On Video

By Vernon W. Smith

Marty McSorley's lower lip is cut and bleeding.

His face is red and bruised and his white Edmonton Oilers jersey is doused with blood. McSorley had just done battle with Joe Patterson of Los Angeles.

The two hockey heavyweights have scrapped for about 90 seconds. And the same people who are standing on their feet cheering will go home in a couple of hours and tell their families how violence is ruining hockey.

Steve Parsons leans back in his easy chair and smiles. He doesn't have to go to the local rink to watch the boys battle it out.

In fact, he spends several hours each week analyzing hockey fights on his video cassette recorder at home.

Collecting ice fights on videotape has become an underground phenomenon among sports collectors. Though hockey officials have clamped down on fighting in recent years, fans are still thrilled when hockey players "drop their gloves."

Equipped with VCRs, fight collectors can be found across North America. They collect the scraps by taping local games, and some even go as far as having satellite dishes. They make trading contacts by taking out classified ads in newspapers.

With more than 160 hours in his violent library, Parsons has one of the biggest collections in Toronto.

"It's all part of the game," said Parsons, a 22-year-old Ryerson business student. "There are a lot of bleeding hearts out there that want to see fighting banned. But, when two guys go, nobody gets up to leave for coffee.

"Everybody's into it. It's not just kids, it's older people — men with their wives," added Parsons.

Parsons should know. He's an authority on fisticology, earning his stripes as a tough guy at the junior level in Newmarket and Brantford.

The 6'3", 210-pound Parsons began battling as a 15-year-old midget. Trying to catch the wonderful eye of hockey scouts, he fought his way through the junior ranks to the university level before quitting two years ago.

"When you win a fight, it's like scoring a big goal," said Parsons.

"It can lift your entire team if you do it at the right time. A lot of people ask, 'How can these goons play in the NHL?' Well, today, there are no more pure goons — guys like Dave Schultz, Steve Durbano and the rest are gone. Today, guys like Rick Tochett and Al Secord will mix it up, but they will score some goals."

When Parsons stopped playing, there was nobody left to swing at. Instead of pulling the wings off small insects, Parsons got his daily fix by collecting fights on video.

He spent more than 15 hours a week collecting and editing fight tapes.

A season ticket holder to Toronto Maple Leafs games, Parsons does manage to see some live fights. But that doesn't mean he misses taping the heavyweights. Equipped with three VCRs and televisions, he makes certain he doesn't miss a hook or a jab.

For scraps aired in the U.S., Parsons trades tapes with guys south of the border. His collection also includes clips from minor and junior hockey.

"When I played, fighting was part of the game and it still is today," he said. "I enjoy watching fights so I make tapes.

"It's no different from somebody collecting autographs or hockey cards. A lot of people don't understand it because they don't know how hard it is to play. It's something that happens in the heat of the moment — spontaneous."

His most prized videos are from the mid-70s when the Philadelphia Flyers were known as the "Broad Street Bullies."

When his tape reaches one of these classics, he interrupts the conversation and replays the Flyers' Dave Schultz and the Maple Leafs' Dave (Tiger) Williams thrashing each other.

"It's when two guys get loose, give each other that look and go toe to toe," he said. "You wait to see who is going to land the haymaker that puts the other man out."

Parsons got into the fight memorabilia game when he answered Sandy Vigilante's ad in The Hockey News two years ago.

Vigilante, known as the "Godfather of Hockey Fights," was looking for people in the Toronto area to tape Canadian broadcasts in exchange for American ones. A native of Nutley, N.J., the 34-year-old postal worker has turned the habit into an obsession.

Along with more than 300 hours of hockey fights on video, Vigilante has a written record of every regular season NHL fight dating back to the early 1970s. Currently, he's dating fights back to the 1960s. Vigilante compiles his forgotten fight record by studying newspaper clippings in libraries.

"He started it all," says Todd Cummer, a fight devotee from Oshawa. "Anybody who collects fight tapes knows he's the main man. If you're looking for anything in the last 10 years, he probably has it."

Cummer and Parsons are Vigilante's two contacts in the Toronto area. Vigilante has at least two people taping and trading with him in every NHL city and one in every minor league city.

He started the phenomenon in 1978 when VCRs became popular.

"It's my life," said Vigilante, "Just getting games in this part of the country wasn't enough. I would pick up the morning paper to look at the summaries, and it would make me sick to find out about the heavyweights going the night before, and I couldn't see them."

Vigilante, who never played hockey as a youngster, won't stand for anyone using the word "goon" to describe one of his favorite brawlers.

"Never use that word. They're human beings, and good ones at that. The media does not have the knowledge to judge the fighters. They pay attention to players like Wayne Gretzky and other finesse players," says Vigilante.

Vigilante's favorite hockey hitman is Steve Durbano, a defenseman who played in St. Louis, Pittsburgh and the now defunct Colorado Rockies.

"He was a wild man," said Vigilante. "He knew the importance of setting the pace of the game and what intimidation could be used for.

"He wasn't a pretty player, or even a great fighter, for that matter. But he was tough. He would just keep coming."

While Vigilante and thousands of others are collecting and trading tapes, some enthusiasts are pirating the tapes for money, and the networks aren't pleased.

It is illegal to tape broadcasts even for personal use, they say, and the infringement of copyright could land a collector or pirate in court.

Frank Selke, business coordinator for Molstar, the company that produces Hockey Night in Canada, said there isn't much to discourage collectors.

Advertisements to buy and sell tapes, he said, are common in classified ads of every newspaper. Even if a bootlegger is convicted, fines are usually less than $45.

"It's illegal, and still there are all kinds of unauthorized fight tapes or highlight tapes around," said Selke. "We've got a constant eye on it, but it's fruitless for us to prosecute because the penalties don't even approach what they should be. The pirate is just going to turn around and open up the next day."

Vigilante said he's been told the league isn't thrilled about traders and collectors, but insists he isn't doing anything wrong.

"They say they don't like it, but I've never been threatened and they're well aware of what I'm doing. I'm not selling tapes at $50 or $60 a crack. I just trade. There's a ton of money in it, but I'm not interested in selling out."

Parsons is also aware of the money that could be made by peddling tapes but he wants no part of it.

"If you sell them, you're asking for trouble," Parsons said. "I don't like the idea of making a business out of it. But as far as recording and taping, that's no worse than you borrowing a record from me and taping it."

Just then, Parsons turns toward one of his three televisions. "Watch this," he said, rewinding the tape.

When he stops, Montreal's Chris Nilan is being thrown out of a game at Boston Garden. As he passes the Boston bench he takes a swipe at Ken Linsemen. Players and fans follow Nilan into the corridor beneath the stands and one can only guess what's going on.

Parsons leans back in his chair and smiles. — Vernon W. Smith, Feb. 17, 1989

* * *

John Bucyk

"I think the worst thing I ever did, in my book (Hockey In My Blood) I mentioned that I do read all my mail. I always have and I still do and I send stuff back. Then all of a sudden I got tons of mail requesting pucks, hockey sticks, gloves. That's something I just can't do. Most of the time the requests are for pictures, a lot of times they'll want a puck or something like that.

"There's some funny requests — people will request three or four team pictures like they grow on trees, but those are the type of things you can't do. If you start doing those you're going to be spending a fortune, but my own personal pictures I do mail out to anybody who asks for them." (Don't forget the SASE.)

Bucyk remembers an occasion when he visited a sick youngster who provided an emotional moment for the hockey star.

"I went to see one kid who had leukemia and it was a sad thing," Bucyk said. "We went to his house and we visited him there for a while, we took pictures with him. And then about a month later he passed away. I got a letter from his mother thanking me and she sent me the picture of the two of us and stated that he'd want me to have it. That kind of choked me up a bit."

Bucyk, like many former pros, has saved a great deal of memorabilia with which to remember. "I have enough plaques and trophies and stories that I could wallpaper a whole house. My most precious ones are the replicas of the Stanley Cup and the Prince of Wales (division trophy) and of course the Lady Bing Trophies and the Three Star Award in Boston, the Dufresne Trophy (for the Boston player who was most outstanding in home games). I won the Lester Patrick Trophy; that was a nice honor." — Douglas A. Letch, Jan. 12, 1990

* * *

Gordie Howe

According to Howe, at the age of 9 he began practicing his autograph signing along with his hockey skills. Clearly, the budding superstar had a keen sense of his destiny.

"As a young fellow," he recalls, "I received autographs from a local team in Saskatoon and I went home and I started practicing for the day that I would be asked for an autograph. I all but drove my mother crazy pulling at her skirt long enough to get her attention so she could pick which autograph she liked best. The one she chose is still the one that I use today. I like to think of my signature as a legacy of my mother."

To Howe, autograph signing should be an obligation among athletes.

"I feel everyone should sign autographs, because it's a real privilege to be asked. You strive all your life to gain recognition, and one of the most important ways people recognize you is to ask for your signature.

"Sports stars should always remember that the better the player the more autographs you be asked for. So it's a real pat on the back, one that most will never get again when they retire."

Sometimes a simple autograph can transcend fan worship and hobby collections. Through his long career, Howe has made a considerable impact on the lives of many people, including one Korean War veteran.

"I suppose a lot of signatures get thrown in the trash can but I've heard so many stories about an autograph really cheering somebody up. A few years back, for instance, a man walked up to me as I walked along the beach and asked me to stay put while he ran to get his two sons. When he returned he told me that, at the request of his mother several years previous, I had written him when he lay wounded in the war. He proceeded to tell me how much it meant to him and how it helped lift his spirits. He assured me that if I followed him to his car he'd show me that letter — a letter that he goes nowhere without."

While he is accommodating to a fault, there are certain times that Howe will refuse an autograph request.

"Fans have to look at things from the players' view," Howe emphasized, "such as what a loss does to him or because of a poor performance he might not want to talk with anyone. Or in the case of Wayne Gretzky or Mark Howe, they choose not to sign certain cards because they have reserved that card for their children only. Personally, I don't sign when I'm out at dinner.

"Some people even wave me over to their table when they are eating, but I'd never respond to that. I also no longer stop to sign when I'm with my wife and being seated at a table. I had done this in the past, but it shows poor taste towards my family." — Mark Willand, Nov. 23, 1990

* * *

Bobby Hull

Was Hull a card collector as a kid? "God no, I didn't" he says. "When we were kids growing up — I came from a family of 11 — we didn't have any extra money to buy bubble gum and what-have-you, so I never thought of collecting. Hockey was my dream and that's what I concentrated on."

Does Hull accept autograph requests through the mail? "Absolutely, I get autograph requests all the time," says Hull. "I'd be more than happy to help them (autograph seekers) out. Sometimes I get a little behind in my mail, but if they have patience, I'll get it to them."

Even though he doesn't collect cards, does Hull have a favorite of himself that he likes the most? "I think that card back close to my rookie year (1957-58) was pretty good," he says.

As far as personal mementos that Hull has saved over the years from his career, he says he has "almost a thousand of them." They include the Avco Cup (WHA playoff championship cup) that was won a couple of times in Winnipeg; the Canada Cup from 1976; the Art Ross Most Valuable Player trophy; the Prince of Whales trophy; the Lester Patrick award; a Father of the Year award which was presented to him by the Canadian Society of New York; pucks that reminded him of certain milestones he achieved, such as his first NHL goal, first hat trick, 50th goal (1962), 51st goal (1966) and his 100th, 200th, 300th, 400th 500th and 600th NHL goals, along with his 1,000th Major Pro Hockey goal.

He says they all mean something to him, not one any more than the other, because they all go into making a 23-year career — if he hadn't scored the first goal he wouldn't have been able to score the 51st.

Hull also owns mementos from other players, such as hockey sticks from Gordie Howe, Stan Mikita, Bobby Orr and Phil Esposito, along with hockey sticks from sons Brett and Bob.

Even though Hull doesn't collect cards, he does say that he has attended several card shows — Chicago, Detroit, Ottawa, Toronto, Smith Falls — as an autograph guest. Hull likes the card show circuit and would like to do more shows in the future. "You betcha, I'd be more than happy to go to any card shows that might be in easy traveling distance to Toronto," he says.

The reason he enjoys the shows, he says, is along with getting to see the different pictures of himself and other hockey players, he also gets to meet the people who supported him as fans during his career. — Fluffy Saccucci, Oct. 20, 1989

* * *

Eric Lindros

SCD: How did you react when you first saw your picture on the Score hockey cards?

Lindros: Overwhelmed. I was just overwhelmed and flattered.

SCD: Do you collect hockey cards or any other trading cards?

Lindros: No, I really don't. To tell you the truth, I don't understand why people collect things, whether it is cards or stamps or coins. If you want to save something as a reminiscence of an event or something you go to, that is one thing. But just to collect things, I don't understand. However, I have bought some packs of Score hockey cards.

SCD: Why?

Lindros: To see if I could get some Eric Lindros cards.

SCD: But didn't Score give you some?

Lindros: Yes, but I understand they are going to be valuable some day and I figure I can't have enough. I intend to get as many as I can. — Rick Firfer, March 21, 1991

* * *

Bobby Orr

Like other former NHL players, Orr knew about the explosion in sports cards. Another connection with Lindros led to Orr actually becoming involved in cards.

"There's a friend of mine, Ricky Curran, who happens to be Eric Lindros' agent," Orr says. "When he was a kid, he worked for me when we had our camp — he was a camper, counselor, and ran the pro shop. I've known Ricky a long time.

"He was friends with the people at Score. I hadn't really thought about the cards that much. Obviously, I followed how popular they were getting, what kind of business it was becoming. But Ricky called me and asked if I would be interested.

"I thought it might be fun, so I met the Score people. I enjoyed them. I believe they do a quality job. When I go into business with people, I like to enjoy them, and I do enjoy the Score people and we did the cards."

Score's proposal was to do a limited-issue Bobby Orr subset, randomly issued in wax packs of its 1991-92 hockey product. Orr signed 2,500 of the six-card black-bordered set. A total of 1,238 are issued in U.S. edition, with 1,238 issued in Canadian packs. The other 24 cards will be offered through a mail-in sweepstakes.

The six cards trace Orr's career through his childhood, junior days, early years with the Bruins, and Stanley Cup wins. Orr took an active part in the making of the cards.

"We looked at all the photos," he says. "I came up with some photos, and they tracked some down. We went over the info, stats and so on. It was fun."

Orr's first involvement with cards came when Topps shot photos for its hockey cards.

"I remember in Boston Garden the setup in the hallway outside our dressing room doorway, where we had to go for our photo shoot," Orr says of those early photos. He doesn't remember how much or even if he was paid for the photo.

"I think most of it was through the league or through the players' association," he says. "I don't remember being paid a fee. I think it was as it is now, with the exception of a few players. They might have paid us, I don't remember. It couldn't have been too much. I think between the league and the association, you might have been paid a flat fee."

His main involvement with the memorabilia hobby now is, of course, signing autographs.

"I don't do card shows and charge the kids for autographs," he says. "But I'm out and doing a lot of autographs. Sometimes there are 'collectors' — actually investors — expect so much. A lot of time there's a lot of people around, and you just don't have the time. Then they get upset with you. Some people just want the item signed, and you know they're going out and selling it.

"In many cases, it's messing it up for the person who just wants an autograph," he says. "They're in business and most of them are very enterprising people. It's a business. But sometimes I think they expect too much when there's large crowds around.

"I do not like to go to card shows and I just could not handle sitting there behind a barricade and seeing some little fellow not being able to afford an autograph. I find that a very difficult thing to do."

Orr admits he's still swamped for requests. "It's not bad at all," he says, laughing. "But we do a fair amount.

"Obviously, now we get a lot of cards. Everyone's gone into their basements and attics. We do sign a lot of cards now. We used to get the cards in the mail, but now you don't get many cards in the mail. I think they're afraid you won't send them back. I try to send them back."

Orr handles autographs the way he has handled everything — his on-ice play, his conduct with other people, his business ventures — with grace, style and class. — Don Butler, June 12, 1992

* * *

Jerry Roenick

Roenick thinks highly of the collectibles hobby, and he recently signed a deal with Fleer Corp. to autograph 2,000 cards for random insertion in Fleer's new Ultra hockey cards. "I think the collectibles hobby is a good thing," Roenick said. "It's challenging for kids and adults, and it's something the players also enjoy." Though not a serious collector, Roenick admitted to keeping cards of star players such as Wayne Gretzky and Mario Lemieux.

As for signing autographs, Roenick said he signs "whatever is put in front of me. I have no preferences about what I sign." The oddest thing he's ever signed? "A little kid's fire engine."...

...Roenick's signature is also highly sought by other NHL players. "I sign items all the time," he said. "A lot of the guys have friends at home and charities they're involved with. A lot of the players also like to collect." — Bob Cycon, Dec. 25, 1992

* * *

5 Is Easiest And Nicest, 0 Is Never Signs

Basketball 5s: J. Drew, D. Roundfield, G. Huston, A. English, B. Davis, T. LaGarde, J. Spanarkel, D. Thompson, C. Murphy, D. Bradley, J. Edwards, P. Ford, O. Birdsong, S. Wedman, S. Moncrief, Marques Johnson, M. Newlin, B. Cartwright, M Webster, J. Erving, W. Davis, A. Adams, R. Kelley, M. Gale, Mychal Thompson, Freeman Williams, S. Nater, J. Sikma, A. Dantley, D. Griffith and E. Hayes.

Basketball 4s: K. Vandeweghe, J.B. Carroll, J. Wilkes, J. Bridgeman, M. Lucas, D. Dawkins.

Basketball 3s: L. Bird, B. Robinzine, Larry Smith, L. Free, B. King, Q. Buckner, S. Lacey, N. Nixon, K. Washington, J. Silas, K. Porter, M. Brooks.

Basketball 2s: Eddie Johnson, R. Parish, K. Abdul-Jabbar, Truck Robinson.

Basketball 1s: John Johnson, Bob Lanier, George McGinnis and C. Maxwell.

Basketball 0s: Tiny Archibald, Moses Malone, Magic Johnson.

My All-Star team of nicest autographs is as follows: F) J. Erving, F) Marques Johnson, C) Bill Cartwright, G) P. Ford, G) C. Murphy, G) W. Davis. — Bill Dod, No Dod About It, June 20, 1981

* * *

Architectural tours with the 1973-74 hoops cards: A quiet mist had settled on Iola, like a pitcher of maple syrup spilled on a checkered tablecloth in a forlorn, rotted log cabin somewhere in the spruce-infested Northwoods...or an invisible fear wafting down from an alien space ray...One of the two, it's tough to decide...when Slothar and I left for a show in Throkk, N.Y.

I was representing Krause Publications' sports department; Slothar, an elephant pelt dealer, was not. However, we both were attending the 23rd annual Basketball Card/Endangered Animal Skin Traders Conference, annually held at the luxurious Sven's Boarding House.

The night before the conference began, Lothar and I stopped in the dining car, where he had roots and berries while I had a delicious meal consisting of chocolate mousse, chocolate cake, and chocolate ice cream. With our fair-skinned waitress delivering libations consisting of pureed chickpeas and chocolate soda, I would rate this as one of the least whimsical feasts I have ever engaged in at this convention.

Slothar and I parted ways the following morning, when the sun was bursting upon our mauve and wood-panelled walls like a supernova signalling the death of yet another solar system...Or the flashlight of one of our diligent police officers discovering a critical clue to a kidnapping case in some murky and wind-swept bushes one dark and stormy night...One of the two.

For breakfast I was served Little Round Crunchy Things That Are Bad For Your Health But Advertised Otherwise; I enjoyed the meal immensely but wished there was more chocolate topping. I traversed the hall in search of some, but my Sherlockian inspections of other room service offal left me feeling a bit peckish.

My conference began shortly after in the Main Conference Room, a gaily-lit edifice thanks to the large hole in the aluminum roof. Sven had once again thoughtfully remembered to remove the cattle from the set-up area, so we knew right away this convention would be a success.

The autograph guests included Bob Feller, Jose Canseco's manager and Honus Wagner (who used a special autographing device attached to his right ulna; flat items only). I had to skip this exciting fare for the conference, however.

One of the first topics at the seminar was "The Silliest Looking Basketball Set of All Time." One of the sets was the 1973-74 effort rendered by Topps.

I could barely believe my sensory input devices. This, one of my favorite basketball sets of all time, being cut down like so much pork gristle!

Bad photography, they said. One of the worst cards of all time in that set, they said. Few action shots, they said.

It all depends on how you look at it. Here, then, is my defense of that important basketball issue, which should stand as a cultural milestone instead of being trussed up like a Thanksgiving Day pilgrim.

The '73-74 basketball set can be divided into three major subsets: Architectural Tours, Adam West Tributes, and the Ansel Adams Collection.

Some might call the '73-74 set unsophisticated — thoughtless, blurry and indistinct action shots and bad posed shots. It should actually be seen as high art and we should be grateful Topps thought enough to bring a taste of different artistic schools to card collectors who live with their parents at age 40. The set takes us through architecture, acting, and, yes, inspired photography.

Architecture: This unique service offered by Topps features a number of ABA and NBA players modeling in front of their favorite indoor support structures (commonly called walls). We see no fewer than 20 different structures, though it's difficult to tell if any were the brainchilds of the likes of Frank Lloyd Wright or Eero Saarinen, since most are just walls.

But what walls! There's half the Blazer team, strking fearsome poses before a fieldstone number. And there's future coach Don Nelson, representing the Celtics, poised in front of some good ol' painted brick. Fred Hilton of the Braves finds the drywall behind the baseline to be worth defending; the Rockets' Julius Keye thinks the same of the sideline wall. The Milwaukee Bucks appreciated the netting at their nearby racquetball club enough to enshrine it on their cards; the Kings found the bathroom tile to be more to their liking.

Phil Chenier of the Bullets prefers the wood paneling look. Cliff Meely, breaking the mold in singularly spectacular fashion, seems to seek solace in the great outdoors as he assumes a Johnny Unitas pose against a lazy summer league sky.

Acting: As commanded by those fearsome Topps photographers — many of whom have gone on, I presume, to direct such Hollywood classics as Friday the 13th Part V — A New Hibachi — the subjects of the Topps set brought forth all their dramatic abilities to simulate a real-live NBA game.

There's Toby Kimball, assuming his dangerous one-handed set shot. And Otto Moore, straining mightily to stuff a basketball through an invisible square. And Roland Taylor, doing the fabled ABA Bunny Hop/Watusi in obvious glee. And Mack Calvin's All-Star card is taken from a real-life situation as he completes a 100-yard dash moments before being closelined by a Virginia Squire.

Discovering the aesthetic interplay of light and dark photography: Look at all those background photos. Aren't they great? Dwight Davis even has two shadows on his card. So that's my defense of that remarkable set. I'm glad it's had an influence over such outstanding sets as the King B Jerky baseball set. — Don Butler, The Butler Did It, Sept. 15, 1989

* * *

The Worst Card Ever Made Straight From That '73-74 Hoops Set

It's probably the worst-conceived, worst-executed card in basketball history. Kind of like Plan Nine From Outer Space of the card world. Or "In the Navy" of the card world. Or People Magazine Salutes 50 Years of Television. Except this card was never popular.

In the middle of the run of ABA All-Stars in the 1973-74 Topps basketball set is #220, Warren Jabali. Cards in front of his and in back of his feature grainy, unfocused, poorly-done action shots; but action shots nonetheless. There was no action shot of Jabali in the Topps files, evidently, so instead of doing the intelligent thing and simply featuring him on a posed shot, Jabali was cropped from a posed photo (presumably standing in front of a blue wall in a cramped gym, as commanded by the Topps photographer) and placed in the middle of an action shot.

That's not the best part, even though poor Warren appears to be holding up the game while he poses for the camera. The best part is that the Denver Rockets guard has been placed in the middle of a game between the visiting Indiana Pacers and the New York Nets.

It's classic stuff. It really is. — Don Butler, The Butler Did It, Sept. 15, 1989

* * *

Collecting Kareem And Kareem On Collecting

From the March 17, 1989, SCD:

Abdul-Jabbar has never been known as an easy autograph. Here are a few quotes detailing Kareem's view from the other side of the table:

"It's strange but when I sign 'Kareem' people get upset. 'Kareem Abdul-Jabbar' is so long it cuts down on the number of autographs I can give by half, so now I sign 'Abdul-Jabbar' and everyone seems to be happy." — (Giant Steps, 1983)

"Signing and signing is OK for a while. But you know something about autographs? You know where they end up? Under the couch, in the desk drawers, stashed away in files and between letters and odd stuff. That bothers me." (Sports Illustrated, March 1969).

"I never used to get a lot of autographs, could never really understand the appeal of my signature on scrap paper. (Once when I was in grade school I had waited on an autumn Sunday outside the Yankee Stadium locker room door and gotten a whole sheet full of football Giant autographs. I took them to St. Jude's the next day. By the end of the week they were lost, and I found them that summer stuck down inside the couch.) Often people are incredibly inconsiderate, interrupting meals and conversation to plunk down paper and make rude demands. A lifetime of this kind of interruption — constantly, at every public meal every day, year in, year out — will make the most even-tempered person abrupt. Plus I felt like signing autographs somehow acknowledge a lack of their own significance. Cheryl told me that no matter how commonplace the experience was for me, these people were showing gratitude and admiration, and it was insulting to ignore them when they were honoring me. I'd never thought of it that way; I'd thought of it as an inconvenience imposed by pests. From then on I tried to be easier about it." (Giant Steps, 1983).

* * *

Stacey Augmon

SCD: Have you saved any special memorabilia from your career?

Augmon: Yes. I have a team ball signed by the 1988 Olympic basketball team that I played on. That was a special time for me and the ball brings back memories. But I don't need a lot of mementos. What I really appreciate is the recognition I get for my skills. I especially like when we are seen on national television. — Rick Firfer, March 20, 1992

* * *

Rick Barry

Presently, Barry does not collect cards of any kind at all, but he does relate a story with a strange twist to it. According to Barry, he said that while he was working in the booth for TNT, a card depicting him as a broadcaster was issued in limited edition and that people had told him that each card was worth up to $1,000.

"I had a bunch of them that were given to me and people were sending me requests for autographs. I had been sending out those cards with my signature on them for autograph seekers free of charge, so some people were getting incredible gifts from me in the mail," joked Barry.

As for his personal favorite card of himself, Barry claims that he doesn't have one. However, there are two that he particularly dislikes.

"I only had a moustache for about 30 days in my life and the photographers took two pictures of me sporting a moustache one year while I was with the Warriors. One card is a full-length shot and the other is a head shot, and I don't particularly like them," said Barry. — Fluffy Saccucci, June 19, 1992

* * *

Lou Carnesecca

Carnesecca wants his ugly sweater back. Little Louie may not get it back...ever. But Louie may be the first person ever to get into the basketball shrine after his sweater got there. The sweater made it in 1985 after he led St. John's to the Final Four. The body gets there on May 11.

"How would you like a sweater to beat you out?" asked Carnesecca. "Isn't that amazing? I'll tell you, it's a wonderful feeling to be voted in, and the sweater thing is a fun thing. I think people can relate to Lou Carnesecca when they look at the sweater. That's important. It's just not the wins and losses, it's the atmosphere. It's not just a basket made here or there, there is something beyond that.

"It was the ugliest sweater. I pulled it out of the closet and put it in my valise and went out to Pittsburgh. I put that thing on, we hit a shot at the end of the ball game...I had to wear it. If I didn't wear it, the kids would start looking at me. It became a signal or something. But don't knock it, I got a lot of wins out of it." — Evan Weiner, April 24, 1992

* * *

Bob Cousy

If you expect to see Cousy as a special guest at card shows, forget it. He says that he has never done them and doesn't expect to do any in the future either. Confesses Cousy, "I've turned down every request up to now because I don't feel that I want to get up before an audience of fans and charge them for autographs."

He does, however, respond to autograph requests through the mail. "I respond to all of the autograph requests just as long as there is a self-addressed stamped envelope. I have the 8x10 photos that I send out, and I also sign cards and everything else that is sent to me and then I send it back, free of charge," he says.

"You know it sounds corny, but I still feel privileged, especially after almost 30 years of not having played, that I still get the number of (autograph) requests that I do (get)," he adds...

...As for his thoughts on athletes charging for autographs at card shows, Cousy says that he doesn't like it. "I have even less tolerance for athletes who are earning two or three million dollars a year and charging for autographs. I think this is unconscionable," he adds.

He concedes, however, that he does think it's more justified for old jocks who are still out there grinding out a living to charge money for autographs and sincerely adds, "If this is an opportunity (for them) to earn some needed dollars, then this would have an impact on my feelings." — Fluffy Saccucci, July 19, 1991

* * *

Kendall Gill

SCD: What's the most unusual item you've ever been asked to sign?
Gill: (smiling) I can't tell you that.
SCD: (laughing) How about one that can be printed?
Gill: A guy asked me to engrave my name in his car dashboard panel. — Tol Broome, Nov. 29, 1991

* * *

Larry Johnson

"Larry said he has been kidding Dikembe Mutumbo because it took Mutumbo and Dominique Wilkins to do the subset last year, and he is doing it all by himself this year," said Ted Taylor, Fleer director of hobby relations.

Being involved with this subset has given Johnson, who never collected cards, a taste of what the hobby is all about.

"I feel honored," he said. "They could have picked all these other guys, and they chose me. It's something you have to take in stride. This is a great time for me to start collecting cards. I could start investing in myself." — Tom Hultman, Sept. 25, 1992

* * *

Michael Jordan

Jordan's attitude refreshing

It was refreshing to recently read a baseball hobby show promoter's retraction in the Chicago Tribune that Michael Jordan would appear at his show for the purpose of signing autographs for a rather hefty stipend. An annoyed Mr. Jordan stated that he never charged for his autograph and would not appear at the show.

An autograph used to be a memento of a priceless moment when one met his sports hero and obtained his autograph as proof of that priceless moment.

Baseball card collecting is no longer a hobby or fun, for even the youngest of collectors has baseball cards taken from him and placed in a plastic sleeve to avoid the wear and tear in the expectation that the cards will soon be valuable.

It is the same with autographs, which are only regarded as an investment that is expected to rise in value with the passing years.

In this day of money-grabbing sport show promoters and baseball card dealers, it is indeed refreshing to find someone like Michael Jordan who doesn't put a price on everything in life. — Lionel Carter, Evanston, Ill., Reader Reaction, May 13, 1988

* * *

Bob Lanier

Bob Lanier's sneakers aren't in Springfield. They should be, since he wore a size 22...the largest in the NBA throughout his 14 years. The largest until Alton Lister came around. When Lister came, Lanier knew it was time to leave.

"You know what happened?" asked Lanier. "The joker came in (to Milwaukee), and that's when I knew it was over. He fit in my sneakers and started to use my sneakers to practice because he didn't have any sneakers at the time."

"When you got a big foot like mine and someone comes around to fill it, you know it's time to leave. He stole my shoes and he is still going strong. And there was nothing for me to do. He filled my shoes."

Until Lister came around, no one came close to filling Lanier's shoes. "A lot of people put their two feet in my shoes, but no one came close."

Lanier still had those big feet and cannot buy shoes in the normal manner; all of his shoes were custom made. — Evan Weiner, April 24, 1992

* * *

"Easy Ed" Macauley

It was during his sophomore season that "Easy" became a part of Macauley's moniker. He explains how it came about.

"We had rotating captains, so we didn't have the same captain for each game. I think it was the first game of the season and Coach Flanigan said, 'You're the captain for the night.' Literally, my only job was to take the team from the basement dressing room at the SLU gymnasium on West Pine up a spiral staircase, through a door and out onto the basketball court. The other guys were supposed to follow me.

"So I went out of the dressing room and up the staircase, through the door and dribbled down to the other end of the floor and took two or three shots. I suddenly turned around and looked and nobody had followed me. The reason they hadn't followed me is the national anthem was being played and I didn't even hear it. I'm down there shooting and they're playing the national anthem.

"The people in the stands started yelling, 'Take it easy, Ed, take it easy. The game hasn't started.' Well, we had a very bright sports information director by the name of Warren Boecklen, and he liked the term and he started using it in press releases. The greatest thing that can happen to you in sports is a nickname...Stan the Man, the Rocket Richard, etc.

"We go to some Hall of Fame golf tournaments and the hockey players never say Maurice or Richard, they always say The Rocket. Anyway, it caught on and it fit my style of basketball, because that's

the way I was. A lot of people thought that's why I got the name, because of the way I played. But I got it because of my stupidity, rather than my grace or skill." — Rick Hines, March 15, 1991

SCD: You've seen basketball cards of yourself. What was your reaction the first time you saw one?

EM: I thought, wow! It kind of takes you to a new plateau of importance. Golly, they've got a card about me. It's like seeing your name in a crossword puzzle. It's flattering. — Rick Hines, March 15, 1991

* * *

George Mikan

While Mikan became the Cadillac by which other college and pro players were measured before he was through, he started out as a jalopy.

"When I used to take the floor they'd kid me; I used to trip over the lines...they were too high. We jumped a lot of rope and (De Paul Coach Ray) Meyer put me running on the track team for confidence.

"One of the things that we always laugh about, he'd have me go to all of the dances and he'd keep sending all the short girls up to dance with me so I'd learn how to move around and not step on their toes. It was all confidence-building kinds of things...jumping rope, boxing, doing rebounding drills, doing the Mikan drill (figure eights) and all those kinds of things."...

...SCD: So you don't mind signing autographs for fans?

GM: Not really. The only thing I object to is the fellows that are charging and making money off the situation. Vern Mikkelsen (former teammate of Mikan's at Minneapolis), myself and some of my friends gave some memorabilia to a fellow from New Jersey and the next thing we knew the guy sold it in an open auction and picked up a lot of money. This is sort of repugnant to myself and my friends. We didn't do it for that basis. Here's a fellow that really took advantage of us. I'm careful now...

SCD: What's the most unusual thing you've been asked to sign?

GM: Toilet paper. People run out of material and they grab anything available, like hand towels. We autograph a lot of shirts, hats, just about anything.

SCD: Is there you won't sign?

GM: Well, everything has to have a little dignity to it. Like gals come up and say, 'sign my brassiere.' That isn't my kind of stick. One of my theories is that I don't like to disillusion the youngsters. We try to do everything with dignity and above board. We follow out on that...

...SCD: Your 1948 Bowman card is valued at $2,500. Do you have any cards of yourself?

GM: I had an unfortunate thing happen. Ten or 12 years ago we had a fire in our house and I lost a lot of that stuff. So I don't really know where there are any cards. I don't have any. I checked with my relatives and no one seems to have one.

SCD: What was your reaction the first time you saw a card of yourself?

GM: Well, you know, you're always flattered. It's a touch of immortality. You know that people do collect them, and at the time we didn't put any significance to it about values and that. And then as time went by we saw the great following for trading cards and keeping the cards and having these collections. So if I'd only known, I could have gotten a case of them. But I guess that's why they're valuable. — Rick Hines, July 19, 1991

* * *

Chris Mullin

SCD: What's your attitude toward basketball cards today?

Mullin: They're nice. They give people something to do. I think one thing it's done is brought a lot of notoriety to everybody.

Now everybody, they see you on these cards, and then you've got a lot of autographs to sign, so it's good and bad.

SCD: How do you feel about signing autographs?

Mullin: They're all right. One per, you know. As long as they just want your autograph and are not running to the card shop to sell them. — Tol Broome, Dec. 11, 1992

* * *

Shaquille O'Neal

SCD: How do you view your role off the court, as opposed to your role on the court?

O'Neal: Athletes like me are viewed as role models. We should live up to those expectations but not carry it too far. It is good to be able to set a standard for the kids to look up to, but we are not their parents. They have to look to their parents for what is right and wrong, but we should help with that standard in the way we act. If it wasn't for my parents, I wouldn't be where I am now. — Rick Firfer, Aug. 7, 1992

* * *

John Paxson

SCD: Are there any particular instances of fan interaction that stick out in your memory?

Paxson: I remember getting a letter from a young guy when I was in college. I've lost touch with him now. But his brother had been killed in an accident and we sent him some practice jerseys because he followed the team and it lifted his spirits. Sometimes these things mean more than we really know.

On the other hand, I have seen some situations that weren't so nice, like the time Michael Jordan was getting on the team bus and he really didn't have time to stop for anyone, and some woman started yelling at him. It wasn't pretty. Some people just have their own agenda, I guess. But when people are polite to you, you like to be nice to them, too. — Rick Firfer, March 20, 1992

* * *

Scottie Pippen

Scottie Pippen still remembers the first time he saw his picture on a basketball card.

It was his second year in the NBA, and the card was his 1988-89 Fleer rookie card.

Since then, Pippen has won two NBA championship rings and an Olympic gold medal. But he still fondly remembers the thrill of seeing himself on a simple piece of cardboard.

"It was really neat," says the Chicago Bulls superstar. "You always look forward to the opportunity to be on your first card. Once you get on one, you think it's the neatest thing." Tony Prudom, Dec. 25, 1992

* * *

Jim Pollard

"Today, some of these athletes won't walk across the street unless they get paid for it. I think that's a lot to do with the agents they have. The agents are always looking to pick up extra money and they get a percentage any time they can arrange a speech or go to a card signing place or something.

"To me, I think it's ridiculous to go to a card show and charge a youngster five bucks for your autograph. They must have a guy standing behind you counting every time you write your name. I think it's ridiculous, but there's still big money in it. People are willing to pay. The attitude today, get what you can." — Rick Hines, Sept. 27, 1991

* * *

Terry Porter

SCD: You mentioned all the sports collectibles that are on the market these days. Did you ever see the 1989 Starting Lineup Kenner figure of yourself?

Porter: (laughs) Huh? I've never seen this one! Geez, is this supposed to be me? This guy has too much hair! See, NBA Properties comes out with so much stuff the players don't have a chance to keep up.

SCD: Kenner puts these out every year. Your Kenner statue was real tough to find. It might be one of the rare ones.

Porter: I'd say it's rare! I never saw it before! Nobody ever came up to me in Portland and asked me to sign one or anything...

...SCD: With any kind of luck, maybe you'll be on the cover of SCD with this interview.

Porter: That would be great. I've never been on the cover of anything.

SCD: At least you're in Sports Illustrated a lot.

Porter: I'll tell you, you're right. (Laughs). I'm in Sports Illustrated quite a bit. My mug's been in there now and then, but I'm usually a victim. — Tim Sullivan and Randy Wievel, Nov. 22, 1991

* * *

David Robinson

Robinson has mostly good things to say about the basketball card hobby, particularly for kids.

"As long as they don't get too caught up in the whole thing as a business, it's a positive thing," he said of younger collectors. — Tol Broome, June 19, 1992

* * *

Oscar Robertson

SCD: How do you feel about signing autographs?

Robertson: If people are nice, I don't mind. Sometimes people think you owe them something and you don't. As an athlete you don't owe them anything, but a great performance.

People have to understand it's a two-way street. I know a lot of athletes now are nasty and don't understand what it's all about. But people can provoke them, too.

Once you understand it's a two-way street you get a better understanding about signing autographs. I don't mind signing autographs — I've signed them all my life.

A lot of people complain about certain players who won't do this or that. It's up to the individual player, I guess.

SCD: Do you sign through the mail?

Robertson: (laughing) Every day! It's a funny thing about that. You find out who the real collectors are with that. Guys who send eight or nine different pictures to sign, I send them back unsigned.

I think if it's a true collector who wants one for a collection, then I'll sign for him. But if he sends eight or nine I know he wants to sell them.

I was in Memphis and a guy asked me to sign his cards. I said, "Fine, what's your name?" He said, "No, don't put a name on it." You see, he wanted to sell them. I said, "Here, take these back. I won't sign them because I know what you're trying to do with them."

But normally I don't mind signing. I know people enjoy it, so it's fine with me. — Jeff Schaefer, Jan. 3, 1992

* * *

John Stockton

SCD: Did you collect trading cards or autographs as a kid?

Stockton: No, I didn't collect cards or autographs. I did collect beer cans for a while, though. Probably because my dad owned a bar.

SCD: Do you collect anything now — cards, autographs or memorabilia?

Stockton: I don't really collect anything, but I do have some signed balls and things from my teammates for the rec room. Mainly, my wife saves these things. I know some of the other players are more serious about trading and collecting things. I'm happy to oblige when someone asks. — Rick Firfer, June 19, 1992

* * *

Isiah Thomas

"When people write in and ask for autographs, I sign them and send them back," Thomas said. "Most of the time I answer them, even if they don't send an envelope." — Sean McDevitt, Aug. 17, 1990

* * *

Jerry West

SCD: You mentioned the card memorabilia business. What is your attitude toward the card memorabilia hobby? How involved are you in it?

West: Well, really not any. I do not go to autograph card shows. Obviously, I get a lot of stuff sent to me here at the Forum, which I do sign, but I do not go to the card shows.

SCD: What's your reasoning behind that?

West: It's just my personal feeling. I don't know, it's just something about if a kid comes and asks you to sign something, I just have a hard time...I have a different feeling about that. I think that this has become a business that people freely trade and sell. It's my personal feeling.

SCD: Have you ever personally collected anything or saved anything from your playing days?

West: I have some memorabilia obviously, but it's not prominently displayed in my house. I do have some things — uniforms, stuff like that. I don't have any of my old cards, but I do know the value of some of them. — Don Butler, April 24, 1992

* * *

John Wooden/Dale Brown

I wrote to Coach John Wooden in early November 1990, asking him for an autographed picture. I included a sports article that I'd written as a gift for him, and asked him to answer two questions — what he enjoyed most about coaching at UCLA, and what values he attempted to teach his players.

About three weeks later, I received a letter from Wooden, with an autographed 4-by-6-inch color photograph.

His letter answered my questions.

"My greatest enjoyment in teaching was in working with young people and in seeing them graduate from school and on into productive lives," Wooden explained.

"Love and balance are the values that I tried to teach. Be considerate of others; do not be disagreeable when you disagree; listen; do not worry about the things over which you have no control; be more concerned with your character than your reputation; make every effort to do the very best of which you are capable in everything you do."

"No written word, no spoken plea can teach our youth what they should be, nor all the books on all the shelves," Wooden added. "It's what the teachers are themselves."

Coach Wooden included a creed that his father gave him when he was 12. He said he's tried to live by this creed ever since.

"Be true to yourself; make each day your masterpiece; help others; drink deeply from books; make friendships a fine art," Wooden quoted. "Build a shelter against a rainy day, and pray for guidance, giving thanks for your blessings every day."

With his letter Wooden also included a chart called "The Pyramid of Success." He defined success, too.

"Success is a peace of mind which is a direct result in self satisfaction in knowing that you did your best to become the best that you are capable of becoming," Wooden explained...

...A familiar participant at NCAA basketball tournaments for many years, Coach Dale Brown of Louisiana State University has coached his team to the "Final Four" once and the Southeastern Conference championship and SEC tournament championship several times.

Many of his players have excelled in the National Basketball Association, including center Dwayne Scales.

I wrote to Coach Brown in late November 1990. I also sent him an article that I'd written as a gift, and asked him for an autographed photo.

I posed some questions, too, inquiring about which of his victories was the most difficult to obtain.

About two weeks later, I received a 10-by-8-inch color photograph which included two pictures he had signed and inscribed for me, "Pride, never give up, and remember God doesn't make any junk. Dale Brown."

That day I received a letter from Coach Brown, an LSU bumper sticker, a schedule and an inspirational essay.

"You asked me which of my victories was the most difficult to obtain and why. I suspect our win over Kentucky on Feb. 11, 1978, was the most difficult when they were ranked #1 in the nation, went on to win the NCAA title, and we beat them 95-94 with all of our starters on the bench," Brown said.

"Also, you inquired about what values do you attempt to teach your players. I guess it's very simple; to have confidence, work hard, persevere, and follow the Lord's plan and everything will work out fine."

I found the inspirational essay, "Keeping Christmas," that Coach Brown shared with me, meaningful. An excerpt follows in the next paragraph.

"Are you willing to stoop down and consider the needs and the desires of little children; to remember the weakness and loneliness of people who are growing old; to stop asking how much your friends love you, and ask yourself whether you love them enough...are you willing to do these things even for a day?

"Then you can keep Christmas, and if you keep it for a day, why not always? But you can never keep it alone. It must be shared like love."
— Pride Sherrill, Jan. 18, 1991

* * *

James "Buster" Douglas

Although Douglas doesn't collect much of anything, he has, however, saved a few mementos from his boxing career. Included are the boxing gloves that he used to defeat Tyson with, trunks, shoes, and his World Heavyweight championship belt. He also has hung on to many awards and plaques that he has received during his career. — Fluffy Saccucci, Nov. 2, 1990

* * *

George Foreman

Even though Foreman is not a card collector, to say the least, he does claim to have a personal favorite card. He describes it as an Olympic series of small-size cards that told a little bit about Olympic history and which pictured all different sport athletes. Foreman says that he really enjoyed that set, and in particular the card that shows him hitting the punching bag on the front of the card with a small biography of him illustrated on the back.

Also a part of Foreman's personal collection are boxing gloves that he has kept from his previous fights, a boxing glove that was personally hand-signed by former heavyweight legends Muhammad Ali, Joe Frazier and Larry Holmes, and a baseball bat inscribed with the signatures of future Hall of Fame slugger "Mr. October," Reggie Jackson. — Fluffy Saccucci, March 29, 1991

* * *

Evander Holyfield

Even though Holyfield has accumulated 25 pro victories in the ring, he has yet to collect a single card of any kind. However, he does say that he has unautographed photos mounted on his wall at home which depict pro players from the Atlanta area, such as former Brave slugger Hank Aaron, former Falcon running back Dave Hampton, and others...

...Although not a card collector, Holyfield has saved many things that he has used during his career. Included are all of his Olympic gear, gloves and all the gear that was used in every championship fight that he appeared in. However, Holyfield adds that he hasn't saved any gear from any other athletes. — Fluffy Saccucci, March 29, 1991

* * *

Floyd Patterson

Although never a collector of cards, Patterson said that when he was young he had a scrapbook filled with newspaper and magazine clippings of heavyweight great Joe Louis. "I don't have that Joe Louis scrapbook anymore and I don't know what happened to it," he says. He does have his pre-Olympic Golden Gloves robe, Olympic robe and gold medal — all from his amateur career.

From his pro career he has his two world heavyweight title belts, "one when I first won the title and the other when I regained it," along with the Everett J. Neal Award which he received twice, in 1956 and 1960, for being named the best fighter of those two respective years.

As for having collected memorabilia from other boxers, Patterson says that he hasn't, "although if I had Joe Louis' trunks I would be delighted."

The eloquent-speaking Patterson says that he does not sign autograph requests from collectors through the mail, and he states valid reasons for not doing so. "I don't sign the requests because I suspect the collectors are selling my autographs for money and I don't like that," states Patterson.

He elaborates on his suspicions by saying that in the past he has received 10, 15 or 20 different items to sign from the same people and has even written down their names to keep track of them. Patterson goes on to single out one collector, whom he refuses to name, who really irks him.

"Every month he sends me a form letter and he requests from me three or four things to be signed, so I'm under the impression that he does it with a lot of other celebrities because he uses a form letter. What I do is read the letter and then disregard him," says Patterson. — Fluffy Saccucci, May 15, 1992

* * *

Bill Shoemaker

Forget all the #1 draft picks, the top prospects and the future stars. The top rookie card of 1991 features a legend.

Six decades and 8,933 victories later, Hall of Fame jockey Bill Shoemaker is finally featured on a trading card.

Shoe is the subject of seven cards in the recently-released Jockey Star Cards set. He is featured on the promotional card and six cards, from the regular issue, honoring his six decades of competition.

This 220-card set is more than just a nice collectible for Shoemaker and all jockeys, past and present; it commemorates the 50th anniversary of the Jockeys' Guild.

The royalties from this product will benefit the Jockeys' Guild Fund for Permanently Disabled Riders. Shoemaker, who served as president of the guild for 15 years, and the other jockeys in the set, receive no proceeds.

They welcomed the opportunity to appear on cards for a cause to benefit predecessors, peers and, unfortunately, possibly even themselves in future years...

...When asked how it feels to be featured on a card, he simply replied, "It's always nice," referring to publicity in general.

Shoemaker serves as the spokesman for the Jockey Star Cards. While many of the present jockeys are excited about seeing themselves on a card, Shoemaker is focused on what the card set can do for the guild.

"We hope to get better insurance and a pension. Right now the IRS considers us independent businessmen," he explained.

Jockeys do not receive the many benefits that athletes from other sports enjoy, yet the physical demands of a jockey and the risk of injury are much greater than many other sports. — Jeff Kurowski, May 10, 1991

* * *

Top row, left to right: Alan Rosen, Joshua Evans; Larry Fritsch; Gloria Rothstein; "Red" Wimmer. Middle row: Bill Goodwin; Eileen and Lou Brown; Tony Galovich; Rich Hawksley. Bottom row: (clockwise, from left) Bill Mastro, Walter Hall, Alan Rosen and Frank Nagy; Jim Hawkins, Red Wimmer; Mark Jordan, Dick DeCourcy; Ron Lewis.

Right off the bat, we'll start with the complaints: 1) Dealers are just in it for the money. I would never consider selling a baseball card to make a profit. 2) Dealers are crooks. You're lucky if they pay you 60 percent of book value for a card. 3) I just bought a wax pack from that dealer over there and didn't even get a single card worth over a dollar. He must be opening and resealing the packs. 4) Dealers are ripping us collectors off. I had to pay $33 for a box of '88 Fleer wax today.

In an April 1, 1988, Designated Editor column, dealer Robert Hershaw offered his rebuttals to these generalizations made by collectors about dealers. His responses, in part: 1) "Aren't dealers basically doing the same thing as grocery, bulk, and convenience stores are when selling baseball cards? You never hear people say, 'K-Mart sets should be banned from the pages of SCD because K-Mart sold Donruss cards last year at retail price, and made a profit at the expense of the hobbyists.'"

2) "The dealer is buying with intent to make a future profit. Second, at a typical show, the dealer can expect to pay for: at least one table,

food, gas, maybe a hotel room, and possibly even airfare."

3) "Collectors who like to gamble on older wax packs (and even the newer ones) just don't seem to understand that the chances of getting the key card from a set in ONE pack are pretty slim...what collectors don't realize is that, for most dealers that are in the hobby to financially succeed, it is not worth the while to tamper with unopened packs. The reason for this is that it would be simply too time consuming to go through each pack, take out the stars, replace the stars with commons, and then reseal them with some villainous device, to be profitable. There also is the risk of actually being caught at the practice, too, and the chance of tarnishing one's reputation is generally recognized as not worth the risk."

4) "Buying a box of Fleer for $30 to $35 is just assuring the dealer that the price should stay up. In effect, you ARE being ripped off. But the truth is, you are ripping yourself off. Do you honestly think that if collectors refused to pay anything above retail price for current year cards that dealers would still expect to get up to $35 a box? No way!"

The Sad News Came In A Phone Call

By Lionel Carter — Jan. 21, 1983

The sad news came in a phone call from Bill Mastro on Nov. 27: Buck Barker was dead.

This was truly sad news, and especially so, following so closely on the heels of the passing of Bob Jaspersen. I wrote Alice Barker, who I had met on several visits to the Barker home, for further details. Buck had gone to the hospital for a gall bladder operation on Nov. 24 and, to quote from her letter: "One day he is doing fine, and the next morning at 4:30 they called and said he died." And her letter continues: "We all loved Buck so much. He was good to everyone and everything."

The obituary was all too brief: "Barker, Charles C., Wed. Nov. 24, 1982, beloved husband of Alice M. Barker (nee Wiethuechter), dear father of Patricia J. Eberhardt, dear brother of Constance Amsinger, grandfather of Elaine Sparks and Michael Eberhardt. Funeral from Drehmann-Harral Chapel, 7733 Natural Bridge, 1 p.m., Sat. Nov. 27. Interment New St. Marcus. Visitation after 4 p.m. Fri."

Irving M. Lerber's Who's Who in Card Collecting lists Buck's date of birth as May 14, 1911, so Buck was 71.

But we feel that we know Buck a little better than that, although we have been unable to determine just when our card collecting paths first crossed. A search of Jeff Burdick's early Card Collectors Bulletins failed to turn up Buck's name, so he had not been as lucky as I had been in finding Burdick in 1938 and having a whole new world of card collecting and card collectors opened up for me.

Perhaps it was not until I returned from World War II in the Pacific that we began to correspond. He was what might be termed a "card collector's card collector." He was about as interested in adding to your collection as he was in adding to his own. Send him a want list, and he'd mail back a stack of cards along with his want list and write: "Send me some of my wants in return when you come up with some?"

But I always seemed to have stacks of his duplicates on hand just waiting to become part of my collection if only I could find some cards he wanted. Often it became a rather complicated deal of swapping my duplicates to other collectors for Buck's wants so I could swap them to him. The point was finally reached when I reluctantly returned the remaining cards I had which he had sent, as I just couldn't come up with any of his wants. Buck wouldn't have cared, he would have given them to me. But that would ruin all the fun of swapping and with it collecting as well.

It must have been in 1954 that we first met. He paid me a visit, bringing more baseball cards in his suitcase than clothes. I invited Bob Wilson over for an evening of fun. Each of us was assigned a room in our three-room apartment and over the bed, sofa, or table (depending on which room one had) we spread our duplicates and whipped out our want lists. From room to room the three of us would go, swapping cards until the wee hours of the morning, experiencing the true joy of card collecting. None of us was trying to get the best of each deal for himself, but trying to see that the other person got the best of the deal. It was truly great.

Then there was July 9, 1958. I don't know who had written first, but suddenly I had lined up Charles Bray of East Bangor, Pa., the publisher of the Card Collectors Bulletin, Preston Orem of Altadena, Calif., and Buck Barker of St. Louis, to which I added local collectors Bob Wilson, John Sullivan, Bill Leonard and Bob Solon. Four members of the "Sport Collectors Hall of Fame" together for the same evening! That has always remained my "most wonderful evening of card collecting." Maybe this was the "first convention."

Although I've had a lot of fun and excitement at conventions in Los Angeles, Detroit and Chicago, none of this ever reached the pinnacle attained by this evening. It was the first time I'd ever seen a Hans Wagner in T206 and a Ty Cobb card issued by Ty Cobb Cigarettes, both the property of Charles Bray. When Bill Leonard, who wrote a column for the Chicago Tribune for so many years, saw his first large Kalamazoo Bats he nearly had a stroke. Oh, how he wanted them!

I remember one visit Buck made a few years later. I had to work that day, so to give Buck something to do, I gave him a list of old book stores on North Avenue to visit where I had previously found old baseball cards. I was really upset when Buck came back with stacks of Old Candy and Gum Cards, and my mouth watered as I went through them seeing player after player that I needed for my collection. Luckily I had a good supply of duplicates that Buck needed that night, and we were soon making deal after deal.

Later we went through album after album of some of my scarce sets, talking about this player and that player as we went, for Buck was a fountain of information that spouted continuously from his mouth, but always in an interesting and informative manner and never in an "I know everything" style. Even in such good company, the working man must call a halt and bid his guest "good night." The next morning at breakfast I asked Buck how he had slept. "Fine," he said, "but I didn't get much of it. I went through all your albums of Early Candy and Gums until 3 a.m.!" That was Buck.

We paid Buck a visit during one of our many trips to the western part of the United States, stopping off overnight in St. Louis. We wanted to take Buck and Alice to Stan Musial's for dinner, but Buck kept objecting, saying that he knew a place with better food at half the price. But we wanted to say that we had eaten at Stan Musial's, and eventually we won. But Buck was never satisfied with our decision.

It was odd that Buck and I were such good friends, as our collecting methods differed so much. I was always known as the most particular collector in the hobby, I only wanted mint, well-centered cards, and I would keep replacing them and replacing them until I got them in that condition. Preston Orem once said, quite disgustedly: "You mean you sort through thousands and thousands of Topps cards, looking for the one that is the best centered?" We had to admit that we did, and for once the very talkative Orem was speechless.

We mounted our cards in albums, Book Shelf Albums that were not looseleaf, much to Buck's disgust as he named me "King of the Mounties." You see, Buck liked to sort through his cards, handling them, wearing off the corners, sometimes carelessly bending them. He liked to group them by team rosters in 1922 or in 1927 or 1933, mixing and interchanging the sets to get the proper players with the proper team for that certain year.

He didn't care if the card was issued with gum, cigarettes, candy or whatever. He kept his cards in his dresser drawers so he could get at them at a moment's notice, the cards contesting with sox, handkerchiefs, and underwear for space. One wouldn't have to think about it too long to realize who got the most fun out of their cards; me with my cards stuck in albums or Buck with team and lineup changes.

One point we did agree on was that we would rather have six different players who had just come up to the majors for one cup of coffee than to have six different cards of Babe Ruth or Mickey Mantle! Who wanted all those cards of the same star player? Give us variety instead. We both, however, collected complete sets, and it was always a thrill to complete yet another set or to swap a card that gave the other fellow a complete set. But we never swapped cards from our collection just because someone needed it to complete a set, as so many collectors beg you to do today; only duplicates got traded and no one begged and pleaded for cards from someone's collection. It just wasn't done.

For many years Buck wrote interesting, informative, yet humorous articles for many hobby papers that were a pleasure to read rather than a chore. For almost as many years he was the hobby's recorder of new issues, both sport and non-sport, giving each new issue a catalog number and, from time to time, publishing a list of the new issues to keep everyone's card catalog up to date. Who donates his time and efforts to such a project today, a project more for the benefit of others than for self? But that, too, was Buck Barker.

I believe it was in 1975 that I planned to attend one of the conventions organized by the St. Louis Cards. I had made my table reservation and had been delighted by the response of the fellows who were organizing the show; they had given me a table next to Buck Barker! How I looked forward to that show and spending so many happy hours with my old friend. But a pinched nerve in my neck just a few weeks before the show negated my trip. It was a cruel disappointment, even more cruel now that I realize I was denied my last-chance to see Buck.

Recently l had been trying to decide if I would invite Buck Barker or Bob Jaspersen to be my house guest during the National Convention in Chicago in July, and finally I had decided to invite both! Now that would have been a time to remember, but it was only a dream, for now both are gone!

Not only has the hobby lost grievously with the passing of Buck Barker, but perhaps the world itself; I know the world must be a better place to live because Buck Barker passed through it, for he was that kind of a person. Goodbye, Buck. Perhaps we'll meet again. I hope so.

* * *

Meet Mike Berkus Frequent Hobby Moderator Is Co-Founder Of National

By Tom Mortenson — April 17, 1992

If you've been around hobby circles for any length of time, it's likely you've met or heard the name Mike Berkus.

Berkus, the 46-year-old lifelong sports fan, has been active in organizing shows, including (along with Galvin Riley and Steve Brunner) the very first National Sports Collectors Convention in Los Angeles in 1980. He also served on several terms on the National Convention Committee (NCC).

The smooth-talking Southern California resident often serves as a spokesman, panel moderator or master of ceremonies at hobby-related events. Berkus' sense of humor helps to make these functions lively.

Originally from St. Paul, Minn., Berkus has fond memories of his early days as a baseball card collector.

"I have the sweetest memories of collecting in the 1950s," he told SCD. "After I started high school I lost a little interest in collecting. Back then girls didn't think highly of you if you were still collecting baseball cards. I found out that women were neat, but that they cost a lot of money. You couldn't just put a rubber band around them and keep them in the closet," he says with a laugh.

Berkus said that for him the decade of the 1960s was a blur. Fortunately his childhood card collection survived. "After I finished with high school, the Army and college, my parents had moved to Nevada and, lo and behold, they had hung onto my baseball card collection," he continued.

Mike Berkus

When he was growing up in St. Paul, Berkus spent a lot of time at Lexington Park watching his heroes, the St. Paul Saints of the old American Association.

"My fondest enjoyment was with a best friend that I grew up with," he recalls. "He and I would go to as many of the Saints games as possible. The Saints were my heroes. They were a Dodger franchise. We'd go out to the games early. As soon as they'd open the gate and let us in we'd head to the left-field bleachers. My favorite player was an absolute unknown, he never made it to the bigs. We were 10 years old and he was the nicest guy we'd ever met. He was a left fielder by the name of Bud Hudson. I've never seen a card of Bud Hudson, but if there was one, I'd probably do anything for it. I do have a team picture with him on it. I have all the Saints team pictures. But anyway, Bud was the friendliest guy. We'd go get him Cokes and things. He'd sign all the autographs anyone wanted. He'd screw around with us. He'd grab your cap and wear it around for a while. He was just the type of guy that would make you feel good about rooting for the team."

Berkus recalls that through Hudson, he had a chance meeting with someone who would go on to be one of baseball's biggest stars of the 1960s.

"One day he (Hudson) pointed out a young guy sitting in the bleachers and said, 'If you want a great autograph, you ought to get that kid's autograph. He's going to be a great pitcher.' We said, 'Who's he?' and he said, 'Sandy Koufax.' Sandy Koufax had a sore arm and the Dodgers hid him in St. Paul for a couple of weeks in 1955. He didn't suit up. We walked over to him and he looked like one of our older brothers or something. He was just a kid. He was about 18 years old at the time, a skinny young kid. We asked him, 'Are you a baseball player?'

and he said, 'Kinda.' He was quiet, very quiet. He wasn't very talkative. But we did get his autograph. I don't know what ever happened to that. I lost a number of important mementoes of my childhood."

As much as Berkus enjoyed collecting, he says it really wasn't difficult for him to get unusual items that would assuredly bring top dollar today. "My dad and uncle were president and vice president of Snyder Drug," relates Berkus. "One day in 1956 my dad came home with about 50 uncut Topps sheets with Mickey Mantle in the middle. I went out in the garage with my lifelong buddy Mike Appelbaum, who was a fanatical collector. There was no way we could cut the Mantle card out without ruining the sheet. We tried to trim the card out with scissors, razor blades, whatever. We destroyed every sheet and threw the cards away. We didn't care."

Mike's father realized the joy that his son got from baseball cards and was supportive of the youngster. "My dad bought me the first issue of Sports Illustrated, the one with the cards in it," said Berkus. "It was in 1954. He bought it for me because my dog got run over the day before. He knew how much I loved cards. I've still got it," says Berkus of that first issue of SI.

A few years ago, after an absence of nearly 30 years, Berkus returned to his old neighborhood and tells the following amusing incident: "We used to buy penny packs of cards with one card and a piece of bubble gum in the pack at a little neighborhood grocery," he relates. "A very young guy and his mother owned the store. The fellow's name was Larry, a heavy-set guy. I went back there about seven years ago with my kids. I walked in and there's Larry. I hadn't seen him in about 30 years. He had the new baseball cards out and I said, 'How much are these per pack?' He didn't look up. He just said 40 cents, or whatever they were selling for in the mid-'80s. I told him I'd like to buy the penny ones. He looked up at me and said, 'Hey, you're that Berkus kid!'"

Berkus moved to California in 1969, where he worked for Dancy Waters Inc., building, installing and operating water shows at Disneyland and throughout the world. It was around that time that he got back into sports collecting with one of the early card collecting clubs in the country, the Southern California Sports Collectors Club. "The shows were incredible," he says of his early days at the card club shows. "People saved money all year long for those shows. They'd come in with thousands of dollars to spend. It was an incredible sellers market. We had a Memorial Day show and a Labor Day show. They're among the longest running shows around. In 1990, Gavin (Riley), Steve (Brunner) and I sold our interests in the shows to Jack (Petruzzelli). It was the first time in years on those holidays I wasn't involved in the show. So what did I do last Labor Day? I went to the card show!"

Berkus says that the idea for the first National Sports Collectors Convention was suggest by Gavin Riley. "Gavin came to Steve (Brunner) and I with the concept of a National Convention," he said. "He had thought about it. It took him about 13 seconds to explain it. He felt that it was the right time. Steve and I both felt that it was a good idea but we didn't think it would fly. We were against it at first. We felt there were established shows in places like Plymouth, Willow Grove, Cincinnati and Chicago and that those promoters may not accept the idea of a National Convention. Steve and I felt at the time there was a delicate balance with shows and we didn't want to upset anyone's feelings. We enjoyed going to those shows and those people were our friends. Then we decided that if the show moved around to different parts of the country each year that it could be done." Needless to say, Berkus' and Brunner's fears were unfounded as this year will mark the 13th National in Atlanta. It's testimony to their foresight. Of the three original founders, Berkus is the only one who has remained active politically in the hobby.

Some prized possessions in Mike's collection came from renowned collector Barry Halper. "Barry showed up at one of our shows once and we were sitting together at a table," says Berkus. "A guy walks up and said, 'Would you like to buy these?' He had two photographs. One was a team picture of the 1919 Gonzaga University baseball team and the other was a single picture of one of the players. It was Bing Crosby in a baseball uniform. I gave the guy I think 50 bucks and Barry said, 'I want it.' I said, 'I want it too.' About a year later Barry sends me an 1889 St. Paul Saints Cabinet. Needless to say, I parted with the two prints of Bing Crosby. To this day, Barry thinks of me whenever he comes up with any St. Paul Saints stuff. He sends me something and I send him something out of my collection. Money has never changed hands with Barry. Of course, I can't keep up with him."

These days Mike Berkus is kept busy with three different business ventures. He has an independent firm that does consulting for installing and operating water shows across the world. He's had a marketing and telemarketing firm since 1973 known as PTS. In addition, about a year and a half ago, Berkus started DeCinces Sports Productions, along with former Orioles and Angels third baseman Doug DeCinces. According to Berkus, that business is his true love. "We did a lot of work at the National last year," he said. "We designed the promo cards for Disneyland and tied it in with Upper Deck."

Berkus says that his four children, ages 20, 14, 11 and 10, are also keen collectors who keep up on all the latest prices and products in the hobby. "The only hobby publication I have a subscription to is SCD," he said. "I enjoy going through all the articles and ads. I find that if I put it down for a minute, I won't get it back. They'll run off with it."

Upon meeting Mike Berkus, you'll find an astute guy with a passion for sports collecting. "I've never seen any other hobby that renews itself like sports collecting," he says. "It's a great time now for collectors with all the choices and opportunities we have. With sports we have live heroes and new rookies that are coming along all the time. It's great, it's the real American way."

* * *

For This Father/Son Team, Sports Is A Snap
Vern And John Biever Have Captured Some Of Sports' Most Memorable Moments On Film

By Don Butler — March 31, 1989

Only in the past century have we had the capacity to accurately retain the images of sports. That's as good a reason as any for the boom in sports interest over the past hundred years — almost any play from any year can be retrieved, relived, scrutinized, and compared by looking at the films.

Sports photography provides inroads to our perception of sports. It can be something as simple as a glare from Charles Barkley, a cheerleader in tears after a win (or loss), or a howl of delight from Kirk Gibson. The emotion captured on that bit of emulsified silver strikes a responsive chord in everyone.

The photography industry has seen drastic changes over the years. New equipment and new developing techniques seem to come out by the day. But the bottom line is still creating memorable pictures that strike at the core of sports — images of competition, of winning and losing, of the characters involved.

Two extremely successful sports photographers have been around to see their interest and profession grow in stature. They're two of just eight photographers to cover every Super Bowl.

Meet Vern Biever, the Green Bay Packers' official team photographer for more than 30 years, and his son John, a photographer for Sports Illustrated.

Vern, now in his late 60s, runs a travel agency with his son Jim in Port Washington, a quiet city north of Milwaukee on the Lake Michigan shoreline.

You may recognize his name. His work has appeared in the NFL Hall of Fame and in dozens of publications and books on pro football. On up to 11 weekends (not counting special assignments) in late summer and early fall, he'll travel a hundred miles north or 25 miles south to capture the ups and downs of the Packers at Lambeau Field and County Stadium.

Vern has taken some shots that can best be described as the K2s of sports photography. Perhaps the best-known one is Bart Starr's plunge into the end zone to beat Dallas one frigid Sunday in 1967. He gets a lot of requests for that.

Vern understands the collector's appreciation for this photography, but he doesn't try to encourage it. It's just too time-consuming to try to accommodate photo requests while running a business full-time.

"By the time I spend the time looking for the negative and everything else, the cost really adds up," he says.

But most of the people with requests "I don't think are true collectors at all," he says. "I think they're just football fans who remember the Lombardi era and want to bring back some memories to hang on their walls."

And of the requests he gets, "almost all are from the Lombardi era," says Vern, whose first experience in covering the Packers was in 1941, when Curly Lambeau was still a coach.

Mass marketing eight-by-10s might become a possibility, he says. There are about 15 shots that always seem to be popular. "One shot I could print by the dozens — that's the one of Bart Starr sneaking over the goal line in the ice bowl game," he says. "Another is the picture of Lombardi being carried off the field after Super Bowl II."

Since his first day in 1941 roaming the plush sidelines of Lambeau Field, Vern has always had a plan of action.

"When I go to a football game in general — and the Super Bowl is nothing compared to that — we're looking for good pictures," he says. "We really are not concerned about who wins or loses. That we can read about in the paper the next morning. And in fact that's when we really find out who wins or loses, because we're so concerned about the photograph at that point that the game itself doesn't mean a heck of a lot."

Because the action is always unpredictable and hectic, photographers never have time to compose a shot, Vern says. "With the motor drives on cameras nowadays, you just shoot and shoot and shoot and hopefully in the film that comes back to you there's going to be something there. It's pretty much, I should say, an accident."

Well, not completely an accident. There's more to just loading up a camera and standing with a horde of other photographers, waiting for a game-turning pass, fumble or run.

"You have to understand football, first of all," says Vern. "Third and nine means pretty much a pass. So you've got to set yourself to that location.

"You can try to compose for future shots on the bench area during the regular season, but at the Super Bow it's just shoot, shoot, shoot."

Since he's been at it for the better part of 40 years, Vern has eased off on his Packer responsibilities somewhat.

"Up until about three years ago I used to travel with the team," he says. "If I came back from a trip from, say New Orleans, and got back here around 10 or 10:30 at night, I would still develop every film to see what I had."

Vern, who has a contract with the Packers, freelances his work everywhere else. Ray Nitschke's Packer Report and SI are two publications on Biever's regular route. He's covered he Super Bowl for the Bear Report. A selection of shots from every game is sent to the National Football League Properties in Los Angeles, the publishing arm of the NFL. (NFL Properties has a photographer for every league city). He submits to other magazines and some hardcover books. In just about every book on the Packers, in fact, you'll find one or more Vern Biever photographs.

The Hall of Fame Photo Contest is the creme de la creme for the sport's shutterbugs. Initiated in 1968, there are four categories: Black-and-white and color feature photos, and black-and-white and color action photos. Vern, who has entered the contest every year, is one of two men to win the contest four times.

"A photographer looks for one picture a year to have a good season," he says. And the season is capped off by sending it to the HOF contest.

The first year of the contest, Vern took honors in the color feature category — a picture of Packers Lionel Aldridge and Henry Jordan sitting on the bench in Milwaukee during a night game, in pouring rain.

Vern won two first-place awards in 1969. One was a black-and-white shot of Green Bay's Dave Hampton celebrating after he scored a touchdown. The other was a head shot, in color, of the Packers' Lee Roy Caffey with blood on his face.

The real award winner came in 1984, which depicted Dallas defender Everson Walls making an interception over Green Bay's Philip Epps.

Getting from a high school photography club to the Green Bay sidelines within six months was more than just a drive north. In 1941, Vern was beginning his freshman year at St. Norbert College in De Pere, a city just south of Green Bay. "Before I went up to Green Bay, I stopped at The Milwaukee Sentinel and said, 'You know, I used to be in the camera club in Port Washington and I'm going to be going to school at St. Norbert,'" Vern recalls. "'The Packers play in Green Bay. Why send your own guy up there when I can do it for you?' They said, 'Well, there's a Bear-Packer game next Sunday, why don't you cover it and put the stuff on the train?'

"Those were the years of the old speed graphic camera, the old four by five press-type cameras, and you had to prefocus the camera onto the field, about 25 yards away," he says. "Only when the action came there could you snap the shutter. So I usually shot about eight or 10 pictures a game. Twelve would be a lot.

"Anyway, that night I put the film on the train. I couldn't sleep of course, thinking that maybe I didn't have anything or it didn't come out. But I picked up the Sentinel Monday morning and it was in there."

Vern did his part when the Second World War rolled around, serving as the Army photographer in Germany and France for a couple of years. By the time he got back, he found the Sentinel, Journal and United Press International had chartered a plane to cover Green Bay games, effectively ending Biever's newspaper job. Again taking matters into his own hands, he knocked on the Packers' door and told the brass he'd like to be the team photographer, and that way the team would have documentation of every game they played. The team agreed.

Taking pictures in the old days was always an adventure, Biever says. "You had to prefocus pretty much," he says. "I could roam the field — and I did, quite a bit — but you always had to be focused on one spot and wait until the action arrived there.

Tripods weren't allowed on the field. "I had to hold this four by five speed graphic, this big box," he remembers. "There wasn't any motor at that time, there weren't any telephoto lenses."

John Biever accompanied his dad on several of those Packer game shoots, eventually becoming his assistant at age 14. He's now a staff photographer for Sports Illustrated. More and more of his pictures are beginning to appear on the magazine's cover. He was the subject of SIs "From the Publisher" section in the Nov. 21, 1988, issue.

Requests for John's work are few, and thankfully so right now, he says. "It would take a lot of time and I'm not around too much anymore," he says. "It would take a personal secretary or a lab man.

John picked up photography at a young age, since his father was shooting for the Packers. John was on the Green Bay sidelines at age 14. While at the University of Wisconsin-Madison, John worked as a summer intern for The Milwaukee Journal for two years and remained with the paper after his graduation. He worked for the paper for nine years as a staff photographer and the last five there as an assistant manager of the photography department. During this "management" period, he found himself with more time on weekends, and brought some of his samples to SI. They liked his work and began assigning him to games. Gradually, the magazine gave him enough work to force a decision three years ago — stick with the paper or work as a freelancer for Sports Illustrated.

"That's always the dream a young sports photographer — to work for Sports Illustrated," John says. Earlier this year, the magazine signed him to a contract.

Though it didn't make the magazine's cover, one of his best pictures from this year's Super Bowl was a shot of the winning catch. "I'm glad I got that," John says. "Up to that point things weren't hitting too well. But that last drive turned out really well."

Sports Illustrated had 11 photographers at the game. Nine were positioned at different spots around the field and stadium. John was one of the two who were allowed to roam around the field, so he followed the action along the Bengals' sideline.

"In past years I've had one of those positions where you just stay in an area. You try to carve out a little spot and just stay there because it'so crowded."

Vern and John never anticipated what a hype-eating media monster the Super Bowl would become. The first Super Bowl didn't command a lot of attention from sports pages. "You could move around very easily back then," Vern says. "Now you sometimes find yourself in the third row.

"Since about four years ago, they divided the field into quadrants. They allow so many photographers between the goal line and the 30 on one side and between the 30 and the goal line. There are four different areas and you have different colored vests, which indicate to the security guys where you belong. And you're supposed to stay there."

Coverage of the Super Bowl has changed as well, according to Vern.

"Even though you do have roaming passes, when you get to the point where you might want to sit, there might be four guys in the same area because that's a popular area. It's difficult — a free-for-all — but you find your way around. You've got to be an acrobat.

"You don't have too much time to work on features on the sidelines around the bench area because your time is spent finding the right spot for action film," Vern says.

The earlier Super Bowls were easier to shoot, says John, now 37. "But for me, I was floating on Cloud Nine. I wasn't really realizing what was happening. I was so young that I was just glad to be anywhere at the game.

"I think the third Super Bowl, which featured Joe Namath, was when they started getting crowded," he says. "The New York media showed up, and have shown up ever since. At the first two, the Packers didn't have quite the media following as the Jets."

Because photographers watch the game through various-sized aperatures, it's like trying to appreciate the rest of the peacock by looking at one feather.

"You're looking at a small portion of the game through your viewfinder, and we ended up going back to the hotel after the game and watching a replay of it, saying 'That bappened?' or 'This happened?' or 'I wonder if I got this?'" John says. "It's amazing how little of the game you see."

John has a set pattern when shooting the Super Bowl.

"At the start of the games I usually focus on the quarterbacks," he says. "You always try to get a good shot of who you think the most valuable player is going to be. Generally it's been quarterbacks, so at the start of the games you zero in on him. Then you're cognizant of how the flow of the game is going — if the defense is doing well. What I do with all football pictures is try to watch the quarterback's eyes and see where he's looking, and that's how I got the winning touchdown pass this year.

"Montana was scanning the field. At first I thought he was going to come to my corner, but then he looked back over the middle. He cocked, and I knew it was going to be a pass over the middle so I looked for a receiver, and that guy ended up as the only one."

The equipment has had to improve over the years at the Super Bowl because the light has gotten so much worse, John says. It's got nothing to do with the deteriorating ozone layer, but with the deteriorating game times enforced by the league. As the starting time of the game has been pushed back more toward prime time, better and faster camera equipment is needed to document the game in worse lighting conditions.

John usually shoots about 20 rolls of film for a regular game; for the Super Bowl, he shoots 45. "You want to shoot everything, because anything could be important at the Super Bowl." John says.

John has also logged time at every sports event imaginable, from the World Series to the PGA tournament to college basketball. Most of his SI covers have been football shots, and John admits a special affinity for the game he grew up with, but he enjoys the variety and the challenge of finding workable angles in each sport.

John, like his father, is looking for something more than just action when he presses the shutter.

"Generally, I look for faces and emotions," he says. "I try to shoot real tight. A lot of newspaper and wire service people are there to record the play. Although I'm there to also do that, I try to see somebody's face — a grimace under a helmet, an expression here or an expression there. So a style I try to develop is a in-tight action picture."

Most pictures, he says, are a matter of being in the right place at the right time.

"I'm sure a lot of that happens subconsciously," John says. "After 20 years of doing this, you tend to figure where things are going to happen. And that experience pays off."

Basketball, despite its grace, is a tough challenge for a photographer. "You can shoot five games and not see anything but the normal basketball rebound shot," John says. "You want to get something more than that."

Baseball is probably the most difficult sport to shoot for photographers, John says. "You have a hard time getting anything very different. You see all the second base slide pictures...Baseball is the most challenging sport. There may be only one or two things a game where the really good action picture would be. Once you get a good baseball picture, you're very proud of it," he says.

Photographers such as John — who uses only about 12 rolls of film at a typical baseball game — don't use much film because they're waiting for that one action shot that doesn't always happen. Basketball also requires about 10 to 12 rolls, so football becomes the winner of the All-Film Sweepstakes.

"There's constant action on every play in football, which is not the case with baseball and basketball," John says.

Golf is a totally different branch of the sports photography genre, John says. He's shot the U.S. Open, the Masters and the PGA Invitational, among others. "It's a lot of work, because you have to try to be at the spot where the guy takes the lead and it's a big course. Plus the golfers are so attuned to cameras that if they hear any kind of noise on the backswing...They're touchy that way. You have to be careful when you shoot them."

Photographers have been thrown off the course, he says, for not waiting until a golfer's follow-through before pushing the shutter.

More and more sports fans are finding pleasure in high-quality photography. Vern and John Biever have been two of the best at providing it — and hopefully will be for years to come.

* * *

Only 600,000 Dwight Gooden Cards?

By Steve Ellingboe, The Coach's Box, Nov. 8, 1985

How many cards do you suppose Topps prints of each player in a given year? Would you believe about 600,000?

The exact number is one of the things that Topps likes to keep secret, but based on recent comments made by Topps Vice President Sy Berger, the 600,000 figure seems like a reasonable estimate.

Berger was a guest Oct. 8 on the Art Rust Jr. radio talk show on WABC in New York. The Topps V.P. was there primarily to promote the giant new book which celebrates Topps' 25 years in the baseball card business by picturing every card made by the company from 1951 through 1985; but he also fielded a number of questions from listeners.

At one point, he told a caller that Topps prints "More than 500 million baseball cards a year." That's when I got out my calculator. Let's see, there are 792 cards in a set. Divide that into 500 million, and that comes out to just over 600,000 of each card.

That's assuming, of course, that Topps does print the same number of cards for each player; and Berger assured the caller it does.

"Every single card in our series is produced in the exact same number," he said. "There is no way we can possibly make more of one card and less of another."

Berger has been personally involved with Topps baseball cards since the first red backs and blue backs rolled off the assembly line back in 1951. He, no doubt, has more knowledge of the business than anyone else alive. Unfortunately for collectors, though, lots of questions regarding Topps' products remain a mystery to this day. Berger did address a variety of questions during his two-hour radio stint, but he never actually revealed anything new. Most of what he said was already common knowledge in the hobby.

Still, Berger is an interesting guy, and it was good to hear the stories firsthand. Included among the topics discussed were:

How much do players get paid by Topps? Berger answered this one rather specifically. "The players share in a royalty," he explained. "They have a fixed sum they receive if their picture is printed or they're on a major league roster the first 31 days of the season. Then, based upon our sales, we pass a royalty along which is divided among the players based upon the number of days they spend in the majors." He said a player who stays up for the full season makes about $2,000.

Berger's own collection — This one may surprise you. You'd think the vice president of Topps, a man who's been there since Day One, would have the most fabulous collection in the hobby. Not so. Berger told one caller, "I am not a collector. I have never really saved the cards that I produced."

Topps card designs — Believe it or not, Berger said that Topps considers 30 to 35 potential card designs each year before selecting one. That makes you wonder. If those are the best out of 35 designs, what in the heck do the 34 rejects look like?

But Berger defended Topps' designs, calling them "innovative," and he said they were based upon research with youngsters, who are their primary customers. "The bulk of our sales is to youngsters," he said, "the 10-year-old boy or girl who goes to the store clutching their coins and reaching for our package." He also said Topps' research includes testing potential card designs on youngsters at shopping centers, etc. And he implied that Topps may experiment a little with its non-baseball sets to see how those designs are accepted. For example, if the reaction to this year's radically-designed football cards is favorable, Topps may use a similar design for a future baseball issue.

Topps' contract situation with current players, some of whom are not renewing — Not surprisingly, Berger chose not to comment on this one. "At the present time we are in litigation," he said, "and based upon the advice of counsel it's something that I really can't discuss." Berger did add, however, that "our 1986 series is in the works and will consist of a full 792 cards and will be as complete as ever, despite the many things you read."

The 1985 Gary Pettis error (the card actually pictures his younger brother) — Berger said the error resulted from a trick Pettis played on a Topps photographer who had the misfortune of showing up to take Pettis' picture on "Family Day" at the ballpark. Pettis, himself, pointed to his younger brother and told the confused photographer, "That's the Pettis you want over there." Berger said the photographer took the picture and Topps printed it. "Later, when I encountered Gary in spring training, he laughed like hell and ran," Berger said, then added, "The players wouldn't 't try to kid us if they weren't so fond of us."

Berger also said he was responsible for the "Washington, N.L." cards in the '74 set. "I had the information from a reliable source that the Padres were moving to Washington," he said. "Sure enough, after a small quantity were manufactured and distributed, boom, we found out they weren't going to move, so we changed the plates."

Ted Williams and Stan Musial — Berger said at the end of the '53 season, Topps decided it needed someone "to keynote the '54 series." Berger chose Williams and signed him to an exclusive contract. "It was the only time we ever payed one player more than another," he said. "When Bowman found out that this happened, they withdrew the Ted Williams card from their series," resulting in the scarce Bowman Ted Williams card.

Berger recalled that Musial consented to appear on cards only after Topps agreed to contribute to one of the Cardinals' favorite charities.

* * *

222

He's The Owner Of Some 30,000 Player Photos Baseball Photographer George Brace Profiled

By David Craft — Jan. 5, 1990

In a manner of speaking, George Brace knows' the whereabouts of nearly every major league ballplayer, past and present.

They're in any one of his 57 file cabinets.

More than 9,000 photo negatives — some in color, some in black-and-white, are filed alphabetically in those cabinet drawers. JUST as impressive is the fact that Brace himself took those shots.

Altogether, his "treasure chest" includes photos of some 30,000 players, acquisitions over the years.

George Brace

If you're an eager collector of baseball cards or, if you own any number of baseball books or periodicals, you're likely to possess some of Brace's work. The man has been around.

For the past 60 years, photographer George Brace has attended at least one game of every home stand of the Cubs or White Sox. That, friends, translates into a lot of photo opportunities. And at age 76, Brace continues to make the most of them. He still gets around.

When he met George C. Burke, the Cubs' official photographer, in the late 1920s, Brace had already taken photographs of his own amateur baseball team from Chicago's South Side. Brace was answering Burke's ad for buying or trading copies of Spalding's Official Base Ball Guide.

Brace at the time was compiling — on file cards — data on pre-1900 ballplayers. The two men hit it off, and did a little more trading after that initial visit. On one occasion, Brace identified the players in several photos in Burke's possession, identities Burke himself was unable to pin down. That so impressed Burke that he offered the teen-aged photographer a job.

"I was put in charge of filing," Brace told Sports Collectors Digest, "but eventually he began breaking me into the business by taking me out to the ball parks and letting me assist him."

Although most of their work took place at Wrigley Field or Comiskey Park involving major leaguers, there was the odd junket out of town. One time, Burke sent his young protege to Milwaukee for three days. Brace took about 126 shots and brought them all back to Chicago for developing. But by misunderstanding Burke's instructions, Brace accidentally ruined all 125 shots during the developing process.

That unfortunate episode notwithstanding, the two men worked well together for some 20 years, right up until Burke's death in 1951.

"In the first few years, we went out there every day, Mr. Burke and I did," Brace said. "In addition to shooting the players before the game, we used to shoot from the coaching box during the game. We were allowed on the field back then, which enabled us to get shots of players sliding into third, or get shots of a play at the plate.

"In some cases we trailed the play or tried to anticipate when there would be a play at the plate and move down the line, about 10 feet from home plate. We did that for about five years before we were barred from being on the field once the game started.

"I always preferred the action shots myself, but for autograph purposes people usually want the head shots."

The tandem of Burke and Brace were much in demand. For years, their work graced the pages of Who's Who In Baseball, Spalding's Baseball Guide and the pages of newspapers and magazines nationwide. Collectors who own copies of those various publications are undoubtedly familiar with the two Georges.

Also, Brace's individual credits include The Sporting News (for many years its official photographer) and Baseball Digest.

Card collectors may be familiar with George Brace's name through his contributions to SportFlics' "Decade Greats" set or, TCMA's "Hall of Fame" set of a few years back. Brace also served as baseball card consultant for Post Cereals in the early 1960s.

"They sent me three-foot square cards with all the baseball players and their names on the back, and all I had to do was check to see if the pictures matched the name on the card and the stats and everything.

"They used a few of my own photographs for those players they didn't have, but I honestly can't tell you which ones because I don't remember. I don't even have a copy of the set."

For "baby boomers" who may have started collecting baseball cards with Post's colorful back-panel efforts, it may be interesting to note that it was about that same time that Brace began shooting strictly with color film and using a 35mm camera. Up until then he'd been filming in black-and-white using a Speed Graphic camera that, while offering magnificent photos also was heavier and less manageable than a 35mm.

In fact, one time Brace was using a Speed Graphic to take a picture of Roy Cullenbine near the dugout. Brace slipped and fell, landing on the camera as he hit.

"I just kept on shooting all day, but when I got back to develop 'em I saw about an inch on each side, along the border, where the light had broken through," Brace recalled. "I had to shoot 'em all over again.

"After photographers were barred from the field, Mr. Burke and I stopped taking those great action shots. Now, I mostly take shots before the game — all the new players — although I do take some shots from, say, the dugout, once the game has started."

Brace says it didn't take long for him to establish credibility with the ballplayers, despite the fact that he was a teen-ager when he first approached those uniformed idols of millions. Part of that was because of Burke's on-field presence as the Cubs' official photographer, but part of it was the result of Brace's ability to engage in intelligent conversation with players.

When he was 15, Brace entered the visitors' locker room at Comiskey Park and talked with Babe Ruth and Lou Gehrig during a White Sox home stand.

Brace claims Ruth was a braggadocio; the usually quiet Gehrig, the "nicest guy you'd ever want to meet." Gehrig, in fact, remains Brace's favorite ballplayer of all time. The Iron Horse had a favorite photo of himself that Brace had taken, and over the years ordered hundreds of copies from him.

"I remember when they came out with Pride Of The Yankees," Brace recalled. "I was in the Army at the time, stationed in Denver. I went to see the movie and cried. It was a good movie; they did a nice job.

"Gary Cooper played the part perfectly. The only thing that didn't look right was that Gehrig had big legs and Gary Cooper was lanky. I think they should've padded his legs to make it look more real."

Brace also saw action during World War II as a surgical technician serving in New Guinea and the Phillipines. He oversaw the ward housing the seriously ill and injured. Once, more than 800 patients were brought in during a very short period of time and Brace worked for 72 straight hours without sleep.

"Situations like that kind of put everything in perspective," said Brace, who offered an anecdote about a soldier suffering from a serious head wound.

The chief surgeon indicated the man was "too far gone — let's save some of the others." So George wheeled the man back out into the rain and confusion and voices, where a younger doctor asked George why the wounded man wasn't going into the operating room.

"Nobody's too far gone as long as he's still breathing," the doctor snapped. "Get that guy in the operating room."

"Well," Brace recalled, "he operated on him and that night the guy was the life of the party, cheering everybody else on. I saw a lot of miracles; that was one of 'em.!"

In the mid-1930, Brace and Burke learned that plans were being made for a national shrine to the game of baseball that would include all types of mementos, icons and historical papers. Burke instructed his young colleague to "print up an extra picture for this Hall of Fame" every time he printed an order of a specific player photograph.

"They have thousands of our photographs there now," Brace said. "Ken Smith, who was the Hall's curator for many years, is retired now, but I see him whenever I visit Cooperstown. He sings in the opera there."

In addition to supplying photos to a myriad of publications, and retired and current ballplayers, too, Brace helps out with other requests.

"Relatives whose grandfathers or great-grandfathers played back in the 1890s have called me up," Brace said. "I get calls from all over the place. One time I got a long distance call from Amsterdam from some lady who wanted to get a photo of her namesake, (Roy) Sievers."

Brace himself collects little in the way of baseball cards and the like. He does keep up with team sets, however, and at one time was an avid Topps collector.

Brace is also a writer. His column, "The Evolution of Baseball," has been a regular feature of Oldtyme Baseball News, a quarterly publication based in Petoskey, Mich.

He says he works so fast that oftentimes he'll have the players photo taken before the player realizes it. Brace always takes two photos of each player — one head shot and one action shot. His photo files now include shots of non-playing personnel such as umpires, coaches, managers and club officials.

"Friendship with the players...that's what has meant the most to me over the years," Brace said. "I've had a few run-ins with people over the years, but nothing too bad."

"Knowing all these players and getting along with them has been great. And everywhere I go I see people who either know me firsthand who tell me that a mutual friend asked them to tell me 'hello.' That means a lot to me. It's nice to be remembered."

* * *

The Nostalgia Factor: How A Major Coin Dealer Was Hooked By Baseball Cards

By Paul Green — Dec. 30, 1988

Brigandi is a name synonymous with coins both in New York City and on the national level. That's because three Brigandis (Donald, Robert and John) have made their mark in the coin business as members of the Professional Numismatists Guild, on bourse floors around America and in their store in New York.

But look carefully in that store window — Brigandi also deals in baseball cards.

Standing on the floor of one of the nation's largest coin shows watching the opening of a 1960 Topps pack, there too is John Brigandi, sometime coin dealer, but increasingly a dealer in top quality baseball cards. We discussed this interesting transition recently.

SCD: How did you get started in cards?

Brigandi: At a coin show in the Orient, believe it or not.

We traveled to the Orient on rare coin business which we do two or three times a year. We were at an international coin show in Singapore and looked at a dealer's case and he had a bunch of T206 cards there. I looked at them and thought they were really intriguing. On the way back from Singapore I was at our semi-annual national convention and was doing business with a fellow, and in his briefcase there were a bunch of baseball cards. I spotted a 1954 Bowman Mickey Mantle and he ended up selling me the card for $50. It was the greatest thing I'd ever seen. I looked at it for months on end. Everybody who walked into my office, the first thing they would look at was the card. So we were all interested.

A few months later, Don Lepore, who is a real pioneer in this business, responded to one of our rare coin ads in Numismatic News. He wanted to buy a coin, but I kept him on the phone for about an hour talking about baseball cards. He wanted to talk about coins, but I said the heck with the coins, I want to talk about this baseball card thing. We subsequently became the best of friends and still are. He has taught me a great deal about baseball cards.

For the first six months, he basically spoon-fed me the business. I amassed a six-figure collection and he suggested I should start selling them in the store. I was apprehensive about doing that, but Don and my family thought it was a good idea so we did it...

...SCD: What sort of cards are you handling?

Brigandi: We deal only in pre-1970 superstar cards, generally in Near Mint or better. We may, for a 1933 Goudey superstar like Ruth or Gehrig, go below that threshold, but normally they are Near Mint or better. We do handle a small amount of new material for our clients who actually demand it, although that has actually grown into quite a big business.

SCD: OK, you're a coin dealer first. How does a card business really fit in with a coin business?

Brigandi: We do about $20 million a year in coins. Obviously cards are just a little part of what we do, but we enjoy it and it probably brings us more joy than any coin we sell. If we sell $1,000 worth of cards, we get more enjoyment out of that than we do when we sell a $25,000 coin.

SCD: You're selling expensive cards. What sort of people are buying these cards?

Brigandi: We're talking very expensive cards, generally $100 and up. There are several groups buying. The first are collectors — either mail order or walk-in. Don't forget, there's only one real store in New York dealing in high-grade cards so there aren't many alternatives here.

The second group are investors who feel cards are a great hedge against inflation. Those are the customers who we wish would get more involved in what they're buying. I think everyone should take the time, buy a book, go to shows and read, read, read. That's how I learned. Why buy because it's a hedge against inflation? I can think of millions of things I could buy as hedges against inflation.

The third group are people who just walk by the store, see some cards in the window, get totally intrigued. You can watch them. It's like a magnet; they do a complete reversal and walk right up to the window to look at the cards. On any given day there's always five to 10 people who stop at our window to look at cards. It's just amazing. If they come in to look at a card, nine out of 10 times they'll buy a card, so there is a certain amount of impulse buying, and from those people collectors grow.

I watched the coin business in the 1960s and 1970s, and I honestly believe this is no different from the coin business in the 1960s and 1970s. I think it's really in its infancy...

...SCD: Are you having trouble getting the cards you need?

Brigandi: It's tough. I'm constantly in need of rare old high-grade cards...

...SCD: And in the older cards you probably have to drop a little in grade to have much of anything.

Brigandi: Sure, in Cobbs, Ruths, Gehrigs, DiMaggio, early Williams you have to make the threshold grade Excellent and there's absolutely nothing wrong with buying an Excellent Ted Williams 1940 Play Ball or an Excellent 1939 Joe DiMaggio or Goudey or Ruth or Gehrig. That's because the Mint or Near Mint are almost non-existent. If you look at the Excellent prices of Ruth or Gehrig, you see they're $1,700 or less while the Mints are $5,000. You always try to go with the best, but sometimes it isn't available.

One question I always get, and it bothers me, is what's wrong with a card listed in an ad as Near Mint. The answer is there is nothing wrong with the card; it's a fantastic card. It's Near Mint due to a minor flaw, not a hole in it. Not all cards come in perfect Mint condition and people have to realize that. I would estimate that less than 6 percent of the cards out there are in Mint condition and it's probably less than 10 percent in Near Mint. Once you get above Near Mint these cards are really rare, where the Excellents from the 1950s are really abundant. If you try to put together a set in Mint from the 1950s the chances are you won't do it, and if you do, the prices will probably be five times higher than they were when you started. You just can't expect to run around and get a 400- or 500-card set in Mint...

...SCD: Grading services are the big thing in coins right now. Do you expect to see something similar in cards?

Brigandi: I don't think this market is ready right now. One of the differences between the coin and card markets is that the card market still has collector base. People who buy cards want to collect them for the sake of collecting. Since the 1970s, coins have become an investment vehicle, and I think that's really hurt the coin business. When you sell a coin like an IBM stock, you want to be able to get out like an IBM stock and with that mentality in mind, grading services are required

because they want grading to be standards. In all collectors' markets, there's a subjectivity in grading and once you take that out, it becomes more of an investment vehicle.

I don't see that happening in cards right now. I think it will take a while. Most people love the cards they buy; they're more enthusiastic than I am. They enjoy looking at their cards and holding them. A question I ask people is if the cards they bought six months ago for $1,000 would now bring $1,200 would they sell them? Nine out of 10 people answer that they would not sell them and I think that's very important.

Unless they need the money, people really want to hold onto their cards. They know if they bought high-grade cards, they can always get their money out of them.

I really enjoy the business and have developed a lot of nice friendships both among dealers and customers. My hat is off to all the nice people who helped me.

* * *

An SCD Dealer Profile
Lou Brown:
A New Generation Card Dealer

By Paul Green — June 3, 1988

Lou Brown and his wife Eileen, with Sam

Lou Brown is one of what might be called the younger generation of baseball card dealers. Although young in age, Brown is hardly a newcomer, having been at it for a number of years both at shows and through mail order. He took time recently to discuss some of his observations on the market and hobby.

SCD: What is your business like today?

Brown: It breaks down into a number of different areas. First, there are the shows which I do on a regular basis. I'll do at least two a month. I'll probably set up at two nice-sized shows a month and then I'll probably go to another show or two just to buy.

SCD: Is that primarily in the Midwest?

Brown: The ones where I just go to walk around are, but I do about a show a month in New York or the East Coast and another show each month in the Midwest or wherever else there might be a major show. I've participated in most of the major shows, the St. Louis shows, the Kansas City Club shows, the National and shows like that.

Then I have the mail order and that probably keeps me the busiest. We advertise in Sports Collectors Digest, as from what I've heard the ads there are the most effective. The problem is that there just aren't enough hours in the day. A lot of times I'll find myself staying up until very late trying to keep up with it. Then next year there are plans to open a store in Grand Rapids, actually a small suburb of Grand Rapids. We're working on that now.

SCD: That's got to be a fairly major undertaking.

Brown: Yes it is. You mentioned before the factor of my age and being fairly young. Well, it wasn't as big a deal when I started going to shows, but it sure is today with the store situation. My wife and I probably feel discriminated against every day on the basis of our age alone. There's not much of that in the hobby. Most people don't care. A few are surprised to find out that I'm young.

SCD: But people like bankers are a bit different about that.

Brown: Right, we did the best juggling act I've ever seen just to be able to buy our first home here.

SCD: And things probably don't get any better when you tell them you're a baseball card dealer.

Brown: Exactly. The man we're talking to about the lease on our store has mentioned a few times, "You do understand you'll have to open six days a week," and things like that. A little like do you kids know what you're doing?

SCD: And bad as it is today, it was probably much worse 10 years ago.

Brown: Sure, but I bet just about every day someone who knows our situation says something like, "You really make a living selling baseball cards!" I guess they're just surprised that you can make your living doing something you like so much...

...SCD: One last question, in your ads you have another member of your business, I guess. That's Sam your dog. Does Sam like baseball cards?

Brown: Sam used to go to shows, but Sam got too excited so he doesn't get to go any more. Maybe some day he'll go again.

SCD: Does he like cards?

Brown: Sometimes. He has gotten a few. Sam seems to especially like Topps rookies. I don't know why, but of the seven or so cards Sam has gotten about six were Topps rookies.

SCD: I guess Sam knows what he's doing.

* * *

Pro Set's Lud Denny Talks Football Cards

By Don Butler — Nov. 29, 1989

Pro Set burst onto the football card scene with near-perfect timing this summer. Early in the new year, interest in older football cards began to take hold. When Pro Set introduced its line of cards — creating competition with Topps for the first time in more than 20 years — fans flocked to Pro Set and to football cards in general.

Lou Denny and the Pro Set entourage

Lud Denny, the dynamic president of Pro Set Inc., recently discussed his company's second series of cards, as well as the background of Pro Set.

SCD: Had Pro Set planned to release the Series II set all along or was this a response to sales?

Denny: We had planned to do this all along. (We had set up our production) so that we can have not only good photographs of the first-round draft picks, but low-round draft picks, traded players, Plan B free agents, and guys, for want of a better phrase, who are starring in substitute roles.

It's not only an attempt, it's a reality of making the set better.

SCD: So this second series will continually be a part of the Pro Set line. In other words, you'll come out with your football cards in the summer and your Series II or update set in early fall.

Denny: Right. What we intend to do is issue these new cards with cards from the first series and an announcer card.

In this wax pack, the person will get, instead of a Super Bowl collectible, an announcer card. In the case of those announcers that were players, it'll be a player picture on the front and an announcer picture on the back. There'll be 30 of those. In the case of the first-round draft choices, collectors will see a scouting photo on the front. That scouting photo will be from a highlight in the college career of the player that led him to be scouted high enough to be a first-round draft pick. On the back there will be a candid photo of the player as close to being in the uniform of his pro team as possible.

226

We went to all the minicamps and shot tons of rolls of film to see if we could get action photos of these draft choices and give their new team colors. The problem is people don't suit up into full pads and get into contact drills in minicamps. You would have had to settle for pictures of players in sweats or in jerseys with no pads, and that's not football. So on the front of the first-round draft pick (college) photographs, you'll see a little photo credit running vertically on the left-hand side of the card that says "Scouting Photo."

Aikman didn't get to be the number one pick of the draft because he was a history major. He got there because he played great football for UCLA. So we went into the files and found a great picture of Troy Aikman playing the kind of football that caused him to become the number one choice and called it a scouting photo. Then on the back we put a picture of Aikman and the Cowboys.

On the Pro Set prospects, the only way to make that all-inclusive is to delay until the very last minute the inclusion of those prospect cards. Next year, if possible — and we're shooting for this — we will actually be taking pictures in the first weekend of play and have those pictures result in player cards that will be in that year's set and on the shelves two weeks after the opening of the season.

The third element of Series II is those players that did not get into Series I for one reason or another; for instance, if we didn't have their authorization. There'll be a Tony Dorsett card, a "real" Fridge (William Perry) card, a Steve Largent card — we didn't know if Steve was going to play or not.

What we will also do — and perhaps it's the reason the hobby has decided our errors are valuable — is, just as in Series 1, we will correct any little defect we find immediately so there were never a great volume of any errors. In Series II, we have gone back and done that.

For example, Stacey Toran was killed. The Stacey Toran card now has a black stripe with the years of his life, and the text on the back of the card has been updated to report his death. Tony Dorsett's card has been updated to report on the fact that he blew his knee out in preseason.

As far as errors are concerned, we'd like to have an error-free set. I don't know that anybody can do that. But I think that what makes an error product valuable is the control that spots whatever's wrong and gets it fixed almost immediately so that it doesn't run through the entire set. Obviously, if we printed all of our cards with the wrong player on the front, that card wouldn't be very valuable, it'd just make us look stupid. Maybe someday we'll hit it off and have a perfect set. We feel pretty proud of our efforts in this first year. You can have this promise from us: You ain't seen nothin' yet.

What we've tried to do — and we don't know if anybody else has ever done this — is as things change, we have changed his card to reflect this. So we will make this set as up-to-date as possible. Next year, having learned from this year, we hope to be able to include some players that wouldn't have been in the cards except for their play in the first season game. I don't think anybody's even tried to do that before...

...SCD: What's going on with the commissioner card? It's been reported in your Pro Set Gazette that there was going to be a card of the new commissioner, but obviously one hasn't been chosen yet.

Denny: They haven't selected a new commissioner, so we are still including Commissioner Rozelle. Rozelle was elected to the Hall of Fame, so we have altered his card to recognize his Hall of Fame stature.

Terry Bradshaw's announcer card will recognize the fact that he's in the Hall of Fame.

From the beginning of the competition with Topps, there has never been an ancillary product (a non-player card product that must be included in every card pack because of Topps' exclusivity clause in its contract) that had a collectibility. The Pro Set Series I Super Bowl series — which, true to our word, Series I is the only time Super Bowls I to XXIII were ever printed, they won't be printed again — those cards have a value and a collectibility. We feel that kind of collectibility will apply to the announcer series. Nobody's ever done it before. We had network and talent approval for 30 announcers, because they're a very big part of the game as far as it's presented to the fan...

...SCD: In other words, the distribution and decollation that plagued the early runs won't be repeated?

Denny: Yes, that will not be a problem. In the later cases we tested, we're very happy with the decollation and we don't see that problem happening at all.

In the very early cases we also had some damaged cards and some miscut cards. It was a situation where we learned a lot, and you won't find those problems in Series II.

Also, we're very pleased with our policy of having only a wax pack product. We are not now, nor do we contemplate, ever issuing factory sets. That takes a lot out of what the hobby ought to be. We've had a little problem with some stolen sheets and with some people who've actually made up bogus sheets that we were able to retrieve. We feel good about the integrity of our product.

Part of the story is the Pro Set Gazette. In an industry where kids have either Choice A — one less card in the set in order to get a checklist — or Choice B — mail in a dollar to get a checklist — we've come out with a 16-page color magazine that is free. The response to that is close to 2,000 letters a day. People like it a lot. To date we've had several thousand winners; the highest prize so far is the Super Bowl media pins which have a value of maybe $100 to $200, old Super Bowl programs, and patches. The kids that are winning these things are absolutely ecstatic that besides the package of cards they're getting access to a piece of NFL history. They love this official NFL memorabilia that has never been available to the average fan before.

We're totally committed that people who buy sports collectible cards do it as a hobby and as a value judgement, that the more value you can add into the package, the more reason they make Pro Set the card to buy.

Another thing we've done is to have a single set policy which gets the hobby a uniform distribution of cards with an advance shipment to the regular retail market. We think the hobby is very important. We think it's the expert consumers that drive the market. We're interested in what they have to say, we appreciate their compliments and we listen to their gripes. We're human beings and you can't do a lot of things without making mistakes, but when we can identify them, we fix them. We're trying to position ourselves as a top-quality, long-term player.

SCD: Let's talk about Pro Set in general. Do you approach it as a separate entity, or are you an arm of NFL Properties?

Denny: It's an independent company, a privately-held corporation that has two basic functions. One is the card series; the second is to merchandise sporting events. For example, Pro Set produced all the T-shirts and event merchandise for the American Bowl game in London at Wembley Stadium. Pro Set will continue to merchandise sporting events, and next spring we'll be introducing a complete set of collector's aids. We have some albums, hats, sheets...collector's aids that we feel we can produce as a quality, official NFL product.

SCD: As you go along, then, you will introduce more and more NFL products to go along with your set.

Denny: Correct. And you'll look for that next spring. When the cards are introduced, you'll be able to have all of your collector's aids, which we think have a very good value with very good quality.

SCD: Tell us a little about the inception of the idea for Pro Set cards. Did you foresee the football market getting this big?

Denny: For years I've wondered why baseball dominated the sports card market. About a year and a half ago, I made an agreement with John Bello, the president of NFL Properties. I started studying in-depth the marketplace and why baseball dominated. What we found was that football was roughly two-thirds of baseball in 1980, prior to the competition (when other card companies challenged Topps). But in 1981, with the introduction of Fleer and Donruss and competitive, good products stimulated the marketplace, there was dramatic growth in baseball, and football just kind of plugged along. We feel that 1989 is a growth spurt for football cards, as 1981 was for baseball. And only the collectors will tell us what a fair parity will be between foot-ball cards and baseball cards.

I just got a letter the other day from somebody who told us, "I've never collected cards before. I'm a football fan and I don't really like baseball. I didn't collect football cards before because I didn't like the quality." So not only are we getting crossover collectors who see the value, but we're getting people who didn't collect cards before because they prefer football to baseball.

* * *

SCD Dealer Profile
An Interview With Larry Fritsch

By Paul Green — Dec. 25, 1987

Larry Fritsch

When talking about the nation's largest card dealers, one name which comes to mind is Larry Fritsch. It's not just an 80-page catalog which you can get by writing him in Stevens Point, Wis. It's not just his 35 million-card inventory housed in building after building. It's not the incredibly rare Wagner or Plank cards he owns.

It's a staggering combination of it all. The unopened cases from almost 20 years ago, box after box of treasures to make any mouth water and any wallet dry up. Put it all together and you have Larry Fritsch, the top of the heap in baseball card dealing.

SCD: How did you get started?

Fritsch: The first card I ever bought was a 1948 Emil Verban. In the years from 1948 through the mid-1960s I kept accumulating them. I got married in 1958 and moved down to Stevens Point. There I ran a lot of ads and bought a lot of cards. As a matter of fact, in those days a lot of times you'd run an ad in the local shoppers guide to buy baseball cards and the people would call and say just come and get them.

So I kept acquiring cards and in 1963 or 1964 I physically counted them and found I had over two million. At that time I was working out of the smallest bedroom in the house. I was trading part-time and just accumulating more and more cards. I went through all the different rooms in the house and eventually ended up quitting my regular job and selling baseball cards full time. I was the happiest guy in the world to be selling baseball cards full time.

SCD: At the time, that was unheard of. It was really an adventurous thing to be doing.

Fritsch: I was the first guy to start selling them full time. At the time it was pretty adventurous. I had been in the hospital in February with my heart pounding out of my chest. It wasn't a heart attack, it was overwork, and the doctor said quit the job you like the least. My wife and I talked about it and the job I liked the least happened to be my full-time job as associate director of the community action program. I quit that, remodeled the basement and started selling out of the base-ment. That was May 1, 1970, and it's just continued to grow.

SCD: You must have the largest inventory in the business, right?

Fritsch: I would guess there's nobody close. We've got about 35 mil-lion cards. People say they don't believe it but I just take them in the back and show them. It's a 30-by-60 building 14 feet high and it's just solid right to the ceiling. We don't even count any more. I've got unopened cases from 1968 just sitting there. As we need them we use them. We sell them by series and by set and we open them as we need them. They're obviously not for sale...

...SCD: I would bet you've seen an enormous change in the business over the years.

Fritsch: Oh yes, it's become something completely different than it was even three years ago. When I was advertising in the mid-1960s there were very few people collecting and nobody buying for invest-ment. It was a high percentage of kids that you were selling to and that's all changed today too. Something that hasn't changed is that our philosophy was and will continue to be that we sell sets. Obviously that's only to a point.

We sell singles too, but we emphasize selling complete sets over selling rookie cards of Mattingly. We will not break up our sets. Peo-ple call all the time. This year Mark McGwire is the hot one and we could be breaking sets all the time for him. But five years from now we'd be looking for them. So we have not done that.

In the early years we did some of that and sold some Mays and Man-tles. Since then we've had to re-acquire them so we can keep our com-plete set inventory and that's what we're aiming for. I really believe the backbone of the hobby is the set collector. The guy who buys the good sets and enjoys them. Maybe I'm wrong, but we've kind of stayed away from the rookie thing...

...SCD: What are your feelings about the current market? There's obviously been an enormous influx of people.

Fritsch: There's an old saying, what goes up has got to come down. I'm saying publicly, and I'm saying privately, be ready when it comes down. All these people making all this big money on paper will be wondering how they're going to sell everything when it comes down. Our buying habits have not changed much in the last 10 years.

Obviously as the business has grown, we've bought more stock to take care of our customers, but we are not stockpiling certain items in 1987 that we didn't in 1983. We haven't changed. I'm getting older so

I'm getting more conservative and not doing all the crazy things I used to do. We're currently buying a lot more large collections than we did in the past...

...SCD: What advice do you give newcomers to the hobby?

Fritsch: Buy sets, complete sets in Mint condition. If you want to play with them, buy two sets. Put one away and do everything with the other one. Unless you can get Fleer and Donruss at a very good price, buy Topps and stay with Topps. Topps won't double and triple overnight, but it's a good solid base and Topps will be around forever, don't let anybody kid you. I don't know about the other two and some of the things happening with them are turning people off, especially Donruss and Fleer to a degree...

...SCD: We see a lot of new card sets and the like. Are you concerned about it being too much?

Fritsch: Yes, very, very much. I think we're killing the golden goose. This goes back to my advice to people. Stay with Topps and stay with only the major issues unless you have an interest in a certain team like the Brewers. Then you get your police set, but don't attempt to get every set; it's impossible. I can't even remember every set, or even attempt to get them all.

SCD: So buy them only if it fits your collecting?

Fritsch: Yes, once in a while I help pull orders and we'll get them a Revco boxed set or whatever. I can't tell them apart anymore, and I don't know that the collector can either. How many more different poses do I need of Jose Canseco and Wally Joyner? That's not a slam at them either. It just seems to be what Fleer is doing is part of their philosophy and maybe there's nothing wrong with it. Maybe they're saying they can't beat Topps, can't go head to head in the marketplace with them because they don't have the distributor network. So they can't compete in the regular marketplace with the wax packs so they go for the boxed sets. That may be what Fleer is doing and there's nothing wrong with it. But I'm just saying to myself how many boxed sets at $2.95 or $3.95 or whatever do I want to buy when they're all the same 33-40 players in different poses.

SCD: Overall as you look at the market today do you feel basically good or are you concerned?

Fritsch: I'm concerned that it will burn itself out. It's burning so fast and so rapidly right now. It's almost like a meteor and that concerns me. It concerns me from a business standpoint, but not from a collector standpoint. I think we'll still be in business, but I think some others won't make it.

We have a tremendous stock and we have a tremendous list of collectors, but I think you'll see a big decline in prices, especially in stuff from 1979 on. Before 1979, there isn't a lot of good stuff out there. But after 1979, those prices will drop. It's the guy with 500 Mattingly rookies, real or phony, he's the guy who should be worried.

SCD: So you're strongly emphasizing collecting.

Fritsch: Yes, a lot of people are missing the whole fun of collecting cards. Believe it or not, I'm a collector first and a dealer second. That's what I'm working on now, a museum to display my collection. People must remember, it's fun to collect. I'll tell you a little story which may sound crazy, but when my son Jeff was young we used to do teams. We'd take a Topps set and put all the cards in teams. When players were traded we'd move them around. We'd take the rookie cards which had two or three players on a card and cut them apart and put the parts with the right team.

Two or three years ago we were digging through some cards and found a Seaver rookie cut in half, a Carew rookie cut in half, a Carlton rookie cut in half. We showed them to some people who were shocked. But you know, I wouldn't trade the fun we had doing that for what the cards are worth today. That's what people are missing, the fun. They're worried about what the card is going to be worth next week. That's not the point, the point is enjoy them, have fun.

I sell thousands of sets each year, but I get my own sets by going out and buying wax packs. I put my own sets together card by card because that's fun. I have fun doing it. Too many people are worried that this card or that card is going to be worth five bucks five years from now. That's not the idea. If it's worth that fine, it's a bonus, the important thing is the joy of collecting them. Collect by set or by team or however you want to do it, but enjoy it. If I wanted to invest in something I'd invest in the stock market or something.

SCD: Overall, have you enjoyed it?

Fritsch: Oh sure, I enjoy going into the shows and shooting the breeze with boys I've known 10 or 15 years. That's what's neat about the hobby, you meet a lot of nice people. I like it and it's given me the freedom to work how I want to work. I've probably worked a lot harder than I would for somebody else, but it's a labor of love and it's allowed me to put together a tremendous collection. I still get excited about finding cards. It's getting tougher and tougher to find things like T203s and it's exciting when you do find some.

SCD: You're probably the most successful card dealer and you're also sort of a senior spokesman in the hobby which is no longer the sort of thing you keep quiet about.

Fritsch: There are still a lot of closet collectors. They want to remain anonymous.

SCD: But some seem to be coming out, aren't they?

Fritsch: They're going to shows, but they still want to remain anonymous. I think they're worried about theft and also the old thing that you're a little nuts if you're collecting baseball cards.

SCD: Right. What's a 35-year-old adult doing with baseball cards?

Fritsch: You ask Jeff. He was as embarrassed as hell. I walked into a store and bought 1,200 boxes of Kellogg's cereal for the 3-Ds back in 1971. In the 1960s I was buying 200 boxes of jello at a crack off the shelves. I was trading guys all over the country with them and they thought I was crazy. I remember going into a store in Chicago which had the 1963 Post Cereals with the real hard backs and buying about 15 boxes of them. I asked the girl if she had a scissors and cut off the backs and left her the cereal.

SCD: Those are the fun parts of the hunt.

Fritsch: They are the fun stories.

* * *

Frank Fulop:
The Original Hartland Man
The Creator And Artist Of
Those Treasured Sports Statues

By Tom Mortenson — Dec. 11, 1987

When Frank Fulop came up with an idea to help the company he worked for avoid seasonal plant layoffs, he had no way of knowing he would be making a huge impact on the sports collecting hobby.

Back in the 1950s, Hartland Plastics of Hartland, Wis., manufactured a variety of products for different industries. Point-of-purchase items for breweries were a big part of their business. There were also boat seats for Sears-Roebuck, display cases for Timex, radio and television cabinets, plastic washers for Ford Motor Co., front grilles for American Motors, religious figures of all types and toy western statues, to name a few.

Frank Fulop

"We had a tremendous brewery business in those days. Toys were really a small percentage of our work," Fulop says. "There was enough work in the summer to keep the plant busy, but after Christmas, there was always a lull."

Fulop was supervisor of the assembly and decorating departments of the Hartland firm at the time.

"At one of our production meetings, the boss asked if anyone had any ideas on how we could avoid those winter plant layoffs every year. Since I was a baseball fan, I suggested the possibility of making plastic toy figures of baseball players that we could make in the winter and sell in the summer. We (Hartland Plastics) were a division of Ameriline Corp. of Chicago at the time, so my proposal had to be approved by them.

"They did, and I got stuck with the whole program," recalls Fulop.

The first players selected to be done as statues were Milwaukee Braves stars Eddie Mathews, Hank Aaron and Warren Spahn. "I spent almost one whole summer at the ballpark (Milwaukee County Stadium) observing them and making sketches. They couldn't understand at first what I was doing. Later that year, I sketched Mickey Mantle at Comiskey Park in Chicago when the the Yankees were in town to play the White Sox. After that, we got approval from Babe Ruth's heirs to do one of him."

Fulop designed the statues and Roger Williams and a man from Sweden named Alvar Backstrand sculpted them.

In the spring of 1960, the first line of Hartland baseball statues hit the market. Customers liked the excellent detail of the figures and they sold well at concessions stands. The company then began to sign other players to contracts. They (players) received $500 plus 5 percent of the gross sales, a far cry from what athletes command for endorsements today. "There was no players association in those days," points out Fulop.

Selling retail for $2.98 each, the success of the first five statues indicated that the company could add more. Chicago stars Ernie Banks, Nellie Fox and Luis Aparicio were next. After that, there were 10 more: Duke Snider, Don Drysdale, Yogi Berra, Stan Musial, Willie Mays, Ted Williams, Roger Maris, Harmon Killebrew, Rocky Colavito and Dick Groat. Fourteen of them are in the Hall of Fame.

Except for Ruth, Frank Fulop's sketches were the models for all the statues. Asked why he worked from sketches rather than photographs, Fulop responded, "We didn't have a company photographer and we would have had to send film to Chicago for processing. That would have taken a week to get prints back. With sketches, you could see immediately what you had, plus you could get feedback from the players. The players had a say in what kind of poses we used. Some wanted to be shown as fielders rather than as hitters. You might forget that Fox and Aparicio were considered to be the best double-play combination in the big leagues at that time. They were proud of their fielding. Eddie Mathews wanted to be shown as a fielder, too, because he told me that Henry Aaron was such a great hitter that he (Aaron) should be the one (Brave) to be shown as a hitter."

Production of the statues was in full swing in 1961 and 1962. "Four girls could paint 90 statues in an hour. The biggest sellers were the first five we made, about 150,000 each. The most common today are the three Braves. We made more of them than the others," recalls Fulop.

Most Hartland collectors are aware that the rarest of the baseball figures is the one of Dick Groat. According to Fulop, only 5,000 Groat statues were ever on the market. Today a Groat in Mint condition could fetch $400 or more from the right buyer, while an Aaron probably wouldn't bring much more than $150.

Next to Groat in scarcity is the Rocky Colavito statue. Only 10,000 were sold.

Statues of Killebrew, Snider, Drysdale and the others had approximately 50,000 of each on the market in the early '60s.

"We presented one to each of the guys. When I gave one to Musial, his teammates in the dugout teased him about it. The only one who ever mentioned that he was in any way displeased with it was Aaron. Henry thought that the colors were not quite right and that we had made the skin a little too dark. So after that, I had it lightened up to please him."

A genuine nice guy and true gentleman, Fulop relayed this story about what happened to factory-rejected Hartland toys. "Every year, I used to take the rejects and fix them up. I'd pack them up and send them throughout the country to Indian reservations and orphanages at Christmastime. My son, Don, used to help. It was gratifying to get thank you notes back from the kids. Some of them told us that they (toy statues) were the only Christmas presents they had ever gotten. That made me feel good, knowing I had pleased them."

In all, 18 baseball figures were made, plus a little leaguer and a smaller minor leaguer were added later. Production of two football figures, Jon Arnett (Rams) and Johnny Unitas (Colts), also took place. "We found that the two football ones only sold in Los Angeles and Baltimore. Then we made two figures for each team, one lineman and one running back.

"At that time Bert Bell was the commissioner of football and Roy Rogers and Dale Evans owned National Football League Properties. They were good friends with our sales manager, so they gave us permission to sell all 14 teams. We must have sold 50,000 each. The most valuable today is the Dallas Cowboy running back. Those had the original Cowboys uniform with epaulets on the jerseys. They go for as much as $350. The most common ones are the Green Bay Packer ones. We flooded the market with them."

Despite the success of Fulop's program, production of the statues came to a screeching halt in 1963. Hartland Plastics was sold to Revlon. "One day a short little guy with a big cigar came in. It was Charlie Revlon, who has been dead for a long time. He and his brother owned the Revlon Cosmetics Co. He walked through the plant and demanded that production of all toys be stopped right then and there and every effort be put into making compact cosmetic cases and other things. All the sketches, molds, contracts — everything was taken to the dump. There's a housing project over the top of it all now.

"We had just started selling the Groat and Colavito statues and we got orders to stop. We had gotten permission to do a Casey Stengel and we were just getting ready to start on him. Today, I have the only Casey Stengel Hartland around (a handpainted metal prototype). I was getting ready to begin sketching Jim Gentile (Orioles first baseman) too, when we were told to stop."

Fulop emphasizes that Hartland Plastics never went bankrupt as some people think. A series of sales of the company to different conglomerates took place and Hartland Plastics, as it had been known, closed on June 30, 1978. Company employees also owned the company at one time and they (employees) own the patents to the statues, which run out in 1990.

Somewhat accidentally, the collecting hobby rediscovered the Hartland statue creator eight years ago. "My daughter bought an old building in Oconomowoc (Wis.). She found some old baseball cards in it and sold them to a collector from Jefferson (Wis.) for $400. He asked her if she knew of anyone who might have any Hartlands. She told him she knew someone who had the whole set and the Casey Stengel, too. Well, this really intrigued him, so he came over and invited me to a card show. I decided to go and at one of the tables I saw a box of old, beat up Hartlands. I told the guy at the table that I could fix them up him if he wanted and he said, sure! So I fixed them up and he was so happy with them that he told me I should go into business repairing and repainting them. I thought about it for awhile and said no, I don't think so. He said if I took out an ad in Sports Collectors Digest I could get all the repair work I wanted. Well, I finally agreed. He paid for the ad and everything. I guess I've fixed up thousands of them since then," relates Fulop on how he got started repairing the statues.

Fulop says that he is often questioned about why some of the statues tended to get yellow in time, while others were able to maintain nice whites. He explains, "It wasn't the way they were stored. It was that some of them were made from virgin plastic. Others were made using reground plastic, and they were the ones that yellowed. You couldn't tell it at the time they were made, though." Whiter statues are favored more by collectors and can bring $30 or $40 more each when sold.

When Sports Collectors Digest staff writer Tom Owens asked Fulop recently how it makes him feel to see his creations so popular today, he sat back and thought about the question for a moment before a slight smile spread across his face and he answered, "It makes me feel pretty good, Tom. It's like old times again."

Asked if he is surprised so many Hartlands are still around today, he answered, "Yes, I'm surprised they're here at all. They were meant to be toys. You know what children do with toys?" he answered with a laugh.

"Maybe some were daddy's toys?" said Merian Fulop, who had been listening to the conversation, with a chuckle.

* * *

Celebrity Photographer Ray Gallo
Mantle Photo His "Claim To Fame"

By Tom Mortenson — April 15, 1988

When Rhode Island portrait photographer Ray Gallo got a call from the William Esty Advertising Co. of Oxford, N.Y., in September of 1956, he was delighted...

"They wanted to know if I'd be interested in photographing Mickey Mantle for them," recalls Gallo.

"I was shocked. I couldn't understand why they had singled me out to do 'The Mick.' Just imagine, here I was getting the chance to photograph my hero, the idol of all baseball," he says.

Gallo remembers vividly the night he went to Boston's Fenway Park to take the photograph.

"It was Ralph Terry's debut — he was getting his brains beat out. I remember Casey Stengel was at the top of the dugout, screaming his lungs out. He was saying some words that couldn't be printed in a family magazine," remembers Gallo.

After the game, Sy Mann of the Esty Co. introduced Gallo to his subject, the 25-year-old Mickey Mantle. It was the year that Mantle was tearing up the American League, finishing with a .353 average, 130 RBI and 52 homers (several of them tape measure shots).

He went on to win the triple crown that year.

Yet, despite all the fame, adoration, and media attention heaped on the young Mantle, Ray Gallo knew that the center fielder was a relatively shy, humble subject, someone not always easily accessible for photographers.

Once introduced, Mantle asked Gallo how he wanted him to pose. Gallo responded by telling him to relax. "Just be Mickey Mantle, the ballplayer," Gallo said.

Today, Gallo recalls, "He was in the dugout, and I tried to get him to relax. I directed him to cross his legs.

"I used a 2 1/4 Graflex Speed Graphic press camera. I was getting it focused and (Mantle) asked me, 'What will this picture be used for?' I told him it was going on the cover of The Christian Science Monitor. Well, he breaks out with this grin and I snapped the shutter," says Gallo about his unique shot.

"I only took one exposure...I knew I had it," he beams.

Gallo sent the print to the Esty Co. and received numerous compliments.

"People who saw the photograph thought that it was the best Mantle photo they had ever seen, including The Mick himself," tells Gallo. "He has a print of it in his office in Dallas."

Noted collector Barry Halper also owns a print, according to Gallo.

For 25 years, Gallo himself had an original black-and-white print hanging in his studio. "One day a few years ago someone came in and said, 'that print belongs in the Hall,'" Gallo said. He then contacted Hall of Fame director Howard Talbot Jr. to inquire if they were interested. They were. A 24" x 28" black-and-white print was handpainted in color by Yvette Andreoni and donated to the Hall of Fame in 1982.

Since photographing Mantle in 1956, the 65-year-old Gallo has gone on to produce several award-winning pieces. He has photographed other celebrities, including Presidents Reagan and Kennedy, Robert Kennedy and Eleanor (Mrs. Lou) Gehrig, as well as other ballplayers. These include Joe DiMaggio, Ted Williams, "Pudge" Fisk, Rocky Colavito and Bud Harrelson.

But the Mantle photo is the one that stands out in Ray's mind.

"It's my claim to fame," he says.

* * *

California Dealer Tony Galovich Interviewed
Dealing In High Quality Cards

By Paul Green — Sept. 30, 1988

Mention the highest quality in cards and you almost have to mention Tony Galovich. Mention the highest prices and you must consider Galovich. If you mention investing in baseball cards (not of the 1987 genre) there too, you almost certainly must mention Tony Galovich.

Simply put, if the topic centers around the most extraordinary Babe Ruth, Ty Cobb or Willie Mays card you'll ever see or spend your hard-earned money to buy, Tony Galovich is one of that small group of dealers you'll be seeking.

SCD: Can you describe your business today?

Galovich: I have a reputation for high quality cards. If you're looking for Near Mint to Mint cards, that's what I carry. My specialty is pre-1973 superstars. It's been like that since I started. People are always buying superstars, like Mantle, Mays, Clemente or Koufax. They sell the best. I deal in other things, like tobacco cards, Bowman — always high quality.

SCD: How do you see the market today in these areas?

Galovich: Right now the market is very strong if you're dealing with Mint to Near Mint quality Topps and Bowman cards. It's extremely strong for Mint cards where the demand keeps increasing. Obviously, since they're not making any more Mint cards from the 1950s and 1960s, the prices are continuing to go up.

I see a tremendous demand right now for commons from the early 1950s. It's unbelieveable. I'm basically paying "book" for the common cards right now because they're selling in excess of book, and superstar cards are really bringing big numbers. People are willing to pay big numbers for quality stuff, but it has to be "all there" as they say. Some dealers are still trying to get big numbers for stuff that's average quality, but it's just not happening. The knowledgeable collectors and investors know what they want, and they want the best, be it art, rare coins or baseball cards. The people want quality and they're willing to pay for it.

SCD: What would yon say to the person who just can't believe that people really pay the big prices for top condition cards — often many times the price of the same card in VG or Excellent condition.

Galovich: The person who doesn't buy these cards doesn't understand how scarce these cards are in Mint. Most of these are many times more scarce than the price guides indicate. Before, the low grade for a card might be a dollar, the middle grade two dollars and Mint would be three. You're going to start seeing multiples of 10, 20 or 30 times for Mint cards. You're also going to see much larger spreads between the Near Mint and Mint cards. Until lately, if a Near

Mint card had a price of, say, $100, a Mint version of the same card might be only $110 or $130. You're going to start seeing spreads of maybe 100 to 300 percent on many of these cards.

SCD: In all of this are there things people might be overlooking that are good opportunities?

Galovich: What I would call condition rarities. We hear that in other hobbies, but not too much in baseball cards yet. A good example is the first card in many sets, be it a common or superstar.

I think five years from today those cards will start bringing big numbers. It will be nothing for a card that is currently $20 to go for six, seven, 10 times that. For instance, a 1933 Goudey Bengough is one of the rarest cards in the hobby in Mint. A Mint one will bring just unlimited numbers.

Then there are cards which aren't known in Mint like the T206 Wagner. One sold for $110,000, which I believe was the finest known. Find a true Mint one and you can throw out the book. A quarter million would not be out of the question for that. Handled by a major auction house, I would think $300,000 or $400,000 would be possible. I'm not saying that's what they're worth. I'm just saying that the right card in the right situation could bring big numbers.

When the Wagner sold for $110,000, many people thought that was outrageous, since the old record was about $25,000 four years ago. There's no limit to what prices quality will bring because there are enough people with money and insight who are willing to pay for quality...

...SCD: So there still are some sleepers or overlooked cards.

Galovich: Sure. As much as the 1950s cards have zoomed, I still see some good areas to get into. When you're talking investing, you're talking a minimum of two to five years. Anything less is speculation. If you're talking long term — longer than five years — there are a lot of areas, like key rookies, Koufax, Clemente rookies. Even a Mantle rookie. Those cards are the blue chips of our business. I think any of them have tremendous potential. The Mantle is the key card from post World War II. Anyone who collects key cards will want a 1951 Mantle, so it will always be a very desirable card.

There are still a lot of areas in 1960s cards — a lot of Hall of Famers in the $10-$30 range. Another area that will be coming up next are the early 1970s cards, and there are a lot of good cards there which are inexpensive. After 1973, the cards seemed to see a little more production, so they may be good, but not as good as the earlier years.

SCD: What advice do you give people just starting?

Galovich: If you're a collector, there are really no set rules. Buy what you like; buy what you can afford. If you're a collector, you don't have to buy Mint condition cards. If you're an investor it's just the opposite. If you're a collector and are happy with your card, even if it's in poor condition, then it's fine. But if you're an investor, you have to buy the finest because you have to think about selling it later.

SCD: So there are strict guidelines for investing.

Galovich: Some. You may even have to buy cards of players you didn't like. You might be a Yankee fan and might not like Jim Palmer. Well, a collector wouldn't buy him; but if you're an investor, buying Jim Palmer rookies might make you money. And if they do, then maybe you like Jim Palmer.

SCD: What about diversifying?

Galovich: We do that. We try to put people into as wide an area as possible. We also try to keep them in as cheap an area as possible, because you rarely sell cards over $1,000.

SCD: Do you see the market continuing to attract the new people and new money?

Galovich: Sure, because there is so much opportunity. A Mantle rookie basically peaked out at the end of last year, and what's happening now is that people are looking for other cards. I got a lot of our clients out of the market last year and into 1960s cards. We talked about

1960s cards in my newsletter and showed that things were out of balance, that one card was selling for $500 and another for $10. We knew things would even out in the long run, and that's what has happened. The 1960s cards are starting to catch up now.

Another example is when rookie cards take off and the player's second-year card is selling for maybe five percent of the rookie card. People ask why a 1955 Aaron is selling for $20 when his rookie card is $700? So they catch up quickly.

That's what you look for — things that are out of balance, and sometimes it's real obvious...

...SCD: Are there any things on the horizon which could hold this market back?

Galovich: Counterfeiting is always a potential problem. At this point in time it really hasn't been a serious problem, as far as I can tell. Right now we have a slight problem with cards that have been restored. I can see that as a growing problem if it gets out of hand, especially for the people who are buying only high grade cards. They're taking a VG or Excellent card and making it Near Mint or Mint. You'd better know what an unrestored card looks like if you're buying restored cards because you have the potential of losing a lot of money.

SCD: What advice do you give people as far as dealing with these potential problems?

Galovich: Since some people have neither the time nor the inclination to study these things themselves, then knowing your dealer can become very important. If you're knowledgeable enough you can rely on your own expertise. But if you're coming in with $25,000 and all you know is buying gum packs, then you had better get some investment advice from a professional. You don't want to learn when you go to sell your cards, because then it's too late. Some people are learning already with the cards they put away in collections in the 1970s. They are expecting to get some of the prices they hear or read about, but are disappointed to learn that the cards they thought were Mint may be only Near Mint or even Excellent.

Overgrading is a problem right now with people coming into the market and not really knowing how to grade. So it's important that your dealer be a strict grader, and that he will not only sell you a card, but also be willing to buy it back at the same grade. Get your receipts in writing, so you can take them back to make sure he's fair with you. Also sell a card back to him every six months or so, just to make sure he'll do what he says as far as buying cards back at fair prices and at the same grade. I think it's really important to do that; and it may save you a lot of money in the long run.

* * *

An SCD Dealer Profile
Bill Goodwin:
Car Salesman Turns Card Dealer

By David Craft — June 17, 1988

The words, "Baseball, apple pie and Chevrolet" have long served to describe life in America, and for Bill Goodwin the words hold special meaning.

Goodwin, whose St. Louis Baseball Cards is a nationally-known and trusted mail-order business, recently talked with Sports Collectors Digest about life in America as seen through a successful hobbyist's eyes.

Bill Goodwin and St. Louis Blues player Rick Meagher

"I guess the 1957 Topps baseball card set was so special to me because I was 10 years old at the time and I was just at that age when I was really starting to follow baseball," said Goodwin, who, as a youngster growing up in St. Louis, played in an organized league.

"I used to ride my bike up to a confectionery here in town and buy those one-cent packs and get the '57s. It meant a lot to me. I never was able to get a Ted Williams card, though. One of the kids across the street from us had one.

"Don Blasingame was my favorite player for the Cardinals, and his card had this great action pose. When you're a kid you always preferred those action shots to the portraits. And, like all kids who are beginning to collect, I studied the players' gloves and caps and uniforms shown in those cards."

But, like a lot of kids who all too soon, it seems, grow into adulthood, Goodwin's interest in cards waned over the years.

"I got back into cards going over to my mom's house and finding my treasures," Goodwin said. "I thought back to how much I had wanted to complete the '57 set when I was a kid. So, I decided to do just that. From there, I went on to the '58 Topps set and then back to the '56s until I'd developed a pretty good collection."

The cards and the confectionery take care of the first two words in the phrase. Where does Chevrolet enter into it? (And Buick, too?)

Well, after serving a year and a day in Vietnam with the Ninth Infantry Division, Goodwin returned home in 1970 and began a successful career in the retail automobile business. He started as a salesman and worked his way up the local dealership ladder with Chevrolet and later, Buick.

Around the time he was to have closed a deal that would have given him one of the St. Louis-area's top Buick dealerships, Goodwin decided to use a free airline ticket — awarded him by Buick for having sold "x" number of Rivieras over a specified period of time — to do something he's always wanted to do: attend some major baseball card shows and sell off his doubles.

By then, Goodwin's passion for cards was undermining his zeal for selling cars. As it turned out, the first deal to have his own business fell through, but he was offered what he says was an even better deal elsewhere. He and his family did not want to leave the St. Louis area, however, and Goodwin made his decision.

"I wanted to buy and sell baseball cards," Goodwin said, laughing. "Having worked as a sales manager in cars, a very good professional job, and then say to family, friends and business associates, 'I'm gonna sell baseball cards,' well, some people questioned the move."

One person who did not, however, was Goodwin's wife, Sharon.

"She's always had the confidence in me that I could make money in whatever line of work I chose," Goodwin said. "I guess the biggest question in my mind was, 'would I be able to find enough material to keep the business going?'"

That was a couple of years ago. Today, Bill and Sharon, along with their two daughters, Carrie and Courtney, run a family business out of their home, St. Louis Baseball Cards.

"I knew I could sell the materials and merchandise them," Goodwin said.

"The big thing I had going for myself was that I'd been collecting cards for some time. I felt I knew what collectors wanted in a mail-order business: strict grading, speedy service, professional packaging and fairness."

Goodwin said he tries to have more than one item of everything he advertises in trade publications such as SCD. He knows from personal experience how disheartening it is to call someone who is selling items and learn a particular collectible you want has been sold.

"That's part of collecting," Goodwin said with a shrug. "It's probably happened to most people. But I try to advertise things that I have more than one of in stock."

In addition to a thriving mail-order buiness — the Goodwins average sending out about 20 mail orders a day — Bill does as many as 40 card and memorabilia shows a year. About six to eight of those shows he also hosts, along with show partner and fellow collector Rich Hawksley, at the Holiday Inn North in St. Louis.

"The heart and soul of my business, really, is the mail-order," Goodwin said.

"I do shows mainly to meet people, make contacts and buy material."

Goodwin deals mostly in cards issued prior to about 1973.

"From 1973 on, it's better economically for most people to buy those cards as sets, and those sets are readily available," Goodwin explained. "Consequently, to stock that much inventory...it's probably not going to turn over as quickly as the rest of the cards."

Even casual observers marvel at the quality of baseball cards the Goodwins bring to card shows and conventions. And Bill's reputation for tough grading standards and his easygoing demeanor have brought him customers from all 50 states and such locales as Guam, England, Germany and Puerto Rico.

"I like to think a majority of my customers are collectors and not investors," he said, "but of course, in this day and age, everybody has to think in terms of investment, too, because that's how you justify your purchases.

"Still, I really enjoy the people, the collectors. You know, buying a car is not, unfortunately, a pleasurable experience for most people. Buying a baseball card, on the other hand, is — or should be — a pleasure. I really like that part of my work, being with other people who are as enthusiastic about the hobby as I am and seeing them enjoy themselves.

"At one point I remember thinking that if this thing didn't work out, I could always go back to the car business. I came back from the nationals in Arlington (Texas) a few years ago, and said, 'Nah. I'm not going back. This is too much fun.'

"Plus, I'm home a lot more, and Sharon and the kids enjoy that because I'm around to do different things, such as attend school functions and so forth. It's kind of hard to switch careers the way I did after 17 years in one profession, but selling baseball cards was what I wanted to do."

* * *

SCD Dealer Profile
Walter Hall
One Of The Hobby's 'Giants'
Talks Of Yesterday, Today
And The Future Of
The Sports Memorabilia Hobby

By Paul Green — Sept. 18, 1987

It isn't hard to find Walter Hall's ad in SCD. Try the back cover or one of the first pages and you'll usually find him well-represented. Walter Hall is, after all, one of the nation's largest and most successful card dealers. Like most others, the story of Hall's Nostalgia is the story of a family, their love of baseball and the many types of things which relate to the game. It's also a bit of a story about one of the hobby's modern-day pioneers, as when Hall's Nostalgia started, the landscape was hardly dotted with baseball card stores and shows...

...SCD: How did it turn into a business?

Hall: It wasn't until the middle 1970s. All my life I had collected odds and ends, but that was for myself. In the middle 1960s, when my sons were around their middle teens, they started getting very interested in baseball. Then the Red Sox won the championship in 1967 and that helped to raise their enthusiasm. About that point I started dragging out a lot of my collectibles. Like a lot of boys they started fantasizing about how nice it would be to sell some of them to buy some current items. They started asking if they could sell some of my things and I said "No problem." They started going to flea markets with my supervision and started selling things through the mail. That was really was the beginning of it.

SCD: Of course, back then it was basically unkown to do that full time.

Hall: That's true, but about 1974 we went to our first sports convention. There was a mini-convention in New York City, and we drove down and bought a lot of cards. I remember buying a Babe Ruth card for about $10 and a lot of cards of that vintage at prices which now seems very inexpensive. That was our first show. From that point, my sons really wanted to start a business. They asked me if I could rent a store in town and they could start selling baseball memorabilia. My wife and I talked about it and decided to invest $1,000 in getting them a place to start. That was probably the best $1,000 investment we ever made. That was early 1976...

...SCD: One thing you have which few others have is a regular auction. How is that going?

Hall: It's going very well. Since we started our business we've had four major expansions. One was opening the second store, we've also expanded our current location, going from a one store front to a three-store front. The most recent has been the auctions. On Sept. 11, we'll be having our 31st auction. We got into it when a fellow with a deaf son came into the store. He wanted us to contribute some memorabilia for an auction for a home for the deaf. So we contributed some items

234

and he had a mini-auction. He came back and told me how successful it was and asked if we were interested. My sons and I discussed it and decided that it might be something the hobby could use at the time. So we developed a relationship with this auctioneer 31 months ago. Since then it's taken off really well. We've been interviewed by several television stations and had extensive coverage in all media.

We consider the auctions to be first class auctions. There are no minimum bids, they are quality lots and we make sure that everyone who comes is given a free gift and free refreshments when they enter the hall. I consider it a first-class atmosphere. People feel very comfortable and so far have been very receptive every time. We're not only adding to our business, we're adding to the hobby. We're getting a lot of merchandise out into the hobby which might never have gotten there if we didn't have these monthly auctions. We get people from all over the country. We give away a distance prize and last month we had a fellow from Seattle, Wash., and at that same auction we had people from California and Arizona. People out this way on business or vacations come. They know about the auction because we advertise them.

SCD: What sort of attendance do you get?

Hall: We average about 150 people at each auction. In the 30 auctions we've had we've generated a list of over 2,000 names of attendees, so it isn't the same 150 who come every month.

SCD: Do you think auctions will be a growing part of the hobby?

Hall: Yes, I do. Going back to my coin and stamp days, that was one of the best ways we used to buy coins and stamps. We used to go to auctions. They had conventions and shows, but it seemed like the auction atmosphere was always better for buying merchandise and I enjoyed it more. It's not that I don't enjoy conventions because I do, it's just that auctions are a different atmosphere. It's very interesting just to see what people are paying for a given item and how many are interested. An auction can educate you a lot better than a show does because you can see visually what people are doing...

...SCD: How do you feel about the whole investment aspect in general? Ten years ago it was rarely discussed. Is it healthy to have it assume such a major focus?

Hall: I personally don't like the investment portion of the hobby. I think it's a lot more fun and a lot more healthy when you do it from a standpoint of pure collecting and fun for the individual and family. However, there are good features in the investment attitude. One of them is that it brings many people into the hobby who would have never come into it if that aspect wasn't there. It's made the hobby much more accepted.

Ten years ago, nobody would dare talk about being a baseball card collector. They would be looked down upon. Today, with all the articles in the Wall Street Journal and Time and various others, instead of looking down on you, people look up to you. They say, "Gee, that's great, you collect baseball cards."

So, there is a certain factor in it which is good. I just think that people who are in it strictly for the investment itself will find that they will either have to play it very smart or they're not going to make the money they think they're going to make. Something will happen to eliminate that particular profit. If you expect to make money, you'll have to be very careful.

SCD: How do you see the hobby today?

Hall: I think the hobby is extremely strong, probably the strongest it's ever been. In 1978 when my sons, my wife and I took a tour of the country we went looking for other stores. We found three other stores in the whole country. Today, if you went on that same 8,500 mile tour, I'd guess you'd probably find 8,500 stores. There are an incredible number of stores in every city and in every state now. The hobby itself has just increased phenomenally. Every aspect of the hobby is very strong. Something I've seen, too, is that even four years ago you didn't see girls coming into the store. Today you find not only fathers

and sons, but mothers and daughters and whole families. I think this is extremely good for the family. It gives them something in common, and is extremely good for the hobby. You like to have females in the hobby as well as males, and that's happened.

* * *

Meet Rich Hawksley
This St. Louis Browns Fan
Is A Hobby Circuit Veteran

By David Craft — April 29, 1988

If you want to learn about the St. Louis Browns — the city's other baseball team during the first half of the 20th century — ask Rich Hawksley.

The best place to ask him is at his card shop, Baseball Collectors Corner, a small retail outlet that doubles as a museum of Browns memorabilia...

...Hawksley began collecting Browns yearbooks and baseball cards about 1950. Four years later, his heroes were in Baltimore, and St. Louis became a one-team town.

"I was getting to be a teen-ager by then, and other things were distracting me from baseball, anyway," Hawksley said, "including girls. Later, I joined the service, and eventually I went to work for the Anheuser-Busch Co. I didn't really get back into collecting until about 1975.

"I went to a card show back then, and got wrapped up in it again. I'd forgotten how much fun it can be to collect cards and everything."

Eventually, Hawksley became convention chair of a local sports memorabilia club that hosted card shows and boasted some of the area's top collectors, including Jim Hickerson, Bill Goodwin and Rick Maloney.

Through the business partnership known as St. Louis Sports Collectors, Hawksley and Goodwin continue to host major conventions in St. Louis throughout the year, as well as one-day "mini-shows." For several hours, baseball cards and photos come to life, as some of the great names in the game sign autographs and meet with fans, collectors and dealers from all over the country.

Hawksley maintains a high profile, during these shows, talking with the players, expediting the lines of autograph seekers, and ensuring kids and adults alike come away from the tables happy.

He also helps coordinate the players arrivals and departures from the Holiday Inn North, which is an adventure in itself, since as many as eight players are in any autograph signing.

"I don't know how he keeps doing it," said a dealer who frequently buys a table at Hawksley's shows and who asked SCD for anonymity.

"To some people, he comes off as gruff, and even a little cold sometimes. But that's just because he's busy making sure everything's going OK. The ballplayers respect him and trust him, and he really does put a helluva lot of work into it. And you've gotta remember, he works full time and has the shop open on Friday nights and Saturdays when he's not doing a show."

Does the No. 1 Browns fan ever relax and just enjoy his collectibles?

"Oh, sure," says Hawksley. "Every time I get a new jersey, I feel real good. I collect them by type, because the styles changed over the years. I'm missing only two types of jerseys that I know of — one from the mid-1930s, and one all the way back to around 1910."

Hawksley is also tickled by those things that are locked in his memory. Luke Sewell, who played a few games for the Browns in 1942 and managed the club to its only World Series appearance (against the Cardinals in 1944), was a guest at one of Hawksley's shows.

"He was about 85 or 86," Hawksley said. "That was a big thrill for me to meet him. Luke really had some good baseball stories and I really enjoyed talking with him, before the show and on the way back to the airport afterward."...

...One of the reasons why Hawksley enjoys collecting Browns items is "because they're really hard to find, especially uniforms," Hawksley said. "It's a real challenge, and it's a lot of fun. It's gratifying to know that some of these guys who were tough autographs signed these photos for me."

Hawksley's shows began with one about eight years ago that featured Hall of Famer Johnny Mize. That show's success led to other shows with future HOFers Bob Feller, Enos Slaughter, Lou Brock, as well as shows featuring baseball greats not in Cooperstown.

The popularity of the shows has forced Hawksley to host them more frequently — from one a year to two or three to the present format of several major conventions plus the one-day "mini shows" every year...

...For Hawksley, who pitched American Legion ball ("I had a pretty good fastball and...kind of a curve," he said laughing) putting on successful shows is a business. Yet his biggest thrill is from meeting the ballplayers.

"How many people can say they had dinner with this Hall of Famer or that great player?" Hawksley says. "And collecting their signatures is still fun for me as a fan, just like everybody else. What fan wouldn't find it a thrill to meet and talk with Stan Musial and have him call you by your first name?

"You know, I always said I would quit all this when I turned 50, which is next year. Now that I'm nearing that point, I'm not so sure."

* * *

He Was A True Lover Of Collecting

By Lionel Carter — Jan. 21, 1983

As one grows older and older, he begins to expect these letters with a wife's name as the return address, or these phone calls from a wife when it has always been the husband who did all the calling in the past.

He might expect them, but he is never ready for them, nor does he at first accept them. It is too hard to accept the fact that another old friend has passed away. Today, as I near the retirement age of 65, the calls are more and more frequent; first it is an old classmate, then an old army buddy, and then a card collector.

So it was on the evening of Nov. 18 when Helen Jaspersen called to tell me the sad news that Bob Jaspersen had passed away. How could that be? It hadn't been too long ago that I had received yet another issue of Sport Fan. Why just the night before, when Bill Mastro had purchased my Sport Kings and Football Stars, I had jokingly mentioned to him how I had asked Bob to write my obituary when I died. Bob had agreed only if I would write his if he died first.

And now I am sitting at my typewriter, sad and depressed, trying to write an obituary for Bob Jaspersen, the best friend I ever bad in the hobby.

In writing of Bob Jaspersen and the sport collecting hobby, I think one would have to begin with Sport Fan. This was Bob's main interest in the hobby, and, next to his family, his main interest in life. Although Bob never expressed such feelings to me, I believe that Sport Fan was his big dream. To make it into something big in the hobby so that he could combine his love of sports collecting with his love of writing.

Sport Fan began way back in 1951, when there weren't too many collectors, or if there were, they hadn't as yet crawled out of the woodwork in the closet. Bob never made a profit with Sport Fan, but it was a labor of love and he continued to put not only his time and his labor into keeping it afloat, but also his money. I began writing a regular baseball card column for Sport Fan in 1955, and was pleased when Bob wrote me several months later to report that my column had created a large increase in subscriptions. Even before I joined the Sport Fan staff of writers, Bob was dreaming of a sports collectors convention. The April 1955 issue headlined the idea, and the April 1956 issue of Sport Fan claimed: "Convention To Be Held at Chicago 'Y' July 7 & 8."

Remember, this was 14 years before Jim Nowell hosted the first sports collectors convention in Brea, Calif. A two-day affair, the convention was not planned as a dealers' or selling show but as an exhibitor's show with tables offered to exhibitors for $4.50 and a chance to win prizes for best collections and for $2.50 for non-exhibitors and dealers.

Bob had contacted various companies and publishers for donations of gifts to be given as prizes and had some really excellent prizes. Accommodations at the YMCA were $2.10 to $4.50 for singles and $3.50 to $7 for doubles.

Bob came down from St. Paul, Minn., for the weekend of April 7-8 to push the two-man committee of John Sullivan and myself into action. It was our pleasure to host Bob and his lovely wife, Helen, with that intriguing tilting Irish Brogue, for the weekend. It was a wonderful visit and a whirlwind affair as anyone who has had to try to keep up with the fast-moving, long-striding Bob can testify.

It was also the weekend that Helen asked Irma if she might keep Bob's insulin in the refrigerator and we learned that Bob was not quite as healthy as he looked. We rushed hither and yon as arrangements for the coming convention were made, including a visit to Hobbies Magazine which resulted in articles by Sullivan (scorecards) and myself (baseball cards) being published in that nationally-circulated publication, the first time sports hobby articles had reached such a lofty status, although Jeff Burdick had a previous article published in Hobbies on cigarette cards, and I had written a series on baseball cards for the Kaw Chief Stamp Journal as far back as 1937.

John Sullivan made the arrangements with the YMCA at 1508 N. Larrabee St. in Chicago, obtaining a display room for only $100 for the weekend. With such low rates and excellent prizes, what happened to the convention? Only 10 collectors reserved tables, and Bob dismissed the venture due to lack of interest.

Yet I have always felt that that was not the real contributing factor, and just perhaps Bob also recognized the real reason: one of the members of the committee was not contributing anything. Me. I was all enthused about the idea and wanted to see it happen until Bob mentioned that he would put our collections display for the general public. I just couldn't see putting my mint, well-centered baseball cards in such a precarious position. I just didn't want my albums torn and my cards bent by the careless handling I associated with the general public.

At that point I lost interest entirely. In fact, I was faced with the prospect of refusing to display my collection if the convention had been held. So we only had 10 collectors; how many did Jim Nowell have in 1969? If one of the three organizers had offered to cover one-third of the loss of staging the convention, the other two would have gone along. I considered making that suggestion, but I didn't really want a convention. It was a battle between my friendship for Bob and my love of my mint card collection. Actually it was no contest; Bob and the hobby lost.

If Bob even suspected that I had sabotaged his convention, he never led me to believe that he suspected, as our friendship grew and ripened over the years. In 1958 we paid a return call to St. Paul to spend a wonderful weekend with the Jaspersens, looking over the files of Sport Fan and the sport mementoes that Bob collected. I have always suspected that Bob looked down on baseball card collectors although he never expressed or showed such feelings, and it was surprising we hit it off so well when his favorite in his considerable number of interests seemed to be autographs, a hobby that I have always regarded as silly, an opinion I have often stated in articles and discussions.

I think Bob's highlight of the year was his almost annual pilgrimage to Cooperstown for each year's induction ceremonies, where he would put Helen's good looks and charming personality to work asking and collecting autographs for him. Not that he didn't get his share of autographs, but he was not about to overlook any advantage he could use in obtaining them.

My wife is a true gourmet — if gourmet meals were served at conventions, we would make all of them — and one of the spots she had selected for a visit was the Lowell Inn in Stillwater, Minn. Bob and Helen had often talked of going there for dinner, so it was our lucky privilege to take them for dinner there as it is so often when out-of-towners take local dwellers to places they always intended to visit but never did. As I said, it was a wonderful, wonderful weekend.

Another innovation of Bob Jaspersen was the Sport Fan Who's Who, first published in 1955 and published yearly thereafter until the sixth and final edition which was for 1960-1961. Each edition of Who's Who, which originally sold for 35 cents but was later raised to 50 cents, listed collectors with a short description of the collector, his collection, and his interests, plus advertisements of want lists and items for sale.

Jeff Burdick had published a "Collector's Directory" in the first issue of his Card Collectors Bulletin in January, 1937, but a "Who's Who" was another first for Bob Jaspersen, just as his attempt to organize a convention had been.

Yet another innovation brought into the hobby by Bob Jaspersen, in 1975, was the annual Frank Jock Memorial Award sponsored by Sport Fan as a tribute to the late Frank Jock of Kezar Falls, Maine, and presented to the collector who received the most votes from fellow collectors for his contributions to the hobby. As the proud and happy recipient of the 1979 award, through the persistence of Don Schlaff in nominating me three times, I would like to see one of the hobby publications take over the annual presentation of this award. It is the only one of its kind in the hobby and worthy of being continued. I would suggest that it be renamed the Frank Jock-Bob Jaspersen Memorial Award, and that the 1983 plaque be awarded to Bob Jaspersen posthumously and be given to his widow, Helen Jaspersen.

I would further suggest that if the Sport Collectors Hall of Fame as originated by Irving Lerner's "Who's Who in Sport Collecting" is ever revived, that Bob Jaspersen be considered for immediate induction. Bob gave so much to the hobby and asked so little in return. It is too bad that he was not recognized for what he did while he was still with us to enjoy such recognition.

Bob Jaspersen was a true gentleman, a fine fellow, an honest collector. He put so much time and money into the hobby with no expectation of financial return that it could only be a labor of love. Like this writer, he never went into the hobby with an expectation of financial gain, and, like this writer, he never got into the buying and selling end of the hobby, so that he never knew the value of items in his collection and was often ripped off by those he trusted for an honest deal.

As a true lover of collecting, he was not fond of the commercialism that has invaded our hobby and sent prices and values soaring. He struggled for years with a mimeographed Sport Fan, trying to stay afloat as the hobby became flooded with finely-printed hobby papers drawing away his subscriber and writers alike by writing some of the finest, most interesting, most informative articles in the hobby.

When Bob went to a convention his readers were assured of the finest coverage in the hobby; giving his reader the impression that he, the reader, had just stepped through the door of the convention and was making the rounds of the tables. We tried to emulate this style when we covered a convention. But today no one writes like that, but perhaps no one could write like Bob.

A friendly, easy-going fellow, always interested in anything anyone would say about the hobby, Bob could on occasion rise up to defend his principles for honest collecting, honest dialing, honest reporting. He was my friend, and I have lost him. But the hobby has suffered a grievous loss too; the hobby lost a collector and writer who tried to keep us on an even keel.

Replacing him will not be easy — if it is ever done. Even the word "hobby" can be altered to say: "Hy Bob!" and so it must be now, wherever sport collectors go when they leave this world that Jefferson Burdick is extending his hand and heads a delegation of Walter Corson, Preston Orem, Jake, and James Lacey in saying, "Hy Bob!"

* * *

MARK R. JORDAN — April 15, 1974

Currently a freshman at David Lipscomb College, Mark is actually is actually a veteran sports collector, particularly being active in "I" "E," "R" and regional card collecting.

He has near complete sets in T200, T205, T206 and T201 and has most of the Bowman and Topps issues.

In addition he is a collector of World Series and All-Star game items, player uniforms, yearbooks, guides, press guides, programs, autographs, tickets and ticket stubs, postcards and pins.

He was a sports writer in Hollywood, Fla., and has worked for several big league teams. He has been chairman of three Florida conventions.

His collection is well advanced in most of the issues in card collecting.

* * *

ROBERT LIFSON — Feb. 24, 1974

This 13-year old collector already has over 35,000 cards in his collection. His main interest is in baseball cards, especially from 1933-1941, although he admits to collecting all of the other eras about as much.

A student at Chestnut Hill Academy, Robert has, of late, been working on improving his sample collection with his prize samples including Gypsy Queen, Kalamazoo Bat, Goodwin (cabinet size), Fro Joy, DeLong and a handful of other rare samples.

One of his favorite sets is the 1933 Tatoo-Orbit, which he is just two away from completing. Another favorite set is the 1950 Topps set, which he also intends to complete. He at the present time has 19 different in this set, including five current stars, and all 19 are in Mint condition.

He has also started all of the Goudey sets from 1933-41 (except R325), plus all National Chicle Sets and has over half of the Play Balls issued in 1939-1941. Robert also collects the 1941 Double Plays and many regionals such as Drake's and Tip Top.

He feels that the most interesting characteristic of his collection is its variety with the sample now numbering over 100 different and he is actively collecting to complete those.

* * *

Meet Dealer Don Lepore
He Ran His First Card Show Table At Age 13
Some 16 Years Later, Don Lepore Oversees A Thriving Mail-order Business In New Jersey

By Paul Green — Aug. 19, 1988

Since 1972, Don Lepore has been active in baseball cards. That's some 16 years, meaning Lepore started at a time when there were basically no active dealers and really a rather quiet hobby which very few who are active today could even identify as being the hobby they know. Lepore took time to discuss his activities of the past, of some of his observations on the present and the future...

...SCD: Did you then start collecting?

Lepore: What happened was that I had some cards from when I was young. We looked to see how much they were worth according to this guy's price list and they were worth a couple hundred dollars. If I sold them I could afford everything I wanted — a basketball, a pair of sneakers and a radio. I didn't know what else there was in life other than those three things. There was an announcement about a baseball card show out in Brentwood, Long Island. It was the first show I know of on the East Coast. I went out there and had a table and sold my cards. I made $125. I was a rich man. I was planning on buying the things I wanted, the radio type thing, the basketball and the sneakers figuring I'd be set for life.

SCD: But you obviously didn't stop with that one show.

Lepore: What happened was that I only bought the basketball and sneakers. With the rest of the money, I bought some cards my friends had. I had heard about another show in New York City so I decided to buy cards and bring them to that show. That's what I did. With the $50 I had left over I bought cards from kids in the neighborhood. I'd pay two bucks a box or three bucks a box. I accumulated some cards and took a bus up to the District 65 Center and the next show I took all my cards and can remember coming home with $400. It was amazing.

SCD: So you started a business rather quickly.

Lepore: Yes, I was 13 at my first show...

...SCD: Looking back, you've seen a lot of changes haven't you?

Yes, I'm not shocked, but I'm pleasantly surprised. When I started going to shows there were maybe 200 of us nuts in the world. We actually believed baseball cards were worth money.

SCD: And everyone thought you were crazy.

Lepore: Right, they definitely though it was unusual, but I really believed it. I had no problem buying cards and having my life savings in baseball cards. Now we have maybe 300,000 solid collectors in the country and maybe another half million or a million casual collectors

and I think it will just continue growing. You have 50 million people a year who go to games in person and hundreds of millions who watch on TV.

I think you have a big pool of possible future collectors to draw from and now its a lot easier. When you tell people they should spend $100 on a baseball card, they understand why. A decade ago it was unheard of. There were only a handful of cards worth $100, just the rare classic stuff. A rare card was only worth $20. Now it's a lot easier to get people to spend the money. They see the value there. So, I'm not surprised, I've just had this unusual idea for all of my adult life and since I was 13, that cards were worth money...

...SCD: What advice do you give someone just starting?

Lepore: First, I tell them that before they go out and buy a whole bunch of cards they should define what they are interested in and what is their budget. I recommend they read publications such as SCD or Baseball Card News to find out what they're interested in, see what's out there. Then see what they can actually spend, because everyone has limits. You can't go out and spend millions, so if you go after something you can afford, then you don't get frustrated. So define what you're interested in and be realistic about what you can afford.

SCD: Do you have any advice for people who have been in a while?

Lepore: I think it's good to share with people. Give some time to the new people because they may become a collector and that's good for all of us. The more people collect, the more valuable the cards become, and you're also doing them a favor, because it may help fill a void in their life and give them something they will enjoy.

Many people think that they're not knowledgeable enough to talk to others, but they'd be amazed how much they could help someone who is just starting and really doesn't know anything. I think we should all think about sharing our hobby with others because we'll be doing both the hobby and others a service by sharing it with them.

SCD: You seem optimistic about the future.

Lepore: Oh yes, I'm a positive thinking person. I think this hobby is such a positive thing. Fathers and sons are enjoying their weekends together where otherwise they might not even be spending the time together. It's a natural for the family.

* * *

Sports Artist Ron Lewis Interviewed

By Kevin Huard — May 11, 1990

SCD: Ron, how are things going with the print — the '61 Yankees print?

Lewis: Well, right now the original art is getting photographed and all the transparencies will be delivered to the printer tomorrow morning through Federal Express, so then they have to go about getting the separations, which will be about a weeks worth of work. And then they'll start printing in about 10 days, I would suppose. Everything's right on line.

SCD: Was it a painstakingly big project for you?

Lewis: Yes, it was. I'm used to doing two or three characters, something like that, but 41 characters was more of a challenge than I've ever taken on before, and it proved to be a very long, drawn-out process. I wouldn't want to tackle it again all too soon.

SCD: Maybe four or five years down the road?

Lewis: Maybe a hundred and five years down the road.

Ron Lewis

SCD: Can you tell us a little about all the detail work that goes into each individual player, in terms of things like eyelashes, one little stroke of the brush changes the entire person?

Lewis: I think one thing to take into consideration is that when you take on a project like this you've got some people who really don't have existing photographs in the public domain, and so you have to work from very old poorly lit photographs, and you had to try to draw a rendering from that particular photograph. Sometimes it's really hard to see what the features of the face really are, so that's a major problem right there. That happened on a lot of these guys, because a lot of them I went through yearbooks, baseball cards, old magazines, and I just had a hard time rounding up a lot of photographs on these guys.

SCD: Of course, you're doing a team that was probably one of the most successful of all time, the '61 Yankees.

Lewis: Yes, no doubt about it. There's conjecture about the '27 Yankees and the '61 team, but there seems to be a split halfway between them.

SCD: Unfortunately, there's not too many left from the '27 team, so I don't think anyone will be doing a show reunion with the '27 Yankees.

Lewis: There's one guy left. Actually, we're having this guy sign a piece of my artwork when I did the '27 Yankee card set. He's (shortstop) Mark Koenig, and he's still alive, and he's got my artwork right there that he's going to be signing, so as soon as we get that back then we'll be releasing that.

SCD: That would be an interesting piece for collectors.

Lewis: Yes, he's the last guy remaining from that team.

SCD: You mentioned that you were having a little bit of difficulty finishing up on the pinstripes. Can you explain what the problem was there, you know when people see this and they see all the pinstripe uniforms, they probably just take for granted no big deal doing pinstripe uniforms.

Lewis: Well, you have to figure that for every fold in a uniform, and those were baggy uniforms in the first place, that that line has to follow the contour of not only the fold of the fabric, but also where the body shows through as far as you can see muscularity on the body, so you have to follow the contour.

Plus, not only does the line have to follow the contour of all the folds, it also has to change in value, in color as the light strikes it. So you've got 41 guys with all these tiny little pinstripes that are a 32th of

an inch, maybe less, maybe a 64th of an inch, and they all have to be same degree of thickness, and it's a very time-consuming deal. It took me two solid days of probably 12 hours a day, probably 24 hours just to do the pinstripes alone.

SCD: Who were some of the more interesting, or easier players that you were able to render on your print?

Lewis: I think a face is face for me basically, it just boils down to who I have the best photographs of. And obviously, with guys like Mickey Mantle, Yogi Berra. But Yogi Berra was a little easier because he's got a lot of character in his face. But anybody that I had more access to more photographs I was able to render a little more convincingly, because the more photographs I have the more chances I have to pick out individual characteristics of the face.

SCD: The research on this must have been incredible. If you take into consideration you may have looked at anywhere from 3-20 different photographs of each ballplayer and multiply that time 41, that's a lot of time just looking at photographs, and trying to pick and choose which one, or two or three would be the best to use when you do the particular face.

Lewis: Plus, you also have to take into consideration when you're doing a face or a portrait of a person, the actual shadowing is what makes the characteristics of the face, the way the light strikes the face. So I had to alter almost everybody's faces to make one light source. And so you have to think in your own mind how a nose is going to work, you're looking at one light source in the photograph, and you're having to try to render another light source, so that's a problem in itself right there. I had to keep the actual light source, like a bright sunlit light source all consistent with everybody, with the pinstripe, with the stadium, with everything. That was a problem.

SCD: Let's change the subject just a bit, go back to a time when you first got involved in the hobby. What is some of the work that you're proud of that you created since you first became involved in the hobby?

Lewis: I guess I got started when I showed my portfolio to Bill Hongach, who is at Capital Cards, and he was doing a magazine at the time called Baseball Hobby Card Report. He was using photographic material for the cover and he wanted to use some artwork, so he had me do some artwork for the cover of his magazine. I think the first one I might have done was Ron Kittle. He had been Rookie of the Year that year, and then I did a few other little projects dealing with sports. Then, I did another magazine cover for him, which was Cal Ripken. So through the process of doing those magazine covers, we had other projects crop up, card sets, then we started doing posters, prints.

SCD: Mostly baseball players I take it?

Lewis: Yes, at this point I was working independently doing book cover and magazine covers for other periodicals at the time. It just seemed to be that most of the work was coming through baseball, so I just got to the point where I had to put the other work aside.

SCD: When was this? Probably 1984-85?

Lewis: Yes, 1984.

SCD: The hobby has grown significantly since 1984-85, and it appears your career within the hobby has certainly grown and magnified to the degree that it's at now. You are now one of the top sports artists in the country.

Lewis: You're so kind.

SCD: Have people ever mentioned that you bear a remarkable resemblance to Mike Schmidt?

Lewis: Yes, but until you got up close and noticed all the muscle tone I have compared to what you've seen on Mike Schmidt. At the 500 Home Run show in Atlantic City I wasn't able to get too close to Mike Schmidt. To tell you the truth, it was kind of like passing the item along and get it signed and see you later. But it was a great show, and I think that one particular show fueled this hobby to a degree that has been just amazing. That particular show generated a lot of interest.

SCD: It would seem that two of the most popular pieces are your 500 home run posters, the Yankee Stadium version and the lightning bolt version, have been probably two of the most popular pieces of sports artwork within the hobby over the last year or two. Do you still find that a lot of requests are for your particular rendition of the 500 home run hitters?

Lewis: Yes, as a matter of fact I find it kind of unusual, not unusual, kind of interesting that people would take that to the shows and have me sign the the thing along with the ballplayers, which is extremely flattering for me. Every show I go to I get several of those that I autograph the thing for them.

SCD: Getting back to a thing that happened about two months ago with you and Bill Hongach. Maybe you could talk about the new vehicle for displaying and merchandising the Ron Lewis line. Could you tell us what's going on now?

Lewis: What we've done is we've decided to make a much more accessible display for the public, so they don't necessarily have to go at the table and talk to us. They can just walk by an 8x10 foot display and see what I've done. And we wanted to get a little more professional and clean up the act.

SCD: You're displaying quite a bit of your famous pieces of artwork. Could you give us 10 of your more favorite pieces that you've created over the last four or five years?

Lewis: I think obviously the 500, because it gained such a popularity among the people. It was definitely one of the favorites. My Spahn and Sain, I like that because it's different from anything I've worked on. I've got some Nolan Ryan's that I'm real happy with, that are on display. I did an Ali/Frazier thing that I'm real happy with, and the Seaver, and my Living Legends.

SCD: Within that series the Warren Spahn was magnificent, almost like a photograph.

Lewis: Well, you know Spahn, he's got a lot to work with there. I think that will be true to any artist though, whenever you've got a face that has a lot of character in, not only is it a lot more pleasurable to work on, it's just a lot easier to do, because you have much more chance of making things work, rather than a face with less character in.

SCD: You're on your fourth or your fifth (Living Legends) series now?

Lewis: Fifth. Yes, the fifth just got released two weeks ago.

SCD: So that means that out of the total numbered series, you have 20 baseball players that you've created.

Lewis: Right.

SCD: Are you going to be continuing that even further?

Lewis: Yes. Right now, not only is Bill, who's basically my partner, working on the '61 Yankees show, but he's in the process of getting the new Legends characters lined up, the guys we're going to use this time. I don't know now, but we're working on some real big names this time. Not only this time, but I mean again this time, some real big names. And another thing that would maybe have to be said here, you just don't paint these guys. You have to go and discuss it with them, you've got to pay them, and you've got to get rights to do them.

SCD: Major League Baseball wants a piece of the action?

Lewis: Yes. It isn't like you can just do anybody, or else we would. We have to be very selective as to who will work with us. We have to be very legitimate on this or we can get in a lot of trouble.

SCD: It's better in the long run.

Lewis: I believe so. It's very costly and it's very frustrating working with, not necessarily the ballplayers, but their managers and their agents are the people who really set you off on this.

SCD: You seem to personally enjoy meeting the ballplayers. Do you still get excited to meet a Warren Spahn, a Eddie Mathews, a Mickey Mantle?

Lewis: Eddie's my favorite, put that in there.

SCD: Eddie Mathews is your favorite?

Lewis: Eddie's my favorite.

SCD: Any reason why?

Lewis: I just like the guy's ability to really get down and to be a regular guy. He and his wife (Judy), they're both great.

SCD: Real down to earth people, huh?

Lewis: Yeah, you can sit down and just talk to them and just have a good time with them.

SCD: I'd like to know what the hobby's going to be like in 1995. Are we still going to be doing this, Ron?

Lewis: I don't know. It scares me sometimes.

SCD: It looks like the '61 Yankee Reunion show may be another big show like the 500 home run show.

Lewis: I hope it is, not that I make any money if it is. I just think it's a great time.

* * *

Score's Stand On The 1989 Football Set

By Don Butler — Sept. 29, 1989

Score released its first set of football cards this year — a colorful, exciting, 330-card card entry that features action shots on the front, head shots and biographical data on the back.

Score included several subsets in its NFL football card issue. The most notable — and one that may change football cards forever — is the rookies series, which shows a head shot of each team's first pick in the 1989 draft.

Score spokesman George Martin talked about the production of the 1989 set.

SCD: Can you tell us how Score became involved in producing football cards? In other words, what was behind the decision to produce football cards at this time?

Martin: As you recognize, there's been a tremendous boom in the growth, proliferation and popularity of football cards. Football cards have been sort of a dormant collector's vehicle for a number of years, and we did some fundamental test marketing and analyses of what the market could do if it were stimulated a bit and if people got a little more interested in the collectibility of football cards. Based on our evaluation of the results, we decided to take on the licenses from the Players Association and NFL Properties.

SCD: What time line are we taking about? A year ago, two?

Martin: About a year ago. Within the last year, really. We hammered it out quite quickly once it got started.

SCD: What about the cards themselves? How many photos did (photo editor) Larry Lambrecht have to sort through per player?

Martin: That was an immense task because, as you know, we've really established our reputation in the marketplace on pictoral and editorial content, the kind of card stock we use and the graphics.

In this particular case, we weren't able to send our own photographers out to the training camps and to the games during the season, so we had to purchase our pictures on the market. So the research that went into that was really the major task that we faced. He (Lambrecht) spent a solid week at one location looking at pictures — 10 or 12 hours a day — and I spent two days at another location looking at pictures. So we spent an awful lot of time editing down pictures. It was a rather laborious and involved task.

SCD: Where were these outlets where you looked at football pictures?

Martin: On the West Coast, primarily. There was a place that had a large stock of football pictures, really by the ton. Some of them were good, some of them were not so good, so you really had to sort through and get the best pictures. Everyone appreciated what he (Lambrecht) went through, but I don't think everyone really knew, other than perhaps myself, how difficult a task that really is. You get overwhelmed looking at pictures after awhile. It sort overwhelms your senses. It was a big job and took a long, long time.

SCD: When he started looking through pictures, did he have a player list to choose from or did he pick the photos first?

Martin: We retained a consultant, the well-known writer Paul Zimmerman from Sports Illustrated. I guess he's probably the best-known football expert in America.

First of all, we decided how many cards we were going to have in the series, and that was 330 cards. We have fewer than the competition for a couple of very important reasons: Number one, we wanted to be able to give the consumer more value. We're the only card company that has all the top rookies from each team in the set. And then we have a higher mix of superstars in our series. Since we have 330, it really meant that we had to concentrate on the top eight or nine players on each team. So when the consumer opens up his packs of cards...For example, I have a pack in front of me, and I'll open it up and look through the 16 cards. We've got Mark Bavaro, Ronnie Lippett, Irving Fryar, Steve McMichael, Don Beebe (rookie receiver for the Bills), a Super Bowl card, Bo Jackson, Curt Warner, and another rookie, Wayne Martin (defensive end for the Saints). The one specifically designated as an all-pro card is Deron Cherry. And also in this pack is Anthony Miller, who's part of the Speedburners subset.

That's a pretty good mix of 15 cards. So the consumer is going to appreciate getting that. There are no no-names in there. Getting the superstars, which as you know from baseball cards, kids are interested in the name players and they're also interested in the rookies.

SCD: Speaking of subsets, that seems to be a logical idea that nobody ever attempted before in football cards. What's behind some of these subsets — the rookies, the speedburners?

Martin: I think we have an obligation to ourselves, and therefore an obligation to our consumer, to put out the most creative product, the product that's going to sell in a very creative marketplace. Basically, we don't really think Topps has an edge in the business. The only edge Topps has is they have a franchise name. But I think that our product speaks for itself, both our football and baseball cards.

Obviously, Pro Set doesn't have anything other than a handle that they created for themselves — "The Official Card." What does it mean, "The Official Card?" It's like having "The Official Soft Drink of the Olympics." What does that mean?

So we all started off on equal footing, and the idea here is to deliver the very best product possible to the consumer. When we established with Zimmerman, we tried to analyze what the consumer was looking for. Obviously, he as was looking for rookies. Secondly, he was looking for the top stars of each team. Then he was looking for those recognizable all-pros. Then you break down and look at a football team, and what are the most exciting categories? Obviously the big hitters, the guys that come crashing through the line and are after the quarterback. So we did a series on those guys called "The Predators." Then, of course, the speedburners are always exciting; they're the guys who have the speed, the quickness, so that was another one. And then the

combinations you read about in the newspapers and watch on television — the Mark Brothers, Duper and Clayton. Those combinations always have an appeal, also collectibility.

SCD: I suppose the one you're most excited about is "The Rookies," because you're bringing something that's been very baseball-oriented over to football. Did you have any problems in getting any of the pictures of these rookie players?

Martin: That was a real challenge, because first of all, as you know, the cards are first being issued now (Editor's note: this interview was done in August), and that would have meant that we'd have to back up 60 days ago. We actually had planned on doing the rookies before the draft was done.

We not only analyzed the top players — and that was fairly simple to do — but then the players were unsigned. We had to ask the player's association to make special arrangements for us so that we could actually get the player's agreement to participate in the series, even though they're unsigned. Then how do you get these players' pictures? Deion Sanders — we got him in a hotel room in Milwaukee. He was playing with the Yankees. We had a uniform sent to the hotel to the player director of the Yankees. Then he put on the shirt and hat and we took his picture.

That's the kind of thing, though, that's a difficult objective to accomplish but it's one of the things that we've really been noted for, obviously with baseball cards. We had a beautiful World Series card issued of the Dodgers' surprise win over Oakland.

I don't know how many people are aware of this, but I'm sure the collectors are. On Canseco's card — we did a special 40/40 card — the two photographs we have are of Canseco hitting his 40th home run and stealing his 40th base.

SCD: So you were actually stalking him as he was doing it.

Martin: Exactly. And we did the same thing with Bo Jackson. We're going to have a special card of Bo Jackson for the All-Star Game. We've got the shot of Bo smacking the home run at the All-Star Game. So we're very interested in capturing pictures of players that are historically relevant to their own careers.

In the case of the rookies, we weren't sure how we were going to get it done, but we managed to track some of these guys down, and we shot them in very unusual places. Like Deion Sanders was shot in his hotel room. So that's the way it went. Logistically, it wasn't easy, and of course it was very expensive.

SCD: How long did it take to track down this rookies set? It must've taken a couple of months to do this.

Martin: It did, because I think we had trouble with the rookie from the Atlanta Falcons. It wasn't Deion, it was another rookie. We had trouble even getting his OK, and we wanted to get everybody. David Braxton (of the Minnesota Vikings), I think it was. For whatever reason, as I recall we had problems getting him signed, but he's quite a player.

SCD: But he was the only one you had trouble getting to sign.

Martin: I'm not saying it was trouble, it was a prolonged thing. You don't really talk to the player, you have to talk to his agent. And the agent is going to wonder, "Wait a minute. If you get him to do this thing with football cards, yes, the benefit is he gets exposure as a player, but what if we want to be real harda--es and negotiate?"

SCD: I think a lot of people are going to be excited about these rookie cards.

Martin: I think once the word gets out...It's funny. There's so many things in business and in life that are obvious, and this is an obvious thing to do. Why not do the rookies, and why not spend the money and take all the time and effort and all the complicated situations and make that a part of the appeal to this set?

I think the other thing is that this series we're putting out, the premier edition, if anything has been underproduced. We didn't underproduce it on purpose. We thought that this first year, for football, unlike Score baseball, was going to be a learning experience and we didn't want to put too much product out there. The market right now is not aggressively buying football cards. It's a bit early. But the takeaway at the show (the National in Chicago) from retail has met with our expectations, but as I understand it Pro Set believed the market was going to be incredibly big this first year. I don't think it's going to be this big.

We (Score and Pro Set) differ dramatically — and I emphasize the word dramatically — with the amount that should be available at retail this year, and also the amount of time it's going to take for football cards to become more of an entrenched product in America.

SCD: Could you tell me how many cards you plan on producing this year?

Martin: We never give those numbers away. But knowing the information that's available on what we have done and what Pro Set has done, we have produced a significantly smaller number of cards than Pro Set. Psychologically, just speaking now from the retail standpoint, the retailer doesn't want to end up the season with product in his storeroom. That's very damaging. I can attest to our whole marketing approach in that vein has been one of making certain there's just enough out there to stimulate the marketplace. On the other hand, I think the collectors have responded. We have had a higher incidence of purchases from the collectors than we anticipated. That has been a remarkably positive item as far as we're concerned. I don't know what the competition has done with the hobby. But we have had a very, very brisk report level on the part of the, hobby and we see it increasing although we've actually stopped our sales to the hobby.

SCD: Is there any specific reason why it's picking up? Is it football cards in general, or is there any one thing that's drawing them?

Martin: I think that they sense that football's going to make it. They know our product in baseball, and they know we've done a good job with football. So I think there is just an interest in what's happened with their own customers' reaction in football.

SCD: As long as we're talking about the buyer, who are you looking at as your football card buyer? Are you looking at baseball card buyers who are looking for something less expensive, or the football fan who hasn't yet begun collecting? Do you see them as different markets?

Martin: I think they're similar markets, but I don't think they're the same markets. I think basically out there is a mind set for collecting baseball cards, and I think that football card collecting is an adjunct to it because there are so many superstars out there — Joe Montana, Herschel Walker, Bo Jackson. It's the star system all over again. We've been really encouraged by the reception at the collector level. I think that all these media, the trade publications such as yourself, have been very supportive of what's happened with football cards.

It's been a very enthusiastic response. We think it's going to be a successful business, but we really believe that this is a business that has to be carefully managed from a marketing standpoint. I don't think you can afford to put too much product out there. I think you have to be very careful about maintaining the demand for your product. Rather than have too much out there, I'd rather have too little. And again, one of the things that Score has done with baseball is monitor the inventories of that product at retail, so return has never been a big factor for Score. In baseball cards with all the companies, there's a thing called a guaranteed sale, and that means if the wholesaler doesn't sell it, they can ship it back to you. The better and the more professionally we manage this aspect of our business, the better it is for the collector.

SCD: Somewhere down the road, would you plan on coming out with different types of subsets — following in the footsteps of the baseball card market with update sets? Would you plan issuing update sets in football cards?

Martin: I think it's a smart thing for us to consider. This year, we've got sets out there and Pro Set doesn't have any sets out. We're not going to do it in year one. Basically, we really want to plant the seed out there — introduce the product, create a product that'll capture the attention of the consumer, then next year take it that one step further.

SCD: What's happened with Eric Dickerson? It sounds like it's been a heck of a time trying to sign that guy. Have you signed him to a football card?

Martin: As I understand it, he's going to be in the Topps program. At least that's what I read.

SCD: He'll be on a couple of Topps cards this year.

Martin: He's not a signature on the Players Association agreement. So Pro Set doesn't have him (Editor's note: This interview was conducted before the announcement of Pro Set's Series II, which includes a Dickerson card), and neither does Score. Within the confines of our contract, we're not allowed to approach the players individually. I'm sure that Franco Harris, who's been with our company since its inception despite the fact we were a baseball card-oriented company, could have gotten him to sign, but we were told by the Players Association not to make any direct contact.

* * *

Ray Medeiros:
Preserving Parks On Postcards

By Tom Owens — Feb. 3, 1989

Ray Medeiros has been collecting postcards of baseball stadiums since way back when. In fact, "Way Back When" is the title of a successful series of ballpark postcards Medeiros pioneered for collectors seven years ago.

Medeiros decided to print his own stadium postcards in 1982. Originally he planned to use eight ornately-bordered postcards as a one-time advertising promotion for the sports memorabilia store (named Way Back When) he owned in California at the time. "Initially, they were given away," Medeiros recalls. "They seemed better than business cards. We were amazed at how much people enjoyed them."

After Medeiros closed the store and moved to Wauna, Wash., with Jeanne (his wife and his business partner), he decided to print a subsequent series in 1983. Now, 104 postcards later, "Way Back When" postcards are a collecting staple for many ballpark enthusiasts. Being a 40-year veteran of postcard collecting has given Medeiros the needed determination to uncover many rare, obscure photos of forgotten stadiums.

"I have a strict criterion for choosing photos to be included in the 'Way Back When' series," Medeiros says. "First, the photo has to be at least 20 years old. The majority of photos are 40 to 60 years old. They bring you into the real era of nostalgia.

"Secondly, the ballpark photo has to be something we don't see usually," he says. "I want the photos to show rare parks, like the South End Grounds in Boston. Or, I like photos of better-known parks like the Polo Grounds or Shibe Park, which show unusual camera angles." An example of the unusual types of ballpark photos Medeiros prizes is a shot of a World War II air raid drill at Ebbets Field in Brooklyn. The postcard, number 828096, is found in the ninth series of "Way Back When."

Medeiros says that just more than half of his postcards show interior views of stadiums. "In my 40-plus years of collecting, I've noticed that certain ballpark postcards don't show up in field or outside perimeter views," he says. "A great deal of photos of Yankee Stadium are air views, because New York City is surrounded by airports. Hence, many air and birds-eye views are available."

As an alternative to the traditional Yankee Stadium fare, Medeiros produced a card with a view of the media sitting with fans in the third deck behind home plate with a capacity crowd for a World Series.

Some hobbyists wonder why he never uses color photos in his postcard series, Medeiros says. He says he's never seen color photos of some defunct stadiums like old Braves Field. In order to maintain consistency, he chooses to show all stadiums in black and white.

After producing 10 postcards of various stadiums, Medeiros has needed to tap assorted resources to keep hobbyists satisfied. "I've driven border to border looking for stadium photos," Medeiros says. "I've contacted newspapers, ballclubs, libraries and historical societies."

He says that many big-city newspapers have virtually no photos of old ballparks. "Most don't have any photos of consequence. Some only have one or two stock photos of new cookie cutter-shaped ballparks. Most papers have little regard for the past."

He says that he's only found five useful photos after visits to dozens of historical societies. "These societies seem to exist because of the good will of the local wealthy families, so the organizations often save what's of interest mainly to these people."

Of the many major league teams Medeiros contacted for help, he found that several had only a minimal appreciation of their stadium's history. He says the Yankees and Dodgers are the primary exceptions. In 1984, Medeiros issued a postcard of Dodger Stadium using a 1962 photo. The card shows the right-field half of the Dodgers' new home still under construction.

Through nine series of postcards, Medeiros says that two-thirds of his customers are repeat buyers from series to series. Three of his customers are major league executives and one is a member of an NFL front office. Many national sportswriters have become fans of "Way Back When" too, Medeiros says. "Collectors seem to really appreciate the different views," he says. "I've never had a customer return a card for a refund."

Medeiros is proud that he's kept his postcards affordable yet collectible. Each 12-card series costs $4.35 postpaid. "We're collectors too, so we want to make them affordable," he says. "The average series is produced only in the hundreds. Compare that to the millions of baseball cards which get printed each year. When these are gone, that's it." None of the cards have been, or ever will be, wholesaled to dealers, Medeiros adds. "Because of the small numbers produced, we tell dealers no. We feel an obligation to maintain availability of each series to the many fans who appreciate the ballparks.

Which individual "Way Back When" postcards are Medeiros' favorites? They aren't the typical famous parks like Ebbets Field or the Polo Grounds, mind you. "Washington Park from Los Angeles is one," he says. "It's a famous park in Pacific Coast League. I looked for a view of it for about nine years. It hosted three PCL teams in the 1910s: Los Angeles, Vernon and Venice. A friend had looked about 35 years for any picture of the Venice ballpark. He never saw one. By accident, I discovered that Venice never had its own ballpark during its short existence.

"At a flea market, I found a picture of the ballpark, but I passed it up," Medeiros says with regret. "I thought it was overpriced. It took eight more years to find one."

When it comes to finding rare stadium photos, Medeiros bas been called upon by some famous names. The author of Bowie Kuhn's biography needed the perfect shot of Griffith Stadium for a book.

Medeiros found it. The Boston Red Sox wanted some historical photos for a book commemorating Fenway Park's 75th anniversary. Again, Medeiros assisted. Before the movie Eight Men Out began production, the studio wanted some old historical photos of Comiskey Park and Crosley Field to use as reference when building movie sets. A call to Medeiros was all it took.

The postcard collecting hobby can thank Medeiros for establishing collecting standards. In 1963, he asked the late Buck Barker (one of the originators of stadium postcard collecting) if it would be possible to create a checklist of all ballpark postcards. "He felt it would be impossible, because there are so many different kinds. Many postcards, of different cities and by different publishers, were still undiscovered," Medeiros says. Nevertheless, Medeiros began documenting all his finds for the next seven years. "In 1970, I sketched out a checklist," he says. "I broke it down into three categories: chromes, postcards from the 1950s, and '60s, with a chrome-like finish; linens, postcards from the 1930s through the early '50s with a linen-type finish; and pre-linens, cards published before that."

Barker made additions to nearly 300 entries made by Medeiros. The categories stood, and are used today by all serious collectors. In 1974, a full checklist (29 pages long) was published in a defunct hobby periodical called The Ballcard Collector. The information sparked massive interest in stadium postcards. "In the 1960s, there weren't more than five of us who were full-time stadium postcard collectors," Medeiros says. He says that now, the latest member directory of the Society for American Baseball Research lists more than 2,000 members with interests in baseball stadiums.

Medeiros never profited from his countless hours of research, but proudly notes that no person has ever created, finished and published a more comprehensive checklist. Medeiros says that he has mixed feelings about the creation of a ballpark postcard price guide. "Many feel a catalog could be useful, especially for newcomers," he says. "On the other hand, there's the danger of price manipulation. If the creator is unknowledgeable or unscrupulous, it could do more harm than good."

Who is the typical ballpark postcard collector of today? "Based on the people who've purchased 'Way Back When' cards, they're guys who've collected 10 or more years," Medeiros says. "Most are in their 30s, but a few are in their late teens. They're mature enough to see there are huge differences from old parks and new places in Atlanta, Pittsburgh or Cincinnati. As they learn more about old ballparks, they want more pictures.

"Fans realize we've destroyed nearly the entire second generation of ballparks," Medeiros says. "An alarming amount of old ballparks were demolished in the 1970s. That threat has returned in the late '80s. Fenway Park, Comiskey Park, Tiger Stadium and Wrigley Field are all that's left from that great era. The panic is setting in." Medeiros says that he's corresponded with several collectors who are bringing their cameras to the old ballparks like Wrigley Field and taking photos "while they can."

Medeiros' "Way Back When" postcards are more than just stock shots of stadiums. They're like time machines for old ballpark fans. The postcards show old scoreboards, advertising on outfield walls, views of infields, anything that could be missed by conventional history books. Seeing Crosley Field underwater in 1937, buying $1.10 bleacher seats at Ebbets Field in the '40s or watching a Stan Hack Day celebration at 1948 Wrigley Field are just a few offbeat scenes Medeiros has recaptured in his past postcard series.

"I saw my first ballpark postcard in 1948," he remembers. "It was a view of Sportsmen's Park, and it arrived in the mail. It was different, and it seemed special. It was a neat photo, and was an unusual size in relation to bubble gum cards. It was a ballpark far away for me, living in Massachusetts at the time."

For a young man who took snapshots of Fenway Park and Braves Field whenever he saw a game, the postcards were a natural attraction. During his travels to other cities during the next few years, Medeiros always picked up stadium postcards, and kept them in a shoebox. "At the time, I suppose I wanted a postcard of every major league stadium," he says.

Now, 40 years later, Medeiros has seen the world embrace many of the stadia he grew up with. Researchers write books about stadium histories. The hobby staged "Stadiapex II,'" the second annual Stadium Postcard and Photographic Exhibition, held in Los Angeles in the summer of 1988. While Medeiros openly detests the emergence of hastily-built, ugly multi-purpose stadiums, he still enjoys the challenge of collecting various postcards of any baseball stadium, old or new.

"I continue to enjoy the search for postcards," he says. "You never know what you'll find. I've found them at hobby shops, antique shops, postcard shows, flea markets and garage sales. That bit of mystery provides a continuous incentive for looking. Even just-published postcards, at 25 cents each, may prove to be scarce issues. Some are pulled from the racks before their time."

Medeiros, unlike some veteran collectors, welcomes newcomers to the hobby with a refreshing openness. He says that stadium postcards are still one of the most affordable collectibles available, and the hobby has the potential for more growth. "I don't think that one person could have one each of all the stadium postcards ever made," he says of his hobby philosophy. "It doesn't matter who you are, anyone can have a crack at finding something rare. I know of many new collectors of stadium postcards who found rare and beautiful postcards early on in their efforts to join the older collectors in this facet of the hobby.

"That's what delights me about this hobby."

* * *

A Chat With "Mr. Baseball Card"

By Ted Taylor — Feb. 28, 1981

"Mr. Baseball Card" is 85 now and the years have slowed his pace a bit, but deep down the creative fires that spawned the Play Ball and Bowman baseball sets, the "Horrors of War" sets and many others, still burn brightly.

George Moll lives quietly in retirement now in Bucks County, Pa., with his wife, his antiques and his extensive collections of art and hobby cards, but he stays on top of hobby developements through his subscription to Sports Collectors Digest and rare visits to local baseball card and sports memorabilia shows.

"I'm still amazed that this hobby has grown to such immense proportions," he said in a recent conversation. "Sometimes I find it hard to believe that I really helped get this whole thing started."

Moll, who was honored as a hobby pioneer back in 1978 by the Eastern Pennsylvania Sports Collectors Club, headed an advertising agency in the 1930s whose job it was to promote the chewing gum products of a firm headed by Warren Bowman.

"I had saved cigarette cards as a boy," Moll recalls, "and I told Mr. Bowman that if we flattened his gum and included a picture card with it we'd be able to capture a larger segment of the children who bought such things. He agreed and we started with a cowboy and Indian set."

While Moll doesn't come right out and say so, his early efforts were probably encouraged by the Goudey issues out of Boston who were selling "Indian Gum" at the time he flattened Blony bubble gum and stuffed trading cards in the flat package with them.

His personal collection of hobby cards currently includes quite a number of the Goudey Indian cards, as well as other sample issues of cigarette and candy offerings.

When war clouds started gathering on the horizon in the lale 1930s Moll cooked up the idea of a war theme for the Bowman company and produced the "Horrors of War" set.

"Those cards were really pretty graphic as far as the blood and guts aspect of war went, but we called the issue 'To Know the Horrors of War is to want Peace' and we sold them that way," he recalled.

A LIFE magazine feature at the time labeled George as the "Gum Moll" and held him up to the nation as the leader of the hobby card industry.

By the late 1930s Goudey had all but bowed out of the card market and Bowman jumped ahead with a baseball issue called "Play Ball." This set was issued for three straight years and ended with the beginning of World War II.

While all this was going on, of course, Moll's advertising agency was handling many other accounts as well and not all that concerned with the hobby card market during the war.

In the late 1940s, though, Warren Bowman, again, prevailed upon Moll to create some hobby cards and the baseball, football and basketball issues were reborn, as well as a raft of non-sport offerings.

Again Moll's creative juices were fired and the hobby card industry hummed once again. Success, however, begats copycats and other, sometimes larger, companies jumped into the fray.

Ultimately, Topps forced Bowman out of the marketplace and took virtual control of the industry.

"I understand that Topps is having some financial difficulties of their own now," Moll commented. "Wouldn't it be ironic if they were forced out by one of the new companies in the card market now?"

"I think it is great for the hobby that both Fleer and Donruss are going to produce card sets this year," he continued, "it's just amazing how much a part of America cards have become."

Amazing, yes, but not very surprising when you understand that people like George Moll have devoted a lot of creative energies into making it happen.

An entire hobby owes thanks to the George Molls of the world.

* * *

The Creative Genius Behind Gum Inc. & Bowman George Moll, Trading Card Pioneer, Dies

By Ted Taylor — Sept. 2, 1983

George Moll, the guiding creative force behind Gum Inc. and the Bowman Gum Co., of Philadelphia, died in the Philadelphia suburb of Abington on Saturday, July 23. He was 86 years of age.

Dubbed "The Gum Moll" by Life magazine in the late 1930s for his "Horrors of War" set, Moll was a lifelong card collector himself and owned an extensive collection of British turn-of-the century cigarette cards...

...It was in the early 1930s when the owner of Gum Inc., Warren Bowman, engaged Moll to market Bowman's Blony bubble gum. It was then that Moll recalled his own fascination with cards as a youth and suggested that Bowman flatten his gum to the size of a card and insert it in a package with some sort of trading card.

In later years Moll said that he had also drawn inspiration from the Goudey Indian Gum series of cowboys and Indians for his marketing ploy. In his own personal archives Moll retained a set of the Goudey Indian cards and, when he discovered that I also had a fondness for those cards, gave me a large supply of his duplicates.

It was his "Horrors of War" cards that created a market for Bowman's gum and a furor among the parents of America. The cards graphically depicted war, and it was not unusual for the illustrations to include murdered children, dismembered arms and legs and an ample supply of blood and gore...

...During the second World War Moll ended his association with Bowman and didn't return to the card business until 1948 when Bowman, again in business trouble, needed some marketing help.

Moll reminded him of the success of the Play Ball series (1939-41) and suggested a 48-card offering in 1948. This set was the first commercial baseball card set in seven years and opened the door to today's hobby.

A chronic saver, Moll's Churchville, Pa., home still contained many of the original photos and much of the original artwork from the hobby's pioneer days.

The 1950 Bowman set, for example, was simply copied from promotional pictures provided to the Bowman Co. by the various major league clubs.

One mystery that went to the grave with Moll was the revelation a couple of years ago that there was a move afoot in 1952 to produce larger baseball cards — similar, in fact, to the size used by the upstart Topps Co.

Black-and-white and color proofs of the larger cards exist in several collections today and Moll had once indicated that Bowman used the baseball prototype to enlarge his 1952 football card set mid-way in the year and opted for the black-and-white format for a second baseball set in 1953 when competition from Topps made inroads on his business.

Moll was unsure about whatever became of the missing 16 cards in the 1951 set. As longtime Bowman collectors know, in 1951 the set was advertised as being a 340-card set and yet only 324 were issued. He told me at one time that the cards probably never made the marketplace because of some contractual difficulties with the intended players.

* * *

The Kissing Bandit George Brett And Pete Rose Remain Morganna's Favorites

By Fluffy Saccucci — Jan. 19, 1990

How many times have you seen in the sports highlights a blonde woman, with arms thrashing wildly and front upper torso gyrating vigorously, bolting out onto a baseball field and planting a big smooch on the face of a surprised ballplayer?

I'll bet you've seen it many times.

But, who is this crazed (to some people) female?

Morganna Roberts, baseball's celebrated and controversial Kissing Bandit.

Morganna has puckered up to 37 athletes, including 24 baseball players and the San Diego Chicken.

But being the Kissing Bandit has its pitfalls. She's been arrested 16 times for trespassing on playing fields and arenas all over the country.

Morganna

She's also had numerous run-ins with ballpark security.

Adversity is no stranger to Morganna.

As a 13-year-old runaway from a Catholic boarding school in Mt. Mercy, Ky., the distraught teen-ager was thrust into the harsh realities of adult life.

"About two weeks after I turned 13 years old, I was able to get a job in a nightclub as a cigarette girl and a camera girl," she said.

How did Morganna get a job in a nightclub at age 13 when the legal drinking age was 18?

"I was able to get the job by telling them (the prospective employers) that I was 18 and that I would send for my birth certificate. And it worked; I got the job," she said.

After Morganna spent four years as a nightclub entertainer, the epoch of the Kissing Bandit was born in Cincinnati's Riverfront Stadium during the 1970 All-Star game.

The Kiss List

Who was the first kissee in Morganna's long and illustrious career? "It started with Pete Rose (then of the Cincinnati Reds)," she said.

Why him?

"It was on a double-dirty dare and he was the fans' most favorite player."

Besides Rose, Morganna has kissed George Brett, who she's kissed in Kansas City and in Seattle, Don Mattingly, Mike Schmidt, Nolan Ryan, Dickie Thon, John Candaleria and Fred Lynn.

As Morganna so cheerfully says about her baseball kiss list, "I love 'em all so much."

Morganna considers Fred Lynn to be the funniest baseball player she's kissed.

"After he (Lynn) struck out one day in a game right after I had kissed him, after the game that evening, we (me and Lynn) had a live-at-five interview together on television.

"The interviewer asked Lynn, 'Fred, how come you struck out after Morganna kissed you?' He (Lynn) then told the interviewer, 'Well, I'll tell you, after seeing Morganna run at me, the baseball looked like a pencil dot.'"

Morganna hopes to work Lynn into her comedy nightclub act sometime.

Morganna says the Cubs' Ryne Sandberg and George Brett are the two cutest players.

"I'd have to say that Ryne Sandberg, to me, is one of the all-time best-looking baseball players," she said.

She hasn't kissed Sandberg yet, but "he's still at the top of my kiss list, so I'm going to have to get to Ryne before my kissing career is over."

Regarding Brett, Morganna says, unequivocally, "he's a honey."

Baseball players aren't the only athletes to experience Morganna's lips.

Other athletes include Kareem Abdul-Jabbar, an ex-basketball star for the Milwaukee Bucks and Los Angeles Lakers, Charles Barkley of the Philadelphia 76ers, and Chuck Nevitt of the Houston Rockets.

Two Utah Jazz personalities, former Coach Frank Layden and Jazz announcer "Hot Rod" Hundley, are also included.

But her favorites remain George Brett and Pete Rose "because they are the only two (players) that I actually know. I have kissed them both on the field and been lucky to know them as folks off the field," she said.

Morganna says her hit list includes "Will Clark, because everybody loves Will Clark;

"Orel Hershiser, because he's been the fans' favorite since the ('88) World Series;

"Ryne Sandberg, because he's everybody's favorite, not only because he's cute but also because he's a great player and a wonderful all-around guy;

"Pete O'Brien of the Cleveland Indians, because I've been crazy about him, and so have the fans since he played with the Texas Rangers a couple of years ago;

"And Dave Parker; because I've always been a big fan of his and he's a nice guy who's always treated me wonderfully."

Morganna says Parker "has the prettiest eyes that I have ever seen."

Morganna has targeted players in other sports also, such as basketball stars Michael Jordan, Magic Johnson, and Larry Bird.

Harrowing experiences

Morganna's motivation to run out on fields and arenas to kiss the athletes is "the fans. I like to put a smile on people's faces," she said, adding "the fans always make me feel terrific and that's why I enjoy it so much."

But Morganna gets a kick out of it, too.

"To me, it's (kissing the athlete's) worth all the abuse that I've gotten over the years."

But Morganna has experienced bruising situations involving security guards. The first encounter with security occurred in Cincinnati at the All-Star game in 1970.

The security guards beat her up, she said, and knocked her unconscious, breaking three of her ribs and a tailbone all because a $100 bonus for the guards was offered by the Cincinnati front office to stop Morganna from reaching the athletes on the field.

"They (the security guards) virtually had to kill me and that was the last thought I had right before one of the guards karate-chopped me in the neck," she recalled.

The second meeting with security guards transpired at Chicago's Wrigley Field while Morganna was pursuing second baseman Ryne Sandberg.

"When I went after Ryne Sandberg, it was one of those rent-a-cops and he threw his body weight against me a little harder than he needed to.

"He then quickly executed a chicken-wing maneuver on me by grabbing me behind the arms and he wouldn't let go.

"When he was escorting me off the field, he was also very rough on my wrist" she said.

But, for the most part, Morganna thinks the real police who are now hired at stadiums are very nice, compared to the aforementioned rent-a-cops.

After scurrying onto the field, Morganna has been arrested 16 times, and won all cases in court.

She says, however, after she kissed Nolan Ryan and Dickie Thon in a game at the Astrodome in Houston the Astros front office charged her with criminal trespassing, which carried a maximum one year in jail and a $5,000 fine if she was convicted.

But Texas attorney Richard "Racehorse" Haynes successfully defended Morganna on a charge of unlawfully being on the field.

The acquittal occurred because Morganna says, "I'm top-heavy and gravity took its toll and whipped me out onto the field."

Of all the numerous sporting events that she's uninvitedly infiltrated, Morganna says her most memorable occurred at the Kingdome in Seattle, "when I kissed George Brett there for the second time back in 1980."

It's memorable, she says, because she said in advance that she was going to kiss Brett.

Thus Seattle officials sent out press releases stating that not only would she not get into the parking lot but she wouldn't even make it to the field.

But, Morganna said proudly, "they (the Mariner front office) hired extra security, between 100 and 200 extra officers, and I still made it."

Playboy beckons

Morganna has appeared in three issues of Playboy magazines: June 1983, April 1985, and September 1989.

After persistent phone calls from the publication and at the insistence of her manager, Morganna decided to appear in the magazine, "but only if I could appear in the celebrity section where I would have more control over my choice of poses and photos."

"We (me and Playboy) did it (the photo session) and it worked out wonderfully," she said.

After the first appearance, Morganna's career as an entertainer leaped forward.

"Once I became Morganna in the June '83 issue of Playboy, the phone started ringing off the hook (for bookings). All the personal appearances I had been trying for for years were now happening," she said.

"Now, I'm doing all the things I wanted to do as the Kissing Bandit — including working with children and senior citizens — but couldn't do until I at least appeared in Playboy at least one time," she adds.

Thinking over the whole success story behind the Playboy experience, Morganna says, "It's strange how life is, but whatever works."

As a promotional maneuver, Playboy also printed a Morganna card set featuring Morganna as a baseball celebrity.

The five-card set, often available at card shows, is selling for $45 a pack.

Playboy made only 25,000 packs back in 1983, so the card set is a limited issue.

Autographed cards usually sell for $6 at shows where Morganna appears.

"My cards are pretty high-priced and I've never even hit a home run," she says.

Morganna's memorabilia

Although she's always admired athletes, especially baseball players, Morganna never collected cards as a child.

"When I was a kid, 13 years old, I was working 56 hours a week and when I got older, I started working even more hours. I didn't have much time for collecting."

Morganna's affiliation with many athletes over the years has afforded her the luxury of being able to collect memorabilia from these sports figures. Three items are really special to her.

The first is an 8-by-10-inch photo of Steve Garvey taken when Morganna was playing ring-around-the-umpire at a ball game when she had kissed Garvey. Inscribed on the photo is: "Morganna, your pucker is much prettier than mine,

Love, Steve Garvey."

The second item is a Bucky Dent jersey he wore in 1983, the last year he played with the Texas Rangers. Dent's jersey is now hanging on Morganna's wall, along with some other players' shirts and jerseys.

The Kissing Bandit says Dent's jersey means a lot to her; she considers the current Yankee manager to be either the best or second-best looking baseball player.

Dent, when told about the compliment, presented Morganna with the jersey and said, "Here's the shirt off my back."

The third tidbit revered by Morganna is a poster given to her by George Brett.

It pictures the Kansas City Royals and the New York Yankees engaged in a fistfight

Morganna points out that in the picture she can see George Brett — with his familiar number 5 on the back of his jersey — on top of someone, doling out fisticuffs.

The poster, autographed by Brett, says "Look Morganna, I'm still defending your honor, Love, George."

The card show circuit

Morganna has recently appeared at card shows in New York City and Los Angeles.

She loves to do card shows because "any time I can come into contact with the baseball fans, it's just such a thrill for me because they've always been so wonderful to me.

"They (the fans) have supported me over the years by cheering me on and booing the police when they take me away," she said.

Because of her unique look, does Morganna believe the mothers who bring their children to the card shows will be intimidated by her?

"Oh gosh, no," says Morganna. "The mothers of the children are the first ones to come up to me and introduce their sons in order to obtain autographs for them."

Morganna also says the mothers offer card show programs and practically everything else for her to sign.

In fact, "the mothers tell me that they wished that they had the 'guts' to go out there and kiss the ballplayers. I tell them, instead of you doing it, I'm doing it for you," she said.

Even if she's on the road, Morganna has her mail sent to her every week. When she's home she goes through the mail every day.

Collectors who send for her autograph will also receive a mail order form listing everything she has available for collectors, including a video called "Sports Blooper Mania," available for $9.95.

Morganna's Idols

Morganna, who is five-feet, five-inches tall and weighs 120 pounds, says she keeps her figure (60-22 1/2-39), "and it's totally natural," physically fit by doing a two-hour daily exercise regimen, which includes workouts on a rowing machine and nautilus, aerobics, and fast-walking three to five miles.

Morganna tries to emulate Cher, because she "was my idol because she's a survivor, a lot like I am.

"When people said that she was down and out and would never make it without her ex-singing partner and ex-husband, Sonny Bono, she managed to rebound.

"Look at her now. She's a fantastic actress and a terrific singer. I admire that," she said.

She also idolizes talk show host Oprah Winfrey and Jessica Rabbit, the character from the movie Who Framed Roger Rabbit?

"She's (Jessica Rabbit) built just like me and I know the kind of trouble she can get into (from being built so well). But she remains so naive and unassuming about it."

Business endeavors

While Morganna traipses all over the country attacking unsuspecting pro athletes with a barrage of puckers and works 40 weeks annually on the nightclub circuit, her husband handles all of her business affairs.

She's been married for 13 1/2 years to her husband, Bill Cottrell, her accountant and manager.

Cottrell, who took over for her previous manager after he died a few years ago, has turned out to be a better manager because "he (Bill) actually cares about me and cares about where I go," said Morganna.

Does her husband have any qualms about her kissing and nighclub endeavors?

"No, nothing bad. He has a rather shy personality, as opposed to my outgoing personality, and he tells me that I keep him from getting bored."

Morganna is the proud co-owner of a minor league baseball team, the Utica Blue Sox, a Chicago White Sox affiliate of the Class A New York-Penn League.

"I was doing a press conference in Jacksonville, Fla., and a gentleman who was a part-owner of the Blue Sox was there and he asked me to look into the matter because part-owner shares were for sale," she recalls.

She was further enticed because, "I knew the club's manager, Ken Brett (George Brett's brother), and so I asked the Blue Sox to send me information about the team.

"A week later, I received the information, read about how much money they wanted from me and promptly sent them a check," she said.

Morganna joyfully laments on her current financial status of the team she co-owns by saying, "I still haven't made a penny (on them), but at least we're lucky to be a farm team."

Striving to be an entrepreneur of sorts, Morganna says her own brand name of peanuts will be available at convenience stores all over the country soon. They're called "Morganna the Kissing Bandit Roasted Peanuts."

The peanuts will come in a 3-ounce bag, complete with a Morganna lip print, and will have a suggested retail price of 69 cents.

The producer, Carolina Fine, is the same people who furnish President George Bush with his pork rinds. "As you know, it's a quality company," Morganna said.

Although she's been a show biz personality for so many years, Morganna was not only just a ballpark and nightclub entertainer. She's appeared as a host on two Columbus, Ohio, shows — "Good Morning Columbus" and "Screen Test."

She also hosted a radio show, for six weeks in Houston, as the "Doctor of Love."

In the next few months Morganna will be in comedy clubs all over the country.

"There are a lot of things coming up. I always like a challenge, so when somebody calls me up to do something that I haven't done and it sounds like it's in good taste, I say to myself, 'Well, let me give it a shot,'" she says.

* * *

He Shoots The Texas Rangers
Baseball Photographer Brad Newton Profiled

By Kit Kiefer — July 15, 1988

Brad Newton

Shooting pictures with Brad Newton is like shooting a round of golf with Jack Nicklaus. You know who's going to make all the great shots.

"Did you see that?" says Newton, the Texas Rangers' team photographer. Mark McGwire is hitting off a batting tee prior to a game with the Milwaukee Brewers at County Stadium, swinging, grimacing, swinging, grinning, swinging. The tee is about six feet from a net placed squarely in front of the foul-ball screen behind home plate. Behind the net and the screen kids are crying, "Mark! Mark! Autograph!" It's a feeble cry, like third-world ragamuffins begging for centavos. McGwire ignores it, and keeps swinging off the tee.

Click. Whirr. Click. Whirr. Click whirr click whirr click whirr.

"Did you see that?" Newton asks again. "It was like he was posing for me."

Later on, during the game, Newton is in the third-base photographer's well, a plywood-floored foxhole with padded rails next to the Oakland dugout. Inside are the rest of that day's photo corps, guys with thousand-pocket vests and $10,000 macro-zoom macro lenses the size of 55-gallon drums.

There's a play at third. Paul Molitor tags a runner trying to advance to third on a ground ball.

Click. Whirr.

"I got it," Newton says, picking up a second massive camera, not the massive camera he had been using most of the day. "It's a little soft, though. I had this one focused about a foot in front of the bag."

There's a rundown on the next play. Newton goes back to the big camera.

"Great stuff," he says, click-whirring off a few more frames.

"Did you get it?" I ask.

"Missed it," he says. "The umpire was in the way."

Well, even Jack Nicklaus misses a few.

It's taken a good eight years for Brad Newton to progress from being just another free-lancer who likes baseball and cameras to one of the best young baseball photographers in the business. This year you can see his work on the covers of Baseball Cards magazine and Beckett Monthly, on the Texas Rangers calendar and on a handful of baseball cards. Next year you'll see his work all over the 1989 Score set. Throughout, Newton has combined his love of baseball and his love of photography to produce a product just a little bit beyond the run-of-the-mill baseball photograph.

"I want to show the personality of the players, what the guys are really like," Newton says, as he slides around knots of sportswriters and assorted hangers-on at the batting cage several hours before game time. He moves quietly, like a wedding photographer, but with a little bit of a fashion photographer's grace and experienced style.

"You gotta be unobtrusive; that's the key for me at least," he says, moving in on Jose Canseco, zooming out the sportswriter talking to Canseco, zooming out Ozzie's twin brother, zooming in for a super-close closeup ("A nostril-hair shot," he says. "A good nostril-hair shot") and then zooming back out for a conventional head-and-shoulders informal portrait.

"And, of course, the first time in a stadium — like for me, this is my first time here in Milwaukee — I spend a lot of time just figuring angles, where the sun is, where the shadows are, what I can take where.

"Score loves black backgrounds," he continues. "Tiger Stadium is great for that. Wham! The players just jump out at you out of that background. It's impossible in this park, though."

Newton blows through a roll in the time it takes him to finish the thought. The motor winder does the rewinding — WHIRR whirr whirr whirr whirr and so forth — while he answers the next obvious question.

"When I'm shooting for Score I'll shoot 20 or 30 rolls of film a game," he says, slapping out the old roll and slapping in the new in the time in takes most people to figure out which sprockety doo-hickey the thingamabob goes on.

Film is cheap?

"Right," he says, with a you-gotta-be-crazy glance and a grin. "Only when somebody else is paying for it, man; only when somebody is paying for it.

"I go through about 10-12 rolls of film a game when I'm just shooting for myself, unless I luck into something good — like this thing with McGwire and Canseco and the batting tee."

After McGwire finished up on the tee, Newton said, "Watch this. I'm going to impress the heck out of you."

He walked over to McGwire. McGwire smiled, they exchanged greetings, talked and laughed for awhile and patted each other on the shoulder.

"You impressed?" he said, grinning.

"Aw, he's a super guy. And I feel for him; I really do. He's signed so many autographs, done so many shows. He's just burned out on autographs. That's why he said he'll only sign at the ballpark.

"You know, it comes to a point with a lot of these players where, sure, they can get thousands of dollars to do a card show, but it just doesn't matter to them anymore. I think that's where he's at."

Later on, over in the first-base fox-hole, out of the 90-degree heat, Newton snaps off a few frames of Jeffrey Leonard in the on-deck circle and says, "Most of the players are just super guys. There are only a very, very few that aren't nice guys. As long as you're accredited, as long as the players' association says what you're shooting for is all right, then it's never any problem at all. They may say, 'Not right now; catch me later,' but they're real good about it."

Chumming around with big-league ballplayers may be a kick for the average fan, but for Newton the game has always been the thing.

It was that way even when Newton shot his first big-league game. Newton was fresh out of North Texas State in 1980 and fresh into his first teaching job when he approached the newspaper editor in Carrolton, Texas, and offered to shoot pictures of an old-timers'game at Arlington Stadium. The editor agreed. ("Hey, it was free," Newton says. "What else was he gonna say?"); Newton shot the game, wrote up a story and sent it in.

That led to more occasional assignments for the newspaper. When Newton had enough good pictures of his own, he sent a package of 8x10s to Rangers President Eddie Chiles. Chiles sent back a polite semi-rejection letter, but said the photos would be kept on file.

They were kept on file, all right, but one of them — a "real neat shot" of Jim Sundberg — appeared on the cover of the Rangers' newspaper.

"I said, 'Hey, guys, that's my photo.'" Newton says. "And suddenly I had a little bit of leverage. They let me in.

"There wasn't any money in it, not any at all, but I wasn't interested in the money," he adds. "I'm still not now — not really, even though I'm a school teacher and the other photographers say, 'Oh, he's a schoolteacher so he really needs the money,' you know, and they treat me pretty good. It was just getting my stuff out there. That's the way it is for any young photographer.

There was a baseball strike the next year, and "they must have let everybody who was on the list for even being a free-lancer once have a full-time pass. It was like they were trying to make amends or something. It was nice from my standpoint, because I could go out when I wanted, take more pictures, practice more, get better at what I was doing. It was all night games, of course, but it was nice."

Still, Newton was at least a big break away from making the jump from free-lancer to Texas Rangers photographer. That big break came in 1985, and while it was the most unfortunate sort of big break — the team photographer died at the time of an aneurysm — someone had to get the job. It just happened to be Newton.

"Jim Small, who was in the Rangers front office at the time and now works in the commissioner's office, called Steve Green, who's been the Cubs' team photographer for years, and asked if he knew anybody down here," Newton says. "Steve's sort of been my mentor in this business, and he said, 'Yeah, there's Brad.' And that was it."

Newton's job is complicated — or simplified, depending on how you look at it — by the fact that the Rangers play few day games. Night games are bad for color photography — "You have to use such a fast film, or push the film, and it gets all grainy," he says — and Newton doesn't follow the team on the road. So his shooting is restricted to batting practice up until dusk ("Some nice shots at that time of day," he says. "Some nice shots") at night games, and the seven or eight home day games the team plays.

Newton also makes one trip a year to Chicago, where he shoots National League teams for Baseball Cards and other free-lance assignments.

Last year Newton was in Chicago for the Padres-Cubs game where Andre Dawson was severely beaned.

"I just missed Sports Illustrated on that one," he says, just as a foul ball goes shooting into the photographers' well. A photographer at the end of the well grabs it. "It's like 'Incoming!', you know. Everyone looks out for one another. Someone shouts and you duck. Anyway, I was shooting, and I got the shot but just didn't think of it, and when they called the film was being developed."

That was the second time Newton missed making it in SI, and while SI may not be the penultimate ultimate it, as far as a baseball photographer is concerned, it'll do until something else comes along.

Still, Newton has had his pictures in Inside Sports, which is not bad at all, and he's seen plenty of baseball history made.

"Remember Mike Witt's perfect game, the one he threw at the end of the year against Texas?" he asks. "I was there for that. I saw Phil Niekro's 3,000th strikeout. I was there for the game where Mattingly broke the record, hitting a home run in his eighth straight game.

"Gee; I've seen more baseball history than I thought."

History is nice, but art is just as nice to Newton.

"It's the mood; it's the love of the game," Newton says. "I've read some stuff in other places that sort of suggests that we're only in it for the money. Like I told you before, that's not the way it is for me. It's patterns, spatial relationships, composition. You get into grooves; you see things."

He points to a freshly painted yellow foul pole set off against a deep green wall and a dark blue billboard.

"Like that. You see that?" he says. "It's just a combination of things. A lot of times I look for what I want to see, and I'll shoot it. It's not for Score, it's not for you guys, it's just for me, just things that suggest to me what the game is all about. Jose Canseco signing autographs for kids back there. That bat rack. A glove. That's baseball. Babe Ruth surrounded by kids. Ty Cobb sliding into third. It's the same thing. That's what I have up on my wall at home."

While Newton's pictures had appeared on several cards (a 1985 Rod Carew was his first) he hadn't progressed beyond a don't-call-us-we'll-call-you relationship with any of the card companies until Score called.

"I think it's hard to become a baseball card photographer," Newton says, "but I don't know why. I guess it's because there are only so many that can do it.

"I don't think there are too many photographers complaining about all these new card sets," he adds, glancing away to watch Teddy Higuera spit sunflower seeds from the corner of the Brewer dugout. "And it's not just cards; there are all these new magazines covering baseball, and so much of a need for different pictures."

While an amateur photographer may never be as consistently successful as a professional — though even a hacker can hit a shot now and then that would do Nicklaus proud — Newton says amateurs can still take some good pictures at a baseball game.

"Do what those guys do," Newton says, pointing to a bowknot of box-seat photographers with long lenses. "Buy a long lens. The Instamatic over there? Probably not. Some of these guys set in the front row with one of these cheap $500 mirror lenses, and take some pictures that are all right. Get here for batting practice."

Newton uses a third-hand macro-zoom lens about the size of an Oster Kitchen Center. It looks tiny next to the 55-gallon-drum lenses of the other photographers in the well.

Is it necessary?

"Just take a look," he says. Suddenly faraway things aren't very far away at all. "And with one of those really big lenses, we're talking nostril hairs from a mile away."

Newton hasn't let his success as a baseball photographer drive him away from his day job. He teaches gifted and talented students during the baseball off-season. During the teacher off-season, he becomes a photographer again. When he isn't doing either one, he practices t'ai chi and plays blues guitar.

"It's all creativity," he says. "That's what life's about. That's what keeps me going.

"Baseball is different every day, fresh," he adds. Paul Molitor pops out. "You're outdoors; it's timeless."

He turns around and fires off three or four shots of Robin Yount, eyes greased up with lampblack, kneeling in the on-deck circle.

"Get tired of this? Never," he says. "Not when you can get a picture like that."

Click. Whirr.

* * *

It Sounds Like A Good Life!
Fort Wayne's Bob Parker Tells His Story

— Nov. 30, 1977

My baseball interest began in 1928 when Fort Wayne fielded a strong team in the Central League, winning the championship. Big gun in their batting attack was outfielder Chuck Klein, who was sold to the Phillies in August for $7,500. Elon Hogsett pitched in two play-off wins for Fort Wayne (it was a split schedule, with Fort Wayne taking the first half, Erie the second) and Si Simon, an ex-St. Louis Brown, held forth at third base.

This team held a mighty attraction for an 11-year-old boy who belonged to the "knothole gang," an organization of Fort Wayne grade school children who were privileged to see games free of charge after classes were dismissed in mid-afternoon. We would walk to the ballpark (two miles or so) and sometimes see the last two innings of play as all games were afternoon games in 1928. Many times the walk was for naught as the game had ended shortly before our arrival. What wonderful memories!

By the time I was a high school senior, a local newspaper started running sports cartoons by Pap (Tom Paprocki, Associated Press). I recall the first one I ever viewed was of Wally Berger, Boston Braves, and I still have the clipping. Being an art student (not a very good one at that time) I was suddenly engulfed with an overwhelming desire to draw sports people. Of course, I thought that I could just sit right down and do it...what a laugh!

My father brought home a Chicago Tribune whose sports pages included a fine picture of Burleigh Grimes. I sat on our front porch, paper and pencil in hand, and struggled with reproducing that photo. I ended up with a very crooked Burleigh Grimes...learning quickly that I was no Pap. I tried drawing from the thumbnail-sized photos in Reach and Spalding Guides and still have many of these early attempts...not too bad, but far from professional.

Then working a part-time grocery store job which turned into a full 60-hour per week effort (15 cents per hour in 1934)...the only time left for cartooning was Sundays and holidays. I did manage time to prepare several drawings, took them to the Fort Wayne Journal-Gazette and the sports editor finally published my first one in February 1935...what a thrill...spent almost all my pocket money (probably 35 cents) on extra newspapers that morning. That led to a long relationship with that newspaper which published hundreds of my cartoons through the years. They were not all baseball, covering almost any sport that was popular in the 1930-1960 era of sports.

* * *

SCD Dealer Profile
A Veteran Shop Owner Recalls "Good Old Days" Of Early Card Collecting

By Paul Green — Sept. 4, 1987

At Ball Four Cards in West Allis, Wis., Frank and Steve Pemper have built one of the nation's leading card and supply stores. Whether it's a single card holder, an autographed ball or a minor league set, Ball Four Cards is one place where you are likely to find what you need. Frank Pemper took time out from work to discuss the business and the hobby...

...SCD: You've always been fairly active in terms of supplies.

Pemper: Yes, with supplies nobody ever tells you the source. They always just tell you to buy from them, but we got started with supplies and our secret has always been variety. We don't just carry one type of album or card holders. We may have seven or eight different.

SCD: Is there demand for that many different types?

Pemper: When it comes to supplies a lot of collectors and dealers are set on a particular one. It might be lucite, or a top load or whatever. Most like a specific type of holder and it's hard to convince them to try something else so we have plastic and poly and so on. We want to satisfy the customer.

SCD: Do you have any other particular guidelines for running the business?

Pemper: We try not to hold on to anything too long. Let's say you have a 1986 Topps Update. You buy it for maybe $6 and sell them for maybe $7.50-$10. Some people might think the price is going to go up so they can make more on them. They're afraid that if they sell it, someone else might double their money on it. But as I've talked to dealers around the country, most of the really successful ones tell me the same thing, buy something and sell it. Get out of it and get into something else.

SCD: So you don't worry about getting every last possible dime out of something?

Pemper: Right, it ties up too much money, just to sit and hold something. Most successful dealers just buy a card like Eric Davis and then they get out of it.

SCD: The point can also be made that some profit is better than none and cards can go down in price too.

Pemper: Right. People don't always understand the cost of a business. For example, you have to advertise and you have to do it regularly. You can't just take out one ad a month and get discouraged because you're not selling something. People can look at your ad one time and forget about it. The second time they see it, it stays subconsciously in the back of their minds. The third time they see it they decide they want to order something but forget to do it. Then the fourth time they see it and remember they need some sheets, they order from Ball Four. That's been another secret to our success, our advertising. We put our name before the public....

...SCD: Have you seen a lot of changes in the supply business and the types of supplies available?

Pemper: Definitely, there is always somebody coming out with something new which is one of the important reasons for going to a show and reading the hobby papers. You have to stay on top of things. What was popular four or five years ago might have been replaced by something new which has come in. Take card holders. When lucite first came in they were 60-65 cents. Then somebody invented a holder that sells for about half so that you're seeing more inexpensive things on the market and taking over a bigger portion of the market.

SCD: Have you seen many changes in cards and card collecting?

Pemper: You have so many more cards today. And people want more than one of them, they want 100 Eric Davis cards...

...SCD: You mentioned all the different issues, regionals, minor league sets, and so on. Do you have too many or are they filling a need?

Pemper: We're a distributor for minor league sets. We've already doubled what we sold last year and the cards aren't even out yet. The demand is tremendous. But take police sets. We used to sell a lot of Milwaukee police sets around the country and we don't sell so many today. I think there is a demand, but there are so many cards. People have a hard time collecting all the new sets without also collecting the regional sets...

...SCD: Are you pretty optimistic about the future in terms of the hobby and your business?

Pemper: Oh yes, I'm very optimistic about it. I would think that as long as the economy is good and people have money to spend it will be good. It's a good thing to do with the kids. It's a good hobby. It brings families together. I've seen it happen. You see the father bring the son in so much or the son brings the father in because the son is interested in collecting. That happens all the time and the father will remember the Braves and he'll start getting into it a little bit. It's a way for the father and son to do things together.

SCD: Have you enjoyed the business?

Pemper: Yes, I love the business. In fact, next to my faith and my family, this is my greatest love. People come in all the time and say they would love to have a business like this, so we can see how fortunate we are to be able to go into work. It's really something you love to do. I really enjoy it, I've been blessed in a sense.

* * *

An In-Depth Interview With Jack Petruzzelli

By Scott Daloisio

...SCD: Were you a collector when you were growing up?

JP: I started collecting as a five-year-old and this is a very true story. My very first card was a 1954 Willie Mays. We used to flip them up against a wall. Every time I won with my Mays card, I would put a mark on the back. I still have that card to this day. It probably isn't worth $30 because it is just brutal. The corners are gone and there isn't a condition to name it. Fair would be giving it a Mint grading. The thing is just brutal.

SCD: Of everything you own, it probably means the most to you.

JP: Yes, because that is one of the very first things I ever had...

...SCD: Being the promoter of the National is like being the manager at the All-Star game.

JP: Being part of the one in '85, I got an idea of what it was like to be part of a big show. Every year since then I have participated in some way. With that five years behind me, I took something from everyone and said, "You know what, something has got to be done to improve this?" That is where we came up with the booth concept, different ways for corporate sponsors to get involved and ways to treat corporates and treat dealers.

SCD: What have you seen at other Nationals that you want to be sure to incorporate in Anaheim in 1991?

JP: Professionally-done seminars is one. I have seen some Nationals where they throw together some guys that can go in and talk to some people for an hour. That was supposed to be a seminar. I have been to some other trade shows, Hawaii being one of them, where I learned a lot. I learned a lot from Kit Young's trade shows. Bruce Paynter had some great seminars in 1989 and Wanda (Marcus) had some nice stuff last year, too. Seminars are important to people. A lot of people want to learn, and they want to see stuff at seminars.

The autographs have always been a pet peeve of mine. I refuse to charge a lot of money for autographs. There are going to be about six to eight Hall of Famers at our show, baseball, hockey and football, that we are not charging for autographs. There are going to be the prime guests, the big guns, so we are going to charge for those. I feel bad charging people the exorbitant amounts you have to charge for autographs nowadays but it is almost a way of life. People know that if they are going to go to a show and see an Aaron, Williams, Mantle or DiMaggio, they are going to have to pay a premium for the autograph. The way we handle autographs is another thing. We have an organized way of doing things. We will make an announcements, "Please don't get in line until your numbers are called." The people appreciate it, because nobody likes standing in a line a long time...

...SCD: Can you give an estimate on the amount of hours you have put in prior to the doors opening?

JP: You have got to be kidding! Let's put it this way. I put in a minimum of four hours a day, either mailing stuff out to people who did not get their hotel reservation envelope or mailed their application to the wrong place. Checking, double checking and triple checking the work to make sure we did not screw up along the line somewhere. Thousands and thousands of hours. Easily...

...SCD: Right now it is the big build up. You are looking forward to the National. Then comes the ultimate let down when it is all over.

JP: You know what? Monday morning, July 8, as I am lying in bed not being able to move, it will be one of those, "is it over?" I am really looking forward to it. My family is pumped. Southern California just buzzes about it. I probably get 20 or 30 phone calls a day from interested people coming in from all over. It is going to be fun.

* * *

Artist Finds His Niche Creating Bowman Portrait Cards

By Ted Taylor, Off the Cuff, Sept. 14, 1990

Craig Pursley? Who is Craig Pursley?

I'm sure many of you were wondering just who he was when you opened your first packs of 1990 Bowman baseball cards and discovered a 1950s-like baseball portrait card included with the rest of your cards.

Compounding the question might have been Bowman's sweepstakes offer on the back of the Pursley cards. Those entered were eligible for a drawing to win all 11 artist-signed lithographs "valued in excess of $440."

My first thought was that perhaps Pursley was an old-timer who, like Gerry Dvorak, was making a comeback in the baseball card art world. But, no, that wasn't it.

It turns out Pursley is the very capable sports artist on the staff of the Orange County (California) Register. He's also a longtime baseball fan.

"Being an illustrator and a baseball fan, I've long admired the 1950-52 Bowman cards," Pursley explained recently.

"Last year I started doing a series of paintings in that style of one player from each American League team.

"I sent photos of these to Topps and the idea for the Bowman inserts was born" he went on.

Interestingly, Pursley turned out all 11 insert paintings in just one month.

"I did them on my days off from The Register, quite a busy month," he added.

Actually, Pursley had to do 12 paintings; Topps didn't like the first Will Clark painting he submitted.

"They felt he had kind of dumb look on his face...I felt it was accurate," he recalled.

In addition to his Bowman inserts, Pursley also did a prototype 1955 Topps Mickey Mantle card that the company used as a two-page illustration in its mid-summer Topps Magazine.

"No one at Topps seems to know why there wasn't a 1955 Mantle card," he added. (As an aside, there was a 1955 Bowman Mantle card. It is likely Topps did not have Mantle under contract for that year. It's not an uncommon happening during the mid-1950s Topps-Bowman player wars.)

The similarity between the Bowman 1990 inserts and the original cards of the 1950-52 era is intentional.

For example, Pursley notes the background in the Kevin Mitchell card is identical to that in the 1951 Lou Boudreau card. The artist also used the Boudreau background on a prototype Ken Griffey Jr. card that never made it to the final set.

The original of the Bo Jackson card in the insert set was drawn from a picture of the Royals star in an Auburn uniform.

In the original painting, Jackson appeared with the same background as the 1951 Bowman Johnny Vander Mere card. By the time the card hit production, however, Jackson was posing in Anaheim Stadium.

"One could only conclude that this painting was done at the 1989 All-Star game," Pursley said. Which, of course, it wasn't.

* * *

Meet Alan "Mr. Mint" Rosen

A Former Copy Machine Dealer, Rosen Is Busy With Card Sales On A Full-time Basis
Now Learn How "The Buying Machine" Got Its Start

By Paul Green — July 22, 1988

"The Million Dollar Dealer." That's Alan Rosen, the man whose name is synonymous with big. When it comes to baseball cards, he's always pursuing the spectacular.

Alan Rosen

Actually, few have been more successful or had a greater impact on both the hobby and the baseball card market than Rosen. Whenever you mention the leading dealers in the country, his name will be at or near the top of the list, and his activities continue to expand. His auctions have quickly become a place to find the true treasures in cards and memorabillia.

He did this interview only a few days after hosting his first baseball card show at Madison Square Garden, and the list of Rosen activities just goes on and on.

SCD: How did you get started collecting? As a kid?

Rosen: No, I went to a baseball card show in 1980. I bought my first baseball card that year. I bought a 1953 Mantle, which happens to still be my favorite card, and I caught the bug. I picked up all the years following the next couple shows, and started buying sets of cards, 1979, 1978 and 1977.

When I got back to 1975 and 1974, I couldn't find Mint sets that were to my liking, so I pieced them together. I was everyone's best customer. In the space of two years I accumulated $40,000 or $50,000 worth of cards. Then I started buying 10 or 20 of a set, keeping the best two or three and selling the rest off.

SCD: You were perilously close to being a baseball card dealer.

Rosen: I was selling copying machines. I had my own business selling them and typewriters and had a part-time antique store. Before I knew it, I had more cards in my home than anything else, more cards than towels. I had the bug and started placing ads in local papers to buy. I started buying large quantities of tobacco cards Topps cards, boxes of 1973s, 1974s or whatever I could buy. I was making more money buying cards than I was selling copying machines.

I got my hands on a Sports Collectors Digest in 1981, and started advertising as "Mr. Mint." I was backed, I had money to buy and started really buying. I had ads in for "Mr. Mint the Buying Machine" and that kind of thing with unlimited funds. I was the only one doing it at that time in that boisterous way. I was making thousands of dollars a week buying cards. By the end of 1982 and early 1983 I sold my other businesses to do this on a full-scale basis. It's just snowballed into what it is today.

SCD: Can you describe your business today?

Rosen: I try to handle Mint sets and Near Mint sets from the 1950s and 1960s, to tobacco cards, older memorabilia. I really deal in deals. I have built a reputation through Sports Collector's Digest, which I give all the credit, because if it wasn't for SCD, I don't think I or anyone would be where they are now. I think SCD has been instrumental in making the hobby what it is today, and I have probably been instrumental in raising the prices to the levels where they are today. What I mainly do is buy large collections of baseball cards. I keep the cream for the auctions and sell the rest off to other dealers. I process some at shows, sell others off to flea market dealers...

...SCD: But in fairness, you've made some of the most impressive buys in the decade. The 1952 Topps, the Paris, Tenn., find, which was a favorite out of the top few spectacular ones?

Rosen: Of course, the 1952 find. Honestly, when I found them, I thought they were fake. I kept smelling them and touching them. I just couldn't believe my eyes. Then I had buyer's remorse. I laid out a lot of money for them, more than a lot of people make in a lot of years of working, and I came home in a van with just a little box of cards. I didn't have any money left and I honestly thought the end of the hobby was coming when I was sitting there with 50-75 Mantle rookies, 140 Mays; it was unbelievable. I had 5,500 high numbers. I thought the end of the world was there. I put the first ad in and sold less than $10,000 worth of cards. Then I started giving them away to dealers cheap. I was charging $2,100 for Mint Mantles, $50 for Mint high numbers. Then right after I sold my last card, that's when they started to hit. As a matter of fact, I just bought back one of the Mantles I sold from that time. I paid $7,500 for it after I had sold it to him for $2,000...

...SCD: Was there another special buy?

Rosen: The Paris, Tenn., find. I walked into that room in the one-horse town of Paris, Tenn., in that little Holiday Inn, in the meeting room and saw seven tables filled with unopened boxes. I was actually trembling, I couldn't believe it. Then when I got close I saw all the damage from bug infestation and water.

But when you're looking at 50 boxes of 1955 Topps and 130 boxes of 1954 Bowmans, I mean that's scary.

SCD: But what a shame, so many were ruined.

Rosen: We held packs up to the light and you could see bugs crawling right through them, right through holes in the cards. We threw away at least 100 boxes of cards, right in the garbage. I took abuse for that, got some letters about not all collectors collect Mint. But the people don't understand. In most of those cards you couldn't even see the face. They were destroyed by gum damage, bug infestation.

SCD: So these cards weren't even fillers.

Rosen: No, the fronts of the cards were totally ruined, like a burnished orange from the gum, with holes and like sandpaper finish. They were just horrible. If I tried to sell those cards people would have laughed at me....

...SCD: I would gather that overall you've enjoyed it (the business).

Rosen: What else could I do that I'd enjoy more? The only thing is pitching for the Yankees. I work hard, 60-70 hours a week minimum, but I enjoy it. I enjoy it when the phone rings the first time in the morning. I want to get up and go to work.

To make the money I make and enjoy what I'm doing. How many people can say they enjoy what they do? Not many. I know when I was in the copier business I had every minute of it. But you know how it is; you have to work to support the family. There is nothing I can do with education to make the money I make and enjoy myself.

Now that I'm on top it's even better. Everything seems to work out. I try to keep a high profile, but I try to make sure that what I do is right, what I sell is right, how I come across at shows is right. I try to be professional, avoid controversy while keeping my advertising positive and over the years, I think I've done a good marketing job.

* * *

Queenpin Promoter Rothstein Started With Antique Shows

By Rich Marazzi — Batting the Breeze, April 5, 1991

I'm sure you've seen "A Gloria Rothstein Show" Inc. advertisements in this publication.

You've probably wondered about the path a woman would take to rise to such a high level of promotion in this hobby/business.

I was curious, so I tracked down the queenpin of the East Coast promoters at one of her shows in the Westchester County Center in White Plains, N.Y.

Gloria Rothstein

The show, by the way, is one of her smaller shows, attracting "only" 175 dealer tables.

SCD: How did you get started?

Rothestein: We started doing flea markets, antique shows, gem and mineral shows and street fairs in 1971.

In 1978 a young man named Gary Pecora came to me and asked if he could have a booth at one of the antique shows. I didn't know if he would fit in. I wanted him to dress like my other antique dealers.

Gary came in with baseball signs. I told him that he would have to take the signs down. It was Gary who influenced me.

He said, "You're a great promoter, why don't you do baseball shows? There's no professionals. Nobody knows what they're doing. I'll get you dealers."

SCD: So what was your next step?

Rothstein: Well, it was my idea to kick off the show with a big name baseball player at the show and we got Hank Aaron to appear.

Unfortunately, six months before the show, Gary Pecora died from a rare form of cancer. I didn't know where I was at with the dealers.

As I walked around and introduced myself, people said, "Who are you?"

SCD: How did your first show go?

Rothstein: We had 120 tables. It was the start of something very big. The show was such a huge success that everybody was talking about it. It was like the New York area was waiting for this to happen.

SCD: Did you make an evaluation of your shows after a certain period of time?

Rothstein: Yes. After three years we sat down and took a look at things. At the time we were running shows twice a year.

We were not happy with the star players making appearances because we weren't making money. All of the profit was going into paying the stars.

So we decided no more stars. The dealers loved it because the customers where there to buy. The only time we have stars is at the East Coast National. We do it once a year in August.

At the Pier 92 show (Feb. 9-10) we had names like Bobby Thomson, Johnny Podres, Johnny Vander Meer and Marv Throneberry. Autographs were free.

SCD: So your policy is that certain shows you bring in star players to sign autographs while other shows you don't?

Rothstein: That's right. For instance, we're initiating a huge Memorial Day weekend classic (May 24-27) at the Raritan Expo Center in Edison, N.J.

We have already booked 20 Hall of Famers for the weekend. There will be 700 dealer tables at the show.

SCD: How many dealer tables will there be at the East Coast National in White Plains Aug. 15-18?

Rothstein: There will be 582. In addition, we have card flipping contests, Stratomatic, etc.

The dealers tell me they make more at the East Coast National than at the so-called National show.

SCD: How did your East Coast National show come about?

Rothstein: I refused to bid for the National because I don't want committees telling me how to promote a show on the East Coast. How could a committee from the Midwest tell me how to advertise in the East?

All the dealers asked why I wouldn't bid for the National. We found out that we had to live by so many rules and regulations.

SCD: Apparently, you have some concerns about the National.

Rothstein: That's right. When I read about a professional firm taking over the promotion of the National, I was very disheartened. I don't think this industry is ready for that.

I've been promoting antique shows for 20 years and never heard of a promotion firm promoting for retail public shows. They use promoters for trade shows.

SCD: How many people usually attend your East Coast National?

Rothstein: In excess of 20,000 people.

SCD: Do you, like some promoters, have the baseball stars sign personally for items to be sold at future shows?

Rothstein: Never.

SCD: As a result of all your shows, have you developed a personal collection?

Rothstein: Yes. I have a hat signed personally from Mickey Mantle. Reggie Jackson once gave me a T-shirt he was wearing. And I have various bats and balls signed to me personally.

SCD: Do you consider yourself a collector?

Rothstein: I was an antique collector. I collect cut glass, tiffany and antique jewelry.

SCD: You have a reputation among dealers as a promoter who runs a tight ship. Is that true?

Rothstein: Let's put it this way. If I find any dealer to be misrepresenting his merchandise, I put him out immediately.

Also, I expect the dealers at my shows to dress appropriately.

SCD: It sounds like you have a good rapport with your dealers.

Rothstein: I think so. Once it was very warm and they couldn't get the blowers to work properly. One of the dealers complained.

Another one yelled from the back of the room, "If she ran a show in hell, I'd follow her and buy a fan."

SCD: How do you see this hobby developing?

Rothstein: It's a hobby for some but for the dealers it's big business.

SCD: Do you have a feel as to what type of clientele are drawn to your shows?

Rothstein: I'll tell you this. At my January show, one of the dealers had a heart attack. I requested help, and would you believe that 14 doctors came forward.

SCD: About how many shows do you promote each year and where are they held?

Rothstein: Twelve shows. From September 1990 to August 1991 four of the shows were scheduled for Giants Stadium, five for the Westchester County Center in White Plains, N.Y., two for the Raritan Expo Center in Edison, N.Y., and one for the New York City Pier 92 on 52nd Street and 12th Avenue in New York City.

* * *

A Talk With Rick Salvino

By Paul Green — March 3, 1989

When you're talking quality cards or the increasingly influential Southern California Baseball Card Dealers Association, one name that will crop up in both areas is Rick Salvino. Week in and week out, few advertise more nice cards in SCD than Rick and Carol Salvino. Rick gave us some background on their business...

...SCD: Do you see more people coming in?

Salvino: Every day. It's unbelieveable, and I see a lot of professional people coming in, a lot of doctors, attorneys and they spend a lot of money. At first, I think it's for investment; then they become attached to the cards. A few months go by and pretty soon they are 100 percent collectors. I do not see a lot of investment in the old card market, I really don't. I know there's a lot of speculation in new cards, but I don't think that's true with old cards. And when they say they're investors, they end up becoming collectors...

...SCD: What's drawing them all in?

Salvino: There's not one thing that I can see. It's a combination of things. Articles draw them in, getting publications on the newsstands is another. The two papers out here have had articles on the top investments and every time in the last year baseball cards were number one. That's pretty amazing to see in the business section of the paper.

SCD: Do you think people are well advised to look at it as an investment or should they strictly stick with collecting?

Salvino: With the amount of money that's in it now, there's no way around the investment. They're like pieces of art at this point. On their own they will always be worth something, but I don't think you should buy them figuring you'll make a fortune. I disagree with that theory. We haven't seen a down since it's been recognized as a market. There was a down when I was collecting but I don't think it was really recognized as a market back then. I think it's just now being recognized as a market and we haven't been down yet. They say there's a down in every market, although I'm not sure. I don't think we've really scratched the surface in the market yet. If there was a big down in the economy I think the new stuff might have a little trouble, but I suspect the old stuff would stay fairly solid. Even in a slow economy you don't see too many doctors and lawyers out of work. I have a stockbroker who sold all his and put the money into baseball cards. He said the baseball cards are a solid investment.

SCD: It's probably no worse than stocks and has to he a lot more fun.

Salvino: I think it's better, baseball cards are legitimately rare items. Any time you get into legitimately rare items like paintings, they usually stay in down periods. I know stamps and coins have gone down and I think baseball cards have a lot to do with that, but I've never heard of Picassos going down...

...SCD: I would gather you're pretty optimistic?

Salvino: Oh yes. I hear predictions of gloom and doom from some but I'd like to see those people make me a list of five reasons why this hobby is going to crash; I'd even like to hear one solid concrete reason. Some have been doing it so long they can't say they were wrong. Are they expecting baseball to die? Is roller derby going to become bigger than baseball or something? I just don't see it. I can see prices leveling or dipping and things like that, but the percentage of collectors to investors is about 90 percent to 10 percent.

SCD: Overall, I would imagine you're pretty happy doing this for a living.

Salvino: Oh yes, I love business and the challenges of business. I'm not as much of a collector as I used to be because I see everything, and they're in and out every week. I think the most enjoyment I get is putting some of my clients into pieces I would have been so thrilled to get when I was a collector. That's probably where I get my thrills now. I think the hobby is in a great state. Over the next few years I look for it to grow tremendously. I think we're just getting started. We have just scratched the surface as far as national attention.

I expect we'll see baseball cards advertised on TV, and shows dedicated to baseball card collecting. That's where we're headed. This is going to turn into a major thing and when it happens, for the stuff I deal in, the prices are just going to go out of sight because there is not a big enough supply. That's why we'll all have to consider expanding our horizons because the stuff we deal in now just won't be available. I've been in promotions all my life, and so far we haven't done anything really.

* * *

An SCD Dealer Profile Ohio Dealer Kevin Savage Interviewed

By Paul Green — May 20, 1988

Kevin Savage of The Sports Gallery in Sylvania, Ohio, is known to dealers and collectors around the country as one of the nation's leading dealers. He took time from his store recently to share his ideas on the business and the hobby with SCD readers.

SCD: How did you get started collecting? As a kid?

Savage: Yes, I collected as a kid. When I was a sophomore in college my father bumped into Tom Noe, who is in the rare coin business but who had accumulated a lot of baseball cards. They bumped into each other on an airplane and they got talking and that type of thing. Then I met with Tom and we went to lunch and he hired me to work for him during the summer selling baseball cards. He sent me to Plymouth, the National and all the shows and then we started a little mail order business under the company name Numismatic Investment of Ohio. That was in 1981 and it just kind of mushroomed. We started doing real well and I liked it. Then when I got out of college we opened a store, The Sports Gallery.

SCD: Can you tell us a little about the business today?

Kevin Savage

Savage: Basically we deal in older and newer issues, along with collecting supplies like plastic sheets, boxes and all the different card holders there are.

SCD: So it's basically a little of everything.

Savage: Yes, we handle all the different things that come up from Donruss, Topps and Fleer, and whatever we can pick up of the older stuff, whatever we run across at shows or whatever walks into our store. It's getting harder and harder to find those cards. We just don't have as many older cards as we used to have.

SCD: Is that in large part a function of the supply just drying up on them?

Savage: I think so. I also think the guys who are putting all their interest and time into finding the older cards and dealing the older cards are just outhustling us. It's harder for guys like us who are trying to handle everything. They come across bigger deals, they advertise more to buy older collections and they're able to offer the collectors more than the guys who have the hobby shops which also carry new cards, card supplies and the whole bit.

SCD: Based on what you're saying, I would gather that any notion that the market is strictly active when you're talking Eric Davis rookies would be a wrong conclusion.

Savage: Oh yes, definitely. In fact, I'm seeing a renewed interest in collecting older cards, especially in the last six months. Even our regular customers in the store that were collecting the Eric Davis rookies and that type of thing are going back and trying to collect 1960s and 1959s sets and they're finding it very hard to find those cards in excellent or better condition. So our supplies are drying up all the time. You can't have enough older cards.

SCD: Why are people suddenly switching? Are they comparing the prices of modern rookies to cards of the 1960s or what?

Savage: I think that's part of it. Look at an Eric Davis card for $15; for that you can buy Duke Snider from 1962, 1964 or something like that. Then you think is Eric Davis ever going to be as good as Duke Snider? And even if you think he will be you have to consider scarcity and figure that there have to be a lot more 1985s than there are 1962s and 1964s, especially in Mint condition.

SCD: How would you characterize the market in general today?

Savage: The last year has been incredibly strong. Our sales more than doubled in the last year. I think part of that is that we're getting more established in the market, but a lot of it is just due to a huge influx of collectors. We used to have 50 people in the store and now we have 100-150 in a day.

SCD: Does that make you wonder how much it can grow?

Savage: Well, it does. At times you say it can't get any better than this, but other days you realize it's just a small part of a growing collectible market and that some day it might get bigger and bigger. I think the National last year was living proof of that. They probably had twice as many people there last year than they did any other year I've been there.

SCD: What's really hot right now?

Savage: About one out of every three people who came up to our table at the National asked for Mark McGwire rookie cards. It was unbelieveable. Of course we were right across the bay from Oakland.

SCD: Even so, that's pretty hot. What else?

Savage: In unopened material I think the 1985 Topps, Donruss and Fleer are all very good right now. There are a lot of good rookie cards in those sets. Also the 1984 Fleer material is hard to find and a lot of people think it is underpriced.

SCD: What about older material?

Savage: I think 1968 is kind of a break year. Anything before 1968 that is in Excellent or better, especially Near Mint to Mint cards, is just really good right now. It seems like you can just throw out the price guide on some things. I'm afraid it's confusing for collectors. For example, at the National we were looking for Mantle cards and by the end of the show there wasn't a Mantle card in the room that was Mint for less than $100 and some of them book for $30 to $40. But none were less than $100. So there is great, great strength in that market, especially the superstars. Mantle is probably the most popular right now in the older players.

SCD: Sounds like that market is getting like rookies.

Savage: That's right, it's starting to simulate what the rookie market has done in the last couple years where a Mark McGwire card could have been $3 a month ago and is $10 now. So I think the older cards are starting to come around now, too.

SCD: Sounds like it's getting to be a wild, whatever-the-market-will-bear situation.

Savage: It kind of is that way, which is what I think it should be. Prices should correct when there's a drop off in demand or an over-abundant supply.

SCD: Are there any areas people are overlooking that might make for good collections?

Savage: I see a lot of people searching for that. I personally think, among the newer cards, players like George Bell and Jesse Barfield, people who have legitimate big-time numbers but who aren't playing in large metropolitan areas. I think they have a lot of potential price wise.

SCD: Although finding any quantity of their rookie cards isn't that easy either.

Savage: Even the other cards which aren't their rookies will grow in price. In the older cards, I like some of the lesser-known Hall of Famers; players like Billy Williams are a good bargain. I like Harmon Killebrew and think even Gaylord Perry, who doesn't seem to be very

popular, has some potential to grow. I especially like cards from the first five or six years of their career when their cards are a little harder to find. Once you get up into the 1970s they are a lot easier to find.

SCD: So you're looking at older cards of lesser-known Hall of Famers.

Savage: Yes, guys who started in the late 1950s and early 1960s who are certain Hall of Famers but who are not at prices like Yastrzemski, or Mantle or Rose. I like some of the early Marichal cards even though the rookie card is way up there now. I think those cards have a lot of growth potential.

SCD: What advice do you give new people to the hobby?

Savage: We get tons of them. You get a lot of new people every day. We try to steer the new people into buying complete sets, especially the current year set. Of course, it depends what they're in it for, but even if you're in it for investment it's the best hedge; you're getting one of everybody. If you're a collector it saves you all the time of trying to put the set together and buying all the packs, although that can be a lot of fun. Economically it's the cheapest way to complete a set and you're getting one of all the players. I think you can get a lot of enjoyment just out of looking through those cards.

SCD: Do most of them then stick with sets?

Savage: Some will go back and collect things like Tigers because we're near Detroit. Some want particular players, as many people are superstar collectors. Maybe Hank Aaron is their favorite player, so they'll go back and try to get all the Hank Aaron cards. You must remember it's rather cost prohibitive for many of the people who come in to try and go back and complete the 1952 Topps set because you're talking a huge chunk of money there. That just rules out a lot of people who would really love to have a 1952 set, the price just scares them away. Even trying to collect it doesn't seem to make a whole lot of sense for them unless you want to make it a lifelong journey.

SCD: And it could be. Are you seeing more of the guy buying 1,000 or maybe 10,000 of one player as a penny stock type deal?

Savage: Yes, there's some of that, but we're not geared for that. We don't have the sorters so we're not really able to offer someone 1,000 Eric Davis rookies. But if you go through SCD you see there are more and more people doing that. I see a lot of investors buying that kind of thing. I don't really know how good an investment they are. They can certainly be good, but I think liquidity is the problem when it comes time to sell. Who is really going to buy at some super, super price? If you really know your baseball and get in on the ground floor and can tell who the next superstar will be, even though a lot of the scouts can't, then you can certainly make money. I think that's separate from collecting.

SCD: Are you at all concerned about the number of card sets at present?

Savage: From a business standpoint, it's advantageous to have more products to sell. I'd have trouble staying in business if all I had were the Topps sets every year like it used to be. There just wouldn't be enough products to sell to make a living selling baseball cards. After you bought that year's set, then you might go back to earlier sets, but I don't think we could possibly come up with enough older cards to do a large amount of business. We are getting to a saturation point, though. Collectors are coming in saying "Geez, another set. Do I really want this or don't I?" I don't know how many issues there have been this year; I quit counting them.

SCD: I wasn't that good in math. I don't know that I could count them.

Savage: There are a lot of them and I like a lot of them so I can see why they're bringing them out. But there is going to be a point where it's too much. Like the Donruss "Opening Day" set — I don't think a lot of dealers are going to order them; I've had a number tell me that they've had enough. Pretty soon it will be like a set-of-the-month club and a lot of the dealers are scared about being stuck with worthless inventory, which I think happened somewhat with 1986 Donruss highlights.

SCD: Are there some things you'd like to see change in the hobby or business?

Savage: I'd like them to let the dealers buy all their cards and cases directly from the company. I think they'd really be shocked how many orders they'd get from just the hobby dealers and they'd save the money we're spending with the candy wholesalers now.

SCD: What cards do you always need?

Savage: A problem in our area is Al Kaline cards, especially the first five or six years. Any older Tiger card and really anything that's older and in nice condition. Any of the older sets, anything from 1952 to 1973, is something we always need. People are always coming in and asking for something like a 1968 set and we don't always have it because those older sets are getting harder and harder to find. If it continues, you're going to see prices rise.

SCD: Also sounds like you're getting increasing emphasis on condition.

Savage: Yes, condition is important. People who are buying are looking down the road and if they want to sell, they want to have a card that's easily saleable and they know the mint condition cards are tougher to find, so they'll probably be easier to sell down the road. Increasingly, I think the collectors are looking at resale when they're buying cards.

SCD: What changes have you seen in the business that stand out?

Savage: I've seen a big growth in full-time dealers, especially in the last two to three years. It used to be that the guy taught school and did shows in the summer, but more and more people are quitting their regular job and are buying and selling baseball cards for a living. I've also seen the shows grow. I've been going to the National since the second one in Plymouth and it seems like it's grown threefold since then. I also think things are getting better organized and I think within a year or two there will be a national dealer organization which should help.

Another thing I'd like to see is grading become more consistent. I don't know what the answer is there. I know we buy things through the mail and it seems like everyone is grading cards differently. I don't know if we need a more exact grading system or just better guidelines as to what the grades really are. There's also no way to enforce standards on anyone so that's a problem, too.

SCD: Are you enjoying the business?

Savage: Oh, yes, I'm just happy to be able to do something I enjoy for a living. It's a fantastic way to make a living. I think that's why more people are getting into it. You may not make as many dollars as your brother who is an attorney, but probably have a lot more fun. You get to travel and meet a lot of people and you can't beat a job where you just sit around and talk sports all with customers.

* * *

Talking Cards With Ray And Peggy Schiflett

By Paul Green — Sept. 8, 1989

It's pretty hard to miss the advertisements of Ray and Peggy Schiflett. They are among the most humorous in all of baseball cards. If there are any advertisements where the cards are almost eclipsed by the way they're described, it's Ray and Peggy Schiflett who did it.

SCD: How did you get started?

The Schiflett clan

Peggy: We got started because Ray collected cards as a kid. I was a tomboy who adored baseball and also collected cards as a kid although I traded all mine away for Civil War cards. That's where all my Mantles went.

SCD: Ah, but you got General So-and-so.

Ray: She got "Death Barges In" and things like that.

Peggy: Yes, I traded off all those guys who I figured would never amount to anything. When we got married, I told him I was going to turn him into a baseball fan because he was just an Astros fan, where I liked baseball for the sake of baseball. I didn't care who was playing, the Little Sisters of the Poor or whoever.

Ray: She's right. As far as I was concerned, if the Astros lost, the game just wasn't worth going to. But now I can truly enjoy a lot of games. She's converted me to a Cardinal fan, a Ranger fan. I can even tolerate the Dodgers and have developed an excellent attitude toward the Mets.

SCD: So the cards were a logical out-growth of all this.

Ray: After we'd been married about a year or so my grandmother called, explaining she had found the old tobacco humidor I had stuck my cards in and that they were still there. They had been there for 20 years, nice 1960-63 cards in Mint condition. I guess I was a real retard as a child and didn't flip them, I didn't do anything except look at them and eat the gum.

Peggy: You know, one of those smart-aleck kids who memorized all the statistics.

Ray: Anyway, we took them to a show figuring if we could get a couple bucks out of it, that would be great. Some guy offered me $70. I figured they were worth $100, but that I'd sell at $75. He said it was $70 or nothing, and that's what sparked us getting into it. So for $5 we probably would have never gotten into the hobby. But they blew it, so we've inflicted ourselves on the hobby for almost 10 years now.

Peggy: And we have a lot of fun going to shows. We never get a table because we enjoy going to other tables too much.

SCD: Now, about these ads.

Peggy: Yes, the two of us put them together, and Ray is probably the funnier of the two of us.

SCD: We'll discuss them a little more later. First tell us a bit about your business.

Ray: First off, unlike most people you interview, we really don't view ourselves as dealers. We view ourselves as collectors who have an incredible amount of turnover in our collection. We get a lot of thrill in the chase, but once it's complete, I automatically shift gears and start thinking about what I can sell to chase something else. We aren't collectors who write saying all dealers should be shot. We really like dealers, but don't view ourselves as dealers, I guess, because we don't take tables.

We do buy collections, but what ones have been offered either have had the quality not there in the cards or in condition. We don't deal in only Mint cards. In fact, we love VG and Excellent, but there's an awful lot of Good and Fair stuff that's pushed at us and we just won't deal with that because it doesn't move. We have everything from cards to uniforms, bats, a little bit of everything, but not a lot of anything. We do like consignments in our ads and are getting into that a little more.

Peggy: Let's face it, we do have fun with our ads and we have people who have called us up to say we don't have anything in particular they want but that they just wanted to tell us how much fun they had reading it.

Ray: Yes, usually there are two or three with each ad and we like that a great deal.

SCD: Has anyone ever taken offense at them?

Ray: Someone last year was upset that we made fun of the Astros and what you must remember is that the Astros are our team — except maybe this year with Ryan gone — but we're still negotiating that. But at the time we were committed to the Astros.

Peggy: Yes, we did a wonderful tongue-in-cheek ad making fun of the Astros, whom we love dearly.

Ray: And someone called to tell us it had really upset them a lot and that they were going to prosecute us to the full extent of the law. I'm an attorney and couldn't figure out what that would be, but you can't please everybody.

Peggy: We do all this in good fun and most people pick up on that. But it did kind of upset us that someone took it so seriously.

SCD: Do you have fun putting them together?

Ray: Oh yes. See, I have a bizarre sense of humor; I love any kind of comedy.

Peggy: And I'm a high school English teacher so once he gets it basically put together, I go back and make sure it fits in the English language.

SCD: Do you have favorites you've done?

Ray: We were talking about it, and I only wish we had saved some of the old ones we have done. We've done several movie theme ones. We've always had a wonderful time with our little girl, who is about 6 now. When she was about ready to be born we had baby sales and once she was born, baby ransoms which was basically "Save Our Daughter From A Life of Poverty."

SCD: Are you surprised more people don't use humor like you do?

Ray: Very frankly, we've been amazed there hasn't been more of it in SCD because anybody can just put "Sale" or "Clearance" and there are a lot of people in this hobby who are very imaginative. Maybe they're not comfortable doing it or whatever.

Peggy: And some people are just so serious they never relax.

Ray: The hobby has gotten so serious as the money has gone up in it. I realize the economics are important, but you can still have a light-hearted approach to it, can still treat it as a hobby which is what it supposed to be. I guess if it ever gets to be a slabbed coin situation we'll probably back out of it completely because then it will cease to be fun. I can see the place for slabbed cards, but I would hate to see the hobby go 100 percent in that direction.

SCD: Certainly there are still going to be lots of cards that are not economically feasible to have graded.

Peggy: Right, and we have some cards like a 1952 Mantle, but we also have VGs and had in one a whole shoebox full of cards that were only worth a nickel each and we had a contest giving it to any young person willing to pay the postage and who wrote the best story and why they should get a box for free.

Ray: That was tough. We got about 20 letters and it was real tough to pick the winner.

SCD: What changes have you seen in the hobby since you started?

Ray: Cards are more accessible. When we started, it was real hard to find a given card you wanted. Now with all the shows and SCD having flourished as it has, the hobby now has most of the cards which have come out of the attic. You may have to pay the price for them, but you can now get most cards, especially if, like Rosen says, "You're Mint sicko." I like that a lot. When we first got in it was kind of maddening trying to complete sets. The source has only been drying up for Mint and Near Mint cards. If you're willing to settle for Excellent, you can still find them.

SCD: And Excellent is not an ugly card.

Ray: Right. Now VG can start getting unattractive. I've never liked creases, but have never minded rounded corners that much.

Peggy: We go by strict grading criteria and I'm always tickled when one calls and asks if an Excellent card has any creases.

Ray: Right, and Excellent with creases is a little like Gem Mint except cut in half.

SCD: What changes haven't you liked?

Ray: It's become too serious. It's always been a little serious, but has gotten hyperserious in the last couple years. I just want to say come on, lighten up. We ran an ad a couple years ago directed at that called "This Ad is More Serious Than The U.S. Constitution and Bible Put Together." Everyone laughed, but I think some missed the point that things were getting a little too serious. Our favorite people are ones who smile and laugh and enjoy what they're doing.

We just really enjoy the hobby and especially the friends we've made. We've probably made more friends through this than through any other medium I can think of and we've done lots of different things like work, EMS service and things like that. This, by and large, gets us more consistent friends who we can converse with and go to shows with and things like that.

SCD: So you're definitely collecting?

Ray: Oh lord yes.

Peggy: Sometimes we make up our own sets we want to do.

Ray: Yes, we decide that we don't want to just collect a 1972 or 1966 set. Like right now we're trying to collect a card of what we consider to be the 100 greatest players of all time. We've compiled those 100 names and are trying to collect a set with one card of each of those people. That's something that takes a little work.

SCD: That could be a lot of fun.

Ray: It is and we've got about 10 cards that are always in the collection, like a Ruth card. I don't think we'll ever part with that.

Peggy: Or my N-28 Annie Oakley card because that's me.

* * *

"Smalling's Guide" Now In 5th Edition Collecting Addresses Is A Challenge For R.J. Smalling

By David Craft — Sept. 30, 1988

For its authors, the biennial book is a fascinating hobby.

For collectors and fans, the book is an essential reference book.

For the baseball players, managers and umpires whose names are listed in its pages, the book is a valuable source of information on the whereabouts of friends, acquaintances and former teammates.

The book is The Sport Americana Baseball Address List, now available in its fifth edition. As with its previous incarnation — published in 1986 — the Baseball Address List includes more than 2,000 additions and corrections. One of the book's co-authors, R.J. "Jack" Smalling, says this new edition promises to be the most popular one yet.

"I don't think any one of the first three issues sold more than 10,000 copies," Smalling told Sports Collectors Digest. "No. 4 is going to sell about 30,000 and the new one, I imagine, will do better than that."

The marketing of the book has started to pick up, Smalling says, and cites a recent phone call from his sister as proof.

"She told me she saw it listed in the JC Penney's catalogue for Christmas," Smalling said. "I think it'll be in the (Montgomery) Ward's catalogue, and Sears has bought some copies of the book, too."

The paperback can still be found in the local bookstores, of course, and can also be ordered directly from Smalling by sending a check or money order for $12.45 ($10.98 for the book plus $1.50 to cover shipping charges). Smalling's address is 23008 Van Buren Ave., Ames, Iowa 50010.

The new edition of Baseball Address List provides a handy, alphabetically-arranged directory of nearly every player to debut in the major leagues since 1910. There are also special sections listing major league umpires, and coaches and managers (with no major league playing experience). Addresses of the living and date and place of death of the deceased are given.

Also included are hundreds of autographed photos (and illustrations taken from what Smalling and co-author Dennis Eckes believe to be authentic signatures) to serve as guides. They also provide helpful tips and common-sense measures on how to acquire signatures.

Most of the additions to the new Baseball Address list are the 1986 and 1987 rookies. There are, however, a few names from the more distant past — men who, Smalling says, have been "missing" for years.

"That's part of the fun in updating the book," Smalling said. "I really made a concerted effort this time to look for a lot of players we hadn't located for a long time. One of them is Joey Jay. Another is Ken Burkhart, the pitcher-turned umpire.

"Then there are still those people who either don't want to be found or are so far gone that you can't find them."

Some people can be found but don't want to respond to fans and collectors. Mail will be returned to sender, often with the word "Refused" written on it.

Among the former greats whose signatures have been tough to get in recent times are Harmon Killebrew, Lefty Gomez, Pee Wee Reese and Joe DiMaggio.

People who've used the Baseball Address List to contact an individual and gotten their correspondence returned to them unopened have criticized the book for being "inaccurate," but Smalling insists his "blanket approach" to gathering the addresses, combined with cross-referencing and occasional contacts with the player's relatives, assures up-to-date, accurate information.

"If you send an address verification to the post office (of the community in which the individual was last known to reside), along with a dollar, they will verify the address is good, or tell you the forwarding address, or tell you they don't have it," Smalling explained.

"Once I started sending a dollar along with the information I was requesting, my percentage of replies increased greatly."

Although the information is public record, Smalling admits he gets "one or two" complaints a year from current or former ballplayers who resent having their address listed in the Eckes/Smalling paperback.

"On the other hand," Smalling said, "I have lots of players who send me their new address and say, 'Here's where I live now, be sure and get it right in your next edition.'

"I also sell the book to current and former ballplayers. They're anxious to get it. Ken Keltner has bought nearly every edition that's come out."

The book also serves as the most accurate source available for who's living and who's deceased among baseball men, Smalling says.

"By the time an edition is two years old, the information is two years old," Smalling said. "But, when each new edition first comes out, it is as up-to-date as you'll find anywhere."

To illustrate Eckes' and Smalling's devotion to accuracy, and the humanistic aspect of their work, there was the case several years ago of Bob Rothel, a third baseman who played briefly for the 1945 Cleveland Indians.

Smalling felt Rothel was "in Ohio somewhere," and sent out about 15 or more inquiries to postmasters, city officials, local newspapers and other possible sources.

"I got a letter from his daughter, who told me her father was deceased," Smalling said. "I didn't know that, of course, but she wrote that she had received four or five letters saying I was looking for her dad. She wrote to me and said she was really appreciative that people had contacted her about her dad, of whom she was very proud but who was now gone."

Smalling, who starred for the Ames (Iowa) High School baseball team and then followed that year with a successful 13-year semi-pro career, served several years as a high school teacher and coach. His athletic activities include 20 years of officiating football, basketball and baseball games.

For the past 10 years he has been in the insurance profession.

For the past few decades he has been an avid collector. He owns more than 9,000 player-signed 3x5 index cards, as well as numerous baseball card sets, sports periodicals and baseball books.

Updating his computer's address is an on going process for Smalling. When it comes time for a new edition of the Baseball Address List, in fact, Smalling simply has to run what's currently on file. (For $17.50 plus $2 shipping costs, Smalling will sell a computer printout of the latest data to anyone who requests it.)

"It's been a very interesting process over the years, collecting the information on the players, coaches, managers and umpires," said Smalling, who met co-authror Eckes at a card show in Indianapolis.

"If the individual has been in two or three different cities over the years, I just have to send out 10, 12 postcards, maybe more, and hope some of them will hit the target.

"The replies have been great, whether they've been from the players themselves, or the players' relatives, or the postmasters, or whoever it might be. People have been very helpful in our efforts to obtain the information needed as we update each new edition of the book."

* * *

JOHN SPALDING — March 15, 1974

The administrative assistant to the mayor of San Jose, Calif., is a former reporter for the San Jose Mercury-News (from 1957 to 1970).

He is particularly interested in cards of all types and all years dealing with baseball football and basketball.

John, one of the three organizers of the Northern California Convention last November and also of the upcoming April 6, 1974, get together at Lafayette, Calif., is also interested in guides and needs pre-1937 NCAA college guides.

John is married, and he and his wife are the parents of three children. He is 42 years of age.

* * *

Frank Steele
Meet One Man Who Has Helped Donruss Cards, Sports Artwork Become Popular Collectibles

By Paul Green — Oct. 16, 1987

The name Frank Steele is familiar to many throughout the hobby. In addition to his involvement in the Perez-Steele Galleries, his role as a consultant brought him a good deal of recognition and questions over the years. This time the questions were from SCD.

SCD: How did you get involved with baseball?

Steele: I was born and raised in Pittsburgh and as a kid I collected baseball cards just like I collected radio premiums and tadpoles and whatever else kids collect when they are 14 years of age. That went through a hiatus when I went on to high school and college and graduate school. I always sustained an interest in baseball as a game but did not sustain an interest in collecting.

I am a collector at heart. I think you either have collector blood pumping through your veins or you do not have collector blood. Over a period of years my wife and I have collected various things including antique furniture and early Christian art from the 16th, 17th and 18th centuries. In the past I have also collected coins and stamps. I also had a rather large collection of Little Orphan Annie memorabilia. I thought Little Orphan Annie was one of the all-time gutsy gals. She was a survivor.

One day my wife and I were at a flea market just looking at everything and nothing and I saw a Mel Ott Play Ball card which I remembered as a kid. I asked the fellow how much he wanted for the card and he said a dollar. I thought this was fantastic. I couldn't believe that people still had these things. I gave him the dollar, it was the fastest dollar I ever spent in my life.

SCD: That card just had to seem cheap.

Steele: It was great; I would have given $10. There were no price guides then. It was a case where if I wanted it, I was going to buy it. So I bought it. Mel Ott, I had seen him play. So the next day we went to another flea market.

There I saw an Allen & Ginter card from 1888. It was George Miller of Pittsburgh. I thought, oh boy, what a card. I asked the lady how much she wanted for the card and she said, "Give a dollar for that damn card and get it the hell out of here." That's an actual quote. So I said OK just because she intimidated me. I would have given her whatever she wanted because it was Pittsburgh, it was early and now I had two cards.

The following weekend we went to a large flea market up in northern New Jersey and finally I came to one table where this guy had nothing but baseball memorabilia. I thought I had gone to heaven. He had yearbooks, he had media guides, pennants, cards. I could not believe it. I was looking at the stuff and was so excited. He asked what I collected and I told him Pittsburgh Pirate items. He asked if I had ever seen two players on one card and I told him no. Then he told me that O'Brien twins were on one card. I still have the card here in the office and the story will tell you why. This card is called let's keep Frank humble. I asked how much he wanted for the card and said five dollars. I said great and gave him five dollars and bought some other things. As we walked away Peggy said, "This is going to be an expensive hobby." I thought no, if there's one thing I know how to do, I know how to buy.

We went on and collected some other things, collecting as most do at first, meaning you basically accumulate things. We were buying the good, the bad and the indifferent. Then we shifted to the next phase which is actually collecting. Now, we're in our third phase where we are now editors of our own collection. We have baseball memorabilia in every room, but because it's interesting and it's beautiful. But if we see something at a show, now we ask where is it going to go in the house because if it's just going into the attic that doesn't achieve a whole lot. We already have more stuff in the attic than any normal person should have.

After the purchase of the O'Brien twins card we went to a baseball card show. I couldn't believe all the dealers. Well, I went to one fellow's table and was going through his cards and he had the O'Brien twins. I told him it was exciting and he said, "It is?" I told him it was a rare card and he said, "It is?" That was when I knew I was in trouble. I said two guys on one card is rare and he said, "Big deal." He was great. He said, "How many do you want?" I asked how many he had and he said, "I don't know, I've got about 40 or 50 here and probably a couple hundred more back in the shop."

I asked how much the card cost and I think he said 20 cents. I said "twenty cents!" and he asked what was wrong. I said I was in a world of hurt. Fortunately, five dollars wouldn't destroy me but it certainly hurt my ego. Later I saw that dealer who sold me the card for five dollars and he asked why I didn't come up to his table. I told him I couldn't afford to come to his table.

He asked why and I told him the story and that he was a bad person. He told me I was a big person. I told him I was able to afford the five dollars, but that a young kid might not be able to afford it. When they found out what he had done they might have been driven out of the hobby, which would have been very sad.

I told him I was announcing his demise and that I would drive him out of this hobby. That every chance I had to take a shot at him I would. He got me worked up and he has since left the hobby although I can't honestly say it was because I gave him the gypsy hex. So that's how we got started.

SCD: Where did it go from there?

Steele: We made an early decision to collect baseball-related sheet music because we enjoyed the graphics and because everybody else wasn't collecting. We decided to go down that different path which isn't to demean anyone who collects T206s or Bowmans or anything else. Then we branched off after baseball folk art and statuary. Then came baseball plates, goblets, pewter, ice cream molds and many things outside of the mainstream of the hobby, but which captivated us.

For example, we have two Victorian shaving mugs. During that era, you would go into a barber shop and whatever your occupation was would be depicted on your shaving mug. It might be a farmer, lawyer, baker or whatever your occupation might be. We've been able to find two that have baseball depictions on them. The joy there is that baseball has forced us to cross over into other fields. We've been forced to learn something about shaving mugs, something about painted American toys. We have one of the two known sleds with a baseball depiction on it. They normally have a winter scene, but apparently this grandfather didn't want his grandson to forget about baseball, even though it was winter.

What's important is that it's meaningful and satisfying. I don't like the "you-top-this" attitude some collectors have. It's the wallet syndrome where if Green has more money than Steele, it means Green will have a larger collection. It doesn't follow though that Green will get more satisfaction. I know some people with very modest collections and I dare say that they've probably gotten as much joy from their collections as we've gotten from ours.

SCD: So your roots are collector roots. What happened next?

Steele: We met Dick Perez back in the mid-1970s and developed a friendship with him. He's our partner and our artist and there is no finer man on the face of the earth than Dick Perez. He had been doing all the work for the Phillies since 1972, and for the Eagles since 1971, so he already had established himself as a sports artist in this city. By 1976, he was the competitive winner for the National League Centennial logo.

I had known the president of the Hall of Fame for many years. His offices were on Wall Street where I worked at one time. One day Dick came over and found the Allen & Ginter card and asked why they weren't making baseball cards like this anymore. There is no arrogance in him, but he said he could paint like that.

I told him that if he could, we would do a set of cards which we would sell if I had to go door-to-door to sell them. The rest is history. We had sensed a vacuum in the hobby having a Hall of Fame autograph collection where it was difficult to find photographs or any pictures to frame with those autographs. You could use the Hall of Fame plaque cards but there is a sameness to them. You could use album cards but they weren't consistent. You might find a good Cap Anson, but try to find a good Hoss Radbourn. No one had ever done a consistent high-quality set of Hall of Fame art cards. We seized that opportunity. Dick has now done 199.

SCD: How did the affiliation with Donruss happen?

Steele: That came about in early 1981. Perez-Steele started in 1979 and our first series came out in January of 1980. In early 1981, I got a phone call from a mutual friend who asked if we had ever considered doing with modern ballplayers what we were doing with the Hall of Fame ballplayers. I said we had considered it and he asked which one of the three major card companies I would like to work for. I said that Topps was already dominant in the field so I was not sure I would have a value added to them.

Fleer, a fine company, was in Philadelphia, but I felt that it was in Dick's interest as well as our interest to get a national reputation. I wasn't sure that an affiliation with Fleer would do that. That left Don-

russ, which at that time was owned by General Mills. I was satisfied that they had the financial resources to remain in the business if they chose to do so.

He said that I would get a call from the president of Donruss in a couple of days. In a couple days that's exactly what happened. He asked if we'd like to work for him and I said I didn't think we'd like that at all, but that we might work with him. I loved him, he said, "OK, that's fine with me." He said he'd send his top two men up to see us. Sure enough, they came on April 8, 1981. We sat in the living room and talked about philosophies and reached an accord which we wrote up on a yellow pad. The rest is history. We started out to do a major star for each of the 26 franchises.

SCD: As opposed to just the major star without regard to their team.

Steele: Right, I know from having grown up in Pittsburgh, which had some bad teams, that despite being bad, to a kid in Pittsburgh they are the only heroes he has. Some people have told us we're doing it wrong, that we should load them up with Phillies because the time they had Rose and Schmidt, but we only sold so many cards in Philadelphia and that seemed to me to be overkill. They said load them up with Phillies and Yankees, which obviously we didn't do. Donruss had also wanted a relationship with the Hall of Fame as a point of difference with their competitors. So we and they struck on the idea of a jigsaw puzzle, because you have to have an insert with the cards and only Topps can do a confectionary product. The product must also be meaningful, it cannot be a sham product.

That began the Donruss Hall of Fame puzzle with Babe Ruth being the first. I guess we've done about nine now.

SCD: And the relationship has grown from there.

Steele: Over the years Donruss has become comfortable with us and we've become equally comfortable with them, so the relationship evolved beyond just doing the artwork. We're also consultants to them on their baseball card program and have been involved in the evolutions which have taken place over the last four or five years.

SCD: Do you get much feedback from the hobby?

Steele: Oh sure. I talk to hobby dealers all the time. We are the bridge from one division of a very large company to the hobby, so I have to be tuned to what is going on and then translate that into English. There is a great diversification of personalities in this hobby and you also get a diversification of attitudes and perceptions. Some are very far reaching in their perceptions and some are rather myopic in their perceptions and all that must be filtered in.

SCD: What are your feelings about the state of the hobby today?

Steele: I think the joyous thing is the ease of entry through wax packs. It's not an elitist hobby or collecting field. If you and I set out to collect antique toys, we had better have a lot of money. Because of the economic consideration you will not see many people at the entry level of that hobby each year. But you can get into baseball cards for 40 to 50 cents.

Relatively speaking, you might be an inordinately modest collector, but for that small sum of money you are a collector. It's a strength we have which no other hobby has. We also have constant media coverage. This hobby is blessed with unheard of free media exposure. There's no other hobby I'm aware of that gets this kind of media exposure. Stamps or coins don't get a fraction of the coverage. It's a marvelous gift that we have all been given.

The vitality of the hobby is through the ease of entry the constantly changing cast of characters we get in. The disturbing thing is that the hobby as such has become very commodity oriented. It doesn't have the nostalgic grab to it that it had when we came into it 12 years ago. When I was at the National, kids would come over and ask the price of a Mickey Mantle or Rickey Henderson card and I found that to be kind of sad because it's unimportant. The cards are meant to be toys, but there was a kid in fourth grade asking me the prices of cards and that was sad.

We tell them to collect the cards because they enjoy it or because they like the cards or the photography or information on the back. You use them to make you happy. The disturbing element is that the hobby has become a commodity and that means it loses a lot of its sweetness and a lot of its joy.

SCD: It this a permanent state of affairs?

Steele: Like all commodities, like the stock market or silver or gold, these things go through cycles. At times certain commodities get over-heated and there will be corrections. The Pete Rose card got hot, then it got cold. That's going to happen.

I remember a 14-year-old kid coming up to me at a show a few years ago asking if he should pay $450 for a Pete Rose rookie card. I asked if he had $450 and he said yes. I asked where he got that kind of money and he said from his father who was a surgeon. I told him I would not pay $450 for a rookie card. His response to me was, "Do you own it?" I said no and that I probably wouldn't. He said, "You're just frustrated because you missed it."

I told him I didn't know I missed it and asked where it was going. He told me to $750. I asked how he knew that. He told me that a dealer told him. It was the dealer who was trying to sell him the card and caused me to ask why the dealer was so kind to sell it now when it was going to $750. His response was that the dealer was just trying to help him out. I told him I wouldn't buy it and he told me that he was going to buy it. I thought it sad to be having this conversation.

SCD: What advice would you give someone who is new to the hobby?

Steele: Basically, one should collect for the joy of it. One should always collect quality and condition because history has proven that's your best insurance if you're ever in an economic condition where you have to sell your collection. Buying quality in life is like having friendships. The higher the quality of your friendships the better a person you're going to be. By the same token, the higher quality of person you are in what you bring to those relationships, the better those relationships are going to be.

SCD: Do you think people in the hobby are overlooking the aesthetic aspects or value of the cards?

Steele: Yes, and in many cases through no fault of their own. People aren't born with this knowledge, it's an acquired knowledge. There's such an incredible emphasis on the economics of baseball cards as we see in the publications, so that exposure is lacking. It can be kind of a Catch-22 sort of thing.

The dealers don't put it out because they feel there is no interest in it and the collectors express no interest because they don't know it's there. I'm not saying anybody is wrong, but in response to your question I think it would be marvelous if there was a great appreciation of the issues which have brought us where we are today. The original Turkey Reds are one example. I think they are absolutely beautiful cards, yet at the National I'd bet you wouldn't find six tables with Turkey Reds. You must remember that the very idea of our set was to bring a 1911 art form into modern idiom.

SCD: Overall, have you enjoyed your time in this area?

Steele: Oh yes, it's the best work I've ever done. It's very satisfying to us at Perez-Steele. We communicate through the artistic word. It's very satisfying to us that we've created literature in a broad sense which will outlast us and will forever be collected, revered and respected. That's a very delicious feeling and that's what fuels us.

* * *

Robb Wochnick
Meet A Full-time Jersey Broker

By Don Loving — Sept. 12, 1986

It's 8:45 on a Thursday evening at Robb Wochnick's house.

The telephone rings, and a man inquires about the availability of a Bobby Grich uniform. But the Grich jersey is apparently out of his price range, so he proposes a trade for a 1979 Ferguson Jenkins Texas Rangers shirt.

"[Mike] Flanagan for Jenkins?" Wochnick (pronounced WALK-nick) asks increduously. "No, I can't do that." A pause as he listens. "No, no, that won't do either. I'm sorry."

He returns to his family room, laughing.

"That guy wanted to trade a 1979 Mike Flanagan for my '79 Jenkins, straight up. Can you believe that? Flanagan had some good years, but really, he's a .500 pitcher. Jenkins won 20 six years in a row. He's a future Hall of Famer.

"Then," Wochnick continues, still chuckling, "he said he'd throw in a Len Barker shirt from Cleveland. What would I want with that? Sure, he had the no-hitter once, but the Braves waived him out of the league."

This is a typical night in Wochnick's life. Operating from his suburban home in Portland, Ore., Wochnick has been a full-time jersey "broker" for nine months now. He deals with people nationwide every day, as one of what he figures to be 10 or 12 "major" brokers of professional sports uniforms in the United States.

"I don't consider somebody with a card shop and three or four jerseys a major dealer," Wochnick said.

Wochnick, 39, has called himself "a serious collector" since 1970. A Portland native, he collected "everything" as a kid, and never threw anything away.

"I just hoarded it," he recalled. "I was definitely a pack rat."

Like most baseball collectors, Wochnick started out in cards. He still has a large personal card collection, and he stockpiles sets of the newer cards for future profit. But he readily admits a disenchantment with cards.

"I use to deal in cards a lot, but I don't mess with them too much anymore. Everybody's got cards. Collecting jerseys is much more a challenge.

"There are just so many cards now that I've become real turned off," he continued. "There's too much 'junk' out there. I still purchase lots of new cards every year. Someday they'll put my kids through college. But that's why I went to uniforms over cards — they're a lot more unique."

Wochnick has dealt in uniforms on the side for a number of years, but in late 1985 he retired after 20 years as president of a small Portland trucking firm to devote full attention to his uniform brokerage, which is simply named "Sports Warehouse." In December 1985, he bought out the entire stock of noted California uniform collector Dick Dobbins. Dobbins' material accounts for a large share of Wochnick's for-sale stock, which numbers over 950 jerseys and uniforms.

"I bought my first jersey from Dick Dobbins many years ago," said Wochnick. "A 1963 Boog Powell. That's part of my personal collection."

Wochnick's personal collection also includes autographed jerseys of many former and current baseball stars, plus familiar-looking autographed basketball jerseys of Celtics' #33 (Larry Bird), Philadelphia's #6 (Julius Erving) and a warm-up cape and trunks of Muhammad Ali, both autographed.

But his personal favorite is a 1956 Milwaukee Braves jersey that belonged to Wes Covington. The Covington flannel shirt includes the Braves' old tomahawk logo across the front and a five-color Indian headdress patch on the sleeve. The jersey is in excellent shape, showing little wear.

"I figured it's worth $1,200, but I'd never sell it," said Wochnick. "Most of my personal collection includes either Orioles items or baseball flannels, plus anything that's been a gift. I figure if someone gives me something, I can't, in good conscience, turn around and sell it."

And just where does Wochnick get all of his material?

"Well, that's a hard one," he said. "I really can't tell you in any simple way. You have to develop your contacts and then pursue them. Keeping in touch with your contacts is very important. Equipment managers, bat boys, umpires, administrative personnel, general managers, clubhouse attendants — I have a whole network of sources that I keep up with. Many of them I've cultivated as they pass through Portland at the Triple A level. I call them every now and then asking, 'What do you have for me?' And I send them all Christmas cards.

"I don't do a lot of traveling. I've attended the winter baseball meetings before — that's good for making contacts. I've never been to spring training, but I intend to try that next year. Spring training is an excellent time and way to pick up material.

"But that's the key. Develop contacts and keep up with them. I got a Dan Quisenberry jersey from Kansas City's chief scout, for instance. That was a nice one."

Jersey collectors use the same terminology as card collectors, though Wochnick has some problems with that.

"I'm real suspect of the term 'mint' for jerseys," he said. "I mean, if a jersey's been worn and washed once, how can it be mint?"

There are two basic "types" of baseball uniforms — flannels and knits. Flannels have become increasingly popular with collectors in the past two years, and their rising prices reflect that trend.

Wochnick recently acquired an Enos Slaughter New York Yankees jersey from the 1940s which was worn in the World Series.

"It's a nice, old flannel," said Wochnick. "He's a Hall of Famer, you know. I've already had an offer of about $2,000 in trade for it. I think I'll probably go ahead and do it.

"There's a lot of demand for flannels from defunct teams, too. Basically, there's demand for anything that nobody else has."

Demand for the newer jerseys — the knits — goes pretty much like you'd expect, according to Wochnick.

"Everybody wants Dwight Gooden," he said. "Darryl Strawberry, too. Those are tough. Mattingly, Ripken, Hershiser, Murphy — everybody wants those, too.

"The teams that consistently win always sell. The Dodgers, Yankees and Orioles — those three are always in demand. The Braves and the Cubs sell well because of their national exposure on cable. Especially the Cubs' road jerseys, because they have the name on the back."

The name sewn on a jersey's back is an important factor in jersey pricing. NOB (name-on-back) shirts are always relatively more valuable than NNOB (no-name-on-back) shirts, provided you're talking about the fairly recent era where shirts have the names included.

And there are jerseys that won't sell quickly.

"Cleveland and Texas may be the worst," said Wochnick. "They never win, and they never sell."

There's a big demand for Toronto Blue Jays uniforms simply because they're not available.

"There are none on the market," said Wochnick. "Their ownership doesn't believe they should be out in the public, and they destroy their old jerseys. I don't know anybody with a Blue Jays jersey in stock right now."

The availability of counterfeit jerseys is a minor problem for Wochnick.

"There have been instances of bogus Goodens and Strawberrys showing up," he said. "You have to be careful. I basically deal with people I know. If you're buying something very expensive, I'd check with independent sources first to make sure it's the real thing. I think that's important."

If you work as hard as Wochnick does at his job, sometimes you get lucky. A few years ago, Wochnick purchased a #9 Orioles jersey at a swap meet. He kept it over a year, and noticed one night there was something under the jersey's nameplate.

"I don't even remember what name was on it now," Wochnick said. "The Orioles had been using it as a AA jersey before I bought it. But as I held it up to the light one night, I realized there was another name sewn on the jersey. So I ripped the plate off and almost dropped over."

What caught Wochnick's eye was the name "Jackson." For $50, he had purchased one of the few Reggie Jackson Orioles jerseys in existence. Jackson spent a portion of the 1976 season with the Birds, and any Reggie items associated with Baltimore are in high demand. Wochnick sold the Jackson jersey for $850 at a Portland card show last year.

"The guy got a bargain," said Wochnick. "I probably could have got more for it. But he bought a Garvey and a Joe Morgan at the same time, so I gave him a break.

"I'm not a big Reggie fan personally and I have one of his orange Orioles jerseys in my personal collection, so it wasn't too hard to part with. But it goes to show you that you never know."

Wochnick said that dealing in baseball uniforms accounts for 90 percent of his business. Only the superstars in basketball or football move, and there is virtually no market for hockey jerseys. He did recently purchase an autographed Magic Johnson Lakers jersey for $175, which he promptly sold for $1,000. And he says the San Francisco 49ers — Joe Montana, in particular — are fairly hot these days. But still, baseball jerseys are the backbone of Wochnick's enterprise.

Uniform patches are also a highly sought-after collectible, both on and off the jersey. Dodger patches, which are rare, are wanted by everybody, as are the 100th anniversary Major League Baseball patches worn by teams in 1969.

As you might expect, Wochnick has developed a distaste for some "unfavorites" over the years.

"Boston is not popular at all," he said. "Of all the knits, they sell the worst. Nobody wants them. They're too simple, and there's no name on the back.

"The Mariners' firelt-year uniforms were brutal...real ugly. The Yankees' road jerseys were — and still are — basically ugly. I don't like the Milwaukee Brewers uniforms either; they're ugly too."

Wochnick's business keeps growing. He's a regular SCD advertiser and virtually all of his business is mail order. He also does some business through the classified sections of collector periodicals. He says there are no real secrets to his success.

"Develop your contacts and stay with them," he repeated. "That's number one.

"You've also got to have cash available up front. That's important. I have the contacts, and I have the capital.

"But there's really no wrong or right way," he continued. "Any way you can make money is the best way to do it, from the business side. I just try to provide a service. I stress the term 'broker' over dealer. 'Dealer' has some connotations I don't like. I'm a broker. I have a large want list file. I'm always looking for certain things for people. Again, I'm providing a service."

But is he working?

"No, I don't work," Wochnick quickly remarked, laughing. "I figure if this ever goes haywire somehow, I can always go out and get a job again.

"This is a labor of love. It's not work."

* * *

Meet A Card Maker
For A New Sports Magazine
Or A New Baseball Card Set,
Les Woodcock Makes It Happen

By Tom Owens, — May 20, 1988

It was April of 1954.

The New York Yankees were World Champions, the New York Giants were preparing to win a record 111 games, and Les Woodcock had won a triple crown.

"Three major events happened then," says Woodcock, now the public relations director for Score and Sportflics baseball cards. "My first child was born, I knew that I would graduate from college, and Managing Editor Sid James told me that I'd be listed as a reporter in the masthead of the first issue of Sports Illustrated."

Woodcock is the biographer who writes the backs of Score and Sportflics cards. But in 1953, he was working in the Time Inc. "morgue" (the publication's archives) while attending college classes in the evenings. He got wind of a new sports publication beginning within the company and jumped at the opportunity. Eight months later, a new sports tradition was born.

Les Woodcock

"Our staff was very small the first year," Woodcock says of the beginning of Sports Illustrated. "I covered both baseball and horseracing." His first bylined article covered the "new" Phillies Whiz Kids of 1957.

Woodcock believes the first of many player features he wrote for SI profiled Milwaukee Braves catcher Del Crandall. In a premium booklet published by Phillies Cigars entitled Big League Secrets from Sports Illustrated, "Del Crandall on the Art of Catching" appears with a "told to Les Woodcock" byline. The introduction of the Crandall piece, a typical tribute to Woodcock's devotion to detail, reads:

"Few players run on Crandall — his arm is outstanding (he led league catchers in assists in three out of the last five years). Big, strong and highly intelligent, Crandall at 29 is acclaimed one of the finest catchers in baseball."

One hobby-related memory Woodcock has of his early SI days is of receiving free sets of baseball cards from Topps executive Sy Berger. "He'd bring one by for everyone in the office," Woodcock says. "I never kept them. I gave them to my kids."

Woodcock vaguely remembers the Topps baseball card inserts in the first two issues of SI. He gasps when told that the first issue now sells for more than $100 in mint condition. Some collectors are still puzzled about the inclusion of baseball cards in the early magazines. "We hadn't found our focus in the first few years," Woodcock says of the card inserts. "We lost a lot of money in the beginning."

Woodcock concluded his SI career in 1968 under the title of senior editor. From there, Woodcock was involved with many new publications as both editor and publisher, including Jock, New York, Sporting Guide, Turf and Sports Digest, Classic and Long Island Life.

Robert Creamer, SI editor and Babe Ruth biographer, was a long-time co-worker of Woodcock's. "Les Woodcock is a dynamic editor who is a first-rate idea man, planner, organizer and administrator," Creamer says. "He has a rich background in all aspects of magazine publishing."

Considering his background, Woodcock's new position writing Score and Sportflics cards is only natural. "The demand for me was in sports," he says. "That was my love." He compares his current job to his former post as an SI editor. "This is just like putting out a magazine," he says. "It involves photos, writing and proofreading." The only difference is that Woodcock now has to confine his descriptions of each player to a 2 1/2-by-3 1/2-inch cardboard slab.

"The longer a player's career has spanned, the less space I have," says Woodcock, noting that the statistics will seize most of the available space. "I may have only two lines to write up Pete Rose, but will have 20 lines available for, say, Chris Sabo. It's a reverse challenge, but it's kind of fun that way." He says it's difficult to find correct past statistics for many players, because various references books won't agree.

Woodcock's player descriptions on the back of the cards sparkle, giving new insight to the person behind the player.

For instance, the Score card of Franklin Stubbs (#147) begins: "Franklin, a tremendously strong power hitter with surprising speed, became the Dodgers' first-string first baseman in 1987 when Greg Brock was traded to the Brewers."

Other times his comments are wry but always on-target. For Charlie Kerfeld, the erratic Houston Astros relief pitcher, Woodcock writes on Score card #479: "Charlie, the Astros' blithe spirit, managed to keep his wonderful sense of humor in a less-than-wonderful 1987 season ...Yet he did get his weight down below 250 and is hoping to return to his sensational rookie form of 1986."

"I try to personalize the cards," Woodcock says. "I point out things when I think they are relevant. I find certain things interesting."

Woodcock's card-back commentaries involve time-consuming research. For at least an hour a day, he'll update his index card file of each player, on which he notes interesting happenings in each player's career. He'll peruse numerous other sports publications to monitor relevant comments made by and about the player.

Writing his newest set, "Young Superstars II," (which is available as rack-pack inserts or in complete set form by sending in wrappers and money to the company) was a new challenge for Woodcock. Each of the rookie cards contain comments from various general managers about the player's abilities and accomplishments. "All of the GMs got a set of the first series," Woodcock says. "They're all cooperative. They're aware we're out there."

It seems fans are beginning to know that Woodcock is out there, too. He laughs when he tells that, during a recent visit to Cooperstown, fans actually wanted him to autograph the backs of Score cards.

Personally, Woodcock says that he's enjoyed working on the Sportflics "Decades Greats" set the most. "It was the most fun, even though not as many people saw it," Woodcock says. "We went through a lot of trouble to produce the set, paying royalties to the player's pension fund. I enjoyed helping choose the greatest players from each decade." In this year's Score set, Woodcock liked the five-card tribute to Reggie Jackson. None of the cards used statistics, so Woodcock had suitable space to honor the retiring star.

Looking at the future, Woodcock says that he'd be delighted to finish his career working for Sportflics and Score. Concerning his past, the Woodcock name at Sports Illustrated will be preserved by daughter Susan, who now works as a member of the SI photography department.

Naturally, Woodcock feels the future of Score and Sportflics cards are bright. He says that he'd enjoy getting to some card shows in the future to meet collectors of the sets and "talk baseball" with them. As one of the game's most knowledgeable observers, Woodcock has high hopes for the future of the sport. He sees inter-league play, expansion and divisional realignments as future happenings.

"Baseball just keeps getting better and better," he says. "But it's still a kid's game. Maybe that's why everyone loves it so much."

* * *

Candid Comments From Kit Young A Major Dealer Speaks Out

By Paul Richman — May 28, 1982

...Kit Young is 35 years old and resides in San Diego where he runs one of the leading card dealerships in the nation, from his home. He came from a family of bankers, doctors, and "Ivy League degrees." Indeed, he, himself, was a vice president of a bank in Washington state, until about four years ago when he took the plunge into the hobby.

"I started collecting cards as a kid in Peoria, Ill., in 1953," he said. "Selling my original 1953 Mickey Mantle from that '53 set was one of my toughest deals once I became a full-time card dealer. I also had trouble parting with a stack of doubleheaders I had collected but it became obvious that I couldn't afford to have an elaborate collection, and have a nice business inventory as well," he explained to me...

...SCD: The life of a dealer — a boyhood fantasy for many collectors. Traveling to card shows, running big display advertisements, and owning a store. But is the life of a dealer really that glamorous?

Young: Making a living selling cards does sound like something out of Fantasy Island. My travel schedule this year sounds like that of the Indiana Pacers — or Toledo Mud Hens. Cards took me to New York, Philadelphia, Chicago, Atlanta, K.C., St. Louis, San Francisco, Detroit, Phoenix, Seattle, Los Angeles, and Denver; not to mention

such garden spots as Des Moines, Indianapolis, New Haven, Bakersfield, Scranton, and points in between. I imagine that sounds glamorous — more than analyzing financial statements, digging ditches, or pulling teeth.

The big display ads you mention are fine — even better when people order cards. It's also nice being known. I admit that I still enjoy it when I'm at a show in Cincinnati or Portland and people know me. But being known as "that nice West Coast dealer," or "that so and so from San Diego" does me little good unless people buy my cards.

I'm not knocking this noble profession, but it is a business. And just like the auto parts store or the shoe-shine stand, I have to make money to pay my bills.

SCD: The traveling schedule of a full-time dealer could indeed be compared to that of an NBA team. But do you enjoy this aspect none the less?

Young: I've heard athletes say that travel is a drag. It's hardly glamorous sleeping in a Sheraton one night, a Hilton the next; O'Hare airport one day, Logan the next; a steak sandwich today in Philly, a porterhouse on the run in K.C. tomorrow.

They are partly right — it's not all its cooked up to be. The names aren't the same, since Motel 6 and The Colonel are more standard fare for the typical baseball card dealer, but the effect is the same. Once you've wrestled for your luggage once or twice in the Detroit airport, or repeatedly tried to get towels in a hotel room in Seattle, you begin to understand the true glamour of traveling.

SCD: There have to be some good things about the road?

Young: Traveling on the baseball card circuit is not without its redeeming features. Travel is also sitting in our favorite watering hole in Philly swapping tales with Denny Eckes, or listening to Barry Halper talk about the Yankees. It is also munching pizza in Detroit with Tony Galovich and Randy Archer, or playing poker all night in K.C. — and losing — with Tom Notestine and Jerry Clark. Somehow this all makes up for the occasional surly waitress or dirty motel room one encounters in his wanderings...

...SCD: Kit Young is definitely reknowned in the hobby for unique buying trips. What really goes on in these setups?

Young: I think you're asking the wrong man that question. The real pioneers were guys like Pat Quinn, Gar Miller, Jay Barry, Eric Lange, and others. I would have loved to travel in the old days when no one cared about baseball cards, when TV shows didn't feature cards, when there weren't five or six price guides for sale in every bookstore, when there must have been Goudeys or Connie Macks in every other attic.

SCD: Do you still find a lot of people with walk-in material, who are willing to sell at low prices?

Young: No, the walk-in material is pretty limited, and half the time the seller is carrying a price guide with him. Guides have their place, but in the hands of non-collectors, a little knowledge is dangerous.

We've had people call in with a 1970 Bench in nice shape asking $48 because some "pocket guide" suggests that price. The same for a '61 All-Star Mantle — asking $90-$95 for it.

It's hard to convince a teen-ager in Fort Wayne, Ind., whom you've never seen before, that his '72 Carew is not a $45 or $50 card, and that besides, if I wanted to pay retail, I'd go up to the card show in Detroit and buy to my heart's content.

I guess it's the thrill of the chase in the elusive Wagner or Lajoie that keeps me cruising the countryside. Someday I'll find one...

...SCD: Two other complaints that I constantly hear lodged against dealers are: 1) They never trade, especially at shows, and 2) They usually never bother to answer inquiries, and if they do, almost always belatedly. What's your defense?

Young: You're taking some good shots at dealers. Anyway, you're right. I don't trade at shows. First, it takes time and prevents me from selling cards, which is why I go to a show. Don't forget that shows aren't cheap unless they're in your backyard. ($100 for tables, $300 airplane tickets, $150 for meals, motels and so on...) Secondly, I have virtually all cards from 1953 to present, and most stars 5, 10, or 20 deep. Why would trade? Why trade a '64 Mays for a '65 Mantle if I have 10 of each? Do you think your drug store is going to take some sun-tan lotion in trade for deodorant? That store and the card dealer both need to constantly produce cash to pay bills and expenses. It does no good to trade apples for oranges — or Clemente for Koufax.

It's a different story when someone wants to trade a card that a dealer can sell very rapidly — '65 Carlton or '72 Rose — for a less popular, but equal value card — '59 Clemente or '57 Banks. Some dealers will also trade $1 for every $2 worth of cards. This is lopsided, but remember he has to sell the cards, and secondly, you trade some duplicates for the cards you wanted. Overall, trading with your friends is the most productive, and the most fun.

About your second volley about inquiries; if your dealer won't answer your questions, you're dealing with the wrong fellow. However, don't feel your inquiries are the main priority of the dealer. If you approach him at a show, do so when no one is at his table. Don't block off his display items from collectors, and step aside when someone else approaches.

More than once I've had people approach my table at 10:30 on the first morning of a big show, wanting to swap stories or ask questions about his cards. It's hard to be polite while collectors around him are bumping each other trying to see my cards. Usually I just ignore him, or ask him to get together later.

Mail inquiries are different. We answer all inquiries, as long as they include a self-addressed stamped envelope. This SASE may seem insignificant to some, but we receive 100 to 150 letters a week — and some high-volume dealers receive much more. It's plain discourteous to not include an SASE. After all, the dealer is taking his time to answer your questions and help you with your needs.

How often do I get a postcard saying, "Do you have Hostess panels #3, 8 and 42 from 1976?" That's all it says. You can guess where that postcard ends up.

Also, please don't forget that the mail order dealer has ads to prepare, orders to fill, and inventory to attend to. So, allow about 10 to 15 days for a response...

...SCD: All right, let's talk about memorabilia shows. They occur weekly at many different places across the country. Being a top dealer, how do you choose which shows you'll work when there are more than one supposedly "big" shows on a given weekend? In other words, what makes a good show or a bad show?

Young: Two words — cash sales. A dealer goes to sell cards; if he doesn't, it's a bad show. I usually try to hit the major shows in the country — L.A. Marriott, Philly, Plymouth, St. Louis, King of Prussia, K.C., Chicago and others.

SCD: It'still doesn't seem to make sense. How in the world can a guy travel from San Diego to Philly with the skyrocketing prices of traveling, and the luggage limitations, and still make enough money to be worthwhile?

Young: Well, Philly has been the biggest show in the country for some time. Usually, I try to do some East Coast buying on the same trip, which spreads the cost. But overall you're right — it's becoming uneconomical to travel to shows across the country. If you don't sell $1,500 to $2,000 or more, you may as well stay home.

What I see as the real obstacle in the future trips I make is not the expenses, but the rising number of shows. What that has done is offer collectors a sometimes bewildering array of shows to attend. Most collectors no longer wait for the "big" shows. An area like L.A. offers so many shows that a collector hardly knows which one to attend. It's

an unfortunate trend for collectors. The so-called "major'" dealers can't afford to attend so many shows. Most shows now have local dealers only.

I attended a recent show near L.A. and found a room only half-filled with tables. There were virtually no out-of-town dealers, and worse, there weren't many collectors. The reason, is obvious — there was a show scheduled there two weeks earlier; and a show scheduled a couple weeks later, with many more on the calendar. The quality of material at the show wasn't very good, and I imagine most collectors were disappointed.

I think you'll continue to see more disenchanted collectors who find most shows won't offer the great opportunities of the past. More is available in stores and through the mail.

* * *

Card Dealer Kit Young Speaks Out — Again! Whose Cards Are Hottest?

By Paul Richman — Nov. 25, 1983

...SCD: If I may backtrack a minute, you said earlier that Rose cards are no better than your 9th or 10th best-sellers. I think collectors would be amazed to know your top seller.

Young: Number one is Roberto Clemente. My top sellers in order are: Clemente, Mantle, Aaron, Mays, Carew, Maris, Stargell, Berra, Brooks Robinson, Rose, and Yaz.

SCD: Seriously?

Young: I imagine the typical dealer who sells at shows is going to think I'm reading the list backwards, or that I've been out in the sun too long.

Clemente is a big seller because he was a tremendous, colorful player. Who doesn't like Roberto Clemente?

There is a tremendous regional interest in Clemente, too. Invariably, orders from Pennsylvania — outside of Philadelphia — will request Clemente. The only other regional favorite to compare with him is Yaz, with his well-known following in New England.

Also, Clemente cards are still reasonably priced in relation to his greatness. You can still buy most of his cards for $5-$15. The same can be said for most cards of Mays, Aaron, Brooks Robby, Maris, and Berra.

SCD: What about some of your other top sellers?

Young: Well, Carew's popularity can be traced partially to his good season, but he's been a good seller in past years.

Sales of Rose and Yaz, as well as Schmidt, Carlton, and Yount, suffer because of the sky-high prices I've had to put on the cards to prevent the investor-speculator crowd from buying them.

SCD: There are three Yankee players in your top 10. Any comment?

Young: This is no coincidence. There may be legions of Yankee haters throughout America, and books on the same, but card buyers buy more Yankee cards than the next three teams combined.

Richardson and Kubek easily outsell Oliva and Morgan. Same for Elston Howard and Don Larsen, each of whom easily outsells the likes of Bunning, Burdette, Gilliam, Doby, Santo, Schoendienst, Sutton, Billy Williams, etc. Not surprisingly, the Dodgers are number two in popularity.

SCD: One thing I noticed about your top sellers is that all the players appeared on cards during the 1960s. Last interview you told us that the 1950s were still great sellers, despite what was being said about the '50s boom dying out. What is the story on '60s cards? Are they dying out in favor of current rookie cards?

Young: On the contrary, 1960s cards are terrific sellers — particularly 1961-1965. In fact, on balance, the early '60s might, by a narrow margin, be our best sellers.

Most of the action continues to be in the '50s and early '60s with the exception of a few rookie cards like Schmidt, Carew, Ryan, Murphy, Jackson, and a couple others. Demand for late '60s and early '70s cards is more for sets, with sets from 1973, 1974, and 1975 being surprisingly good sellers.

* * *

I Had My Commission And A Heck Of A Story To Tell!

By Paul Richman — Dec. 8, 1983

...SCD: Getting back to buying cards a second. Do you buy a lot of cards at shows?

Kit Young: Oh, a fair amount. I only get to three or four shows a year now.

SCD: What do you look for at other dealers' tables?

Young: Usually I look to fill holes in my inventory. At the National Show this year that included many cards of Maris, Berra, B. Robinson, Stargell and Snider. I used to buy every Mantle, Mays, Aaron, Clemente, Yaz and Rose I could get my hands on, but I stopped that because I've ended up with 20-50 of every Aaron card, and virtually none of Brock or Banks.

I guess you could say I do selective buying. I also look for large quantities of the '50s cards if they're available at decent prices.

SCD: All right, it was reported a while back that you handled the sale of a T206 Wagner card for $10,000. Would you be willing to talk about the sale? Most hobbyists are spellbound by details of a Wagner deal.

Young: Why not? I think "deal" is the proper word — it was an interesting transaction.

A couple of years ago I talked to a collector who I knew had a nice Wagner. He wasn't looking to sell the card, but I told him to let me know if he ever decided to sell because I thought I might be able to help. That was the last I thought about it until a year later when a collector-client of mine dropped me a line with his latest wantlist. Leading it was a fellow named Wagner. Did I mention this man was an advanced collector?

Well, I didn't happen to have Honus in my current inventory of star cards, but I thought about the Wagner card I'd seen the year before. So what the heck, I called the guy and asked if he had any interest in selling his Wagner. To my surprise, he said "Sure, if the price is right."

Now, determining the price of a T206 Wagner is comparable to buying a mansion on Sunset Boulevard — each is a rare jewel of sorts, and like many things, value is in the eye of the beholder.

And worse yet, in this case, buyer and seller live a couple thousand miles apart and had never met before. I wasn't about to introduce them, either, because that would eliminate the need for me.

My first step was to establish with each party what my fee would be if I would put together a deal — needless to say, I was planning to make a few bucks on the deal. Both men agreed to my proposed fee, so we started talking price.

To no one's surprise, the seller had somewhat different ideas about price than the buyer. The last known Wagner sale was the one Lew Lipset sold for $25,000 in auction. That was by far the highest price ever paid for a Wagner, but that card was said to be in terrific condition. Our card was pretty nice — slight corner wear, no creases. I described it to the buyer as near-Excellent.

Well, to shorten the story, after a series of calls to each collector, we found a price that was agreeable to both. Success! Well, almost — we still had the matter of payment, delivery, and ultimately satisfaction on the buyer's part.

Next came a cross-country wire of the funds to the bank. I think the tellers are still shaking their helds watching grown men exchange $10,000 for a small piece of cardboard.

The seller and I agreed that the sale wasn't final until the buyer was satisfied with the card. We transported it across the country by insured courier, although a Brinks armored truck wouldn't have been enough security for me.

Finally I got my call from the buyer — the card was every bit as nice as described — he was happy as a clam. The deal was over; buyer and seller were happy; and I had my commission and a heck of a story to tell.

SCD: The Wagner deal makes me think, Kit. Being a dealer you have had to sacrifice your personal collection to keep your inventory up. Is there any special card, say maybe the Wagner, that you would buy and keep instead of selling?

Young: Nope. Even though I love cards, I just have handled too many to get excited enough to keep some.

The same thing happened to my right-hand man Scott Cowan. You remember him, don't you? The man who is so blase he throws '52 Mantles in the garbage. When he first started working for me, he was an avid card collector. But working around cards all week long I guess takes some of the fascination away. As Scott says, it's tough to lay out $60 for a supposedly tough card like a '57 Koufax if you look in a notebook around here and find two or three sheets of them.

Very few cards turn me on enough to collect, because with some exceptions — Honus for one — they are so plentiful and easy to replace.

* * *

It's The People That Make This Hobby Great

By Ted Taylor, Off the Cuff, Dec. 21, 1990

The other night hobby veteran Larry Fritsch and I were discussing the hobby's good old days and the fun we've had during our decades of card collecting.

We recalled the joy of finding a new series of cards on the drug store counter or finding that missing player to complete this set or that. We agreed that the collecting aspect was rewarding.

But while we talked, it occurred to us that what we, a guy from Pennsylvania and a guy from Wisconsin with nothing else in common, were doing was talking about the hobby and sharing our experiences.

It became clear to us that the friends we've made and the people we met along the way have as much to do with the ongoing fascination of collecting cards as the cards themselves.

You can find out the value of a 1951 Bowman Mickey Mantle by checking the price guides. But how can you put a value on a friendship? In what book do you check for that?

I started thinking about the people I've gotten to know, and made a long list.

When I met Dick Sisler at a Willow Grove show I was in awe of the man who gave Philadelphia the National League pennant in 1950.

My mother (Helen) said to Sisler "you were handsome then and you are just as handsome now."

Mom was in her late 30s when Sisler hit his homer and now, in her 60s, she still knows a good looking guy when she sees one.

Sisler, conversely, wondered "if anybody will remember me?"

They did, of course.

I can remember most of the dealers who signed up for that first Philadelphia show at Spring Garden College in 1975. President Bob Thompson believed the show was a great idea to help promote the institution.

After three years, we outgrew the place and moved to Willow Grove.

Thompson retired and moved to Alabama.

I still have memories of Lee Elia asking my wife (Cindy) if the college offered any courses in the evening so he could have something to fall back on if his managerial career went south. That was in 1977.

There was a guy who came along at one show. He wanted to use the logo to sell T-shirts. We said OK but we wanted a cut.

The poor guy didn't sell much at all (it would be cruel to say he lost his shirt, but he did). Bob and I ended up buying his leftovers for peanuts.

(The shirt featured the '52 Topps Mantle, but Mickey looked more like Yul Brynner — no hair — and nobody was all that thrilled with the idea.)

The dealers and the collectors I've met have been a legion.

I once answered a person, who had asked if you enhanced the value of a baseball card by laminating it, by telling him that the only worse thing you could do was set it on fire.

My friend, Ernie Montella, who has made quite a nice little business laminating things, was not amused. But he understood where I was coming from.

I remember folks such as Ted and Linda Pina, now long gone from the hobby, who sold Roman Pro baseball caps and other souvenir-type memorabilia long before that aspect of the hobby became lucrative.

What follows, though, are brief cameo descriptions of 30 interesting people I've gotten to know and enjoy in the hobby.

If I skipped a dear friend, please accept my apologies.

Rob Lifson: He's now a major player in the advanced segment of hobby collectors.

As a youngster, Rob used to phone me every evening (usually in the middle of dinner) to find out if I had gotten anything new that day.

Years later Rob told me he was so excited about baseball cards that he thought I went out every day and got new things.

Joe Dugan: I became aware of Joe in the 1970s when I discovered he possessed multiple Philadelphia Athletics uniforms and I, an "expert" on the team, didn't have even one.

Joe, feeling sorry for me, loaned me one. He always seems to have a nose for finding older collectibles.

John Scott and Nick Schoff: I have fond memories of the old show they used to run in Wheaton, Md., which always came right after our Willow Grove show. It was a great place to unwind.

I can recall hesitating on a 1948 Leaf Babe Ruth because the dealer wanted $20 for it. (I paid it, though.)

I also remember Bob Schmierer buying a 1967 Topps set for $65 but passing on a second set at the same price because "who needed two of them?"

And at that time, who did? What I could never get straight about John and Nick was who was who. That used to break up Bob.

I think I have them straight now, though.

Allen Becker: He's one of the pioneers of the EPSCC show movement at old Spring Garden College. Allen loved sports and the hobby.

He was a brilliant math professor, but what he really wanted to be was the public address announcer for the Sixers.

God rest his soul.

Frank Steele: He's the business half of Perez/Steele Galleries. I first met him at an early Spring Garden show.

He told me the first things he ever bought were over-priced 1954 Topps cards of the O'Brien twins.

He has since discovered what's valuable and what isn't.

Alan Rosen: I first met "Mr. Mint" in Ocean City, N.J., back in 1981 as he was just getting involved in the hobby. At that time the only mints he was interested in had chocolate coatings and went for a nickel each at the checkout counter.

Alan is truly a revolutionary character in the hobby. Some people love him, some people hate him, but almost everyone will agree that he had made money for most of us with his aggressive marketing tactics and flamboyant syle.

Howard "Smitty" Smith: He's the San Antonio auctioneer who has probably bought and sold more off-the-wall hobby-related items than anyone living (or dead).

Howard is one of the most "up" people I've ever met. Every contact with him is a breath of fresh air.

Paul Hill: He's one of the least-known major collectors who ever lived. He's that way by choice.

Paul's collection may not rival Barry Halper's (but then neither does his bankroll), but Paul was out there collecting stuff (uniforms, bats, caps, trophies, etc.) when most of us didn't even realize things like that were worth collecting.

Bob Schmierer: Contrary to popular belief, Bob and I are not (and never were) joined at the hip. He is a longtime friend with whom I pioneered a lot of hobby things (the Philly Show, countless card sets, auctions).

We share a love for the New Jersey community of Ocean City and we're both longtime Philadelphia baseball fans.

His collecting tastes run toward autographs, mine toward cards. We've had a lot of fun together — and apart — in the hobby.

Dick Perez: I may have known Dick before he knew Frank Steele. Had I been clever enough, you might, today, be ordering Perez-Taylor Galleries art postcards.

The last joint venture I had with Dick Perez was a 3-D campus map of Ursinus College back in 1968.

Is Dick a great artist or what? Is grass green? I love his work.

Larry Fritsch: He's one of the few dealers who even existed when I started collecting cards seriously. Guys like him, Woody Gelman and Bruce Yeko really got me hooked on filling in my stash with older cards.

To this day, Larry remains a purist and leaves the day-to-day hobby adventures to his son Jeff.

Don Lepore: He's another one of the hobby's solid dealers who I feel like I helped raise. Don was just a teen-ager when he started doing the Spring Garden shows.

What I liked most about Don, though, was that he was always accompanied to the shows by attractive friends of the opposite sex.

Al Sweigart: He's one of the most dedicated collectors I've ever had the pleasure of knowing. I've never seen Al sell anything. To my knowledge this gentleman from Cressona, Pa., has never set up anywhere as a dealer.

Al likes quality things, especially turn-of-the-century stuff. It is always a joy to exchange collecting stories with him.

Irv Lerner: I envisioned Irv as the "enemy." When Bob Schmierer and I decided to go with "Philly I" back in 1975, I had the distinct impression Irv was not an ardent supporter.

Back in those days guys like Irv used to set up "buying" trips in local motels to pick off quantities of good gtuff. He was high profile in Philadelphia, while Bob and I were the new kids on the block.

However, after one late-night meeting at Irv's house (that interrupted a Mah Jog game) the air was cleared, and we've been friends ever since.

Unless I'm mistaken, Irv has never missed a Philly show since they began back in 1976.

Donald Peck: When I met Don he was president of the Fleer Corp. He had me subpoenaed to appear as an expert witness in his antitrust suit against Topps.

When I arrived in Judge Clarence Newcomer's courtroom it looked like an extension of the neighborhood candy store and Don looked like a guy who was going to win big! He did.

Kit Young: When you call Kit "one of the hobby's biggest dealers" you just aren't kidding. Kit is a big man, with big ideas and a big business in baseball cards.

I've known Kit for longer then we both care to remember, but the I thing I remember about him most is that he once threw away a 1952 Topps Mickey Mantle with a bunch of old pizza boxes. He climbed inside a dumpster to retrive the card which he did find, pizza-stained though it was.

He's now the driving force behind the latest effort to organize the hobby. I'm not so sure it'll work, but if it doesn't it won't be because Kit failed to do something.

Dave Miedema: He's not the hobby's biggest dealer, but certainly the hobby's tallest dealer.

Dave once called me the "Pete Rose of card collecting," which at the time was flattering.

Now I'd prefer to be known as the "Dale Murphy of card collecting;" I don't gamble and I pay my taxes.

Dave is oh so serious about the hobby and that's the fun about him. If there's anyone who knows more about collecting uniforms I haven't met him.

Bill Henderson: Bill and I share a love of the South Jersey shore and I dearly love to camp out in front of his bargain boxes at whatever show I happen to encounter him.

He calls himself "King of the Commons," but there's nothing common about Bill. He's a class act.

Bob Lemke: The first time I ever met Bob he was wearing a baseball shirt and acting like he knew what he was talking about. Later I found out that he did.

What I like about Bob (and what a lot of people don't like) is that he says what he thinks.

I was really impressed when I learned he owned a piece of the Wausau (minor league) Timbers. That told me he was a baseball guy for real.

Krause Publications recently recognized what Bob has meant to the company and made him a vice president. Was anyone surprised?

Paul Mullan: It was in Memphis, Tenn., where I first met Paul, who was then in the process of getting Donruss into the baseball card field in a big way.

He was a Donruss vice president at the time and wanted me to join his team as marketing manager — however, a house under construction, an ill mother and kids who didn't want to leave the school's they were in kept me from moving to Tennessee.

Paul is now making things happen for Fleer — as if that came as any surprise to anybody!

Jeff Rogovin: Jeff was knocking on my door when I first met him. He was a printer at a little shop in Collegeville, Pa. He had this set of Reading Phillies cards he wanted me to see.

He thought minor league cards could be done better and more successfully, and eventually restructured the entire concept.

Perhaps he did it too well and made it look so attractive; now there are more people making minor league cards than are consuming them. Or at least so it seems.

John Metzger and Julian McCracken: They're the other two-thirds of the Pro Cards ensemble (Rogovin's creation) known as "The Three Amigos."

I've seen John selling hotdogs at Reading Stadium (where Julian was a longtime employee, onetime general manager) and I know how much he loves minor league ball.

Julian, by the way, is a pretty good golfer. You don't ever want to bet against him on the links.

Mike Aronstein: He's the guy who invented minor league baseball cards as we know them. His innovative ideas helped shape the future of the hobby we now enjoy.

Mike's SSPC set in 1976 was the first substantial challenge Topps had to face. Although Topps out-bankrolled him, Mike showed the way for the minor league card explosion of the 1980s.

George Moll: He's the brains behind Gum Inc. and the early Bowman card sets. Moll's intellect was tapped to help Warren Bowman sell bubble gum, pure and simple.

Lucky for all of us, George collected tobacco cards as a youngster and thought that concept would sell gum, too. As you know, it did.

John Stommen: John was the publisher (and owner) of SCD before Krause Publications took over many moons ago. John is the one who got me on board at SCD for a year as a news editor.

John had promised me we'd talk about a partnership. He was coming to Atlantic City and would call me when he got there. I could drive down to meet him.

Hey John, I'm still waiting for the call.

George Lyons: George was Alan Rosen before somebody invented Alan.

A major influence in the early days of the hobby, George's "Lyons Roar" column in the hobby press struck fear in the hearts of many people.

Bob and I often did battle George over long-forgotten things, but we buried the with hatchet with him once and for all at an early Philly show when we gave him a birthday cake.

Friends later told me George was afraid we had either poisoned the cake or, at the very least, were going to hit him with it.

Tom Reid: He's a longtime hobby dealer and resident good humor man.

Tom is proud of his background as a sheet metal worker. He's often said that if the bottom ever fell out of the hobby he'd still be able to put food on his family's table.

Don't worry, Tom, the hobby is doing just fine.

Brian Schaefer: This is probably the first name that at least somebody hasn't recognized as an influential hobbyist of one sort or another, but don't sell Brian short; he's the future of this hobby.

Brian, 12, truly loves collecting baseball cards like I truly loved collecting baseball cards.

He can't buy everything because his paper route (and his parents) doesn't provide him with that amount of money. But he buys what counts and he's careful about every purchase.

I get a real kick out of talking baseball cards with Brian. His enthusiasm is contagious.

* * *

269

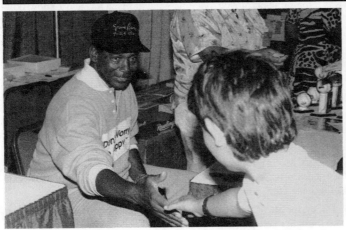

Ernie Banks makes an appearance at the National Convention.

A scene from Bill Goodwin's show in St. Louis.

"Memorabilia-seeking fans have always been ready to converge on big league real estate when it is known that a team is playing its last game ever at that park. Whether the cause is a newly-constructed stadium or franchise shift, the grand finale usually turns into a collector's party. Things such as home plate, the pitcher's rubber and even clumps of sod are hot items that are usually ripped from the stadium tundra the moment the game ends, or sometimes before," wrote Rich Marazzi in his June, 7, 1985, Batting the Breeze column.

Such was the case when the Washington Senators played their last home game at RFK Stadium Sept. 30, 1971, against the New York Yankees before more than 14,000 fans. Some of the overanxious fans would do most anything to take home a souvenir, including disrupting the game before the final out, resulting in a Yankee 9-0 win by forfeit.

When Senators slugger Frank Howard launched a home run in the bottom of the sixth inning, fans celebrated in wild jubilation. "Hondo" responded by "tossing his baseball cap into the crowd before he entered the dugout. The screaming fans refused to let the moment die. Howard subsequently came out of the dugout three times before he finally threw his batting helmet into the stands, his second collectible contribution of the night. By the time the inning was over, the Senators had tied the score and eventually took the lead, 7 to 5," wrote Marazzi.

"Washington chucker Joe Grzenda was called on in the ninth inning to finish the game. 'Shaky Joe,' as he was sometimes called because of his nervousness, remembered, 'I was told to warm up. I was afraid to get into the game realizing the fans would be coming onto the field to collect memorabilia. They told me after I got two out to hesitate and let the bullpen clear out.

"'Bobby Murcer made the second out. I still have the ball. The fans poured on the field in all directions. Some hairy-looking guy came at me. He touched me, but didn't do any harm. Frank Howard had three guys on his back. He knocked them off like little toys. There was a guard at home plate. Somebody picked him up like he was a pole and put him aside. Fans then dug out home plate with their bare hands,'" Marazzi wrote.

Fans attending the first night game ever at Wrigley Field on Aug. 8, 1988, had plenty of souvenirs to choose from too, as Donn Pearlman reported in his Sept. 2, 1988, story.

"Not only would Thomas Edison have been proud of the efforts to produce the first night game at Wrigley Field, so would P.T. Barnum. Buttons, shirts, pennants, souvenir books, posters, even a commemorative Postal Service cachet (decorative envelope) were hawked outside the ballpark on the historic night of 8/8/88," he wrote.

Among the commemoratives for sale were special feature sections from the Aug. 8 editions of the Chicago Tribune and Chicago Sun Times for 35 cents each; one-ounce silver medallions at 24.95; 60-page programs for $5; "Let There Be Light" pennants for $4, and T-shirts; blue-and-white cigarette lighters which said "I got lit at Wrigley Field," for $2; baseball caps saying "Opening Night" for $12; and posters which said "Chicago's Northern Lights, August 8, 1988," for $10.

Although the two previous examples involve obtaining souvenirs at the old ball game, sometimes attendance isn't always possible. But, as Chapter 9 traces the proliferation of card shows, perhaps you'll get the feeling that the next best thing to being at your favorite ball park is being at a card show.

Young Collectors Learn 'Show' Business

By Pete Dobrovitz

Sometimes, I think we all forget. You move up to the table because you've spotted that rare 1953 Bowman you've been scouring for, and they seem to be taking up space. Walk down an aisle and you're likely to be buffeted by a cluster, like Fagan's urchins running through the streets — about to be trampled under foot! But "they" are really what this hobby is all about and sometimes, we just plain forget that.

Bill James of Baseball Abstract fame has said baseball cards are "the greatest teaching tool" for young kids in America. He wondered aloud if schools might consider ways of peddling other subjects (Robespierre for RBI? Charles for Danny Darwin?) with cards.

Kids are learning about the game and its legends, but what other lessons are they picking up along the way? When they venture into a card show, what are the adults who run the hobby teaching them about business and fair trade, by action and example?

I decided it was time to find out. Standing by the entrance at a local show and sale, I found a few subjects — youngsters who let me tag along as they went shopping for cards. To watch what and how they bought, and to overhear just how they were being treated.

Desperately Seeking Mr. Boggs

It was a typical card show; a rented hall, 40 dealers, free admission. Mostly local dealers had set up shop for this Sunday sale. But for 12-year-old Jason Terena, it was Opening Day, the Candy Shop, and a bit of Christmas all rolled together. Jason had just walked into his first card show. "I had seen a flyer for it at the neighborhood store," he noted.

Stopping into that store "once every two weeks" was one thing; this was something else altogether. Two steps behind — Jason's dad, John. "I'm not up on the cards...I work B shift (4-midnight) so by the time he's out of school, I'm working. And there's been a lot of overtime. But I asked for this day off — so we could spend the time together."

Like every good hitter stepping up to the plate, Jason took his time to "dig in." The moves were methodical — first the outer perimeter. Flip through a book display. Explain the "Opening Day" set to Dad. At first, he was just another one of those faces, left alone to wander. Finally, by the fourth table, the object of the quest began to crystalize.

In two words — Wade Boggs. It made sense. After all, Jason was a third baseman himself. And while Wade delivered on his promise of more power from 1986 to 1987 (from 8 to 24 homers), Jason was cranking them out of the park, leading his town's Little League.

He spots a Boggs Fleer rookie. The dealer quotes "$14" and you could see the slight gulp. That was about 10 percent of the value of his total collection to date! Father and son discuss purchasing an 1988 Donruss wax pack box for $14 instead, but Jason decides "no" and moves on. Rounding the corner, he spots a binder with a page of Boggs cards.

A couple catch his eye, but the dealer is busy. Jason doesn't speak up to get some service, rather he just moves on and spots another Boggs across the aisle. 1985 Donruss. It's fairly priced at $5, and Jason doesn't haggle; he hasn't checked a price guide. All he knows is his first show purchase is being slipped into a sleeve and he's getting change from a $10 bill which was "Easter money." He has $5 left, but Dad has already offered to buy a higher-priced box. What next?

Heading into the home stretch of lap #1, Jason's eye flashes to a cork display board. He seems to like those — a chance to gaze without getting up too close. Here, it's not the vintage Marichal or Killebrew catching his eye — it's Wade Boggs on a Slurpee coin. But he passes.

It's been a half hour. Lots of browsing, but only one buy. Suddenly, the tempo changes. A Boggs poster. $4.50. "Who'd ya get?" asks the outgoing dealer. Jason's too shy to answer, but flips the rolled-up poster to the name. "Hey...great!"

The vendor's words are like a slap on the rump from his coach after one of those home runs. Jason was "in the groove." This time, there's no resin bag — it's some coins clutched in that fist. Coins about to be redistributed into the economy. Fifty cents for a Score wax pack.

"I don't get sets," Jason comments — even though Dad has offered to buy one. "I trade cards with friends — the doubles." No doubles when you buy the whole set. So it's "no" to that Opening Day, an 1988 Fleer and an 1988 Score. But "yes" to two Fleer wax packs — 80 cents each. Remember, Jason doesn't study price guides.

John spins quickly only to see his son bolt. He's torn off into the crowd, with all the confidence of a show vet on the prowl. He's back at the table with display books — the one with the page of Boggs cards. Panic! He can't find the Wade he wants and is still not ready to ask.

He's just about to step away when a young dealer says those magic words, "Can I help you find something?" Like a big brother, the dealer quickly zeroes in on the right book and pulls the right card. A 1988 Fleer — #345 — Wade Boggs. It's a dollar over budget, but by now Dad has already staked Jason to another $5.

Jason and John, check that, Jason has been wandering for about an hour. John has followed along patiently — asking questions, discussing choices. He's spent $12.60; bought exactly the things he wanted. More important, after two years of collecting, he's finally walked into a show and come out alive! You get the feeling Jason and his Dad may be doing this again some Sunday.

Tannous, Tannous & Olsen

No, it's not a law firm, but no sooner did Jason walk away, than Eric Tannous (he's almost 13), his brother Adam (10) and partner Erik Olsen (he is 13!) descend on the show with mother Elaine Tannous close behind. They're all "pro."

"I didn't really push them," says Mom, who grew up with a brother who taught her the "Importance of Being Mickey Mantle." "It just sort of happened. We get the price guide every month. It's a nice sort of social thing — all his friends are into it and I think it increases their social circle."

There's no slow waltz around the show floor here. These guys dart, cutting in and out of tables quickly. The two Eric(k)s call each other by their last names. Tannous dives headfirst into a book of older cards. He's looking for "Yankees," but when he spots a 1965 Dick Howser in an Indian uniform, he doesn't see an ex-Yankee skipper, but a guy who died of cancer.

Meanwhile, Olsen has eyed an Elston Howard, but went for a 1962 special card — Babe Ruth's Twilight Years. He's taken it out of the sleeve, and stands ready — apparently to buy — but the dealer is taking a box order from some Big Kid (adult). He puts it back. No sale.

Olsen vacates, but Tannous catches the dealer's eye and pays $4.50 for a 1961 Lou Gehrig special card. It's a steal. The card "books" for $6 and has been getting "heavy action" typical of all early 1960s material. Will these guys haggle? You bet. Olsen adds, "Yeah...sometimes a guy will knock 75 cents or more off a price. I just ask. 'How low will you go?'"

Where's statistician Bill James when you need him? Fleer team sets at a table are marked 10 percent off. The sticker says $5.50. So, what's the sale price? It takes a couple of stabs, but the trio finally decides it's under "five bucks."

Skip that — Tannous has just won the day's first door prize! A Donruss wax box. And Mom has just returned with a 1988 Score set! "It's a birthday present." "I think Score's a good looking set," Eric says, managing an editorial comment amid the excitement.

Twenty minutes in and time to bargain. But not with this dealer. "Look at that Maris — mint." He rattles off a litany of other mint stars in the heavy plastic cases. "My prices are outrageous, I admit it, but these are the best. Like they just came out of the pack. I can't 'deal' with you guys. I'm selling these to the guys who come in here with big money."

On that note, Olsen stuffed his wad of $24 back into his pocket. The dealer didn't even try to direct them to another display, where more reasonably priced recent stuff was waiting for business. Could Olsen have purchased a Kal Daniels? We'll never know, but we do know Tannous went next door and plunked down $9 for a Fleer Seitzer rookie. The same card was sitting in Mr. Outrageous's display! Did he miss the sale with his high-powered "I can't be bothered" pitch? You decide.

There would be more buys. Olsen scarfs up a 1960 World Series card; Mantle's 2 Home Runs. Another steal. Book price — $4.25. Olsen pays just $2. Eric's mom points out a 1960 Batting Leaders card. "Look. Mays AND Clemente. You're never gonna get your hands on Clemente." Tannous sidesteps that insight and buys an 1988 Donruss team set instead. ("It's got Boggs, Burks, Clemens, lotta great cards.")

Elaine Tannous figures she spends $150 every six months on cards for her son. "At Christmas, it was the 1985 Olympic set. All the relatives have been instructed to buy cards as gifts, too." Elaine won't allow trading. She says she's afraid dealers might try to pull quick deals and knew trading was out the day her son traded away a Mattingly card. "Besides," she adds, "I tell them not to get a nasty reputation taking advantage of younger kids just starting out either."

Tannous, Tannous & Olsen know the hobby's inside game. It's hard to ignore when the $15 Mantle you buy now books for $175! But Mom sums it up best; "It's just a real healthy hobby — there will be financial payoff someday, like people say there will be, that's secondary."

And what about junior partner Adam Tannous? "I kind of got disinterested and gave all my cards to my brother."

The Post-Show Game

What lessons do we Big Kids learn from all this? I think there are a couple.

First, kind words and a helping hand go a long, long way. For some kids, cards sell themselves. But for the countless new Jasons, just getting the hang of "show business," the right word means a happy kid and a sale.

Second, don't underestimate the spending power of the little guys.

In following three buyers for just under two hours, I witnessed nearly $50 in sales! Granted, one mint 1968 Seaver can command that price in the flash of a checkbook. But, it's the Erics and Jasons who'll be back time and again for all the new issues and all the latest cards.

And finally, don't think you can over-price every kid who comes along. Sure, some newcomers might fork over 80 cents for a wax pack, but you're just as likely to alienate a kid who knows his stuff. The same wax pack dealer who sold to Jason didn't even get the time of day from our other trio, even though his table was filled with books of 1960s and 1970s Yankee cards!

As I left, I kept remembering a couple of really great images. John being taught the card business by his son, Jason. Elaine artfully dropping a few well-placed suggestions into her sons' deliberations. Teaching. Learning. It was clear in both cases, cards were a vehicle for parents to talk to their kids about something that mattered to them!

That kind of communication could only help when it came time to discuss the other stuff — the things important to parents! — Pete Dobrovitz, May 13, 1988

* * *

$278, But It Felt Like $1 Million

Thank you Pete Dobrovitz! Finally, someone tells what baseball is supposed to be about. Kids.

I whole-heartedly enjoyed your story in the May 13th issue of SCD entitled "Remembering the Young Collector."

Being a dealer myself, I travel to shows quite often, as well as operating a business full time. Dealers and kids have one thing in common. Both are accused of taking advantage of each other.

Dealers are said to over-charge on their merchandise or are ripping off customers, mostly kids. Kids are often accused of shoplifting or stealing.

The truth is, most dealers and kids are wrongly accused. In fact, most are incredibly honest.

I've lost count on how many times I've helped "Johnny" find the perfect card and it may be 35 cents. Problem — Johnny only has 25 cents. My answer — "catch me later," and they usually do, like the young man this past weekend who handed me a nickel and said "I owe you this." It had been four months since I had sold him his perfect card — 1985 Topps Bret Saberhagen.

Honest, responsible kids will grow up to be honest, responsible adults. But what about the dealers? The majority of dealers I've met are doing it for the enjoyment of the hobby.

I used to think business owners were rich. I was wrong. Sometimes I wonder if it's worth it — between the bills, rent, stock, mail (my cards are where?) and millions of other headaches.

But then I see those big, wide "in amazement" eyes and smiles — it was worth it.

I, too, have had experience with the "don't bother me, kid" type of dealer and I pity them. For they have missed the true value of the hobby.

This past month we were set up beside a "mega" dealer. I'd never seen so much stock. All day I watched him make "mega" deals with well-dressed men and shun and shoo the kids.

The kids came to me and I helped most of them. If I couldn't fill their orders, I sent them to someone who could.

At the end of the day the "mega" dealer sat counting his sales for the day. "Not bad, but should have been better," he said.

He later told me his total for the day — $9,367.52.

"How'd you do?" he asked.

"Terrific," I responded, knowing that I had $278 in my pocket.

But the smiles and looks of those kids made me feel as though I'd made a million. Maybe two. — Kelly Harinck, Round Rock, Texas, Reader Reaction, June 3, 1988

* * *

Hey, Let's Have A Baseball Card Show!

By Steve Ellingboe

Have you ever thought about promoting your own baseball card show? You know, rent a hall some weekend, get a retired player to sign autographs, charge dealers $40 or $60 each for a table, and then collect a buck or two from every anxious hobbyist who shows up.

Sounds easy enough, and profitable, too. The only problem you might have is finding enough time to count all the money coming in. What an easy way to make some big bucks! Right?

Think again. There's a lot more to running a baseball card show than the average collector might realize.

I've been to a lot of shows the past few years, including most of the major ones and many of the smaller ones. And in nearly every case I just assumed the promoter — whether it be a club or an individual — was making a profit. What made me think again was the March issue of the Twin Times, the fine newsletter of the Twin Cities Sports Collectors Club in Minneapolis/St. Paul.

As part of his monthly financial report, club treasurer Jack Fei presented a detailed summary of the club's show at the Metrodome the weekend of Jan. 28-29, with Harmon Killebrew, Johnny Logan and Dave Nelson as guests. The figures are very interesting — and enlightening. Here's the report:

Estimated Expenses: Metrodome rental $1,800; Security $780; Table rental $550; Insurance $427; Admissions tax $205; Killebrew fee $1,250; Logan fee $680; D. Nelson fee $200; Advertising $900; Publicity $150; Salaries/misc. $225; Total Expenses $7,167

Estimated Income: Dealer table fees $3,650; Admissions 3,500; Total Income $7,150

It's not often that a show promoter opens up his books for public inspection in this manner, and, as you can see from the figures, the Twin Cities club — one of the largest and best organized in the country — just barely broke even. They lost 17 bucks, as a matter of fact.

In his follow-up report, Treasurer Fei told club members that "several lessons can be learned" from the experience. "First," Fei said, "the 'bargain' Metrodome rental wasn't. The rental fee was less than half the real cost of holding a show at the Metrodome. We must be careful about hidden costs when holding a show in a new location," he warned.

Fei also learned a lesson about bringing in celebrity autograph guests, too.

"My guess is that Harmon Killebrew drew more than $1,250 in additional admissions," he wrote, "while Johnny Logan did not draw $680 in additional admissions. We must be more certain of our ability to recoup expenses before inviting out-of-town celebrities," he cautioned.

And finally, Fei concluded, "Even though we broke even, we took a big risk; worse, we did know the size of the risk we were taking. We must do a better job of estimating projected expenses and revenues when promoting large shows."

It's good advice for those who may be planning a show — and just plain interesting for the rest of us. (Makes you wonder, if a guy like Johnny Logan gets $680 for a few hours work, what kind of money do you think Aaron and Mantle get for a weekend of signing? — Steve Ellingboe, The Coach's Box, April 27, 1984

* * *

Suggests A "Show" Without Dealers

Dear Ted:

I have dreamed up an idea which I would like some feedback from you.

My idea — a convention without dealers, just collectors like myself and most of your other readers. A convention without thousands of dollars changing hands and where everyone who wants to attend would not need the almighty dollar, except maybe admission to pay for use of the facilities.

I think this convention should be centered around people just bringing their duplicates, meeting each other and just doing some old-fashioned "hoss trading." I have attended many shows and the dealers who

will trade still want to make a 100 percent profit on the deal. I understand that that is their livelihood, but for the simple collector we lose out on deals like that.

So, what do you think?

Sincerely, Kent Ritchie, Baraboo, Wis.

Editor's Note: That's a tough one, Kent. It is almost impossible to answer without sounding flip, but here goes. Without dealers there would be no conventions. It is that simple.

Major shows, especially, recapture a huge percentage of their expenses — building rent, advertising, printing, personnel, security — from dealer table fees. Without them, admission to such a dealer-less convention would cost you $20-$25.

Dealers often catch it in the neck for their policies, etc., but let there be no doubt about it that without them shows cease to exist. As an aside, at a couple of the early Philly shows "trading rooms" were established with the ground rules that no cash could change hands. Likewise, a flea market room where hobbyists could set up their wares without table fees, etc.

Both were horrors in that no one bothered using them. In fact, you could have driven a Greyhound Bus through either room without hurting a soul. The crowd, by the way, could always be found back at the dealer tables. — Letter to the Editor (Ted Taylor), June 20, 1981

* * *

What Is Going On?

Please help! What is going on in this hobby? Why are shows so expensive to get into? Why are people being charged for autographs? This has to stop! I urge you to print this letter and generate some dialog on the subject.

The consumer isn't the only one getting shafted by this new surge of carpet-bagger shows. The dealers are also getting the shaft. If a kid pays three bucks to get into a show and then, say, another six bucks for a superstar autograph, that's nine bucks spent. How much more do you think the poor kid has to spend?

Here is what I purpose and, in fact, will try to do. Shows should never cost more than $1.50 to get into. There should never, never be a charge for an autograph. Shows should also have some creativity to them. Show a free highlights film or get some local high school coach to put on a clinic.

Let's get back to basics. Not all pro players are mercenary swine who have to make five grand to get out of bed and sign a few autographs. — Tony Akey, Metuchen, N.J., Reader Reaction, April 15, 1983

* * *

A Revolutionary Idea

By Jim Hawkins

There are, it has been said, no truly new ideas — only old ideas that have been reborn. However, I have one here, I must admit, that I have never heard before.

I wish I could tell you with a straight face that it originated with me. In fact, it is the brainchild — whether brand new or reborn — of Mr. Don Mathews, longtime collector, former confidant and roommate of Denny McLain, and now Florida greenskeeper extraordinare.

"The day is coming," Don declares, "when your superstars, guys like Joe DiMaggio, Mickey Mantle and Willie Mays, will pay promoters for the privilege of selling and signing autographs at their shows."

Don't laugh. At first I thought it was a rather ridiculous notion, too. But the more I think about it, the more sense it makes. And, as a promoter, I'm liking the idea better and better.

Think about it. Superstars such as the men named above virtually always sell out at shows. Invariably, in city after city, there is more demand for their autographs than the athletes are willing or able to fill. There is also a growing concern on the part of these superstars, and many others, that they are being "ripped off" by avaricious promoters and dealers who, these athletes believe, are making small fortunes off of their signatures.

So why shouldn't these superstar attractions go into business for themselves? Our hobby's appetite for autographs has grown to the point where that seems to me to be the prudent thing to do.

A ballplayer or ex-ballplayer, anxious to make some extra money and capitalize on the burgeoning autograph market, could contact the promoter or promoters of his choice, perhaps basing that selection on the promoter's reputation and past performance record in running shows.

The player would agree to pay the promoter a fee, dependent upon the player's presumed ability to attract a crowd to the show. The promoter could then use that money to offset the costs of renting a hall and advertising the show.

The player would then function in much the same manner as a dealer does under the present set-up.

The player would pay his own travel expenses to the show. It would be his responsibility to make certain he arrived there, and on time. If he didn't, it would merely be money out of his — the player's — pocket.

The player would set his own autograph fee, as high or as low as he pleased. It is, after all, the player who is attracting people to the show, and it is his image and reputation that are at stake.

The player would also decide how many autographs he wanted to sign. He, or an associate, would be the one selling the autograph tickets. All autograph money would go directly to the player. He could pack up and leave early — as dealers sometimes do — or he could stay late. It would be entirely up to him.

The more autographs the player signed, the harder he worked, the more money he would make. Since he alone was in control of the number of autographs sold, and since he had set the price, there is no way he could ever feel cheated.

And why, you might ask, would an athlete, who is already getting a guaranteed fee for appearing, without putting a penny up front, agree to such a revolutionary arrangement under which he, like every other independent businessman, would actually be at risk?

Profit, my friends. That All-American password: Profit.

As I mentioned earlier, at almost every show where a superstar is involved, many people go home empty-handed or disappointed. In most cases, it is because the superstar, ever-suspicious — sometimes with good reason — of promoters and dealers and collectors capitalizing on his signature, simply refused to sign anything more.

But I have a hunch if the player could be confident that all of that extra money, indeed all of the autograph money period, would be coming directly to him, he might be far more obliging.

I know for a fact that many athletes take note of the price being charged for their autograph at a particular show, then keep a rough mental count on the number of autograph tickets sold and items signed. When that price, multiplied by the number of tickets sold, reaches their agreed-upon fee, some players will begin to slow down, drag their pens, or even refuse to sign many more.

If they were in business for themselves, they would certainly have the incentive and inclination — as some conscientious players do even under today's set-up — to continue signing until there was no one left standing in line.

And what assurance might the player have that the promoter wouldn't simply pocket the money, forget to advertise, and therefore fail to produce a crowd?

The very same assurance each every dealer has when he pays his table fee for a show.

It might happen once in a while. But that promoter wouldn't be in business very long. News travels fast. And players would quickly learn which promoters they could count on, and who was likely to stiff them, just as dealers do now.

I don't know about you, but I think it sounds like a great idea. Let the revolution begin! — Jim Hawkins, Eye of the Hawk, May 19, 1989

* * *

Scenes From A Typical Mini-show "If Nothing Else, Come Over To My Table, And Just Chat"

By Lionel Carter

...Meanwhile, down at the other end of the table, a young collector had whipped out a checklist and was working his way through the excellent 1971 Topps I was selling for 10 cents each. He was busily pulling out the cards he needed and crossing the numbers off his list, and I gloried in his activity.

Here was a real card collector; a fellow who collected complete sets. Is there really any other way to collect cards? "Go to it, young man," I thought, "I'd rather see the cards go into your collection than to sell them to some dealer who would only resell them for two or three times what I was asking. What a nice kid! No need to watch him that closely; anyone with a checklist is a real collector."

I busied myself with other duties, and when I looked at that end of the table again, the kid was gone, the checklist was gone, and the cards he had selected were gone! Why that dirty little thief! You can't trust anyone these days!...

...A little boy inquired if I had any Mike Schmidt cards.

"Have I got the Mike Schmidt card for you," I said, "I got one for 25 cents that none of your friends will have!" And I pulled out an O-Pee-Chee card.

"Look," I said, "it's printed in French and English. It's a Canadian card called O-Pee-Chee!"

A big smile began at his lips and spread up through his eyes which sparkled with excitement.

"And it's only a quarter!" I added. Never had any quarter parted company with a little boy so quickly. "Gee, thanks," he said, his voice trailing off as he was already moving so fast. That's the fun of collecting...

...If you have never attended a mini-show, come out and see for yourself; you won't find many scarce items, but you can bring along your checklist of recent issues and fill in some missing numbers or, if nothing else, come over to my table and chat. — Lionel Carter, March 16, 1984

* * *

Feeding your face: Part of the fun of traveling around the country to various shows is sampling the local cuisine. Most of the dealers on the show circuit enjoy trying new and unusual restaurants.

Over the past five years, it seems like I've tried every restaurant in the United States, so I thought I would share with you some of my favorites. If you folks like to eat, these places are outrageous:

Durgan Park, Boston: The best lobster in the world, but the waitresses abuse you — all in fun, of course.

Original Bookbinders, Philadelphia: A fine eatery with a nicely varied menu; very classy.

Carson's, Chicago: Really good ribs and, oh, that anchovy salad dressing!

Bomber Squadron, St. Louis: On the runway at the airport; great food, great service, great view.

Precinct, Cincinnati: The best steak I have ever eaten; and when Brian can't finish it, you know the portions are huge!

Montgomery Inn, Cincinnati: The best ribs in the world, bar none.

Leon's, Milwaukee: The best custard in the world, bar none.

Scoma's, San Francisco: Everyone's been talking about; we're going to try it this summer. — Alan Rosen, Mint Matters, June 26, 1987

* * *

Leaving Shows Early

I experienced something this past weekend that has happened to me before, and I'm tired of it! I attended a pretty well-established card show this past Sunday — one that is usually well attended and advertised in SCD. I wasn't able to arrive until 2 p.m., which normally still gives me plenty of time at the show. To my surprise, dealers were packing up and leaving! As I heard one explain, "There weren't enough customers."

I tried to ignore it, but by 2:30 I couldn't even move through the aisle any more — not because of crowds, but because of so many dealers packing up their boxes and loading them onto carts.

At that point I decided leave. If dealers didn't want my money, then I would keep it. Believe me, I had money and was prepared to spend it. I paid the same admission fee as those arriving at 10 a.m., but somehow I felt cheated. I'm just glad I hadn't traveled far to get there.

This was not the first time this has happened to me. I've attended shows in California, Colorado and Illinois and have seen it every time.

I have had tables myself at many shows and I know the frustration of just sitting when the show begins to wind down. But because I enjoy the hobby so much, and really enjoy being one of those "dealers" whenever I can, I feel it is important to live up to my commitment and stay until the show's advertised closing time.

From a financial angle, if I spent $35 for a table and the crowd was very low, every dollar I make adds to the small profit. And you never know who was delayed for some reason and couldn't make it to the show early. Maybe it's someone who loves the hobby enough to even come late — and has money to spend.

Such was the case with me this past weekend. I guess the dealers didn't want to help empty my wallet. Wake up, dealers, you're losing a profit! And, hey, promoters, how about free admission after a certain time? That might encourage those who can't arrive until late to come anyway, and encourage the dealers to stay longer because the crowds would be picking up at the end of the day. — Mike Buckley, Arlington Heights, Ill., Reader Reaction, July 24, 1987

* * *

To Close Or Not To Close

By Jim Hawkins

To close or not to close, that is the question.

It happens every weekend, at show after show, all across the country. Saturday morning, or sometimes Friday evening, the dealers arrive, brimming with optimism. By Sunday afternoon — if not earlier — that optimism, that enthusiasm, has waned. Sales have been slow, or there's a plane to catch, or that seven-hour drive home is looking longer by the minute.

Inevitably, at every show I have ever attended, there have been some dealers who have packed up early and said adios. I would be less than honest if I did not confess I have done so myself, on more than one occasion.

Years ago, when shows were little more than small swap sessions, when admission fees were minute, if indeed any fee was charged at all, early exits did not pose much of a problem. If a dealer wanted to leave early, he left. See you next time.

But, as I have said so many times, our hobby is now big business. Promoters have to pay top dollar for extensive advertising and adequate, often elaborate, halls. The dealers, who must bear much of the brunt of this increased cost, understandably demand nothing less. They also expect huge crowds.

Collectors also have seen their admission fees rise, to help defray the additional costs. They, too, when they pay their admission, have a right to expect to see a full show — not a half-empty room as indifferent dealers wheel their wares out the door.

There are three distinct sides to the controversial matter of dealers closing early. And each side can cite valid arguments to support its case. Unfortunately, I don't have a clear-cut answer.

Frankly, I tend to agree with my colleagues who decree that dealers closing early forsake their table privileges at future shows. If a show is advertised as open until 5 p.m., it is the promoter who comes under seige from irate customers who arrive to find half the booths closed. Dealers who sign up for a show should make a commitment to stay for the duration.

As a dealer, I can empathize with the weary merchant who, seeing little hope of many future sales, or faced with the necessity of being at work by the next morning at 9 a.m., elects to exit early. All too often, it is the only move that seems to make sense.

I certainly can also sympathize with the customer who comes to a show with high hopes of finding a few choice items to add to his collection, and pays his admission only to find dealers left and right abandoning ship.

If the customer gets disgusted and refuses to return, the promoter and the dealers all suffer. If enough people feel that way, of course, there is no more show.

By way of comparison, I annually set up a booth at the Michigan State Fair, an 11-day ordeal that ends at 10 p.m. on Labor Day. Dealers at the fair don't dare begin tearing down their displays until that 10 p.m. closing. Even if they do, they aren't allowed to leave the grounds. So we sit around the final three or four hours, which are invariably dead.

This year, my son and I watched the Michigan State/Southern Cal football game on TV in our booth. The only interruptions came from other bored dealers, seeking to know the score. But everyone stayed.

As I said, I don't know the answer. Kicking dealers who close early out of future shows can be self-defeating unless a show is extremely well-established with a long waiting list. But allowing dealers to depart at will, thereby turning off customers, can be equally damaging to a show.

What do you think? I would like to hear from you promoters, collectors and dealers alike. Hopefully, there is a solution that can satisfy all three sides. — Jim Hawkins, Eye of the Hawk, Nov. 27, 1987

* * *

One of the first charity shows SCD reported about was the Jimmy Fund Benefit Sports Collector's Convention, in Chicopee, Mass., in October 1977.

More than $175 was raised through admission fees and table rentals. Proceeds were donated in memory of Mr. Tom Yawkey. Persons who donated $5 were given a 45-card set of Red Sox players from 1933-1938, the Oct. 15, 1977, SCD reported.

Another first was reported in the March 15, 1978, SCD: the first convention to be co-hosted by a major league baseball club, the Houston Astros. The event, held in the Astrohall in July, was billed as the largest sports memorabilia convention.

Yet perhaps another first in the hobby was reported in the Feb. 26, 1988, SCD:

Shane Rawley Meets The Hobby Phillie Co-hosts Card Show

By Tom Penzkowski

On Jan. 23, there was a unique card show put on in Racine, Wis. What made it different was that it was put on with the help of a Major League baseball player.

Sports and Entertainment of Greater Racine co-hosted the weekend show at Shane Rawley's Sports Club, Rawley's own state-of-the-art softball facility.

The Phillies' talented left-hander was born and raised in Racine, and wanted to bring his hometown a first-class facility to enjoy summer's favorite pastime in these parts.

Shane appeared at the show, along with his friend, Milwaukee Brewers superstar Paul Molitor, to sign autographs and to pose for pictures. Card show promoter Jerry Tapp is somewhat of a celebrity himself. Tapp writes a "Stats on Tapp" column for the Washington Post and several other newspapers.

The staff of Rawley's Sports Club were very pleased with the turnout of nearly 500 people for their first card show endeavor, while the players truly enjoyed talking to the fans who braved a near-zero degree Wisconsin morning to attend the event.

There are more plans for the future of this fine establishment, which currently rivals any sports complex you can find in the area. These plans include the possible addition of more volleyball courts, miniature golf, soccer fields, indoor batting cages, and, hopefully, more card shows.

Several of Rawley's teammates have made personal appearances at the complex when the Phillies road trips have made a stop at Wrigley Field. Mike Schmidt, Von Hayes and other Phillies stars have made the trek north to inspect Shane's "softball paradise."

Inside, any collector would be impressed by Rawley's display of an impressive variety of major league equipment and photos, many autographed by other National and American League stars.

Located at the Highway 11 exit of the I-94 Expressway, it is approximately halfway between Milwaukee and Chicago. The sports club draws quality softball players from many surrounding cities to play at its fabulous diamonds. So if you're passing through, stop by and take a look. You'll be glad you did. — Tom Penzkowski

* * *

In the Jan. 31, 1981, SCD, editors John and Phil Stommen offered proof of how the hobby was growing. In their Our Hobby column they apologized for an oversight when they wrote: "Even though on the occasions we have a Convention Calendar in SCD, we list up to as many as 75 such events, and thereby include just about every one around, we have somehow failed to this point in getting in the notice of the 4th annual Arizona Sports Collectors Association Show information."

Eight years later, in a June 16, 1989, article, Rusty Morse documented the hobby's continued growth.

Baseball Card Shows Document Hobby Explosion
A Couple Reasons Why This Hobby Seems Certain To Continue Its Growth

By Rusty Morse

Between August 1973 and February's final show in 1989, 15,444 shows featuring baseball cards and sports memorabilia were reported in the pages of SCD.

By actual count, more than a third of these — 5,235 — were held in 1988. More than a third of all reported shows by December 1987 had been held during that year.

Tabulation of the first two months of 1989 indicate that the number of scheduled shows is still rising. More shows were reported in the first two months of 1989 than in all of 1984, eclipsing the number by 50.

As with the stamp and coin shows, activity is seasonal, with spring and fall being the peak times. Mid-summer and the Christmas/New Year holiday season are periods of decline, but monthly figures from year to year show steady rises.

To gain a better picture of what this means, selected tallies of the reported table size of the shows reported over the past few years reflect that within plus or minus 5 percent, the shows reported an average of 40 tables per show, with better than 85 percent reporting this information along with show dates.

Based on a 40-table average, the 5,235 shows in 1988 translates to 209,400 tables for rent to market sports memorabilia and sports cards. As not all shows are reported in SCD, the additional shows could well offset or exceed any unrented or non-sports tables at shows.

The bulk of the shows listed are billed as strickly baseball/sports cards and memorabilia. The few combination events with stamps or coins are a very small portion of the total shows.

If each of the tables had an average sales volume of only $25 at the show, that would yield a show sales volume of $5,235,000. A $100 per table sales average would be $20,940,000 and, of course, multiples could be calculated.

Attendance figures could be estimated as well. A 100-person attendance per show would average out to 523,500, based on the number of shows. If one calculated that for each table in the show, 10 people came (400 average), the total attendance might be 2,094,000. — Rusty Morse

* * *

Shows in the late 1970s were drawing record crowds, generally 4,000 or more collectors, to each event. One of SCD's first show recaps appeared in the Oct. 15, 1977, issue and summarized the third annual show in Philadelphia.

Philly III Drew Record Crowd Of 4,736 Persons

The third annual Philadelphia Baseball Card & Sports Memorabilia Show, held on Sept. 23 and 24 at Spring Garden College, drew a record crowd of 4,736 people despite a cool, rainy weekend, according to co-chairman Bob Schmierer.

More than 102 dealers did a brisk business during the 15 hours the show was open, as hobbyists and the local curious gathered in one of the largest such shows ever held in the United States.

Walk-in items, which started arriving a full month before the show, brought $5,944 in three frantic auctions of a variety of baseball material.

Co-chairmen Bob Schmierer and Ted Taylor, fearful that bad weather might hold down the crowd from the 3,100 who attended the 1976 show, attributed the record numbers to the tremendous amount of publicity given Philly III by the Delaware Valley area newspapers, radio and TV during the week before the show. Besides major features in the Philadelphia Inquirer and Bulletin the day of the show, two TV stations covered the show on the 6 p.m. and 11 p.m. news the day the show opened.

The scene of thousands of people sorting through dealers' wares or just taking a nostalgic trip through their childhood of baseball cards was highlighted by three auctions that drew $5,944 for 90 lots of walk-in material. The varied items, auctioned by Taylor, ranged from Howard Ehmke's personal baseball collection, through sizeable lots, ranging from T206s, Play Balls, Bowmans and Topps, to several uncut mint sheets of Bowman non-sport cards brought in by a man whose father had worked for the Philadelphia-based gum company.

Guest former major league players Del Ennis, Lee Elia and Doug Clemens spent hours signing autographs and talking baseball with those attending. Former A's player Al Brancato was a surprise visitor but was only able to stay a short time. Another unexpected visitor was an executive from the ABC television network who, after taking in the sights, expressed interest to Schmierer and Taylor in doing a network feature on the hobby for network showing.

Attendees were given a free, 28-page program, free baseball cards, and a ticket that pictured Ennis' 1951 Bowman card. The supply of 3,000 programs was gone by noon Saturday...

...Dealer Jim Barnes donated the unsold Statis Pro games from his table to a local boys organization when the show ended, a noble gesture on the part of the Asheville, N.C., game manufacturer.

* * *

Attendance at the Philadelphia show continued to grow — from 1,200 people in at the first show in 1975, to 11,102 at Philly 7 in 1979, when Mary Sue Styles, the Philadelphia Phillies' left-field ball girl, signed hundreds of autographs and posed for countless pictures. Buddy Harris, a hurler with the Astros in the early 1970s, visited the show while his wife busily bought as many Harris cards as she she could find at dealer tables. By 1981, the Philly show was drawing more than 13,000 collectors.

Shows in Cincinnati were drawing well in the late 1970s, too, as Tim Turner reported in the Dec. 31, 1977, SCD:

Cincy Convention Crowd Hit 4,000 Persons

By Tim Turner

A record crowd, estimated at 4,000 persons, and several new hospitality room ideas highlighted the 5th Annual Cincinnati Area Sports Collectors Convention held in Sharonville, Ohio, over the weekend of Nov. 4-6, 1977...

...A total of 112 table holders enjoyed a busy weekend of buying/trading/selling. An unusually warm-weather weekend helped attract the large crowds that were elbow-to-elbow during Saturday and Sunday activities.

The committee for the event, which was held at the Hilton site for the third consecutive year, included Jeff Valentine, Bob and Karon Rathgeber, Phil and Damie Lachmeier, Rich and Suzanne Barkalow, Ray Carson, Stan McClure and myself...

...The hospitality room served many purposes again this year with two concepts (movies and worship service) taking a step forward. The movies were shown twice on Saturday (a 2:00 matinee and an 11:00 feature). Provided by Bob Rathgeber and cinema projected by Jeff Valentine, the movies included the following: 1) 1956 All-Star Game, 2) 1961 World Series highlights, 3) 1975 World Series highlights, 4) 1976 World Series highlights, 5) Tools of Ignorance (about catching), and 6) The Sport of the Century (about baseball)...

...The hospitality snack room was open Friday and Saturday evening after the auction and featured a menu of roast beef and ham sandwiches, a delicious relish tray, potato chips and beverages. A table hockey game, television pong game and plenty of hobby chatter helped keep the hospitality room open to past 3 a.m. both nights. — Tim Turner

* * *

Things were happening on the West Coast, too, as Bob Keisser reported in the Dec. 31, 1979, SCD:

Over 4,000 Attended West Coast Convention

By Bob Keisser

Move over, Mickey Mantle. You've got company at the top of the inflationary baseball card heap.

Without question, the hottest card in the hobby recently has been the 1952 Topps Mickey Mantle, old number 311. And that fact was borne out at the 11th annual West Coast Convention.

But Mickey has some competition, in the form of the rare 1954 Bowman issue of Ted Williams.

Two years ago, the expensive Mantle could have been had for around $75. Lately, he's been going for upwards of $1,000. The card was sold by Garden Grove, Calif., collector/dealer Tony Galovich for $1,400 and just after that at the New Jersey show, the card went for $1,750.

Equally stunning, though, was the price a gem-mint Williams brought in a walk-in auction at the West Coast Convention. The Williams card had been hovering around $150, but when it showed up for the auction, it sold for a whopping $435.

Earlier in the convention, a dealer had sold the card in excellent shape for a reported $300. The same dealer was seen frowning by the time the three-day show came to an end.

The '52 Topps Mantle, '54 Bowman Williams and '53 Topps Willie Mays were the cards in biggest demand at the show, with the Williams the rarest and the Mays the most prolific. It seemed as if every other dealer had a Mays for sale, ranging in price from $750 (good shape) to $250 (excellent). A good-plus Mays went for $219 in the last day auction.

The three-day meeting drew in excess of 4,000 patrons, including a handful of sportswriters from local newspapers and TV crews from KTTV (a local independent) and KNXT (a CBS affiliate), with Brent Musburger of football/basketball fame dropping by with his sons.

The comments from the dealers were all favorable, most of them praising the show organizers — Gavin Riley, Mike Berkus and Steve Brunner — for running a nice show that featured a separate trading/auction room away from the hubbub of the dealing floor, convenient auction hours for dealers, refreshments, and better security. The Memorial Day convention held earlier in the year at the some site was marked by a few incidents of theft, a problem that wasn't as prevalent this time around.

Other auction items included a large lot of cards, which featured complete Topps sets from 1958 through 1966, for $3,600; a 1954 Topps Hank Aaron for $110; and numerous Hartland statues, which averaged at around $85-plus per sale.

* * *

By the end of the 1980s, SCD was still reporting record attendances, but show reports had a new twist — who was signing autographs, and how many autographs they were signing. As the Aug. 5, 1988, SCD reported, a famous trio of outfielders appeared at a card show for the first time together.

Willie, Mick & Duke Appear In Georgia

By Bill Ballew

Baseball card show history was made over the July 4 weekend as Willie Mays, Mickey Mantle and Duke Snider headlined the Cracker Jack Classic Baseball Cards Show in Marietta, Ga., near Atlanta.

The two-day show, held in the Cobb County Civic Center, featured the three baseball legends together for the first time at a card show. Nearly 9,000 people attended the July 2-3 show, promoted by Baseball Buddies Card Shop in Marietta.

The Cracker Classic featured 96 tables and more than 50 dealers from throughout the United States, including national dealers Alan Rosen and Dick DeCourcy. Merchandise for sale had a heavy emphasis on older baseball cards with numerous uniforms and new cards also available.

"We attracted a lot of people who had never been to a card show," said Chip Nelson of Baseball Buddies. "Mantle, Mays and Snider were many of the older collectors' heroes. Hopefully we've raised interest and drawn more people into the hobby."

Planning and arranging for Mantle, Mays and Snider to be at the same time was no small feat. In fact, the show took nearly a year to put together.

"Duke and I have the same agent, Greer Johnson, and Baseball Buddies got in touch with her. Then they worked it out with Carl Kiesler about Willie," said Mantle. "Anyway, they got us all three together and we're all real pleased with it.

"I was afraid that it might be too close to the Fourth of July and that everybody might be going out fishing or to the lake," added Mantle. "But evidently they did a pretty good job."

According to Morris Nix, promoter of the show and owner of Baseball Buddies, another show is in the planning stages for next year.

"I believe this was one of the largest, if not the largest, regional card shows in the country this year," said Nix. "We learned a lot this year so next year will be even better.

"People have asked me what it's like to promote a show," Nix continued. "I tell them it's like a blind date. You get real excited but you don't know whether it will turn out to be Christie Brinkley or the Wicked Witch of the West." — Bill Ballew

* * *

Attendance records continued to fall, switching from coast to coast. The Sept. 23, 1988, SCD reported California show promoter Bob Lee drew 34,055 paying customers to his four-day September show at the Moscone Center, making it the largest event ever staged in the hobby to date. The Oakland A's "Bash Brothers" — Mark McGwire and Jose Canseco — appeared as autograph guests, as did Lou Brock, Willie McCovey and Bobby Thomson.

"As promoter of the hugely successful 1987 National Sports Collectors Convention in San Francisco, Lee says he was motivated by a few comments that he heard after the '87 National. Those comments implied that the only reason the '87 show was so popular was that it was the National, and that it would be successful no matter when or where it would be held. He then set out to disprove any doubts. An aggressive promotional and advertising campaign would be the key to another success, Lee reasoned," reported Tom Mortenson in his Coach's Box column.

In January 1989, the 11 living members of the 500 Home Run Club helped draw a record crowd to Atlantic City for "Supershow 1." The Feb. 10, 1989, SCD reported attendance was between 35,000-38,000.

In addition to the home run sluggers, all-time hit king Pete Rose (a co-promoter of the event along with Bill Hongach), Tony Perez, Bobby Murcer and Hall of Famer Duke Snider signed autographs.

The show, however, did have a downside: "the longest autograph lines ever seen — resulting in the most unruly autograph crowd ever. On the show's first day, the mob knocked down the barricades and swarmed the tables at which the players were signing, almost causing a player walkout. Reggie Jackson made one of the most dramatic pinch-hit appearances of his career, grabbing a microphone and restoring order. The autograph situation greatly improved over the next two days of the show," SCD reported.

* * *

Tino Martinez And Ty Griffin Olympians' Golden Path Leads To Card Show Appearances

By Mike Payne

Even now, out of uniform and months after the 1988 Olympic Games, they're often recognized.

Most people just want to talk. Talk baseball. Talk Seoul. Talk gold medal.

And Tino Martinez and Ty Griffin are loving it.

"I go out and sometimes people I've never met before will come up and say 'congratulations on winning the gold medal,'" said Martinez, Team USA's first baseman and the Seattle Mariners #1 pick.

"I think that's nice. I really do. That means I get to meet them, and I like meeting people. I'm just glad they appreciate what we've done," he said.

What Martinez and the rest of the Olympic baseball team did was barnstorm through a summer tour of the country last year playing several exhibition games and traveling to the World Amateur Championships in Italy, where they finished second to Cuba.

Then it was on to the Olympics, where they downed Japan 5-3 in the gold medal game. Martinez homered twice in that game, including a 410-foot shot which cleared the center field fence at Chamshil Baseball Stadium.

It was America's first Olympic baseball gold medal in the demonstration sport, which will achieve full medal status in the 1992 Barcelona Games.

When they returned to the states, the Olympians began to realize just how popular they had become. More and more people wanted autographs.

Topps included several team members in its 1988 Traded Series, bringing speculators out of the woodwork and still more notoriety to the players. Some were used to the national attention and international attention, particularly University of Michigan pitcher Jim Abbott and Oklahoma State third baseman Robin Ventura.

But a few, like Martinez, who attended Division II University of Tampa, were not.

"I could never have imagined this five years ago," Martinez said.

"When I was a junior in high school it was the Olympic year (1984) and I remember thinking I wanted to go out for that team. But it was nothing more than a dream back then.

"About that time people started telling me I could be eligible for the '88 Olympics and I said, 'yeah, right.' I never really thought it could happen," he said.

"But it did and it was so...I just couldn't believe everything happened so fast."

Fellow Tampa native Ty Griffin, the Olympians' second baseman whose cumulative .416 summer average led the Americans, actually had made a bit of a name for himself a year before the Olympics. He hit a dramatic ninth-inning home run which helped the United States beat Cuba in the first round of the round-robin Pan Am Games Tournament.

The U.S. eventually lost to Cuba in the gold medal game, but Griffin's homer continued to be played and replayed on sportscasts weeks later.

And why not? The loss had been Cuba's first in Pan Am competition in 11 years.

"That opened a lot of eyes," Griffin said of the homer. "Not only in Tampa, but all over."

Griffin and Martinez are among the handful of Olympians who have been touring the country as autograph guests at card and memorabilia shows.

Martinez made his first appearance in Rhode Island in January. Boston shortstop Jody Reed, who was also born in Tampa and raised in nearby Brandon, also attended.

They met the morning of the show and, naturally, Reed wanted to talk about the Olympics.

Griffin is also new to card shows this year. His first was a Tampa show.

"They approached me and said they wanted me to be a guest at an autograph session," said the former Georgia Tech standout and #1 pick of the Chicago Cubs.

"I thought it would be a great opportunity to get a little exposure. It's nice being around people who want your autograph. It kind of puts you on a natural high, like I used to get playing the game in the summer," Griffin said.

Both players immediately worked five shows into their schedules and had other offers pending.

Griffin admitted he was surprised when he was initially contacted.

"I thought they would probably want Ventura, Martinez, or Jim Abbott," he said. "I didn't think anyone would want Ty Griffin to sit in on one."

Griffin, who studied industrial engineering in college, has spent part of the offseason working as a substitute teacher at Tampa's King High School.

Imagine walking into class and seeing the Olympic second baseman preparing the day's plans at the front of the class room.

"It's mostly math," Griffin says. "Algebra II and Trigonometry. I've got some English classes, too."

"When I walk in the kids say, 'where's the teacher?' I say, 'I'm right here.' But they tell me I look more like a student."

Martinez, who was added to the Mariners' 40-man roster, spent some of the spare offseason hours working at his father's cigar plant in Tampa. He spends most mornings hitting with his former UT teammate, then hooks up with Toronto Blue Jays first baseman Fred McGriff and others in the afternoon to work out with his former college teammates on the UT campus.

Extra time on the weekends is used for commitments, including show appearances.

"So many people are into autograph and card collecting," says Martinez. "There's so many people at those shows. I thought maybe I would sign a little bit and then just sit and relax, but the lines have been pretty long," he said.

But the exposure to the autograph-for-sale part of the hobby has hardly dimmed Martinez from signing when approached off the field.

At the mall? Fine, although he's still embarrassed that people think his signature is worth having. "I don't mind it," he said.

"I just don't want to make a big scene because some people will ask and I'll sign and then other people walk by and say, 'who's that, who's that?' And no one really knows. So I just sign it and keep going. But I really don't mind it."

Martinez said the extra money earned from show appearances is nice. But he placed a limit on the number he would appear at before spring training. And he still makes time for workouts.

"If I'm doing a card show in New York on Sunday I'll try and fly out Saturday night," he said.

"That way, I can work out Saturday afternoon, do the show Sunday, then come back Sunday night. I don't want to be out of town too many days in a row.

"There was a show I was asked to do the weekend of Feb. 12 that I wouldn't do. That was just too close to spring training."

Griffin continues to work out regularly, and has become comfortable, and certainly appreciative, of the positive press he's received since the homer that knocked out Cuba.

"I don't think it's surprised me as much as if I didn't know about the continued success of the '84 team," said Griffin, who has taken pride in his success with handling the media. He's really become quite good at it.

"That just comes with time and experience," he said. "At first I guess everybody gets nervous when they do their first interview because you want everything to be perfect.

"But then you realize that some of the questions can be tricky and you've just got to learn how to answer them."...

...In a year that's produced a gold medal and a professional baseball contract, both Martinez and Griffin have gotten just as big a kick out of being included in the Topps Traded set.

"When you're little and you collect cards you never really imagine being on one. You just think, wow, that must be pretty nice," Martinez says.

"Now I'm on one, even though it's not really a pro card. I used to collect a lot of baseball cards growing up but I think I threw a lot of them away," he added.

Griffin still can't believe he was included in the Topps set.

"Sometimes I sit back and look at it," he said. "I never thought I'd be on the front of a baseball card."

Griffin has already passed out several of the complimentary stack of the complimentary stack of cards Topps supplied to the team members. Of course, some went to the same King High students he was substitute "teacher" to.

"I get asked, 'you got a card? You got a card?'" he said. "I find that very exciting."

* * *

In September 1989, Bob Lee was at it again, breaking his own record for attendance at the Moscone Center, as reported in the Sept. 22, 1989, SCD:

More Than 41,000 Appear At Hobby Show San Francisco Show Sets Hobby Attendance Record

By Don Butler

"I left my cards in San Francisco."

That was the theme, at least, for many of 440-plus dealers who appeared it Bob Lee's 1989 All American Sports Collectors Convention, held Sept. 1-4 at the mammoth Moscone Center in San Francisco.

Between 41,000 and 44,000 visitors trooped through the doors at the four-day Labor Day weekend show, making it the largest-ever convention in the history of the sports collecting hobby.

Through Sunday night, 28,000 collectors had streamed through the doors to see the 840 dealer tables and have memorabilia signed by autograph guests such as Reggie Jackson, Catfish Hunter, Will Clark, Willie Mays, Steve Carlton and Willie McCovey.

Monday's autograph guests included Rickey Henderson, Roger Clemens, Mike Greenwell, Willie Stargell, Walt Weiss, Jose Canseco and Mark McGwire. The day's total of between 13,000 and 16,000 visitors would certainly rank it as one of the most successful one-day show totals of all time.

Hot items included Nolan Ryan, any football and basketball, and 1989 Upper Deck factory sets. Nolan Ryan rookie cards began the show at around $350, and toward the end were commanding considerably higher (one dealer reported selling a perfect Ryan rookie card for $1,500). Upper Deck factory sets — with the 100-card update set — were selling well at $85 on Friday, and prices soared to $125-140 per set by the end of the show.

In football, anything was up for grabs — stars, rookies, sets, Hall of Famers — as football cards continue to take up more and more space in dealer display cases. O.J. Simpson rookie cards sold for $75-95; Joe Namath's rookie card sold for anywhere from $750 to $1,600; 1984 Topps football sets, which include rookie cards of Marino, Elway, Dickerson and Warner, rose to a high of $54 (most sets were around the $20 range just a few months ago); a 1965 Topps football set fetched $1,490; 1975 Topps football sold for $260; and Walter Payton's rookie card, at $75 just four months ago, was selling for $175.

In basketball, the Fleer 1986 set rose steadily throughout the show from $100 to a reported high of $175. Michael Jordan's card from that set brought up to $100. The Chicago Bulls set from Star's 1985 release — only a few of the only basketball set Star produced were seen at the show, reflecting the scarcity of the sets — commanded healthy prices, as well, anywhere from $125 to $200. Julius Erving rookie cards appeared to settle in at the $95 range, while any Kareem Abdul-Jabbar cards continued to be good sellers.

Some of the show visitors brought in material to be priced or sold. Among the more interesting of the walk-in material were at least two T206 Honus Wagners in reported VG condition. At least one of them was sold.

* * *

Willie, Mickey and the Duke rang in the 1990s by appearing together again, this time in Atlantic City for a show sponsored by Big League Promotions in January. As Jim Kelly reported in the Feb. 2, 1990, SCD:

Shows in Atlantic City tend to cater to spectacular. This is where Mike Tyson turns opponents into notches on his boxing gloves. This was the city that gave birth to the 500 HR show, a theme which shows no sign of slowing down.

So it shouldn't have been any surprise that baseball fans camped out at 4 a.m. on Saturday to wait the arrival of New York Yankee great Mickey Mantle. "I can't understand it," Mantle would tell me later, when asked about his continuous and, might I add, growing popularity...

...Saturday's portion of the show went "according to plans," said (promoter Fred) Davies, having ironed out the wrinkles by now. The only disappointment on this day may have been to the public when Spencer Ross made the announcement at 9:13, "There are no Mickey Mantle autograph tickets available for today."

Just 13 minutes into the show, The Mick was sold out. It seems as though he's appeared everywhere — twice — but this man is the exception to the card show rule. He's a legend.

And not surprising, most of the sales activity was tied to Mantle material. Dealer Scott Goodman, dressed in tux and outfitted with National-type material, sold a Mickey Mantle game-used bat for $3,000.

"I'm a BIG Mantle collector," said 36-year-old John Taube, who purchased the bat. "It's a K55 from the 1965-71 period. It's nice...I have other mementos, more game-used bats and Mantle memorabilia." The price is believed to be the highest paid for a Mantle bat.

One dealer had the famed 500 HR poster (blank) for sale for $20. These were the ones given out by promoters of the Tropworld show for autograph purposes. Completely signed and framed, this item is now in the $1,000 range...

...Duke Snider, always a congenial guest, signed and smiled without incident for the next several hours, as did Willie Mays. Now there's news. Apparently Willie is doing his best to change his card show image, tarnished by several incidents of grumbling and rudeness. Mays posed for pictures, smiled and was even cordial at times. On to my hero.

Mickey Mantle, who will be 59 this year, is still the main attraction. Co-promoter Tom Catal, who has worked with Mickey over the years, says, "I love 'em. He's still the greatest."

It's odd. Aaron has 755 home runs, the most of any major league player, but it's the man listed number seven on the list that everyone seems to flock to.

"I can't explain it," said Mickey.

Dressed in a jogging outfield complete with fresh Nike sneakers, #7 went through the day-long process of putting his signature on everything placed in front of him. Baseballs, 8x10s, posters, books, whatever mementos of the kids you wanted signed. Well, almost everything. "No bats" was obvious, but one customer was miffed when Mickey refused to sign a replica uniform. Why not?

"Because I don't want to," drawled Mickey as those nearby cracked a smile. Hey, he's the Mick.

"There's a time factor involved," said number seven. "You have to have two people stretch out the material so it doesn't bunch up. And while they're holding it, I've got to sign it. It takes too much time and it costs these guys (pointing to Catal) money. It hurts the promoter."

* * *

At the Madison Avenue 25 show in November 1990, another former Yankee slugger, Reggie Jackson, signed a record amount of autographs by any guest ever appearing at any of the nearly 30 shows sponsored by the National Pastime over the last six years. As Robert Obojski reported in the Dec. 21, 1990, SCD:

Reggie Jackson Sets Show Record For Signing Autographs

By Robert Obojski

"All right, already. I just can't move my left arm anymore...we'll just have to finish this some other time," declared an exhausted Reggie Jackson after signing almost 3,500 autographs during a marathon two-day autographing stint at the "Madison Avenue 25" card show.

The show, sponsored by the National Pastime, was held in New York City's Armenian Church Ballroom Nov. 17-18 (Saturday and Sunday).

Jackson, who signed for just over six hours on both days, admitted "a six-hour autographing stretch is my limit."

"If I was ambidextrous, and could also sign with my right hand, maybe I could go on a bit longer. But I believe most fans want a left-handed signature, my natural side," he said.

Harvey Brandwein, who operates the National Pastime with his partner Steve Hisler, said the lines of fans were so long that Jackson could have signed at least 500 more autographs.

But Brandwein ordered his staffers to stop selling autograph tickets when he realized "Mr. October" was "running out of gas."

"The human arm can take only so much," he said.

The relatively high rates for Jackson's signature apparently had no real effect in deterring his autograph-seeking fans.

The rates were set at $20 for any flat item, $25 for a baseball, and $80 for a bat. (While Jackson indicated he would not sign more than 100 bats per day, he went a bit over that number to satisfy the great demand.)

Those who learned that Jackson's rate for autographing a bat is $80 wondered if Jackson supplies the bat. No, he doesn't.

You've got to bring your own baseball bat; all Jackson does is sign it for you.

Brandwein said Jackson's 3,500 signatures is a record for any autograph guest at the nearly 30 Madison Avenue card shows sponsored by the National Pastime over the past six years.

The previous record was Johnny Bench's 1,850 autographs, signed at the Madison Avenue #24 show on Oct. 27. Bench, however, was there only one day.

In commenting on Jackson's performance as a whole, Steve Hisler said, "Though the lines of fans were long, Reggie took the time to personalize items, posed for photographs, shook hands, chatted briefly with the fans, and seemed to enjoy himself enormously."

"He seemed to be happy to be back in New York because some of his greatest successes in the game came with the Yankees."

Hisler also said the majority of the autograph fans apparently wanted Jackson's signature on various types of memorabilia, or on an array of memorabilia pertaining to his being a member of the very exclusive "500 Home Run Club."

* * *

Madison Avenue 27, in March 1991, marked the return of Pete Rose to the card show circuit after spending five months in a federal penitentiary for income tax evasion. As Robert Obojski reported in the April 5, 1991, SCD:

Pete Rose Returns To The Card Show Circuit

By Robert Obojski

Pete Rose returned to the show circuit March 9, as one of the featured autograph guests at the Madison Avenue 27 baseball card show sponsored by the National Pastime and staged at the Roosevelt Hotel in New York City.

As most everyone knows, Rose served five months at the Marion, Ill., federal penitentiary for income tax evasion, receiving his release on Jan. 7.

The courts ruled that Rose must perform a minimum of 1,000 hours of community service, an obligation that will require another several weeks to complete. While performing this service (which entails assisting physical education teachers in the Cincinnati public school system in carrying out various programs), Rose is being confined in a Cincinnati "halfway house."

In order to get the weekend off, Rose needed court approval...and after completing his engagement at the Madison Avenue show, he went to Waterbury, Conn., to do another card show on Sunday (March 10). He then flew right back to Cincy. He was accompanied by his wife Carol and his agent Cal Levy.

Rose's handlers made it a strict rule that the all-time base hit king was not to talk to the press. Surrounded by a squad of local security men, Rose left the Roosevelt Hotel. He brushed by a group of reporters from New York, Cincinnati, Boston and Washington, D.C., newspapers.

Reporters from many radio and television stations, as well as from CNN, were also on hand to cover the event, but through it all Rose didn't say a single word to any of them and came to be dubbed by the press as "Silent Pete."

When it came to signing autographs for the fans, however, Rose was extremely coordial as he exchanged quips and pleasantries.

Rose signed approximately 1,200 autographs, including mail orders — and apparently not too many collectors seemed to be deterred by the $20 price tag for items and balls, and $50 for bats. He signed 1,100 flats and balls, and about 100 bats.

One source mentioned that Rose "netted" more than $20,000 for his stint that lasted approximately five hours (including the mail order work that preceded the public appearance.)

Rose graciously signed anything and everything that was placed on his table, including copies of the Dowd Report, the 235-page printed document revealing the findings of the special commission formed by the late baseball Commissioner Bart Giamatti as to Rose's alleged gambling on major league baseball games, including those played in Cincinnati, when Rose was the manager.

One collector brought along two copies of the Dowd Report to be signed. There was Rose's big, bold, black signature on the front cover of both copies. The collector quoted Rose as saying: "Why don't you read the eight evidence volumes that go along with the Dowd Report? Those will show I'm in the clear."

Throughout the signing session, Rose was the picture of charm, and he didn't even flinch when several collectors placed before him the July 3, 1989, copy of Sports Illustrated with the front cover showing a juxtaposed photo of a glum Rose alongside some damaging testimony from one of his alleged gambling companions from Cincinnati.

Commented the New York Times' George Vecsey, who was standing with other reporters trying to get a statement from Rose: "It took a certain amount of gall to place that magazine in front of Pete Rose, given his current status as a resident of a halfway house."

Steve Hisler, who operates the National Pastime with his partner Harvey Brandwein, held a mini-press conference with writers on hand to report the Rose autograph session.

Emphasized Hisler, "the collectors attending this show treated Pete Rose with great respect...and you've got to keep in mind that New York area collectors are as sophisticated and as knowledgeable as they come."

Hisler added, "it appears to us that most of the autograph seekers believe that Pete will get into the Hall of Fame eventually, despite the fact his name won't be appearing on the ballot because he's on the ineligble list, at least for the time being. Collectors we talked to regard Pete Rose as a Hall of Famer in every respect."

* * *

In his March 13, 1987, and May 15, 1987, Off the Cuff columns, Ted Taylor presented results from his reader survey on their favorite baseball card shows, based on availability of material, cost of autographs from featured guest, aisle space, number of dealers and the performance of the host promoter.

The EPSCC Willow Grove Show finished first, followed by the Madison Avenue (New York Show) and the Levittown, Pa., shows. The White Plains/Yonkers Show finished fourth, followed by the Mid-Atlantic Show in Richmond, Va., and the JFK Airport Show in New York, in a fifth-place tie. Wayne Miller's Columbia, Md., came in seventh, followed by the Mid-Atlantic Show in Alexandria, Va., the Plymouth, Mich., Summer Show and the Charlottesville, Va., Mid-Atlantic Show.

The second 10 included a four-way tie for 11th place between Black Sox Enterprises (Toledo, Ohio); Middletown, Ohio; Denver, Colo.; and Ocean City, N.J. In 15th place came a six-way tie, including Cincinnati; Los Angeles/Memorial Day; Bishop Guertin in Nashua, N.H.; York, (Pa.) Vo Tech; Cooperstown, N.Y.; and Meadowlands, N.J.

Others receiving votes, but not finishing in the top 20, included the Annual Kansas City Show; Freehold, N.J., Austin Prep in Reading, Mass.; the Manchester, N.H., Boys Club; and the Armenian Church Show in New York City.

Reader Frank Whelan, Wallington, N.J., said the Willow Grove show is "the King of shows for me (and I've been to the New Jersey and Texas Nationals)...great merchandise...gets very crowded but usually you can find exactly what you wanted in the condition you wanted."

Al Sweigart from Cressona, Pa., attended 18 of the 21 Willow Grove shows. "The shows are well planned...well run and enjoyable...the autograph fees are most reasonable and the promoters have always been friendly and helpful to the hobby 'small fry.'"

Bob Strait of Wareham, Mass., said his top choice is Wayne Miller's Columbia, Md., show. "There is always a large variety of high quality items and a lot of turn-of-the-century material at Wayne's show," he said.

An Ohio dealer commented on the policy of the Black Sox Enterprises Shows in Toledo who have, on occasion, refunded both admissions and dealer table fees when a scheduled guest failed to appear. "It is the most honest and fairest show I've ever been associated with," the dealer wrote.

* * *

Large Turnout For The National Convention At Los Angeles
Collectors Enthusiastic About Big Five-Day Hobby Event

Collectors, dealers and visitors to the First Annual National Convention held at the Airport Marriott Hotel in Los Angeles Aug. 28 through Sept. 1 were high in their praise of convention co-ordinators Gavin Riley, Steve Brunner and Mike Berkus for their efforts in organizing the five-day event.

Close to 50 persons gathered for an informal reception and round table discussion the first night of the get together, mulling over dishonesty in the hobby in particular, that subject coming almost immediately to the fore when three reprints of 1952-53 cards were displayed and passed around those in attendance. Discussion then bypassed such scheduled topics as prices, future trends and hobby education to dwell on the dishonesty topic and how it could best be remedied.

Convention workshops the following day were well attended. The session on storing, protecting and displaying was particularly interesting and there were also workshops on regionally issued and unusual sports collectibles and money-saving tips and other hobby shortcuts.

Some 100 persons gathered for the Convention Banquet that second night of the convention during which Denny Eckes and Jim Beckett were honored with presentations for their respective and collective contributions to the sports collecting hobby. Co-convention coordinator Mike Berkus used his many talents toastmastering the banquet. The banquet was then followed by a hospitality room get together to close out the evening.

The opening day of sales portion of the convention, Saturday, Aug. 30, was the busiest of the three days the remainder of the convention operated. We enjoyed visits with very many of our hobby friends then and throughout the remainder of the Labor Day Weekend. — Oct. 31, 1980

* * *

Draws Hobbyists To Plymouth Second National Convention

By Ted Taylor

The 2nd National Sports Collectors Convention was held in Plymouth, Mich., July 9-12, and drew a considerable number of dealers and hobbyists to a well-run, if not too lengthy, series of seminars, autograph sessions and auctions.

With 215 tables in a convention room of approximately 10,000 square feet, dealers and potential customers were often forced into uncomfortable quarters to try and complete transactions.

When Hall of Famer Al Kaline appeared on Saturday to sign autographs, almost one-half of the room was rendered useless for a period of time for dealers unfortunate enough to be located in that sector. The situation was almost as bad during the auctions and when other guest signers made their initial appearances.

Show promoters Lloyd and Carol Toerpe did an outstanding job of arranging the affair but obviously miscalculated the floor space requirements and admitted later that the whole concept of in-the-hall autograph signing at future shows there would have to be reconsidered.

While no accurate count of attendance was kept, Lloyd guessed at "between 8,000 and 10,000" — which seemed on the high side given the floor space available at any period of time.

At any rate, dealers on the floor reported brisk business in the morning hours both Friday and Saturday with afternoon and evening lapses mostly dictated by other related activities in progress in the room at the time.

Guest autograph signers Ned Garver, Paul Foytack, Billy Rogell, Jim Northrup and Kaline were all most congenial and spent a great deal of time accommodating their many fans.

A "ground swell" of dealer interest in forming a national-type organization began on Thursday evening, sparked by Kit Young, Jeff Goldstein and Denny Eckes, and ended with a lengthy meeting Saturday evening at which Dr. Jim Beckett agreed to compile data for a later presentation.

It was obvious, however, that there were as many detractors as there were supporters among dealers for such a group and it is probably too soon to even speculate on what the result of this effort will be.

In many respects it was reminiscent of the 1977 Detroit convention effort that spawned the ill-fated "national card collectors association" with a body of prominent dealers as the guiding force.

Several dealers told SCD that they feel one thing that might be a factor in the success of the new group is that "there are just too many shows" and the number of shows held in any given location during a year eventually dictates the success or failure of all of them.

"We would like to see a grading system in effect (like the one suggested by SCD in the Jan. 31, 1981, edition) for shows so that dealers working nationally would have a better handle on what's good and what isn't," said Young from Washington state.

"There are just too many shows being run by inexperienced kids or opportunists that don't pay a bit of attention to the needs of either the collector or the dealer," Young added.

The four-day National Show was seen by several as, at least, one day too long and the show hours were criticized as being too many per day.

"When you are in a room from 9 a.m. until 11 p.m. for two days of a four-day show, it is just too long to be practical," said Walter Hall of Hall's Nostalgia in Arlington and Lynn, Mass. "I don't really think it

matters much after 9 p.m. and, frankly, when we opened our tables at 9 a.m. there were fewer than half the others open and ready for business."

In fact, one of the major complaints by consumers at the Plymouth Show was the fact that many tables were closed during long periods of time and several dealers packed up and went home at or near the conclusion of business on Saturday.

The show's seminars were well thought out and well attended. "That's one of the things I like about this kind of show," Walter Hall said, "we did get a chance to sit in on some seminars and to exchange ideas with fellow hobbyists in something other than a buyer-seller arrangement."

Carol Toerpe is also to be congratulated for arranging women's activities throughout the convention and for running a top-flight and well-stocked hospitality suite during off-show hours. — Ted Taylor, Aug. 20, 1981

* * *

National Brings Thousands To Anaheim

By Steve Ellingboe

The sponsors of the event — and the hobby — can be proud of the 6th National Sports Collectors Convention held in Anaheim, Calif., the weekend of July 11-14.

Because of deadline restrictions, a full report of the convention (with photos) will have to wait until next issue. But here are a few of the highlights.

This year's National was the largest ever — 450 dealer tables offering every kind of sports collectible available anywhere in the hobby. Attendance on the convention floor was strong and steady throughout the three days of the convention. By Sunday morning, attendance had reached the 10,000 mark with a full day still remaining.

(I had to leave the show Sunday morning because of deadline requirements, but it appeared almost certain that the final attendance figure would top the previous high for a National Convention set in Chicago two years ago.)

The Thursday evening banquet was a first-class affair and was very well attended. Guest speaker Joe Garagiola delighted the crowd with dozens of stories about his career as a ball player, a broadcaster and a collector.

"I'm a collector and I'm proud to be a collector," Garagiola said. "Collecting lets the little boy in you jump out!"

The former catcher remained at the convention through Friday, circulating through the room, talking with dealers and hobbyists, adding to his collection of tobacco cards and Goudeys and graciously signing autographs.

All the while, his NBC camera crew followed along, taping a special segment on our hobby for future use on the NBC "Game of the Week." Garagiola, in his commentary, always emphasized the fun and nostalgia aspects of the hobby, rather than the financial and investment potential. He is, indeed, a true collector, and we appreciate his efforts to promote our hobby and put it in the national spotlight.

Also on the banquet program was Hall of Famer Roy Campanella, who had appeared earlier Thursday at an informal seminar where he answered questions from fans and collectors.

"I loved the game," said the former Dodger catcher. "I'd have played for nothing. I'm so proud to have been a Dodger — the only team that gave me a chance to play." The crowd responded to Campy's appearance with a warm standing ovation.

Garagiola and California Angels third baseman Doug DeCinces officiated at a special charity auction Thursday night that raised over $5,000 for the March of Dimes.

DeCinces returned on Friday as an autograph guest at the show, along with future Hall of Famer Rod Carew. Bob Feller and Chuck "Rifleman" Connors also had tables at the show and signed hundreds of autographs for collectors.

The meeting Friday night to select the site of next year's National Convention attracted about 400 dealers and hobbyists. In a three-way race, voters awarded the 7th National to veteran show promoter Wanda Marcus, who will host the 1986 show in Arlington, Texas.

At the same meeting, hobbyists elected two new at-large members to serve on the National Convention Committee. Chosen from an impressive field of eight candidates were Barrie Sullivan of Denver and Bob Wilke of Phoenix.

Other candidates on the ballot were: Tom Daniels of Richland Center, Wis.; Jim Herron of Westchester, Ill.; Steve Pemper of Milwaukee, Wis.; Barry Sanders of Atlanta, Ga.; Allan Schwartz of Rockville Centre, Md.; and Tom Wiley of Florissant, Mo.

Voters at the meeting also agreed to extend the terms of previously-elected at-large members Bill Mastro, Larry Dluhy and Walter Hall from one year to two; and approved a measure that will require all future National Convention promoters to give $5 per table to the National Convention Committee to help cover operating expenses.

The convention also included the traditional softball games, Strat-O-Matic tourney, seminars and card flipping contest, along with a baseball trivia contest.

Our congratulations to the promoters of the Sixth National — Bill Heitman, Steve Brunner, Jerry Williams, Mike Berkus, Jack Petruzzelli and Gavin Riley — for a job well done. — Steve Ellingboe, The Coach's Box, Aug. 2, 1985

* * *

A Report From The 7th National

By Bob Lemke

I had fun at the 7th National. Wanda, John and the City of Arlington spoiled us rotten.

We've never seen a National convention with so much room in the aisles for the public to browse and so much room behind the dealer tables for them to stretch out. The only way the hotel, convention center and ballpark could have been any more convenient would be to have them under the same roof.

And really, a short walk — no more than 100 yards — between facilities in the 104-degree Texas sunshine only served to remind us of how well the air conditioning was working in the convention center.

Sure, the show had its problems, but I think all prospective future National promoters learned from them so I'm not going to dwell on them here. The important thing is that all the problems were quickly resolved and, I'm proud to say, the solutions quite often reflected a cooperative attitude on the part of the promoters, the dealers and the collecting public. I saw several cases of where a helping hand was offered or given to get the show over a rough spot.

Just prior to the National, the year-long hassle about where the 1987 shindig will be held had gotten particularly nasty. An unsigned poison pen letter was sent to supposedly influential hobbyists in an effort to denigrate one of the bidders for next year's event. That struck me as a new low in what has been a one-sided war against our host for next year's National.

However, by the time the actual voting for site selection was held, it was remarkably devoid of the expected sound and fury. Our hobby is made up of many strong personalities, some of whom have been butting heads for the past 12 months over the 1987 National. However, at the 11th hour, these parties were able to sit down and put their heads together and come up with what is evidently a satisfactory understanding of their respective positions.

We now know we're going to San Francisco in 1987, let's just sit back and enjoy it. Or better yet, let's pitch in to see what we can do about making it every bit as successful as the past seven affairs.

I'd like to share with you a few of the special memories of the Arlington National that will linger with me.

* The stadium. Ballparks are magical places. It was always a treat to walk out of the hotel or convention center and see the stadium just a stone's throw away. We were literally close enough to hear the crack of the bat during BP. By the same token, it was exquisite torture to have to "go to work" at the show, and not be able to catch a game until Saturday night.

* And what a game! Old-timers game. The convention floor was shut down an hour early on Saturday because virtually all of the dealers were headed for the old-timers game. It was a leisurely stroll over to the Stadium and then we took our seats in the shade, a good thing because at game time the temperature read 103 degrees. The humidity was low, however, so it was not at all uncomfortable. When Johnny Logan stepped to the plate in his Milwaukee Braves uniform, I got all misty. With Lew Burdette on the mound, I flashed back to County Stadium in the days when it was a National League park.

* Old-timers everywhere. We were fortunate enough to be lodged on the same floor at the host hotel with most of the old-timers who were participating in the game. There was a special lounge on our floor where you could grab a quick coffee and doughnut in the morning or a drink during cocktail hour. The lounge almost always had between two and six former ballplayers present. I wish there had been more time to sit in and listen to the great stories, but, again, the press of business beckoned.

* They're only human. I especially enjoyed "catching" a couple of ballplayers just being normal human beings. There was a former pitching great who we saw nodded off at his table in a nearby steakhouse...- we're talking chin-on-chest asleep. And a currently-playing favorite of mine from the Cleveland Indians who shared an elevator with us. He'd spent several hours in the hotel bar and was feeling no pain. We had an enjoyable couple of minutes of animated small talk...not player and fans, just four guys on an elevator.

* Where were you when the lights went out? And they did on Friday morning just as convention business on the floor was getting brisk. All of the lights suddenly went out. Unfortunately, the lights are the type that take 15-20 minutes to reignite, so we were kept in the dark. Quick-thinking dealers near the doors opened them and we were able to get some light from the hallways and outside, and a few dealers who had lighted exhibits which remained illuminated until the emergency lights came on.

How would you like to be a dealer sitting behind your table with a stranger in front going through your stack of Gem Mint 1952 high numbers when the room suddenly goes black? Philly area dealer Jeffrey Miller, always ready with his horn, gave a soulful rendition of Taps as the room went dark...it certainly helped lighten mood.

I was at a coin show once when the room went dark for a few moments. All you could hear was "click, click, click" all around the room. When the lights came back on, more than half the dealers were sprawled protectively across their display cases with pistol in hand. — Bob Lemke, The Bleacher Bum, Aug. 29, 1986

* * *

8th National Convention Report Card

By Alan Rosen

Attendance: 21,776, and they said it couldn't be done!

Well folks, the National is history. The above figure represents actual turnstyle count. The total attendance figure was well in excess of 26,000 people.

All I can say to this is some of us in the hobby owe Bob Lee an apology. Other hobby publications, dealers and even some of my own friends were beginning to doubt the efforts of Mr. Lee prior to the show.

I'm not saying that Bob adhered to all the rules, which of course, must be obeyed. However, he is the consummate professional and show promoter par excellence. Luis Oliviera, his able assistant, and his entire staff should take a bow for a job well done.

In this column, I would like to cover the National in its entirety on a report card-type basis. Hope you enjoy. Let's begin with:

Attendance: The largest attendance of any National and as far as I know the most people for a three-day attendance in our hobby's history. Mike Berkus said it when he said it was the largest show he has ever seen in his life. Tony Galovich added, "beyond my wildest expectations." Grade: A+.

Sales: I asked approximately 45 dealers and almost all of them responded the same way — best show they ever had! Here are some quotes from some major dealers attending the show:

Bill Henderson, "Extremely happy, sales were my highest ever." Barry Saunders, "Best I've ever done at any show." Joshua Evans, "My greatest National ever." Rick Salvino, "Greatest thing I've ever been involved with."

I guess you get the idea folks. Tens upon thousands of people spending, at my estimation, close to five million dollars on the floor. Grade: A+.

Moscone Center: The ultimate professionals who, along with United Exposition Services, made sure the show ran like a clock. When a piece of equipment was needed — a table, pegboard, etc. — a radio dispatch was sent out and in minutes it appeared.

The 575 tables were set up efficiently, spaced perfectly with 14-foot aisles and 10 feet behind each one. The only two minuses I noticed were long lines to set up and two slight hassles with unions. Both were solved rather quickly.

When you gather together this many people in one place for an event of this magnitude, I think all in all a damn good job was done. Grade: A+.

City: As Walter Hall of Hall's Nostalgia put it, lots of people, a fabulous city. Most people I spoke to thoroughly enjoyed their visit to this quaint and clean city. Lots to see and do, great restaurants, natives exceptionally friendly. All in all, a great place to visit. I'd love to go back. Grade: A.

Host hotel: Only negative of the weekend as far as most were concerned. Long lines to register, most rooms small and shoddy with paper-thin walls. Garage parking that cost $7 a day (and that was a special rate), hotel coffee shop extremely overpriced — and they say New York is expensive. Grade: C-.

Future: As Gavin Riley so aptly stated to me, "a quantum leap for the hobby." I firmly believe that our hobby is on fire and growing with leaps and bounds. With all the newspaper and television coverage we continuously receive, along with the unbelievable attendance at this year's National, our future looks extremely bright.

Next year's National, which was awarded to Ron and Maureen Durham to be held at Resorts International in Atlantic City, N.J., will, in my estimation, draw over 30.000 people. I wish the Durhams lot of success and pledge my support. I hope the support of all of you out there is with them for the advancement of our hobby. Grade: A+++.
— Alan Rosen, Mint Matters, Aug. 7, 1987

* * *

In Atlantic City July 6-10
9th National Show Draws Corporate Sponsors

By Mark K. Larson

The Atlantic City Convention Center will be more than just a flea market with a bunch of sports fanatics who are collecting cardboard...

During the National Sports Collectors Convention July 6-10 at the center, the sports collecting hobby "will be elevated to the next plateau" because, for the first time ever, corporate sponsorship has been secured, says the show's promoter, Ron Durham, president of Durham Associates, a sports marketing firm in Dumont, N.J.

The significance of corporate sponsorship, he said, is "it takes us out of the flea market mentality and puts us into the corporate world."

Durham said he encouraged corporations such as Warner Books and Parker Brothers to sponsor the show because they could not afford to not be there. They would receive corporate exposure to the "hard core" collectors, he said.

Warner Books will display its best sellers, Classic Baseball Cards: The Goldern Years, 1818-1956, and Topps Baseball Cards: 1951-1985. Parker Brothers will unveil its new "Starting Lineup Talking Baseball" electronic game.

Durham expects to attract 50,000 to 75,000 collectors, topping last year's record of about 25,000 people who attended the eighth annual show last year in San Francisco. The show will have more than 500 exhibitors, Durham said.

"We have advertised it to be conducive to someone who has $5 in his pocket to someone who has $5,000 in his pocket," he said.

Particularly on the east coast, "People are recognizing the vulnerability of our Wall Street stock market and its instability at the moment. What we have tried to do is point out the solid investment value of baseball collectibles," Durham said.

During the convention, representatives from Las Vegas and Chicago will present bids to host next year's convention. But Atlantic City offers the nightlife, entertainment and casinos to those who attend the show, Durham said.

The convention center, the site of the Miss America Pageant, is centrally located and has undergone multi-million dollar renovations, he added.

"It has a nice impact on the hobby. It looks brand new. It's just a gorgeous facility," he said.

The roomy, 12- and 16-foot-wide aisles won't create a sardine effect where everyone is jammed, he added.

"People won't feel rushed and will have time to stop and look and purchase," he said.

Tentative seminars on Thursday, July 7, through Saturday, July 9, cover topics including hobby courtesy, press pins, 19th century cards, uniforms, baseball music, running a baseball card shop, regional cards, pricing, ticket stubs, computers in the hobby and autographs.

Joe DiMaggio, Ralph Branca and Bobby Thomson will attend the show to sign autographs, and Chicago Cubs stars Ernie Banks and Billy Williams are being lined up.

Though the details are still being worked out, the autographs will be free. However, due to the expected crowds, not everyone will be able to attain the autographs.

Under a lottery-type system, each convention ticket buyer will receive an envelope along with the ticket. Only some attendees will receive notification in the envelope that they are entitled to autographs.

Former Negro League stars Ray Dandridge and Lou Dials will test their coaching skills during a first-come, first-serve softball tournament. Arm-chair managers will have a chance to test their strategies in a Strat-O-Matic Baseball Tournament. Trophies will be awarded to the top finishers, as they will be in the card flipping contest.

Winners in the adult and children categories for a trivia contest will leave Atlantic City with all three of New Yankee Don Mattingly's rookie cards.

Yankees Magazine will produce the convention program, which will include a 10-page supplement from its "Old-Timers" issue.

Tickets for the Friday through Sunday show are $3.50 plus tax for one day and $7.50 plus tax for the weekend and are available through Ticketron outlets. The show hours are from 9 a.m. to 9 p.m. each day.

A kickoff banquet is slated for Wednesday night and features an auction to benefit the Jackie Robinson Foundation, which grants scholarships to needy students. Celebrity guests will highlight the hall of famer's career. Banquet/auction tickets are $50.

Representatives from various Krause Publications sports periodicals will be attending the convention. — Mark K. Larson, May 13, 1988

* * *

Atlantic City Convention Reviewed

By Tom Mortenson

Atlantic City is now just a memory.

Crowded gambling casinos with little old ladies in tennis shoes...glitzy hotel cocktail bars with local "lounge lizards" providing music...yuppies and winos passing one another while blending together on the oceanside boardwalk...open-air food stands...giftshops that sell T-shirts and "naughty" novelties...seagulls swooping down annoyingly close to pedestrians...all this and sports memorabilia, too.

These are a few tidbits dealers and collectors at the 9th Annual National Sports Collectors Convention might remember about the events of July 6-10, 1988. This year's National got underway for sports memorabilia dealers the evening of July 6. A dealer banquet and charity auction honoring the late Jackie Robinson was held at the Resorts International Hotel, the official headquarters hotel.

Here's to you, Mrs. Robinson

Honored guests at the banquet/auction were Mrs. Jackie (Rachel) Robinson, along with her children and grandchildren. Several dealers and individuals donated collectibles to be auctioned off for the benefit of the Jackie Robinson Foundation, which is headed up by the athlete's widow.

Former Dodgers pitcher Ralph Branca, a teammate of Robinson's, paid tribute to the man by stating, "Jackie was the greatest competitor I've ever seen. If anyone ever got him mad, the adrenaline would really flow. He was such an intense competitor."

The keynote speaker at the banquet was New York Times sports columnist and Pulitzer Prize-winning author David Anderson. Anderson was a writer for the Brooklyn Eagle in 1951 and he also shared some of his memories about Robinson.

"When a clutch play had to be made, Jackie was the one to make it," Anderson said. "If you needed one man to win a ball game for you, it would be Jackie Robinson."

Anderson went on to mention that one of the fondest memories he had of Jackie Robinson was that they both shared a common bond that involved an item of memorabilia.

"In 1953, when the Dodgers became National League champions, Charlie Dressen gave all the players and writers who followed the team a special pin with their initials on it. I remember that Jackie and I were the only ones to use it as a tie clasp. It was one little thing that we shared in common," Anderson said.

Rachel Robinson also addressed the audience, telling them how the Jackie Robinson Foundation has provided scholarships for over 300 students.

"We want the foundation to be here for a long time, to help to contribute leaders for America" she said.

WFAN sports announcer Spencer Ross was the auctioneer for the event, which brought in more than $25,000 for the Foundation.

Texas dealer/show promoter Wanda Marcus was presented the Buck Barker Award for meritorious service to the hobby by Baseball Hobby News publisher Vivian Barning.

Setup day

Thursday, July 7, was a day filled with dealer seminars and highlighted by a softball game with former Negro League stars Lou Dials and Ray Dandridge as coaches.

Seminars were held on 19th-century cards, press pins, uniforms, baseball music, regional cards, ticket stubs hobby press, running a baseball card store, autographs, computers in the hobby, hobby courtesy and card pricing.

Thurday was also dealer setup day at the Atlantic City Convention Center. Dealers could be seen parked for several blocks around the building waiting their turn to unload their merchandise.

A bebop cruise up the Atlantic completed the day's activities for those dealers not already too exhausted from the day's events.

The show must go on

Friday, July 8, marked the official opening of the National to collectors. Two lines of people were waiting outside the Convention Center for doors to open at 9 a.m. Pennslyvania publications dealer Jeffrey Miller, as he so often does, announced the official opening by blowing his trumpet.

558 dealer tables were ready for the hubbub of activity.

Corporate sponsors set up at the show included Parker Brothers, Warner Books, Score/Sportsflics, Nike, Collectible Resource Group, REL Travel, Yankees Magazine (who also provided the official convention program), Chicagoland Processing, Lelands, Sports Net, Consumer Guide, and Lin-Terry Trading Corp.

Card-flipping contests and collecting seminars by James Beckett and SCD columnist Marv Mallon took place.

Autograph guests included Hall of Famers Ernie Banks and Billy Williams (who also had their own table for the first two days of the show), Ray Dandridge and Joe DiMaggio.

Collector attendance and activity on Friday easily surpassed the following two days.

Many types of collectibles were being offered at the tables. Offhand, there seemed to be an abundance of autographed items, especially Roger Maris items and Perez-Steele cards. — Tom Mortenson, July 29, 1988.

Bruce Paynter Planning Chicago's National Convention

By Paul Green

Bruce Paynter promoted the 10th National Convention .

It's national convention time again. This year's festivities might have a hard time living up to the advance billing, but if anyone can pull it off, it's probably Bruce Paynter, the man responsible for this year's show.

Paynter has all the qualities you'd want in the man responsible for the hobby's most important show. Hard-working, knowledgeable and creative, Paynter has the added plus of having been through it all before.

He knows what a National means, and he's done it successfully. Hopefully, when the doors open this year, Paynter will do it again, and if he does, it couldn't happen to a nicer guy.

SCD: How did you get started in promoting?

Paynter: I started by running the Chicago club. That was back when a club meant 150 people and everyone had a great time getting together. Our club president was working his way out, and the club

was something I wanted to keep going. So I started promoting shows in Chicago, and was about the only person really promoting shows in Chicago.

SCD: What about the National?

Paynter: At first, I was a skeptic about the concept and whether it added anything, but we decided to put in a bid, which we did. We would run it on our own, but had the blessing of the local club. That was in 1983.

SCD: Are you doing much dealing with cards these days?

Paynter: Until about 1980, I was dealing in everything, but then I made a conscious decision that it was getting ridiculous lugging all that stuff around. I made a decision to just start focusing on the stuff that was of the most interest to me, which was basically from 1952 to 1968.

For about seven years, that was what I sold, although I never have had a store, never have left my job, but still managed to do 10-15 shows a year, usually outside the Chicago area. Since the National in San Francisco, much of my energy has gone into seeking the National.

We were unsuccessful the first time, so it was a two-year run for the National. In the past year, I haven't sold a card. When I've gone to a show it's been strictly to promote the National.

SCD: How much has changed since you last ran the National?

Paynter: It's really not even the same thing, it's a completely different creature. That was not a surprise, but how totally different it has been a surprise. See, I take this obligation very seriously, whether it's to collectors coming to the show or dealers expecting the greatest show ever financially.

I take it seriously. That's what keeps my energies going, but at the same time it provides a lot of anxiety. I wake up in the middle of the night regularly with some detail I could be doing. I wake up and have one foot on the floor when I realize it's three in the morning and have to say, "Sleep four more hours and then take care of it." I really get that kind of drive going.

When we had it in 1983 it was 270 tables. Now it will be over 600. It's gone from being one very nice-sized hotel ballroom and now it's a convention center where you have to deal with unions of all descriptions.

The show in 1983 was still a show where we could actually make everybody's hotel reservation. In the days after we won the bid in Atlantic City, we reserved more hotel rooms than we totaled at the Holiday Inn in 1983, so right away you knew something was going on.

The table applications in 1983 trickled in mostly from the Midwest. Contrast that to this year where something like 98 percent of the people eligible for tables took them. We also had 700-800 written applications from people who cannot get tables. Those are just the ones who choose to defy the odds and write in. It doesn't count the ones who have called and found out there is no way they realistically can hope to get in.

There is also the autograph situation. We had the fourth National. To my recollection, the first had no autograph guests other than speakers. The second had Al Kaline. The third had four or five players, which was thought to be great.

When we had it, we had free autographs for everyone and that included Ernie Banks. To be honest, my whole approach to autograph guests hasn't changed much. It can easily become the tail wagging the dog.

Now you could say your guests are Mantle, DiMaggio, and Gehrig and some would ask who else. While 75 percent of the calls may be about who the guests will be, my theory is that they only represent 5 to 10 percent of the people.

287

It just gets very easy to get wrapped up in it based on the calls and the mail. Yet in all my contacts with tableholders and potential table-holders, not one has asked who the autograph guests will be. To me that says that while the autograph thing is fun, and great for media relations outside the hobby, it's not the be-all and end-all.

SCD: And it probably takes an enormous percentage of your time.

Paynter: That's what I found out doing my own shows. It just takes a huge amount of time.

SCD: All that said, you have put together some pretty interesting promotional plans.

Paynter: Yes, we started with the premise that most people would come if they possibly could, as the practical reality is that it will probably be the only National in the Midwest for a long time.

In my mind the crowd is made up one-third of people who always come to the national wherever it's held. Another third are local collectors who will come if it's within a day's drive.

Then the remaining third are people who are out there waiting to be convinced it would be interesting, and to me the real challenge is the number of people you can bring in from that last group. They may not be the big spenders, but they are the people who come in and create that mood of excitement, which I think still returns periodically, especially at the National Convention. From the start we were looking for those people.

One of the first things we did was something that goes back to what St. Louis did with their National. In Chicago, although he's been retired for years, no one is in the same league as Ernie Banks, the man who loved to play.

So we made arrangements with Ernie so that he is working as the host of the National. He's going to be promoting the show, appearing at every radio and TV station that will have us to talk about sports collecting and the National Convention.

In my opinion, having Ernie Banks, someone so associated with nostalgia in this city, should result in an outpouring of publicity and people acting on that publicity.

We also are working on the corporate sponsorship. We had an experience in our family which led me to believe that we could get a publicity boost out of a charity auction which would benefit a worthy cause.

We approached the people at McDonald's and their childrens' charities, explaining to them they could control all the books, all the money.

Their organization funds charities, the most prominent of which is the Ronald McDonald House, which is sort of a halfway house for parents of children who are seriously ill in the hospital. It allows the parents to stay near the hospital without the expense of a hotel or commuting.

Without getting into it, because of an experience we had, I believe this charity is important. I was standing in line at a McDonald's one day and started wondering what it would take to get a sign up there.

That developed into an agreement between me and McDonald's where for three weeks before the convention, two cases of special placemats will be delivered to every McDonald's in the Chicago area. That's some 340 stores from the Wisconsin border to northwest Indiana.

The only subject on that placemat is going to be the convention and the fact that we're doing a charity auction for the benefit of the Ronald McDonald Children Charities. The actual number is approximately one million placemats.

We've also borrowed an idea Alan Rosen used when he promoted his Madison Square Garden Show. There, on Friday, I was struck by how many people in business suits came into Madison Square Garden.

I asked how it happened, and I forget exactly how, but he had boy scouts or someone pass out flyers to people as they came out of the train station.

There you are putting something in the hands of the right demographic group and a group that probably has a lot of income and are in need of things to do with that income. So, we're going to do that, but also may have done Alan one better by getting permission to hang banners all along Wacker Drive and Monroe Street, which is where the people walk from the train stations to downtown Chicago. So that's another way to get the information to people who otherwise wouldn't know much about baseball cards.

SCD: So you're really spending money and using aggressive approaches to promote this show?

Paynter: I hope so. The time has passed when you could drop a press release off at the Chicago Tribune and expect someone to come and cover the show.

Baseball card shows are not unique anymore. You need to promote in a novel way or to come up with a novel aspect of the show which is so unique that the press has to sit up and take notice, and I really think we've done both. I think the biggest mistake you can make is to figure you've got so much table money and can just sit back and take it and never do anything to promote the show.

I prefer to be more innovative. That money is a given; I'd rather take it and plow it back into these promotions, some of which may work, while others may not. But I think enough will to have it pay off for me and for everyone else as well.

SCD: How much pressure do you feel in terms of expectations for the National? That first time, I don't think anyone had any real expectation at all, but that must be changed too this time.

Paynter: I think you're absolutely right, there were no expectations. People were a little concerned, it was the third year in the Midwest and we all hoped to do well. I still remember, I opened the door and saw 270 tables and that's when I started to get cold feet.

What happened was, and with all due modesty, that's still a show people talk about. They still talk about the crowds that came and feeling people had and all that. Now I think they've taken whatever money they made at that show or the good times they had and multiplied by about 10 times and they're expecting that sort of fantastic show and that's the expectation we have to meet now.

I fully expect two to three times the attendance we had at that show; we've got better than twice as many tableholders to make happy. And there's pressure on the National. If the hobby is in a down time they look to the National to pull it out and if it's in an up time they expect the National to be even greater.

The real pressure I feel, though, is from the administrative responsibilities. I'm confident if I do my job, the attendance and the spending of the crowd will take care of itself. It's tough. Everybody wants a big crowd, but then you start to think, "But maybe we don't want a crowd that big," and people want larger aisles, more space, the creature comforts.

So there's a delicate balance and now you have the added matters of unions, set up times and so on. But I must say, the pressure has been pretty much internal and those who have called seem pretty confident we'll be able to overcome any problems.

SCD: What can people, either dealers or collectors coming to the show, do to help you pull this off?

Paynter: The biggest thing everyone can do to help is follow the rules and procedures that are established. For instance, on move-in day we'll have roughly 425 different tableholders with between 600-625 tables. It used to be you drove up to the Holiday Inn, pulled stuff from the trunk, brought it in and talked for a while.

Then you went back and got some more. It's not practical to do that when people now bring semi-truck loads. You can't bring everything you own and try to place it on a six-foot table.

We have tried to set up a schedule which will make that day work, but if people choose to disregard the rules, it could be an impossible day. We must remember, we are now dealing with unions, with fire regulations, with tax regulations. We can no longer slide into town and have no one notice us. It's wrong to try to do that and it's silly to think it can happen.

SCD: How much work has this been for you?

Paynter: Since we got the bid, I don't think there has been a day when I haven't thought about the National. Since December, it's been five or six hours every night, and all that effort has been put into efforts to let the whole world know that we've got a national convention and that baseball card collecting is big time, is for real.

If we're successful that means we have to deal with the real world, which means unions, taxes, security, that the promoter will not be able to allow you to bring 50 people in, all of whom say they are your table helpers, that you can't bring for six feet of space enough stuff to fill 30 feet just so you can say you've got something there. It's a situation which we will all face and all have to make adjustments, and some haven't adjusted to it yet.

SCD: Certainly on move-in day, that whole thing will be done in downtown Chicago, where you just can't have semis and station wagons backed up for five blocks.

Paynter: Right, and I'm concerned about that. This will be the most dense downtown area where we've had a show, so we have to have a system and you can't just junk the system the first time it's going slower than you might like.

People will have to give me credit for putting together a system which will work and then they're going to have to be a little patient as far as being responsible themselves for implementing that system, which means if we're running 10 minutes late, you can't come to the conclusion that the whole system will get junked.

We're trying as best we can to do everything we can to recapture the spirit we had in 1983. That is everybody just feeling good about what we are doing.

Administratively, through the systems, we're trying to allow people to do that. We're putting an emphasis on the seminars, on the program, putting emphasis in a very real sense to a worthy social cause while getting a benefit for the hobby.

What I'd like to say is that I'm very grateful for the support and encouragement we've had up to this point. I feel real good about it. I think the show has a good chance to be a tremendous success, not just financially. I feel a mood growing of tremendous enthusiasm.

Rarely does a night go by when I don't get a call from someone in a distant part of the country who is planning on coming and bringing their whole family. You know the big dealers and buyers will come in. What's amazing and encouraging to me are the high school teachers and factory workers taking their entire vacations to come up and see this. The letters from kids on notebook paper asking for directions on how to drive in from Manitowoc, the car pooling. It's real astounding, it really is. — Bruce Paynter, June 30, 1989

* * *

Chicago National Convention In Review

By Mark K. Larson and Tom Mortenson

The 10th National Sports Collectors Convention is history. The beautiful Hyatt Regency Hotel in the beautiful city of Chicago was the site.

And it went off beautifully, too, thanks in no small part to hosts Bruce and Bonita Paynter. Collectors and dealers on hand were hard-pressed to find any fault in the organization and attention to detail the Paynters demonstrated for this year's event.

Oh sure, there was a little grumbling about the inability to find parking near the Hyatt. There was some mumbling about the overcrowded elevators and the heat on the show floor. But all in all, when you put some 30,000 people together at one event, you probably won't reach the state of Nirvana. It was as good as it could possibly be.

Dealers came with plenty of sports memorabilia. Collectors came in droves. The autograph guests made it. Ernie Banks was there. The tempo was definitely upbeat.

These are a few tidbits exhibitors and collectors at the 10th National Convention might remember about the events of June 28 through July 2, 1989.

During seminars on Wednesday and Thursday, dealers told secrets of the trade. Topics included security problems, hobby publications, price guides, uniforms, card grading and hockey collectibles.

Dealer Tim Turner, speaking on the topic "Running a Hobby Store," plugged offering grab bags for $2. "That grab bag pays the rent and utilities each month...it's a great way to get rid of your commons. People love them. Grandmothers buy them," he said.

Dealer Stan Marks, discussing "Hobby Ethics and Its Future," said a satisfied customer will tell three people, but an unhappy one tells 25.

Tom Dreesen roasted Ernie Banks at the National Convention .

Since hobby ethics starts with word of mouth, tell someone about bad experiences, added dealer Miles Locke. Word will get back to the dealer, who "will realize 'hey, nobody wants to deal with me. Maybe I should change my act,'" said Locke.

One class act, Ernie Banks, was the roastee Wednesday night during a dealer banquet/charity auction held at the Hyatt Regency Chicago. Distinguished panel members included Steve Carlton, Billy Williams, Minnie Minoso, Monte Irvin, Jack Brickhouse and show promoter Bruce Paynter.

Host Comedian Tom Dreesen, making light of the doldrums experienced by past Cub teams, recalled the time just 45 fans attended a game at Wrigley Field. They didn't sing the "Star Spangled Banner" together; instead, they sang "Feelings."

The P.A. announcer, he said, asked the mother with the nine lost children to please claim them; they were beating the Cubs.

And, Dreesen quipped, the vender, who had just one hot dog, instructed each fan to "Here, take a bite."

Dreesen, taking a few pokes at the eternally optimistic Banks, said if Banks were in hell, he'd still say "It's all right. It's going to get cooler down here."

Banks also had no bad habits.

"Ernie Banks' idea of a good time is to sit on a toilet until his legs get numb," Dreesen quipped.

And Ernie, as a young produce department worker, could also think fast on his feet. Once, a 6-foot-9, 300-pound man wanted a half of a head of lettuce.

Banks, not knowing the customer had followed him, went back to tell his boss that some "big jerk" only wanted a half of a head of lettuce.

Upon seeing the customer, Banks quickly added, "and this man would like the other half."

Monte Irvin told Banks that instead of playing two games, "let's play one, and win it."

Longtime Cubs announcer Jack Brickhouse recalled two of the most memorable events he's broadcasted — when Banks was involved in a play during which two balls were in play, and when Banks hit his 500th home run.

Also during the banquet, Baseball Hobby News' The Buck Barker Award, signifying the spirit of the hobby, was awarded to Franklin Steele.

During a three-hour charity auction Wednesday night, more than $16,000 was raised to benefit the Ronald McDonald Children's Charities.

Items garnering the top bids included:

An autographed Roy Campanella Perez-Steele postcard ($375); a baseball signed by the 11 living members of the 500 Home Run Club ($500); a set of 18 Hartland statues commemorating the 25th anniversary of the originals ($470); and five original 10th National Sports Collectors Convention banners, displayed along the streets of Chicago ($475 each).

On Thursday, Score Inc. had a reception for its line of Scoremasters, 42 oil paintings which will be made into a limited-edition card set to be released in September.

Among those present included artist Jeffrey Rubin, former Pittsburgh Steeler great Franco Harris, and Kansas City Royals pitcher Tom Gordon, the only rookie included in the set.

Gordon, quite delighted to have had a painting done of him, said "I'm thankful. It's a big honor to be in a room with these guys. There are some classy names in here."

Thursday night was a sneak preview from 6 p.m. to 9 p.m.

On Friday, Philadelphia Eagles quarterback Randall Cunningham presented officials from Pro Set and NFL Properties his helmet and jersey, which will be given away as prizes for winning game cards in Pro Set card packs.

Tom Gordan with his Scoremasters card and Jeffrey Rubin.

Autograph quests Friday were Brooks Robinson, Sandy Koufax and Steve Carlton.

Among the large sports-related corporations set up at the show, there were booths for: Leaf-Donruss, Upper Deck, Pro-Set/Hot Cards, Major League Marketing, Hartland Plastics, Scoreboard, Baseball Card World, Collectible Resource Group, Chicagoland Processing, ALS-Lou Gehrig's Disease, Sports Poster Impressions, The Sporting News and others.

Friday evening was the National Convention Committee's annual meeting. The big topic of the meeting was the presentations for the proposed sites for next year's 11th National Convention.

The winning bid came from Wanda and John Marcus, who proposed the Arlington, Texas, Convention Centre. The Marcuses, who were hosts of the successful 1986 show, proposed July 4-8, 1990, for the dates of next year's event.

There will be 556 dealer tables (8 foot) at next year's convention. The fee for a wall display unit space is $190. Aisle tables will be $170. Arlington's Sheraton Centre Park Hotel will be the host hotel.

Election of three National Convention Committee (NCC) at-large members also took place Friday evening. Incumbent member Bob Wilke of Arizona, along with Clayton Pasternack of Ohio and Frank Pemper of Wisconsin, were elected to seats on the NCC among a total of 10 candidates.

A formal invitation only affair, with Mickey Mantle, was hosted by Collectible Resource/Sports Impressions on Friday evening.

Dealers were lined up early Saturday morning at the Marcus' table to make reservations for next summer's National in Texas.

Donn Jennings of Huntsville has already begun circulating flyers advising dealers of his intentions of offering Nashville, Tenn., to voters for the 1991 Convention.

Jack Petruzzelli of California was also verbally stating his intentions of proposing Anaheim for '91. Other unconfirmed bids for 1991 were coming from Indianapolis and North Carolina.

Autograph guests on Saturday included pitching greats Steve Carlton and Sandy Koufax again, along with new Hall of Famer and former Red Sox great and Carl Yastrzemski.

Pro Set, the new maker of football cards, brought in celebrity guests all weekend, too. "Mr. Cub," Ernie Banks, could be found signing and selling autographs on his Fotoballs — baseballs with pictures of Banks and other baseball stars on them — for $12 each.

Former Cleveland Indians pitching star and HOFer Bob Feller could be found at Cowboy George Dickstein's table. Former Negro League star Lou Dials was set up in the middle of the room selling photos and card sets.

On Sunday, the final day of the convention, attendance was still strong. Comments from numerous dealers at the show ranged from "I've been doing good" to "this is my best ever."

Vancouver, Wash., dealer Kit Young summed up his feeling about the '89 Chicago National this way: "The preparation (by the Paynters) is without comparison. Everything has been very thoroughly thought out, from the seminars to the roster of nationally-recognized speakers.

"Bruce exhibited an innovative approach to marketing (the National). I made 41 big buys the first day. I've had people at my table non-stop."

Drexel, Pa., dealer Tony Carrafiel echoed Young's sentiments. "I think they (the Paynters) have done a fantastic job. I can't say enough about it. It's as good a job as you could do," he said.

Sunday's autograph guests included Yastrzemski, ailing Yankee slugger Dave Winfield and former two-time batting champion Bill Madlock.

A crowd gathered for the drawing of the '52 Topps Mickey Mantle card donated by Alan Rosen. The lucky entry was from T. Batman, 13, from Decatur, Ill.

When asked for his comments on the 10th National, a visibly exhausted, smiling Bruce Paynter said "I think it was successful. It exceeded every expectation we had as far as attendance and in terms of business that was done. People came here intent on having fun, and they did have fun.

"The level of cooperation from everyone has been great," he continued. "It feels great."

The 1989 National Sports Convention is over...now let's see, there are only 350 some days until next year's. — Mark K. Larson and Tom Mortenson, July 21, 1989

* * *

Sittin' In With The Duke Snider's Anecdotes Keep The Fans Laughing

By Mark K. Larson

At about ten minutes to eleven, the show promoter walked his guest to the conference room where fans, sitting against the walls and leaning on baseball bats, had lined up outside, waiting to reminisce with their hero and take home a prized signature or two.

"Don't worry. It's a National League ball. It's just in an American League box. We didn't screw up," a father told his son as the two waited to meet Brooklyn Dodger Edwin "Duke" Snider in Plymouth, Mich., July 24.

After the 11 a.m. starting time had passed, some fans, holding ticket numbers up to 200 and now sitting in an adjacent room, grew impatient as the door remained closed and Snider signed mail order requests.

But the boy in the Pepperdine shirt still looked excited — the look of a kid who was going to meet a big league star, but he wasn't exactly sure who.

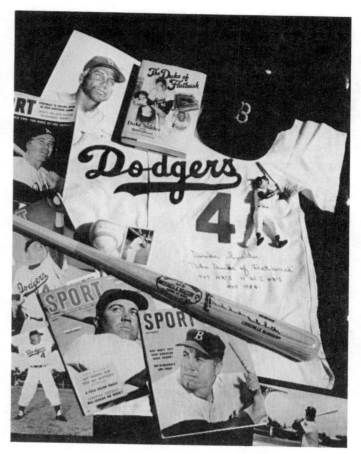

Duke Snider kept the fans laughing in Plymouth.

At 11:25 a.m. the door opened and the fans snaked through a maze of chairs into Snider's room. The first man in line snapped a photograph, while the hotel manager's son was allowed to sneak through the exit door for an autograph and a moment with the Duke before the others.

Outside, in the hall, promoter Jim Hawkins was holding a walkie-talkie with an antenna so long it looked as if it needed a fishing lure on the end of it.

"OK. Call the 300s. OK. Also, the hotel manager is going to get you some singles. Can you get me a Diet Coke and two regulars?" he radioed back to his wife, who was running the card show inside. Later, Snider had the Diet Coke.

At 11:30 a.m. Snider, wearing a comfortable blue shirt with white whales on it, told a fan carrying a baseball bat — the size of the pink, big barrelled bats tots are using for wiffle ball these days — "You shouldn't be able to miss many with that thing, if you can get it around."

Snider was flanked at the autograph table by Jim Hawkins' son Mark and Dan Ewald Jr., the son of the Detroit Tigers public relations director. Two guys, about in the sixth grade and both sporting baseball caps, approached the table. To their surprise, the Duke was talking to them — even asking them a question.

"Do you guys know what ground rules are?" the former outfielder asked, explaining to them that those are the particular rules used at each stadium. Snider proceeded to tell the youngsters about a game being played in the farmyard, with chickens, cows and pigs grazing about the outfielders.

One batter, Snider said, hit a ball into center field. But "a pig ate the ball. What would the ground rule be? What would the ruling on that be?" he asked the youngsters.

"A double, I'd say," offered one puzzled youngster.

"That's a good guess...But it's an inside-the-pork home run," said Snider, to which the people in the first two rows burst out laughing.

Snider continued to sign items — a $1 bill, and a Pete Rose Louisville slugger signed by Johny Mize, Lou Boudreau, Brooks Robinson, Ray Dandridge and Enos Slaughter, among others.

"Don't you want to shake his hand?" one woman asked her husband, who then shook hands with Snider.

"I've never seed a bat with so many signatures as this guy's got. That's neat," said Snider.

One gentleman had Snider sign a few items, but had a special request for the last 8-by-10-inch photograph. "On this one, could you put 'From one Duke to another Duke'?

As Snider signed, the gentleman explained there were two Deans at work and he needed a nickname, so he picked Duke. "You don't have that copyrighted, do you?" he asked.

"I don't believe so. But there's a fellow running for president that's trying to steal it," replied Snider.

Snider continued to sign and make small talk.

"I heard a game the other day and the score was 10 to 8. Not a man touched home plate. Why?" he asked.

"It was a football game?" answered one boy, not too sure on his answer.

"No, it was a baseball game. 10 to 8 was the score...It was a womens' game. The women were playing," Snider said with a chuckle.

Snider continued to autograph items — a portrait of Mickey Mantle, Willie Mays and himself, a 1951 Topps baseball card in the Topps book featuring all that company's cards up to 1985, a September 1955 Sport Magazine with Snider on the cover, a just-taken polaroid of himself in his blue shirt with white whales.

Snider began to tell those around him about the game of logic.

"There's a guy who gets up every morning. He lives on the 28th floor of the high rise. He gets up, gets on the elevator and goes to work everyday.

"When he comes home, he gets on the elevator, gets off on the 13th floor and walks up to the 28th floor where he lives. Why?"

"I know this one," yells a youngster from the second row.

"You know this one?"

"Yah. Because the guy's a midget."

"He couldn't reach any higher than the 13th floor," says Snider, who then tells about former Milwaukee Braves General Manager Donald Davidson who, when he got into the elevator with the team, would say "'would you please push 5?' 'Push it yourself.' He couldn't get up there.

"So, finally, he'd get one of the bellmen to push the button for him. Finally, he outsmarted them. He got rooms on the first and second floor."

At about 11:45 a.m. Mark Hawkins and Dan Ewald decide it's time to recycle Duke's jokes. "Every 20 minutes we tell the same jokes," said Snider.

At 11:51 a.m., a Hall of Fame, limited-edition bat from Aug. 3, 1980 — when Snider and Al Kaline were inducted into the Hall of Fame — was thunked onto the table. The brown bat had signatures in gold.

"You have to shake it a bit," said the gentleman who owned the bat as he handed the Duke a special marker with gold ink.

Duke later offers a story about teammate Jackie Robinson.

"The one story I have in my book is Jackie Robinson had a death threat at the Polo Grounds. It said if he played in this game at the Polo Grounds, he'd be shot. So the FBI was there.

"At the Polo Grounds the clubhouse is in center field, so we had to walk down over these steps and walk out on the field. There's Jackie, standing there waiting for all of us to go out on the field with him."

"I said, 'You've got to be crazy Jackie. You could get shot.'

"Before we went out, one of our outfielders, named Gene Hermanski, decided that he had it all figured out. Jackie was number 42, the only black man on our team.

"And he (Hermanski) said 'we'll send all of our uniforms out and have number 42 put on all the uniforms so he doesn't know which guy to shoot.' Smart guy."

At about 11:53 a.m., the excited, and now awed boy in the Pepperdine shirt was approaching the table.

"Pepperdine, huh?" asked the Duke.

"Yeah," said the timid youngster.

"Just the shirt. Can't afford to go to school there," chipped in the father.

"Pepperdine? Why not?" Snider asked.

"I can only work two jobs at one time," he replied.

As the two left the table, the youngster, who had received an autograph and had exchanged in some small talk with a big league star, whom he will now never forget, offered a polite, quiet "Thank you, Mr. Snider." He left with a smile.

Snider, who played from 1947 untill 1964, finished his career with 407 home runs, 2,116 hits, 1,333 runs and a .295 batting average. He hit .300 in seven seasons, led the league in runs batted in and home runs once. He also hit 20 or more home runs in 10 seasons, including five consecutive seasons with 40 or more home runs.

Snider, an intense player with exceptional defensive skills, played on three pennant-winning and one World Series-winning Dodger teams.

As Snider signed "To Donald" on a "Duke of Flatbush" plate, Donald noticed the DUKE bracelet and the Hall of Fame ring Snider was wearing.

"Do you still have all your World Series rings?" someone inquired.

"I've got them. But I don't wear them," he answered.

At 11:55 a man, who looked like Wade Boggs, only he was wearing a Brooklyn Dodgers shirt, asked Snider "Could you make it out to Stan?"

"Dan?"

"Stan. S-T-A-N."

"Oh, Stan. Most of us are hard of hearing," replied Snider, who was known as the Silver Fox because he had premature grey hair.

"What did you say?" kidded Stan.

"Hugh?" replied Duke.

Snider, still in a jovial, silly mood, decided it was time for another joke.

He asked, "How many Marichals did the Giants have?"

"Three," some yelled out.

"No," corrected the Duke, "that's the Alous. How many Marichals did they have? Just Juan (one)."

"Thank goodness," someone said.

"Thank goodness is right. If there'd have been three Marichals, then we'd really have been in trouble...Juan's a nice guy — when he's not on the mound he's a nice guy."

"Did you have trouble with him?"

"He was tough."

At 12:03 p.m., after he signed a ball right above Stan "The Man" Musial's autograph, a photograph was put out in front of him.

"Nice pop-up there, isn't it," noted Snider. "The catcher's looking up at it too. He's going to catch it."

At 12:06 a Red Man chewing tobacco card is placed on the table and Snider notes he doesn't see many of those any more.

As Hawkins, Ewald and Snider examined a National League baseball, the Duke said, "Do you know what Ron Perranoski of the Dodgers does when he signs the ball? He writes Perranoski under there," pointing just below the RO-N on the ball.

At 12:09, a boy in a blue Tiger shirt is apparently holding his 8-by-10 too loosely. Father brings his son's arm in closer to his body, so no one would bend the picture from a special occasion to be remembered, and perhaps boasted about, in the future. — Mark K. Larson, Aug. 19, 1988

* * *

Chapter 10
Memories

Remember back in the good old days, the 1960s, when the fastest way to build your collection was playing "topsies" and "leaners" — two classic forms of card flipping confrontations?

In the Aug. 2, 1985, SCD, Robert Segal describes the game of "leaners:" a "youngster sends a bubble-gum-fresh baseball card slicing through the air in frisbee-like fashion. With a cardboard sounding 'ping,' the four-cornered projectile stikes the creased and battered 'veteran' card propped against the playground wall. As both cards topple to the blacktop, an eight-year-old sharpshooter gleefully scurries over to collect a jackpot of baseball cards strewn about. That done, he withdraws a crisp new card and positions it at a 45-degree angle against the wall. Soon, a flurry of baseball cards again fills the air until one carefully aimed offering inevitably finds the mark."

In "topsies," "two marksmen took turns flinging cards toward the wall until one player became the first to have his card flutter down atop any part of a card already lying on the ground. The winner was then entitled to all the baseball cards that had been thrown."

But as time went on, not as many kids were flipping their cards or putting them in their bike spokes. Card collecting was emerging on the scene as a "real" hobby, with monetary values being placed on cards. Even Major League teams added to their legitimacy by picturing cards on team yearbooks and media guides. The Pittsburgh Pirates 1977 yearbook, the Minnesota Twins 1980 media guide and the 1978 American League Red Book all used cards for their covers, while the the New York Yankees 1978 yearbook included a pullout of 27 cards. And the Los Angeles Dodgers held perhaps the first "baseball card night," in 1980.

But Chapter 10 is an anthology of stories which brings us full circle — back to the good old days, when people collected things just for their sentimental values and the priceless memories they held.

Above: Kermit Kiecker mans his booth at Twinfest in the Metrodome. Below: The Famous Chicken and the Gorilla in action.

293

The Great Hostess Card Caper

By Eugene Wood

Way back there in the spring of 1975, I found myself wandering through the aisles of the local Piggly Wiggly Store while my wife was filling the basket from her list. I had already checked out the cereals and found nothing except the #*% Kellogg Frosted Flakes with 3-D cards.

Suddenly, a softball-sized sign proclaiming that specially-marked Hostess boxes contained three baseball cards caught my eye. My heart leaped for joy and then just as suddenly almost stopped when I remembered what Hostess was: a manufacturer of products for women. That's what I thought and I knew my wife wasn't going to let me go around the neighborhood asking the housewives to save them for me.

But I did have the presence of mind to look past the sign and there were the Twinkies, Ding Dongs, Suzy Q's and Cup Cake boxes all proudly bearing three cards apiece. Boy, was I ever relieved. Quickly, I bought a box with Lolich and a couple of other guys on it and I was hooked. I visited the stores that we traded at and asked the clerks who bought family-size Hostess products. They couldn't name anyone specifically, but all said that lots of people bought them. This wasn't exactly true because lots of people DIDN'T buy them.

I watched the shelves closely and determined that about 20 boxes a week were all that were sold at Madill. It didn't take much to determine that if I was going to get my share I was going to have to work hard. I ran an ad in the local weekly paper about seven times during the year. This brought only two responses, one of which got me three panels. The other response was much better. It was from a youngster from Tulsa who visited his grandmother here at various times during the summer and she bought him the stuff. He called me three different times and I got a total of 20 panels from him.

The local radio station (KMAD) has a program they run at 8 o'clock each morning called "Want Ads on the Air" in which you can run your 20-word blurb for four consecutive days for a dollar. I invested in that once, but it was a total failure. I also ran an ad twice in the daily paper in a larger town about 25 miles from Madill with no luck. Apparently the Northern Texas and Southern Oklahoma Card Collectors and Cattle Rustlers Club didn't see that ad as I never found any burning crosses on my front lawn.

I made homemade signs which I placed in one grocery, a barber shop and a laundry. The grocery ad brought me three panels, the barbershop brought me three or four from the wife of one of the barbers, and the one in the laundry brought me some cut cards from the daughter of the laundry owner. I must say that for a 12-year-old, she sure hadn't passed a course in card cutting.

Before next season starts, I'm going to give her a call and impress on her that it's whole panels or nothing. The laundry owner said a lady visiting from California saw the sign and told him that when she got back to California she would send me lots of cards. Obviously, she never made it home.

I made sure that the fellows I work with all knew what I was collecting. This got me half a dozen or so panels. I also notified several other railroaders that I worked with at other stations, but they weren't any help.

My steady source of supply was a local bakery. This fellow made delicious donuts and other pastry, but he ate only Twinkies, none of his own stuff. He saved me a box a week throughout the summer.

Every garage sale I heard about called for a visit, but got me only one box. Naturally, I also asked about other baseball cards and a dozen times I got this heart-breaking answer: "My boy had a big box (or closet, or trunk) full but I threw them all out about a week (or month, or year) ago." Late in the summer I found out about a neighborhood grocer, who opened boxes of Ding Dongs and sold them individually and threw the boxes away, naturally. I got to him only in time to get three or four panels.

It didn't take me long to find out that grocery store checkers got their kicks out of crushing Hostess boxes in both hands, then scooting them face down along their sticky counters. After those wrenching experiences I would place everything but the Hostess stuff on the counter.

The Hostess I would hold in my hands where they could see the price and then sack it up myself. After a few days of eyebrow raising they learned to accept my odd habit.

Asking strangers in stores to keep their Hostess boxes for me was rather difficult, but I tried it three or four times. The first time was a young lady with a baby. When I asked her if she saved the cards for anyone she admitted that she didn't even know there were any cards. I asked her if she would save them for me and she agreed. I wrote my name and phone number on the top of the box and that was the last I ever heard from her, nor did I ever see her again. I guess the store is still wondering what happened to run off such a good customer.

Getting my car serviced one time by a youngster turned out to be profitable for me. When I asked if he ever saved cards he volunteered that he had nine Hostess boxes at home. He agreed to sell them to me, and with another later sale I got a total of 17 from him.

How many boxes did I buy from stores? I didn't keep count, but I would guess about 30. The last box that appeared in Madill was on Oct. 3. A week later we were in Kansas City and cards were still on boxes of Ding Dongs there. However, Ed Brooks was in Orlando, Fla., late in August and couldn't find any cards.

Somewhere in this great land, some guy may dash into a store on Christmas Eve looking for a present for his wife and find a box of Twinkies with baseball cards.

Cards that appeared late in the season sometimes had a more brilliant color than earlier ones. Hostess corrected the Bill Madlock error and I was able to get both cards of him, as a pitcher and as infielder. I never did see a correction of the Nettles card or the one that pictured Lee May as Milt May.

What will 1976 bring? Can a poor boy from a small Oklahoma town collect 300 cards and not go mad? A year from now you'll know the answer.

Anyone like to make a bid on four dozen frozen Twinkies? — Eugene Wood, Dec. 12, 1975

* * *

The Ultimate Collectible

By Bob Lemke

Just about a year ago, three of us here in Iola bought into the ultimate sports collectible — a professional baseball team.

Doug Watson, former SCD publisher, Bruce Meagher, our company attorney, and I bought a small interest in the Wausau Timbers, the Midwest League (Class A) affiliate of the Seattle Mariners.

For those unfamiliar with minor league baseball, the Midwest League is organized baseball's largest circuit, with 12 teams (scheduled to expand to 14 for 1987). It's a full-season league, where the quality of play is highly rated, perhaps lagging behind only the California League among Class A minor leagues.

The Midwest League has sent more players to the major leagues than any other minor league. In 1985, some 150 players appeared in major league uniforms who had received part of their baseball experience in the Midwest League. Among the more familiar names: Harold Baines, Vida Blue, Cecil Cooper, Chili Davis, Carlton Fisk, Terry Forster, Rich Gossage, Orel Hershiser, Kent Hrbek, Tommy John, Ron Kittle, Gary Matthews, Paul Molitor, Dan Quisenberry, Ted Simmons, Bruce Sutter and Willie Wilson.

Wausau is certainly one of the smaller cities in the U.S. to boast a professional baseball team; current population of the city and surrounding "suburbs" is about 50,000.

While the roots of minor league baseball in Wausau go back to 1905 and the old Wisconsin State and Wisconsin-Illinois Leagues, modern minor league ball in the city traces its history to 1939 and the Northern League. From 1946-1953 Wausau was part of the Class D Wisconsin State League. For the last couple of seasons before the league went defunct, Wausau was an affiliate of the Detroit Tigers.

In 1956-1957, Wausau was a member of the Northern League, as a Reds farm club that final year.

Wausau has been part of the MWL since 1975, first as an affiliate of the N.Y. Mets; as a co-op team in 1979-80, and since 1981 — when the Timbers won the league championship — as a farm club for the Seattle Mariners.

Among Wausau's more distinguished alumni now active in the major leagues are: Neil Allen, Juan Berenguer, Ivan Calderon, Kelvin Chapman, Darnell Coles, Roy Lee Jackson, John Moses, Edwin Nunez, Jim Presley, Harold Reynolds, Alex Trevino, Dave Von Ohlen and Mookie Wilson.

To me, that's probably the greatest thing about being a minor league baseball fan — watching youngsters, some fresh out of high school, and picking out the superstars of tomorrow. I could have told you back in 1981 that when Jim Presley finally made the major leagues, you'd want to start hoarding his rookie card.

Or that Edwin Nunez had the "stuff" to bring him to the brink of becoming one of baseball's best short relievers. By the same token, there's nothing like a first-hand look to see if there is really a ballplayer behind all the hype that sometimes precedes a youngster into pro ranks.

Shawon Dunston, for example, simply did not look like a major league prospect when he was making the circuit of Midwest League teams in 1983. He batted .310 (5th best in the league), but he looked awkward around the infield and on the basepaths and fielded in the bottom half of the league's shortstops, at .914.

As far as I'm concerned, Dunston is still only a major league prospect — I'm certainly not hoarding his rookie cards to see me through my golden years.

But then, what do I know about scouting major league talent? I'm the guy who picked Razor Shines for stardom in 1981. As this is written, he's been released by the Expos and is looking for a new gig.

Being a minor league fan is one thing; being a part-owner is a whole 'nother ball game. As small as our percentage of ownership is, and as low on the ladder of organized baseball as a Class A team is, there is immense pride in being part of baseball's "family."

I bought into minor league baseball for many reasons. There are the aspects of bragging rights — owning something that very few other collectors will ever have the opportunity to have; jock-sniffing — being welcome in the locker room and on the field, meeting future superstars and faces that I remember from my baseball cards who are managing or instructing or scouting for teams around the league; and, there's an ego thing — believing that I have something to offer to America's great national pastime, even if it's only as a minority shareholder on a Class A team.

Our stock purchase was the least of our contributions to the team. Bruce has become the team's secretary-treasurer and legal counsel, Doug and I have worked with the GM in putting together the team's '85 program and in boosting souvenir sales dollars, and from time to time all of us have left our box seats to draw beers or slop mustard on hot dogs when we get a really good crowd at the game.

You may have noticed an ad in SCD several issues back offering Wausau minor league jerseys for sale. Previously, the team just let these collector's items slip away from the locker room and storage closet, or sold them for a couple of bucks apiece to local softball teams. We sold out 27 of the 29 jerseys we had left over from the 1980-1982 seasons at $25 apiece. A nice piece of income for a minor league team.

For next season, I hope to find time to be even more active with the team. There is a real challenge to trying to raise money or cut costs that will help the team's bottom line. At this level, minor league baseball ownership is not a money-making proposition. About the best you can hope for is a break-even year or maybe just a few dollars in the black ink column.

Doug, Bruce and I are at a bit of a handicap, being located some 60 miles away from Wausau, but we do the best we can to get to as many games as possible. We've got a pair of box seats among us, and SCD has a pair. If you're ever going to be in the area and want to catch a ball game, drop me a line or give me a call; chances are the tickets are available — maybe I can even meet you over there.

Speaking of tickets, that's another advantage of being part of baseball's official family. Any time the Mariners are in Milwaukee, or any other place I happen to be, a call to the front office in Seattle will net some freebies. Like Bob Uecker says in the commercial, "Bingo. I must be in the front row."

I'll be going to spring training for the first time ever this year, down in Arizona. Besides watching the Mariners system in action, I'll be spending some time with three of my other favorite teams, the Cubs, Indians and Brewers.

Then there are the team and league meetings. I love 'em. Many of our stockholders and advisory board members have been associated with the Timbers for the team's entire 10-year history. And around the league there are people who have been part of other teams for 25 or 30 years. That makes for some great baseball talk — and really juicy gossip.

Like which All-Star infielder left more than one unwed mother when he moved up, and which popular rookie left one local girl literally standing at the altar. Or which of baseball's new millionaires stuck his MWL club with a $100 bill for bats. Inside baseball tidbits like these really make the guys on the baseball cards come to life.

"How did the Wausau Timbers do in 1985?" you ask. Don't ask. We finished 32 games out (52-85). In all of organized baseball, only one team was worse — another minor league team, the Pittsburgh Pirates.

But there's hope for '86. In the last half of the season we began to get some better players from the June draft, and Seattle has semi-promised to leave half a dozen of them here for '86, so we have the nucleus of a good team before we even get to spring training. I'll keep you posted next season. — Bob Lemke, The Bleacher Bum, Jan. 3, 1986

* * *

Card Set Brings Back Memories Of The Summer Of '71

By Scott Blanchard

Rainy spring days are natural invitations for us to browse through our collections. Today is one such day when I pull a binder from the shelves in my "memorabilia room."

Ah, my 1971 Topps set. Paging through those black-bordered beauties brings back memories of how I assembled this set, but I also recall the summer of 1971 with friends and marathon baseball games. These cards, simple pictures of boyhood idols, allow me to return to a time when the only worries I had were over having enough money for more packs of cards or having enough guys for a baseball game.

During the summer of '71, I was 10 and my brother Todd was 9 — ripe ages for card collecting and game playing. We lived about five miles outside of Marinette, Wis., in an area where a dozen other kids our age shared our interests — frogs, turtles, forts, popsicles, cards and sports. Playing sports, especially baseball, allowed us to enter a fantasy world, to become our favorite all-stars and to conveniently forget that we had chores to do back home.

To prepare for that particular summer, the gang — Mike, the two Steves, Chopper, Mark, Chuckie, my brother and I — decided to develop our old ballfield into something more professional. You see, the field we played on was just that — a field. But by 1971 we felt that we were no longer "kids" just playing with a whiffle ball, and we felt we needed a field that better reflected our maturing talents as ballplayers.

After some planning about how we were going to complete our undertaking, we were ready to go. Even though we were supposed to dust the furniture, shake the rugs, trim the bushes, or mow the lawn, we were all eager to really work on our field. With the help of Chopper's lawn tractor and a couple of push mowers, we cut down the tall grass and straw and raked the area into respectable shape. Since we didn't have chalk or lime to mark the foul lines we didn't mow outside of fair territory. Our foul lines were two feet tall!

Next, we dug sliding pits around the bases and created a pitcher's mound; a chunk of two-by-four served as the rubber. Our field was starting to take shape.

Unfortunately, since we never had enough guys for full, nine-man teams, the batting team usually supplied the catcher. However, the "catcher" was often reluctant to tag out his own teammates at home and he never chased wild throws. So, we felt a backstop was in order. After secretly "borrowing" a saw and an ax from Mark's house, we set out to cut down three poplar trees about 12 feet tall.

After doing this and stripping the trees of their branches, we dug three holes several feet behind home plate, stuck the trees into them, and filled the holes solidly with rocks, leaves, and dirt. To complete our backstop, we nailed chicken wire, "obtained" from the local lumber yard, onto the trees. Presto!

Even after all this work, something was still missing. If we were going to consider this field a professional diamond, we needed an outfield fence and a dugout! So, we took a roll of snow fence that the county road crews had conveniently left from the previous winter and installed it in straightaway center field.

For the dugout, Todd and I dug a 10-foot-by-3-foot trench, about two feet deep, inserted a pine bench, again courtesy of the lumber yard, and we were all set. Our field, after a week's worth of hard work, was ready for official games. Not bad for a bunch of 9- to 11-year-olds!

What a beautiful field it was, too. There were still some natural hazards that we couldn't do much about — the line of 40-foot willows behind first base that took away most of right field, the mass of raspberry and blackberry bushes in center, the creek that ran deep in left, and, of course, the natural bumps on the field that made any grounder an adventure. We didn't despise these hazards, though, but accepted them as challenges. Besides, these gave our field a personality, sort of like the ivy on the walls at Wrigley.

Our work completed, we couldn't wait to play our first game. Typical games were not simply nine-inning affairs. They often went 25 or more innings, six or seven hours long. And the days that we had doubleheaders — wow! We were always well-prepared, though. Each of the guys came supplied with peanut butter sandwiches, chips, and canteens full of Kool-Aid.

With our lunches packed and our gloves well-oiled, the gang assembled at the field promptly at 10 a.m. every day. Sides were quickly chosen, although teammates seldom varied. Todd led the Braves and I captained the Pirates. The home team was chosen by the traditional tossing of the bat ("Eagle's claw — we take last raps").

On a typical day, it wasn't Todd versus Chopper or Steve, but Phil Niekro versus Steve Blass or Dock Ellis ("Niekro's knuckler's workin' today! Another one's gone!"). Who pitched rarely mattered though, since the defense consisted of the pitcher, two or three outfielders, and one or two infielders. Because of this, runs were scored in a hurry and in bunches; 60-53 scores were not uncommon in our games.

There was usually a great long-ball contest each game, too: me, Willie Stargell, versus Mike, the Hammer, Hank Aaron. ("Stargell puts another one over the fence...you go get it — it's in the creek again.")

The action, the camaraderie, the talk was all big league. ("Perez to Millan to Cepeda! Double play!" "No way! Tie goes to the runner!") We were not just the neighborhood kids playing sandlot ball, but the incarnations of our heroes performing in our home park. ("Sanguillen slaps another double into the gap...Garr drills one down the line...Clemente makes the throw...Oh, what a peg!")

In between the action and the banter was talk of the current major league standings, records, who was hot and who was bombing (I constantly got into heated arguments with Steve about his Reds and my Bucs). We compared our stats to our heroes, of course. We also discussed who was getting doubles in their packs of cards and who we'd be willing to trade (Steve always hoarded the Benches and the Roses).

Much of this occurred not during the seventh-inning stretch, but in the 15th- or 16th-inning stretch, when we attacked our food in the dugout. The combination of peanut butter, sand and sweat made for some interesting sandwiches, but we didn't care.

After a little break, we again took to the field for a couple more hours, or until we heard the dreaded, "Mark! Steve! Mike! Come on home!" or my mom ringing our supper bell (specially installed since we'd never acknowledged her call from a quarter-mile away).

The victors would saunter away gloating about how many home runs they had hit or about the rifle throws that nailed runners at the plate. The losers, well, they'd walk away mumbling something about, "Wait'll tomorrow." Sometimes the wait seemed like forever.

The tomorrows did come, though — 15 years worth. Skimming through these cards now brings Mays, Aaron, Clemente, and Gibson back to live action, not to mention the likes of Aurelio Monteagudo, Bill Zepp, Woody Woodward, and J.C. Martin. The '71 Series flashes through my mind, too — Clemente's outstanding performance, Sanguillen bearhugging Blass, and Blass, in turn, sharing a special moment with his father in the clubhouse. This particular set of cards, though, also lets me escape back to simpler times with the gang on our field.

While the 1971 Topps set may be tough to find or keep in Ex-Mint condition, on this fall rainy day the condition is the farthest thing from my mind. These simple cards have helped me recall a precious summer and are worth more to me than the value listed in any price guide.
— Scott Blanchard, May 8, 1987

* * *

Whatever Happened To #755?

By Tim Sullivan

July 20, 1976. Milwaukee County Stadium. Dick Drago is on the mound for the California Angels. It's the seventh inning, and Drago tries to sneak a fastball past the Milwaukee Brewer batter, Henry Aaron.

The move backfires on Drago. The 41-year-old Aaron, he of the infamous quick wrists, calmly unleashes his patented power swing and drives the pitch over the left-field fence. Milwaukee goes on to win, 6-2.

History will show that Aaron's blast on that fateful July evening in 1976 was the last home run that Aaron would ever hit in a major league game. His drive off Drago was home run #755.

In case any of you have been living in caves for the past 12 years, it should be pointed out that Hank Aaron is the all-time career home run champion in the history of major league baseball. Numero Uno. Nobody has hit more major league home runs than Henry Aaron.

Did anyone ever wonder what happened to that baseball? Whatever became of Hank Aaron's #755 home run baseball?

To find out, Sports Collectors Digest contacted Tim Sullivan, a freelance sportswriter from Stevens Point, Wis. It was a good decision. Sullivan is also the agent of the fellow who caught the historic baseball.

In what might be considered a journalistic "first," writer Sullivan will now interview agent Sullivan to get a rundown on the entire matter. In other words, he agreed to interview himself.

SCD: Let's start from the beginning. Is there a beginning to this episode?

Sullivan: Sure. The whole thing started on July 20, 1976, when Henry took Dick Drago over the wall.

SCD: Fair enough. What happened next?

Sullivan: Well, a member of the Brewers' grounds crew, Dick Arndt, was sitting with two other workers way down the left-field line. Arndt was assigned to be a spotter for the bullpen. He was supposed to watch for a pitching change. Once a change was made, he'd open the gate so another guy could drive a car to the bullpen and get the relief pitcher. After that was done, he'd wait until the guy got back with the car and shut the gate again.

Anyways, Aaron's homer, a line drive, went about 10 feet over Arndt's head. It hit the seats and fell back down. Arndt went over, picked it up, and took the ball back to where he was sitting.

SCD: That sounded pretty easy. What happened after Arndt came back with the ball?

Sullivan: A few minutes later, Arndt's boss, Harry Gill, came over and told Arndt that the Brewers wanted the ball. Apparently, they were giving all of Hank's later home run balls back to him. Arndt asked Gill if he could give the ball back to Aaron himself, and Gill said sure.

So, after the game, Arndt walked to the Brewers' dugout hoping to find Aaron so he could give him the ball.

Unfortunately, Aaron wasn't in the dugout. Instead, Arndt was confronted by the Brewers' equipment manager. The equipment manager told Arndt that he couldn't meet with Aaron because the Brewers were busy packing for a road trip the next day to Kansas City.

However, the equipment manager also said that Arndt should give him the ball. Then, when the Brewers came back from the road trip, they'd take a picture of Arndt giving the ball to Aaron and they'd give Arndt one of Hank's bats and an autographed baseball.

SCD: Wow! The Brewers were really giving up a lot, eh?

Sullivan: Well, there's something we must remember here. This all happened in late July. The season still had a couple of months to go. I don't think anybody knew that ball would be Aaron's final homer.

At any rate, Arndt told the guy that he'd have to think about it. The equipment manager told Arndt that he better decide what he wanted to do before the night was over.

SCD: So what did Arndt decide?

Sullivan: Arndt decided to take the ball home with him. He didn't think it was a really big deal.

SCD: What happened next?

Sullivan: The Brewers fired Arndt the next day for leaving the ballpark with club property. They also deducted $5 from his final paycheck to cover the cost of the ball.

SCD: Would it be accurate to say that the Brewers and Dick Arndt don't quite get along?

Sullivan: I think that's a pretty fair assessment. You could take it to the bank.

SCD: OK. So Arndt took the ball home and got fired the next day. What was the next development?

Sullivan: I really give Arndt credit for this. The guy had just been fired. He felt that he had to document the fact that he had one of Aaron's home run balls, so he went to the Milwaukee Journal. They ran a story about it three days later, and the headline said "Groundskeeper Fired Over Aaron's Home Run."

Up to then, there's a major irony about all this that seems to escape everyone. See, the number one Henry Aaron fan during this time was probably Mr. Dick Arndt. The only reason he signed up that year to be a member of the grounds crew was because Hank was on the Brewers. Arndt was merely hoping that he might stumble across one of Hank's bats or something.

SCD: If Arndt was such a big fan of Aaron's, why didn't he find some way to get the ball back to him later?

Sullivan: That's the best question so far. Now keep in mind...here's a guy who's just been fired. Arndt obviously didn't have much love left for the Brewers.

Secondly, remember the timing. A few more weeks went by and Aaron was playing less and less. It began to dawn on Arndt that this wasn't just another baseball. It was the final home run. Arndt wasn't about to rush into anything.

SCD: Did Arndt ever try to get in contact with Aaron?

Sullivan: I can tell you something better than that. For a short time, Aaron was actually holding the ball in his hand!

SCD: Could you run that by again?

Sullivan: Later on in the '76 season, Arndt went back for a Brewer game and waited for Hank underneath the stands where Aaron liked to park his car. Dick wanted him to sign the ball and put "755" on it. Hank took the ball, told Arndt that he wouldn't sign it, and gave the ball back. He also told Arndt that he was supposed to have given it to the Brewers, who would then have given it to him.

SCD: That showed some class on Aaron's part. He could've kept the ball right then.

Sullivan: That's right, and don't think that Arndt doesn't realize it. The problem is, Arndt tried to explain everything to Hank right then, but Aaron was with some people and had to go. Arndt has a ton of respect for Hank handing him back the ball.

SCD: Let's take a little break in the action. How did you find out about Arndt, and better yet, how did you become his agent?

Sullivan: OK. I could take an hour alone on this, but I'll try to make it brief. In July of 1985, I met Ron Carlson. He's a cop in Stevens Point. One night we were sitting in the stands at a softball game firing sports trivia questions back and forth. Carlson suddenly stunned me when he asked "Who caught Hank Aaron's final home run?"

I told him I didn't have the slightest idea, and he smiled and said, "Dick Arndt."

SCD: How did Carlson know?

Sullivan: It turns out Ron was also on the Brewer grounds crew that night. He was sitting two chairs away from Arndt when he saw him pick up the homer.

SCD: What happened next with Carlson?

Sullivan: Well, I don't remember which one of us thought of it, but we decided to try to track Arndt down to see if he still had the ball.

Carlson called all the Arndts listed in Milwaukee. He hit a dead end. Then Ron drove to Milwaukee (he's from there) and looked around. The result was always the same. Nobody knew where Arndt was.

SCD: But you must've eventually found him, right?

Sullivan: Yeah. It was a one in a million shot. Pure luck. But before I get to that, there was another deal here. Ronnie and I thought hey, why bother looking for Arndt anyways? Let's do the next best thing and call Aaron.

SCD: Did you?

Sullivan: Yes, and this took some guts. See, Hank was my boyhood idol, too. I called the Atlanta Braves, asked for Hank, and a girl took my number and said he'd call me back. I didn't give it much hope but, sure enough, Hank Aaron called me back a few hours later and I dropped the phone. It was exciting as hell.

Anyways, Hank said he didn't have #755 but would love to get it. I told him we'd keep trying to find Arndt.

SCD: So you found Arndt?

Sullivan: As incredible as it may seem, Arndt found me! See, the University of Wisconsin-Stevens Point Pointer Alumnus paper carried a small story on me about catching four balls or something, and at the end of the story I mentioned that I was looking for Arndt.

The note in the Pointer Alumnus story generated a lot of reactions. In early February of '86, I got a call from Gene Mueller of radio station WKTI in Milwaukee. He went to school in Point, saw the Alumnus thing, and had Carlson and me on the air the next morning. After the show aired, a lady from Milwaukee called WKTI. The lady said she didn't know where Arndt was, but she said she had the bat that Hank hit his home run with!

SCD: Then, the radio show didn't lead you to Arndt, right?

Sullivan: No, but the Alumnus note did. Just when Carlson and I were thinking about giving up our search for Arndt, a guy called me two days after the radio show. He said, "I'm Dick Arndt, and you can stop looking for me in Milwaukee. I live in Albuquerque, N.M."

SCD: You must've been shocked.

Sullivan: Darn right I was. It turns out that Arndt's mother, who lives in Houston, Texas, somehow got a copy of the Alumnus paper, read about our search, and informed Dick in Albuquerque. That's what I mean by a million to one shot.

SCD: OK. You finally made contact with Arndt. What did he have to say?

Sullivan: Basically, he said he still had the ball. He moved to New Mexico shortly after he was fired and was selling office furniture. I told him about my talk with Aaron, and he said he wanted in the worst way to get the ball back to Hank. However, and this is important, he also realized that the ball was very valuable and that he should be compensated in some way.

SCD: So what steps were taken to get Aaron the baseball?

Sullivan: Obviously, the first step was that Dick kept the ball over all those years. He had several chances to sell it to private collectors, but he always refused because he wanted to be positive the ball would end up with Hank. Dick asked me if I'd serve as something of a go-between with him and Aaron so something could finally be worked out.

SCD: What happened out of that arrangement?

Sullivan: Not a hell of a lot, because too many people got involved.

SCD: Please explain.

Sullivan: It gets confusing, but I'll try. See, in the spring of '86, every other two days or so I'd get phone calls for either Hank or Dick. Hank was always asking "What does the guy want for the ball?", and Dick kept saying "Nothing from Hank, but I should get something from somebody."

The whole deal was getting bogged down. Then I found out that the Brewer Old-Timers were going to play the Equitable Old-Timers on June 7 at County Stadium. Hank said he planned on being there, and Dick said he'd love to present the ball to Aaron at County Stadium 10 years after Hank hit the homer in the same ballpark. The situation was perfect.

SCD: So what went wrong?

Sullivan: I still don't know. By this time, Hank got his agent, Alicia Berns, involved. I knew she had a few talks with Arndt and I thought everything was all set. In fact, Dick Hackett, the Brewers' vice president of marketing, already cleared the way for a presentation at home plate. Keep in mind that Hackett and Arndt aren't exactly buddies.

Anyways, the Old-Timers game was on a Saturday, and the thing fell through Friday afternoon. The way I understand it, Arndt was offered $5,000 plus several thousand dollars worth of baseball memorabilia, such as Bob Buhl's Milwaukee Brave uniform. The money was to have come not from Hank but from a collector in New Jersey who is a business partner of George Steinbrenner.

A couple of days before the game, Arndt decided to ask for $10,000 and forget the memorabilia. The deal fell through a short time later.

SCD: So what's your opinion of the Old-Timers' fiasco?

Sullivan: I wanted it to go smoothly, and it obviously didn't. However, the more I think about it, the more I think Hank and Alicia blew it. Dick Arndt is no dummy, and he still has the ball.

Also, he knows that the guy who caught Roger Maris' 61st homer in '61 received $5,000 from a restaurant owner. $5,000 in 1961 is worth about $25,000 today.

SCD: Did the Old-Timers' Day leave a bad taste?

Sullivan: You better believe it. I understand Hackett went through the roof, and so did Alicia Berns. On the other hand, let's be reasonable. Arndt wasn't exactly asking for the moon, either.

SCD: What happened after the deal fell through?

Sullivan: Arndt called a few days later and said, "Listen, I tried my best, but it wasn't to be. Since you've been behind me from the beginning, I'm willing to make you my agent. Let's try to sell the ball."

SCD: What was your response?

Sullivan: I told Dick I'd love to help him sell the ball. Heck, I'm not sure what an agent does...all the ins and outs...but if he says I'm his agent, then I'm his agent. Other than a few phone calls, I wasn't out anything anyways.

SCD: So how is your "agenting" coming along?

Sullivan: The first thing I did was tell this whole story to a friend of mine who's a huge collector. He said, "Call Arndt. I might be interested."

Hey, what's an agent for, right? So Arndt and my collector friend talked a few times. They kicked around a certain figure but nothing ever really happened.

SCD: Then your first attempt as an agent was a near miss, correct?

Sullivan: A very, very near miss. But that's fine with me. It's a serious situation, but I've had a lot of fun doing it. This has come a long way since my trivia session with Ron Carlson.

SCD: Have you made moves?

Sullivan: Sure. A year and a half ago, Dick and I took out an ad right in SCD. We got 10 replies.

SCD: Were they favorable?

Sullivan: Yes and no. Based on that ad, you better believe me there's a ton of people out there who want that baseball. Unfortunately, they can't meet the price.

SCD: What's the price?

Sullivan: 25 big ones. As long as I'm Arndt's agent, nobody is getting that baseball for less than $25,000.

SCD: $25,000 is a lot of money.

Sullivan: That's right, but we're talking about a lot of baseball here, too.

Out of the 30 or so replies I received, at least 10 of the collectors thought my price was in line. None of them had the money, but they didn't think it was unreasonable. They were merely inquiring.

On the other hand, a few of them hit the roof. I'm not mentioning any names, but New Jersey comes to mind immediately. You never know about these things. One guy offered to trade a Ty Cobb uniform for the ball. No way.

The funniest call I received came from a guy who said he was calling from Atlanta. He said right off the bat, "Listen, I don't think your man even has the ball." I said, "If he doesn't have it, then you tell me who does." The guy hung up.

SCD: Have you tried any other avenues as an agent?

Sullivan: Yes. I sent a letter to Ted Turner. A Mr. Kasten of the Braves wrote back saying that Turner wasn't interested. Then I tried Howard Cosell. No answer. Same with Steinbrenner.

We figure, what the hell? If you're going to shoot big, then go to the big guys, right? They got the money. Look at what they pay the players. Right now, we're trying to get ahold of Bill Cosby. We're also thinking about trying Jerry Lewis or Sammy Davis Jr.

SCD: One final question. Do you think you'll ever sell the ball?

Sullivan: Probably not with me as an agent, but you never know. There must be someone out there. Maybe the ball will end up in Japan, but I know Arndt wouldn't want it to happen that way. Geez, the ball is part of Americana. I really don't care if the ball stays in Albuquerque. As long as Dick still has it, the ball ain't hurting anybody. — Tim Sullivan, April 29, 1988

* * *

See How A Baseball Team Responds To Fans, Collectors

By David Craft

In his four years as the St. Louis Cardinals' director of promotions, Dan Farrell has never collected an autographed baseball or card or photo, yet he's well aware of the value people attach to such things.

"I've just never been inclined that way," Farrell recently told Sports Collectors Digest. "I own a set of the Surf (detergent) books put out by the clubs for that particular promotion last year, but I'm looking at giving them to a charity. I know it would be a major auction item for them."

Marty Hendin, on the other hand, may never have to repaint his office walls for the simple reason you can't find the walls.

Hendin, the Cardinals vice president of marketing and a club official since 1973, has accumulated so much Cardinals memorabilia that visitors wonder if they've walked into the St. Louis Sports Hall of Fame, which is actually located a few doors down in Stadium Plaza.

Posters, prints, mugs, baseballs, bats, ashtrays, Cardinal mascot "Fredbird" in various configurations — perusing Hendin's office from floor to ceiling leaves little doubt who's the chief collector among the club's front office people.

Farrell and Hendin provide a study in contrast as far as collecting goes, yet the two men and their colleagues team up to develop a series of popular promotions and giveaways throughout each baseball season. Some items are presented to people as they enter the ballpark. Others are distributed through the sponsor of a specific item, such as a fast-food chain or local service stations.

The ones who benefit the most from these promotions are the young fans and collectors.

Dan Farrell, director of promotions for the St. Louis Cardinals.

"That's probably one of the drawbacks as far as collectors go," Farrell said. "For example, this year's 25-player 'Smokey Bear' card set will be for the kids, 15 and under.

"It's our opinion that this is the kind of thing we'd like to have in the hands of youngsters. The fire tips from the U.S. Forest Service are obviously geared toward the younger kids, and that's the market we're going after with this giveaway."

The set of 3-by-5 player cards will be given away only at Busch Stadium the night of July 19, when the Cardinals take on the Dodgers.

Farrell suggests that adults who want to collect a set of the "Smokey" cards "round up a couple of kids and come to the ball game that night."

The U.S. Forest Service and Harry R. "Punky" McClellan, the man with whom Farrell corresponds on the "Smokey" project, get rave reviews from the Cardinals' young administrator.

"They did an outstanding job in connecting Smokey the Bear, fire tips and Major League Baseball," Farrell said. "We had the cards done for each individual player and gave them to the players to use in autograph sessions and fan mail. The players went through them like crazy and were continually coming back to us for more cards."

Several hundred complete, 25-man sets were left over, however, and once people learned of their existence the remaining sets were gone with the mail-order wind. The club, Farrell emphasizes, never intended the set for mail-order sale, adding that the Cardinals made no profit from the secondary distribution.

The ballclub has no intention at this time of selling this year's "Smokey" set after the giveaway, either, although an arrangement might be made with the Forest Service that would turn over the revenue to the Missouri Department of Conservation.

Another alternative for the older collector is to invest in this year's black-and-white card set, which will be available sometime in June. The collector, regardless of age, can purchase this card set that features head shots of the Cardinal players. This type of black-and-white postcards have been distributed by the club for more than 30 years.

The club does not make any money off the sale of these black-and-white sets, Farrell says. Last year's sets cost $3.50 each, but that to-be-determined cost may slightly increase due to higher postal rates. The postcard set price covers the cost of printing.

Fans who write in to request such items as a decal, a schedule, a list of upcoming season promotions or a Cardinals gift guide are likely to get a positive response in short order.

Other than that, however, the Cardinals — and most likely, other Major League clubs as well — don't sell collectibles through the mail.

"Basically, we just don't sell any of our promotional material," Farrell said. "For instance, we do calendars at the beginning of the year with the Hardee's name on them, but we won't sell the excess number of calendars. We give them to Hardee's with the very strict restriction that they do not sell them.

"We don't sell anything with the sponsor logo on it, nor do we sell anything featuring the likeness of the ballplayers without first reaching an agreement with them."

One thing the Cardinals do sell to the public is the team's media guide. As Ed McMahon might say of it, "Everything you'd ever wanna know about the Cardinals franchise is in that $6 book."

Approximately 10,000 Cardinals media guides were sold last year, a figure likely to be repeated this year in the wake of the team's 1987 success.

As for player fan mail sent to Busch Stadium, Farrell says all of it is turned over to the individual players. The volume of mail, he adds, is tremendous, and people should not be too disappointed if their letters and requests are not answered.

Certainly, sloppy form letters from collectors are likely to get pitched in the wastebasket without guilt. Joe Cunningham, a Cardinal first baseman outfielder from 1954-61 and now the clubs's director of community relations and group sales, showed Farrell a form letter that began: "Dear -----," with the blank filled in with the player's name and the body of the letter asking the player to "please sign the enclosed cards and return them to me in this stamped, self-addressed envelope."

It has gotten to the point where players are having difficulty separating the true fans from the people who hope to resell the autographed items at a profit, Cardinal officials say.

"I know the ballplayers want to be more responsive to their fans, especially the kids," Farrell said. "If I were a kid wanting some player autographs, I'd make my favorite player a John Morris or a Jose Oquendo or a Curt Ford — guys who aren't getting reams of mail.

"Then, I would write them a personal letter. Write them something that shows you're interested in their careers and hope they do well, and then ask them if they would sign that item you'd like signed."

Ah, signing. The concept takes on special significance for Farrell, who has accompanied Cardinal players on several caravans that featured autograph signing. In the past the club has tried to adhere to its policy of one autograph per person, but some people have taken advantage of situations by foisting numerous cards, baseballs or photos on the players.

That has led to stalled lines and unhappy fans toward the back who failed to get their collectibles signed because time ran out.

Sometimes, the sheer number of fans who show up for a signing, even if the rules are followed, means a last-minute change in plans.

Farrell recalls the time when several Cardinals, including former second baseman and current coach Red Schoendienst, arrived at a gymnasium to find 300 people in line inside and another 2,000 in line outside. The temperature was at or below the freezing mark.

"We brought everybody into the gym, all 2,000 of them, and sat them down and had a question-and-answer session," Farrell recalled. "While some people may have been disappointed they didn't get any autographs, many more were delighted they could see the players and ask them questions directly. It really turned out well."

The Cardinals, incidentally, are considering dropping the autograph sessions from their future caravans because of logistics and time constraints. A final decision has yet to be made.

In addition to the yearly caravans, the ballplayers make a substantial number of guest appearances at other functions.

"It varies from player to player," Farrell said, "but each one, on the average, makes about five appearances every year. We probably book more than a hundred appearances each year just through our offices here."

Some collectors focus their attention on player equipment. The Cardinals used to have a well-defined sales outlet for old, used jerseys and the like via distributors who were friends with the clubhouse manager, but Farrell says that pipeline has pretty much dried up.

"We'd get a nice little resale off the jerseys and just put that money right back into the system here," Farrell said, "but I don't think that's going to be done anymore. I'm pretty sure the club's just going to recycle the jerseys into the minor league system or give them away to charity. Other clubs, too, are probably either doing that or heading in that direction."

The Cardinals, like other clubs, already do a lot of work with charitable organizations and causes. Fund-raising efforts by the Pinch-Hitters Association — a group of ballplayers' wives and the wives of front-office people and local journalists — have brought in tens of thousands of dollars over the past couple of years.

The Pinch-Hitters' main event every year is the "Ball-B-Que," held at Grant's Farm, a 281-acre tract operated by the Anheuser-Busch Co. Inc. It's a first-class banquet that features participation by many of the Cardinals players who take part in a fashion show and sign autographs. And, Farrell says, the club auctions off "an awful lot" of merchandise.

"That's basically the way the club handles it," Farrell said, referring to excess collectibles and promotional items. "We just don't have enough to ship it off to various charities around the country, but the ballclub can focus on one or several local charities and help out in that way."

Promotions geared for the adult fan are part of the Cardinals' game plan too. On specified nights at Busch Stadium this year, the club will offer to the first 35,000 fans age 21 and older with a paid admission a free thermal beer mug, a rally towel, a coffee mug and other useful collectibles.

Another night with the older fan in mind is Redbirds book night, when the first 30,000 fans age 16 and older with a paid admission will receive a free copy of the 1987 revised edition of Bob Broeg's history of Cardinals baseball. And, of course, the club has planned several promotions for the whole family, such as the Equitable Old-Timers Game/Six Flags Over Mid-America day.

"We have a heavy promotion schedule," Farrell said, "and one of the things we strive for is giving away items with a higher perceived value than say, a paper item such as a poster. Premium items are what we look at, things that people will want to keep rather than toss in the trash."

With all the promotions Farrell's involved in during the season, he has little time to follow the team's ups and downs.

"When the team's at home I'm so busy I rarely see a ball game," he said. "Oh, I might have the radio on in the office or something, but I love when the team's on the road because then I can sit back and watch it (on TV) as a fan would, and just enjoy the ball game." — David Craft, April 29, 1988

* * *

In Search Of The Elusive Hartlands

By Tim Sullivan

Everything started in the summer of 1984. A normal day was about to turn into an obsession.

Back in the summer of '84, I was at my neighbor's house watching a Cubs' game on television. Actually, my neighbor, Bob "Ma" Pesch, was the one interested in the game. My eyes were glued to his baseball statues on top of the set.

When Bob left the room, I walked over to the television set for a closer look. Suddenly, I stood face to face with three eight-inch plastic statues of Hank Aaron, Yogi Berra, and Harmon Killebrew.

It was uncanny how those statues looked exactly like the players they were supposed to represent. You could almost imagine Berra telling Aaron that his bat label wasn't facing up, and if you listened closely, you could also hear Aaron reply that he wasn't up there to read.

A few minutes later, Pesch came back into the room and saw me staring at his statues. Before I could utter a single word, he snapped, "Yes, I know those are great and no, you can't have any."

Of course, he had read my mind. No true-blue baseball fan could look at a bunch of Hartland statues without wanting a couple for himself.

The minute I walked out of Pesch's house, I knew I was hooked. Somehow or another, I had to get my hands on some Hartlands.

This wasn't easy. I soon found out that Hartland statues are very difficult to find. A person doesn't simply walk into a local dime store and tell the clerk that he'd like to buy a Roger Maris statue. Those days were over in 1963.

The reason that the Hartland statues aren't available in stores is because the company stopped making them over 25 years ago. From 1958 to 1963, the Hartland Plastics Co. of Hartland, Wis., produced a series of baseball, football and TV western star plastic statues.

In 1960, the first line of Hartland statues to be sold at concession stands included figurines of Eddie Mathews, Hank Aaron, Warren Spahn, Mickey Mantle, and Babe Ruth. The sales were so successful that the company later added statues of Chicago stars Ernie Banks, Nellie Fox, and Luis Aparicio.

Following that, Hartland also cranked out statues of Duke Snider, Don Drysdale, Yogi Berra, Stan Musial, Willie Mays, Ted Williams, Roger Maris, Harmon Killebrew, Rocky Colavito, and Dick Groat. For anyone who might be wondering, there were no Hartland statues made of Bob Uecker.

The Hartland statues ingeniously portray each player in a nostalgic and characteristic pose. Ernie Banks stands proudly upright with his bat cocked as he prepares to launch one out of Wrigley. Willie Mays is positioned to snare a routine fly ball (probably hit by Uecker) with his patented basket catch. Don Drysdale is captured in his follow-through motion which suggests that he just drilled some poor clown in the leg with a blazing heater.

I'm telling you, those statues almost seem to come to life.

In 1963, Hartland Plastics was sold to Revlon and the short but glorious statue-making production came to an end. The world said hello to compact cosmetic cases and goodbye to the little Duke Sniders and Ernie Banks. A great era had ended.

However, in the few years that the statues were made, Hartland pumped out about 150,000 each of the three Milwaukee Braves, Mantle, and Ruth. One hundred thousand statues of Williams, Mays, Aparicio, and Fox came down the line, and 75,000 figurines of Berra and Maris saw the light. Approximately 50,000 statues of Banks, Drysdale, Musial, Snider, and Killebrew were made.

At the other end of the lineup, only 10,000 Rocky Colavito statues were sold, and only a mere 5,000 Dick Groats ever went on the market. Obviously, because of the numbers, the Groat statue is the toughest one to find.

Not that any of this made any difference to me, you see. By 1963, there were about 1,632,500 Hartland statues out on the market, and as recently as 1984, I didn't have a single one.

So how did Ma Pesch get his? Simple. His parents bought a few Hartlands over 25 years ago at County Stadium when the Braves were still in Milwaukee. Each statue, which came in a small cardboard box, retailed for $2.98.

In the back of my mind, I seemed to remember that another guy in town, Donny Lind, used to display some baseball statues in his front bay window during our Little League days. I got on the phone and asked him if he still had the statues.

Lind replied, "Sure, I have the complete set. All 18."

A start for me perhaps? I cleared my throat and asked, "Uh, Donny, what are the chances of you selling some of them to me?"

He answered, "Well, I'll sell them to you as soon as I'm done looking at them."

That was fine with me. "When," I asked, "would that be?"

Donny didn't hesitate. He replied. "Oh, in about another 50 years."

Terrific. My "collection" was still holding at zero. Pesch and Lind weren't selling, so I had to start looking someplace else.

A few months went by, and a different plan of attack was in order. Back then, I didn't know that people advertised Hartlands in Sports Collectors Digest, so I decided to try finding some of these things in a toy store. After all, they used to be sold in novelty shops, too. Better late than never.

With visions of old Hartlands hiding in a remote corner, I walked downtown to a small toy store. The manager's name was Bonnie, and I got right to the point.

"Bonnie," I asked, "do you sell small plastic baseball statues?"

Bonnie said no. Then she added a shocker by saying, "But my son has one of them at home."

Hallelujah! Maybe the kid wanted to unload it.

With a pounding heart, I gave Bonnie a description of the Hartlands I saw at Pesch's (he had five more in a closet) and asked her if any of them rang a bell.

Apparently, something got lost in the translation when I gave a description of the Hartlands because Bonnie said "From what you've told me, I think my son has either Eddie Mathews or Hank Aaron. Whoever the player is, I know he still wants to keep the statue."

Man, was I doing great. I'm not sure how anyone could confuse Hank Aaron with Eddie Mathews. For one thing, Mathews is in a fielding pose while Aaron is shown batting. However, I did know that I still didn't have any Hartlands.

Since toy stores were now ruled out, it seemed like the next best bet was garage sales. Unfortunately, I bombed out twice, 0 for 2...just like Germany in world wars. At the first stop, the only item that remained were some sewing machines, luggage, books, and an old canoe. No Stan Musials were lurking anywhere.

The second place wasn't much help, either. I explained to a nice gentleman everything there was to know about Hartlands. He thanked me and said he'd keep an eye out for them. It turned out the guy was only browsing around looking for a used bowling ball.

My search for the elusive statues was getting nowhere. Donny Lind owned a complete set, Ma Pesch closely guarded seven or eight, and a little kid had one that maybe was a Brave. Meanwhile, I was still shut out. It was ridiculous.

The next possibility was a flea market. A freezing rain was falling as I drove to my destination. It was early in the morning and the place was already crowded. A 30-minute walk around the floor followed, but no Hartlands were sighted. Just when I was ready to leave, I suddenly spotted a table with a bunch of dolls on it.

The lady behind the table was friendly. I approached her and mumbled, "Uh, would you happen to have any small plastic baseball statues?"

The lady replied, "No, but I just bought one from here today."

My hand started to shake. I asked her if I could see it.

"Well," she explained, "I don't have it right now. I bought it earlier from that little boy at the next table, and he still has it for now."

I thanked her and raced over to the next table. The kid looked up and asked if he could help me. I replied, "Yes. Do you have a small plastic baseball statue?"

The kid said no. I asked him again. He still said no.

Frustrated, I walked back to the lady at the first table. She asked, "Did he show you the player?"

I answered, "No. He said he didn't have one."

The lady gave me a quizzical look and said, "You wanted to know about a small football statue, didn't you? The one with the bobbing head?"

I politely nodded and headed out the door.

Finally, the tide turned late in the winter of '84. Randy Wievel, a local collector, told me to check out Larry Fritsch. Fritsch has two warehouses full of baseball cards and other baseball memorabilia. His warehouses were only 15 minutes from my house.

When I reached his office, I asked Larry if he had any Hartlands for sale. Fritsch walked into a small room and came back holding statues of Warren Spahn and Eddie Mathews.

"These are the only two I have right now," he said. "You can have them for one-fifty."

"Boy," I thought to myself, "If I ever heard of a great deal, this is it!" I reached into my wallet and pulled out two dollars.

Fritsch let out a tremendous belly-laugh. "Uh, I meant one hundred and fifty dollars," he said.

My wallet fell to the floor. Remember, this was back in 1984. "Do you mean that each one of these goes for $75?" I asked.

Fritsch nodded and said, "Hey, these things are true collectors' items. They stopped making them over 20 years ago."

No wonder I was having trouble finding the Hartlands. I left his warehouse and returned 30 minutes later with the loot. Eddie Mathews and Warren Spahn were now part of my personal collection. Finally, I was "on the board."

A few months after I'd purchased my first two Hartlands, Eddie and Warren were standing on top of my dresser while I was watching television. My mother came up and said, "Say, I noticed those two baseball statues. Where did you find them?"

"Oh, I just bought them a short time ago," I answered. "Paid one-fifty."

"A dollar-fifty!" she exclaimed. "Gee, those things actually went down. The one you had before cost me about three bucks."

I didn't bother to explain that we weren't talking about three bucks. Instead, I wanted to know what she meant about "the one I had before."

"Oh, my," she reflected. "We bought you a Henry Aaron statue when you were about 10. I think it cost about three bucks. It's probably still around here somewhere in the house."

It wasn't. For two solid weeks, I combed every inch of our house looking for little Henry. No luck.

In the spring of '85, I did a story for the "Green Sheet" section of the Milwaukee Journal describing how I almost tore the house down searching for a Hank Aaron statue that I might've had back in the early '60s. Looking back, I think I might've lost little Henry in a marble game.

Ethel Klein, a sweet lady from Wauwatosa, Wis., saw the article and immediately sent me a letter. It read: "You can stop tearing your basement apart looking for little Henry. I remembered I had him in our attic."

How about that for luck? Mrs. Klein was a complete stranger. She sent me her Hank Aaron statue for free.

I now had all three Braves and, two weeks later, I picked up another Spahn from a local collector at a very reasonable price.

A few months later, Randy Wievel and I took a trip to Rhinelander, Wis. An older couple saw the article and remembered that they had several Hartlands when they used to own a tavern in Milwaukee. Following our trip, Mays, Banks, Drysdale, Mantle, and Fox were added to my collection.

Wievel also bought five Hartlands from the Rhinelander couple. The price was very fair, but there was one slight catch. All of the statues from Rhinelander were in excellent shape, but the color was definitely not pure white. We imagined the statues took on their caramel color from all those years in the Milwaukee tavern, but the couple insisted that was the way they came as new.

At any rate, we decided to see what we could do about changing the colors from caramel to white. For our first move, I took a bucket, filled it with soap and water, and let Mickey Mantle swim in it overnight. The plastic Mantle was floating on the top, but we thought something good might happen.

The next morning, it was discovered that the little Mick had drowned. The statue was laying on the bottom of the bucket. It turned out that there was a very slight hole under his baseball cap. We also found that Mantle's overnight plunge didn't affect the caramel color one bit.

Our next experiment involved toothpaste. We went down to a drugstore and picked up a tube of Topal toothpaste and brushed the heck out of little Nellie Fox. After a few hours of that, little Nellie smelled really good but was still caramel.

Not to be denied, our next step called for drastic measures. We bought a can of some high-powered industrial cleaner and rubbed down certain parts of Ted Williams. If these statues could talk, little Splinter would've screamed! The best way to describe this is that little Teddy now looks like a rainbow. It was a very bad move on our part.

We ceased with our experiments and in 1987, I sent a letter to Mr. Frank Fulop explaining the caramel situation. Mr. Fulop, of course, was the creator of the Hartlands and is a beautiful guy besides. Frank wrote back saying that the golden color will always remain because the white colorant has dissipated from the reground plastic used. In other words, nothing will ever make a caramel Hartland white. But that's OK with us. A Hartland is still a Hartland.

Although it took me almost half a year to get my first Hartlands, the wait was certainly well worth it. Three years after my collection began, I'm proud to say that the number of my personal Hartlands is now up to 18. The nifty part is that I can glance at all of them, recall the memories they give, and immediately recall where each one came from.

I fell into a nice groove after the first nine. A local retired restaurant owner, Pete Redfield, called out of the blue and gave me Aaron, Spahn and Mathews. A dealer in Springfield, Ill., sent me another Fox, Musial and Berra. Another Berra came in the mail from La Crosse, Wis. A package arrived from Phoenix. A trip to a card show in Plover, Wis., netted Babe Ruth.

If anyone ever wanted to start a collection, try the Hartlands. Collecting them is a labor of love. — Tim Sullivan, June 3, 1988

* * *

Autograph Hound Ralph Winnie Usually Gets His Man

By Rich Marazzi

He behaves like a private eye, pursing perhaps a cancelled check from baseball's midget, Eddie Gaedel, or a scribbled note from pitcher Bill Froats.

Ladies and gentlemen, boys and girls, meet Ralph Winnie, the owner of the second largest baseball autograph collection in the world.

Winnie's stockpile of signatures places second only to Jack Smalling of Ames, Iowa.

Winnie, a 62-year-old Boeing engineer in Seattle, Wash., has been digging for baseball John Hancocks for 54 years, dating back to his childhood days in Norton Hills, N.Y., near Albany.

A graduate of Clarkson College in upstate New York, the personable engineer almost signed a baseball contract with the Pirates as a first baseman prior to World War II, but elected to join the Navy instead. He served on an aircraft carrier during the war.

Winnie currently has 9,500 autographs. That's not too shabby, considering approximately 13,300 players have appeared in the big leagues since 1871.

To put it in a more modern perspective, Winnie said, "From 1930 to the present, 7,231 players have debuted in the majors. Of those players, I have 7,148 autographs."

Winnie's impressive collection is housed in 60 large 3-ring binders. He also has about 1,000 8-by-10-inch autographed photos of the top stars.

"I have only a few autographed balls and bats because they're harder to store and handle," he said.

In today's market of $10 and $15 autographs, building a massive collection could get pretty expensive. But Winnie's method of obtaining signatures is very inexpensive and practical.

"As a kid, I drifted around dugouts and dressing room doors. But the bulk of autographs were solicited by writing to players in care of their teams or by writing to the player's home.

"In 1936, I started sending penny postcards to the stars of that era in care of their teams and requested signed photos or autographs.

"The first photo I received was from Yankee shortstop Frank Crosetti. By the early 1940s, I started to send to everyone on the team rosters.

"In 1948, I began to acquire ex-stars such as Ty Cobb, Honus Wagner, and Nap Lajoie. Old Ernie Lanigan, the former historian of the Baseball Hall of Fame, would sell 100 addresses of old players for $1," Winnie said.

Perhaps Winnie's most successful and unique method of snaring signatures is to get them before the player makes it to the majors.

"Each spring I mail latters to several hundred minor leaguers at the various training camps, requesting their autographs. About 80-90 percent comply on the first try.

"It's easier to get a player to sign while he's still an unspoiled minor leaguer or a rookie. That's how I got Ted Williams, Mickey Mantle, Hank Aaron, Stan Musial and Fernando Valenzuela, among others," he said.

The beauty of that system is that if tragedy strikes, such as in the case of former Cubs' infielder Ken Hubbs (1961-63), who was killed in a plane crash, Winnie has the autograph since he corrals most of his autographs while the players are in the minors.

But there are some situations when a player dies at an early age before Winnie gets his autograph.

"In the case of Charlie Peete (1956, Cardinals), who died in a plane crash, and that of Dick Wantz (1965, Angels), who died of a brain hemorrhage shortly after his debut, I did not have their signatures.

"I finally got Peete's in an auction and obtained Wantz's, after a 15-year search, from a minor league collector who had a Wantz autograph on a Hawaii program."

Persistence is a prerequisite for an autograph hunter. The expert philographer wrote to ex-White Sox and Twins' catcher Earl Battey about 50 times during his playing days. The golden-armed backstop finally signed after he had retired.

Another tough one involved Leo Norris, an infielder with the Phils in 1936 and 1937. But after years of searching and waiting, the Norris autograph turned up.

"Leo spent the last 40 years of his life in a mental institution and couldn't sign. One day I had my autographs on display at a Seattle card show when a lady came in with a stack of Minneapolis (American Association) programs containing Norris's signature. So you never know," Winnie said.

Some of the people Winnie seeks have defined ground rules before signing.

Others have idiosyncracies worth mentioning.

Winnie explained, "Phil Wrigley, the ex-Cubs' mogul, would not sign for me until I promised in writing not to sell his autograph.

"George Twombly (1914-19 Reds/Braves) would sign only if I bought his book, which he had written about raising pigeons and his World War I exploits."

As for the strange signing habits of players, Winnie added, "Lou 'Doc' Legett, who caught with the Braves and Red Sox in the late 1920s and early 1930s, drew a picture of a leg in his signature.

"Many players sign a religious verse. A few guys will not sign a blank card because they think you convert that into a check. One player put X marks all over the card and kept the middle open," he said.

A member of the Society for American Baseball Research and the Hall of Fame Research Committee, Winnie collects biographical data on big leaguers. He is listed as a contributor in all three baseball encyclopedias: The MacMillan Baseball Encyclopedia, The Sports Encyclopedia of Baseball, by Neft and Cohen, and The Encyclopedia of Baseball, by Turkin and Thompson.

In cases where a player is deceased, Winnie tries to get a living relative to complete the information. This has frequently resulted in obtaining an obscure autograph for his collection.

The clever engineer once designed a swap in which he exchanged a batch of 78 RPM jazz records for the signatures of Hall of Fame umpire Bill Klem and former White Sox owner Charles Comiskey.

Winnie's oldest autograph is that of Adrian "Cap" Anson, who played from 1871-97. His most prized signature is that of Rube Waddell, the former eccentric pitcher who spent most of his career with the Athletics.

Good things sometimes come in small packages. He once purchased a child's autograph book in the late 1940s for $50.

It had hundreds of autographs, including two Ruths and two Gehrigs. Winnie calls it "my biggest bargain."

A lot of leg work is involved in compiling more than 9,000 signatures. Winnie often goes to the downtown library to check phone books and city directories of places where the player he is tracking down is known to have lived.

"Maybe there's a name of a relative and then I go from there. I do the same thing exactly as a private eye does.

"For instance, I might write to every Joe Smith in the Detroit phone book and that's a lot of letters," he said.

Relatives of former players are often flattered by Winnie's autograph requests.

He elaborated, "I couldn't believe it when Walter Blair's daughter sent me her fifth grade report card, signed in five places by her dad, who was a catcher with the New York Highlanders/Yankees from 1907-15.

"I received the autograph of Edward Eiteljorg (1890-91 Chicago/Washington) from his granddaughter, who cut the signature from Eiteljorg's own personal Bible.

"John McGraw's widow sent a cut signature from one of his checks. Hanson Horsey sent me an old postcard written by Horsey (1912 Reds) on the honeymoon," he said.

The joy of collecting is when the unexplained occurs.

When Winnie learned Hack Wilson had died destitute, he sent a small check to Wilson's widow.

In return, Mrs. Wilson sent Winnie a cancelled check with her husband's signature.

Some autographs warrant a desperation gimmick if a player refuses to reply. Pete Gray, the one-armed St. Louis Brownie (1945), is a good example.

The only way to obtain his signature was to send Gray a registered letter and wait for its receipt. Mission accomplished.

In Winnie's pursuit of autographs, he put together a handsome baseball book library.

"I've accumulated about 2,000 hard and soft cover books because of my search for players. I've got all the Baseball Digest issues except five, dating back to 1942.

"I have all the Spalding Guides, Reach Guides, and Sporting News Guides ever printed and have a complete set of Baseball Registers.

"I also have all the National League Green Books and and American League Red Books. In addition, I have about 2,000 various baseball magazines," he said.

Autograph collecting 1990 style is a radical departure from Winnie's creative, traditional methods.

"Everything is for profit today. Forgery is probably more prevalent today than it was in the 1930s and 1940s because the hobby has grown so much.

"Kids in general don't collect common players. They look for the stars.

"To avoid forgery, you've got to get the guys to sign while they're in the minor leagues or get them in person," he said.

But forgery is nothing new in the world of autograph collecting.

"Over the years I think it's been common to have clubhouse boys of the major league teams sign for players. Also, Christy Walsh, Babe Ruth's agent, used to sign many things for the Babe. I believe Joe DiMaggio's sister used to sign his autograph," he added.

Krause Publications has published a baseball autograph handbook that carries examples of autographs of all Hall of Famers. Winnie has mixed emotions about the book.

"The book will allow autograph collectors to compare signatures, but it will allow unscrupulous people to forge," he said.

Winnie believes the current flood of card collectors shows has fostered the autograph hobby because of the players signing at the shows. This has increased autograph seekers throughout the country.

He remembers a time when you could count the major autograph collectors on one hand.

"In the 1940s and 1950s, I could name all the major autograph collectors. Guys like Roy Pitts from Alabama, Dick Jeffery (New Jersey), Dr. John Davis (Kansas) and Conrad Anderson (Massachusetts)," he said.

There is another baseball dimension to Ralph Winnie. A few years ago he published his own book, titled What If?

He explained, "Over the years I fooled around with statistics. I looked back and found that Bob Feller would be the leader in most pitching categories if he had pitched in the war years.

"Feller had my material printed in a 1985 Cleveland Indians program. It made Feller, DiMaggio and Spahn look good.

"I decided to put it in the form of a book and have self-published three different editions."

Winnie's roster of names would dazzle even the most advanced autograph collectors. But there are a few who have eluded the master.

Bill Froats, a one-game Detroit Tigers pitcher in 1955, is high on Winnie's want list.

Winnie has also failed to obtain the autograph of Eddie Gaedel, the 3'7" midget who went to bat once for the St. Louis Browns in 1951.

Apparently the only person who has the extemely rare midget's signature is Smalling. If you can help, give Ralph Winnie a holler. And yes — be sure to sign your name! — Rich Marazzi, Batting the Breeze, May 11, 1990

* * *

Maris Fan Will Always Be Remembered For His Catch

By Frank P. Henry

Have you ever gone to a baseball game and dreamed of catching a foul ball, or maybe even a home run ball?

Almost 29 years ago, a 19-year-old kid from Brooklyn, N.Y., caught one of the most famous home run balls of all time, one that's in Major League Baseball's Hall of Fame.

On Oct. 1, 1961, Sal Durante wanted to attend a game at Yankee Stadium. But not just any game.

This game would be the last chance for Roger Maris to become the first major leaguer in history to hit more than 60 home runs in a season.

Durante persuaded his fiancee, Rosemarie Calabrese, to buy the tickets.

"I was broke. We went to the Yankee Stadium box office and asked if there were any tickets available in right field.

"I couldn't believe that we got the tickets, right in section 33. Being at this game was very important to me, especially since I had been at the game when Maris hit his 60th home run," he said.

The 23,154 fans in attendance in the Bronx Bombers' home that day saw the count run to 2 and 0 in the fourth inning when Boston's rookie right-hander pitched Maris a fast ball.

The ball sailed into the right field bleachers of the "House that Ruth Built."

Durante reached for the ball, catching it in his bare hands.

"The security guards rushed to my aid and escorted me to an area under the stadium near the dugout. Roger Maris walked over to me and congratulated me on catching the ball.

"I said, 'This belongs to you, Mr. Maris.' He said 'No, you keep it! You can make money from it.' He was a real gentleman."

Durante spent four hours after the game posing for pictures while holding the ball and giving interview after interview.

"I can remember meeting Elston Howard and Johnny Blanchard that day in the clubhouse. Blanchard said, 'Hold on to that ball. It may be worth 10 grand,'" Durante recalled.

Durante's wife, Rosemarie, remembers how fans at the stadium were pleading with her to obtain anything that belonged to Sal.

One man offered her $10 for a picture of him. Another fan offered Rosemarie $10 to send her Sal's shoes.

When Durante was about to leave the stadium, someone told him the ball would be safer if it was locked up at Yankee Stadium. He agreed, but first he put his initials on the ball.

Durante recently visited the Hall of Fame in Cooperstown, N.Y. He was allowed to examine the ball and yes, his initials were still there.

The weeks that followed that infamous catch would be a tiring experience for Durante, who made countless appearances, personal, and on national television.

He said, "I picked up the ball from Yankee Stadium on Oct. 28, 1961. Rosemarie and I were married on Oct. 29, 1961, just one month after I caught the ball."

Sacramento businessman Sam Gordon had offered $5,000 to the person who caught Maris' 61st home run ball, so the Durantes went to Sacramento, where they were presented with a $5,000 check.

"That $5,000 was like getting one-and-a-half years salary. I was making $60 a week back then," Durante said.

Roger Maris, who was also there, was presented the ball.

This is Durante's first interview since he caught the ball in which he has expressed his feelings regarding the fact that Maris has not been inducted into the Hall of Fame.

"For what Roger Maris has accomplished, he should be in the Hall of Fame. I wish someone would tell me why he isn't.

"He did something no one else has ever done. I think it's long overdue," he said.

Durante thinks an awareness campaign, by fans writing to the Hall of Fame and to the commissioner to state their reasons why Maris should be inducted into the Hall of Fame, may make Maris' induction a reality.

Durante is a private man. He never asked for any compensation for any of the interviews he has given in the past 29 years.

"There is nothing special about me. After all these years, someone will hear my name and say, 'Hey, aren't you the guy who caught Maris' home run ball?' I just say 'Yes, that's me.' I guess its something that will always be remembered," he said.

Durante was at a New York Rangers hockey game not too long ago and, yes, you guessed it, he caught a hockey puck. — Frank P. Henry, Nov. 16, 1990

* * *

Kiecker's Walnut Shop Shows Father's Woodwork Ability

By Dave Miedema

Remember those nostalgic 1976 and 1985 Topps sets with the "then and now" cards depicting baseball's father/son duos?

Gus and Buddy Bell were in both sets, while most, such as Jim and Mike Hegan, Bill and Jeff Kunkel, and Bob and Joel Skinner, appeared in only one.

Nonetheless, the cards were a pleasant addition to the rookie, Super Vet and League Leader cards in these sets.

Last January, I was privileged to meet another father/son baseball combo.

This pair won't make it on a baseball card; only the younger one appeared in a major league game. Yet, the love and appreciation they share for baseball makes this pair unique and just as interesting as any combination of Smalleys, Averills, or Virgils.

The player is Dana Kiecker, a 29-year-old pitcher with the Eastern Division Champion Boston Red Sox this year.

The extended preseason and shortened exhibition schedule prompted teams to add pitchers to their staffs when they eventually headed north.

Kiecker, who nearly retired out of frustration at being stalled in the minors so long, finally made it up. By season's end, the Boston brass was thanking the stars.

Most of the 1990 season was a series of ups and down for Kiecker, a native of Sleepy Eye, Minn. Although his record entering early September was a mere 6-9, Kiecker lost a few wins to leads that evaporated after he left the game.

Then, the Red Sox found the Toronto Blue Jays breathing down their necks on the pennant ladder, and the situation developed into a nip-and-tuck battle for the division crown — one that some critics felt neither team seemed particularly anxious to wrap up.

But if that was the case for the Red Sox, someone forgot to tell Dana Kiecker.

At one point, the Sox went into a major tailspin. The nosedive reached eight losses in 11 games — not the stuff first place finishes are built upon.

Yet, Kiecker, for the most part, suddenly showed the baseball world what the tough do when the going gets that way.

Kiecker was credited with two of the three wins during the tailspin. Another game later that month Kiecker again departed from the mound with a marvelous performance and a win there for the taking.

The latter, however, was not meant to be that night. But no one could deny Kiecker credit for another gritty and successful outing that any hurler on the staff, Roger Clemens and Mike Boddicker included, would have been happy to claim as their own.

Then, the baseball world was treated to one more helping of Kiecker's Krunch. The Oakland A's, Boston's nemesis in the postseason and the prohibitive favorites in this clash of champions, turned a tight Game One affair into a laugher with a late offensive deluge on the Boston bullpen.

Boston needed to win to avoid trekking to the West Coast with a 2-0 deficit staring the team in the eyes. But the Red Sox didn't get that must win.

However, a peek at the box score will show that Kiecker, opposed by Cy Young Award winner Bob Welch, nonetheless battled the Oakland hurler to a standstill until his sixth inning departure.

The Boston pen again failed to contain the Oakland Bash Bunch, but, before that point, Dana Kiecker had pitched the game of his life. He matched the league's best starter pitch for pitch in a pressure cooker situation that has wilted many seasoned veterans.

Kiecker, the rookie, was tougher than titanium steel that October evening, and gave Red Sox fans everywhere a moment of pride in an otherwise-gloomy postseason.

A tough cookie like the younger Kiecker has a source to draw upon for his fortitude and grit — his dad, Kermit Kiecker.

A longtime farmer who recently retired from working the fields, Kermit Kiecker's profession required toughness, too.

The physical work the American farmer undertakes, and the concerns farmers have had in recent years as rural economies have sometimes suffered, evidences the sharing of determination and fortitude that both Kieckers possess.

The game of baseball also forms a bond between the two men. Although Kermit never donned a major league uniform, he does have a niche in baseball that will be good news to many equipment and other sports collectors, even if it doesn't get him a standing ovation from the Fenway Park faithful.

Although farming was his main pastime until recently, Kermit Kiecker had a fondness, and a talent, for woodcrafting and carpentry.

That fondness of working with lumber, combined with his Heartland-style hard work ethic, and his connection with and enjoyment of baseball, bring us to his part of the father-son equation.

Kiecker has an expanding business of handcrafted bat racks, ball holders, and other quality display materials that collectors seldom find at shows of any size.

Kiecker's Walnut Shop, in Fairfax, Minn., began with other woodcrafts, but Dana's involvement in professional baseball soon changed that.

"He (Dana) brought home broken bats, and other items, and you know how one thing leads to another," related the elder Kiecker, a pleasant, relaxed fellow.

"As Dana's career progressed, all of us (including his wife Gladys) saw our interest in baseball grow, and there was more of a focus on baseball...we gave it lots of attention."

The wide-open country spaces give the Kieckers added opportunities to follow Dana's career by radio, and baseball in general.

"We can pick up WMAQ (the White Sox Chicago-based radio outlet) and other clear-channel stations here at night," he said.

The process for preparing the wood can take a long while, up to five years if airdry procedures are used, to allow the wood to be at top quality for the eventual crafting.

"And that's with a low rainfall," Mr. Kiecker adds.

"The drying process should result in having the wood carrying only 6 to 7 percent moisture," he continued. "Humidity can wreck a crafted item when too much moisture is present. At about 15 percent, the wood will splinter and crack.

Kiecker's Walnut Shop produces a variety of display items, starting out with a basic single-bat wall holder.

"Most of the items are made with walnut, but I also use oak when the situation warrants, such as a brown or black bat," Kiecker said.

"The oak is a lighter color, and helps provide a better contrast to the darker colored bat."

The nice thing is, however, that because they are personally crafted items, not mass-produced factory productions, the possibilities for combinations and sizes are numerous.

"I made a mini bat rack for a lady in Wisconsin," Kiecker recalls. "At her request, I told her I'd give it a try. I ended up producing a rack that could hold up to 26 miniature bats. She was very happy."

Then there's the other end of the scale — racks that could hold a dozen or more pro sticks have been made for collectors, fans, and even some of Dana's teammates and friends in the Red Sox organization.

Citing another craft project in his resume, Kiecker recalled an item for another baseball Dana.

"Back when they were with New Britain (Red Sox farm club), Dana Williams (1990 Fleer rookie card) wanted a bat lamp, and we made a real nice one for him."

"The bat lamps tend to surprise some people who think it's too high priced," he continued. "You have to remember, though, that, in addition to the craftmanship involved, there's the cost of electrical parts, the actual lamp itself, and the cost of obtaining the players' bats."

One lamp he made has a walnut home plate for a base, and a gold glove ball holder prominently located on the base.

Considering all of that, the $150 price tag suddenly seems a lot more understandable. Kiecker maintains that most people appreciate the quality they get for the price they pay. I know I do.

Another Kiecker's Walnut Shop specialty is a bar stool that is comprised of four bats, which, as is the case with most bat crafts, can be personalized or left plain.

The seat part of the stool is a regulation base that is produced by Rawlings. If $200 seems a bit steep for this unique item, just go to the next card show in your area, ask an equipment dealer for four unbroken bats of any major star, or even minor star, never mind the base, and see how much it tallies up to.

For those with fewer funds, but a desire to obtain quality workmanship for displaying special collectibles, there is plenty available.

At $5.50, there is a hand-crafted walnut baseball card holder, and for $7.95 there's a baseball holder with a walnut base, using a gold glove as the holder.

If you want to combine the card and ball holder, it will run you $10. That's not a whole lot more than your standard mass-produced ball-and-card holder. And these are made with personal precision and a lot more style.

The single bat racks mentioned earlier are $25. For $40, a walnut coat rack, or a coat/hat rack made out of a half of a professional bat, can be yours.

The hooks, depending on the item, may either be mini bats or knobs of regulation bats.

A prized item is the lighted bat case, made in either walnut or oak. Such cases can hold either a single bat ($225) or two sticks ($250).

"I did a few for the state tournament, and added an engraved metal plate, as well," Kiecker said.

Kiecker also mentioned the increasing challenge in obtaining bats for his projects.

"Louisville Slugger is running short on the white ash wood needed to make bats," he said.

"Brown ash is also used for bats, but the brown variety tends to break more easily. Cooper bats are well made, but I have no idea how much white ash is available up in Canada (where Coopers are made)," he adds.

How does Kermit Kiecker perceive his bat rack, bat rack and ball holder crafts and bat lamps these days?

"It's been basically a hobby for me up 'til now," he explains. "And it's been fun helping people and providing them with something nice to show off a prized bat or ball.

"Now that it's full time, I'll be able to expand things, and give more people a little something special."

And, being an owner of one of Kiecker's bat racks, which contains a bat of family friend and Oakland catcher Terry Steinbach, I think the work and the quality is something special indeed.

In the meantime, both the Kiecker baseball men are already planning their 1991 activities.

Kermit's expanding his woodcrafting business, and Dana hopes to avoid the sophomore jinx, a task that will be a certainty if he can continue to do what he did in September and in Game 2 of the American League Championship Series.

This father/son tandem may never end up on a Topps subset card or on a Fleer Super Star special card, but they both do what they do well, and both have the old-fashioned work ethic as the backbone for their successes, whether that pertains to going toe-to-toe with Bob Welch and matching him in a pressure-cooker playoff game or tinkering in the wood shop back in rural Minnesota with an eye on good old-fashioned American values and quality.

They're a father/son duo that you can appreciate and like. I know I do. — Dave Miedema, Up Autograph Alley, Jan. 4, 1991

***

What Was It Like Growing Up With Nolan Ryan?

By Linda Brown

"What was it like growing up with Nolan Ryan?" is a question the former Nolan Ryan Fan Club president is frequently asked.

Nita Lutz, a member of the board of trustees for a proposed Nolan Ryan museum in Alvin, Texas, still helps out with fan mail, but her parents are now officially in charge of the fan club.

Lutz says that back in high school Ryan was just one of her classmates.

"He was a pitcher on the high school baseball team and he pitched a bit wild back then," she said.

None of his classmates could have imagined the phenomenal success he has achieved in his career.

The girls in school didn't follow his every move because he was, even then, dedicated to his childhood sweetheart, Ruth, who would later become Mrs. Nolan Ryan after high school.

Lutz, a longtime resident of Alvin, says Ryan draws more attention and people to the area than one would think.

The town of 19,000, home to the future Hall of Famer, and the Nolan Ryan Historical Foundation, hope to draw more visitors with the proposed museum. The museum, in Ryan's honor, would chronicle his life and roots in Alvin and provide interactive exhibits.

A bond election held in December 1990 to finance a joint effort of a community center/Ryan museum complex didn't pass, but the Ryan foundation stated earlier it will build a museum, whether or not the bond passed.

Although the bond didn't pass, the admiration the hometown hero receives was evident, in full force, on July 31, 1990.

The whole town of Alvin gathered at Joe's Barbeque, a bastion of Ryan sentiment festooned with posters of Alvin's favorite son, to watch history being made.

The fans who couldn't be with him were glued to TV screens fed by a satellite dish as Ryan entered the history books again, recording his 300th win in baseball.

Lutz lamented that it was the first record setter she had missed; she'd made all other record-setting performances by her old schoolmate.

"We saw the first game he played in the Astrodome in 1968, when he pitched against the Mets," she said.

Lutz watched the game at Joe's and was overwhelmed with the media attention. She was interviewed and photographed by The Post and USA Today.

Lutz, a travel agent in Alvin, has an extensive collection of Ryan memorabilia displayed at her office. She has been collecting since Ryan started with the New York Mets.

Her most valuable items are the three 1968 rookie cards of Ryan, who's pictured with fellow Mets pitcher Jerry Koosman. The Sports Collectors Digest Weekly Price Guide from Jan. 11, 1991, lists its value at $1,500, but Lutz has been offered up to $3,800 for each card.

"Those cards and my other memorabilia are my retirement nest egg," she said.

A stroll into the office that houses Lutz's baseball treasures is like attending a baseball game. Posters of Ryan line every inch of the walls.

A glass case holds about 20 autographed baseballs, and there are framed pictures of Ryan and other baseball players on furniture tops and shelves. Baseball gloves and bats are scattered about the room.

A television sits in one corner of the room, while a radio sits nearby. This allows for watching or listening to the game, or both. All that's missing are the peanuts.

Lutz said Ryan gave her many of the pictures and baseballs, but she has purchased many of the posters, which date to the 1960s, when Ryan started his career with the Mets. Ryan was part of a World Series win with the Mets during the beginning of his career.

Lutz and many others in Alvin are working hard to make the Ryan museum a reality.

"Our big thing now is getting the museum and having people come and visit the city," said Patricia Greer of the Alvin Chamber of Commerce.

"We already have people come who want to see where Nolan played (now Nolan Ryan Field) and where he lived and grew up."

Greer says one woman in Massachusetts called wanting to know how she could invest in Ryan's bank in Danbury.

Ryan is the lifeblood of Alvin, a true hometown hero who is well-respected. Even those in Alvin who don't follow baseball — yes, there are few — respect Ryan in some way.

"He's our friend. He's the father of our kids' friends," Greer says. "When he comes back, we allow him a lot of relaxation. You see him at the Dairy Queen and Baskin Robbins."

Barbara Moore, a nearby neighbor and a friend of the Ryans, says "They're good parents who raise their kids the old-fashioned way. The kids have good manners and are clean-cut."

Ryan's eldest son, Reid, will try to follow in his father's footsteps. He is attending the University of Texas on a baseball scholarship.

Lutz said that among Alvin folks, Ryan prefers to talk about anything but baseball.

"If a kid asks for his autograph, he'll ask the kid his name and how he's doing in school." — Linda Brown, Feb. 8, 1991

***

A First-Hand Look At The 1991 Cracker Jack Set

By Tol Broome

OK, here's a jeopardy answer for you: "Sugar, corn syrup, popcorn, peanuts, molasses, corn oil, salt and soya lecithin."

Give up? How about, "What are the ingredients in a box of Cracker Jack?"

In the past few weeks this combination has become a staple part of my diet.

307

Why? Well, it's not because I've had a sudden insatiable craving to consume as many cracker jacks as one human can possibly eat. No, the reason is simple. It's the toy surprise inside the package.

But we're not talking about miniature magnifying glasses and tiny story booklets that have caught my eye. Cracker Jack, in conjunction with Topps, has been giving away little baseball cards in specially-marked packages.

It all started innocently enough. A couple of months ago I was standing in line at a discount drugstore purchasing various and sundry items when I noticed a box of Cracker Jack with something unusual on the packaging. Right at the top were the words, "Free! Cracker Jack/Topps Mini Baseball Card Inside!"

"I wonder what they look like," I thought. I quickly deemed it worth the 28 cents price tag to find out and purchased a box. Once in my car, I opened the box, popped a few cracker jacks into my mouth and pulled out the card, which was protected by the paper wrapper usually reserved for the magnifying glasses, booklets and stickers.

Tearing off the paper, I nearly ripped the card in half, but caught myself just in time to salvage the borders of the card.

The card inside the wrapper was unlike any I had ever seen. Yes, the picture of Cecil Fielder was the same as the photo used for the front of his 1991 Topps card, but this little sucker was small! I mean really tiny.

I chuckled to myself that Cracker Jack should consider putting a magnifying glass in with the card. Still, the card looked pretty attractive having been modeled after one of Topps' better looking sets of the past 10-15 years.

I didn't think much more about my purchase until a few days later when I was back in the same drugstore buying more drugstore-type stuff. There were three boxes of Cracker Jack left at the checkout counter.

Deciding that my wife and children really would appreciate my thoughtfulness, I tossed all three onto the counter to take home for dessert. The treat was well received even though my hidden motive soon was discovered.

The aforementioned promo on the outside of the package was a dead giveaway, but no one seemed to mind, although they might have if they had known what was in store.

This time I paid a little more attention to the package and cards. Before opening the boxes I noticed another promo on the packaging cover — "Collect All 36 Cards, See Side Panel." The side panel revealed a checklist of all the players in the set. As with most food issues, it was chock full of superstars with a few 1990 rookies sprinkled in (Alomar, Justice and Maas).

The three cards I received were Rickey Henderson, Ryne Sandberg and Doug Drabek. For some reason the Henderson card with the neato photo of him sliding headfirst into second looked even better on the mini Cracker Jack version. It also prompted me to do a little more investigation.

I measured the four cards and discovered the tale of the tape to be 1 3/4 x 1 1/4 inch. Comparing them to a "normal" sized Topps card which measures 2 1/2 x 3 1/4 inch, I found that the mini version is four times smaller than its big brother.

I also checked the card backs and learned that they differed from the backs on the regular Topps cards, which made a lot of sense. It would be difficult to imagine trying to read the microscopic type that would have to be used to print a player's entire major league record on a 1 3/4 x 1 1/4 inch sized issue.

The designers of the Cracker Jack set wisely decided to put only 1990 and career totals on the back, and even these are barely legible despite the royal blue lettering used on a bright red paper stock.

The backs also contain the card number, player's name and position, the player's biographical information, several trademarks and a couple of career highlights. For instance, Sandberg's card back reads, "Ryne was NL Most Valuable Player in 1984. He led NL with 40 Homers in 1990."

From Fielder's we learn that "Cecil led both leagues with 51 HR and 132 RBI in 1990. Three HR, May 6, 1990." Just good 'ol information.

The cards really were beginning to peak my interest the more I studied them. What's more, I had forgotten how much I love cracker jacks. Eating them was kind of like getting reacquainted with an old friend.

When I was little, there was a nice elderly lady who lived down the street from us. My sister used to visit her regularly, and she would always give us a box of Cracker Jack. For that reason we called her Nanny Cracker Jack, and I still remember sitting on her front porch steps with my sister and eating cracker jacks.

I also have fond childhood memories of eating cracker jacks with my dad at Washington Senators games. In fact, the cracker jacks are the only affirmative recollections I have of going to see the perennial cellar-dwelling Senators.

Eating Cracker Jack again was conjuring up some happy childhood moments. So not only was I becoming enamored with the cards, but also I was experiencing some major nostalgia. Consequently, I really didn't have much choice but to try to complete the set.

When I explained this reason to my wife she just rolled her eyes. I guess I couldn't blame her. Having heard similar arguments in the past for why we should drink 7-Eleven slurpees or eat Kraft macaroni and cheese, she was weary of my proposal.

I tried to ease her apprehension by explaining that there were "only" 36 cards, and that it wouldn't be any big deal to complete the set. These turned out to be words I would later have to eat, along with enough Cracker Jack for the company to double its sales during 1991!

Now I was committed to collect a set of cards that could fit in the palm of my hand. For that matter, they could fit in the palm of my 4-year-old daughter's hand, but their smallness was part of their allure.

So, what would I do next to help expedite the set completion process? Call my sister, of course! Over the past few years she had been one of my greatest helpers in collecting food issues such as Kraft, Cap'n Crunch, Post and Bazooka.

I know I can always count on her for a couple of reasons: 1) both my brother-in-law and nephew are sugar freaks and 2) she actually enjoys buying stuff with card giveaways. And why not?

She had learned this as a kid when she would somehow get to the box of Kelloggs cereal first and abscond with the 3-D cards. She would then taunt me with them until I agreed to trade her something like one of my Green Lantern double secret decoder rings.

As expected, my sister Laura was excited to hear of yet another food issue set. She enthusiastically agreed to start buying Cracker Jack whenever possible. After we reminisced for a minute about our visits to see Nanny Cracker Jack, I reminded Laura to be sure and buy the specially marked packages and thanked her for her willingness to help.

Over the next couple of days, I talked my wife and kids into helping me eat six boxes worth. New cards included Bonds, Griffey, Thigpen, Raines, Jackson and Parker. So far, so good. I had bought 10 boxes and had gotten 10 different cards.

I knew that the law of averages would begin to catch up to me, but that didn't dampen my spirits. Not at this point, anyway. Little did I know that there was plenty of rain in the set completion forecast!

As I began to bring boxes home to my family, I learned a valuable credo to apply to the eating of cracker jacks by young children. Any child under the age of 4 should not be allowed to eat more than seven cracker jacks in only one sitting.

The eighth cracker jack tends to set off a chemical reaction within a child that causes his/her energy level to increase exponentially. I learned this the hard way when I gave my 20-month-old son half a box one day and he ran what must have been a sub-four-minute mile as he raced around from room to room inside our house!

At first my wife was very helpful in the set collection process. Throughout the eight years of our marriage she had developed a very thoughtful habit of asking if I needed anything before leaving for the grocery store. With my new quest, my standard response had become, "Cracker Jacks. Three boxes. Make sure you get the specially marked ones."

Three boxes seemed like an appropriate number to buy. They were only a dollar, and I found that I couldn't eat more than three boxes in one sitting.

My wife was surprisingly tolerant and even laughed the first couple of times I explained that eating cracker jacks would enable me to get my US RDA daily allowance of soya lecithin. However, my joke began to wear thin, and about the fourth time I asked my wife to bring home my snack of choice, she began to get a little testy. In fact, she threatened to start collecting the toy prizes found in the "regular" boxes of Cracker Jack.

Despite my wife's waning interest in helping me, things were going very well. My sister had called in a couple of acquisitions, and after 21 boxes I had 17 different, nearly half the set! At this point I decided to try and speed up the process by purchasing 18 boxes in one trip.

The first obstacle I faced was the lady at Woolworth's checkout counter. For a second I thought she wasn't going to let me buy the six three-box packages with the strange look I received. After assuring her that the purchase was for a noble cause, I faced my second dilemma. What was I going to do with all those cracker jacks?

I realized at this point that I just couldn't bring myself to buy the cracker jacks only for the cards. I'm still not sure if it was the nostalgic bond I felt with the product or just a general aversion to throwing away something I have purchased, but it simply seemed wasteful to toss out the caramel-coated popcorn and peanuts.

So, I had to find creative ways to entice others to help me eat the cracker jacks. Work cohorts couldn't understand my sudden generosity as I passed them out. They also looked a bit puzzled when I handed them an already opened box.

"Hey, where's the prize?" was the typical response. I finally had to fess up to what I was up to in order to squelch the commentary. After opening and disposing of the 18 boxes, I had a total of 40 cards with 27 different. One of the boxes had actually included two cards — Viola and Griffey.

Being three-quarters of the way to a complete set, I felt I was on a roll and went out the next day and bought 15 more boxes. In addition to making still more friends at work, I picked up four new cards giving me 31 of the 36. I also received another box containing two cards — Thigpen and Viola again, strangely enough.

With only five cards (Molitor, Gwynn, Puckett, Guerrero and Alomar) needed to finish the set, it seemed I had several options. I could:

1) Buy a case of Cracker Jack — this option didn't fall within the confines of our budget and actually would not guarantee me that I would pick up all five cards needed anyway.

2) Go to a store and open boxes there until I found the five I needed — the problem with this option was that I really had no desire to spend a night in jail.

3) Shrink some regular issue Topps cards by washing them in hot water and then drying them for two hours — I might have tried this if not for the different card backs.

4) Write the company — I had had some success with this tactic in collecting past food issue sets.

5) Purchase them from card dealers — that is, if I could find any who had them.

6) Trade with someone else collecting the set — this would require an ad in a hobby publication, an expense that at first seemed excessive just to acquire five cards (I later wished I had tried this much sooner!)

I actually wound up trying a little of everything (except options two and three.) Given that my last 14 cards purchased had been duplicates it was apparent that the law of averages was nipping at my heels. With this in mind and with the aforementioned hope that I could avoid the expense of a classified ad, I figured I would unleash a two-pronged assault — by trying to obtain the five cards from card dealers and/or Borden Inc., the parent company of Cracker Jack.

First I tried calling a few shops, but found very few shop owners who even knew about the 1991 Cracker Jack set. Several thought I was inquiring about the Cracker Jack sets issued in 1914 and 1915, although most didn't have any of those cards either.

Next I tried a card show, hoping I might find just one out of a couple dozen dealers who had some of the cards. Unfortunately, however, my questions about the set were met with one of three reactions: 1) a simple "no", 2) a blank stare, or 3) laughter. The show's promoter (who with six tables must have been selling every type of sports card other than the Cracker Jack set) did politely interject that he thought the set could be a good one because of its uniqueness and alleged difficulty in assembling it.

I was encouraged by his remarks about the set's potential and explained to him that I was living proof of the set's elusiveness.

Having pretty well exhausted the "dealer option," I proceeded with Plan B. I decided to cover all the bases in contacting Borden by communicating my request by phone and by mail.

Having already dashed off a letter explaining how much I loved Cracker Jack and that I would appreciate their sending the five cards that I needed, I called Borden's customer service department.

When I told the person on the other end that I had a question about Cracker Jack, she asked, "Do you want to talk with someone about the product or the baseball cards?"

As I dialed the number she had given me, I thought to myself, "Hey, this is great. Borden has set up a hotline for collectors to complete their sets." However, after several busy signals, I finally got through to a tired-sounding live voice.

When I introduced myself and indicated my reasons for calling, she politely responded that the cards would only be available through product sales.

A response to my letter arrived from Borden's Consumer Response Department shortly thereafter. After the standard customer service introduction, the letter indicated that the cards were being distributed "exclusively in boxes of Cracker Jack," and "all of the cards in the set are mixed on a random basis in equal quantities."

Borden also included a coupon for 50 cents off any size package of Cracker Jack — a very nice gesture but, nevertheless, I was still five cards shy of a complete set.

I now had to rethink my strategy. The only other two viable options at this point were: 1) keep buying boxes of Cracker Jack until I got the five cards I needed, and/or 2) place a classified ad in a hobby publication and hope for good response. I decided to do both. First of all, I designed an ad for the SCD classified section that was short, but to the point:

Cracker Jack (1991) traders needed. Send wantlist to Tol Broome, 1508 Colonial Ave., Greensboro, N.C. 27408.

It still seemed a bit expensive to spend $4 to try to get five Cracker Jack cards, but at this point I was willing to try just about anything. Yes, four bucks would buy 12 boxes of Cracker Jack, but with the law of averages working against me, I had figured that it would take 83 boxes to obtain the five remaining cards!

Eighty-three boxes would run me about $28 with tax, a figure which roughly equated to our son's monthly diaper bill. In fact, I was beginning to measure everything in terms of Cracker Jack boxes.

For instance, our $100/month utility bill would buy 300 boxes while our $1,000/month house payment would buy 3,000 boxes! I could surely complete my set by foregoing these obligations in lieu of Cracker Jack purchases; however, I knew my family would not appreciate being without power and/or shelter!

So, this slightly warped reasoning had led me to run a classified ad for the five cards I needed, but there was one problem. The ad would not appear for nearly three weeks, and I was itching to complete the set. While I couldn't justify the $28 needed for 83 boxes, I could still buy a few at a time and hope for a little luck.

About 10 boxes later, I still didn't have any new cards and discouragement began to set in. I also was beginning to believe a theory that my wife had put forth.

When I explained to her that I had purchased more than 60 boxes and still lacked five to complete the 36-card set, she speculated that those five cards had probably had their printing delayed or had been issued in limited quantities to make it more difficult to complete the set and to entice people to buy more boxes.

As my sources of specially-marked boxes began to run thin, I was just about ready to accept her hypothesis until I stumbled across an interesting find. One day after having struck out at several discount stores, grocery stores and drugstores, I was making my last stop.

Buy me some peanuts and Cracker Jack...

Discouraged from not being able to find any of the cards, I dragged into a discount drugstore into which I had not been before. To my delight I not only found specially marked Cracker Jack but also a special promotion — Buy 10, Get 2 Free. And all for only three bucks.

Feeling like I had found the proverbial pot of gold at the end of the rainbow, I purchased one of the special packages and raced to my car. The first box I opened had a Gwynn — one of the five I needed! One of the other boxes contained an Alomar, another of the missing five.

With only three left, I was feeling refurbished. Heck, I was even ready to take on my 30th birthday, which was coming up in a few days. I used the opportunity to put the word out that I wouldn't mind having a cracker jack birthday cake. Fortunately, no one complied with this request, but I did receive enough boxes to make one.

I think my wife was trying to put me out of my misery, but it backfired.

Counting the 12 boxes she gave me (wrapped up and everything) I received a total of 27 boxes for my birthday. With plenty of tupperware containers on hand for storage, I opened all 27 boxes in one sitting.

Despite the fact that I had opened nearly as many boxes as there were cards in the set, I got exactly one new card — Puckett. Twenty-seven boxes, 28 cards (another two-for-one special) and all I had to show for it was a Puckett and 27 duplicates. Actually, as if to add insult to injury, I got three Pucketts, but no Guerreros or Molitors.

And then depression set in. I had somehow hoped to overcome the law of averages, but it seemed to be holding true to form. A week went by without any Cracker Jack purchases. I knew the Sports Collectors Digest issue containing my ad would be out soon, and the birthday debacle had sufficiently dampened my spirits to keep me out of the discount drugstores.

I celebrated the arrival of the SCD with my ad in it by going out and buying nine new boxes. I really didn't expect to get any new cards, but somehow it seemed an appropriate celebratory action. And, I got lucky to boot. The ninth box I opened contained a Molitor! So, after 108 boxes I was now down to one card — Pedro Guerrero. I now had 10 Ken Griffeys, six Mark Graces, and five of Jose Canseco, Tim Raines and Rickey Henderson, but not a single Pedro Guerrero.

"Why Guerrero," I thought? Was my wife right? Had the company delayed printing Guerreros to ensure that nuts like me would buy 108 boxes trying to complete the set?

Or maybe Pedro was a modern day Honus Wagner. Maybe he was allergic to sugar or soya lecithin and had demanded that Cracker Jack pull his card out of production.

I broke into a cold sweat as I contemplated these horrible possibilities. Reminding myself that I probably would begin hearing from other collectors within a couple days, I was able to calm myself down enough to read the rest of the SCD issue.

Despite my initial apprehension over the cost, the money spent on the classified ad turned out to be the best four bucks I spent in the whole process. As expected, I received a number of responses to my ad within three days of its release.

The five prospective traders who responded the first day all indicated that they were collecting the cards in the unopened toy box prize wrapper. This seemed kind of pointless to me. I mean, what's the point in collecting something like baseball cards if you can't take them out and look at them up close and personal?

Fortunately, the three letters I received the next day were from collectors who also prefer a more meaningful relationship with their cards. The first two, however, did not have any Guerreros to trade. Just as I was ready to hire a private investigator to solve the mystery of the missing Guerrero card, I begrudgingly opened the third response.

And there it was! Right there at the top of the list of this collector's cards to trade was that elusive name — Guerrero. And he had three of them to trade.

I quickly dashed off a note and packaged up one of my Griffeys (from his wantlist) inside a couple of Donruss puzzle pieces (isn't this what they were invented for?).

Then I impatiently waited several days for my reply from my new trading partner. My wife threatened to have our home phone number changed if I called one more time to see if the mail had arrived yet.

It took about a week, but the reply finally came. With excited anticipation I carefully opened the envelope, which contained the same two Donruss puzzle pieces in which I had sent the Griffey.

After removing the tape from the sides of the puzzle pieces with deliberate speed, I gingerly separated them to reveal something I had waited more than two months to see — a tiny cardboard rendition of the Cardinals' first baseman.

Guerrero was pictured in a classic pose — bat in hand, down on one knee with the grandstands for a background. Flipping the card over I expected the caption to read, "Guerrero's 1991 Cracker Jack card is the most elusive in the whole set."

But instead I learned that "Pedro set the NL mark with 15 HR in June, 1985." At any rate, I was ecstatic to say the least.

And so, after 108 boxes of Cracker Jack, numerous phone calls to dealers, two different contacts with Borden, one trip to a card show, a $4 classified ad, one very important mail trade and enough soya lecithin to last me a lifetime, I finally had completed the Cracker Jack/ Topps set.

Epilogue

A couple of days ago, I stopped off at the grocery store to pick up some bread and milk. By force of habit, I strolled by the section with Cracker Jack noticed that they still had a few baseball card boxes. Only they somehow looked different.

A closer look indicated a bright yellow promo in the upper left revealing that these boxes contained one of 36 baseball cards in a 2nd series! Oh well, here we go again... — Tol Broome, Aug. 23, 1991

* * *

Giannoulas Sets Standard For Mascots

By Ross Forman

Ted Giannoulas is living proof that laughter is the universal language.

Giannoulas, the 36-year-old man behind the beak, has set the standard for all mascots.

Without a doubt, Giannoulas, er, the Famous Chicken, is the top jester of the jerseys.

The Famous Chicken, as he is now known after dropping "San Diego" from his title several years ago, is in his 17th season.

He has performed in 47 of the 50 states. He has not strutted his stuff in North Dakota, Rhode Island and Delaware.

He also has appeared in eight foreign countries, including Italy, Spain, Holland, Australia and Japan. In addition, he has been to Puerto Rico, Mexico and Canada.

The Chicken's international response is "wild and crazy," Giannoulas said.

Especially in Latin American countries.

"Those Latins see me walking into the ballparks with these wild colors and they think I'm a walking pinata," Giannoulas said. "They go nuts. It's just incredible. The audience in most foreign countries wears their laughter and their hearts on their sleeves. And they cut loose.

"I've performed at winter ball (stadiums filled to) 98-percent capacity, and that's stunning because some of these towns are dirtpoor so they have attendance problems.

"But when they announce the Chicken is coming, they pack the stadium.

"It's crazy down there...it'll be the ninth inning and you've got 10,000 people, standing on their feet chanting: 'Pollo, pollo, pollo.'"

But, the Chicken knows things can quickly turn nasty in some Latin countries.

"The players have told me that if they don't like you, they'll let you know it — by throwing things at you, such as bottles, bottle caps and limes," he said.

Luckily, Giannoulas said, he has never had problems. In fact, "I think they're great down there and they seem to really love me," he added.

The Famous Chicken is on the road 250 days of the year, including 125 consecutive nights during the baseball season — a pattern Giannoulas has followed each year since the Famous Chicken was hatched in 1974.

He appears at shopping mall openings, trade shows, parades, conventions, restaurant openings and has even been a banquet speaker several times.

"This might sound corny, but I tap into the energy of the people who come out (to the event) because that's the real show — watching them respond to me," said Giannoulas, whose excitement for performing today is as evident as it was when he accepted the job in 1974 while earning $2-an-hour as a one-week promotional stunt for a San Diego radio station.

"I've always been an energetic person. I just get excited when I'm performing," he said. "It really excites me to know that the audience responds as they do, whether it's at a sports memorabilia show or a stadium of 40,000."

Or, as was the case July 4, 1987, when more than 72,500 fans crammed Cleveland Stadium when the Indians played host to the Kansas City Royals on Chicken/Fireworks night.

"That was a real exciting game" Giannoulas said, "just to hear the roar of the crowd...it was like you could hear the earth tremble when 70,000 fans all laughed at once.

"Performing for large crowds is always exciting on the Major League level because the intensity of so many people laughing at once is truly unique."

Giannoulas said he doesn't get nervous with large crowds "because I'm very cognizant of what I have to do — I'm very aware and very confident that I can do it.

"I've got 90 seconds out on the field to make people laugh. And I do it.

"I tackle my job with the same intensity Roger Clemens has when pitching, that same kind of vigor."

The Famous Chicken uses more than 100 routines, and there's no set show.

The Chicken visits many Major and Minor League teams several times during a season, "and the shows are never the same.

"The way a singer comes out with albums every year I'll try to come out with a new show every visit," Giannoulas said. "People know they'll be getting a different array of material and I'm very proud of that. This is my own origination and my own creativity at work.

"It's a tremendous thrill knowing I can walk onto a diamond with a sight gag that I created. Then, 90 seconds later, the place is laughing and applauding. I suppose that's what every entertainer strives for."

Giannoulas said the most popular routine this year has been a parody of rap singer Vanilla Ice's song "Ice, Ice, Baby," adapted to Chicken lyrics.

Topping the all-time favorite list of Chicken acts is when he dresses youngsters as baby chickens and they parody Giannoulas' everymove, including the raised-leg salute to the umpires.

"People never seem to get tired of that (baby chicken) routine," Giannoulas said. "In fact, if I don't use it, fans always ask me why I didn't (use it).

"The Pete Rose imitation around the bases is always a classic because that involves a slow-motion replay with the catcher a la Pete Rose and Ray Fosse in the 1970 All-Star Game."

The Famous Chicken often aids the home team between innings — he replaces the first baseman during infield warm-ups.

CECIL FIELDER

The Famous Chicken and Cecil Fielder pose for Upper Deck.

"I really enjoy doing that," Giannoulas said. "In fact, this summer I took a lawn chair, a drink, a towel and a magazine out to Cecil Fielder. And to see him squeeze into the lawn chair was the funniest sight - even Lou Whitaker was busting up at second base, watching Cecil ease himself into that lawn chair. It was hysterical.

"Upper Deck has a picture of (the Famous Chicken/Fielder act) and they're going to use it for a 1992 card. I'm really looking forward to seeing that card."

San Diego is still Giannoulas' home, as well as his test site.

He often performs new skits there — "the same way a stand-up comic would go and break-in material at a local club as a surprise...I do the same with gags at Jack Murphy Stadium."

Not every routine is a first-time hit, Giannoulas said. Often, he has to refuse a skit before taking it to the rest of the world.

"If something doesn't work, I listen to the audience as my editors — they'll tell me if it's a keeper or a throwaway," Giannoulas said. "I would say about 80 percent of my gags have been successful. And the 20 percent that don't work...I'll polish them and then they'll work."

As for total rejects — "maybe one out of 10. Maybe."

Giannoulas, who never takes pictures out of costume, says he has "the best of both worlds."

"I love being public when I want to be public and private when I want to be private," said the 5-foot-4 Giannoulas, whose cartoon favorites are Batman, the Green Hornet and the Three Stooges.

"No one knows me out of character and I don't mind — I want the Famous Chicken to get all of the attention. I'm happy to stay low profile.

"If I was in this for personal ego and glory, I would let Ted Giannoulas take all of the photographs and shoe the Chicken aside. But that's not what I'm about."

The Famous Chicken had his own cards in the Donruss sets from 1982-84.

"My cards get a very good response from collectors and I'll be honest, that surprises me," Giannoulas said. "I thought the purist (collectors) would be up-in-arms because those Chicken cards were precedent-setting...they were the first cards of a non-purely-baseball personality to appear in a company's major card set."

One of the major attractions of the Famous Chicken cards was the opportunity to get them personally autographed, just by mailing them in to Donruss.

And yes, the Famous Chicken did, and still does, sign each one!

"I still, even to this day, have Donruss send me the cards to be autographed," Giannoulas said. "And for all of the cynics who think it might be a machine or a rubber stamp signing them, they're wrong!

"I sit and sign every one."

The Famous Chicken receives about 100 fan mail letters per week.

"I always get a kick out of the mail, especially when kids send letters," Giannoulas said. "I've gotten letters from some real serious collectors, who have gone through painstaking means to send their cards, such as sending them in plastic cases."

Although unique, the Famous Chicken cards haven't sky-rocketed in value.

"I enjoy the fact that the most I've seen my Chicken card priced at is $1.25," Giannoulas said. "I'm happy because that means everyone can afford them, especially the little kids.

"I like to see the Chicken cards affordable and at...chicken-feed prices."

Giannoulas isn't a card collector, although he wishes he was — especially since he was a collector while growing up as a child in London, Ontario, Canada.

"I admire collectors, but I'm just too far along (in life) to go back and start," he said. "Plus, I devote so much time to the betterment of the Chicken's act. I have very little time for myself personally."

Giannoulas said his favorite set is the 1962 Topps, "although I'm partial to it because it was my first set."

"Those wood-grained '62 cards...I think those are the nicest cards I've ever seen, even to this day."

Giannoulas said he still "kicks him self time and time again" for not having the collection he had as a kid.

Giannoulas calls himself "a collecting purist" because he doesn't like seeing players photographed for cards while wearing their practice uniforms as opposed to their game uniforms.

"I loved seeing the Roger Maris shot in his game uniform, or seeing Willie Mays with the word 'San Francisco' across their chest," Giannoulas added. "But now you see the multi-colored practice jersey and that passes as their main card...and I don't like that."

Giannoulas, who was born in Canada, became a dual citizen (U.S.-Canadian) in the early-1980s. He grew up "on hockey and hockey cards — although I never kept them."

His favorite team was, and still is, the Montreal Canadiens.

"One thing I wish I could do is perform at the Montreal Forum for a Montreal Canadiens game. That would be a thrill," said Giannoulas' whose favorite hockey players were Glenn Hall, Gump Worsley and Rogie Vachon.

Giannoulas' favorite baseball team while growing up in Canada was...the San Francisco Giants.

That's right, Giannoulas idolized Willie Mays and the San Francisco Giants, "and don't ask me why — other than to speculate that when I was a kid, no one in London, Ontario, Canada, would cheer for this lowly-team out on the West Coast."

"I always wanted to be a shortstop for the Giants," Giannoulas said. "In fact, I remember telling my mom, 'One day you'll see me in uniform at Candlestick Park.'

"Well, I got to Candlestick Park and I was in uniform...it was just the wrong colors."

So what's next for this fine-feathered-friend?

Perhaps a whirl as a stand-up comedian, Giannoulas said.

"A hotel in Las Vegas approached me several years ago to be a stand-up there," he said. "They said they'd get me writers and do everything necessary, but my schedule didn't allow.

"But I think now might be the right time, and a neat career challenge to see if it would work." — Ross Forman, Nov. 21, 1991

* * *

This Gorilla Is No 'Dumb Monkey'

By Tom Hultman

You have seen apes at the zoo throw basketballs through old automobile tires.

And that's no big deal. In fact, it gets rather boring after awhile.

That's not the case with the Phoenix Suns Gorilla mascot. This is one animal which is no dumb monkey. And he is by no means boring.

With the help of a trampoline, the Gorilla can do unbelievable dunks — ones that even Michael Jordan, Dee Brown or Dominique Wilkins can't match.

The Gorilla is in a class by itself. Even the man who wears the suit doesn't like his name to be used. For convenience's sake, we'll call him Steve.

"It's the Gorilla and the guy behind the mask," he said.

The man inside the suit, however, does have an interesting story to tell.

"I was busy coaching kids in a gymnastics center and finishing off school at Arizona State. A friend of mine told me I'd be perfect for the job (as the Gorilla)," he said.

"He just kept after me, and finally talked me into it. Both of us ended up trying out for the job. I found it kind of intriguing — the whole aspect of the Gorilla and how he did it."

The man behind the mask was the lucky one chosen out of 525 persons who tried out for the position.

"Once I started doing things and experiencing what I could bring and add to the Gorilla I realized this was for me," he said. "Being an ex-gymnast, we had trampoline acts and gymnastics, and I was just retiring as a gymnast and I felt that my talents could come out in the Gorilla.

"I was really excited about not getting a full-time job behind a desk. I wanted to enhance my gymnastics skills and to entertain people for 5-10 years. I wanted to develop my skills and not put them to rest."

The Gorilla has been in existence for 12 years. The 27-year-old Steve, who is only the second person ever in the suit, has spent four years behind the mask.

Steve was a high school All-American gymnast while growing up in Montana. He then became an All-American at Arizona State, where he competed in all six events in the all-around.

However, basketball was never really in his blood.

"I grew up with a basketball hoop in my yard," he said. "I tried playing basketball, but I was a little short and slow. I did shoot around a lot, but I never did pursue it. I tried it in junior high, but things didn't work out for me."

Oh, but how this furry suit turns him into a basketball whiz. He said once he puts the mask on, he becomes a different person.

"I didn't think I was at first, but everyone from my mom down to my best friends say, 'I cannot believe that's you in the suit,'" he said. "It's two completely different people. It really is. I get into a whole new character once I'm inside the Gorilla suit.

"That's good because the Gorilla has its own character. In fact, I talk about him as a third party because he is so different. I'm proud to be the driving factor behind it all."

It wasn't always great times for Steve when he first started as the Gorilla.

"I had to work into it. No matter what covered my face and body, it was still me inside. If people booed me, it was still me being booed," he said. "It helped me a little bit because I stepped into someone else. I, myself, could not go on the court and do those things, but as a character, yes, I can.

"The mask helped, but if someone booed, it didn't hide everything. I never get booed on the road. When I say booed, I don't mean that in a bad sense. Our audience back home (in Phoenix) likes to let their emotions go. If I miss a dunk, whether it is on purpose or not, they just let the Gorilla have it — more in fun than anything else. They just love to razz the Gorilla, but they like the Gorilla a lot."

This Gorilla is a jack of all trades — from cheerleader to spectator to entertainer.

"We go up and mess around with the kids and the older people," he said. "We do it all. People talk to me a lot. There are only three or four times that I actually have downright laughed hard in my suit."

Basically, the Gorilla is in the same league as the Famous Chicken and the Phillie Phanatic. However, there is one major difference. The Gorilla said he is more family-oriented than the chicken.

"The Chicken goes out on the limb a few times, but that is his character. The big difference is that the Gorilla is so mobile and easy to get around," he said.

"One minute he is on the floor flirting with the cheerleaders and the next minute he's up in the rafters. The Gorilla can do gymnastics and he can do flips."

"The Gorilla wants to be like a human being, but he can never quite get to that point. He's either falling or tripping or messing up somehow. He can never do things right, except when it comes to dunking."

And how.

When it comes to dunking there is no one better. The Gorilla has plenty of dunks in its repertoire.

It'll flip in the air once or twice before a dunk. It will electrify the crowd with a 360-degree slam. And, of course, its famous dunk where it flies parallel to the floor and slams it home. Let's see Jordan do that.

How does he come up with these dunks?

"Dunking comes naturally to me. We don't work too much extra on dunks in rehersals. We just set up the trampolines and let her go," he said. "Whatever we feel like we want to do, we just do it. We have three solid dunks and we throw in others as we go along.

"It started out that the Gorilla was mostly known for its dunking ability. Right now, I enjoy the entertainment part of the show as much as the dunks. I also like working with the younger kids. The toughest part of my job is to get the adults up to the level where I want them.

"I want the adults to say, 'Oh, Wow! That guy was really cool.' Dunking has brought the Gorilla to where he is right now. It's one of my favorite points of my job."

With the type of reckless abandon the Gorilla has in his dunking act, it is a miracle that he has never been seriously hurt.

"Fortunately, I haven't been hurt that bad. A few years back I did a school dance and I hit the stage," he said. "I cut my head open and received 22 stitches. The tricks that you would think I would get hurt on I really don't. That comes through my gymnastics background — how to fall, how to land, how to hit something. I'm sort of like a stuntman.

"It's an illusion to the people in the audience. It looks worse than it really is."

He said he rarely practices his dunks — maybe once a month on a new style dunk. For road shows, it is mostly mental work for Steve.

"You are always trying to get new skits, new ideas and a new way to entertain the crowd," he said. "It's a lot of creative work. In the summertime, I train to stay in shape."

Steve's manager, Kenny Glenn, has been with the Gorilla since the first day.

"He's resurrected the Gorilla. He has made the Gorilla what it is today. He has been the powerhouse behind everything," Steve said. "I'm the man behind the suit, but Kenny has come up with a lot of skits and ideas and a lot of the pencil work behind the Gorilla."

Road manager Bryan Larive does everything which has to be done away from home.

"The three of us usually get together to brainstorm and get everything in order," Steve said.

According to Steve, he expects to be in the Gorilla suit for another seven or more years.

"Honestly, it's a tough question. I would like a good 10-year career," he said. "It's very much year-by-year with the Suns. I hope to be doing it as long as I can."

The Gorilla's workload has increased dramatically over the past four years. In Steve's first season, he did five away shows. He is now up to 40-50 away shows, not including all the Suns' home games. There are also plans to do 20 baseball games this summer.

With all these gigs, you would think Steve would get burned out. But that is not the case.

"I don't have to worry about getting pumped up for a game, especially when there is 10,000-15,000 people in the crowd. It just comes," he said. "The people come with it. Once you are out there, you go with the flow. But when I am performing before 1,500 people, it is a challenge. You want to get these 1,500 people as loud as you can.

"The bottom line is whether it is 1,500 or 15,000 people, I still enjoy what I do. I do it 100 percent everytime, no matter what. Hopefully, it works out both ways."

A goal in Steve's life is becoming a pilot in the National Guard.

That's still a possibility, but now he's flying through the air in a different fashion. — Tom Hultman, Feb. 7, 1992

* * *

Gorilla A Card Collector At Heart

By Tom Hultman

The man behind the Phoenix Suns Gorilla mask may look like any other mascot, but, in reality he is a card collector at heart.

Steve, the man inside the suit, who does not want his real name used, said he collected cards before he became the Gorilla, but since has been buying cases of various basketball cards.

"I've got the set from every year since I started (four years ago)," he said. "I think it's great. I also have saved the press clippings of the Gorilla. Between my parents, girlfriend and me, we have quite a portfolio made. I don't get into it so much, but my mom and dad do. They really enjoy doing that. Also my girlfriend and her mother.

"We have a stack of clippings and a stack of photos. We have a lot of old memorabilia that we started with."

The Gorilla has never been featured on a major card company's card. However, Steve said he has signed possible Suns team-issued Gorilla cards, which were released before he started.

"I have signed some (Gorilla) cards that were at least six years old," he said. "I knew it wasn't me on the card. I thought those cards were put out by the Phoenix Suns.

"We're looking for the day to be put on a card. I'm just holding my breath right now. I would love to."

Steve said before he became the Gorilla, he was collecting cards. But he never did realize how big the hobby had become.

"Card collecting is one of the biggest things that I have ever been associated with," he said. "We do a lot of card shows every year. We sign a lot of autograph cards at these shows. I just cannot believe how big this industry and business is.

"I think it is really exciting."

The Gorilla said he enjoys signing autographs. However, he said signing autographs in the eight-pound Gorilla suit isn't easy.

"Signing autographs in the Gorilla suit is probably just as tough as going out there and entertaining," he said. "It is very hot and I sweat quite a bit (he loses between four and seven pounds at every game). I think it is so neat that the kids want to stand in line and get the Gorilla's autograph.

"I love doing it and I'll do it anywhere I go. Autographing is a way we can give something back to the kids. They can get one-on-one with the Gorilla. It's neat for a kid to walk away with a signed Gorilla photo in his hand."

Steve said the Suns receive many requests for Gorilla autographs through the mail. He said he signs all requests which come to the team's office.

"We have received things from all over the world, including Europe and Hawaii," he said. "It's incredible the number of fans who get a glimpse of the Gorilla and the Suns. We send them all back. However, many are from local schools and charities."

The Gorilla has been a signing guest at many card shows around the Phoenix area. It is something he never turns down.

"I think they are great," he said.

"Sometimes I wish I could be a part of the shows by being out there buying and having fun with the card collectors, instead of signing autographs as the Gorilla.

"I love to see card shows and I like to see how popular they are getting."

You probably won't believe what the strangest thing the Gorilla has signed.

And, believe it or not, it is not below the neck.

"I signed someone's forehead once with a permanent magic marker," he said. "Actually, when a younger kid about six or seven years old comes up to me to sign a $120 ski jacket, I just can't do it. His mom would kill me when he got home. I have a hard time doing that when I know his mom would kill both of us."

After all, when is a mother happy when her child brings home a gorilla? — Tom Hultman, Feb. 7, 1992

* * *

Wrigley Field Ballhawks' Experiences Told

By Dave Miedema

To some, it would seem to be a grand waste of time...spend four hours of a summer afternoon outside Wrigley Field, hoping that maybe a ball would soar over the chain link fence, land below on the street and somehow end up in your clutches.

To others, it would be a case of misappropriated funds and priorities.

After all, who would be daft enough to buy a bleacher seat at Wrigley, watch batting practice and then leave the park and stand outside for the duration of the game?

Rich and Mark and Andy. That's who.

And Mo, Bruce and Yimmie, too.

Let's not forget the three Mikes — Railroad, Black and Bike, as their handles go.

Then there's Cabbie and Jim and Husker.

Regarding the fun-over-funds part, those guys you see on TV running around on the street after home run balls are up to their earlobes in enjoyment.

These guys are far from anonymous, of course. Once or twice a year, a local paper will run a feature on the Ballhawks, with the slant of the article varying from free-wheeling fun to kamikaze competition for a round, white object.

Even TV advertising has noticed their part in Wrigley Field lore.

As seen in the 1990 Levi jeans commercial starring John Witt, himself nearly a victim of his own enthusiasm some seven months prior to that ad shooting on that same stretch of driveways outside the left-field bleachers.

Regardless of the ups and downs, though, many of these guys have careers on the streets around the park that have lasted longer than the fellows in doubleknits patrolling the grass and dirt inside the stadium.

Many have a wound, scar or a visit to first aid to show or tell of in the pursuit of their craft.

A few have been hassled by police and security for the most mundane of reasons, either at Wrigley Field or on one of numerous trips around the midwest.

To the fan who considers snaring a foul ball one of life's major highlights, the numbers these men have rung up over the years would numb the mind.

At the top of your list, you have two Hawks of over 20 years standing, Rich Buhrke and Mo Mullins.

Buhrke, active in this pursuit of joy since 1959, has caught over 2,400 baseballs in that time span, and, even more amazing, has snagged at least one regular season game home run every year in that time frame.

The streak reached 32 straight years last April, when Rich, playing a hunch, stationed himself in an unoccupied area down the left field foul line at Milwaukee County Stadium and chased down a blast by Dante Bichette in a Brewer win over the Chicago White Sox.

Mo, meanwhile, is the only other active Ballhawk over 2,000 catches for a career. The pair were both featured as guests on Oprah Winfrey's "A.M. Chicago" show in 1984.

With over 4,500 baseballs in their combined ownership, what do these two men do with them all?

Buhrke, a uniform collector and bat saver in his other hobby endeavors, swaps some to collectors for items he seeks, and donates others free of charge to the Little League programs at his place of employment. Mullins, likewise, gives many of his catches to various youth programs.

Game home runs are another story, however. Very rarely will a Ballhawk let go of an actual game homer he has caught, and the dingers snagged by Rich, Mo and the others have sometimes been of very notable proportions.

Buhrke, for example, caught Ron Santo's 300th career home run, swapping it to Santo for a bat afterwards. He also snared one of Ryne Sandberg's shots during the 1990 Home Run Hitting Contest the day prior to the All-Star Game.

Mark Didtler, now a sports reporter in Houston, also has procured a four-digit total of catches, foremost of which was the grand slam Will Clark bashed against the Cubs in Game One of the 1989 NLCS.

Didtler and a passerby hopped the fence into a yard along Sheffield Avenue, the thoroughfare outside Wrigley's right field wall, to chase the sphere into a clump of bushes at the rear of the yard.

Didtler's response to repeated requests to sell the home run ball typify the fun-over-profit mindset that is the Ballhawk norm.

One Chicago area Cub collector has repeatedly indicated a willingness to pay a large amount of cash for the Clark ball, all of which Didtler has turned down.

"Money I can replace, but not the ball," Didtler said.

He said the only scenario that would pry his prize loose would be "if Clark wanted the ball, say to give to his mom or dad, then I'd consider letting it go."

Even then, the asking price would not be dollar and cents.

"A jersey of his would be nice, but I wouldn't put a dollar amount at him," Didtler said."You can't put a price on memories."

Andy Mielke is an assistant to Buhrke at his park district workplace, and has also done everything from bartend to act (a brief appearance in "Major League") in his young adult years.

He has snagged over 900 baseballs in a hawking career dating back to grade school.

He enjoys being able to keep in touch with the sport.

Mielke is also a frequent traveler to other area stadiums, and snatched two homers last summer at Tiger Stadium, a favorite destination for the impromptu trips many of the Hawks take on weekends or vacations.

The Cecil Fielder and Tony Phillips taters he caught are definite keepers.

Of course, keeping any home run can be a problem at Wrigley Field, where the tradition for several years has been for fans to fling a visiting home run ball back onto the field, usually at the intimidating urge of bleacher diehards screaming "Throw it back."

One photo sequence in the local papers a few years ago showed a diehard stuffing money into a fan's hand, then wresting the enemy homer out of the stunned fan's other hand and flinging it back onto the field.

To a Ballhawk, throwing back any home run, even one from a despised rival player or disliked opposing team, would be tantamount to a collector buying an unopened wax pack of 1973 Topps cards, receiving a Schmidt rookie and then giving the Schmidt card back to the dealer because he doesn't like the Phillies.

To that end, Ballhawks have become adept at pulling a switcheroo that pacifies the raging crowd and keeps the prized catch in the catcher's possession.

Usually with the help of a fellow Hawk, a catch from batting practice is substituted clandestinely, so that the bogus ball being flung back is presumed by the crowd to be the offending score.

"The guys have had to be more adept at pulling a switch lately," Buhrke said, citing mentions by both TV telecaster Harry Caray and radio announcer Ron Santo last season of the decoy practice on their broadcasts.

While many of the best memories are reserved for game catches, the Ballhawks place great importance on batting practice, as well.

Often, several Hawks will buy bleacher tickets and go after homers that land in the outfield seats, also serving as signalmen to the contingent on the street as to whether lefties or righties are hitting, and just whom is taking their cuts in a given group. Often, hand signals or charades-style gestures are used to identify a hitter.

Once in a while, they'll get lucky. Far more often than not, though, the ball will end up nestled in the mitt of one of the 15 or so fellows who are, for all practical purposes, the Ballhawks.

Such signals will reveal the identity of a batter, and the Hawks will then know whether said batter is a dead pull slugger, or one who slams them towards the power alleys.

The Ballhawks are as scientific in playing batters as the guys getting paid to do it inside the walls are. Wind currents are observed, as even casual fans are usually aware that the wind blowing out generally translates into a higher-scoring affair.

A pitcher's stuff is duly noted...is he a speed pitcher or a junkballer? The strengths and weaknesses are assessed.

The bottom line is, most of these guys are far better prepared for the opportunities that come their way than the out-of-town person who has seen these pros at work on TV, and figures that he'll stroll right up and do the same thing.

That isn't to say that the novice has no chance at all, but those chances are few and far between.

As was the case once last summer when the Hawks played the Mets' lefty sluggers out on Sheffield, and a blast off the bat of Howard Johnson descended onto the street.

Instead of taking a natural bounce, though, the ball hit a piece of debris in the street, took an unnatural bounce and deflected off a parked car back towards the stadium wall, where a 7-year-old being walked by his parents casually picked the ball up off the ground with all the effort of a couch potato flipping the remote control channel selector on his TV set.

"Those bounces happen," said Buhrke.

Of course, what constitutes a great day for a normal fan may be an average or even poor day for a Ballhawk. Most fans would consider it a major event to snatch one baseball.

For a Ballhawk, one baseball caught can often be a slow day at the office, depending on the circumstances.

The competitive urge that the Hawks possess is one that has sometimes not endeared them to casual fans or stadium personnel.

Witt tells of a time at old Comiskey Park when he was "playing the lines," Ballhawk-speak for waiting down the left or right field foul lines, usually alongside a low retaining wall such as the one old Comiskey Park had, and scooping rollers and bouncers down the line off the field by leaning over the wall.

"I had gotten five already," Witt said. "And just reached over and grabbed my sixth, when some young usher comes by and tells me I'm gone (ejected from the park). I asked why, and he said 'You went over (the wall).'

"I hadn't even set foot on the field! I leaned over, picked up the ball and came back in without ever having more than my arms and upper body over (the plane) of the wall."

Witt eventually pleaded his case to the snippety usher's supervisor, who let him off the hook.

Rarely does the activity get into physical mayhem, but most Ballhawks acknowledge that a thick skin helps when fans verbally harass them for having the audacity to catch more than one baseball on a given day.

"I caught two in the right field at Wrigley, and had some guy all over me after catching the second one," one Ballhawk said. "Never mind that this fool never moved out of his seat to attempt to catch one. He apparently expected that a baseball would land in his lap, which it didn't, and took offense that I had caught two, fair and square."

One Hawk said he took a trip to Milwaukee where an usher told him that he couldn't continue shagging after he caught his third of the day.

Their travels take them all over the country.

Favorite stops on the Ballhawk itinerary are (in addition to Wrigley Field), Tiger Stadium and County Stadium.

New Comiskey Park is not well-loved because "the gates open too late (90 minutes before the game, as opposed to two hours earlier at most parks) and there's too many people, meaning you have no room to manuever" gaid Garza.

The Metrodome was once a popular Ballhawk destination, but the Twins' success has left that off-limits, for the time being.

Minor league parks are often enjoyed, but they can sometimes become a hassle due to penny-pinching attitudes by teams operating on a low budget.

The home of the Midwest League Kenosha Twins is an example of stingy management, according to Buhrke.

"I've actually had to bring disguises when I've hawked there — different hats, different shirts and the like because anything that leaves the stadium is pursued by an old security guy who demands that the ball be returned, or else."

The Ballbawks are a diverse bunch who all enjoy the sport.

The group knows no occupational or elitist restrictions.

"We're regular guys that enjoy a regular game," said Garza.

Railroad Mike works in one of the southwest suburban rail yards. Black Mike is a Chicago cop, as is young Buhrke, but Mike has many years of experience in the force.

Bruce Snyder, when he isn't overseeing a repair crew, is a hobby dealer specializing in Sports Impressions and related figurines.

Jim Dlask gets his "Cabbie" moniker from longtime employment as a computer specialist with a city taxi firm.

Most Ballhawks are also collectors of some sort.

Whatever they collect, the balls which come flying at them on the street or in the seats are their common bond— their main hobby love.

While the Ballhawks are an "all for one/one for all" bunch, to describe them as one big happy family would be somewhat extreme the other way.

Some members of the group have been known to ruffle the feathers of their cohorts for varying reasons, be it overzealousness in chasing down baseballs or eventually proven embellishment of individual exploits.

The Ballhawks may occasionally bicker, argue and snip at and about others in the group.

Yet when the going gets tough, they will set those disputes aside and get going for each other, as Witt learned in October 1989.

The young Ballhawk, several months before being filmed in Spike Lee's jeans commercial for Levi Strauss, nearly became a victim of his own hawking success, and was rescued by the intervention of others in the group, by a variety of means.

In the 1989 NLCS, late in Game One, a three-run blast by Kevin Mitchell sailed onto the milling crowd on Waveland Avenue, and pursued by young Buhrke and Witt.

A bounce off the rooftop of the parked bus puts Buhrke out of the catch, which is ensnared by Witt, in full view of the crowd on the street, most of whom are irritated over the local team's drubbing at the hands of the Giants.

Too few Cub runs began to spell trouble for Witt, who would not throw back the Mitchell homer, and who began to be approached by several members of the crowd intent on making trouble.

Buhrke, at the time in the midst of his police studies, used a form of rescue-style escort to bring Witt back to his comrades, most of whom then surrounded Witt, willingly, if necessary, to defend him.

"I really thought we were gonna have to fight our way out of there," Didtler said.

Jim's father, meanwhile, thought and acted quickly to try and stave off the potential small-scale street riot that was brewing.

The crowd continued to remain ugly, and the day was only saved when Chicago police patrolling the area, by now convinced that Witt was at a safety risk, intervened and Jim Buhrke gave Witt an automobile ride out of the area, depositing him at an intersection over a mile away.

One of the Ballhawks' chief concerns and sore spots is much of the media coverage they receive.

They realize that what they do, and the way it has been included in the nostalgic atmosphere of the Wrigley Field experience, is going to bring attention. It's the types of attention — and the angles some of the print and electronic media types use in their coverage — that makes the Ballhawks see red.

"You know you're going to get shown on TV, and have writers approach you for stories," Buhrke said. "But a lot of times, these TV and radio and newspaper types, from the word go, do their piece with a bias against us. They make us look either like total idiots, or else barbarians that try to hurt each other."

Indeed, the media types who have drawn the Ballhawks scorn are numerous.

A popular TV sports anchor was a longtime object of the group's wrath after a TV piece that portrayed these men at play as being a few rookie cards short of a complete set.

To his credit, though, the sports anchor made amends.

"(He) came out here (to Waveland Avenue) the next year, and wanted to do another piece on us, and we let him have it," Buhrke said. "We told him that we didn't like the way he was trying to make us look, and told him that we wouldn't cooperate with him at all.

"(He) was stunned by our response, and seemed genuinely sorry that he had offended us. He asked us to work with him, and promised that he'd make the piece a far more balanced and less ridiculing one.

"We agreed that we'd give it a shot, and (he) was true to his word. He gave us a fair shot then, and has continued to do so since."

Buhrke, the guru of the group, has seen his share of media attention, with the Oprah appearance, several 6 p.m. news features, and several requests for interviews from the print media.

Buhrke was the subject of a three-page article in a summer 1977 issue of Sports Illustrated, and, while the article, he felt, was a good one, some of the ensuing attention left a bit to be desired.

"My wife is a nurse, and often had to work odd hours back then," he said. "Meanwhile, I usually turn in late, and wake up late, as well. After the SI piece hit print, we were getting phone calls at all times from other magazines, and radio hosts wanting to chat."

The straw that broke the camel's back came at about 5:30 a.m. one day.

"We're both sound asleep, and the phone rings," he said. "I pick it up, still pretty much out of it, and some bozo says, 'Good Morning! You're live on' what-ever-it-was radio station he was the morning drive DJ for. This guy worked for a New Orleans station, and was too dumb to acknowledge the early hour, plus he called out of the blue."

Rich read him the riot act, hung up, and then secured an unlisted phone number, still in effect today.

Although some of the Hawks' publicity is endearing and positive, the Hawks are pretty sensitive about some of the coverage they get.

The Ballhawks usually get focused on their chases.

Buhrke was given a fractured cheekbone when a competitor nudged his arm aside chasing a ball, with the ball crunching into said cheekbone.

Mike White (Black Mike) has ripped open his trousers and has crawled underneath idling busses to retrieve baseballs.

Hegel has dove for a ball, and come up with a smearing of doggie-do on his jacket for his trouble. Several have come this close to being hit by, or running into, moving vehicles.

Nonetheless, the game continues, and the guys keep on plugging, keep coming back for more.

And, occasionally, their escapades are recognized and even admired by WGN viewers picking up the games on TV in other ports of call.

"The first time we went to Arlington Stadium, we saw few people that could be considered serious ballhawks, and most of them did nothing more than chase a ball that had already landed in the seats," Didtler said. "Later on, though, we saw some of these fans wearing fielders' mitts, and trying to catch the baseballs on the fly.

"I asked one of them what caused the new approach, and he said something about watching the Cubs games on TV, and seeing how the guys standing out on the street did it, and figuring they'd try to imitate them. Never mind that one of 'them' was the person he was explaining this all to."

What Ballhawks do may, indeed, seem pointless and time sadly wasted. But, hey, isn't that what most people said about collecting baseball cards 30 years ago?

The camaraderie is akin to the barnstorming days of big league baseball, and the rewards are measured in enjoyment, not economics.

"You can't put a price on memories," Didtler said.

And nothing gets these guys rolling like talking about a successful day at the ball park. Pure fun, clean competition, and true collecting.

Lots of sharing, plenty of story swapping, and nobody gives a darn about what the price guide says a Sandberg rookie is going for.

Isn't that the way collecting should be? — Dave Miedema, May 8, 1992

* * *

Last Autographed Ball Has Special Meaning To Hardin's Family

Editor's note: Ted Simendinger spent time on Friday, March 8, golfing with former major league pitcher Jim Hardin. Among the topics the two discussed were Hardin's career, his shoulder injury, the Baltimore Orioles and the sports memorabilia collecting hobby. On that day, Hardin also autographed a baseball for Simendinger, who, for this story, has recalled parts of their conversations from that day. After Hardin was killed in a plane crash Saturday, March 9, Simendinger gave the ball to Hardin's daughter, Gina, and interviewed those who are also quoted in this story.

By Ted Simendinger

The last baseball Jim Hardin ever signed was on my shelf, resting between Stan Musial and Joe Sewell, when news of Hardin's tragic plane crash flashed across my television.

The announcers didn't identify the three victims by name, but the sight of the strewn Beechcraft wreckage, coupled with the flight plan, "the trio left Key West bound for West Palm Beach," — hit me like a thunderbolt.

Hardin had signed the baseball for me Friday, March 8, the day before his death. We played golf together and had lunch at Mayacoo, the West Palm country club where Hardin was reigning club champion.

From there, he flew to Key West to fish on Saturday. He planned to fly home Saturday evening to spend Sunday with his wife and infant son.

Hardin was the least-known player I had. When he died a scant 24 hours after we rekindled our friendship, the baseball in the closet instantly grew exponentially in importance.

But as important as the ball was to me, I also knew it belonged in his family, not mine.

The magic threads connecting collectors to their autographed baseballs is invisible, but strong. The strength of that bond often stems from the fiber of the man who pushed the pen.

Collectors don't sell friends and heroes, but family is the strongest bond of all.

Hardin was a journeyman pitcher for the Baltimore Orioles, New York Yankees and Atlanta Braves in the late 1960s and early '70s. His career statistics are good (43-32, 3.18 ERA) but not overly impressive.

What is impressive, however, is the obstacle he overcame to pitch in the big leagues and his travels along the way. In collector parlance, this fellow was a very uncommon common.

To reach Hardin's birthplace in rural Tennessee "you take a paved road to a gravel road to a dirt road to a path," his daughter Gina said shortly after the March 9 accident. "That takes you to the doorstep of a house with no running water."

317

Hardin was hospitalized and crippled by polio as a young boy. Since Hardin's family was poor and couldn't afford proper medical care, the Memphis March of Dimes provided leg braces so Hardin could walk.

In his will, Hardin remembered the March of Dimes, specifically asking for donations to that charity in lieu of flowers.

Twenty years after the leg braces, Hardin graced the cover of The Sporting News.

Hardin outgrew the polio but wasn't allowed to play football as a child. He played baseball and caught throughout Little League. He often wheeled his baby sister to practice in her stroller while his mom worked.

The switch to pitching came in high school when the team ran out of pitchers, forcing him into action. Among the big right-hander's high school competitors was four-decade big-league star Tim McCarver.

The expansion New York Mets selected Hardin in the 1961 draft. He signed out of high school, received "about $10,000, in increments," recalled his first wife Donna, "and thought he was rich."

Hardin spent two seasons in A ball in Auburn, N.Y., before graduating to Double A Williamsport in June of 1964.

He saved on meal money and supplemented his income by eating peanuts, drinking water, and hustling pool in bars after games.

"In the minors, they only paid for one meal a day," noted Donna.

In Williamsport, Hardin was a teammate of future Met Ron Swoboda. Five years later, Swoboda's big catch in the 1969 World Series catapulted the Mets to a 3-1 lead en route to their five-game upset over Hardin's heavily-favored Baltimore Orioles.

"That (catch) won the Series for them," Hardin said during our conversation on the golf course that day before his death. "If he misses that ball we win the game and tie the Series 2-2 and we'd have won it. When they went up 3-1, it was over."

Hardin never made it to the majors with the Mets. Earl Weaver of the Orioles made sure of that.

"I was responsible for drafting him from the Mets," Weaver said shortly after Hardin's death. Weaver selected Hardin when the Mets left him unprotected in the 1965 winter draft. "He ended up giving us two great years," Weaver said.

"For whatever reason, Jim always pitched well against the Orioles," recalled Donna Hardin. "Going to the Orioles was a big break for Jim."

Hardin pitched at AA Elmira during 1966 and then made an extra $1,000 pitching for manager Ronnie Camacho and Hermosilla in the Mexican Winter League.

Hardin went to spring training, spent two months with AAA Rochester and was called up to the majors in June 1967, replacing an injured young right-hander named Jim Palmer.

"They told us it was only for 10 days," said Donna. "But it never occurred to us he wouldn't stay with the Orioles."

Hardin's contract was the league minimum, "about $8,000" Donna guessed, but with their first child on the way the money came in handy.

Hardin had good control, threw hard and depended a lot on his slider. He kept his roster spot by going 8-3, with two shutouts, five complete games in 14 starts, and an excellent 2.27 ERA. He had earned a permanent spot on the team.

The next year, 1968, was Hardin's best, when he went 18-13 with 16 complete games and a 2.51 ERA. He surrendered seven hits per nine innings and graced the cover of The Sporting News.

Fifth in the American League in wins and ninth in innings pitched, Hardin was a major reason for the Orioles' rise from sixth place to second.

Another reason was Weaver, who took over the team at mid-season and went 82-48 over the second half.

After the season Hardin headed to Puerto Rico for winter ball. He roomed with Palmer and learned self-hypnosis at a San Juan nightclub.

"He thought it would help his concentration," Donna said.

Hardin then began sticking pins through his pinched skin and convinced himself it wouldn't hurt. He abandoned the practice a few years later.

Several years ago, Hardin scrubbed up and followed a surgeon friend into a Miami hospital operating room to watch surgery. At the first sight of blood he passed out and had to be dragged out from the O.R.

Other people, doctors, stuck pins in him during the 1969 season. Hardin, not quite 26, lost his spot as a starter.

He developed shoulder soreness for the first time, took cortisone shots, and pitched through the pain. Sliders, shoulders and cortisone don't mix, however, so Weaver yanked Hardin from the rotation.

Hardin finished the year 6-7 and his ERA jumped up a run a game. He did, however, win a game with his bat — quite an achievement for a .105 hitter.

His home run off Moe Drabowsky in extra innings silenced the radio broadcasters, who had just said "I can't believe they're letting him hit."

Weaver's first pennant in his first full season came on the strength of other arms; some young, some old. Palmer, then 23, went 16-4, while veteran lefty Mike Cuellar went 23-11 and shared the Cy Young Award with Detroit's Denny McLain.

"Cuellar deserved it outright," said Hardin emphatically. "No way he should've had to share it. We beat them (Detroit) by 19 games."

Hardin had great respect for Cuellar. He recalled the great left-hander by his nickname. "Crazy Horse would throw that slow stuff and junk the first two times through the order.

"Third time around, he'd set up the hitter then zip that fastball right past him. They could never catch it."

I saw Cuellar at a card show in Ocala, Fla., Sunday, March 10, and relayed Hardin's story. He listened, smiled and softy said, "Yes, that's right."

I had given Cuellar Hardin's home number and suggested he call. "I will," he said, and slipped the card into his left jacket pocket.

He never had the chance. Hardin's plane had crashed hours before.

Cuellar and the Orioles pitched around Killebrew and handcuffed A.L. batting champion Rod Carew into a 1-for-14 playoff series.

The three-game Twins sweep followed a 109-win regular season and sent Baltimore into the Series as prohibitive favorites against the Miracle Mets.

Hardin did not pitch in the playoffs or World Series but put his $14,000 losers share to good use. He and Donna bought a home, their first, in Miami.

He was not bitter about not playing. "My shoulder hurt too much," he said. "I didn't expect to play."

The Orioles rebounded from their stunning autumn defeat to power their way through the American League again in 1970. Hardin, whose problems with Weaver began when he was yanked from the rotation in 1969, fared no better in 1970.

"When he got pulled out of the rotation he never got into top form again," said Donna Hardin. "Earl lost confidence in him."

With shoulder problems and cortisone his daily partners, Hardin became a spot starter and an occasional reliever. He went 6-5 on a team that went 108-54, beat the Yankees by 15 games and crushed Minnesota three straight again in the playoffs.

"That year was my greatest year," said Weaver. Weaver won four pennants but only one World Series, in 1970 against the Big Red Machine in what became known as the Brooks Robinson Series.

The Orioles won 17 straight at the end of 1970, including the last 11 of the regular season, three against Minnesota, and the first three against Cincinnati in the World Series.

Hardin watched from the dugout as Cuellar pitched a complete game 9-3 win in game five to lock up the world championship.

Nine Orioles pitched in that Series. Hardin couldn't.

"But I sat 40 feet from Brooks Robinson the entire series," he said. "Best seat in the house. None of the plays he made surprised me, nothing was different. What was unusual was that he had a lot of chances for a five-game series."

Robinson, Davey Johnson, Dave McNally and Andy Etchebarren were some of Hardin's closer friends on the team.

"We all got along fine," he said. "Winning takes care of that. Shoot, we went a-year-and-a-half without a roster change. We were the best team in the world and we knew it."

Hardin had an estimated 40 cortisone shots fired into his damaged right shoulder during his career. He'd had the majority of them when Weaver finally gave up on him in May of 1971 and traded him to the Yankees for a big right-hander named Bill Burbach.

"He had bad-mouthed me when I traded him," Weaver said. "He bad-mouthed me. He got traded, that's all. Traded."

Hardin learned of the trade on a plane bound for Minnesota. When the plane landed, he left the Orioles in the airport and flew off to join the fourth-place Yankees.

Besides his ego, Hardin was also hurt in the pocketbook. "He was bitter because he knew the Orioles would win again," Donna said. "He also missed out on a trip to Japan. That bothered him a lot."

Hardin went 0-2 for the Yankees and was released at age 28. Burbach never made it back to the big leagues after the trade.

The Orioles, meanwhile, won their third straight pennant but lost the Series in seven games to Pittsburgh.

Hardin's last season in baseball was 1972. He signed on as a free agent with the Braves, becoming a teammate of the great Henry Aaron.

"How good was Aaron? A quiet man, very unassuming and professional. Just look at his record. His record will tell you how good be was," Hardin said.

Hardin never faced Willie Mays but idolized Mickey Mantle. Frank Howard scared him, which put Hardin in rather large company, and was roughed up by Reggie Jackson for a multi-homer game.

We also argued about Yastrzemski. "A real professional hitter," Hardin called him, "a great player."

The longest home run he ever gave up exploded off the bat of Toronto Blue Jays Manager Cito Gaston.

"It was in the minors," Hardin recalled. "It went into the next county. He hit it so far I turned around to watch it to see where it would land."

After baseball, Hardin joined the Xerox Corp. and spent 17 years with the company. He hoped to join the Senior Golf Tour in 1993.

Hardin had financial backers at Mayacoo, and deservedly so. He could hit a golf ball a country mile with robotic precision.

In addition to his club championship, he was proud of his Major League Alumni tournament title, too.

He was happy for the players sky-rocketing salaries but just as happy with his $1,500 monthly pension check.

"It's great," he said "It's nice to get in the mail each month."

Hardin returned to Baltimore in the summer of 1989 for a 20-year reunion of the 1969 team. He took to the mound, painfully lobbed two pitches, waved his arms in the air and walked off the field.

"That's it, I'm done," he said. "I want to sit in the dugout, watch, and have a beer."

"I was proud of him," said daughter Gina. "I was so afraid he'd be a 45-year-old man trying to recapture his youth."

Hardin discussed Jim Palmer's attempted comeback bluntly. "More power to him. I think he's nuts. I can't even shave."

He then had me feel his shoulder socket, which ground bone-to-bone when he mimicked a throwing motion.

Every week Hardin received cards and autograph requests through the mail. He was a bit amused but signed freely and sent them back.

He was considering doing a card show, but never did. The day we were together I gave him the artwork from his 1973 Topps card cartoon.

I had obtained it from the R.M. Smythe auction last year through SCD and wanted him to have it. He got a kick out of it.

I gave him two copies of the card, too, so he could frame the pieces together.

Hardin was a Mr. Fixit who couldn't see spending money on someone if he could do a job himself.

"Meticulous to a fault," said Donna. "Then he'd be walking down the street and give a homeless person fifty bucks," daughter Gina added. "He'd look at me and say, 'don't tell Susan.'"

Susan, his second wife, married Jim 12 years ago, just six weeks after Jim and Donna divorced. Susan and Jim had a son, Michael, who's 2. Gina, 24, also works for Xerox and Jim's other son, JJ, is 20 and in college.

Hardin loved his family, friends, flying, fishing and golf. He took up flying in 1985 after cars bored him.

"He had at least 25 cars," his daughter said. "He had one of everything. And the Beechcraft was his second plane. His Cessna was too slow."

Unofficial reports indicate a propeller pin may have sheared and caused the propeller to stop spinning shortly after a windy early-evening Key West takeoff March 9.

Hardin was buried at sea two weeks after the crash six miles off the southern Key West coast. Longtime friend Bill Kielsden, a Key West charterboat captain, used a LORAN to take his boat with 11 family members and friends to the precise spot Hardin last fished.

The last baseball Jim Hardin so carefully signed is now where it belongs. His daughter Gina has it in a display case in her home. She also wears her mother's 1970 World Series ring.

Every son and every daughter should have a baseball signed by their father, whether or not he ever played baseball. We're all here on borrowed time, as the tragic accident once again illustrates.

"I don't have much from my dad," she told me. "I really appreciate the baseball very much. It means a lot to me.

"I don't have anything like that. It means a lot to me now and I'm sure it'll always mean a lot to me.

"And I'm sure he'll like the story, too. He loved publicity." — Ted Simendinger, May 31, 1991

* * *